The Eighties
in America

The Eighties in America

Volume III
Recessions—Yuppies
Appendixes
Indexes

Editor
Milton Berman, Ph.D.
University of Rochester

Managing Editor
Tracy Irons-Georges

SALEM PRESS, INC.
Pasadena, California
Hackensack, New Jersey

Editorial Director: Christina J. Moose
Managing Editor: Tracy Irons-Georges   *Production Editor:* Joyce I. Buchea
Copy Editors: Andy Perry, Timothy M. Tiernan,   *Acquisitions Editor:* Mark Rehn
and Rebecca Kuzins   *Research Supervisor:* Jeffry Jensen
Editorial Assistant: Dana Garey   *Research Assistant:* Keli Trousdale
Photo Editor: Cynthia Breslin Beres   *Graphics and Design:* James Hutson

Title page photo: *The space shuttle* Discovery *lifts off at Cape Canaveral, Florida, on September 29, 1988.* (AP/Wide World Photos)

Cover images (pictured clockwise, from top left): Michael Jackson, 1988. (Hulton Archive/ Getty Images); Ronald and Nancy Reagan, inaugural parade in Washington, D.C., Jan. 20, 1981. (AP/Wide World Photos); *Pac-Man* video game, 1980. (Ullstein Bild); Mount St. Helen's eruption, May 18, 1980. (AP/Wide World Photos)

∞ The paper used in these volumes conforms to the American National Standard for Permanence of Paper for Printed Library Materials, Z39.48-1992 (R1997).

Library of Congress Cataloging-in-Publication Data

The eighties in America / editor, Milton Berman.
    p. cm.
Includes bibliographical references and indexes.
  ISBN 978-1-58765-419-0 (set : alk. paper) — ISBN 978-1-58765-420-6 (v. 1: alk. paper) — ISBN 978-1-58765-421-3 (v. 2 : alk. paper) — ISBN 978-1-58765-422-0 (v. 3 : alk. paper)
  1. United States—History—1969- —Encyclopedias. 2. United States—Social conditions—1980- —Encyclopedias. 3. United States—Politics and government—1981-1989—Encyclopedias. 4. United States—Intellectual life—20th century—Encyclopedias. 5. Popular culture—United States—History—20th century—Encyclopedias. 6. Nineteen eighties—Encyclopedias. I. Berman, Milton.
  E876.E347 2008
  973.927003—dc22
                                       2008005068

First Printing

■ Table of Contents

Table of Contents

■ Complete List of Contents

Volume I

Volume II

Volume III

The Eighties
in America

■ Recessions

Definition   Sustained declines in economic activity
  lasting six months or longer

*The recessions of the early 1980's resulted in the highest un-
employment rates in forty years, causing millions of workers
and their families to experience substantial declines in their
standard of living.*

There were two recessions during the 1980's. The
first occurred from January to July, 1980. The second began in July, 1981, and lasted through November, 1982. Following a period of little economic
growth in 1979, overall economic activity declined in
early 1980. Because of the high rate of increase in
consumer prices (inflation), the Federal Reserve imposed severe restraints on the availability of credit.
Partly as a result, interest rates rose rapidly to peaks
of 14-20 percent in March and April, 1980. Consumer spending fell drastically and gross national
product declined at a 10 percent annual rate in the
second quarter of 1980. When the Federal Reserve
became aware of the negative economic impact of
very high interest rates, it removed the credit constraints beginning in May, 1980. The decline in economic activity came to an end in July, 1980, and
for the remainder of the year retail sales (including
automobile expenditures) and home construction
gradually increased. Because the recession lasted for
only six months, its overall impact was moderate. For
example, industrial production declined 8.5 percent and unemployment rose by two percentage
points. Of the seven post-World War II recessions up
to that time, the 1980 recession had the smallest effect on the economy as a whole.

The recovery that began in August, 1980, was
one of the shortest on record, lasting only eleven
months. Because it was a relatively weak recovery,
unemployment barely declined from the recession
peak. Reaching a level of 7.8 percent in July, 1980, it
had fallen only to 7.4 percent by July, 1981.

The rate of inflation remained above 10 percent
in 1980 and early 1981. Partly because of high inflation, monetary policy remained restrictive. The combination of high inflation and restrictive monetary
policy pushed the prime interest rate to 20 percent by
spring, 1981, compared to 11 percent in mid-1980.

The high interest rates were responsible for a
sharp decline in purchases of new homes and auto-
mobiles. Consumer spending on such items as furni-

ture and household equipment (durable goods) as
well as home construction is responsive to interest
rates. These expenditure declines were major causes
of the sixteen-month recession that began in July,
1981, and resulted in an increase in unemployment
to the highest levels since 1941.

The 1981-1982 Recession   The second recession of
the 1980's was among the most severe of the post-
World War II period. By November, 1982, twelve million people were unemployed. This level was 50 percent more than in the third quarter of 1981 and
nearly double the number of unemployed at the beginning of the 1980 recession. Industrial production
fell 12.5 percent during the 1981-1982 recession.
Home construction in 1982 was 50 percent less
than between 1977 and 1979, the most recent period
of general prosperity.

By the fall of 1982, the prime rate of interest had
fallen to just over 13 percent. The interest rate decline was the result of easier monetary policy, somewhat lower inflation, and a decline in demand for
business and consumer loans. Moreover, in August,
1981, the Economic Recovery Tax Act became law.
One major feature was a 25 percent reduction in individual income taxes consisting of a 5 percent cut in
October, 1981, a 10 percent reduction in July, 1982,
and a further 10 percent cut in July, 1983. The tax
cut, plus increased government purchases of goods
and services and the rise in transfer payments, led to
substantial increases in disposable income. This factor, combined with lower interest rates, led the economy out of recession.

From 1983 through 1985, the economy experienced substantial growth. Employment increased by
more than nine million, and business investment experienced the largest increase of any comparable
period in the post-World War II period. Interest
rates declined five percentage points from their
peaks in 1981, and home mortgage rates were down
by seven percentage points. Inflation was only about
one-third of the level reached in the early 1980's.

There were no periods of economic decline from
1985 to 1989. The next recession, a relatively mild
one, did not occur until 1990-1991.

Impact   Frequently, a decline in economic activity
has a political impact. For example, when President
Jimmy Carter ran for reelection in 1980, the effects
of the 1980 recession were still occurring. This con-

tributed to Ronald Reagan's victory over Carter in the 1980 presidential election. By contrast, when President Reagan ran for reelection against Walter Mondale in 1984, the economy was expanding vigorously and the 1981-1982 recession was a fading memory. This contributed to Reagan's reelection.

The major economic impact of the 1980 and 1981-1982 recessions was the rise in unemployment, particularly in the manufacturing and construction industries. Manufacturing unemployment was 5.6 percent in 1979 and 12.3 percent in 1982, an increase of 6.7 points. In construction, unemployment rose from 10.3 percent in 1979 to 20.0 percent in 1982. Because most of the workers in these highly impacted industries were men, the female unemployment rate rose more slowly than the male rate from 1979 to 1982. Thus, for women the rate rose from 6.8 percent in 1979 to 9.4 in 1982. Among men, the rate rose from 5.1 percent in 1979 to 9.9 percent in 1982. Among all workers, African Americans suffered the greatest increase in unemployment. In 1979, the unemployment rate for African Americans was 12.3 percent; it rose to 18.9 percent in 1982 and 19.5 percent in 1983. For white workers, the unemployment rate was 5.1 percent in 1979, 8.6 percent in 1982, and 8.4 percent in 1983.

Further Reading

Glasner, David, ed. *Business Cycles and Depressions: An Encyclopedia.* New York: Garland, 1997. An exhaustive study of the history of business cycles and the economists who wrote about them.

Kurian, George, ed. *Datapedia of the United States, 1790-2005.* 2d ed. Lanham, Md.: Bernan Press, 2005. Extensive statistical information on the impact of business cycles. Contains important data not readily available elsewhere.

Samuelson, Paul, and William Nordhaus. *Economics.* 17th ed. New York: McGraw-Hill, 2001. Excellent discussion of the causes of business cycles. Written at a basic level.

Alan L. Sorkin

See also Business and the economy in the United States; Economic Recovery Tax Act of 1981; Inflation in the United States; Reaganomics; Unemployment in the United States; Unions.

■ Regan, Donald

Identification   Secretary of the Treasury, 1981-1985, and White House chief of staff, 1985-1987
Born   December 21, 1918; Cambridge, Massachusetts
Died   June 10, 2003; Williamsburg, Virginia

As President Ronald Reagan's first secretary of the Treasury, Regan was a major architect of the supply-side economic policies that became known as Reaganomics.

Donald Regan graduated from Harvard University in 1940. He served in the U.S. Marine Corps in World War II, attaining the rank of lieutenant colonel. After the war, he joined the Merrill Lynch investment firm, where he rose eventually to become president of the firm in 1968 and chairman and chief executive officer of Merrill Lynch, Pierce, Fenner and Smith in 1971. From 1973 to 1975, he also served as vice chair of the New York Stock Exchange.

At the Department of the Treasury, Regan helped to craft the Economic Recovery Tax Act of 1981 and what became the Tax Reform Act of 1986. These bills

Secretary of the Treasury Donald Regan listens as President Ronald Reagan whispers in his ear in the White House Rose Garden in June, 1981. (AP/Wide World Photos)

provided significant tax cuts, which, according to the supply-side economic theories favored by the Reagan administration, were believed to benefit the economy by stimulating spending and investment by businesses and wealthy individuals. Overall, Regan generally pursued policies of business deregulation and the promotion of competition that exhibited his deep faith in the free enterprise system.

In 1984, Regan decided to leave the Treasury Department because of his concerns about leaks to the press from within the White House and an atmosphere of mistrust among the president's major advisers. The president urged him to stay on, and in an unusual maneuver, Regan and White House chief of staff James Baker switched jobs in early 1985—Baker became secretary of the Treasury, and Regan became the new White House chief of staff. At the White House, personality conflicts soon emerged between Regan and First Lady Nancy Reagan. More serious, Regan was soon dogged by the Iran-Contra affair. In late 1986, news reports revealed that members of Reagan's administration had sold arms to Iran and funneled the proceeds to the anticommunist Contras in Nicaragua. Regan was accused of trying to obstruct the investigation into the Reagan administration's involvement in these arms sales, and he resigned as chief of staff in February, 1987. After leaving the White House, he published his memoirs, *For the Record*. His allegations that both Ronald and Nancy Reagan consulted a personal astrologer before making major decisions (widely denied by the Reagan family) further estranged him from the First Family.

Impact   Although he left the chief of staff position under a cloud, Regan had a major impact on the economic policies of the Reagan administration because of his leadership in the Department of the Treasury during Reagan's first term as president.

Further Reading

Noonan, Peggy. *What I Saw at the Revolution: A Political Life in the Reagan Era.* New York: Ivy Books, 1990.

Regan, Donald T. *For the Record: From Wall Street to Washington.* New York: St. Martin's Press, 1989.

Mark S. Joy

See also   Business and the economy in the United States; Iran-Contra affair; Reagan, Nancy; Reagan, Ronald; Reagan Revolution; Reaganomics; Tower Commission.

■ Rehnquist, William H.

Identification   U.S. Supreme Court justice, 1972-1986, and chief justice of the United States, 1986-2005

Born   October 1, 1924; Milwaukee, Wisconsin

Died   September 3, 2005; Arlington, Virginia

Rehnquist was a conservative Supreme Court justice who favored federalism, states' rights, business, and religion.

President Richard M. Nixon appointed William H. Rehnquist to the U.S. Supreme Court on December 10, 1971. As an associate justice of the United States, Rehnquist quickly established himself as the most conservative justice on the Warren E. Burger Court. Unwilling to concede on many issues, he consistently found himself as the lone dissenter. Rehnquist could be counted on to vote in favor of states, business, religious freedom, capital punishment, and antiabortion policies, and against the expansion of the Fourteenth Amendment guarantee of equal protection for all citizens.

President Ronald Reagan nominated Rehnquist to fill the chief justice position when Burger retired in 1986. The Senate confirmed his nomination on September 26, 1986, by an overwhelming majority. His successor, Antonin Scalia, has been viewed as more conservative than Rehnquist.

With his ascension to chief justice, Rehnquist was able to shift the ideological focus of the Court. Between 1986 and the end of the decade, Rehnquist slowly drove a wedge between the public's expectations that the Court would continue to deliver liberal-minded decisions and the reality that it was becoming increasingly conservative. It should be noted that the true extent of the conservative revolution in the Court was not fully witnessed until Clarence Thomas was appointed in 1991.

In spite of his conservative views, Rehnquist was not afraid of joining and occasionally writing considerably liberal decisions. For instance, in *Meritor Savings Bank v. Vinson* (1986), Rehnquist wrote the majority opinion, which expanded the Civil Rights Act of 1964 to cover hostile-environment sexual harassment and include protections against the psychological aspects of harassment in the workplace.

Rehnquist was also an advocate for patriotism. He wrote the primary dissenting opinion in the highly controversial flag burning case *Texas v. Johnson* (1989), in which he argued that the flag was

Chief Justice William H. Rehnquist. (Supreme Court Historical Society)

much more than a symbol. He drew inspiration from the records of the Continental Congress, American flag history, the national anthem, and the "Concord Hymn" when articulating his disgust for flag burning. His arguments resonated with the American public in a way that few Court opinions or decisions have managed to achieve.

Impact Rehnquist was a strong influence on the U.S. Supreme Court. He advanced a conservative approach to interpreting the U.S. Constitution and urged the Court to follow. After becoming chief justice, he sought to make the Court more collegial in an effort to decrease the number of split decisions, thus increasing the legitimacy of the Court's decisions.

Further Reading

Galub, Arthur L., and George J. Lankevich. *The Rehnquist Court, 1986-1994.* Danbury, Conn.: Grolier Educational Corporation, 1995.

Hudson, David L. *The Rehnquist Court: Understanding Its Impact and Legacy.* Westport, Conn.: Praeger, 2006.

Tushnet, Mark. *A Court Divided: The Rehnquist Court and the Future of Constitutional Law.* New York: W. W. Norton, 2005.

James W. Stoutenborough

See also Abortion; Conservatism in U.S. politics; Flag burning; Liberalism in U.S. politics; *Meritor Savings Bank v. Vinson*; O'Connor, Sandra Day; Reagan, Ronald; Religion and spirituality in the United States; Sexual harassment; Supreme Court decisions.

■ Religion and spirituality in Canada

Definition Spiritual belief and practice by Canadians expressed in both formal and informal ways

Through the decade, Canada witnessed a decline in the relative proportion of its "big three" Christian groups, the Catholic, Anglican, and United Churches; growth in the proportion of non-Christian groups and new religious movements (NRMs) such as paganism; and a growing secularization consistent with trends in other industrialized countries.

Canada is a predominantly Christian country with guaranteed religious freedom and a pluralistic nature consistent with its political philosophy. In 1981, Canada was 90 percent Christian; another 7.4 percent were atheist or agnostic or had no religion, and the remaining 2.6 percent were Muslims, Jews, Hindus, Buddhists, Sikhs, or other.

Immigration played a major role in increasing the religious diversity of Canada through the decade, with the newcomers holding mostly non-Western, non-Christian belief systems. Catholics, the largest single faith group, exhibited modest growth, largely due to immigration, while non-Christian groups like Muslims, Buddhists, Hindus, and Sikhs showed much greater percentage increases. In 1975, Catholics worshiped in twenty-one languages, the United in fourteen, Anglicans in twelve, Baptists in thirteen, Lutherans in nine, and Presbyterians in five. Clearly the church played a part in supporting multilingualism and the preservation of ethnic identities.

Canada's religious pulse has been less fundamentalist and moralistic than that of its U.S. neighbor, and sectarianism has not played a prominent role in Canada's religious history. The mainstream Catholic, Anglican, and United Churches are hierarchical, ritualistic, and dedicated to continuity through tradition.

Most Canadians were not regular churchgoers in the 1980's, however, and about 12 percent of the population during the decade was classified as nonreligious, the largest share on the west coast. Quebec experienced the most obvious secularization after the Quiet Revolution of the 1960's, yet religious identity remained strong in the province with the Triune of French ethnicity, French language, and Catholic religion. Indigenous peoples continued to practice animistic spiritual traditions, Christianity, or a blending of animistic and Christian.

Impact   Unlike U.S. groups, Canadian faith groups after World War II drifted to the left in support of the country's social welfare policies, including guaranteed universal health care. The United Church, created from a merger in 1925 of Methodists, Congregationalists, Brethren, and most Presbyterians, represents an unusually successful ecumenical and cooperative effort among Christians, and this group has been particularly effective in the promotion of civil rights for groups such as indigenous peoples and prison populations. The Canadian Council of Churches, a Christian ecumenical umbrella organization, offers leadership and support for its member denominations.

Further Reading

Hewitt, W. E., ed. *The Sociology of Religion: A Canadian Focus.* Toronto: Butterworths, 1993. Essays on diverse topics such as new religious movements, nonbelief, religion and multiculturalism, and the influence of religion on national identity.

Menendez, Albert J. *Church and State in Canada.* Amherst, N.Y.: Prometheus Books, 1996. Addresses the impact of religion on politics, law, education, and national identity, drawing comparisons to the United States.

"Religion in Canada." *Journal of Canadian Studies* 22 (Winter, 1987-1988). A summary of religious patterns supported by official data.

Ann M. Legreid

See also   Immigration to Canada; Minorities in Canada; Religion and spirituality in the United States; Televangelism.

■ Religion and spirituality in the United States

Definition   Organized and nonorganized expressions of spiritual belief and practice among Americans

During the 1980's, debates on several questions that had been a part of American religious history for decades became increasingly heated in religious denominations, in politics, and even in the realm of popular culture. The decade was marked by calls for religious pluralism and tolerance for underrepresented groups—especially in ordained ministry—but also by a gradual and powerful shift to the right in terms of social and cultural activism and the promotion of a Judeo-Christian worldview. These debates were featured not only in internal dialogues among religious and spiritual leaders but also in political debates (including all three presidential elections of the 1980's) and popular culture.

The early 1980's saw the growth and development of opportunities for women, minorities, and others who had been traditionally excluded from certain roles within U.S. religious denominations. The Civil Rights and women's movements of the 1960's and 1970's opened up doors for participation in many positions not only in political and corporate leadership but also for leadership in religious communities. During the 1970's, mainstream Episcopalian and Lutheran churches had voted to allow the ordination of women. Reform Judaism had ordained its first female rabbi, Sally Priesand, in 1972. During the 1980's, other denominations followed this trend. In 1984, the Reorganized Church of Jesus Christ of Latter-day Saints (now the Community of Christ) began to ordain women. Conservative Judaism began ordaining female rabbis in 1985.

In 1983, the U.S. Conference of Catholic Bishops issued a pastoral letter titled *The Hispanic Presence: Challenge and Commitment*, which addressed the Catholic Church's relationship with believers of Spanish and Latin American descent. The letter reaffirmed the need for Church ministries that would address this rapidly growing segment of the Catholic population and encouraged young men in this demographic to consider serving in the priesthood.

Pluralism and Ecumenism   The changes that were begun in previous decades and the opening of ordained leadership positions described above were reflections of larger trends of broader participation within U.S. religious denominations as well as greater participation among the groups. Since the establishment of the National Council of Churches (NCC) in 1950, many denominations had continued to work together to find points of agreement and common areas of interest. One example of this kind of collaboration was the publication in 1989 of the New Revised Standard Version (NRSV) of the Bible. Under the supervision of the NCC, a group of scholars from Protestant denominations joined with Roman Catholic, Eastern Orthodox, and Jewish scholars to produce a version of the Scriptures that included more gender-inclusive language and updated other archaisms. The NRSV was widely endorsed by larger Protestant denominations and is an accepted translation in the Catholic and Orthodox churches.

Though the NCC is a broad alliance of churches representing members of various theological inclinations, it has been criticized by liberal Christians for its exclusion of the Metropolitan Community Church (MCC), an organization that formed during the late 1960's but grew in both membership and national recognition during the 1980's. Throughout the decade, the MCC, with its explicit mission of ministering to gay and lesbian Christians, became a voice for AIDS awareness and in support of church-ordained marriage ceremonies for gays and lesbians. Between 1983 and 1992, the MCC sought membership in the ecumenical body. In 1992, it was denied not only membership but also the opportunity to apply for "observer" status.

The Rise of the Religious Right   The decision by the NCC to deny the MCC's membership resulted in part from tensions at the other end of the political and theological spectrum. The NCC's decision to appeal to more conservative members represented the council's own acknowledgment that conservative Christians were playing a larger role not only in American religious life but also in politics at the local, state, and national levels.

The 1980 election of Ronald Reagan (and the defeat of Jimmy Carter, a self-professed born-again Christian) was a political victory delivered in large part by Christian activist groups that had been mobilizing throughout the 1970's in response to the Supreme Court's 1973 *Roe v. Wade* decision and to the proposed adoption of the Equal Rights Amendment (ERA). Singer Anita Bryant's crusade to repeal a 1977 civil rights ordinance in Florida that included

protections for gays and lesbians is often marked by historians as the birth not only of the current struggles for gay and lesbian rights but also of what is sometimes referred to as the New Christian Right or the New Religious Right. Opponents of the ordinance were quite successful in their use of grass-roots-level organization strategies to influence voters to vote according to their religious principles.

The 1980's thus saw a dramatic increase in participation in conservative religious organizations. Opponents of the ERA—including the Concerned Women for America, founded by Beverly LaHaye, and Eagle Forum, founded by Phyllis Schlafly—helped ensure that the 1982 deadline came and went without the required number of votes for ratification to the U.S. Constitution. Other groups that gained status and popularity during the decade were the Moral Majority, founded by Jerry Falwell and others in 1979, and the Christian Coalition, established in 1989 by the Reverend Pat Robertson.

Reagan's election marked an important victory for the Religious Right. The president rewarded his base by appointing activists to national leadership positions. His tenure in office was marked by social and economic policies that derived from his engagement with what a future presidential candidate called the American "culture wars." Reagan often invoked rhetoric associated with Judeo-Christian principles and frequently referred to America as God's "city upon a hill," a reference to John Winthrop's 1630 sermon "A Model of Christian Charity." Reagan proclaimed 1983 the "Year of the Bible," arguing: "Of the many influences that have shaped the United States of America into a distinctive Nation and people, none may be said to be more fundamental and enduring than the Bible." The proclamation ended: "I encourage all citizens, each in his or her own way, to reexamine and rediscover its priceless and timeless message."

Christian conservatives continued to work on social and political issues. Though there has been fragmentation and some division among conservative leadership at the national level, activists remain united in at least one area—their crusade to end the legalization of abortion in the United States. The Reagan years were a period of great political mobilization for conservative Christians. Many activists joined in Robertson's 1988 failed run in the Republican primary election for the presidency. Robertson, an ordained Southern Baptist minister, was not the only minister in the election. One of the candidates in the Democratic primary was the Reverend Jesse Jackson, a Baptist minister and civil rights activist.

Religion and Popular Culture　While the 1980's saw the development of tensions within various religious communities and the rise of religious conservatism in politics, it was also a time of memorable religious expression in the realm of popular culture. Janette Oke, a Christian romance writer, followed her 1979 best-selling novel *Love Comes Softly* with seven other popular titles in the Love Comes Softly series during the 1980's. Jewish rabbi Harold Kushner published his best-selling book about faith during periods of grief and loss, *When Bad Things Happen to Good People*, in 1981. In 1988, Martin Scorsese directed a film adaptation of Nikos Kazantzakis's novel *O Teleftaíos Peirasmós* (*The Last Temptation of Christ*, 1951). The film included footage of Jesus' crucifixion and, more controversially, hypothesized about the inner nature of the temptations he experienced during his final hours. Conservative Christians organized protests against the film's nonbiblical portrayal of a conflicted Jesus who imagines, and is tempted by, the idea of a fully human existence.

Another source of debate that involved religion and the media was the release in 1989 of Madonna's *Like a Prayer* album. The album featured her popular hit "Express Yourself" along with the title song, which compared the ecstasy of religious expression with the ecstatic feelings associated with love and sex. The "Like a Prayer" video included an image of the singer receiving a sort of stigmata (a rendering of the wounds Christ received during the crucifixion) as well as embracing a black man who appears to be a religious figure. The album, the song, and especially the video mobilized Christians in a boycott against the singer and the products she endorsed.

Impact　The social and cultural questions that emerged in mainstream American culture during the 1960's and 1970's continued to affect conservative and liberal religious denominations alike during the 1980's. The question of women's ordination opened opportunities in progressive and moderate communities while strengthening the resolve against these kinds of changes in more conservative communities. Lingering related questions about the role of minorities in the denominations continued to be debated in broader coalitions such as the National Council of Churches. The political winners during the decade were definitely the Christian conservatives, members of the New Religious Right, whose campaigns for national attention culminated in the election of Ronald Reagan in 1980. Their campaigns against the Equal Rights Amendment and the legalization of abortion translated into large, politically powerful organizations that dominated the Republican political agenda both during the 1980's and beyond.

Further Reading

Ammerman, Nancy Tatom. *Bible Believers: Fundamentalists in the Modern World*. New Brunswick, N.J.: Rutgers University Press, 1987. Ammerman's ethnographic study has inspired many subsequent investigations of religiosity among evangelical Christians.

Gaustad, Edwin, and Leigh Schmidt. *The Religious History of America: The Heart of the American Story from Colonial Times to Today*. San Francisco: HarperCollins, 2004. An overview of American religious history.

Jorstad, Erling. *The New Christian Right, 1981-1988: Prospects for the Post-Reagan Decade*. Studies in American Religion 25. Lewiston, N.Y.: Edwin Mellen Press, 1987. Jorstad's study investigates the social and cultural influences behind the rise of the Religious Right.

Nall, Mark A. *A History of Christianity in the United States and Canada*. Grand Rapids, Mich.: Wm. B. Eerdmans, 1992. An older, but still widely studied, history of Christian events, movements, and leaders.

Jennifer Heller

See also　Abortion; Bakker, Jim and Tammy Faye; Conservatism in U.S. politics; Elections in the United States, 1980; Elections in the United States, 1984; Elections in the United States, 1988; Evangelical Lutheran Church in America; Falwell, Jerry; Feminism; Grant, Amy; Heritage USA; *Hustler Magazine v. Falwell*; Last Temptation of Christ, The; Moral Majority; Nation of Yahweh; Religion and spirituality in Canada; Robertson, Pat; Swaggart, Jimmy; Televangelism.

■ R.E.M.

Identification American rock band
Date Formed in 1980

Despite beginning as a "college radio" group, R.E.M. became one of the seminal bands of the 1980's.

When R.E.M. formed in Athens, Georgia, in 1980, there was little indication of the superstardom the group would achieve. Composed of vocalist Michael Stipe, guitarist Peter Buck, bassist Mike Mills, and drummer Bill Berry, the band was vastly different from the artists that dominated the commercial charts. R.E.M.'s sound was characterized by Buck's jangle-pop guitar, the driving rhythm section of Mills and Berry, and Stipe's cryptic, garbled lyrics.

R.E.M.'s first single, "Radio Free Europe," aired extensively on college radio stations and garnered substantial critical acclaim. After signing with the in-dependent label I.R.S. Records, R.E.M. released the extended play (EP) album *Chronic Town* in 1982. This was quickly followed by the band's full-length debut *Murmur*, which *Rolling Stone* magazine named the Best Album of 1983.

In 1984, the band released *Reckoning*, also considered a critical success. The hypnotic single "So. Central Rain" received considerable airplay on college radio stations, increasing R.E.M.'s cult following. In addition to building their careers, the band members' early success underscored the viability of college radio and helped spotlight scores of alternative artists producing quality music—many who sounded very similar to R.E.M.

The band's next albums, 1985's *Fables of the Reconstruction* and 1986's *Lifes Rich Pageant*, maintained the core sound that had come to define R.E.M.'s musical style and also expanded the band's fan base. Although each successive album earned the band

R.E.M. in 1984. From left: Michael Stipe, Mike Mills, Bill Berry, Peter Buck. (Paul Natkin)

more renown, 1987's *Document* was deemed R.E.M.'s first mainstream success. *Document* reached the top ten in large part because of the breakthrough singles "The One I Love" and "It's the End of the World as We Know It (And I Feel Fine)." Heavy airplay on top 40 radio, coupled with frequent rotation of the videos on MTV, moved R.E.M. closer to superstardom. The band's most successful album up to that time was also the last it would record with I.R.S. Records. *Green*, released in 1988, was the first album of R.E.M.'s record deal with Warner Bros. No longer darlings of college radio, R.E.M. moved to the corporate label, signaling major changes for the band. Every single was played on commercial radio and had an accompanying video on MTV. Also, although the band had toured extensively since its formation, the *Green* tour marked the first time that R.E.M. played in larger stadiums instead of concert halls. R.E.M. returned to the studio in 1989 to begin work on what would be one of their most successful commercial albums, 1990's *Out of Time.*

Impact Although R.E.M. began the 1980's in relative obscurity, by the end of the decade the band had laid the groundwork for its continued success and was poised to become one of the greatest rock bands of the later twentieth century.

Further Reading

Fletcher, Tony. *Remarks Remade: The Story of R.E.M.* 2d ed. New York: Omnibus Press, 2002.

Rolling Stone. *R.E.M., the "Rolling Stone" Files: The Ultimate Compendium of Interviews, Articles, Facts, and Opinions from the Files of "Rolling Stone."* New York: Hyperion, 1995.

Matthew Schmitz

See also MTV; Music; Music videos; Pop music.

■ Retton, Mary Lou

Identification American gymnast
Born January 24, 1968; Fairmont, West Virginia

Retton captured American's attention by becoming the first American woman to win an Olympic gold medal in gymnastics.

In 1981, Mary Lou Retton, age thirteen, competed regionally and nationally in gymnastics while training in Fairmont, West Virginia, a coal mining town.

Mary Lou Retton competes on the balance beam at the 1984 Summer Olympics. (Hulton Archive/Getty Images)

Recognizing Retton's potential, Bela Karolyi, coach of the 1976 Olympic gold medalist Nadia Comaneci, offered to train Retton for free at his gym in Houston, Texas. Only fourteen years old, Retton moved to Texas without her family on January 2, 1983. By the end of the year, she had achieved the number one senior-class ranking in the nation. Although a broken left wrist prevented her from competing in the World Championships that year, she won the American Cup, the U.S. Gymnastics Federation American Classics, and the Chunichi Cup in Japan—the first American woman to do so.

In May, six weeks before the 1984 Olympics in Los Angeles, doctors determined that Retton would have to undergo arthroscopic surgery to repair damaged cartilage in her knee. After only one day of rest, Retton returned to the gym and worked hard at rehabilitation. She defied her doctor's expectations and recovered in time for the Olympics. In the individual competition, Retton scored a perfect 10 on her floor exercise. She then sealed her all-around gold medal with a perfect 10 on her final apparatus, the vault. Retton performed her second vault, although it was not necessary, scoring another 10. She became the first American female athlete to win a gold medal in gymnastics. She also took home two silver medals, in team and vault, and two bronze medals, for uneven bars and floor exercise. Her five medals were the most won by any athlete at the 1984 Olympics.

Retton, dubbed "America's Sweetheart" by the media, capitalized on her fame with national endorsement offers and appearances. Retton's endorsements for companies such as McDonald's and Vidal Sassoon hair products earned her an estimated $1 million in the year following the Olympics. She also became the first woman to appear on a Wheaties cereal box. She briefly continued to compete in gymnastics, winning her third American Cup in 1985. In 1986, however, she retired from gymnastics to attend the University of Texas.

Throughout the 1980's, Retton remained in the public eye working as a sportscaster, including acting as commentator for the National Broadcasting Company (NBC) at the 1988 Olympics in Seoul, South Korea. She also appeared in the film *Scrooged* (1988). Her numerous accolades during the 1980's included 1984 *Sports Illustrated* Sportswoman of the Year and 1984 Associated Press Female Amateur Athlete of the Year. In 1985, she became the youngest person ever inducted into the U.S. Olympic Committee's Olympic Hall of Fame.

Impact Mary Lou Retton inspired a generation of Americans with her perfect performances in the floor exercise and vault, which won for her the all-around gold medal at the 1984 Los Angeles Olympics. One of the first female athletes in America to earn significant fame and endorsement revenue, Retton paved the way for future female athletes with her success.

Further Reading

"Gymnastics: Pathways to the Olympics—The Golden Girls." *Sports Illustrated* 88, no. 23 (June 6, 1988): 61-68.

Hoobing, Robert. *The 1984 Olympics: Sarajevo and Los Angeles.* Washington, D.C.: U.S. Postal Service, 1984.

Malana S. Salyer

See also Advertising; Olympic boycotts; Olympic Games of 1984; Sports.

■ Reykjavik Summit

The Event Meeting between U.S. president Ronald Reagan and Soviet general secretary Mikhail Gorbachev over arms control and other issues

Date October 11-12, 1986

Place Höfði House, Reykjavik, Iceland

U.S. and Soviet leaders met at this groundbreaking summit that many participants believed was a key turning point in the Cold War. While in the end the two sides were unable to agree upon final terms for the elimination of nuclear weapons, the negotiations at Reykjavik eventually led to crucial agreements on intermediate-range and strategic nuclear force reductions.

The summit meeting in Reykjavik, Iceland, between U.S. president Ronald Reagan and Soviet general secretary Mikhail Gorbachev on October 11-12, 1986, followed from their first meeting in Geneva, Switzerland, in 1985. Though no arms control agreements were initialed at Geneva, the two leaders of the world's most powerful states did declare that a nuclear war could not be won by either side and that such a war should never be fought.

After President Reagan made an impassioned speech for a nuclear arms reduction accord before the United Nations in September of 1986, General Secretary Gorbachev extended an offer for the two leaders to meet in October, 1986, in either Iceland or the United Kingdom. In the end, Reykjavik was established as the meeting place for what was billed as an informal tête-à-tête.

The talks began early on the morning of Saturday, October 11; as agreed, the negotiations were to be wide-ranging, covering four major thematic areas: arms control, regional issues, bilateral issues (such as Jewish and dissident emigration from the Soviet Union), and human rights. However, in the final analysis, most commentators and journalists would report that the primary importance of Reykjavik was the sweeping deliberations over nuclear arms control issues.

Indeed, Gorbachev came to Reykjavik having realized the need to end both the superpower arms race and the ideological conflict with the Western Bloc, as the rapidly declining Soviet economy was in dire need of reform. Gorbachev soon showed his hand, arguing in the opening sessions that the two countries should agree to a 50 percent reduction in strategic nuclear arms, a total elimination of all intermediate-range missiles deployed in Europe, compulsory nonwithdrawal from the Anti-Ballistic Missile (ABM) Treaty for a period of ten years, and a complete ban on the testing of space-based antiballistic defensive weapons, except in laboratories. On October 12, Gorbachev sweetened the deal by proposing to limit all intermediate-range missiles in the Soviet and American arsenals to one hundred.

In the final, dramatic hours of the summit, Gorbachev remarked to Reagan that he wanted to rid their countries' nuclear arsenals of all strategic forces, not merely ballistic missiles. To that, Reagan responded that he would agree to the elimination of all nuclear arms, be they strategic, intermediate-range, or tactical nuclear weaponry. It appeared that a major, far-reaching compact on nuclear disarmament was within sight.

Negotiations Break Down   In the final hour, however, the talks collapsed when Gorbachev insisted that Reagan's Strategic Defense Initiative (SDI)—a space-based, antiballistic defensive weapons system unveiled in March, 1983, in order to make nuclear weapons "impotent and obsolete"—be limited to research and testing in a laboratory setting. The Soviet leadership believed that the SDI program was being developed in order to give the United States a first-strike capability and to take the arms race into outer space, not to provide a protective shield against nuclear attack as the Reagan administration claimed. Reagan would not agree to limiting research, development, and testing of the system within the framework of the ABM Treaty, arguing that the SDI program was the best insurance policy against the Soviet Union reneging on arms reduction commitments. Thus, the failure to find common ground on defensive antiballistic systems caused the summit to end without any agreement on nuclear arms control.

Impact   Although the Reykjavik Summit ended without the signing of an arms control treaty, the meeting was of fundamental importance, as the sweeping negotiations advanced the arms control agenda significantly. Important breakthroughs made at Reykjavik enabled the two leaders to sign an Intermediate-Range Nuclear Forces Treaty the following year at their third summit meeting, in Washington, D.C. This accord was groundbreaking: For the first time ever, an entire class of nuclear weapons was eliminated from U.S. and Soviet arsenals. Likewise, the Reykjavik discussions on strategic nuclear forces eventually culminated in the first Strategic Arms Reduction Treaty (1991), the first arms agreement signed by the two superpowers that eliminated strategic nuclear arms.

Another rarely discussed outcome of the Reykjavik Summit—one secured by the United States—was the commitment made by the Soviets to have an ongoing discussion on human rights issues. Perhaps the most significant result of Reykjavik was that the meeting led to a greater level of trust between the two superpowers; indeed, Gorbachev later claimed that Reykjavik was the key turning point in the Cold War, as it was the first time the leaders of the two states met over an extended period of time and talked about all outstanding issues of concern.

Further Reading

Beschloss, Michael R., and Strobe Talbott. *At the Highest Levels: The Inside Story of the Cold War.* Boston: Little, Brown, 1993. A historian and a journalist team up to examine the causes, consequences, and denouement of the Cold War.

Goodby, James E. *At the Borderline of Armageddon: How American Presidents Managed the Atom Bomb.* Lanham, Md.: Rowman & Littlefield, 2006. As a participant in the arms control negotiations between the United States and the Soviet Union in the early 1980's, Goodby examines the negotiating positions, strategies, and achievements of past U.S. presidents.

Gorbachev, Mikhail S. *Memoirs.* New York: Doubleday, 1996. In this wide-ranging autobiography, Gorbachev discusses his rise to power, meetings with global leaders, and the fall of the Soviet Union and communism.

Shultz, George P. *Turmoil and Triumph: My Years as Secretary of State.* New York: Charles Scribner's Sons, 1993. As secretary of state under Reagan, Shultz played a significant role in the five summit meetings held between Reagan and Gorbachev.

In this book, Shultz recounts his role in these negotiations and the opportunities that were opened by them.

Thomas E. Rotnem

See also Foreign policy of the United States; Intermediate-Range Nuclear Forces (INF) Treaty; Reagan, Ronald; Reagan's "Evil Empire" speech; Shultz, George P.; Soviet Union and North America; Strategic Defense Initiative (SDI); Weinberger, Caspar.

■ Rice, Jerry

Identification American football player
Born October 13, 1962; Starkville, Mississippi

Rice came out of a life of obscurity to become one of the greatest wide receivers in football history.

Jerry Rice established himself as a college sensation at Mississippi Valley State University, where he was named an Associated Press (AP) All-American and finished ninth in the Heisman Trophy voting in 1984. Drafted by the San Francisco 49ers, he quickly ascended to the premier receiver spot and remained a dominant force at that position for sixteen seasons in the National Football League (NFL).

Each year in the league, Rice set new records for achievement. In 1987, he was named Player of the Year. The 1988 season proved to be one of his best, as he caught 64 passes for 1,306 yards and 9 touchdowns. That season, Rice helped propel the team to a narrow Super Bowl victory over the Cincinnati Bengals, 20-16. His 11 pass receptions for 215 yards and a touchdown set Super Bowl records and earned him the Most Valuable Player (MVP) honor. The next year, Rice helped the 49ers advance once again to the Super Bowl, and his team beat the Denver Broncos handily, 55-10.

Impact Jerry Rice set more records than any other receiver in the history of the game. To date, he owns

San Francisco 49er Jerry Rice makes a reception while being tackled by Cincinnati Bengals Lewis Billups, left, and Ray Horton, during the 1989 Super Bowl in Miami, Florida. (AP/Wide World Photos)

the records for most receptions (1,549), most receiving yards (22,895), most touchdown receptions (198), most yards from scrimmage (23,540), and most rushing/receiving touchdowns (208). Experts believe many of these records will never be broken.

Subsequent Events In 1994, Rice and the 49ers were Super Bowl champions again. In 2001, he left the 49ers for the Oakland Raiders, and in 2002 he returned to the Super Bowl; although the team lost, Rice became the first player to catch touchdown passes in four Super Bowls. He played with the Raiders until 2004, went to the Seattle Seahawks for a year, had a brief stay with the Denver Broncos, and retired in 2005. In 2006, he signed a one-day contract to end his career as a 49er.

Further Reading

Dickey, Glenn. *Sports Great Jerry Rice*. New York: Enslow, 1993.

Rice, Jerry, and Brian Curtis. *Go Long! My Journey Beyond the Game and the Fame*. New York: Ballantine Books, 2007.

Rice, Jerry, and Michael Silver. *Rice*. New York: St. Martin's Press, 1996.

Stewart, Mark. *Jerry Rice*. New York: Children's Press, 1996.

David W. Madden

See also   African Americans; Football; Sports.

Lionel Richie. (Paul Natkin)

■ Richie, Lionel

Identification   American singer and songwriter
Born   June 20, 1949; Tuskegee, Alabama

Richie was the most influential songwriter and singer of the romantic ballad in the 1980's.

Lionel Richie achieved international success during the 1970's as a lead vocalist, saxophone player, and songwriter for the band the Commodores. The 1978 single "Three Times a Lady," which Richie composed, reached platinum status by selling more than one million copies, highlighted the artist's songwriting talents, and put him on the path to a very successful solo career during the 1980's.

In 1980, Richie wrote and produced the song "Lady" for Kenny Rogers and the following year wrote, produced, and recorded the duet "Endless Love" with Diana Ross for the film of the same name,

starring Brooke Shields. In 1982, under the Motown label, Richie produced his first solo album, *Lionel Richie*. From that album, the ballad "Truly" topped the pop charts and marked the beginning of a successful solo career. Two other hit songs from the album were the ballads "You Are" and "My Love." Richie's second album, *Can't Slow Down* (1983), sold more than eight million copies and included the dance hit "All Night Long" as well as the hit songs "Hello," "Stuck on You," and "Penny Lover."

In 1985, Richie and Michael Jackson cowrote the single "We Are the World" to help raise money for famine relief in Africa. Produced by Quincy Jones, the song was recorded on January 28, 1985, at the A&M Recording Studios in Hollywood, California. Forty-five musicians participated in the project—known as United Support of Artists for Africa (USA for Africa)—including Kenny Rogers, Billy Joel, Bob Dylan, and Bruce Springsteen. The song debuted on March 7, and on April 5 more than five thousand radio stations played the song simultaneously. In total, the single sold more than 7.5 million copies, raised more than $50 million for famine relief, and won three Grammy Awards, including Song of the Year, Record of the Year, and Best Pop Performance by a Duo or a Group. That same year, Richie composed and recorded the ballad "Say You, Say Me" for the movie *White Nights*, starring Gregory Hines and Mikhail Baryshnikov. The song won Richie an Academy Award for Best Original Song. His third album, *Dancing on the Ceiling* (1986), proved just as popular as his others and included such well-known songs as "Dancing on the Ceiling" and "Ballerina Girl." In 1987, the singer wrote and recorded the song "Deep River Woman" with the country band Alabama.

Impact During the 1980's, Lionel Richie's name became synonymous with the romantic ballad. His songwriting and singing talents led to the recording of numerous award-winning songs. From 1977 to 1985, the popular singer had a song reach number one on the pop charts each year, making him the only performer in music history to do so consecutively for nine years. In total, he won three Grammy Awards, six American Music Awards, one People's Choice Award, and one Academy Award. Richie enjoyed phenomenal success as a performer in the 1980's and his romantic lyrics defined romance for a generation of people.

Further Reading

Nathan, David. *Lionel Richie: An Illustrated Biography.* New York: McGraw-Hill, 1985.

Richie, Lionel. *Lionel Richie Anthology.* Milwaukee, Wis.: Hal Leonard, 2004.

Bernadette Zbicki Heiney

See also Academy Awards; African Americans; Jackson, Michael; Music; Pop music; Shields, Brooke; Springsteen, Bruce; USA for Africa.

■ Richler, Mordecai

Identification Canadian author
Born January 27, 1931; Montreal, Quebec
Died July 3, 2001; Montreal, Quebec

Richler wrote two acclaimed novels and served as a critic of Canadian culture and politics, particularly within Quebec.

During the 1980's, Mordecai Richler published two well-received novels, *Joshua Then and Now* (1980)

and *Solomon Gursky Was Here* (1989), as well as the popular children's book *Jacob Two-Two and the Dinosaur* (1987) and the book for the failed musical adaptation of his earlier novel *The Apprenticeship of Duddy Kravitz* (1959). *Joshua Then and Now* was a modest success, but it was *Solomon Gursky Was Here*, released nine years later, that had the greater literary impact. The picaresque novel about an alcoholic Rhodes scholar who spends his life chasing down leads related to Solomon Gursky, the deceased middle brother of a trio of bootleggers, is considered to be one of Richler's best.

While Richler was popular with Americans—Morton Ritts of *Maclean's* noted that he was "the one to whom editors of *The New York Times* and *The Atlantic* turn when they want a Canadian perspective on this country"—some Canadians took offense at that perspective. After a September 29, 1985, *New York Times* sports piece on Wayne Gretzky in which Richler described Edmonton in an unflattering light, columnists and city dwellers cried foul, with Canadian publisher Mel Hurtig complaining that "Richler now makes his living knocking Canada." Perhaps this sentiment was felt most in Richler's native Quebec, where he frequently commented on the Parti Québécois and strained English-French relations in the province. In the essay "Language (and Other) Problems" published in *Home Sweet Home* (1984), Richler critiqued the province's Charter of the French Language (Bill 101), noting that the government's zealous attempts to eradicate the English language from any signage—going so far as to confiscate fifteen thousand Dunkin' Donuts bags—made Quebec a laughingstock internationally and threatened to destroy Montreal's unique cultural balance. In a summary of the 1980's he wrote for *Maclean's*, Richler decried the underfunded hospitals and universities in Quebec and voiced his displeasure over the government's concerns over bilingual signage: "Soon otherwise grown men will be out measuring the size of English letters on indoor commercial signs, crying perfidy if they measure a tad over half-size." Richler's voice in the English-French debate in Canada increased in the following decade.

Impact Despite his literary achievements in the decade, for many Richler is remembered in the 1980's for his role as the critical voice of Canada for American and Canadian publications such as *The New York Times*, *GQ*, *Newsweek*, *Esquire*, and *Maclean's*. Many of the essays he wrote during this time can be found in compilations such as *Home Sweet Home, Dispatches from the Sporting Life* (2002), and *Broadsides* (1990).

Further Reading

Richler, Mordecai. *Dispatches from the Sporting Life.* Guilford, Conn.: Lyons Press, 2002.

_____. "The Eighties: Decade in a Hurry." *Maclean's*, December, 30, 1989.

_____. *Home Sweet Home: My Canadian Album.* New York: Alfred A. Knopf, 1984.

Julie Elliott

See also Children's literature; Literature in Canada; Meech Lake Accord; Quebec English sign ban; Quebec referendum of 1980.

■ Ride, Sally

Identification Scientist and pioneer in the U.S. space shuttle program

Born May 26, 1951; Encino, California

Ride was the first American—and the world's third—female astronaut to fly in outer space. Only two other women, Soviets Valentina Tereshkova and Svetlana Savitskaya, preceded her.

In 1978, Sally Ride became one of six women in the National Aeronautics and Space Administration's (NASA) eighth astronaut class. There was some initial animosity within the program when women were chosen, but Ride found NASA's attitude toward her and her fellow female trainees straightforward.

Ride was involved in the first three flights of the space shuttle *Columbia.* Her first assignment was as mission specialist. Her tasks included working as capsule communicator (capcom), the only person on Earth allowed to talk directly to the space shuttle crew during a mission. Ride was the first woman to hold this position. She also participated in the development of the remote manipulator system (RMS), the robotic arm used on the space shuttle.

Ride's rigorous training for space included running four miles a day, playing tennis and volleyball, and weightlessness training. She also received training in all shuttle systems, including mechanical, electrical, and propulsion. NASA believed that it was important that each astronaut learn the tasks of the other crew members, in case of an emergency.

Sally Ride. (National Aeronautics and Space Administration)

On June 18, 1983, Ride became the first American woman in space while aboard the space shuttle *Challenger* on mission STS-7. One of her jobs during the six-day trip was to deploy two satellites into space using the RMS. She also worked on forty experiments, including studying the effect of weightlessness on carpenter ants.

Challenger returned to Earth on June 24, 1983. Ride received a lot of media attention before and after the historic mission. She also received a number of honors and awards and even made a guest appearance on the popular children's television series *Sesame Street.*

As Ride was preparing for her third flight, the shuttle *Challenger* exploded on January 28, 1986, killing all seven crew members on board. She was appointed to the Rogers Commission to investigate the explosion. Following the tragedy and her work on the commission, Ride decided that she was not ready to fly again and retired in 1987, having logged more than 343 hours in space. She took a teaching position at Stanford University, then went on to become a physics professor at the University of California, San Diego.

Impact By recruiting six female candidates, NASA demonstrated its commitment to adding women to the space program. Women proved that they could work as efficiently and effectively as their male counterparts. Though Ride did not like being the center of the media's attention, she understood the importance of being the first American woman in space and how that would affect the future of the space program.

Further Reading

Fox, Mary Virginia. *Women Astronauts Aboard the Shuttle.* New York: Simon & Schuster, 1984.

Holden, Henry M. *Pioneering Astronaut Sally Ride.* Berkeley Heights, N.J.: Enslow, 2004.

Orr, Tamara. *Sally Ride, the First American Woman in Space.* New York: Rosen, 2004.

Maryanne Barsotti

See also *Challenger* disaster; Feminism; Science and technology; Space exploration; Space shuttle program.

■ Rivera, Geraldo

Identification American broadcast journalist
Born July 4, 1943; New York, New York

A controversial but accomplished broadcast journalist during the 1980's, Rivera became a popular talk show host.

Born Gerald Michael Riviera, Geraldo Rivera was raised by his Puerto Rican father and Jewish mother in West Babylon, New York. He earned a law degree from Brooklyn Law School in 1969 and a journalism degree from Columbia University. During the 1970's, he worked as an investigative reporter for WABC-TV in New York City and hosted the late-night television show *Good Night, America.* From 1978 to 1985, he worked as a special correspondent for the American Broadcasting Company (ABC) news magazine *20/20.* His subjective, often opinionated style of reporting made him popular with television audiences. Rivera also won numerous awards for his reporting and became a role model for the Latino community.

In 1986, Rivera hosted the documentary *The Mystery of Al Capone's Vault,* a live television broadcast in which he opened what was purported to be Al Capone's vault and found nothing. Although Rivera was embarrassed by the outcome, his popularity soared. Under contract with Tribune Entertainment, Rivera filmed seven additional documentaries during the 1980's, including *American Vice: The Doping of America* (1986), *Innocence Lost: The Erosion of American Childhood* (1987), *Sons of Scarface: The New Mafia* (1987), and *Murder: Live from Death Row* (1988).

In 1987, Rivera began hosting and producing the syndicated daytime talk show *Geraldo.* The show, which remained on the air until 1998, often featured controversial guests and tabloid theatrics. One of his most famous episodes involved neo-Nazi skinheads and black and Jewish activists and ended in an on-air brawl, with Rivera receiving a broken nose. The talk show continued to provide Rivera with a forum to share his personal opinions with the American public. The show also joined a growing roster of other talk shows, such as *The Jerry Springer Show* and *Sally Jessy Raphael,* which became known in the television industry as "trash TV." The controversial and extreme nature of Rivera's talk show, however, earned him the reputation as the "King of Tabloid TV."

Impact During the 1980's, Rivera became a popular investigative reporter and broadcast journalist known mostly for his unorthodox style of subjective reporting. While he won numerous awards for his work and became a role model for Latinos, many of his professional peers were critical of his opinionated reporting style. As his popularity grew with the American public, Rivera catered to this fame by moving away from legitimate reporting and toward entertainment reporting through a series of investigative documentaries and, eventually, to his successful talk show. In the late 1990's, Rivera returned to reporting as a war correspondent for FOX News.

Further Reading

Langer, John. *Tabloid Television: Popular Journalism and the "Other News."* New York: Routledge, 1997.

Rivera, Geraldo. *Exposing Myself.* New York: Bantam Books, 1991.

Bernadette Zbicki Heiney

See also Cable television; Journalism; Talk shows; Television.

■ Roberts v. United States Jaycees

Identification Supreme Court decision
Date Decided on July 3, 1984

The Supreme Court determined that the application of the Minnesota Human Rights Act, which prohibited gender discrimination in many public contexts, to the Junior Chamber of Commerce did not violate the group's right to freedom of association.

During the 1970's, the Minnesota Junior Chamber of Commerce (Jaycees) began to admit women as members, in violation of the national Jaycees' by-laws. When the national organization threatened to revoke the charter of the state organization, the Minnesota Jaycees complained to state authorities that the national organization's actions were in violation of the Minnesota Human Rights Act, which prohibited gender discrimination in places of public

Associate Justice William J. Brennan delivered the opinion of the Court in Roberts v. United States Jaycees. *(Library of Congress)*

accommodation. When state authorities, including the Minnesota Supreme Court, agreed with this conclusion, the U.S. Jaycees appealed to the U.S. Supreme Court, arguing that the state's actions infringed on its freedom of association.

The Court, in an opinion written by Justice William J. Brennan, distinguished between two forms of freedom of association—one centering on intimate activities such as marriage and procreation, and the other finding its roots in freedom of expression. The Court concluded that the freedom of association claimed by the Jaycees was expressive in nature. The Court had previously recognized that freedom of expression included a freedom to associate with those with whom one shared common expressive purposes. This freedom, however, was not absolute. According to the Court's opinion, it could be infringed upon if the government had a sufficiently compelling purpose for doing so, unrelated to the suppression of speech, and could not accomplish this purpose in a manner less restrictive of freedom of association. The Court concluded that the state's interest in prohibiting gender discrimination was sufficiently compelling to justify overriding the Jaycees' freedom of association and that the state had no means of accomplishing this end in a manner less restrictive of the Jaycees' freedom of association.

Justices William H. Rehnquist and Sandra Day O'Connor concurred in this result. Chief Justice Warren E. Burger and Justice Harry A. Blackmun did not participate in the case. In a separate concurring opinion, Justice O'Connor argued that the Jaycees were more a commercial form of association than an expressive one and that their rights to freedom of association could be more readily regulated than if their identity were less commercial in nature.

Impact In the last quarter of the twentieth century, the U.S. Supreme Court had several occasions to resolve conflicts between efforts to prevent certain forms of discrimination against individuals and constitutionally protected rights such as freedom of religion, speech, and association. The Court's decisions in this area generally shielded groups whose identities were closely associated with the exercise of these freedoms from the effect of antidiscrimination laws. It permitted, however, the enforcement of antidiscrimination laws against groups that could be characterized—as Justice O'Connor did in this case—as more commercial in nature.

Further Reading

Rosenblum, Nancy L. *Membership and Morals: The Personal Uses of Pluralism in America.* Rev. ed. Princeton, N.J.: Princeton University Press, 2000.

Warren, Mark E. *Democracy and Association.* Princeton, N.J.: Princeton University Press, 2001.

Timothy L. Hall

See also   Feminism; Glass ceiling; Supreme Court decisions; Women's rights.

■ Robertson, Pat

Identification   American television personality and conservative political candidate and activist

Born   March 22, 1930; Lexington, Virginia

Using his prominence as the founder of the first Christian television network and the host of a conservative Christian talk show, Robertson led many conservative Christians to become involved in the political process during the 1980's.

Pat Robertson came to prominence as a television personality in the United States in the 1970's, the decade after he founded the Christian Broadcasting Network (CBN) and began hosting its most influential television program, *The 700 Club*, a Christian talk show. In the 1980's, Robertson, along with many other conservative Christians, turned his attention to politics. In his book *America's Dates with Destiny* (1986), he argued that America had drifted from the Christian and moral values that had animated its founding. Two years later, Robertson made an unsuccessful attempt to capture the Republican nomination for president of the United States. He lost to George H. W. Bush, who won the Republican primary and went on to win the presidential election of 1988. Undeterred by the loss, Robertson thereafter turned his attention to grassroots political action by founding the Christian Coalition in 1989. The purpose of this organization, he explained, was "to mobilize Christians—one precinct at a time, one community at a time—until once again we are the head and not the tail, and at the top rather than the bottom of our political system."

Pat Robertson celebrates placing second in the Iowa caucuses, ahead of Vice President George H. W. Bush, on February 9, 1988. (AP/Wide World Photos)

The Christian Coalition remained active in American politics during the following decade. Robertson himself continued to use his television prominence to comment on American political and cultural affairs; however, by the beginning of the twenty-first century the influence of conservative Christians such as Robertson in the American political process appeared to have waned somewhat from its height in the 1980's.

Impact   During the first three quarters of the twentieth century, conservative Christians tended to avoid interaction with the American political process. In the last quarter of the century, however, they reemerged on the national political stage. Along with televangelist Jerry Falwell, Pat Robertson was a key architect of conservative Christian activism. This activism was at its height during the 1980's and continued into the twenty-first century. Robertson never claimed the political prize to which he aspired, the presidency of the United States, but he had a profound impact on the American political process by persuading many conservative believers that they should be active participants in this process.

Further Reading

Boston, Rob. *The Most Dangerous Man in America? Pat Robertson and the Rise of the Christian Coalition.* Amherst, N.Y.: Prometheus Books, 1996.

Harrell, David Edwin. *Pat Robertson: A Personal, Religious, and Political Portrait.* San Francisco: Harper & Row, 1987.

Robertson, Pat, with Jamie Buckingham. *The Autobiography of Pat Robertson: Shout It from the Housetops!* Rev. ed. South Plainfield, N.J.: Bridge, 1995.

Timothy L. Hall

See also Conservatism in U.S. politics; Elections in the United States, 1988; Falwell, Jerry; Moral Majority; Religion and spirituality in the United States; Televangelism.

■ *RoboCop*

Identification Science-fiction action film
Director Paul Verhoeven (1938-   )
Date Released July 17, 1987

RoboCop, *a violent social satire on big-business capitalism, features a cyborg police officer seeking revenge while trying to regain his own humanity in gritty, near-future Detroit.*

At the time of its release, Orion Pictures' *RoboCop* was one of the most graphically violent American films ever to make it to theaters. The Motion Picture Association of America originally gave the controversial film an X rating, but Dutch director Paul Verhoeven trimmed enough graphic violence to earn it a strong R rating. The film was a box-office success, grossing almost $54 million in the United States.

The film is set in a futuristic, dystopian Detroit where crime, drug abuse, and unemployment are pervasive. The city employs the megacorporation Omni Consumer Products (OCP) to take over the police department, replacing traditional patrolmen and methods with new, high-technology weaponry to cleanse and eradicate "Old Detroit" and to create a utopia called "Delta City." Police officer Alex J. Murphy (Peter Weller) transfers to an exceptionally dangerous precinct in Old Detroit and is viciously killed by a gang of thugs on his first assignment. He is officially dead, but OCP finds him to be a "prime candidate" for its experiments, and it fuses his body with cybernetics to create the cyborg RoboCop. RoboCop inflicts swift justice on the lawbreakers of Detroit, and crime is reduced to a standstill. However, soon RoboCop begins dreaming of his former life and discovers that his killers are working for the president of OCP. He ultimately turns against both his murderers and his creators, killing them all, and regains a semblance of his former identity.

Verhoeven brought to *RoboCop* a European sensibility previously unseen in American action films. *RoboCop* is not only an incredibly violent film but also an intelligent social satire, especially toward the overarching economic policies of the time, known as Reaganomics, which resulted in a recession in the early 1980's and in a drastic reduction in social services. The villains in the film, members and employees of OCP, represent big business, and the downtrodden denizens of Old Detroit clearly represent the middle and lower classes. RoboCop acts as a champion for the common people, overthrowing the evil empire of OCP, and as a liaison between technology and humankind. There is also a current of criticism running through the film regarding new technology's trend of dehumanizing individuals and eroding conventional social structures, of which RoboCop himself is a prime example.

Impact *RoboCop* raised the bar for shocking and graphic violence in American cinema, formally launched Verhoeven's career as an American director, and spawned two less successful and poorly received sequels, neither directed by Verhoeven: *RoboCop 2* (1990) and *RoboCop 3* (1993).

Further Reading

Duncan, Paul, and Douglas Keesey. *Paul Verhoeven.* Los Angeles: Taschen, 2005.

Van Scheers, Rob. *Paul Verhoeven.* Boston: Faber & Faber, 1997.

Alan C. Haslam

See also Action films; Blade Runner; Consumerism; Cyberpunk literature; Film in the United States;

Income and wages in the United States; Information age; Reaganomics; Science-fiction films; Special effects; Unemployment in the United States.

■ Robots

Definition   Machines devised to carry out a series of actions automatically or with minimum external impulse

The advancements made with robots during the 1980's led to the development of robots that could replace humans in performing many routine and dangerous jobs with speed and precision.

By the late 1970's, new technologies were emerging that made the production of personal mobile robots feasible. The development of computer processing technology and storage in the 1980's was the vital link needed to implement simple and more complex actions in robots. The processing power necessary to develop artificial intelligence became available in smaller packages. Developing software interpreted signals from sensors that controlled where the robot was going and what it was doing. Through the software, robots could interact to some extent with humans in a reasonable, predictable manner.

In 1983, a robot dubbed TOPO-I was released by Androbot. TOPO-I was designed as a mobile extension of the home computer. Standing three feet tall, it could be moved with a joystick or with software control. Improved versions of TOPO-I in the 1980's included a bidirectional infrared link to the host computer, some speech support, and an onboard vacuum cleaner.

The Heathkit HERO robot of the mid-1980's contained sensors for sound, visible and infrared light, and motion detection. It utilized an 8-bit 6808 processor. A significant improvement in the HERO series was the HERO 2000, a multitasking robot that had a robotic arm and utilized eleven 8-bit peripheral microprocessors. Each microprocessor performed separate tasks and activities that were all coordinated by the main processor.

The breakthrough robot of the 1980's was the Gemini. It stood four feet tall and weighed seventy pounds. Three onboard computers, all CMOS chip devices, provided artificial intelligence, voice and speech synthesis, and propulsion control. The robot could respond to voice commands and be navigated by using infrared beams. During the 1980's, the public perception of robots was heightened in numerous television episodes and films, including the Star Trek and Star Wars series, *The Terminator* (1984), and *RoboCop* (1987).

Impact   Personal mobile robots built in the 1980's became the prototypes for the evolution of robots in the 1990's and into the twenty-first century. During the 1980's, the evolution of computer processing technology led to mobile robots that possessed artificial intelligence. Mobile robots can free workers from dirty, heavy, dangerous, and mundane labor. The implementation of robots by industrial companies provides improved management control, better productivity, and consistent production of high-quality products. The military uses robots to clear mine fields and survey battlefields. About a dozen small robots were used as part of the rescue and recovery operations after the 2001 World Trade Center disaster. Personal mobile robots are being designed to provide entertainment, education, communications, security, and other useful functions.

Further Reading

Gutkind, Lee. *Almost Human: Making Robots Think.* New York: W. W. Norton, 2006.

Patnaik, Srikanta. *Innovations in Robot Mobility and Control.* New York: Springer, 2006.

Spong, Mark W., and Mathukumalli Vidyasagar. *Robot Modeling and Control.* Hoboken, N.J.: John Wiley & Sons, 2006.

Alvin K. Benson

See also   Apple Computer; Computers; Inventions; *RoboCop*; Science and technology; Science-fiction films; Space exploration.

■ Rock and Roll Hall of Fame

Definition   A repository dedicated to the rich heritage of rock and roll
Date   Created in 1983

The establishment of this institution exemplified the trend toward the preservation of heritage that marked the 1980's.

In 1983, Ahmet Ertegün, cofounder of Atlantic Records, decided to establish an organization that would recognize those who had created rock-and-roll music and those who had propelled it to the

The Rock and Roll Hall of Fame, designed by I. M. Pei. (Jason Pratt/cc-by-a-2.0)

height of popularity. After meeting with attorney Suzan Evans about the concept, Ertegün brought together a group of music industry professionals including *Rolling Stone* publisher Jann Wenner, attorney Allen Grubman, and a handful of record executives. After numerous discussions, a nominating committee was formed to select inductees into the Rock and Roll Hall of Fame. The criteria established by the group included three categories for induction: performer, nonperformer (including producers, journalists, and music industry executives), and early influences.

Once the criteria were established, the search began for a home for a major museum that would include a library, archives, educational facilities, a performance venue, and a permanent museum collection of rock-and-roll memorabilia. The first location was to be a brownstone in New York City, but other cities began to submit requests to be considered for the honor. Philadelphia, New Orleans, San Francisco, Memphis, Chicago, and Cleveland all made offers to the Rock and Roll Hall of Fame Foundation.

The first inductees were honored at a dinner at the Waldorf-Astoria Hotel in New York City on January 23, 1986. The inaugural class of the Rock and Roll Hall of Fame performers included Chuck Berry, James Brown, Ray Charles, Sam Cooke, Fats Domino, the Everly Brothers, Buddy Holly, Jerry Lee Lewis, Elvis Presley, and Little Richard. Robert Johnson, Jimmie Rodgers, and Jimmy Yancey were honored in the early influences category, and the first inductees in the nonperformer category were legendary producer Sam Phillips and disc jockey Alan Freed, who was credited with first using the term "rock and roll."

On May 5, 1986, the foundation announced that

1980's Inductees into the Rock and Roll Hall of Fame

Year	Performer	Early Influence	Lifetime Achievement	Nonperformer
1986	Chuck Berry James Brown Ray Charles Sam Cooke Fats Domino The Everly Brothers Buddy Holly Jerry Lee Lewis Elvis Presley Little Richard	Robert Johnson Jimmie Rodgers Jimmy Yancey	John Hammond	Alan Freed Sam Phillips
1987	The Coasters Eddie Cochran Bo Diddley Aretha Franklin Marvin Gaye Bill Haley B. B. King Clyde McPhatter Ricky Nelson Roy Orbison Carl Perkins Smokey Robinson Big Joe Turner Muddy Waters Jackie Wilson	Louis Jordan T-Bone Walker Hank Williams		Leonard Chess Ahmet Ertegun Jerry Leiber and Mike Stoller Jerry Wexler
1988	The Beach Boys The Beatles The Drifters Bob Dylan The Supremes	Woody Guthrie Lead Belly Les Paul		Berry Gordy, Jr.
1989	Dion Otis Redding The Rolling Stones The Temptations Stevie Wonder	The Ink Spots Bessie Smith The Soul Stirrers		Phil Spector

Cleveland, Ohio, had been selected as the permanent home for the Rock and Roll Hall of Fame and Museum. Once the site had been selected, an exhaustive search was held for a designer, and world-renowned architect I. M. Pei was chosen. He created a building that reflected the energy of rock and roll. The hallmark of the building was a dramatic triangular glass "tent" that served as the main entrance to the museum. The groundbreaking ceremonies for the museum took place on June 7, 1993. The Rock and Roll Hall of Fame opened its doors on September 2, 1995, with artifacts of John Lennon donated by Yoko Ono serving as one of the primary collections.

Impact   The Rock and Roll Hall of Fame Foundation created an enormously successful location for the preservation, commemoration, and promotion of rock and roll. It provides a place for the narrative of rock and roll's history.

Further Reading

Juchartz, Larry, and Christy Rishoi. "Rock Collection: History and Ideology at the Rock and Roll Hall of Fame." *Review of Education, Pedagogy, and Cultural Studies* 19, nos. 2/3 (May, 1997): 311-332.

Manzel, Kevin. "Cleveland's New Museum Celebrates Rock and Roll." *Historian* 58, no. 1 (Autumn, 1995): 29.

Amanda Bahr-Evola

See also   Architecture; Lennon, John; Music; Pei, I. M.; Pop music; Women in rock music.

■ Rose, Pete

Identification   Major League Baseball player and manager

Born   April 14, 1941; Cincinnati, Ohio

In 1985, Pete Rose broke Major League Baseball's career record for hits, but four years later he was banned from baseball for life for gambling.

The 1980's were a decade of triumph and tragedy for baseball great Pete Rose. As a member of the Philadelphia Phillies, he led the National League in hits in 1981 and played in the World Series in 1980 and 1983. The Phillies won the series in 1980, marking the third time in his career that Rose had played on a world championship team.

As the decade opened, Rose, at the age of thirty-nine, began an assault on one of baseball's most important career records: the career hit record held by National Baseball Hall of Famer Ty Cobb. Rose broke the National League career hit record, held by Stan Musial, in 1981. Playing for the Montreal Expos in 1984, Rose recorded his four thousandth career hit. Later that season,

he returned to his beloved Cincinnati Reds, with whom he had begun his Major League Baseball career, as a player-manager. Rose topped Cobb's mark of 4,192 hits on September 11, 1985, in Cincinnati. He retired after the 1986 season with a total of 4,256 hits and a .303 career batting average. He was a sure bet for baseball's hall of fame.

After his playing career ended, Rose encountered problems as manager of the Reds. He did not bring a pennant to Cincinnati; in his first three full seasons as manager, the team finished in second place. During the 1988 season, Rose was suspended for thirty days after an argument and shoving match with an umpire. Even more serious problems surfaced during the next season. Rumors circulated that Rose had a significant gambling problem, that he had encumbered substantial illegal gambling debts, and that he had even bet on baseball. Since the great World Series betting scandal of 1919, Major League Baseball had implemented a zero-tolerance policy for illegal gambling. Rose denied the allegations and threatened to sue Major League Baseball for besmirching his character. In late August, 1989, baseball commissioner Bart Giamatti confronted Rose about his gambling issues. Giamatti agreed not to publicize the evidence that his office had gathered about Rose's gambling provided that Rose agreed to drop his lawsuit and agreed to a lifetime ban from

Montreal Expo Pete Rose hits his four thousandth career hit, a double, while playing against the Philadelphia Phillies on April 13, 1984. (AP/Wide World Photos)

Major League Baseball—meaning that Rose could never again play or manage and that he would not be eligible for membership in the National Baseball Hall of Fame. Although he claimed not to have gambled illegally, Rose agreed to the commissioner's deal and left the game that he loved.

Impact   The gambling allegations that surrounded Rose at the end of his career damaged the reputation of one of baseball's best and most colorful players. Baseball fans and players continue to debate whether Rose's lifetime ban from Major League Baseball—and from the National Baseball Hall of Fame—should continue. A week after imposing the ban, Giamatti died, but his successors have kept the lifetime ban on Rose in place.

Further Reading

Rose, Pete, and Rick Hill. *My Prison Without Bars.* Emmaus, Pa.: Rodale Press, 2004.

Shatzkin, Mike, ed. *The Ballplayers.* New York: Arbor House, 1990.

James Tackach

See also   Baseball; Baseball strike of 1981; Sports.

■ Run-D.M.C.

Identification   African American rap/hip-hop group

Date   First single released in 1983

In addition to bringing hip-hop into the cultural mainstream, Run-D.M.C. is responsible for one of the most successful rap-rock crossover songs of the 1980's.

Rap/hip-hop juggernaut Run-D.M.C.'s lyricists, Joseph "Run" Simmons and Darryl "D.M.C." McDaniels, met while growing up in Hollis, Queens, and started performing together in high school during the late 1970's. Following the addition of fellow Brooklyn native and turntable wizard Jam Master Jay several years later, Run-D.M.C. began recording and releasing albums.

After signing with rap and hip-hop label Profile Records, Run-D.M.C. released a self-titled debut album in early 1984. The breakthrough single "It's Like That" helped propel sales of the album, which was certified gold. Although groups such as the Sugarhill Gang had pioneered rap, Run-D.M.C.'s

unique, interlaced lyrical style helped define the growing genre and established key vocal and musical components that became the backbone of early rap and hip-hop. Other groups and solo artists quickly followed, but Run-D.M.C. undoubtedly set the bar in the early 1980's. The group also separated itself from its contemporaries visually, with each member dressed in a black fedora hat, laceless white Adidas shoes, and a leather jacket—an ensemble that would quickly become the group's trademark wardrobe.

Less than a year after *Run-D.M.C.*, the group's sophomore effort, *King of Rock*, was released, charting even higher and selling more copies than its predecessor. The trio was enjoying moderate success both on radio and on the fledgling cable network MTV, exposure that helped increase Run-D.M.C.'s fan base. However, the success was moderate compared to the superstardom that the group would experience upon release of the third album, 1986's triple platinum *Raising Hell.*

In addition to the popular singles "It's Tricky" and "My Adidas," the album's—and group's—most successful hit was "Walk This Way," originally recorded during the 1970's by the veteran rock band Aerosmith. This was more than just a traditional cover song, however; Aerosmith's lead singer Steven Tyler and guitarist Joe Perry collaborated on the track and music video with Run-D.M.C., creating the first rap-rock crossover. The success of the song was unparalleled; not only was there significant radio airplay, but the accompanying music video was also in heavy rotation on MTV. The album gave the group its highest commercial success to date, reaching number one on the *Billboard* Top R&B/Hip-Hop Albums chart.

While it seemed impossible to match the colossal success of *Raising Hell*, Run-D.M.C.'s fourth album, 1988's *Tougher than Leather*, was issued to critical and commercial acclaim. The album, benefiting from the hit single "Mary, Mary," eventually reached number two on the *Billboard* Top R&B/Hip-Hop Album chart and was certified platinum. The decade ended with the group in the studio, recording 1990's *Back from Hell.*

Impact   Although the group's members would achieve success in later decades both collectively and individually, Run-D.M.C.'s accomplishments during the 1980's cemented the group's status as rap/hip-hop icons. The group's popularity also brought rap and hip-hop into the cultural mainstream, one of Run-D.M.C.'s greatest accomplishments.

Further Reading

McDaniels, Darryl, with Bruce Haring. *King of Rock: Respect, Responsibility, and My Life with Run-D.M.C.* New York: St. Martin's Press, 2001.

Ro, Ronin. *Raising Hell: The Reign, Ruin, and Redemption of Run-D.M.C. and Jam Master Jay.* New York: Amistad, 2005.

Matthew Schmitz

See also   African Americans; Hip-hop and rap; MTV; Music; Music videos; Public Enemy.

■ Ryan, Nolan

Identification   Professional baseball player
Born   January 31, 1947; Refugio, Texas

Because of his record-breaking accomplishments as a baseball player, Ryan is recognized as one of the greatest pitchers in the history of Major League Baseball.

After graduating from high school in 1965, Nolan Ryan signed a contract to pitch for the New York Mets. After pitching for the Mets from 1966 to 1971, he played for the California Angels from 1972 to 1979. He pitched two no-hitters in 1973 and two more in 1974. Ryan became the first professional baseball player to sign a million-dollar contract when he joined the Houston Astros in 1980. Ryan, whose fastballs often exceeded 100 miles per hour, was dubbed the "Ryan Express" by the media and other players.

In 1981, Ryan led the National League with a 1.69 earned run average, and he set the Major League Baseball (MLB) record for no-hitters when he pitched his fifth on September 26, 1981. He registered his second career postseason win with a victory over the Los Angeles Dodgers and Fernando Valenzuela in the National League division series. On April 27, 1983, Ryan established the MLB career record for strikeouts when he recorded number 3,509, surpassing the mark long held by Walter Johnson. After battling injuries during two frustrating seasons in 1984 and 1985, Ryan returned to top form in 1986 and struck out 194 batters in 178 innings. He earned his 250th career victory on August 27, 1986. Although he had a poor 8-16 record in 1987, he struck out 270 hitters in 212 innings and became the only pitcher in MLB history to register 2,000 strikeouts in each of the American and National Leagues.

At the end of the 1988 season, Ryan signed a contract to play for the Texas Rangers. On June 3, 1989, he pitched his eleventh career one-hitter. He became the only pitcher in MLB history with 5,000 strikeouts when he struck out Rickey Henderson on August 22, 1989. During the 1989 campaign, he recorded 301 strikeouts, which was the sixth time that he had more than 300 strikeouts in one season. While playing for the Rangers, Ryan pitched his sixth no-hitter in 1990 and recorded number seven in 1991.

Houston Astro Nolan Ryan pitches against the Chicago Cubs on August 23, 1984. Ryan struck out twelve batters during the game. (AP/Wide World Photos)

Impact   After twenty-seven years as a major-league pitcher, Ryan retired in 1993 with an amazing fifty-three MLB records, including 5,714 strikeouts and seven no-hitters. He was selected as a Major League All-Star eight times. He posted a 324-292 win-loss record. His jersey number was retired by three teams—the Astros, Angels, and Rangers. In 1999, Ryan was elected to the National Baseball Hall of Fame, receiving the second-highest percentage of votes in history after Tom Seaver. That same year, *Sporting News* placed him on the list of the 100 Greatest Baseball Players. In 2003, he was inducted into the Hall of Fame of the Texas Rangers.

Further Reading

Anderson, Ken. *Nolan Ryan: Texas Fastball to Cooperstown.* Austin, Tex.: Eakin Press, 1999.

Kramer, Sydelle. *Baseball's Greatest Pitchers.* New York: Random House, 1992.

Ryan, Nolan, and Jerry B. Jenkins. *Miracle Man: Nolan Ryan, the Autobiography.* Dallas: Word Publishing Group, 2004.

Alvin K. Benson

See also   Baseball; Brett, George; Gibson, Kirk; Hershiser, Orel; Rose, Pete; Ryan, Nolan; Sports; Valenzuela, Fernando.

S

◼ *St. Elsewhere*

Identification Television drama series
Date Aired from October 26, 1982, to May 25, 1988

Unlike some previous medical shows that centered on patients, St. Elsewhere *focused on doctors and nurses, who were portrayed as flawed and fallible. One of the major ensemble dramas of the decade, the show often emphasized the medical professionals' career and personal problems and portrayed the workplace as a surrogate family.*

Much like *Hill Street Blues* (1981-1987), *St. Elsewhere* was an ensemble drama with a large cast. There were often four story lines in an episode, and some plots and subplots continued through several episodes. The show treated medical ailments not generally discussed on television or even "polite" society, such as impotence and addiction. In December, 1983, it became the first prime-time drama to focus on an AIDS patient.

The primary characters, each of whom functioned in various ways as a role model, were three veteran physicians: Dr. Donald Westphall, played by Ed Flanders; Dr. Mark Craig, played by William Daniels; and Dr. Daniel Auschlander, played by Norman Lloyd. The show featured a dozen more central characters, including nurses, first- and second-year residents, and other hospital staff. Additional characters for each episode, some of whom were recurring, were often played by actors celebrated for their work in film and television. *St. Elsewhere* began the careers of many major television and film actors and writers. Actors Mark Harmon, Howie Mandel, and Alfre Woodard went on to success in film and television, and both Denzel Washington and Helen Hunt won Academy Awards. Viewers were attracted to the realism of the show, set at a deteriorating hospital, St. Eligius, in Boston. Compelling plots often explored ethical dilemmas. The series was also characterized by dark humor that mixed the real with the surreal—and by a series of in-jokes and puns. In 1993, the editors of *TV Guide* named *St. Elsewhere* the best drama of all time.

Impact *St. Elsewhere* had the good fortune to be produced at a time when networks were beginning to care as much about the demographics of their viewship as they did about sheer numbers. The advent of cable television and narrowcasting, in addition to more sophisticated audience analysis techniques, made targeted audiences with expensive tastes and disposable income desirable. The series had dismal ratings: It finished its first season ranked eighty-sixth out of ninety-eight prime-time shows. However, critics recognized the superior quality of its writing and acting, and it was renewed for a second season based on the fact that its viewship was composed disproportionately of yuppies. In addition to its quality, *St. Elsewhere*'s focus on the personal problems of the hospital staff appealed to the so-called me generation.

Over its six years, the show won thirteen Emmy Awards but never reached higher than forty-ninth place out of about one hundred shows in the Nielson ratings; it did, however, make a lot of money for the National Broadcasting Company (NBC). Advertisers seeking to reach wealthy baby boomers paid top dollar to air commercials during *St. Elsewhere*'s time slot. The final episode of *St. Elsewhere*, titled "The Last One," portrayed the entire six-year series as a fantasy, existing only in the imagination of an autistic child. This playful vision of television "reality" made media history.

Further Reading

Thompson, Robert J. *Television's Second Golden Age.* New York: Continuum, 1996.
Turow, Joseph. *Playing Doctor: Television, Storytelling, and Medical Power.* New York: Oxford University Press, 1989.

Marcia B. Dinneen

See also AIDS epidemic; *Hill Street Blues*; Television; Yuppies.

■ San Ysidro McDonald's massacre

The Event A seventy-seven-minute shooting rampage at a fast-food restaurant leaves twenty-one people dead

Date July 18, 1984

Place San Ysidro, California

Because of the high death toll, the familiarity of McDonald's, and the random nature of the attack—the killer had no grudge against the franchise or any of the customers, made no demands, and espoused no agenda—the San Ysidro McDonald's massacre stunned the nation, as it suggested a new kind of vulnerability.

A single gunman—a forty-one-year-old former security guard named James Oliver Huberty—killed twenty-one people and wounded nineteen others during his rampage at a McDonald's restaurant. The dead and wounded, Wednesday-afternoon patrons of the restaurant, included men, women, and children. Huberty, who had graduated with a degree in sociology from an Ohio Quaker college and worked as a welder for fourteen years, had drifted through various menial jobs before arriving in early 1984 in San Ysidro, California, two miles from the Mexican border. He worked as a condominium security guard but was fired ten days before the shootings. Concerned about his own depression and mood swings, Huberty contacted a mental health clinic but never received a call back.

On the morning of July 18, Huberty settled a minor traffic ticket. He took his wife and two children to a different McDonald's (they frequently ate there) and then to the San Diego Zoo. They left early because of the heat. After returning home, he casually informed his wife, "I'm going to hunt humans." He drove to the nearby restaurant, arriving around 4:00 P.M., with a nine-millimeter Browning automatic pistol in his belt and a twelve-gauge Winchester shotgun and a nine-millimeter Uzi semiautomatic machine gun across his shoulders. Once inside, he ordered the stunned patrons, mostly Hispanic, to get down on the floor and began executing them, showering the restaurant with indis-criminate gunfire. When the police arrived, they assumed that there were several shooters (Huberty fired more than 250 rounds). Shortly after 5:00 P.M., an employee escaped out a back door and informed the special weapons and tactics (SWAT) commandos that there was only one shooter and no hostages. Everyone else was either wounded or dead. The SWAT team reacted quickly, and sharpshooter Chuck Foster killed Huberty with a single chest shot.

Impact In the wake of the massacre, McDonald's razed the building and gave the land to the city, which built a community college on the site after erecting a memorial. Investigators never accounted for the rampage. Huberty's widow filed a lawsuit against both McDonald's and the Ohio factory where Huberty had welded. She claimed the food's monosodium glutamate and the factory's airborne toxins had slowly poisoned Huberty. Forensic pathologists, however, suggested Huberty might have been a paranoid schizophrenic.

A blood-spattered woman is led away from the scene of the San Ysidro McDonald's massacre on July 18, 1984. (AP/Wide World Photos)

The shootings were unprecedented in the United States. The closest parallel event had been the 1967 University of Texas clock tower shootings. As a result of the incident, police agencies reconsidered their policy of using violence only as a last resort in hostage situations. California politicians launched unprecedented (and largely unsuccessful) attempts to ban assault rifles. McDonald's set a standard for corporations victimized by random crime: It settled victims' injury claims, covered funeral costs, and provided counseling. Mental health facilities reevaluated overworked clinics, and forensic psychologists examined Huberty's antisocial behavior and his wife's failure to respond to his chilling comment before leaving for the restaurant.

Further Reading

Fox, James Alan, and Jack Levine. *Extreme Killing: Understanding Serial and Mass Murderers.* Thousand Oaks, Calif.: Sage, 2005.

Ramsland, Katherine. *Inside the Mind of Mass Murderers.* Westport, Conn.: Greenwood Press, 2005.

Joseph Dewey

See also Atlanta child murders; Crime; Goetz, Bernhard; Lucas, Henry Lee; Night Stalker case; Post office shootings; Tylenol murders.

■ Sauvé, Jeanne

Identification First woman governor-general of Canada

Born April 26, 1922; Prud'homme, Saskatchewan

Died January 26, 1993; Montreal, Quebec

Sauvé was a trailblazing figure in Canadian politics. She was the first woman governor-general and the first woman member of Parliament from Quebec to be appointed to the federal cabinet.

Jeanne Sauvé was the daughter of Charles Albert Benoît and Anna Vaillant Benoît. She was a brilliant student at a convent school and at the University of Ottawa, and she became active as a teenager in a reformist Catholic students' movement, Jeunesse Etudiante Catholique. As the organization's president at the age of twenty, she moved to Montreal and was soon involved with a group of reform-minded intellectuals that included future prime minister Pierre Trudeau. In 1948, Jeanne Benoît married Maurice Sauvé, who was later to serve as a federal cabinet minister in the 1960's. They went to Paris to study, and Jeanne worked in the youth section of the United Nations Educational, Social, and Cultural Organization (UNESCO); the couple returned to Montreal in 1952.

Sauvé worked as a broadcaster and journalist until 1972, when she was elected to the House of Commons as a Liberal member of Parliament from Ahuntsic, Montreal. She served in Prime Minister Trudeau's cabinet until 1979, first as minister of science and technology, then as minister of environment and communications. As Speaker of the House of Commons from 1980 to 1984 and the member of Parliament for Laval-des-Rapides, Sauvé was criticized for early parliamentary mistakes, and as governor-general from 1984 to 1990, she was attacked for security controls she imposed on public access to the grounds of Government House, Rideau Hall.

Sauvé's most important achievement was her appointment as the first woman governor-general. In that position, her patriotism often caused controversy, especially among Quebec nationalists, who were frustrated by her conviction that Quebec could better achieve fulfillment by personal effort, persuasion, and reform rather than by anger, which she felt only destroyed political and social structures. Opponents disliked her farewell New Year's message to the nation as governor-general at the end of 1989, believing it was an improper interference in politics, while supporters found it an eloquent appeal to keep Canada whole. Although Sauvé had delivered the same message at her installation as governor-general in 1984 and on many other occasions, she was criticized for expressing those sentiments at the height of debate over the Meech Lake plan for constitutional reform. In 1990, Sauvé founded the Jeanne Sauvé Youth Foundation.

Impact Sauvé argued her case for a united Canada at every opportunity. Her political vision went beyond Quebec. She traveled widely and believed that if young people were just given a chance to communicate with other young people—East and West, Catholic and Protestant, French and English—the problems that arose from fear and a sense of foreignness would quickly be eliminated. Shortly before her term as governor-general expired, Sauvé established in her name a $10 million youth foundation to bring together young leaders from around the world.

Further Reading

Sauvé, Jeanne. *Selected Decisions of Speaker Jeanne Sauvé, 1980-1984/Recueil de Décisions du Président Jeanne Sauvé, 1980-1984.* Ottawa: House of Commons Canada, 1994.

Wallin, Pamela, and Tim Kotcheff. *Jeanne Sauvé.* Toronto: CTV Television Network, 1989.

Woods, Shirley E. *Her Excellency Jeanne Sauvé.* Toronto: Macmillan of Canada, 1986.

Martin J. Manning

See also Canada Act of 1982; Canada and the British Commonwealth; Canada and the United States; Meech Lake Accord; Trudeau, Pierre.

■ Savings and loan (S&L) crisis

The Event Deregulation leads to a national banking crisis

The S&L crisis of the 1980's, during which one thousand savings and loan associations across the United States failed, was the nation's largest-ever financial scandal and cost American taxpayers and depositors billions of dollars in bailouts, contributing to large budget deficits and possibly to the 1990's recession.

The events leading up to the S&L crisis began during the Jimmy Carter and Ronald Reagan administrations in the late 1970's and the early 1980's, when the government removed many of the federal regulations on banks in a laissez-faire approach designed to make banks more competitive on the open market. Until then, federal law had required savings banks to maintain maximum interest rates on savings accounts and had prohibited them from issuing checking accounts or credit cards. Savings banks also could not make commercial or nonresidential real estate loans. On the other hand, unlike savings banks, commercial banks could, when necessary, borrow from the Federal Reserve Bank. Under deregulation, savings and commercial banks became almost indistinguishable. One result of this situation was an immediate increase in savings and loan institutions, or S&L's, which, under the supervision of the Federal Home Loan Bank Board and insured by the government's Federal Savings and Loan Insurance Corporation (FSLIC), could for the first time freely venture into lucrative commercial real estate markets and issue credit cards. By 1980, there were forty-six hundred such institutions in the United States. However, this trend quickly reversed when the S&L crisis began: By the end of the 1980's, there were only three thousand S&L's left, and five years later, that number had been reduced to less than two thousand.

The Crisis Looms Deregulation resulted in the growth of the U.S. economy during the 1980's, especially in the real estate sector. This growth enticed many of the underregulated S&L's to invest in high-risk, speculative ventures; it also tempted unscrupulous executives to defraud the regulatory agencies. Thus, when the real estate market faltered and fell, the S&L's found themselves in dire circumstances, because they owned real estate that was worth less than they had paid for it. Numerous bankruptcies ensued, and a great number of S&L depositors lost their money. Indeed, many lost their entire life savings.

In 1988, the Federal Home Loan Bank Board, whose function it was to supervise the S&L's, reported that fraud and insider abuse were the primary causes of the S&L failures. The head of Lincoln Savings of Phoenix, Arizona, Charles Keating, came to be known as the worst of the abusers. With full knowledge that Lincoln Savings was about to become insolvent, Keating removed $1 million from the S&L. He was eventually convicted of fraud, racketeering, and conspiracy and spent four and one-half years in prison. His conviction was then overturned, and he pleaded guilty to bankruptcy fraud to avoid a new trial. Before his conviction, however, Keating attempted to secure the aid of five U.S. senators in avoiding regulatory sanctions for his company. When the relationship between Keating and the senators became public, a national scandal ensued, and the senators became known as the Keating five.

Congress and various states attempted to respond to the S&L crisis during the early and mid-1980's, but their stopgap measures were insufficient. Eventually, in 1989, newly elected president George H. W. Bush engaged in a full-scale federal bailout of the industry. He estimated, to the shock of the country, that the government would have to spend between $50 billion and $60 billion. Congress enacted the Financial Institutions Reform, Recovery, and Enforcement Act (FIRREA). It ensured oversight of the S&L's and eliminated the Federal Home Loan Bank

Three members of the Keating five, from left, Senators John Glenn, Dennis DeConccini, and John McCain, arrive at the Senate Committee on Ethics hearing room in November, 1990. The five faced charges of peddling their influence to help Charles Keating, the man at the heart of the S&L crisis. (AP/Wide World Photos)

Board, which had failed to effectively supervise the S&L industry. The government also created the Office of Thrift Supervision (OTS).

Impact   The 1980's were characterized by deregulation of industry in general, which had been a major plank in President Reagan's platform and was at the center of his economic philosophy. The deregulation of the banking industry that led to the S&L crisis, however, was begun by Reagan's predecessor, Jimmy Carter. The ensuing financial disaster became a major threat to the U.S. financial system. The crisis severely dampened the Republican Party's enthusiasm for deregulation, and it changed the terms of the debate about financial policy in the United States.

It soon became clear that President Bush had grossly underestimated the cost of the S&L bailout. Economists have estimated the final cost of the crisis

at $600 billion. The savings and loan crisis, in turn, contributed to the severe budget deficits of the early 1990's, as well as to a major slowdown in both the finance and the real estate markets, and arguably to the 1990-1991 economic recession.

Further Reading

Adams, James R. *The Big Fix: Inside the S&L Scandal— How an Unholy Alliance of Politics and Money Destroyed America's Banking System.* New York: Wiley, 1990. The author, a well-known freelance journalist, examines the savings and loan crisis by looking at the history of American banking dating back to the Great Depression.

Barth, James, Susanne Trimeth, and Glenn Yago. *The Savings and Loan Crisis: Lessons from a Regulatory Failure.* New York: Springer, 2004. Claims to set the record straight about the poorly supervised banking practices of the 1980's that resulted in the S&L crisis. Includes the contributions of a diverse group of former regulators and scholars.

Calavita, Kitty. *Big Money Crime: Fraud and Politics in the Savings and Loan Crisis.* Berkeley: University of California Press, 1999. Attempts to addresses the often confusing and conflicting accounts of the 1980's S&L crisis and posits effective arguments about its causes.

Talley, Pat L. *The Savings and Loan Crisis: An Annotated Bibliography.* Westport, Conn.: Greenwood Press, 1993. Annotated bibliography that includes more than 360 titles on the S&L crisis published between 1980 and 1992. Includes scholarly and popular articles and should appeal to anyone researching the crisis. Includes dissertations and both author and subject indexes.

M. Casey Diana

See also   Bush, George H. W.; Business and the economy in the United States; Elections in the United States, 1988; Reagan, Ronald; Reaganomics; Scandals; *Wall Street.*

■ Scandals

Definition   Public outcries in response to actual or perceived violations of law or morality, usually by public figures

While still recovering from the demoralizing effect of the 1970's Watergate scandal, the United States was rocked repeatedly in the 1980's with a wave of new scandals. These ongoing scandals deeply affected the nation's economy and government.

The 1980's was termed by some the "decade of decadence," and it was characterized by individualistic greed and selfishness that gave rise to the appellation "Me generation" and the famous "Greed is good" speech in Oliver Stone's *Wall Street* (1987). Actual or perceived greed and self-interest drove many of the political and economic scandals of the decade, including Abscam, and Iran-Contra affair, the savings and loan (S&L) crisis, and various insider trading scandals on Wall Street. These scandals not only brought into question the integrity of the institutions at the heart of the United States' power structure but also hampered the ability of those institutions to function.

Minor Political Scandals   In 1980, President Jimmy Carter lost his bid for reelection to Ronald Reagan. Carter was unpopular in 1980 as a result of domestic economic problems and his inability to bring home the Americans being held hostage in Iran. His reelection campaign was also hurt, however, by a scandal involving his flamboyant older brother, Billy Carter. Billy was revealed to be a paid agent of Libya who had received hundreds of thousands of dollars from dictator Muammar al-Qaddafi. Later, in 1983, it was revealed that President Reagan had "cheated" in his final debate with Carter by obtaining a copy of Carter's briefing notes for the debate. This scandal, referred to as "Debategate" in reference to the Watergate scandal, proved to be relatively minor compared to others that would affect Reagan and other national politicians.

Also in 1983, a particularly lurid sex scandal resulted in a recommendation by the House Committee on Ethics that representatives Dan Crane and Gerry Studds be reprimanded for unsuitable relationships with teenage congressional pages. After his admirable role in heading up the Tower Commission investigating the Iran-Contra affair, in 1987 John Tower was nominated as secretary of defense, but a scandal involving habitual alcohol abuse, womanizing, and questionable financial ties to the defense industry destroyed his chances. That same year, presidential hopeful Senator Gary Hart lost his lead when the Miami Herald printed a photograph of him with model Donna Rice. In 1989, scandal forced Speaker of the House of Representatives Jim Wright to resign after an investigation found financial irregularities centering on improper gifts and using sales of books to bypass limits on speaking fees. Also in 1989, a scandal involving Democratic Massachusetts representative Barney Frank hit the airwaves after Frank admitted his relationship with a male prostitute. These scandals, however, paled in comparison to the major scandals of the decade.

Abscam   In 1981, news broke of a Federal Bureau of Investigation (FBI) high-level sting, code-named Abscam, that had begun in 1978. Undercover agents posing as Middle Eastern businessmen had offered government officials large sums of money in return for granting favors to a mysterious (and fictional) sheikh named Kambir Abdul Rahman. Ultimately, the sting, which was the the first large-scale operation designed to trap corrupt public officials, resulted in the conviction of a senator, six congressmen, the mayor of Camden, New Jersey, and members of the Philadelphia City Council. However, the controversy surrounding Abscam was generated not only by the corruption of the officials but also by accusations of entrapment on the part of the agents.

The Iran-Contra Scandal   During Reagan's second term, White House officials, at the suggestion of the Israeli government, covertly sold weapons to Iran in violation of the Arms Export Control Act (1976). In turn, $30 million in profits were used to fund the Contras, a group of right-wing guerrilla insurgents against the leftist Sandinista National Liberation Front in Nicaragua. The subterfuge was designed to circumvent the will of Congress, which had explicitly prohibited further support to the Contras. In November of 1986, a Lebanese newspaper exposed the operation and claimed that the arms sales to Iran were intended to influence Lebanon to release American hostages. President Reagan appeared on television and vehemently denied that the arms sale had taken place. A week later, he was forced to retract his statement, but he continued to deny that the sale of weapons had been intended to help secure the release of American hostages held in Lebanon.

The scandal gained strength when Lieutenant Colonel Oliver North and his secretary Fawn Hall shredded incriminating documents and U.S. attorney general Edwin Meese III was forced to admit that profits from the arms sales were indeed directed to the Nicaraguan Contras. Faced with congressional wrath, in December of 1986 Reagan was forced to form a special investigative commission with former senator John Tower at its head. In 1987, the Tower Commission criticized Secretary of Defense Caspar Weinberger, Deputy National Security Adviser Admiral John Poindexter, and his deputy, Lieutenant Colonel North, as well as accusing the president of ineffectively supervising his aides.

The S&L and Insider Trading Scandals   The S&L crisis was accompanied by scandals when the depth of the greed and mismanagement that led to it were understood. By the early 1980's, the government had removed many federal regulations from the banking industry in order to make banks more competitive. This deregulation resulted in an increase in the number of S&Ls, as well as a broadening of the scope of their financial activities. S&Ls were allowed to invest in commercial real estate and to issue credit

cards for the first time, and they were eager to do so. The associations invested in high-risk properties, many of which lost their value. Bankruptcies ensued, and a great number of depositors lost their money—many lost their entire life savings. S&L head Charles Keating pleaded guilty to bankruptcy fraud after he removed $1 million from Lincoln Savings before the institution's imminent collapse. In addition, five United States senators were implicated in the national scandal for helping Keating. They became known as the Keating five.

In 1986, the Securities and Exchange Commission (SEC) investigated Dennis Levine, Ivan Boesky, and Michael Milken, among others, for willful violations of securities law and business ethics. The men had set up the greatest insider trading ring in history and in the process nearly destroyed Wall Street. Dennis Levine, a managing director at Drexel Burnham Lambert, led investigators to Ivan Boesky, who had made $200 million by betting on corporate takeovers after acquiring information from corporate insiders. In turn, Boesky informed on Michael Milken, who had developed a fast-paced market for junk bonds.

Entertainment Scandals   Although not nearly as serious as the nation's political scandals, show business scandals during the 1980's also captured the nation's imagination. In 1982, *Saturday Night Live* actor John Belushi died of an overdose of heroin and cocaine. A year later, the Beach Boys' drummer, Dennis Wilson, drowned in a drug-related accident, and in 1984, popular R&B singer Marvin Gaye was shot to death by his father during an argument. Actress Zsa Zsa Gabor was jailed in 1989 for slapping a police officer. The most scandalous crime of the decade, however, was the murders that same year of Kitty and Jose Menendez by their children, Lyle and Erik Menendez, who shot their parents with shotguns while the couple watched television. The brothers were eventually found guilty of first-degree murder.

Impact   The 1980 scandal that became known as "Billygate" helped Ronald Reagan gain the presidency, and the major scandals of the 1980's—Abscam, Iran-Contra, the S&L crisis, and the Wall Street insider trading scandals—resulted in public outrage that led to the enactment of legislation seeking to ensure that crimes such as these would not happen again. Deeply concerned about the possibility of law enforcement officials entrapping individuals and damaging their reputations, the courts harshly criticized the FBI for its use of entrapment techniques in the Abscam scandal and in 1981 prompted Attorney General Benjamin Civiletti to issue *The Attorney General's Guidelines for FBI Undercover Operations.*

The deceptiveness and dishonesty of the Iran-Contra scheme cast a dark shadow on the Reagan presidency and made the American people even more uneasy about their government. The S&L crisis, the largest financial scandal in American history, had an enormous impact on the U.S. economy. President George H. W. Bush estimated that government bailouts would cost the taxpayers $50 billion, but later accounts estimated that the crisis cost between $600 billion and $1.4 trillion. The Wall Street insider trading scandal led to a greater understanding that insider trading was not necessarily restricted to individuals, but that crime networks could also be established. The combined effect of all these scandals was to taint the federal government and corporations in the eyes of the American public, which came to expect a certain level of corruption from its elected officials and business leaders.

Further Reading

Barth, James, Susanne Trimeth, and Glenn Yago. *The Savings and Loan Crisis: Lessons from a Regulatory Failure.* New York: Springer, 2004. Written by a variety of banking industry regulators and business academics, this book illustrates how the inept banking practices of the 1980's led to one of history's greatest financial calamities.

Davis, Lanny. *Scandal: How "Gotcha" Politics Is Destroying America.* New York: Palgrave Macmillan, 2006. In his highly praised book, Lanny Davis, special counsel to the Bill Clinton White House, argues that politics in America have become driven by vicious scandals involving partisan politicians, extremists, and the media, who are bent on destroying public officials. Chapter 4, "The Scandal Cauldron," is dedicated to the political scandals of the 1980's.

Greene, Robert W. *Sting Man.* New York: Dutton, 1981. Provides details of the FBI sting operation and how Melvin Weinberg brought about its successful conclusion.

Kallen, Stuart. *A Cultural History of the United States Through the Decades: The 1980's.* New York: Chicago: Lucent Books, 1998. Discusses the major scandals of the United States in the 1980's and the Iran-Contra affair in particular.

Stewart, James B. *Den of Thieves.* New York: Touchstone Books, 1992. Stewart, a Pulitzer Prize-winning *Wall Street Journal* reporter, utilizes court documents, testimony, and interviews in this comprehensive account of the 1980's Wall Street insider trading scandals.

Troy, Gil. *Morning in America: How Ronald Reagan Invented the 1980's.* Princeton, N.J.: Princeton University Press, 2005. Each chapter focuses on a year, from 1980 to 1989, during Ronald Reagan's campaign and presidency. The book details Reagan's reactions to the Abscam scandal, the Iran-Contra affair, the S&L crisis, and the Wall Street insider trading scandal.

M. Casey Diana

See also Abscam; Bush, George H. W.; Congress, U.S.; Congressional page sex scandal of 1983; Elections in the United States, 1980; Elections in the United States, 1984; Elections in the United States, 1988; Hart, Gary; Iran-Contra affair; Junk bonds; Meese, Edwin, III; North, Oliver; Poindexter, John; Reagan, Ronald; Savings and loan (S&L) crisis; Tower Commission; Watt, James; Weinberger, Caspar; Williams, Vanessa; Wright, Jim.

■ Schnabel, Julian

Identification American artist
Born October 26, 1951; Brooklyn, New York

Schnabel experienced meteoric success in the New York art scene and became a lightning rod for art criticism.

Julian Schnabel received an art degree from the University of Houston in 1973. By 1981, the brash and self-promoting artist had unprecedented parallel shows at the Mary Boone and Leo Castelli galleries in New York City. All of his works were sold before the shows opened. He exhibited intensely in America and Europe throughout the 1980's and had several "retrospectives" before the age of forty. Works that brought three thousand dollars at the beginning of the 1980's sold for upward of sixty thousand dollars only a few years later.

Schnabel's paintings were very large, often ten feet by fifteen feet or more. They combined a return to figuration—often quoting religious or mythological themes—with highly gestural paint application. Both of these characteristics were frequently "appropriated" from earlier works of art. Schnabel emphasized the material nature of his paintings with the supports on which he painted and by gluing objects to the surface. The "plate paintings" (in which he painted over broken crockery attached to a wooden base) became sensationalized in the popular press. These works first appeared at the end of the 1970's, after Schnabel had seen the architectural works of Antonio Gaudi in Spain in 1977, but they became well known in the early 1980's. His work is best compared perhaps with such European artists as Anselm Kiefer.

New York art critics dubbed Schnabel a neoexpressionist, and many credited him with a "rebirth" of painting after the periods of minimalist and conceptual art. In critical writing of the 1980's, he was the focus of concerns about key art issues of the decade: the role of appropriation, the relation of high art and mass culture, gallery business practices and art market hype, the remasculinization of the art scene, and the relation between artistic success and authenticity. In the popular press, Schnabel became the very image of the 1980's artist and of the financial excess of the decade.

Impact   Marketing of Schnabel's paintings brought him spectacular success and fueled a boom in the art market. For many critics and much of the public, such success called into question both Schnabel's sincerity as a creative artist and the basically mercantile nature of the business of art. Full evaluation of Schnabel's work as a painter may fall to future generations. In later years, he became a successful screenwriter and filmmaker as well.

Further Reading

Eccher, Danilo, curator. *Julian Schnabel, 22 novembre 1996-30 gennaio 1997*. Bologna, Italy: Galleria d'Arte Moderna, 1996.

Hollein, Max, ed. *Julian Schnabel: Malerei/Paintings 1978-2003, 29 January-25 April 2004*. Frankfort, Germany: Schirn Kunsthalle, 2004.

Pearlman, Alison. *Unpackaging Art of the 1980's*. Chicago: University of Chicago Press, 2003.

Jean Owens Schaefer

See also   Art movements; Business and the economy in the United States; Consumerism; Neoexpressionism in painting.

Julian Schnabel in 1987. (Hulton Archive/Getty Images)

■ School vouchers debate

Definition   Controversy over a proposal to use tax dollars to subsidize private school tuition

A debate begun in earnest during the 1950's found renewed vigor during the 1980's, as education reformers proposed government-funded tuition payments that would divert public funding to private or parochial schools. Those in favor of vouchers argued that they would provide parents with the financial power to choose the best schools for their children. Those opposed to them argued that they represented an abandonment of already troubled public schools, which could ill afford to lose any federal funding. Although the idea of school vouchers did not gain substantial ground during the 1980's, a confluence of political, social, and economic factors kept the idea alive through the decade.

Proponents of school vouchers saw these government-funded tuition grants as a means of providing choice and competition in education. They believed that the public school system was a socialized monopoly, that its problems resulted from this fact, and that competition with private schools could cure those problems. Opponents warned that diverting tax dollars away from public schools and into the hands of private providers was no way to correct the problems facing the American public school system. The debate was shaped by the fact that it was clearly not possible to fix the U.S. education system quickly, so even parents who believed in improving public schools for future generations might not want to send their children to those schools if they had not yet improved.

Not a New Debate Although the term "voucher" may have been a new addition to the debate, the core idea was not new. In the founding days of the nation, English economist Adam Smith, in his seminal work *An Inquiry into the Nature and Causes of the Wealth of Nations* (1776; commonly known as *The Wealth of Nations*), had called for the government to give money directly to parents. This money would be used to purchase educational services in order to prevent the development of a monopoly over the provision of such services. In 1956, Nobel Prize-winning economist Milton Friedman argued that the existence of the monopoly Adam Smith had predicted two centuries earlier was leading to inefficiencies and a lack of innovation. He believed the quality of education would improve if education was driven by market forces. It was no coincidence that the voucher idea resurfaced in the late 1950's and early 1960's. During the height of the Civil Rights movement, public schools were seen as avenues of opportunity and mobility and had become the major focal point of demands for change, community control, and racial equality. Thus, calls for privatization in education reemerged, both among those who wished to avoid the social and political unrest they perceived to exist in public schools, and among those seeking greating educational opportunities than they believed were available in those schools.

A Flurry of Activity In 1983, the U.S. Department of Education released *A Nation at Risk*, which warned of the impending economic doom its authors forecasted for the country as a direct result of a steady erosion of student achievement in American public schools. The report produced a sense of urgency in education not experienced since the launch of the Soviet satellite Sputnik 1 in 1957. Thousands of initiatives were launched, as educators and elected officials responded to the perceived crisis. Among the resulting reforms were increases in teacher pay coupled with decreases in class size, tougher standards for teacher preparation programs and certification, revamped curricula, district consolidations aimed at efficiencies of scale in management, schools-within-schools programs that reduced the size of student bodies while allowing for larger building sizes, and the revamping of school calendars, including the introduction of year-round education. Missing from all of this activity, however, were the vouchers advocated by Friedman and others. Efforts to bring vouchers into the picture were blocked by school administrators, teacher unions, and liberal reformers unwilling to abandon the public school system to market forces.

The fundamental issue at debate was whether or not public tax dollars should be used to pay for a private education. Conservatives, who were committed to a free market approach to education, supported vouchers as a tool of school choice. Under his economic plan, dubbed "Reaganomics," President Ronald Reagan spoke consistently in favor of school vouchers, private tuition tax breaks, and other public subsidies for private tuition. Religious conservatives and Catholic advocates rallied behind the voucher idea, but the concept was tarnished when pro-segregationists began to support vouchers as a means of avoiding integrated schools. Federal courts ruled against vouchers in several cases, giving the impression that voucher supporters had a racist agenda. In addition, because vouchers might be used to pay for parochial, as well as secular, private schools, some opponents believed that they would violate the separation of church and state.

Shift in the Late 1980's Calls for privatization reemerged as more demands were placed on public education to address social inequalities related to race and class. Many social programs resulting from the Civil Rights movement and put in place during the late 1960's and the 1970's had focused on public schools. Federal, state, and local funds were directed at reducing the degree of inequality, and public schools became the focus of these efforts. During the Reagan era, most of these programs were ended.

The call for a voucher system continued, but the arguments shifted. During the 1980's, many in the American middle class continued to rely on public education. "White flight" from major urban centers into suburbia allowed public education to provide for middle-class needs, because the concentration of relative wealth in the suburbs meant that public schools located there were better funded than were schools in urban, working-class districts. As long as the educational needs of the middle class were met, the perceived need to privatize education was minimal.

During the 1980's, the Reagan and George H. W. Bush administrations pushed for educational reform. Since their conservative, middle-class supporters continued to be served by public education, reform efforts shifted away from privatization. Still, the concept of a voucher program fit well into some versions of the political ideology advocating reduced government involvement in family life—despite the fact that it entailed more federal intervention in local affairs. Vouchers were seen as a means of enabling parents to send their children to whichever schools would best meet their children's needs, regardless of whether or not those schools charged tuition. However, during the 1980's, little action was seen on this front. Congress rejected Reagan administration plans to grant tuition tax credits, and the school choice movement remained primarily active only among ultraconservatives.

Impact Many opponents of voucher programs pointed to educational funding gaps as the principal reason for American educational woes. Public schools were thought to fail poor and minority schools for a number of reasons, including the national structure for allocating public school resources between and among schools and school districts. Voucher programs, according to the critics, would have further exacerbated the situation. The worst schools, those most in need of resources, would be the least attractive to potential students. Therefore, they would be the schools most likely to suffer low enrollments and financial cuts if parents were able to use vouchers to send their children to private schools. Thus, it was argued, by channeling money away from the poorest public schools and instead providing public subsi-

dies to private schools, vouchers would help individual students at the expense of the overall system. The parents of those individual students, however, were likely to support the voucher idea, because their first loyalties were to their children, not to their public schools.

Further Reading

Friedman, Milton. *Capitalism and Freedom.* Chicago: University of Chicago Press, 1962. Friedman's seminal work provides the definitive statement of his immensely influential economic philosophy.

Gross, B., and R. Gross. *The Great School Debate.* New York: Simon & Schuster, 1985. Claims the popular notion that current education reforms such as privatization, vouchers, and charter schools are responses to an identified crisis in public education requires further scrutiny.

Kirkpatrick, David. *School Choice: The Idea That Will Not Die.* Mesa, Ariz.: Blue Bird, 1997. Detailed overview of the history of the school voucher concept, including an examination of the various iterations of voucher programs and plans.

Levin, Henry. *Privatizing Education.* Boulder, Colo.: Westview Press, 2001. Explores the voucher debate from a perspective at once domestic and global, demonstrating how it is uniquely American while not necessarily based on educational philosophy.

National Commission on Excellence in Education. *A Nation at Risk.* Washington, D.C.: U.S. Department of Education, 1983. Landmark study of American education during the early 1980's. Decries the state of education and warns of a "rising tide of mediocrity that threatens our very future as a Nation and a people."

Ravitch, Diane. *Left Back: A Century of Failed School Reforms.* New York: Simon & Schuster, 2000. Provides an overview of a century of "progressive" reforms in the K-12 educational sector.

Rick Pearce

See also Consumerism; Education in Canada; Education in the United States; Magnet schools; Mainstreaming in education; Multiculturalism in education; *Nation at Risk, A*; National Education Summit of 1989; Reagan, Ronald; Reaganomics.

■ Schreyer, Edward

Identification Governor-general of Canada from 1979 to 1984
Born December 21, 1935; Beausejour, Manitoba

Schreyer was Canada's ceremonial vice-regal head from 1979 to 1984, years that saw two general elections and the patriation of Canada's constitution.

Edward Schreyer, a Manitoban who had served as premier of that province as a member of the leftist New Democratic Party, was appointed governor-general by Prime Minister Pierre Trudeau in 1979. Unusually, Schreyer was not a member of Trudeau's own party, the Liberals, but he had given key support to Trudeau during the 1970 crisis over invocation of the War Measures Act against Québécois sovereignists, and he was trusted by the prime minister. Trudeau's party was defeated by the Conservatives in 1979, and Joe Clark began a brief tenure as prime minister, but nine months later, a resurgent Trudeau led his party to victory and regained the prime ministry. As a result, Schreyer and Trudeau served jointly during most of Schreyer's tenure as governor-general. Schreyer was the youngest governor-general appointed up to that point, and was only the fifth to be Canadian-born. He was the first governor-general from Manitoba and the first of Ukrainian or German descent.

Rideau Hall in Ottawa, where Schreyer and his wife, Lily, resided during Schreyer's term as governor-general, is nominally the official Canadian residence of the monarch of Canada—Queen Elizabeth II, during Schreyer's term—and Schreyer hosted Queen Elizabeth twice, in 1982 and 1983. The first visit was the most important, as the Queen was visiting as part of the patriation of Canada's constitution as proclaimed by the Canada Act of 1982, spearheaded by Prime Minister Trudeau. On April 17, 1982, the queen proclaimed the act, and Schreyer thus became the first governor-general to preside over a completely self-governing Canada.

Schreyer participated energetically in the cultural role of the governor-general, which included sponsoring awards and prizes for achievement in the arts, sciences, and other areas of public life. Among the writers who received the Governor General's Award for Fiction during Schreyer's term were George Bowering, Mavis Gallant, and Guy Vanderhaeghe. Schreyer also concerned himself with the culture of his own Ukrainian heritage, presiding over the founding of the Center for Ukrainian Studies at the University of Toronto in 1983.

Impact Schreyer was a pivotal figure in the transition of the governor-general's office from a symbol of authority and precedence to an expression of the multiplicity of Canadian life. Schreyer, in standing for the whole of Canada, made clear that the whole of Canada was an abstract concept that could be sustained only by the sum of its parts. This position paralleled a growing sense in the 1980's that the nationalism of the 1960's and 1970's, which had replaced colonial allegiance to Britain with a monolithic vision of Canadian identity, had run its course. Canadians instead began to embrace a spectrum of national identities, while striving to find and subscribe to fundamental values held in common. Schreyer's combination of energy, modesty, populism, and moderate liberalism made him an apt representative of Canada as it passed through the final years of the Trudeau era.

Further Reading

Doern, Russell. *Wednesdays Are Cabinet Days: A Personal Account of the Schreyer Administration.* Winnipeg, Man.: Queenston House, 1981.
McWhinney, Edward. *The Governor General and the Prime Ministers.* Vancouver: Ronsdale Press, 2005.

Nicholas Birns

See also Aboriginal rights in Canada; Clark, Joe; Education in Canada; Elections in Canada; Trudeau, Pierre.

■ Schroeder, Pat

Identification U.S. representative from Colorado from 1973 to 1997
Born July 30, 1940; Portland, Oregon

Schroeder was a liberal representative willing to advocate causes that many of her Democratic male colleagues in the House of Representatives refused to consider. As a member of the House Committee on Armed Services, she regularly challenged the Reagan administration's military policies. She considered running for president in 1988.

Democrat Pat Schroeder was elected to Congress in 1972. Instead of seeking a seat on a committee dealing with women's issues, she requested a seat on the

Pat Schroeder tearfully announces on September 28, 1987, that she will not seek the Democratic presidential nomination. (AP/Wide World Photos)

den Sharing Panel, a task force of the Armed Services Committee. She also introduced legislation to provide women a greater chance of participation in all areas of the military.

In 1987, Schroeder spent five months traveling around the United States seeking support for a possible campaign for president of the United States in 1988. She withdrew from the race at an emotional press conference on September 28, 1987. Bursting into tears as supporters chanted "Run, Pat, Run," she was lampooned on the satirical late-night television program *Saturday Night Live.* On the program, Nora Dunn portrayed Schroeder attempting to moderate a Democratic primary debate, while repeatedly bursting into tears.

House Committee on Armed Services. The House leadership granted her request, and she became the first woman to serve on that committee. In the 1980's, she used her position on the committee to challenge the Ronald Reagan administration's defense policies.

In addition to addressing defense issues, Representative Schroeder worked on issues relating to women and children, introducing bills to eliminate gender inequities in wages and promotions, to provide funds to open shelters for abused children, and to expand Head Start programs. As the chair of the National Task Force on Equal Rights for Women, she advocated federal subsidization of abortions. After a number of women's health clinics were violently attacked by antiabortion protesters in late 1984, Schroeder regularly appeared on television news programs to denounce the violence.

Schroeder used her position on the Armed Services Committee to change the role of women in the military. Her Military Family Act of 1985 helped improve the situation of military families. In 1988, Schroeder was appointed chair of the Defense Bur-

Impact   Schroeder worked to keep the interests of women and children at the forefront of debate in the U.S. House of Representatives. She was one of the cofounders of the Congressional Women's Issues Caucus. She also challenged the Reagan administration, adding the well-known phrase "Teflon President" to the American political lexicon. Frustrated in her inability to make her charges stick, she once described President Reagan, "He's just like a Teflon frying pan: Nothing sticks to him."

Further Reading

Lowy, Joan A. *Pat Schroeder: A Woman of the House.* Albuquerque: University of New Mexico Press, 2003.

Schroeder, Pat. *Twenty-Four Years of House Work—and the Place Is Still a Mess: My Life in Politics.* Kansas City, Mo.: Andrews McMeel, 1998.

John David Rausch, Jr.

See also   Abortion; Congress, U.S.; Elections in the United States, 1988; Glass ceiling; Liberalism in U.S. politics; Military ban on homosexuals; Military spending; Reagan, Ronald; Women in the workforce.

■ Schwarzenegger, Arnold

Identification   Champion bodybuilder and actor
Born   July 30, 1947; Thal, Austria

Schwarzenegger began a career as an action film star in the 1980's, performing in a series of successful films. By the end of the decade, he was poised to become a superstar.

After winning his first Mr. Universe bodybuilding title in 1967, Arnold Schwarzenegger moved to the United States the following year to pursue business opportunities, including a movie career. His first and last movies of the 1970's, *Hercules in New York* (1970) and *The Villain* (1979), were both commercial and critical failures. However, he won a Golden Globe as New Star of the Year—Actor for a supporting role as a bodybuilder in the film *Stay Hungry*

(1976), and he was featured in the documentary *Pumping Iron* (1977).

In 1980, Schwarzenegger won his last major bodybuilding title and was cast as the husband of the title character in the television movie *The Jayne Mansfield Story* (1980). Since Mansfield's husband was born in Hungary and became a champion bodybuilder, Schwarzenegger was an obvious choice. Schwarzenegger finally found success as the male lead of a theatrical film in *Conan the Barbarian* (1982). A series of successful action movies, beginning with *The Terminator* (1984), made him an action star, although none of the films surpassed the milestone $100-million mark at the box office. His only film of the 1980's to achieve that level of success was a comedy, *Twins* (1988).

In 1987, Schwarzenegger received a star on Hollywood Boulevard's Walk of Fame and was named Male Star of the Year by the National Association of Theater Owners. *Forbes* magazine listed him as one of the ten wealthiest entertainers in the United States in 1989. By that time, several of his films had achieved cult status, particularly *The Terminator*, which was initially only a modest success but would spawn two blockbuster sequels in later years.

Schwarzenegger became an American citizen in 1983 and laid the groundwork for his political career when he spoke on Ronald Reagan's behalf at the 1984 Republican National Convention and campaigned for George H. W. Bush in 1988. He joined the United States' most prominent political family in 1986, when he married Maria Shriver, niece of President John Kennedy and Senators Robert and Edward Kennedy.

Impact   Schwarzenegger spent the 1980's building a following among die-hard science-fiction and action fans, earning a reputation as one of the major action heroes of the decade. Each of his films was only a modest success, but he proved to be a consistent leading man and an iconic figure. At the end of the decade, he was poised to achieve superstar status, and during the following decade, he starred in a steady stream of blockbusters.

Further Reading

Andrews, Nigel. *True Myths: The Life and Times of Arnold Schwarzenegger.* Secaucus, N.J.: Birch Lane Press, 1996.

Flynn, John L. *The Films of Arnold Schwarzenegger.* Rev. ed. Secaucus, N.J.: Carol, 1996.

Arnold Schwarzenegger as Conan the Barbarian in 1984's sequel, Conan the Destroyer. *(AP/Wide World Photos)*

Leamer, Laurence. *Fantastic: The Life of Arnold Schwarzenegger.* New York: St. Martin's Press, 2005.

                Thomas R. Feller

See also   Action films; Film in the United States; Science-fiction films; *Terminator, The.*

■ Science and technology

Definition   The physical, biological, earth, and computer sciences and the practical technological innovations developed from scientific advances

In the 1980's, advances in science and technology included the creation and spread of the Internet, biotechnology, and the concept of DNA fingerprinting.

During the 1980's, the implications of advances in science and technology, along with a series of highly visible public disasters, caused the public to question science and technology and led to the growth of the environmental movement, as well as numerous public policy changes designed to protect humans from toxic and radioactive waste. At the same time, advances in information technology changed everyday existence in multiple fields of employment, including education and business.

Computers and Information Technology   Throughout the decade, computing and information technologies rapidly and radically transformed, starting in 1980, when Seagate Technology produced the first hard disk drive for computers. The disk could hold five megabytes of data. In 1981, International Business Machines (IBM) released its first personal computer, which ran on a 4.77 megahertz Intel 8088 microprocessor and MS-DOS system software. The company responsible for designing MS-DOS, Microsoft, was only six years old. Simultaneously, Adam Osborne released the first "portable" computer, the Osborne I. It weighed twenty-four pounds and cost $1,795. That same year, Apollo Computer released the first workstation, the DN100.

In 1982, the popularity of personal computers rose dramatically with the introduction of the Commodore 64, which sold for $695 and came with 64 kilobytes of random-access memory (RAM). The Commodore 64 would become the best-selling single computer model of all time. *Time* magazine named the computer its "Man of the Year," saying "Several human candidates might have represented 1982, but none symbolized the past year more richly, or will be viewed by history as more significant, than a machine: the computer."

At the beginning of the 1980's, the network that would eventually become the Internet was three years old. In 1983, that network split into ARPANET and MILNET, creating a civilian branch as well as a military one. The innovation had been enabled by the introduction of the networking standard Transmission-Control Protocol/Internet Protocol (TCP/IP) in 1980. In 1985, ARPANET was renamed the Internet, and financial responsibility for the network was assumed by the National Science Foundation. The Internet would become a dominant force in both American and global culture, and science-fiction writer William Gibson coined the term "cyberspace" as he explored the possible futures created by advances in information technology. At the same time, in 1983, Microsoft Windows was released, as was Microsoft Word. Some 450,000 floppy disks with demonstration copies of Word were distributed as inserts in *PC Magazine.*

The Parallel Computing Initiative, funded by Livermore Laboratory, redefined high-performance computing, starting in 1989. Using massive, coordinated clusters of microcomputers, the project was able to outperform custom-designed supercomputers. As technology to link computers cooperatively advanced, computer clusters would become preferred over individual supercomputers for most processor-intensive high-performance computing tasks. It followed in the footsteps of research conducted by Daniel Hillis of Thinking Machine Corporation, whose machine used sixteen thousand processors and completed billions of operations per second.

As the popularity of personal computers increased in the 1980's, issues regarding the social and ethical implications of information collection and management came to light. Such issues included privacy rights of consumers and citizens, whose personal information was contained in an ever-increasing number of databases as the decade progressed. The spread of computers also raised issues dealing with intellectual property rights, software piracy, and other forms of computer crime such as "hacking" into private databases and spreading computer viruses. The first such virus, written by Rich Skrenta, was released in 1982. In 1986, the United States passed the Computer Fraud and Abuse Act; the first person prosecuted under the new law was college student Robert Tappan Morris, Jr., another computer virus author. The son of a computer security expert, Morris said he had been motivated by boredom to create the worm and set it loose on the Internet, causing problems for six thousand users of the sixty thousand hosts connected to the Internet.

Biology, Genetics, and Medicine   The face of the biological sciences changed over the course of the 1980's, particularly in the field of biotechnology. In 1980, Stanley Cohen and Herbert Boyer filed a patent application for a process of gene cloning that allowed them to make human insulin from genetically modified (GM) bacteria. In a similar advance, a vaccine for hepatitis B was created through genetic modification.

Genetic modification was not universally popular, and in reaction to its development, an anti-biotechnology movement formed under the leadership of Jeremy Rifkin, who argued against awarding patents for GM bacteria and opposed the transfer of genes from one species to another and the release of modified bacteria into the environment. Rifkin delayed the release of the first GM bacteria into the environment for four years. Eventually, in 1987, the bacteria were released and used to make potato plants more frost resistant.

In 1984, Alec Jeffreys developed a deoxyribonucleic acid (DNA) fingerprinting technique in the course of his research into human genes. The previous year, Kary Mullis had begun research that led to the development of the polymerase chain reaction (PCR) technique, which allowed scientists to amplify or multiply DNA from a single cell in order to replicate a DNA sample. In 1987, police began using DNA fingerprinting to investigate crime. In 1983, the virus that would come to be known as human immunodeficiency virus (HIV) was first isolated. The virus was linked to acquired immunodeficiency syndrome (AIDS). In 1985, the Food and Drug Administration (FDA) approved a blood test for HIV infection that could be used on blood supplies. In 1987, the FDA approved the anti-AIDS drug azidothymidine (AZT).

The decade also witnessed the foundation being laid for one of the most prominent advances in human science, the Human Genome Project. Livermore Laboratory and Los Alamos collaborated to build human-chromosome-specific gene libraries, developing advanced chromosome-sorting capabilities. The project's goal was to map the entire human genome; it was hailed as history's most ambitious biological project. Other advancements in medicine in the 1980's included the first use of artificial skin to treat burns (1981); the first use of a permanent artificial heart (1982); the first release of a patient with an artificial heart from the hospital (1985); the first heart-lung transplant (1987); and the development of Prozac, the first selective serotonin reuptake inhibitor, by the Eli Lilly Corporation (1987).

One notable medical failure of the 1980's occurred in October, 1984, when Doctor Leonard L. Bailey used the heart of a baboon to replace the failing heart of an infant who became known to the media as Baby Fae. The transplant operation was both unsuccessful and possibly illegal. Although Baby Fae seemed to do well for a few days, her body rejected the new organ, and public scrutiny was drawn to the issue of human experimentation.

Energy Crisis and Environmental Movement   Driven by the previous decade's energy crisis, scientists in the 1980's explored alternative sources of energy, including biodiesel, hydrogen fuel, and wind energy. A secondary impetus of this research was the rising risk of environmental pollution and an increasing public awareness of the dangers such pollution posed to human well-being. Antinuclear and environmental activists had also drawn significant attention to the difficulties of safely disposing of radioactive and toxic waste.

The environmental justice movement spread in the United States and across the world, as it sought to combat the social structures that had thwarted environmental reforms in the past. One of the major impetuses of the movement was the Warren County polychlorinated biphenyl (PCB) disaster. The state of North Carolina was forced to create a landfill to contain the more than thirty thousand gallons of PCB-contaminated oil produced by the disaster. The state chose to locate the landfill in a primarily African American county, leading to charges of environmental racism, particularly after it was revealed that the site was not hydrologically suitable for such disposal.

Media coverage of environmental disasters continued to increase public awareness of the dangers posed to the environment by new and existing technologies. It also increased the demand for new technologies that could help prevent further disasters, as well as for new scientific methods for measuring both the risks of disasters occurring and the precise effects of the disasters that did occur. In 1984, a Union Carbide pesticide plant released forty tons of methyl isocyanate into the atmosphere when a holding tank overheated, immediately killing nearly three thousand people in the Indian city of Bhopal and leading to an estimated fifteen thousand to twenty-two thousand subsequent deaths. Union Carbide worked with other companies to create the Responsible Care system, designed to force companies to act responsibly toward humans and the environment.

In 1985, the city of Times Beach, Missouri, was completely evacuated. In 1982, the Environmental Protection Agency (EPA) had discovered dangerous levels of dioxin, which it called "the most dangerous chemical known to man," in the town's soil. The chemical was believed to be a by-product of the production of hexachlorophene. The same year, a hole in Earth's protective ozone layer was discovered by researchers in the Antarctic, whose measurements indicated a steep drop in ozone layers over a span of a few years, far larger than any scientist had predicted. The main source of ozone depletion was determined to be the photodissociation of chlorofluro-carbon compounds (CFCs). In 1987, forty-three countries signed the Montreal Protocol, in which they agreed immediately to freeze CFC production at its current levels and to reduce their production levels by 50 percent by 1999. In 1986, a disaster at the Chernobyl nuclear power plant caused by the explosion of a reactor depopulated areas of the Ukraine and spewed radioactive material into the atmosphere, exposing parts of the Soviet Union, northern Europe, western Europe, and the eastern United States to radioactive fallout.

The emphasis on finding clean forms of energy and ways to reduce hazardous waste in the 1980's sometimes created problems. Eagerness to find alternative energy sources led to results that were difficult to re-create. In 1988, researchers Stanley Pons and Martin Fleischman announced the discovery of cold fusion at the University of Utah. Cold fusion, known to scientists as low-energy nuclear reactions, involved the creation of nuclear reactions near room temperature and pressure using simple, low-energy devices. When two light nuclei were forced to fuse, they formed a heavier nucleus, releasing considerable amounts of energy. After a short period of popular acclaim and widespread media attention, the researchers were accused of being sloppy in their initial research when they were unable to reproduce their results. Efforts by the United States Department of Energy to reproduce the results were similarly unsuccessful, although the department would continue to study the possibility of cold fusion for the next seventeen years.

Space Exploration Early in the 1980's, the U.S. space program seemed to be going strong. On November 12, 1980, the Voyager spacecraft approached Saturn and sent back the first high-resolution images of the planet. As emphasis shifted away from spacecraft for one-time exploration missions, the space shuttle program was created in order to employ reusable spacecraft for near-Earth missions. The following year, on April 12, the first space shuttle, *Columbia*, was launched. In 1984, astronauts Bruce M. McCandless II and Robert L. Stewart made the first untethered spacewalk. Early in 1986, the Voyager 2 space probe made its first contact with Uranus.

However, public fears of "big science"—massive, expensive government programs that were perceived to divert money from social programs—led to the gradual downscaling of the National Aeronautics and Space Administration (NASA). When the space shuttle *Challenger* exploded seventy-four seconds after takeoff in 1986, killing the seven astronauts aboard, public confidence in the merits of such a program was further shaken. Other countries took up some of the slack: In February, the Soviet Union launched the space station *Mir*, the first consistently inhabited long-term research facility in space, and the Japanese spacecraft Suisei approached and analyzed Halley's comet. NASA did not resume space shuttle flights until 1988.

The U.S. space program would receive an unexpected boost in the form of President Ronald Reagan's Strategic Defense Initiative (SDI), first proposed in 1983. Its intent was to use ground- and space-based antiballistic missile weapons systems to defend the United States from nuclear attack. SDI was in part spurred by advances in laser technology made by Livermore Laboratories. In 1984, the world's most powerful laser, nicknamed "Nova," became operational. Ten beams produced up to 100 trillion watts of infrared power. The same year, the Strategic Defense Initiative Organization (SDIO) was established to oversee the program and was led by ex-NASA director James Alan Abrahamson. While SDI was never fully developed, the program's research would provide significant advances in antiballistic technology, and its scientists would explore weapons that included hypervelocity rail guns, spacebased relay mirrors, neutral particle beams, and chemical and X-ray lasers.

In 1988, Soviet and American scientists worked together to conduct measurements of nuclear detonations at testing sites in both countries in the Joint Verification Experiment (JVE). A result of the Reagan mantra, "trust, but verify," the scientists' efforts were intended to develop and improve verification technologies that would be used to monitor compliance with treaties such as the Threshold Test Ban Treaty (1974) and the Peaceful Nuclear Explosions Treaty (1976).

Personal Technology   The 1980's saw the advent of many technological devices that would affect consumers. While the personal computer was one such advance, others included cell phones, compact discs (CDs), and car alarms. Cell phones began to be manufactured by large companies in the 1980's. Motorola introduced its DynaTAC phone to the public in 1983, a year after the Federal Communications Commission (FCC) authorized commercial cellular service. The phone weighed sixteen ounces and cost $3,500.

In 1984, American Telephone and Telegraph (AT&T) was split into seven "Baby Bells" as a result of an antitrust suit brought by the Department of Justice. Each of the seven telephone companies created by the split had its own cellular business, creating difficulties in expansion as well as diminishing the marketing power available to each company to promote cellular phones. The FCC began awarding licenses for the mobile telephone by lottery, rather than by comparative hearings. Many lottery winners chose to sell their licenses to larger companies, which paid well for the acquisition. In 1987, the FCC declared that cellular licensees could use additional cellular services, allowing companies to begin to employ alternative cellular technologies. By the end of the decade, there were over a million cell phone subscribers in the United States.

Another major change in the technology available to private consumers came in the form of CDs, which were introduced commercially in 1982 when the first music album was released on CD, rock band Abba's *The Visitors*. CDs, co-invented by Philips Electronics and the Sony Corporation, would create a revolution in digital audio technology. The discs were enthusiastically received, initially by classical music enthusiasts and audiophiles, and later—as the price of CD players dropped—by music fans in general. CDs were originally marketed specifically to store sound, but their potential for storing other types of digitally encoded data soon became apparent. In 1985, Sony and Philips developed the first compact disc read-only memory (CD-ROM). It stored the entirety of *Grolier's Electronic Encyclopedia*—nine million words—in only 12 percent of the space available on the disc.

One technology that received a legal boost in the late 1980's was the car alarm: The New York State legislature passed a law requiring insurance companies to offer a 10 percent discount to vehicle owners whose car was protected with such an alarm. When other states followed suit, the number of vehicles equipped with this technology rose sharply.

In 1989, Silicon Graphics unveiled the technology of virtual reality—computer-generated, three-dimensional environments containing elements with which users could interact—at a trade show in Boston. First intended for tasks such as flight simulation, the technology was quickly seized upon by game designers as well.

Impact   While many advances in science and technology occurred in the course of the 1980's, the most significant was arguably the steady stream of improvements in information technology. The Internet would become a world-spanning entity allowing instantaneous transmission of information and spurring globalization. At the same time, advances in DNA and gene identification would affect fields ranging from agriculture to medicine. Advances in personal technology would create increasing acceptance and use of electronic devices by consumers, paving the way for the various handheld computing devices of the next two decades.

Further Reading

Allan, Roy A. *A History of the Personal Computer: The People and the Technology*. London, Ont.: Allan, 2001. Sometimes quirky but usually informative look at the figures and technologies of the personal computing movement.

Benedick, Richard. *Ozone Diplomacy*. Boston: Harvard University Press, 1991. Provides a detailed examination of the discovery of the ozone hole and the negotiations that led to the Montreal Protocol.

Cook, Richard C. *Challenger Revealed: An Insider's Look at How the Reagan Administration Caused the Greatest Tragedy of the Space Age*. New York: Avalon, 2007. Traces the history of the space shuttle's development and deployment, describing the equipment malfunctions and internal NASA decision making that led to the crash.

Erickson, Jim, and James Wallace. *Hard Drive: Bill Gates and the Making of the Microsoft Empire*. New York: John Wiley & Sons, 1992. A thorough examination of the company; provides analysis of Microsoft's initiatives and releases throughout the 1980's, including profiles of competitors.

Fitzgerald, Frances. *Way Out There in the Blue: Reagan, Star Wars, and the End of the Cold War*. New York: Touchstone Press, 2000. Explores the history of the Strategic Defense Initiative and President Reagan's attempt to provide the United States with protection from nuclear attack.

Gregory, Jane, and Steve Miller. *Science in Public: Communication, Culture, and Credibility*. New York: Plenum Press, 1998. Discusses the ways in which science came to the attention of the American public in the 1980's.

Reilly, Philip R. *Abraham Lincoln's DNA and Other Adventures in Genetics*. Cold Spring Harbor, N.Y.: Cold Spring Harbor University Press, 2000. Includes explanations of early advances in genetics and DNA, including polymerase chain reaction and mutation analysis, and discusses applications of those techniques.

Shilts, Randy. *And the Band Played On: Politics, People, and the AIDS Epidemic*. New York: St. Martin's Press, 1987. This exhaustive account of the spread of AIDS in the United States discusses how the search for a cure shaped medicine and epidemiology.

Cat Rambo

See also AIDS epidemic; Apple Computer; Astronomy; Bioengineering; CAD/CAM technology; Cancer research; *Challenger* disaster; Cold War; Fetal medicine; Genetics research; Halley's comet; Information age; Medicine; Microsoft; National Energy Program (NEP); Nuclear winter scenario; Ozone hole; Plastic surgery; Prozac; Reagan, Ronald; SETI Institute; Space exploration; Space shuttle program; Strategic Defense Initiative (SDI).

■ Science-fiction films

Definition Motion pictures that focus on the impact of actual or imagined science on society or individuals

Early science-fiction films were associated with unrealistic effects that often made them seem campy, especially to later audiences. By the 1980's, however, computer-assisted special effects made possible a new level of realism that fundamentally transformed the nature of science-fiction cinema. The films of the 1980's thrived on these new effects technologies, which allowed filmmakers to represent the impossible in a realist and compelling fashion.

A new generation of computer-assisted special effects was pioneered in the late 1970's and showcased in such movies as *Star Wars* (1977), *Superman: The Movie* (1978), and *Alien* (1979). As a result, the 1980's began with audiences expecting a high level of sophistication from science-fiction films. Many such films were sequels to the groundbreaking work of the late 1970's, including two *Star Wars* sequels, *The Empire Strikes Back* (1980) and *Return of the Jedi* (1983), as well as *Superman II* (1980), *Superman III* (1983), *Superman IV: The Quest for Peace* (1987), and *Aliens* (1986). It was in the science-fiction genre that Hollywood's twin emerging preoccupations with sequels and effects-driven spectacle reached their height, greatly encouraged by the determination that each new movie's special effects should improve on the standard set by its predecessor.

The success of these series served to demonstrate that the most apt literary models for cinematic science fiction were not literary texts but comic books, which similarly dispensed with both inner experience and explanations. Other notable contributions to the superheroic subgenre of cinematic science fiction included *Flash Gordon* (1980), *RoboCop* (1987) and *Batman* (1989). Animated movies made little progress, although the advent in the West of Japanese *anime* films, with *Akira* (1988), offered a pointer to the untapped potential of that supplementary medium.

Selected Science-Fiction Films of the 1980's

Year	Title	Director
1980	*The Empire Strikes Back*	Irvin Kershner
	Superman II	Richard Lester
	Flash Gordon	Mike Hodges
	Altered States	Ken Russell
	Battle Beyond the Stars	Jimmy T. Murakami
1981	*The Road Warrior*	George Miller
	Memoirs of a Survivor	David Gladwell
	The Incredible Shrinking Woman	Joel Schumacher
	Escape from New York	John Carpenter
	Outland	Peter Hyams
1982	*Star Trek II: The Wrath of Khan*	Nicholas Meyer
	The Thing	John Carpenter
	E.T.: The Extra-Terrestrial	Steven Spielberg
	Blade Runner	Ridley Scott
	Tron	Steven Lisberger
1983	*Return of the Jedi*	Richard Marquand
	Superman III	Richard Lester
	Space Raiders	Howard R. Cohen
1984	*Star Trek III: The Search for Spock*	Leonard Nimoy
	The Last Starfighter	Nick Castle
	2010: The Year We Make Contact	Peter Hyams
	The Terminator	James Cameron
	Starman	John Carpenter
	Dune	David Lynch
	The Brother from Another Planet	John Sayles
1985	*Mad Max: Beyond Thunderdome*	George Miller and George Ogilvie
	Cocoon	Ron Howard
	Back to the Future	Robert Zemeckis
	Enemy Mine	Wolfgang Petersen
	Explorers	Joe Dante
	Trancers	Charles Band
1986	*Aliens*	James Cameron
	Star Trek IV: The Voyage Home	Leonard Nimoy
	The Fly	David Cronenberg
	Short Circuit	John Badham
	Invaders from Mars	Tobe Hooper
1987	*RoboCop*	Paul Verhoeven
	Predator	John McTiernan
	Batteries Not Included	Matthew Robbins

Year	Title	Director
1987 *(continued)*	*Innerspace*	Joe Dante
	Superman IV: The Quest for Peace	Sidney J. Furie
1988	*Akira*	Katsuhiro Ōtomo
	The Blob	Chuck Russell
	They Live	John Carpenter
	Cocoon: The Return	Daniel Petrie
	Alien Nation	Graham Baker
	Earth Girls Are Easy	Julien Temple
1989	*Batman*	Tim Burton
	Star Trek V: The Final Frontier	William Shatner
	The Abyss	James Cameron
	Honey, I Shrunk the Kids	Joe Johnston
	Back to the Future, Part II	Robert Zemeckis
	The Wizard of Speed and Time	Mike Jittlov

Science-Fiction Franchises   The *Star Wars* and *Star Trek* movie franchises—the latter including *Star Trek II: The Wrath of Khan* (1982), *Star Trek III: The Search for Spock* (1984), *Star Trek IV: The Voyage Home* (1986), and *Star Trek V: The Final Frontier* (1989)—reinvigorated space opera as a cinematic subgenre. These series required large budgets, and budgetary constraints limited the ambitions of such second-rank contributions as *The Last Starfighter* (1984), while attempts at serious space fiction, such as *2010: The Year We Make Contact* (1984), often failed to realize their ambition. The new wave of monster movies produced in the wake of *Alien* was more consistently successful in its exploitation of new effects; notable retreads of earlier, low-budget films included *The Thing* (1982), *The Fly* (1986), and *The Blob* (1988), while significant new ventures in this vein included *The Terminator* (1984), *Predator* (1987), *They Live* (1988), and *Tremors* (1989). *The Terminator* was a low-budget film, but it was sufficiently successful to spawn an important series of higher-budget sequels, and it eventually became the archetype of a new wave of exaggerated action movies whose other exemplars included *Mad Max 2: The Road Warrior* (1981) and *Mad Max: Beyond Thunderdome* (1985).

The implicit paranoia of monster movies expressed Cold War fears of the decade. Another more hopeful type of alien-centered science fiction arose during the 1980's, however, to resist the worldview of those films. These films offered more sympathetic accounts of nonhuman characters, while often complaining stridently about human tendencies toward intolerance and exploitation. They included *Android* (1981), Steven Spielberg's *E.T.: The Extra-Terrestrial* (1982)—the most successful film of the decade—*Starman* (1984), *Cocoon* (1985), *Short Circuit* (1986), *Batteries Not Included* (1987), and *The Abyss* (1989).

The difficulties of adapting literary texts to the cinematic medium were amply demonstrated by the Paddy Chayevsky-based *Altered States* (1980), the Doris Lessing-based *Memoirs of a Survivor* (1981), the cinematic travesty of Frank Herbert's *Dune* (1984), and the inevitable remake in its title year of George Orwell's *Nineteen Eighty-Four* (1984). Although it bore little resemblance to its source text and it was initially unsuccessful at the box office, Ridley Scott's *Blade Runner* (1982), based on Philip K. Dick's *Do Androids Dream of Electric Sheep?* (1968), would eventually be recognized as a major and significant work of cinematic science fiction.

The stunning art direction of *Blade Runner* set new standards in the portrayal of fictional worlds, and the film's eventual success as a videocassette rental encouraged further interest in Dick's work. Dick continually questioned the stability of the experienced world, and this concern of science fiction converged powerfully with film's ability to construct visceral illusions in such paranoid metaphysical fantasies as David Cronenberg's *Scanners* (1981) and *Videodrome* (1983). Inevitable delays in production, however, ensured that further Dick dramatizations were postponed until subsequent decades.

The new special effects were also deployed in a new generation of futuristic satires, including *The Incredible Shrinking Woman* (1981), *The Brother from Another Planet* (1984), *Repo Man* (1984), and *Honey, I Shrunk the Kids* (1989). These relatively amiable examples were, however, outshone by the scathing *Brazil* (1985), whose ending was considered too harsh for a U.S. audience that showed a blatant preference for the exuberance of such comedies as *Back to the Future*

(1985), *Innerspace* (1987), *Back to the Future, Part II* (1989), and *Bill and Ted's Excellent Adventure* (1989).

U.S. cinema did make some attempts to address actual trends in science and technology, particularly in computer-inspired movies such as *Tron* (1982) and *War Games* (1983), but it demonstrated no conspicuous understanding of how those technologies actually functioned. By contrast, continued experimentation with the new special effects resulted in some remarkably sophisticated visual representations and strikingly iconic images. Although most of these were contained in big-budget movies such as *Blade Runner, E.T., Brazil,* and *Batman,* it remained possible for enterprising technicians to produce such unique ventures as Mike Jittlov's *The Wizard of Speed and Time* (1989).

Fans wait in line for the premiere of Return of the Jedi, *the final film of the first* Star Wars *trilogy, in New York's Times Square on May 25, 1983.* (AP/Wide World Photos)

Impact It has been argued that, of all genres, science fiction is one of the most consistently allegorical of social and political concerns, and the science-fiction films of the 1950's were frequently interpreted as conscious or unconscious essays on Cold War paranoia. By the 1980's, these interpretations were well known, and science-fiction cinema, while it continued to engage in allegory, also began to comment upon it. Most of the decade's offerings were shaped by the desire of the studios to produce big-budget blockbusters that would draw extremely large audiences away from the competing technologies of television and videocassettes. This desire often meant that the most expensive films were the most simpleminded. However, even these films invented rich visual iconographies, making fantastic worlds believable on screen for the first time in decades. Although the decade was dominated by sequels, remakes, and imitations, it consolidated the innovations of the 1970's and paved the way for further sophistication of futuristic imagery.

Further Reading

Bukatman, Scott. *Terminal Identity: The Virtual Subject in Postmodern Science Fiction.* Durham, N.C.: Duke University Press, 1993. Study of the postmodern examination of identity common to much of the significant science fiction of the 1980's.

Hardy, Phil, ed. *The Aurum Film Encyclopedia: Science Fiction.* Rev. ed. London: Aurum Press, 1991. The chapter "The Eighties: Science Fiction Triumphant" offers a comprehensive chronological survey of titles, with elaborate and intelligent annotations.

Kuhn, Annette, ed. *Alien Zone: Cultural Theory and Contemporary Science Fiction Cinema.* London: Routledge, 1990. Collection of theoretical essays; its key exemplars include *Blade Runner, The Thing, Videodrome,* and *Aliens.*

Landon, Brooks. *The Aesthetics of Ambivalence: Rethinking Science Fiction Film in the Age of Electronic (Re)Production.* Westport, Conn.: Greenwood Press, 1992. Theoretical study that foregrounds the centrality of special effects as a driving force in the genre's evolution, with specific emphasis on the 1980's.

Rickett, Richard. *Special Effects: The History and Technique.* New York: Watson-Guptill, 2000. Topically organized study; many of its key examples are, inevitably, science-fiction movies, but the utility of the book is in filling in the background to the key innovations of the 1980's.

Sobchak, Vivian. *Screening Space: The American Science Fiction Film.* 2d ed. New York: Ungar, 1987. The updating chapter, "Postfuturism," describes the 1980's as a "Second Golden Age" of science-fiction cinema.

Brian Stableford

See also Action films; *Aliens; Back to the Future; Blade Runner; Empire Strikes Back, The; E.T.: The Extra-Terrestrial;* Film in the United States; Horror films; *RoboCop;* Sequels; Special effects; Spielberg, Steven; *Terminator, The; Tron.*

■ Scorsese, Martin

Identification American film director and film preservationist
Born November 17, 1942; Queens, New York

Scorsese belonged to the generation of American auteurs who began making films during the 1970's, and he continued to hone his craft during the 1980's. He directed five very different major motion pictures during the decade, branding each one with his trademark style.

A sickly child from a tough Italian American neighborhood, Martin Scorsese spent much of his childhood going to church and to the movies, then spent a year in the seminary and completed two film degrees at New York University. These seminal experiences shaped Scorsese's fascination with guilt and redemption, with the enactment of masculinity, and with the aesthetic and emotional possibilities of film. In the 1970's, Scorsese made his name as a director with two powerful, urban dramas—*Mean Streets* (1973) and *Taxi Driver* (1976). In the 1980's, he expanded his range of topics, if not his tone, for Scorsese protagonists continued to be men plagued with self-doubt. Thus, Scorsese's films rubbed against the grain of the success narratives typical of 1980's Hollywood.

Scorsese began the 1980's directing a film he thought would be his last. Ostensibly the biopic of a champion boxer, *Raging Bull* (1980) examines how self-loathing drives a man to violence against those he loves. Filmed in striking black and white, edited with great daring, and featuring a bravura performance by Robert De Niro, *Raging Bull* set a 1980's standard for serious American filmmaking. Other commercially risky projects followed. *The King of Comedy* (1983), a dark comedy about celebrity culture, presents another obssesive personality: a crazed fan (again played by Robert De Niro) who captures a television star, portrayed in a surprisingly restrained performance by Jerry Lewis. Next, Scorsese brought his usual paranoia to a common 1980's figure—the yuppie—when he dramatized a misplaced uptowner's terrifying night in lower Manhattan in *After Hours* (1985).

Updating and expanding the 1961 Robert Rossen classic *The Hustler*, Scorsese's *The Color of Money* (1986) again centered on a male world of competition and exploitation. Paul Newman, who had played young pool shark "Fast Eddie" Felson in the original, reprised his role. Twenty-five years older, Felson in Scorsese's film acts as mentor to a cocky newcomer played by Tom Cruise. After numerous postponements, Scorsese worked in the late 1980's to complete his dream project, *The Last Temptation of Christ* (1988). The controversial film was, surprisingly, produced by Universal Pictures. Following the provocative novel by Nikos Kazantzakis, Scorsese and screenwriter Paul Schrader presented a human, sexual, confused Christ who is redemed through suffering. The film sparked controversy, protests, and threats and was pulled from distribution by the studio. Scorsese ended the decade with "Life Lessons," a modest short about an artist and his obsessive loves that was released as part of *New York Stories* (1989), a three-part feature that also included shorts directed by Woody Allen and Francis Ford Coppola. Although Scorsese received two Oscar nominations and numerous directing awards in the 1980's, the Academy Award eluded him.

Impact Scorsese's ability to secure financial backing for innovative projects that resisted popular trends made him an influential bridge figure between mainstream and independent filmmaking in the 1980's. Moreover, along with Allen, Steven Spielberg, and George Lucas, Scorsese contributed to a significant reconception of the nature of film auteurism in general and American filmmaking in particular. In 1989, a poll of American and international film critics ranked *Raging Bull* the best film of the decade.

Further Reading

Nicholls, Mark. *Scorsese's Men: Melancholia and the Mob.* North Melbourne, Vic.: Pluto Press, 2004.

Stern, Lesley. *The Scorsese Connection.* Bloomington: Indiana University Press, 1995.

Thompson, David, and Ian Christe, eds. *Scorsese on Scorsese.* Boston: Faber & Faber, 1996.

Carolyn Anderson

See also Academy Awards; Film in the United States; *Last Temptation of Christ, The*; *Raging Bull*; Spielberg, Steven.

■ Sequels

Definition Narrative work that represents the continuation of a story begun in an earlier work

During the 1980's, as blockbusters became increasingly important to Hollywood's financial model, movie sequels began to drive the film industry's profits. Because large-scale sequels tended to be easier to promote effectively as "event" films, they were among the most financially successful films of the decade, although they were often less successful with professional critics.

The 1980's opened with *Superman 2* (1980), bringing Christopher Reeve back to the big screen for a sequel to the blockbuster *Superman: The Movie* (1978). The sequel proved popular enough to inspire two more, *Superman 3* (1983) and *Superman 4: The Quest for Peace* (1987). The original movie had been a big-budget version of a comic book whose protagonist heretofore had been relegated to inexpensive movie serials, a television series, and the low-budget *Superman and the Mole Men* (1951). By 1989, Superman's comic-book cohort Batman received a similar big-budget movie treatment. That film's success not only led to *Batman* sequels but also legitimized the adaptation to major motion pictures of other comic book characters with appropriate sequels, a trend which would continue.

Another 1980 sequel was *The Empire Strikes Back*, the second installment in George Lucas's trend-setting *Star Wars* trilogy. The final work of the trilogy, *Return of the Jedi*, followed in 1983. Three prequels would later be made as well. The *Star Wars* films were deliberately designed in the style of 1950's movie serials, in which a short chapter would be released each week and each chapter would end with a cliffhanger to draw audiences back the following week. *Star Wars* did much the same thing, only over a period of years instead of weeks.

Steven Spielberg launched another series with a deliberately nostalgic style with *Raiders of the Lost Ark* (1981). That film, the first in the Indiana Jones series, borrowed from the vintage movie serials, but it and other films in the series each featured a self-contained story arc. In fact, the series' second film, *Indiana Jones and the Temple of Doom* (1984), was a prequel rather than a sequel, taking place before the events portrayed in *Raiders of the Lost Ark*. The next film, *Indiana Jones and the Last Crusade* (1989), was a true sequel, taking place later than the first two.

All of these movies showcased the latest in special effects. Such realist effects in science-fiction and fantasy films were initially pioneered by Stanley Kubrick's *2001: A Space Odyssey* (1968) and rejuvenated by *Star Wars* (1977). In 1984, a sequel to *2001* was released: *2010: The Year We Make Contact*. Meanwhile, author Arthur C. Clarke, who had written the books on which both films were based, continued to produce several more literary sequels in that series.

Many other movies that inspired sequels also featured heavy special-effects elements. John Carpenter's *The Terminator* (1984), starring Arnold Schwarzenegger, would be followed by two sequels in subsequent decades. The comedic *Ghostbusters* (1984) was followed by *Ghostbusters II* (1989). The success of *Star Wars* inspired the creators of television's *Star Trek* series to create special-effects driven movies, starting with *Star Trek: The Motion Picture* (1979) and continuing with four sequels during the 1980's. Other science-fiction sequels of the 1980's included follow-ups to *Alien* (1979), *Cocoon* (1985), and *Back to the Future* (1985). Indeed, so sure was Universal Pictures of the marketability of sequels to the latter film that *Back to the Future, Part II* (1989) and *Back to the Future, Part III* (1990) were filmed simultaneously for separate releases.

The James Bond franchise had been a mainstay of the film sequel business since the 1960's, but the 1980's saw no less than five Bond films released. Sylvester Stallone, the star of the *Rocky* franchise, launched a new series featuring a military hero named Rambo with *First Blood* (1982). *Mad Max*, the 1979 Australian movie that introduced Mel Gibson to American audiences as an ex-policeman in an apocalyptic future, produced two sequels in the 1980's: *Mad Max 2: The Road Warrior* (1981) and *Mad Max: Beyond Thunderdome* (1985).

Gibson would also co-star with Danny Glover in the buddy cop movie *Lethal Weapon* (1987), which also became a franchise. *Die Hard* (1988) launched a franchise starring Bruce Willis as a dogged New York detective with a knack for fighting terrorists. Clint Eastwood continued his *Dirty Harry* detective series with sequels into the 1980's. *Beverly Hills Cop* (1984), starring Eddie Murphy, was also successful enough to demand sequels. Police action sequels vied with the fantasy and science-fiction sequels that launched the trend.

Some movies of the 1980's inspired only a single sequel, such as the outdoor adventure *Man from Snowy River* (1982), as well as relatively low-budget comedies including *Airplane!* (1980), *Arthur* (1981), *Look Who's Talking* (1989), *Porky's* (1982), *Revenge of the Nerds* (1984), and *Crocodile Dundee* (1986). There was even a musical sequel, *Grease 2* (1982).

Sequels differ from earlier movie series, which ranged from B-Westerns to mysteries and comedies featuring the same actor or actors, but had plots unrelated from one picture to another. While some movies in series like the Andy Hardy and Thin Man series could be considered sequels in that the characters grow and change from film to film, such others as the Charlie Chan and Bowery Boys series, as well as innumerable Westerns of earlier decades, simply told individual stories featuring the same characters. In this, they resembled television series of the 1950's through 1970's, although in the 1980's some series began to feature significant character development over the course of the show.

Impact During the 1980's, Hollywood became defined by the drive to make a few blockbusters (large-budget films with extreme profits), rather than a greater number of cheaper, more modestly successful films. As a result, studios' interest in high-concept stories (that is, stories that could be easily understood and exhaustively summarized in one sentence) increased dramatically. High-concept films were the easiest to market to a mass audience, and there was no higher concept than "the sequel to *Raiders of the Lost Ark*," for example. At the same time, blockbusters often featured fantastic worlds portrayed by special effects. It was easier to mimic the overall look and feel of an earlier film and invest in more impressive effects than it was to create entirely new art, set, and costume designs from scratch. This fact also drove the trend toward sequels. After the 1980's, movie sequels became a mainstay of the entertainment industry.

Further Reading

Budra, Paul, and Betty A. Schellenberg, eds. *Part Two: Reflections on the Sequel.* Toronto: University of Toronto Press, 1998. Compilation of essays on literary and cinematic sequels, including two essays on cinema of the 1980's and 1990's.

Nowlan, Robert A., and Gwendolyn Wright Nolan. *Cinema Sequels and Remakes, 1903-1987.* Reprint. Jefferson, N.C.: McFarland, 2000. Scholarly overview of both sequels to and remakes of successful films.

Stanley, John. *Creature Features: The Science Fiction, Fantasy, and Horror Movie Guide.* New York: Berkley Trade, 2000. Thousands of capsule reviews of movies from this genre, including sequels.

Thompson, David. *The Alien Quartet: A Bloomsbury Movie Guide.* New York: Bloomsbury USA, 1999. Analyzes different aspects of the *Alien* films, including themes, directors, and the relation of each film to the others.

Paul Dellinger

See also Academy Awards; Action films; *Airplane!*; *Aliens*; *Back to the Future*; Cruise, Tom; *Empire Strikes Back, The*; Epic films; Film in the United States; Ford, Harrison; Fox, Michael J.; *Ghostbusters*; Gibson, Mel; Horror films; Murphy, Eddie; Murray, Bill; *Raiders of the Lost Ark*; Rambo; *RoboCop*; Schwarzenegger, Arnold; Science-fiction films; Special effects; Spielberg, Steven; *Terminator, The.*

■ SETI Institute

Identification Institution established to search for signs of intelligent extraterrestrial life
Date Founded in 1984

The SETI Institute launched the most significant public project dedicated to searching for any evidence that intelligent life exists on other planets.

The stated mission of the SETI (Search for Extra-Terrestrial Intelligence) Institute is "to explore, understand and explain nature and the prevalence of life in the universe." The institute's most recognized project is also named Search for Extra-Terrestrial Life. It is an attempt to detect any radio transmissions reaching Earth from elsewhere that might have been generated by alien civilizations. This project evolved from Frank Drake's original 1960 Project Ozma experiment, which used a radio telescope to examine the stars Tau Ceti and Epsilon Eridani near the 1.420 gigahertz marker frequency. Project Ozma represented humankind's first scientific attempt to detect extraterrestrial intelligence.

The SETI Institute has evolved from its beginning as a systematic search for intelligent extraterrestrial radio sources into a multifaceted organization dedicated to gaining a better understanding of life in the universe. Inspired by its founder Frank Drake and fired by the charisma of astronomer Carl Sagan, the SETI Institute came to employ over one hundred scientists from a wide variety of disciplines at its Carl Sagan Center for the Study of Life in the Universe and the Center for the Search for Extra-Terrestrial Intelligence. Although searching for intelligent extraterrestrial life may be the SETI Institute's highest-profile project, other studies involve more fundamental inquiries into planetary formation and evolution. The institute's projects investigate how life began on Earth and how many other stars in the Milky Way galaxy may have planets that could support life. The SETI Institute's activities were also popularized Carl Sagan's novel *Contact* (1985), as well as by its 1997 film adaptation.

Impact The SETI Institute continued to search for evidence of intelligent extraterrestrial life, employing new techniques and resources as they became available. Detection of radio signals from an extraterrestrial civilization is not an easy task. Radio astronomers first have to determine what types of star systems may have planets. Then they have to decide which radio frequency would be the most logical to listen to. Once these decisions have been made, they listen and wait. Computers evolved to make the job manageable, but even with advances in distributed computing, the task remained daunting.

Further Reading

Ekers, Ron, et al., eds. *SETI 2020: A Roadmap for the Search for Extraterrestrial Intelligence.* Mountain View, Calif.: SETI Institute, 2003.

Shostak, Seth, and Alex Barnett. *Cosmic Company: The Search for Life in the Universe.* Cambridge, England: Cambridge University Press, 2003.

Skurzynski, Gloria. *Are We Alone? Scientists Search for Life in Space.* Washington, D.C.: National Geographic, 2004.

Paul P. Sipiera

See also Astronomy; *Cosmos*; *E.T.: The Extra-Terrestrial*; Science and technology; Science-fiction films; Space exploration; *Star Trek: The Next Generation*.

■ sex, lies, and videotape

Identification American film
Director Steven Soderbergh (1963-   )
Date Premiered at the Sundance Film Festival January 20, 1989; general release August 18, 1989

Along with the films of Jim Jarmusch, Spike Lee, and Gus Van Sant, Soderbergh's sex, lies, and videotape *heralded the birth of what came to be called American independent cinema. Soderbergh went on to enjoy a career bridging the mainstream/independent divide, directing both low-budget and studio films with great success.*

The acclaim heaped upon *sex, lies, and videotape*, a low-budget film by an unknown director and without major stars, at the 1989 Sundance Film Festival is often credited with launching the independent film movement that would become more prominent in the 1990's. To raise the money to make his feature-film debut, Steven Soderbergh made *Winston* (1987), a twelve-minute short intended to be shown to potential investors. When it was completed, *sex, lies, and videotape* proved that American film could examine the mores of the time with subtle humor and understated insight and without the obviousness, didacticism, or sentimentality often seen in mainstream films.

Filmed in Soderbergh's hometown, Baton Rouge, Louisiana, *sex, lies, and videotape* depicts the unhappy marriage of the frigid Ann (Andie MacDowell) and the smarmy lawyer John (Peter Gallagher), who is having an affair with Ann's bartender sister, Cynthia (Laura San Giacomo). The arrival of John's former college friend, Graham

(James Spader), sets in motion changes in the other characters' relationships. The primary catalyst for these changes is Graham's collection of videotapes, each recording an interview he has made with a woman about her sexual experiences. John is typical of the 1980's achievers who care only for their work. Both he and Cynthia, a would-be artist, use each other without any emotional commitment. Ann feels a general sense of malaise, as captured in her sessions with her psychiatrist (Ron Vawter). Graham, who seems to have no direction in life, resorts to his taped interviews because of sexual impotence. In many senses, *sex, lies, and videotape* offers a younger perspective on the issues addressed in Lawrence Kasdan's *The Big Chill* (1983).

Soderbergh was clearly influenced by the films of Woody Allen and perhaps even more by foreign films, especially those from France, that were more

Director Steven Soderbergh holds the Palme d'Or he was awarded for sex, lies, and videotape *at the 1989 Cannes Film Festival, as actress Jane Fonda looks on.* (AP/Wide World Photos)

open than American films in dealing with sexual matters. The director, who was only twenty-six when the film premiered at the Sundance Film Festival, treated his characters—with the notable exception of John—with affection and compassion. He gave considerable latitude to his actors, who found unexpected humor in their characters' aimlessness and self-absorption.

Impact The publicity surrounding *sex, lies, and videotape* gave the public more awareness of the Sundance Film Festival, then a relatively small venue, and of independent film in general. The film's success represented a breakthrough for Harvey and Bob Weinstein's production company, Miramax Films, which had previously distributed primarily foreign-language films. The film launched Soderbergh's career as a major film director. It also boosted the careers of its stars, all four of whom went on to significant careers in film, television, or theater. The film won the Sundance Audience Award, received the Palme d'Or as the best film at the Cannes Film Festival, and was nominated for an Academy Award for Best Original Screenplay.

Further Reading

Biskind, Peter. *Down and Dirty Pictures: Miramax, Sundance, and the Rise of Independent Film.* New York: Simon & Schuster, 2004.

Palmer, William J. *The Films of the Eighties: A Social History.* Carbondale: Southern Illinois University Press, 1993.

Smith, Lory. *Party in a Box: The Story of the Sundance Film Festival.* Salt Lake City: Gibbs-Smith, 1999.

Michael Adams

See also *Big Chill, The*; Camcorders; *Do the Right Thing*; Film in the United States; Generation X.

■ Sexual harassment

Definition Unwelcome sexual speech or behavior, engaged in by someone with institutional power over the recipient

During the 1980's, the U.S. Supreme Court and many lower courts ruled that sexual harassment was a form of sex discrimination. As a result, businesses and academic institutions became more aware of the issue and sought to educate students and employees about it.

Sexual harassment was not a new phenomenon in the 1980's. However, the behavior did not have a legal name until the late twentieth century. Additionally, the public became more familiar with the problem, as the courts established legal definitions and employers became sensitive to their responsibility to prevent the conduct.

Sex Discrimination The Civil Rights Act of 1964 made it illegal for employers and educational institutions to discriminate against a person with respect to "terms, conditions, or privileges of employment because of such individual's race, color, religion, sex, or national origin." In 1980, the Equal Employment Opportunity Commission (EEOC) issued guidelines stating that sexual harassment was a form of sex discrimination. The rules defined the prohibited activity to include unwanted sexual advances, requests for sexual favors, and verbal or physical conduct of a sexual nature. They stated that sexual harassment included giving or removing an economic quid pro quo.

Quid pro quo harassment is the easiest type to identify. It generally involves the attempt by an employer or a supervisor to exchange rewards such as raises or promotions in return for sexual favors. Likewise, it may involve punishing an employee who refuses sexual contact by negative changes to the terms of his or her employment. The second type of sexual harassment consists of creating a hostile work environment. In this situation, there may be no negotiation for sexual favors, but rather the general work atmosphere is infiltrated with sexual content or references, affecting employees' ability to do their jobs.

Meritor Savings Bank v. Vinson In 1986, the Supreme Court heard a case brought by Mechelle Vinson against her employer, Meritor Savings Bank. Vinson claimed that over a period of five years she was continually subjected to fondling, demands for sexual intercourse, and even rape by her boss, Sidney Taylor. Vinson could not report the harassment to her supervisor, as he was the assailant. She also testified that she feared the loss of her job if she told other bank officials. Taylor and the bank management denied any wrongdoing. Taylor claimed the sexual contact was consensual. The bank asserted that Vinson had not suffered any economic disadvantage.

The Supreme Court held that the Civil Rights Act was intended to "strike at the whole spectrum of disparate treatment of men and women." It agreed with the EEOC's designation of two types of harassment, comparing a hostile work environment based on sex to a hostile environment for racial minorities. "Surely a requirement that a man or woman run a gauntlet of sexual abuse in return for the privilege of being allowed to work and make a living can be as demeaning and disconcerting as the harshest of racial epithets." The Court defined a hostile environment as one in which the harassment was severe or pervasive enough to alter the conditions of employment. It left the issue of employer liability undefined, although it did indicate that at a minimum, employers should provide guidelines and grievance procedures to address incidents of sexual harassment.

Widespread Harassment   Feminist scholars and legal experts argued that sexual harassment was incorporated into a social structure of unequal power between men and women. They contended that in a patriarchal society, the behavior had more to do with men asserting control over women than with sexual attraction. In that sense, harassment could be seen as part of a continuum of power and control that involved other crimes against women. Just as domestic violence and rape had often been ignored or distorted by the legal system, so sexual harassment was, until the 1980's, treated as private conduct, "flirting," or "romance on the job." Some commentators noted that sexual harassment helped keep women subordinated in the workplace and that inappropriate sexual comments were designed to remind women of their inferior status.

Numerous surveys showed that sexual harassment was prevalent in many women's experience. Studies of women employed by the federal government conducted in 1981 and 1987 reported that 42 percent of women had experienced harassment on the job during the previous two years. Likewise, reports showed that 30 to 40 percent of women working in private business had been harassed. The most dramatic results came from the military, where 64 percent had been touched, pressured for sexual favors, or—in 5 percent of the cases—raped. Women in the military who reported harassment stated that reporting made their lives worse in every way.

Sexual harassment was an issue in educational institutions, as well as in employment. Studies of college campuses conducted by the National Association for Women Deans, Administrators, and Counselors in the 1980's found that 7 percent of women students said faculty members had made unwanted advances; 14 percent had been asked on dates by professors; 34 percent experienced leering; and 65 percent had been the target of sexual comments. Although a considerable number of them avoided certain classes because of faculty members' reputations, none of the women had reported the offensive conduct to the administration.

Impact   Despite the legal protection against sexual harassment, women only infrequently told their supervisors or authorities about the behavior. Many claimed they feared they would not be taken seriously. Mandated corporate training in regard to sexual harassment became widespread, but it was not always taken seriously. Some comedians even lampooned the perceived oversensitivity that required such training to be instituted.

Subsequent Events   The situation improved slowly and unsteadily in the next decade, particularly after high-profile harassment scandals in 1991 brought further impetus to the national conversation. In that year, Professor Anita Hill testified before a committee of the United States Senate that Clarence Thomas, a nominee for the Supreme Court, had repeatedly sexually harassed her when they worked together a decade earlier. A scandal also resulted from a 1991 convention of the Tailhook Association, an organization composed of naval aviators. Eighty-three women and seven men reported being sexually harassed or assaulted during the convention.

Further Reading

Atwell, Mary Welek. *Equal Protection of the Law? Gender and Justice in the United States.* New York: Peter Lang, 2002. Examines how gendered perspectives have been incorporated into the American legal system.

Forrell, Caroline A., and Donna M. Matthews. *A Law of Her Own: The Reasonable Woman as a Measure of Man.* New York: New York University Press, 2000. Study suggesting reforms that would take better account of women's experience in defining sexual harassment and other such legal terms.

MacKinnon, Catherine. "Toward Feminist Jurisprudence." In *Feminist Jurisprudence,* edited by Patricia Smith. New York: Oxford University Press,

1993. MacKinnon is largely responsible for defining and conceptualizing sexual harassment.

Rundblad, Georganne. "Gender, Power, and Sexual Harassment." In *Gender Mosaics: Social Perspectives*, edited by Dana Vannoy. Los Angeles: Roxbury, 2001. Analysis of sexual harassment emphasizing the extent to which it expresses social power struggles rather than (or alongside) sexual desire.

Mary Welek Atwell

See also Feminism; *Meritor Savings Bank v. Vinson*; Supreme Court decisions; Women in the workforce; Women's rights.

■ Shamrock Summit

The Event A meeting between U.S. president Ronald Reagan and Canadian prime minister Brian Mulroney
Date March 17, 1985
Place Quebec City, Canada

The amicable meeting between President Reagan and Prime Minister Mulroney underscored the growing closeness between their two North American countries.

During the ministry of Prime Minister Pierre Trudeau, which ended in 1984, Canada had often been at loggerheads with its neighbor and closest ally, the United States. When Brian Mulroney was voted into office on September 4, 1984, this situation changed. Mulroney firmly aligned Canada with the United States in geopolitical terms, abandoning Trudeau's fitful attempt to stake out a neutralist position between the Americans and the Soviet Union. Mulroney also redirected Trudeau's interest in developing countries to reaffirm economic and political ties with Canada's large, industrialized trading partners. Though Mulroney did not have a total ideological affinity with the conservative Ronald Reagan—he was much further to the left on issues concerning the welfare state and the environment, for instance— the meeting between the two leaders scheduled for March 17, 1985, in Quebec City was anticipated to be a positive one, and it exceeded expectations in this regard.

The two leaders not only found common ground on policy positions but also formed a close personal bond. The fact that March 17 was Saint Patrick's Day, dedicated to the patron saint of Ireland (whose symbol was the shamrock), underscored the two men's ethnic origins in the Irish diaspora. When Reagan and Mulroney joined in a duet of the song "When Irish Eyes Are Smiling," it was not only a moment of joviality but also a sense of shared identity, a solidarity of both ethnicity and moral temperament that welded the leaders in an affirmation of mutual beliefs. The meeting was also important for Mulroney's international image, as it was the first time most casual observers of world politics had heard of him.

The Shamrock Summit, however, was not popular among many Canadian media commentators and those in the general population who held a strongly Canadian nationalist ideology. They believed that Mulroney had capitulated to the colossus to their south and had relinquished Canada's idealistic and peace-seeking approach to the international situation, as well as the nation's economic independence and the quality of life of its populace.

Impact Many observers, remembering that previous Canadian prime ministers such as Sir Wilfrid Laurier had involuntarily left office because they were perceived to be too pro-American, waited for the meeting to damage Mulroney's political viability. This, however, did not occur. Partially ballasted by Canada's economic boom in the 1980's, Mulroney remained popular enough to lead his party to victory in the next election, retaining the prime ministry in the process. The meeting also helped Reagan at a time when he was beginning to encounter some unusual political difficulties in the wake of his overwhelming reelection the year before, such as the controversy over his visit to the Nazi graves at Bitburg, Germany, two months later.

Further Reading

Martin, Lawrence. *Pledge of Allegiance: The Americanization of Canada in the Mulroney Years.* Toronto: McClelland and Stewart, 1993.

Simpson, Jeffrey. *The Anxious Years: Politics in the Age of Mulroney and Chrétien.* Toronto: Lester, 1996.

Nicholas Birns

See also Canada and the United States; Canada-United States Free Trade Agreement; Mulroney, Brian; Reagan, Ronald.

■ Shepard, Sam

Identification American playwright, actor,
   director, and screenwriter
Born November 5, 1943; Fort Sheridan, Illinois

*Considered one of the most influential playwrights of his
generation, Shepard helped shape contemporary American
theater. In addition to penning numerous plays, the award-
winning dramatist became well known for his work as an
actor, director, and screenwriter throughout the 1980's.*

Sam Shepard began his career as an actor and playwright in the Off-Off-Broadway theaters of New York
in the early 1960's. His work gained critical acclaim
throughout the 1970's, earning him numerous
awards, including a Pulitzer Prize for *Buried Child*
(pr. 1978, pb. 1979) in 1979. Shepard continued to
establish himself as one of the great American dramatists during the 1980's with the publication of
True West (pr. 1980, pb. 1981), *Fool for Love* (pr., pb.
1985), and *A Lie of the Mind* (pr. 1985, pb. 1986). A
theme central to Shepard's work is loss; his characters often suffer from feelings of alienation and

search for connection and identity in an unstable
world. His plays also deal with the notion of masculinity and examine the social role of the American
male. Shepard's works are also deeply rooted in the
myth of the American West and the old frontier, a
landscape that is at once hopeful and destructive,
but is above all distinctly American.

During the 1980's, Shepard's career flourished,
and he became well known as an actor, director, and
screenwriter. Throughout the decade, Shepard performed in multiple films, and it was on the set of
Frances (1982) that Shepard met his longtime partner Jessica Lange, with whom he would have two
children. Shepard's rise to fame in film was bol-
stered by an Academy Award nomination for his performance in *The Right Stuff* in 1983. From then on,
Shepard was known not only as a great American
playwright but also as a prominent presence in American film. Shepard's popularity continued to increase, and in 1984, the Palme d'Or at the Cannes
Film Festival was awarded to *Paris, Texas.* Shepard
had written the film's screenplay, adapting his own
book, *Motel Chronicles* (1982). He participated in
many other films of the decade, including *Resurrec-
tion* (1980), *Fool for Love* (1985), *Crimes of the Heart*
(1986), *Baby Boom* (1987), *Far North* (1988), and *Steel
Magnolias* (1989).

Impact In the span of his long career, Shepard experienced the height of his popularity during the
1980's and was inducted into the American Academy of Arts and Letters in 1986. His works having
achieved national acclaim, he secured a permanent
place in American theater and became one of the
most produced playwrights in America. His influence on stage and screen are evident in the numerous works of scholarship devoted to him, as well as in
the popularity of his plays with modern audiences.

Further Reading

Roudane, Matthew, ed. *Cambridge Companion to Sam
   Shepard.* New York: Cambridge University Press,
   2002.
Tucker, Martin. *Sam Shepard.* New York: Continuum,
   1992.
Wade, Leslie A. *Sam Shepard and the American Theatre.*
   Westport, Conn.: Greenwood Press, 1997.

Danielle A. DeFoe

Sam Shepard. (Martha Holmes)

See also Academy Awards; Film in the United
States; Mamet, David; Theater.

■ Shields, Brooke

Identification American model and actor
Born May 31, 1965; New York, New York

Shields was a 1980's personality icon who gained fame as a result of her modeling and acting career. Because of her numerous magazine cover shots, she is considered to be one of the most photographed supermodels of the twentieth century.

During the early 1980's, it seemed that Brooke Shields was everywhere: She was on the cover of fashion magazines, the subject of newspaper and magazine articles, in advertisements, on talk shows, a costar of several films, and the subject of several books. Shields began her career as a child model, progressing to film roles in the late 1970's. Her controversial appearance as a child prostitute in the 1976 film *Pretty Baby* generated much media attention about her career, her mother, and her looks. She starred in several well-known teen films, including *Blue Lagoon* (1980), costarring Christopher Atkins, and *Endless Love* (1981). She also appeared in fourteen controversial television commercials for Calvin Klein jeans that were censored by several networks. The jean commercials generated much notoriety for Shields with their sensual photography and her statement in one of the ads, "You know what comes between me and my Calvins? Nothing."

Shields appeared in numerous Bob Hope television specials and several of the *Circus of the Stars* television shows. In 1982, a Brooke Shields doll was mass produced in her likeness, as were several outfits for it. Because much of Shields's work seemed to exploit her beauty, critics were quick to accuse her mother and manager, Terri Shields, of pushing Brooke to pursue a modeling and acting career that was not in her best interests when she was too young to make her own decisions. Shields was often noted as being likable and down-to-earth despite her child star status. She attended Princeton University from 1983 to 1987, graduating with honors and a degree in French literature. During her college years, she con-tinued to act in films such as *The Muppets Take Manhattan* (1984) and *Sahara* (1984). After completing college, she appeared in several made-for-television movies. With few exceptions, many of her film and modeling appearances seemed to exploit her sensuality, yet she maintained a wholesomeness that endeared her to many. She received People's Choice Awards for Favorite Young Performer four years in a row, from 1981 to 1984.

Impact Brooke Shields's career as a child star served as an example to others. Despite her fame and public attention, she and her mother both worked hard to ensure that her childhood and education would be as normal and mainstream as possible. Her fame and noted average lifestyle when not working, coupled with her above-average intelligence, beauty, and sensibility, made her an attractive role model to many.

Further Reading

Bonderoff, Jason. *Brooke.* New York: Zebra Books, 1981.

Italia, Bob. *Brooke Shields.* Minneapolis: Abdo & Daughters, 1992.

Brooke Shields poses in a public service image in the mid-1980's. (Hulton Archive/Getty Images)

Simpson, Maria. "Does She or Doesn't She? Revisited: The Calvin Klein Jeans Ad." *Etc.: A Review of General Semantics* 38 (Winter, 1981): 390-400.

Susan E. Thomas

See also   Advertising; Film in the United States; Teen films.

■ Shultz, George P.

Identification   U.S. secretary of state from 1982 to 1989
Born   December 13, 1920; New York, New York

Although Shultz was a staunch anticommunist, he opposed the Reagan administration covert operations that led to the Iran-Contra affair.

On July 16, 1982, President Ronald Reagan appointed George P. Shultz to replace Alexander Haig as U.S. secretary of state. Shultz had a distinguished academic career as a professor and dean of the well-known University of Chicago Graduate School of Business, which included on its staff many illustrious conservative economists. He also had an impressive background in government, having served on the Council of Economic Advisors of President Dwight D. Eisenhower (1953-1961) and as secretary of labor (1969-1970), Office of Management and Budget director (1970-1972), and secretary of the Treasury (1972-1974) under President Richard M. Nixon.

This distinguished record served Reagan's need to find someone with impeccable credentials to replace Haig, but there was nonetheless some feeling that Shultz was more dovish than the rest of the Reagan cabinet. He had a long record as an anticommunist, helped develop the Reagan Doctrine, supported the Grenada invasion, opposed negotiations with Daniel Ortega's Sandinista government, and even advocated invading Nicaragua to get rid of Ortega. Still, he sparred with Caspar Weinberger, the secretary of defense, over the prodigious growth of defense spending, which he saw as reckless. He was also at odds with John Poindexter, the national security adviser, and Oliver North, one of Poindexter's staffers, over various proposed arms deals in the Middle East, especially with Iran.

These deals involved the covert sale of arms to Iran, which just a few years earlier had held American hostages for more than a year, causing a national and international crisis. North and Poindexter used the proceeds from these sales illegally to fund the Contras, a rebel army in Nicaragua to which Congress had banned military aid. When these events became public, Shultz was untouched by the ensuing Iran-Contra scandal, because it was clear that he was opposed to selling weapons to Iran. During the first intifada in Palestine, Shultz attempted without success to convene an international conference to achieve a cease-fire and the creation of an autonomous region in the West Bank and the Gaza Strip.

Impact   In addition to pursuing policies that ended the Soviet Union, Shultz was significant in his resistance to the illegal activities of some of his colleagues in the Reagan administration. He left office on January 20, 1989, but continued to be a strategist for the Republican Party.

Secretary of State George P. Shultz, right, reads a statement to the press regarding U.S. policy toward Central America in November, 1987. The statement represents a compromise with House Speaker Jim Wright, center. (AP/Wide World Photos)

Further Reading

Madison, Christopher. "Shultz Shows How to Survive and Even Prosper in His High-Risk Post at State." *National Journal* 18, no. 7 (February 15, 1986).

Shultz, George. *Turmoil and Triumph: My Years as Secretary of State*. New York: Charles Scribner's Sons, 1993.

Richard L. Wilson

See also Cold War; Foreign policy of the United States; Grenada invasion; Haig, Alexander; Iran-Contra affair; Israel and the United States; Middle East and North America; North, Oliver; Poindexter, John; Reagan, Ronald; Reagan Doctrine; Soviet Union and North America; Weinberger, Caspar.

■ Simmons, Richard

Identification American fitness expert, motivational speaker, talk show host, and author
Born July 12, 1948; New Orleans, Louisiana

Simmons's personal approach toward helping overweight people changed the way people viewed diet and exercise in the 1980's. He promoted not just a weight-loss program but also a positive journey to a healthier lifestyle.

After personally experiencing several failed attempts to lose weight and keep it off, Richard Simmons opened Slimmons, an exercise club for people who were battling weight problems but who felt too embarrassed to join a gym. Simmons was concerned about the many dangerous ways in which people were trying to lose weight. After considerable research and consultations with doctors and nutritionists, he developed a diet plan called Deal-A-Meal. On his Emmy Award-winning talk show, *The Richard Simmons Show*, Simmons inspired others by sharing his own story with his audience and by presenting viewers who had lost weight using his healthy living, diet, and aerobics programs. Interaction with his viewers extended to making personal phone calls or visiting people who wrote to him about weight problems. He also worked to oversee the progress of those struggling with morbid obesity. As an additional aid in preparing nutritional meals, Simmons wrote *The Deal-A-Meal Cookbook* (1987) and *Richard Simmons' Never-Say-Diet Book* (1980).

Since Simmons felt that exercise is a major part of losing weight, he developed the *Sweatin' to the Oldies* series of aerobic exercise videos featuring people in various stages of weight loss exercising with him to upbeat music. His trademark outfit of shorts and a tank top was first worn in these exercise videos. While serving as the chair for the Spina Bifida Association, Simmons saw the need for an exercise program for the physically challenged and developed the *Reach for Fitness* program. The exercises in this program were adapted so people with various types of physical and medical challenges could participate. Simmons further expanded his exercise videos to include seniors and featured his mother, Shirley, along with other celebrities' parents, in *Richard Simmons and the Silver Foxes*.

Impact Simmons's devotion to helping others by providing inspiration, education, and motivation encouraged people in all walks of life to change their eating habits, to follow nutritional guidelines, and to maintain a realistic exercise schedule. In addition, his followers developed a deeper awareness of health issues and the dangers of being overweight.

Further Reading

Simmons, Richard. *Still Hungry After All These Years*. New York: G. T., 1999.

Stearns, Peter N. *Fat History: Bodies and Beauty in the Modern West*. New York: New York University Press, 1997.

Elizabeth B. Graham

See also Aerobics; Diets; Food trends; Home video rentals.

■ Sioux City plane crash

The Event A DC-10 jet endures a severe crash, but 185 people on board miraculously survive
Date July 19, 1989
Place Sioux City, Iowa

The Sioux City plane crash was one of the most famous air disasters of the 1980's, because it was a miracle that anyone survived, because it was captured on film, and because it caught the popular imagination. It was later the subject of fictional motion pictures and television documentaries.

One of the most amazing cases of survival in a commercial plane crash began with United Airlines

Flight 232 from Denver to Philadelphia with a stop in Chicago. The DC-10, a wide-bodied jet with three engines—one on each wing and one in the tail—took off a little after 2:00 P.M. central daylight time. The three-member flight crew consisted of Captain Alfred Haynes; First Officer William Records, the copilot; and Second Officer Dudley Dvorak, the flight engineer. About an hour after takeoff, a fan disk in the center engine broke in two, shattered the engine, blew through the engine case, and tore holes in the tail section of the plane. It punctured all three hydraulic systems, allowing the fluid to run out.

None of this damage was known in detail at the moment of the incident, but the flight crew felt a sharp jolt running through the plane. The copilot, who was at the controls, noticed that the airliner was off course and tried to correct the course with the controls, but he found the plane unresponsive. The crew also discovered that the autopilot was off, that the engine in the tail indicated a malfunction, and that the three hydraulic systems had lost all pressure. Although the three systems were designed to back one another up, their collective failure meant that none of the usual wing or tail controls on the aircraft would operate, creating a severe emergency situation.

The fan blade had broken and locked the controls while the plane was in a slight right turn. The hydraulic loss meant the plane was in a circular pattern while descending about fifteen hundred feet with each cycle. A DC-10 flight instructor, Dennis E. Fitch, was a passenger on board and offered to help. Eventually, he managed to stem the downward cycle a bit by running the two remaining engines at different speeds to steer the plane and gain or lose altitude. He also managed to lower the landing gear, but he was not able to restore the critical hydraulics.

The crew notified air traffic controllers, who indicated that the closest sizable airport was at Sioux City, Iowa. An emergency landing was organized there in the roughly thirty minutes available between the airborne incident and the crash landing. The crew dumped the plane's excess fuel, and everyone took care to avoid allowing the plane to pass over populated areas. This was very difficult, as the plane could make only right-hand turns. On final approach, the crew realized they could not attempt landing on the airfield's longer runway and therefore notified the tower that they would try to reach a

shorter runway on which the scrambled fire trucks had parked. Fortunately, the trucks were able to vacate the runway in time, but this situation delayed their response to the fire that resulted from the plane's impact.

A DC-10 would normally land at a speed of about 140 knots while descending at 300 feet per minute. The best the crew could do was to land their crippled plane at 240 knots while descending at 1,850 feet per minute. This resulted in a crash, but not as severe a crash as one might have expected for such a seriously crippled plane. A strong gust of wind blew the plane to the right of the runway and caused the right wing to hit the ground first, causing fuel to leak and ignite. The tail broke off first, and the rest of the plane bounced repeatedly, eventually rolling over on its back and sliding sideways into a cornfield next to the runway.

Of the 296 people aboard, 185 survived. Most of the 111 deaths resulted from the impact, but some were the result of smoke inhalation as the fire engulfed the section above the wings. Most survivors had been sitting ahead of the wings, and some were lucky enough to walk out of the crashed plane and into the cornfield unharmed.

A number of factors allowed for a better chance of survival than might have been expected from such a seriously damaged plane. The inherent crashworthiness of newer wide-bodied air transports played a part in the relatively high survival rate, as did the shallow angle of descent as a result of the crew's heroic efforts to land the plane as safely as possible. The incident occurred in daylight in good weather on the one day of the month when the Iowa Air National Guard was on duty at Sioux Gateway Airport. It also occurred at a time of day when extra personnel were available at both a regional trauma center and a regional burn center.

The subsequent investigation revealed that the fan blade broke because of fundamental weakness in its design. The weakness was corrected as a result. Additional investigation indicated that the weakness was missed during maintenance checks. The critical hydraulic failure was remedied by installing special fuses to prevent fluid loss in all hydraulic systems.

Impact   The Sioux City plane crash resulted in several engineering improvements for the DC-10 but had an even greater impact on procedures for training flight crews for emergencies. The Sioux City,

Iowa, emergency preparedness procedures were studied after the crash, so emergency responders could improve their readiness for crises.

Further Reading

Faith, Nicholas. *Black Box: The Air-Crash Detectives: Why Air Safety Is No Accident.* Osceola, Wis.: Motorbooks International, 1997.

"How Swift Starting Action Teams Get off the Ground: What United Flight 232 and Airline Flight Crews Can Tell Us About Team Communication." *Management Communication Quarterly* 19, no. 2 (November, 2005).

Schemmel, Jerry. *Chosen to Live: The Inspiring Story of Flight 232 Survivor Jerry Schemmel.* Littleton, Colo.: Victory, 1996.

Trombello, Joseph. *Miracle in the Cornfield.* Appleton, Wis.: PrintSource Plus, 1999.

Richard L. Wilson

See also　Air India Flight 182 bombing; Cerritos plane crash; Pan Am Flight 103 bombing.

■ Sitcoms

Definition　Comic television series in which regular characters and situations recur from episode to episode

Sitcoms in the 1980's focused on humor, friendship, and relationships between friends or family members. They largely discarded the broad physical comedy popular in earlier years.

Early situation comedies, or sitcoms, had filled "family viewing time" between 8:00 P.M. and 9:00 P.M. with lightweight, escapist stories and likable, somewhat predictable characters. When the more irreverent shows of cable television were introduced in the early 1980's, network television programming changed in order to compete for an increasingly sophisticated audience. Fresh and different approaches were needed. Innovative prime-time soap operas, such as *Dallas*, and so-called reality shows appeared, convincing the networks to incorporate serialization and greater realism into their new sitcoms. With continuing story lines, more true-to-life plots, poignancy, and even occasional sad endings, the new shows remained funny but incorporated much less slapstick humor.

The Domestic Sitcom　Almost since the advent of television, the networks had featured family shows such as *The Adventures of Ozzie and Harriet* and *Father Knows Best*. The 1980's family sitcom often retained the depiction of a nuclear family with both parents in the home. There were variations, however, such as *One Day at a Time* (1975-1984), *Who's the Boss?* (1984-1992), and *Diff'rent Strokes* (1978-1986), which portrayed divorced parents or orphaned children. Even these shows, though, used surrogate parental figures, such as a housekeeper or handyman, to maintain the two-parent model. The 1980's family sitcom retained another characteristic of earlier shows: The families always lived in a nice house or apartment with all the necessities for a comfortable lifestyle.

There were several major differences between 1980's and traditional 1950's and 1960's sitcoms, however. Family breadwinners, whether male or female, often worked at unglamourous jobs for little pay. Although *Good Times*, which aired in the 1970's, depicted an indigent African American family, *Roseanne* (1988-1997) was unique in featuring a Caucasian working-class family in which both parents worked at a series of low-paying jobs and were often in dire financial straits. The show's humor often came from the parents' ability to laugh at their circumstances. *The Tortellis* (1987) featured another working-class family composed of a television repairman, his second wife, and his children from his first marriage. It was a spin-off from another successful show, *Cheers* (1982-1993), but it did not capture enough viewers' imagination. *One Day at a Time* portrayed a divorced mother with two teenage daughters, and its plots centered on single parenting and teenagers. *Family Ties* (1982-1989) was probably closest to the American notion of the "ideal" family with its middle-class parents and teenage kids with typical, and sometimes atypical, teenage concerns.

In *Diff'rent Strokes*, a wealthy white man adopted the two young sons of his recently deceased African American housekeeper and took them home to live in his opulent Manhattan townhouse. The show became quite popular in spite of its improbable theme, and it produced a couple of spin-offs, one the highly successful *The Facts of Life* (1979-1988). *The Cosby Show* (1984-1992) was one of the most successful and influential sitcoms of the decade and perhaps of all time. Portraying a middle-class African American family with two professional parents and five generally well behaved, intelligent, and respectful children (ranging in grade level from college to kindergarten), it was a landmark show. Nothing like it had been seen on television before, and audiences loved it. Much of the series' appeal was probably due to the comedic acting of Bill Cosby, who played the father, but audiences could also relate to the parent-child struggles at the center of the show and appreciate the way the two parents stayed in control while clearly loving and cherishing their children. *Married . . . with Children* (1987-1997) rebelled against most other family sitcoms, puting forth a completely different view of American family life. A long-running show, it debuted on the new FOX network after being turned down by the other networks for being too different. It was: The father was crass, the mother was coarse, the pretty teenage daughter was a bimbo, and the teenage son, possibly the most intelligent of the bunch, seemed amoral. This depiction of a dysfunctional family was a hit.

The Singles Scene Another sitcom trend featured the affairs of unmarried people who were either too young to settle down, as in *Happy Days* (1974-1984) or *The Facts of Life*, or too caught up in their careers, as in *Murphy Brown* (1988-1998), *M*A*S*H* (1972-1983), and *Bosom Buddies* (1980-1984). While romance occurred in such shows, it was not usually a major concern. *Cheers* typified this genre with its ensemble cast of partnerless barflies hanging out at the bar "where everybody knows your name" and plotlines revolving around the camaraderie and activities of the bar's staff and regular customers. *Designing Women* (1986-1993) and *The Golden Girls* (1985-1992) followed the lives of single, mature women living or working together with infrequent interactions with men. Romance was occasionally part of the plot, but emphasis was placed more on the way the women enjoyed one another's company and reveled in their ability to make their lives satisfying and fulfilling.

Impact The 1980's sitcoms changed the way Americans viewed life in the United States by addressing more realistic concerns, which were delineated with humor and a frankness in plot, dialogue, and character portrayal far removed from the sugarcoated sit-

Popular 1980's Sitcoms

Program	Airdates	Network
M*A*S*H	1972-1983	CBS
The Jeffersons	1975-1985	CBS
Three's Company	1977-1984	ABC
The Facts of Life	1979-1988	NBC
Gimme a Break!	1981-1987	NBC
Family Ties	1982-1989	NBC
Newhart	1982-1990	CBS
Cheers	1982-1993	NBC
Mama's Family	1983-1990	NBC
Punky Brewster	1984-1986	NBC
Kate and Allie	1984-1989	CBS
The Cosby Show	1984-1992	NBC
Who's the Boss?	1984-1992	ABC
Night Court	1984-1992	NBC
227	1985-1990	NBC
The Golden Girls	1985-1992	NBC
Growing Pains	1985-1992	ABC
ALF	1986-1990	NBC
Designing Women	1986-1993	CBS
A Different World	1987-1993	NBC
Married . . . with Children	1987-1997	FOX
The Wonder Years	1988-1993	ABC
Roseanne	1988-1997	ABC
Murphy Brown	1988-1998	CBS
Seinfeld	1989-1998	NBC

coms of earlier years. With cable television in 50 percent of American homes by 1987 providing largely unregulated programming to an increasingly sophisticated audience, the network sitcoms in self-defense became less puritanical, conservative, and traditional. This situation generated increased controversy over the effect of sitcoms, and Hollywood in general, on the nation's values and moral character.

Further Reading

Brooks, Tim, and Earle Marsh. *The Complete Directory to Prime Time Network and Cable TV Shows, 1946-Present.* 7th ed. New York: Ballantine Books, 1999. Provides details about every prime-time television program shown from 1946 to 1998, with cast lists, airdates, and occasional critical insights into why a show succeeded or failed.

Reddicliffe, Steven, ed. *"TV Guide": Fifty Years of Television.* New York: Crown, 2002. Lavishly illustrated history of significant television programs. Includes photographs of leading actors and performers from the 1950's to the start of the twenty-first century and celebrity commentaries on certain televised events.

Staiger, Janet. *Blockbuster TV: Must-See Sitcoms in the Network Era.* New York: New York University Press, 2000. Analyzes and discusses why some sitcoms achieve much greater success than others, with particular focus on *Laverne and Shirley* and *The Cosby Show.*

Jane L. Ball

See also African Americans; Cable television; *Cheers; Cosby Show, The; Designing Women; Facts of Life, The; Family Ties;* FOX network; *Golden Girls, The; Married . . . with Children; M*A*S*H* series finale; Television.

■ Skinheads and neo-Nazis

Definition Members of white supremacist movements

The skinheads developed into one of the largest and most violent white separatist movements in the United States in the 1980's, a decade characterized by an increase in hate groups nationwide.

The skinhead phenomenon had its origins in England in the early 1970's. The movement generally attracted white, urban, working-class youth between the ages of thirteen and twenty-five. These individuals were concerned about the economic and social obstacles they were encountering in Great Britain because of their limited education and competition from immigrants. Skinheads could be identified by their shaved or closely cropped hair, their tattoos, and their combat boots. Some skinheads were involved in racial attacks against Pakistani immigrants and homosexuals. Over time, the skinhead phenomenon spread from England to continental Europe, where it also attracted working-class youth. By the early 1980's, skinheads began to appear in the United States. While the American skinheads' appearance was similar to that of their European counterparts, their socioeconomic background was more diverse, with the movement comprising alienated middle-class and working-class youth. Many came from broken homes, and becoming a skinhead gave these youths a new identity and sense of belonging.

The American skinhead movement was also more diverse in ideology. Some skinhead groups followed a white supremacist ideology, while others were non-racists. In fact, there were also African American skinheads. The racially oriented skinheads adopted an eclectic pattern of racial beliefs. Some followed orthodox Nazi ideology, while others adhered to a mixture of racial beliefs including populism, ethnocentrism, and ultranationalist chauvinism. The racial skinheads had a special war cry, "RAHOWA," which stood for "racial holy war." These skinheads targeted minority groups, including African Americans, Asians, and Hispanics. They also attacked homosexuals and homeless people.

"White power" music was one of the major recruiting tools of the skinhead movement. The first white power band, Skrewdriver, was started by Ian Stuart Donaldson in England in 1977. Donaldson, who dropped his surname and became known as Ian Stuart, aligned himself with the neofascist British National Front in 1979. In the United States, skinhead music was linked to "Oi," a music form distinct from punk rock, hardcore, or heavy metal. These bands played a type of rock whose lyrics focused on bigotry and violence. In time, a number of skinhead bands emerged in the United States with names such as Angry White Youth, Extreme Hatred, Aggravated Assault, Aryan, Thunder Bound for Glory, RAHOWA, and New Minority.

The skinhead movement was a decentralized movement with no hierarchy or central leadership. Many different skinhead groups operated in the United States, with the greatest concentration on the West Coast. In the 1980's, several neo-Nazi organizations began to try recruiting the racial skinheads into their organizations. The most notable attempt was by former Ku Klux Klan member Tom Metzger and his son, John Metzger. Tom Metzger, a television repairman from Fallbrook, California, was the founder and leader of a neo-Nazi organization called the White Aryan Resistance (WAR). Metzger began actively to recruit skinheads into WAR by portraying his organization as anti-authoritarian and pro-working class. In 1986, he founded the Aryan

Youth Movement, a division of WAR that targeted skinheads for recruitment, and included an Aryan Youth Movement newspaper among his WAR publications.

Metzger also held the first so-called hate rock fest, Aryan Fest, in Oklahoma in 1988. This event attracted skinheads from throughout the United States and served as a recruiting tool for Metzger and his organization. Within a few years, the Aryan Youth Movement successfully formed alliances with skinheads in a number of cities, including San Francisco, California; Portland, Oregon; Tulsa, Oklahoma; Cincinnati, Ohio; Detroit, Michigan; and New York City. Metzger's attempt to control the skinhead movement was curtailed following the murder of an Ethiopian immigrant by three skinheads in Portland, Oregon, in November, 1988. After the skinheads pleaded guilty to murder, the Southern Poverty Law Center brought a civil wrongful death suit against the Metzgers on behalf of the victim's family and won a $12.5 million verdict. This judgment ruined Metzger financially and effectively ended his recruitment of skinheads through the White Aryan Resistance.

Impact The racial skinhead movement in the United States attracted alienated youth during the 1980's. In 1989, the Anti-Defamation League estimated there were three thousand activist skinheads in thirty-one states. Although the movement was small and decentralized, skinheads were responsible for a large number of violent acts. Many of these were crimes of opportunity that were carried out spontaneously by skinheads. From 1987 to 1990, skinheads were responsible for at least six murders in the United States. In addition, skinheads committed thousands of other violent crimes, including beatings, stabbings, shootings, thefts, and synagogue desecrations.

Further Reading

Dobratz, Betty A., and Stephanie Shanks-Meile. *The White Separatist Movement in the United States*. Baltimore: Johns Hopkins University Press, 1997. Analysis of the white separatist movement, including skinheads, based on interviews, movement-generated documents, and participant observation.

Hamm, Mark S. *American Skinheads: The Criminology and Control of Hate Crime*. Westport, Conn.: Prae-

ger, 1993. Sociological analysis of the skinhead movement and hate crimes.

Moore, Jack B. *Skinheads Shaved for Battle: A Cultural History of American Skinheads*. Bowling Green, Ohio: Bowling Green University Popular Press, 1993. Examines the roots of the skinhead movement, both English and American, as well as the ideas, activities, modes of organization, and role of music in the movement.

Ridgeway, James. *Blood in the Face: The Ku Klux Klan, Aryan Nations, Nazi Skinheads, and the Rise of a New White Culture*. New York: Thunder's Mouth Press, 1990. Traces the evolution of the racial Right in the United States, with a focus on racial organizations and their activities in the 1980's.

William V. Moore

See also African Americans; Crime; Domestic violence; Gangs; Nation of Yahweh; Racial discrimination; Terrorism.

■ SkyDome

Identification Major League Baseball stadium
Date Opened on June 5, 1989
Place Toronto, Ontario

When SkyDome opened in 1989, it was the world's first sports stadium with a retractable domed roof.

When the Toronto Blue Jays baseball team entered the American League in 1977, they played their home games in Exhibition Stadium, an old football arena reconfigured for baseball. The team soon began plans for a new home that would become an architectural and technological wonder: the world's first convertible indoor-outdoor sports stadium.

In 1965, the Houston Astros had opened the Astrodome, a covered stadium that made every baseball game played in it an indoor event. The Blue Jays wanted a ballpark that could be closed to protect baseball fans from the often frigid early- and late-season Canadian weather, but they also wanted to allow fans to enjoy baseball outdoors on sunny afternoons and warm evenings. To meet the team's needs, architects Rod Robbie and Michael Allen of the Stadium Corporation of Toronto designed SkyDome, a sports arena with a retractable roof that could be left open during fair weather and closed during foul weather. SkyDome opened for play on June 5, 1989.

SkyDome's roof consists of three interlocking panels that cover the baseball diamond and grandstand when the roof is in place. In twenty minutes, however, a series of gears and pulleys can be engaged to retract the panels toward the outfield perimeter of the stadium, exposing the entire field and more than 90 percent of the fifty-four thousand seats to the open air. Baseball players maintain that a batted ball travels farther when the stadium is enclosed because of a downdraft created by the retracted panels that rest beyond the outfield fences when the stadium is open. Although the roof can be left open to the sun and rain, Sky-Dome's playing surface is covered with artificial turf rather than grass. Besides its retractable roof, SkyDome made another important contribution to sports stadium design. Along with the usual food-and-drink concession stands available in all major sports arenas, SkyDome included a hotel, restaurant, and health club, so fans could spend their entire day—even their entire vacations—in SkyDome. Such auxiliary facilities began to appear in other large sports stadiums built after the opening of SkyDome.

Impact The opening of SkyDome inspired the construction of retractable-dome stadiums in other cities hosting Major League Baseball teams. Moreover, it represented a significant architectural and engineering feat generally, inspiring innovations in the design of other major urban structures. Finally, the combination of several facilities, including a hotel, within SkyDome both anticipated and participated in the movement toward mixed-use and "destination" structures in general, which attempted to draw consumers to a single location featuring multiple types of attractions and spending opportunities.

Further Reading

Gershman, Michael. *Diamonds: The Evolution of the Ballpark—From Elysian Fields to Camden Yards*. Boston: Houghton Mifflin, 1993.

Lowry, Philip J. *Green Cathedrals: The Ultimate Celebration of Major League and Negro League Ballparks*. New York: Walker, 2006.

An aerial view of SkyDome, with the retractable roof closed. (Lee M./ GFDL)

Tackach, James, and Joshua B. Stein. *The Fields of Summer: America's Great Ballparks and the Players Who Triumphed in Them*. New York: Crescent Books, 1992.

James Tackach

See also Architecture; Baseball; Sports.

■ Slang and slogans

Definition Linguistic innovations

New slang and slogans in the 1980's stemmed from marketing and merchandising, social and political life, science, entertainment, and trends among young people.

During the 1980's, marketing agencies reflected in their slogans a no-nonsense, no-frills approach that corresponded to the minimalist movement in literature and music of the decade. Ad campaigns eschewed flowery language in favor of assertive bluntness with such slogans as "Just do it" (Nike) and "It works every time" (Colt 45). Coca-Cola's slogans of the decade were equally pithy: "Coke is the real thing" and "Coke is it." Even when marketers promoted indulgence, they did so tersely: "Reassuringly expensive" (Stella Artois) and "All the sugar and twice the caffeine" (Jolt Cola). Patriotism also featured in 1980's ad campaigns, most notably in the slogans "Made the American way" (Miller High Life) and "Pump your money back into Canada" (Petro Canada). The most famous slogan of the advertising world was "Where's the beef?," croaked by diminutive character actor Clara Peller in a fast-food commercial.

A new word was coined to name a new type of television commercial in the 1980's, by combining two other words. Marketers began to package hour-length promotional films for television as if they were talk shows or news programs, often with a celebrity host. Programmers blended the first two syllables of the word "information" with the last two of "commercial" to yield the format's new name: infomercial.

Politics and Science Such blending of words was also common in political usage in the 1980's. When people with ties to the Reagan administration were found to be trading arms to Iran and funneling the profits to the Nicaraguan Contras, the last syllable of "Watergate," premiere political scandal of the 1970's, was blended with the name of the rebel cadre and the Middle Eastern country to provide names for the new scandal: "Irangate" and "Contragate." A blend of Reagan's name with the last two syllables of "economics" provided the press with a convenient word for the president's financial theories: "Reaganomics."

"Just Say No," the slogan of an anti-drug campaign spearheaded by First Lady Nancy Reagan, was controversial, as it seemed to exemplify the vastly different approaches to social problems embraced by conservatives and liberals. The former applauded the slogan for its suggestion that the answer to America's drug problem was straightforward and involved individuals taking personal responsibility for their actions. The latter derided it as an evasion of the complexity of the drug issue and a refusal to see broad social inequities as contributing to young people's drug use.

One new term that was often used in a jocular way stemmed from a criminal trend of the decade: frustrated postal workers shooting colleagues in a string of highly publicized incidents. Research indicated that stress and resentment lay behind the workers' rampages, so, for most of the 1980's, many Americans used the term "to go postal" to mean "to become violently angry." By the beginning of the following

decade, new policies at post offices had lessened tensions, and the term faded somewhat from the national lexicon. An increase in the number of women in the American workplace in the 1980's resulted in new terms for issues confronting many female workers, such as "glass ceiling" (the invisible boundary that frustrated women's attempts to rise to positions of corporate authority), "mommy track" (work options for women who chose to combine career with motherhood), and "biological clock" (a woman's recognition of the limited time frame within which she could bear children). Both women and men of a certain class and lifestyle were often labeled "yuppies," a term derived from the first letters of either "young urban professional" or "young upwardly mobile professional," combined with the last syllable of "hippie." Many of these terms related to one of the major coinages of the 1980's: "political correctness," an expression originally employed by progressives to poke fun at some of their own orthodoxies. The term was soon appropriated by opponents on the right, who removed the humor from the term while preserving the accusation.

Science and technology contributed numerous neologisms during the 1980's. Undeniably the grimmest was the acronym AIDS, for acquired immuno-deficiency syndrome, the medical scare and scourge of the latter two decades of the twentieth century. To name a popular invention of the era, blending provided "camcorder," a combination of camera and recorder. Conventional derivation (joining existing roots and stems) using the prefix "tele-" yielded "telecommuting" (working from home via telephone and computer), "teleconference" (a conference via phone or computer), "televangelism" (evangelism on television), and "telemarketing" (selling over the telephone).

Entertainment As in previous decades, entertainment and trends among youth affected the national lexicon. Arnold Schwarzenegger's line from *The Terminator* (1984), "I'll be back," replaced Douglas MacArthur's "I shall return" as a common comic rejoinder at any unwanted departure. Probably the most-used catchphrase from television was Mr. T's expression of contempt from the series *The A-Team*: "I pity the fool who. . . ." However, the most talked-about linguistic trend of the 1980's was that originated by "Valley girls," a neologism itself that was in some ways a misnomer, as it did not strictly apply to teens in the San Fernando Valley in California, nor necessarily only to females. Much of what came to be called "valspeak" was typical of many teenagers around North America and exhibited traits that had been common among youth for decades. However, the speech patterns associated with Valley girls were the focus of a hit single by Frank Zappa and his daughter Moon Unit Zappa, "Valley Girl." As a result, the California sociolect (that is, a language variation based on social group rather than region) became famous and provided a name for the speech pattern. Although some phrases from "valspeak" became infamous (including "Gag me with a spoon" and "As if!"), the distinctive aspect of the speech pattern was its intonation—a vaguely Southwestern twang and a tendency to raise the voice at the end of every utterance, as if asking a question.

Impact As with much linguistic innovation, most of the slang and slogans of the 1980's disappeared after a few years. However, certain trends of the era continued in the speech of young people in following decades, especially the tendency toward clipping ("ex" for ex-partner or spouse, for example) and the upraised inflection at the ends of statements.

Further Reading

Bryson, Bill. *Made in America.* New York: Perennial, 1994. Highly accessible and thorough history of American English.

In the 1980's. http://inthe80's.com/glossary.shtml. Excellent on-line compendium of 1980's slang.

Morris, William, and Mary Morris. *Harper Dictionary of Contemporary Usage.* New York: Harper & Row, 1985. Usage dictionary from the 1980's that reflects attitudes toward language change at the time.

Thomas Du Bose

See also Advertising; AIDS epidemic; Biological clock; Glass ceiling; Infomercials; Just Say No campaign; Mommy track; Mr. T; Peller, Clara; Political correctness; Post office shootings; Reaganomics; Science and technology; *Terminator, The*; Valley girls; Yuppies.

■ Smith, Samantha

Identification Ten-year-old American girl who wrote a letter to Soviet leader Yuri Andropov in 1982

Born June 29, 1972; Houlton, Maine
Died August 25, 1985; Lewiston-Auburn, Maine

The correspondence between American Smith and the leader of the Soviet Union became a well-publicized symbol of attempts to improve relations between the two countries.

In 1982, young Samantha Smith, afraid of nuclear war, asked her mother to write a letter to the new leader of the Soviet Union, Yuri Andropov. Her mother, Jane Smith, replied that Samantha should be the one to write the letter. In December, therefore, Smith wrote to Andropov, congratulating him on becoming the head of the Soviet Union and asking him if he wanted nuclear war and why he wanted

A 1985 Soviet stamp commemorating Samantha Smith.

A Historic Correspondence

In December, 1982, Samantha Smith sent this letter to Soviet leader Yuri Andropov:

Dear Mr. Andropov:

My name is Samantha Smith. I am ten years old. Congratulations on your new job. I have been worrying about Russia and the United States getting into a nuclear war. Are you going to vote to have a war or not? If you aren't please tell me how you are going to help to not have a war. This question you do not have to answer, but I would like to know why you want to conquer the world or at least our country. God made the world for us to live together in peace and not to fight.

She received a reply from Andropov on April 26, 1983, in a letter excerpted here:

You write that you are anxious about whether there will be a nuclear war between our two countries. And you ask are we doing anything so that war will not break out.

Your question is the most important of those that every thinking man can pose. I will reply to you seriously and honestly.

Yes, Samantha, we in the Soviet Union are trying to do everything so that there will not be war on Earth. This is what every Soviet man wants. This is what the great founder of our state, Vladimir Lenin, taught us. . . .

In America and in our country there are nuclear weapons—terrible weapons that can kill millions of people in an instant. But we do not want them to be ever used. That's precisely why the Soviet Union solemnly declared throughout the entire world that never—never—will it use nuclear weapons first against any country. In general we propose to discontinue further production of them and to proceed to the abolition of all the stockpiles on earth.

It seems to me that this is a sufficient answer to your second question: "Why do you want to wage war against the whole world or at least the United States?" We want nothing of the kind. No one in our country—neither workers, peasants, writers nor doctors, neither grown-ups nor children, nor members of the government—want either a big or "little" war.

We want peace—there is something that we are occupied with: growing wheat, building and inventing, writing books and flying into space. We want peace for ourselves and for all peoples of the planet. For our children and for you, Samantha.

to conquer the United States. Excerpts of Samantha's letter were published in the Soviet daily *Pravda*, but when the girl did not hear from Andropov himself, she wrote to Anatoly Dobrynin, the Soviet ambassador in Washington, D.C., asking if Andropov would reply.

The Soviet leader did reply in April, 1983, assuring Samantha that his country did not want nuclear or any other kind of war, nor to conquer the world or the United States. It only wanted peace and friendly relations. He ended his letter by inviting Samantha and her family to visit the Soviet Union. Thus, in the summer of 1983, the family traveled to the Soviet Union for two weeks. They visited Moscow, Leningrad, and the children's summer camp Artek, near Yalta. Samantha was impressed with what she learned there and with the friends she made among Soviet children. Afterward, she attended the Children's International Symposium in Kobe, Japan. There, she gave an account of her letters and her trip to the Soviet Union. She proposed an international granddaughter exchange, in which the grandchildren (or nieces and nephews) of world leaders would visit the countries of their adversaries to live with the leaders of that country for two weeks.

Samantha became such a popular and world-renowned figure that she was cast in a television series, *Lime Street*, to be produced in 1985. However, on August 25 of that year, she tragically died in an airplane crash. Samantha and her father were on a small commuter plane from Boston to Auburn, Maine, when the pilot, following a nonstandard radar vector on the approach, crashed into some trees, killing all six passengers and two crew members aboard the plane. In October, 1985, the Samantha Smith Foundation promoting international understanding began. A statue of Smith stands in front of the State Cultural Building in Augusta, Maine.

Impact Samantha's courage and childlike approach to Andropov became a symbol of hope for the peaceful resolution of world problems. Six years after her death, the Cold War ended. Her direct impact on the Cold War is difficult to assess, but she was warmly remembered in both the Soviet Union and the United States, as well as around the world.

Further Reading

Galicich, Anne. *Samantha Smith: A Journey for Peace.* Minneapolis: Dillon Press, 1987. Account of Smith's life for juvenile readers.

Samantha Smith. http://www.samanthasmith.info/index.htm. Web site dedicated to Smith that includes a historical time line and copies of her correspondence with Andropov.

Smith, Samantha. *Journey to the Soviet Union.* Boston: Little, Brown, 1985. Smith's own account of her trip to the Soviet Union.

Frederick B. Chary

See also Cold War; *Day After, The*; Foreign policy of the United States; Military spending; Reagan's "Evil Empire" speech; Soviet Union and North America; Strategic Defense Initiative (SDI).

■ Smoking and tobacco

Definition Production, consumption, and health consequences of cigarettes, cigars, pipes, and chewing tobacco

During the 1980's, an estimated 390,000 people in the United States died from complications due to cigarette smoking. Despite accelerated efforts by the tobacco industry to market tobacco products, the emergence of antismoking efforts—including significant antitobacco legislation—resulted in a steady decline in U.S. smoking throughout the decade.

In 1978, Joseph Califano, head of the Department of Health, Education, and Welfare under President Jimmy Carter, proposed several actions to fight cigarette smoking. These actions included raising taxes on cigarettes, eliminating smoking on airplanes and in restaurants, and ending government subsidies to tobacco growers. With little support for the proposals from others in the Carter administration and strong opposition from the tobacco industry, many of these proposals were blocked. The plan, however, laid the essential groundwork for a more successful campaign against smoking that emerged in the 1980's.

One of the most important steps in the campaign against smoking and tobacco was the appointment of C. Everett Koop as U.S. surgeon general in 1981. Koop emerged as a powerful antismoking advocate, authoring reports on environmental tobacco smoke, nicotine addiction, and the negative health consequences of smoking for women. At a national conference of antismoking groups, delegates developed the "Blueprint for Action," which outlined the necessary steps to build a more aggressive antismoking movement. The following year, the American Cancer Society, the American Lung Association, and the American Heart Association formed a strong coalition called Smoking or Health and launched a rigorous antismoking lobbying campaign in Washington, D.C. In 1985, the American Medical Association called for a complete ban on cigarette advertising and promotion. During the same year, the city of Los Angeles banned smoking in most public places and in many businesses.

Regulating Smokeless Tobacco Although it was slow in coming, strong evidence had accumulated by the mid-1980's that smokeless tobacco also presented significant health risks, particularly that of oral cancer. The evidence mounting against smokeless tobacco worried public health officials, because smokeless tobacco use had been rising among young boys, in part because they thought it would not cause cancer or be addictive. Smokeless tobacco products had not been required by Congress to carry warning labels; however, the state of Massachusetts enacted legislation to require such labels, and twenty-five other states decided to follow suit. The federal government enacted the Smokeless Tobacco Health Education Act of 1986, which required three rotated warning labels on smokeless tobacco packages. The law also banned advertising smokeless tobacco products on electronic media and required warning labels on all packaging and all advertising except billboards.

The Tobacco Industry Seeks New Markets Efforts to educate the public about the risk factors for cancer and cardiovascular disease contributed to an overall decline in nicotine dependence. By the end of the 1980's, more than half of men and more than half of American white adults who had ever smoked cigarettes had stopped. The poor, less educated, and minority groups did not experience the same degree of reduction in smoking rates as did white, middle- and upper-class Americans. Moreover, most new users of cigarettes were female, reversing earlier trends.

The decline in smoking rates within the United States led tobacco companies to expand into new, global markets. Four of the six multinational tobacco conglomerates were based in the United States. In the middle years of the 1980's, the U.S. government—in cooperation with the United States Cigarette Export Association (USCEA)—worked to promote the international sale of tobacco products, especially in Asia. In Asian countries, import quotas, high taxes, and other restrictions were alleged to limit unfairly U.S. tobacco firms' access to the markets they sought. In the face of U.S. threats, however, countries such as Japan, Taiwan, South Korea, and Thailand removed many of their restrictions on tobacco imports, leading to a more than 75 percent growth in cigarette trading in these markets and a rapid rise in smoking rates in those nations.

Moreover, as smoking among U.S. adults declined, tobacco companies also targeted children as potential new consumers. Joe Camel, for example, was adopted as the official mascot of Camel cigarettes, and the character—who had been conceived thirty years earlier—was redesigned to be both more cartoonish and more "cool," in order to appeal to a young demographic. In a series of ads that first appeared in 1987, Joe Camel appeared as a cool party animal, sporting a cigarette, sunglasses, and a tuxedo, and with adoring young women nearby. In the wake of this advertising campaign, the market share of Camel cigarettes among teenagers increased more than twentyfold.

Impact   The 1980's witnessed the emergence of new leaders in Congress with the political skills to guide antitobacco legislation through both the Senate and the House of Representatives. For example, the Comprehensive Smoking Education Act (1984)—which required that four strongly worded warnings be rotated on cigarette packages and advertisements and that the warnings also be displayed prominently on all advertisements—contributed to the decline in smoking in the United States. In 1988, Congress banned smoking on domestic air flights of less than two hours in duration. The ban on smoking in airplanes was later expanded to all domestic U.S.

commercial air travel lasting six hours or less. Reports from the National Research Council and the Office of the Surgeon General promoted the view that passive smoking presented health risks to nonsmokers. They warned that nonsmokers living with smokers had an increased risk of lung cancer, and children living with smoking parents had an increased risk of developing respiratory problems. However, significant legislation to create smoke-free environments would not emerge until decades later.

Further Reading

Kluger, Richard. *Ashes to Ashes: America's Hundred-Year Cigarette War, the Public Health, and the Unabashed Triumph of Philip Morris.* New York: Alfred A. Knopf, 1996. Examines the role of the tobacco industry in promoting cigarette consumption even as the mounting medical evidence pointed to adverse health consequences.

Pampel, Fred. *Tobacco Industry and Smoking.* New York: Facts On File, 2004. Easy-to-read compilation of the important dates and events in cigarette history.

Snell, Clete. *Peddling Poison: The Tobacco Industry and Kids.* Westport, Conn.: Praeger, 2005. Good discussion regarding how the tobacco industry has marketed its products to children and youth. Includes interesting discussion of marketing Joe Camel to children.

Wolfson, Mark. *The Fight Against Big Tobacco.* New York: Aldine de Gruyter, 2001. Documents the governmental and grassroots efforts to limit tobacco use in the United States.

Mary McElroy

See also   Advertising; Business and the economy in the United States; Cancer research.

_____

■ Soap operas

Definition   Television serial melodramas

Reflecting the Reagan era of consumerism and excess, soap operas in the 1980's were heavy on glamour and outrageous plots, fueling the fantasies of audience members who were facing the economic realities of the decade.

Daytime and prime-time soap operas, or soaps, peaked in the 1980's. High ratings led producers to shoot on location, emphasize adventure and boardroom stories, and spend lavishly on costumes and sets. The "supercouple" phenomenon—which had its origin in the 1970's—was fully developed, and "love in the afternoon"—originally a network advertising catchphrase—became a generic term. Celebrity fans of daytime soaps began making cameos on their favorite serials. Prime-time soaps lured many former movie stars to play key roles and made effective use of big-budget cliffhangers. Both daytime and nighttime soap operas featured males and females equally, but the characters remained predominantly white. As the decade closed, daytime serials responded to criticisms of their overt sexual content and made attempts to address contemporary social issues, such as AIDS, lesbianism, cocaine addiction, and interracial marriage.

Daytime Soap Operas *General Hospital*'s Luke and Laura story line began in 1979, and by 1980 the couple was extremely popular. During the summer of 1980, the two were on the run from the mob; the plot presented contemporary twists on old film staples, including a waltz in Wyndham's department store reminiscent of 1930's musicals and an adapted "Walls of Jericho" scene from *It Happened One Night* (1934). The couple's popularity increased until Luke and Laura's wedding photo appeared on the cover of *Newsweek* in 1981, as their plotlines generated more mainstream press coverage for *General Hospital* than any daytime soap had previously received. The wedding of Luke and Laura was also daytime television's single highest-rated event.

Other soap operas also thrived in the shadow of *General Hospital*'s success, as ratings for the genre as a whole climbed. Advertising rates were strong, and production costs (even with the location shoots) were reasonable, resulting in major profits for the networks. For example, the *Soap Opera Encyclopedia* notes that during the Luke and Laura heyday and for a few years afterward, *General Hospital* "alone accounted for one-quarter of ABC's profits."

The star-crossed romance plot was nothing new, but it received renewed emphasis during the 1980's. In addition to Luke and Laura on *General Hospital*, similar story lines involved Greg and Jenny on *All My Children*, Tom and Margo on *As the World Turns*, and Bo and Hope and Steve and Kayla on *Days of Our Lives*. A number of stars noted that they were fans of the soap opera genre and appeared on their favorite shows; examples include Carol Burnett on *All My Children* and Elizabeth Taylor on *General Hospital*.

Daytime soaps also began to feature millionaire families at the center of their narratives. Moguls had already been present in 1970's narratives, and a wider spectrum of economic classes was represented in 1980's daytime soaps than in prime-time narratives, but nonetheless, increasing numbers of corporate capitalists became major soap opera characters, including James Stenbeck and Lucinda Walsh on *As the World Turns*, Victor Kiriakis on *Days of Our Lives*, and Adam Chandler on *All My Children*.

Prime-Time Soap Operas In an effort to rival the success of the 1978 Columbia Broadcasting System (CBS) hit *Dallas*, the American Broadcasting Company (ABC) presented *Dynasty* in 1981. Like *Dallas*, the latter series dealt with a feuding family living together in one giant mansion and a working-class outsider who had joined the family through marriage. *Dynasty*, however, was more elegant, especially after it removed many of its more working-class supporting characters after the first season and brought in Joan Collins to portray the devious Alexis Carrington. In addition to these two shows, other popular prime-time soaps included *Knots Landing* (a spinoff of *Dallas*) and *Falcon Crest*. In the early to mid-1980's, these four shows were near the top of the ratings.

With bigger budgets than their daytime counterparts, nighttime soaps had casts that included former movie stars (such as Jane Wyman in *Falcon Crest* and John Forsythe in *Dynasty*), expensive costumes, and cliffhangers with action-film violence and special effects: Both *Dallas* and *Dynasty* had scenes in which oil rigs exploded, and one *Dynasty* season-ending cliffhanger featured a scene in which Moldavian rebels attacked a wedding party with automatic weapons. Some of these gimmicks were more successful than others. The "Who shot J. R.?" cliffhanger on *Dallas* in the summer of 1980, using no special effects and minimum violence, was a publicity phenomenon. Many critics felt in retrospect that the Moldavian massacre on *Dynasty* in 1985 signaled the beginning of the end for that series.

Nighttime soaps did not broach contemporary social topics as often as did their daytime counterparts. *Dynasty* did feature a major gay character, Steven Carrington, but even though Steven had scenes with male lovers, they were fairly chaste in comparison to the several sex scenes that he had with female partners. Major characters on both *Dallas* and *Knots Landing* struggled with alcoholism, but nighttime narratives usually centered on melodramatic power struggles and glamour.

Impact Daytime and prime-time soap operas in the 1980's relied heavily on romance, action, and glamour, representing a significant shift away from earlier eras in the genre. Escapist fare, soap operas mainly served as glossy entertainment, but the beginnings of more issue-oriented storytelling in daytime soap operas—especially in terms of homosexuality, interracial relationships, and AIDS—picked up momentum as the decade moved forward.

Further Reading

Anger, Dorothy. *Other Worlds: Society Seen Through Soap Opera.* Peterborough, Ont.: Broadview Press, 1999. Explores American and British soap operas and discusses their social significance. Includes an appendix, "Soaps' Most Daring Stories [and the ones where they chickened out]."

Frentz, Suzanne, ed. *Staying Tuned: Contemporary Soap Opera Criticism.* Bowling Green, Ohio: Bowling Green State University Popular Press, 1992. Collection of essays on daytime soap operas, discussing topics such as college students' viewing habits, early AIDS story lines, supercouples, and more.

Schemering, Christopher. *The Soap Opera Encyclopedia.* New York: Ballantine Books, 1988. Excellent concise synopsis of the genre as whole, as well as summaries of every soap opera (both daytime and prime-time) in the history of the genre, including such forgotten curiosities as the Christian Broadcasting Network's early 1980's entry *Another Life.*

Julie Elliott

See also *Dallas; Dynasty; General Hospital;* Television.

■ Soccer

Definition International team sport

Professional soccer suffered a setback in the United States in the 1980's, when the major league folded in 1984. The Canadian national team, however, enjoyed a brief highlight by winning a regional international championship in 1985 and participating in the 1986 World Cup. Throughout the decade, though, soccer remained a marginal spectator sport in North America.

In the United States, the 1980's opened promisingly for soccer fans, with the North American Soccer League (NASL) drawing an average of fourteen thousand supporters for its games. Employing expensive, well-known foreign players, the league modified international soccer rules to encourage more goals and to prohibit ties, which were common in other nations. When top striker Giorgio Chinaglia scored two goals to lead the New York Cosmos to a 3-0 win over the Fort Lauderdale Strikers in the 1980 Soccer Bowl, the American Broadcasting Company (ABC) covered the game watched by fifty thousand fans in the stadium.

Despite this modest success, high spending on star players' salaries, rapid expansion, and a lack of American-born players increasingly endangered the viability and popularity of the sport. At the end of the season, three NASL teams folded. The national team did qualify for the 1980 Olympic Games with two wins, one draw, and a loss against opponents Costa Rica and Suriname, but the U.S. boycott of the Olympics that year deprived the team of its chance to prove its international mettle. Two years later, the team failed to qualify for the 1982 World Cup after losing to Mexico 5-1.

By 1981, the NASL saw an exodus of its European star players, and game attendance fell, adding financial strains to the clubs. ABC canceled its contract, lowering the visibility of the sport. Increasingly, the Major Indoor Soccer League (MISL) was called upon to pick up the slack, together with college level competition. In 1982, Chinaglia's goal won the New York Cosmos its fifth league title in an NASL reduced to fourteen teams. Lack of quality players, fewer fans, and a salary war with the MISL weakened the league. On the other hand, U.S. collegiate soccer teams enjoyed growth, especially women's teams.

In 1983, the idea to let the national team compete in the NASL as Team America failed abysmally, as players showed little inclination to leave their clubs for it. While the Tulsa Roughnecks beat the Toronto Blizzard 2-0 to win the championship, the league experienced a financial crisis. In the 1984 Olympics, the U.S. national team defeated Costa Rica 3-0 in Stanford, California, on July 29 in front of seventy-eight thousand spectators, the biggest soccer audience ever in the United States. Italy then defeated the team 1-0, and Egypt tied it 1-1, preventing the United States from advancing beyond the first round. The same year, the NASL folded, and

U.S. national soccer team striker Paul Caligiuri. In 1989, Caligiuri scored the winning goal in a CONCACAF match against Trinidad and Tobago, thereby qualifying his team to compete in the World Cup. (AP/Wide World Photos)

the United States failed to qualify for the 1986 World Cup.

From 1985 to 1988, U.S. professional soccer was played primarily indoors. Slowly, regional outdoor leagues emerged. On July 4, 1988, the United States won the right to host the 1994 World Cup. In the 1988 Olympics, the national team competed valiantly, tying Argentina 1-1 and the Republic of Korea 0-0 before succumbing to the Soviet Union 2-4 and losing the right to advance.

Rebuilding the national team paid off in 1989, when the United States beat Trinidad and Tobago 1-0 during the Confederation of North, Central American and Caribbean Association Football (CONCACAF) Gold Cup competition. The victory, thanks to striker Paul Caligiuri's goal, qualified the United States for the 1990 World Cup. With profes-

sional outdoor soccer enjoying a renaissance due to regional leagues, collegiate soccer on the rise, and the women's national team emerging, U.S. soccer looked with hope to the next decade.

Canada Professional soccer in Canada experienced a false start, when the Canadian Professional Soccer League folded after its first year in 1983; before the league collapsed, the Edmonton Brickmen won the championship match against the Hamilton Steelers 2-0. In contrast, at the 1984 Olympics, the Canadian team acquitted itself well. It tied Iraq 1-1 after a leading goal by Gerry Gray and came back from a 0-1 defeat against Yugoslavia to beat Cameroon 3-1 with two goals by Dale Mitchell and one by Igor Vrablic. In the next round, Brazil tied Canada at the end of regulation play after a lead by Mitchell. Brazil won 5-3 on penalty kicks.

The decade's highlight for Canadian soccer was winning the CONCACAF Gold Cup in 1985. After tying Costa Rica 1-1 at home, the team defeated Honduras 1-0 in Tegucigalpa, tied Costa Rica 0-0 abroad, and achieved a 2-1 victory against Honduras at home. This victory not only won Canada the cup but also qualified the team to play for the World Cup for the first time in its history. At the 1986 World Cup competition in Mexico, however, Canada failed to score a single goal, losing 0-1 to France and 0-2 to Hungary and the Soviet Union. A post-cup match-fixing scandal in Singapore led to one-year suspensions of four players, including Vrablic.

In 1987, the Canadian Soccer League (CSL) was founded; it survived for five years. The Hamilton Steelers participated in all three finals held in the 1980's but lost to the Calgary Kickers in 1987 and the Vancouver 86ers in 1988 and 1989. The CSL eventually merged with the American Professional Soccer League in 1993.

Impact During the 1980's, soccer endured a roller-coaster experience in North America. After auspicious signs in the early 1980's, the fiscal irresponsibility of U.S. clubs—coupled with a lack of American players, no local roots, and diminishing television quotas—caused the NASL to fold by 1984. However, the large turnout for soccer matches during the 1984 Olympic Games in Los Angeles persuaded international soccer authorities to allow the United States to host the 1994 World Cup. This decision corresponded with a renaissance of professional U.S. soccer, as regional leagues grounded in their communities began to thrive. Moreover, the sport became increasingly popular among young people and college students in the United States, bringing about a resurgence by the late 1980's. In Canada, the successes of the 1984 Olympics and the win of the 1985 CONCACAF Gold Cup notwithstanding, soccer had difficulty attracting significant audiences. The efforts of the CSL ultimately failed and led to a merger with the U.S. professional league in the next decade.

Further Reading

Hunt, Chris, ed. *The Complete Book of Soccer.* Richmond Hill, Ont.: Firefly Books, 2006. Comprehensive compendium of the sport.

Markovits, Andrei, and Steven Hellerman. *Offside: Soccer and American Exceptionalism.* Princeton, N.J.: Princeton University Press, 2001. Study of the U.S. attitude toward the world's most popular sport.

Szymanski, Stefan, and Andrew Zimbalist. *National Pastime: How Americans Play Baseball and the Rest of the World Plays Soccer.* Washington, D.C.: Brookings Institution, 2005. Comparison of different nations' relationships with their sports and athletes.

R. C. Lutz

See also   Olympic Games of 1980; Olympic Games of 1984; Olympic Games of 1988; Sports.

■ Social Security reform

Definition   Attempts to maintain the financial solvency of the U.S. government's Old-Age, Survivors, and Disability Insurance program

The 1980's saw the first major change in the Social Security program: Congress raised Social Security taxes and limited benefits in order to prevent the program from falling into bankruptcy.

Created in 1935, the Social Security program provides insurance for people with permanent disabilities, those reaching old age, and their survivors. It is paid for by taxing wages. The program ran into financial trouble during the 1970's. The twin economic problems marring the 1970's, rising inflation and high unemployment, led to dramatically higher Social Security costs coupled with declining revenues. As the decade wore on, Social Security came closer to bankruptcy. Demographics also conspired against Social Security, as life expectancies began to exceed the retirement age by a decade or more. Instead of retirees claiming benefits for a few months or years, many would receive Social Security payments for decades, putting further pressure on the program. By 1980, those familiar with the program knew that significant changes would have to be made to prevent bankruptcy. Both the president and members of Congress faced difficult decisions about how to reform a program that had defied all previous attempts to change it.

Social Security came to be known as the "third rail" of American politics. Like the electrified third rail of a subway system, the program was thought of as killing the career of any politician who touches it. Thus, few were willing to attempt to change or reform it. The resilience of the program was especially apparent during the Ronald Reagan years: Reagan believed in shrinking the size and fiscal responsibilities of the federal government, but Social Security escaped the budget cuts of his administration, which weakened many other social welfare programs.

The inauguration of President Reagan had marked a sea change in the American perspective on social welfare policies generally. Every such program experienced climbing costs, and the effectiveness of each one was called into question. The programs thus became a target of budget cutters seeking to balance the government budget and change social policy. The only major program to escape major cuts was Social Security, the largest and most expensive in terms of benefits paid and recipients.

As Social Security floundered toward bankruptcy, reform seemed inevitable. Reagan's early attempts to change the system proved controversial, however. His proposed reforms included reducing the quantity of money received by those taking early retirement and receiving Social Security before the age of sixty-five, then 80 percent of full benefits. Reagan proposed reducing the benefit level of those retiring early to 55 percent of full benefits. This proposal would have both reduced the amount of money paid to early retirees and reduced the number of people choosing to retire early. Moreover, those workers choosing to defer their retirement to age sixty-five would both defer the day when they began to draw benefits and continue to pay more money into the Social Security trust fund as they continued to earn taxable wages. The president's plan received little support, and it was unanimously rejected by the Republican-controlled Senate.

After this defeat, Reagan sought political cover, delegating the problem to a bipartisan commission that was to propose changes that the president could reject if he deemed them too controversial. Headed by economist Alan Greenspan, who would later become chairman of the Federal Reserve, the Social Security Commission faced the problem of increasing benefits paid out to retirees and decreasing revenues from workers' taxes. Composed of labor, business, and political leaders, the commission considered many solutions, all with potentially disastrous consequences for any politician who proposed them.

After several months of debate and hearings, the commission offered a plan and several suggestions for stabilizing Social Security. The first was to raise revenue by increasing the Social Security taxes paid by workers and businesses. The commission also proposed adding federal and state employees to the Social Security system, which would raise the number of workers paying into the system but also the number of potential retirees who could draw benefits in the future. A more controversial possibility, raising the retirement age to sixty-seven, was offered as a suggestion rather than a proposal, as members of the commission could not agree to it.

The commission's work, though, would be wasted if Congress did not pass their recommendations. Inclusion of political leaders, including the self-proclaimed defender of Social Security, Florida representative Claude Pepper, eased the political process. Social Security reform bills following some of the commission's proposals and suggestions began to be introduced in Congress. The first bill sought to raise Social Security taxes: It passed easily, as House members realized the boon to the federal purse created by a tax increase.

The second major proposal came from the commission's suggestion to raise the retirement age. The bill, offered by Texas congressman J. J. Pickle, proposed gradually raising the retirement age to sixty-seven. Starting in the year 2000 with gradual increases until the year 2020, retirees would have to work longer before receiving full retirement benefits. Moving the retirement age from sixty-five to sixty-seven in this fashion proved politically palatable, as it would affect only future workers, including many who were not yet of voting age, while not affecting those currently approaching or already having reached retirement. Constituents between the ages of sixty and sixty-seven might otherwise have fought aggressively against the change. Pickle's proposal passed narrowly.

The rise in the retirement age had little immediate impact on the solvency of Social Security, but it was intended to stabilize the system in the future, as more money poured into the system while the number of retirees was reduced. The full reform bill easily passed the Senate and was signed by the president on April 20, 1983. The involvement of Republicans and Democrats, labor and business, had allowed the reforms to be passed with a minimum of partisan rancor.

Impact The Social Security Commission and the legislation it spawned solved the immediate problem of the program heading toward bankruptcy, but it did not solve the longer-term problems of the program, including an aging population, longer life expectancy for retirees, and the baby-boom generation, whose size would entail significant drains upon the program's coffers when baby boomers began to retire in 2013. The decision to raise both taxes and the retirement age may have only pushed the harder decisions into the future, though Congress and the president demonstrated that changes in Social Security could be achieved using a bipartisan approach.

Further Reading

Beland, Daniel. *Social Security.* Lawrence: University of Kansas Press, 2005. Fast-paced book that describes how Social Security evolved from a limited old-age program to a larger social welfare program, as well as summarizing attempts to reform it.

Berkowitz, Edward. *Robert Ball and the Politics of Social Security.* Madison: University of Wisconsin Press, 2003. Describes the life and efforts of the head of the Social Security Administration during the 1960's and early 1970's.

Koitz, David. *Seeking Middle Ground on Social Security Reform.* Stanford, Calif.: Hoover Press, 2001. Analyzes the various approaches to changing the Social Security system in order to solve the financial and other problems with the system.

Douglas Clouatre

See also Business and the economy in the United States; Conservatism in U.S. politics; Congress, U.S.; Demographics of the United States; Elections in the United States, 1980; Income and wages in the United States; Reagan, Ronald; Reagan Revolution; Reaganomics.

■ Soviet Union and North America

Definition   Relations between the Union of Soviet Socialist Republics and the United States and Canada

The 1980's opened with the Soviet Union a bitter enemy of the United States and Canada. By the end of the decade, North American leaders had come to an accommodation with Soviet leader Mikhail Gorbachev, and the Soviet state was on the verge of collapse.

The 1980's witnessed the most dramatic shift in relations with the Soviet Union since Washington had recognized Moscow in 1933, perhaps since the Russian Revolution itself. It started with the 1980 election of Ronald Reagan, a bitter foe of the Soviet Union, to the U.S. presidency and ended with the collapse of the Soviet state. Since 1917, with the formation of Soviet Russia, relations between the countries had run the gamut, from military invasion by American forces in 1918 and 1919 to a firm alliance against Nazi Germany in World War II. After that war, however—beginning in the late 1940's—the two governments were locked in an adversarial Cold War.

This relationship, too, fluctuated, from confrontational during the the last days of Joseph Stalin (whose regime ended when he died in 1953) through the era of peaceful coexistence under Nikita Khrushchev (1953-1964) and détente under Leonid Brezhnev (1964-1982) in the 1960's and 1970's. Relations were complicated with the successful communist revolution in China in 1949. Until 1971, Chinese-American relations were even worse than those with the Soviet Union; Washington refused to recognize the government in Beijing. However, a dramatic reversal under president Richard M. Nixon and Secretary of State Henry Kissinger led to a new Chinese-American accord and placed pressure on Moscow, whose own relations with its Chinese communist neighbor-ally were worse than either nation's with the United States—even exploding into border clashes in 1969.

The Years of Confrontation   A deterioration in U.S.-Soviet relations occurred near the opening of the decade when the Soviet Union helped to overthrow the government in Afghanistan and Soviet troops entered the Central Asian country in late December, 1979, to prop up a more friendly government. Washington reacted with condemnation, and President Jimmy Carter "punished" Moscow by refusing to allow American athletes to participate in the Moscow Olympics of 1980. In 1984, Moscow retaliated by boycotting the Summer Olympics, held in Los Angeles. Carter also announced an embargo on selling grain to the Soviets at a time when they desperately needed it. Canada joined in the Olympic boycott and for a while withheld grain from Moscow, promising not to fill the gap caused by Washington's embargo when it resumed sales.

Much more serious for the Soviets was the long war in which they became involved in Afghanistan, where many casualties sapped Moscow's resources. The war in Afghanistan, in fact, was a major cause of the Soviet Union's demise. Throughout the decade, the new U.S. president, Ronald Reagan, supported the anti-Soviet insurgency against the pro-Soviet Afghani government and the Red Army fighting in the country.

In the early years of the 1980's, Washington and Moscow confronted each other all over the world—in Central Asia, East Asia, Latin America, and Africa. Strategic arms talks begun in the previous years came to a standstill. Reagan wanted to build even more weapons, hoping that dragging the Soviet Union into an arms race would be too expensive for Moscow and force the Soviets to make concessions.

At the same time Reagan won the presidency, Conservative leader Margaret Thatcher became the prime minister of the United Kingdom. Together, Reagan and Thatcher put up a solid anticommunist front against Moscow. In addition to opposing the Soviets in Afghanistan, Reagan led a campaign against Soviet activity in Poland, where the independent union Solidarity was outlawed and where, in 1981, General Wojciech Jaruzelski imposed martial law. Reagan and Thatcher blamed Moscow.

Reagan approached the Soviet Union with strident confrontation. In a speech delivered on June 8, 1982, he declared the country an "evil empire." He funded anti-Soviet movements in developing nations such as Afghanistan and Nicaragua, where the insurgent Contras battled the left-leaning government of Daniel Ortega.

To some degree these efforts backfired. The fundamentalist Islamic Taliban replaced the Soviet-backed government in Afghanistan, which would lead to a brutally repressive regime that later caused problems for Washington. In Nicaragua, the backing of the Contras involved illegal activity that erupted into the Iran-Contra scandal of 1986.

At one point Reagan even joked about his hostility toward the Soviets. While preparing for his weekly radio address to the nation on August 4, 1984, instead of the usual "one, two, three" testing to check the line, the former actor made the statement:

> My fellow Americans, I'm pleased to tell you today that I've signed legislation that will outlaw Russia forever. We begin bombing in five minutes.

The joke, intended to be made in private, leaked, causing an international scandal.

Reagan supported a plan to establish a space- and surface-based antiballistic missile system called the Strategic Defense Initiative (SDI), or the "Star Wars" program. Although this controversial program was never adopted, the U.S. government did fund massive new weapons systems. Reagan pushed for the deployment of Pershing and cruise missiles in Western Europe, for increased allocations in European allies' military budgets, and for their adopting his anti-Soviet policies—with mixed results. Reagan also objected to European Community (EC) contracts with the Soviet Union for building natural gas pipelines. For a while in 1982, Washington banned the use of U.S. technology in such projects, lifting the ban later that year when an agreement with the EC on trade policies was reached.

The United States also resumed grain sales to the Soviet Union and initiated Strategic Arms Reduction Treaty talks (START), first presented by Reagan in Geneva on June 29, 1982. These disarmament negotiations continued off and on. Washington pushed for the so-called zero option, which linked the removal of Pershing missiles from Europe to the Soviets' reduction of intermediate-range nuclear forces (INFs) and mobile missile launchers from the East.

Andropov and Chernenko   As the decade proceeded, the Soviet Union underwent major changes. On November 10, 1982, Brezhnev died after suffering a long illness. A struggle for leadership between Soviet liberals and old-guard bureaucrats continued while two more elder statesmen, Yuri Andropov and Konstantin Chernenko, successively assumed the Soviet leadership role.

Andropov tried to reestablish the era of détente, but Reagan was adamant against any easing of tensions. After receiving a letter from a New England child, Samantha Smith, asking why he was opposed to peace, Andropov responded by saying that he and the Soviet people were in fact eager for peace between the two countries and invited the girl and her family to the Soviet Union for a visit. He tried to divide Western Europe from the United States, with the particular goal of preventing U.S. Pershing missiles on the Continent. However, during his tenure, on September 1, 1983, Soviet warplanes shot down a Korean Air Lines commercial aircraft, flight KAL 007, while it was flying near the border between Soviet and Korean airspace; 269 civilian passengers and crew members died. Moscow maintained that the aircraft had entered Soviet airspace. The Soviets believed that the plane was on a spying mission, in a deliberate attempt on the part of the United States to provoke the Soviets. Andropov died in 1984 after only sixteen months in office. Chernenko succeeded him but died the following year.

Gorbachev   In the subsequent power struggle, the reformer Mikhail Gorbachev succeeded to the Soviet leadership position. A year later, in April of 1986, the Soviet Union suffered a catastrophe when the nuclear plant at Chernobyl in the Ukraine suffered a meltdown, causing explosions and sending radioactive contamination as far as Belorus. After the Soviets briefly denied the accident, Gorbachev realized that he had to appeal to the West for help.

Afterward, Gorbachev introduced the reform policies glasnost (openness) and perestroika (economic reconstruction). Unlike liberalization attempts in previous Soviet periods, Gorbachev's policies were genuine and effective. Eventually, even democratic elections took place in the Soviet Union. Furthermore, Gorbachev began a real policy of cooperation with the West. Gorbachev became a folk hero around the world, a phenomenon called "Gorbymania." Even Reagan came to appreciate his efforts, and in a series of summit meetings in Geneva (1985), Reykjavik (1986), Washington, D.C. (1987), and Moscow (1988) the two leaders put forward meaningful programs, although disagreements still existed. In 1987, the two countries reached an arms reduction treaty. In 1988, Moscow left Afghanistan. Ultraconservative supporters of the president attacked him for his about-face with regard to Moscow, but Reagan counterattacked with the same vitriol he had once reserved for the Soviets.

The last piece of the puzzle was the dismantling of the Soviet's Eastern European empire. Reagan chided Gorbachev for not permitting the final democratic reforms in his "satellite countries." On June 12, 1987, Reagan stood at the Berlin Wall—the symbol of the division between East and West, erected in 1961—and shouted, "Mr. Gorbachev, tear down this wall!" Gorbachev responded by telling his communist allies that Moscow would not interfere in their internal affairs. One by one, the countries of Eastern Europe broke with their communist leadership and introduced democratically elected governments.

Canada   Canadian relations with the Soviet Union after World War II mirrored those of the United States, as both countries were members of the North Atlantic Treaty Organization (NATO). In the early years the Liberal Party prime minister Pierre Trudeau pushed the United States for a more conciliatory tone. He disagreed with Reagan about linking disarmament to Soviet behavior. In 1984, however, the Conservative Brian Mulroney replaced Trudeau and adopted as harsh a stance as that of Reagan. Mulroney was even more reluctant than the American president to come to terms with Gorbachev in the last years of the decade. In 1988, Canada expelled some Soviet diplomats accused of military and industrial espionage. However, both the Soviets and Canadians attempted to exploit differences from Washington's policies. Bilateral talks between Ottawa and Moscow began in 1984 and led to an agreement in 1989 on cooperation in the Arctic and the north, with Canada providing much technical assistance.

Impact   The 1980's witnessed a remarkable reversal of history centered on Soviet relations with the West and particularly the United States. The forty-year-

U.S. president Ronald Reagan and Soviet leader Mikhail Gorbachev relax together during their first summit meeting in Geneva, Switzerland, in November, 1985. (Ronald Reagan Presidential Library)

old Cold War was coming to an end as Gorbachev introduced liberalization into the Soviet Union in part because of pressure from the United States.

Subsequent Events By the end of the decade the whole system was on the verge of collapse, and on December 31, 1991, after a failed last-ditch attempt by communist hard-liners the previous summer to overthrow Gorbachev, the Soviet Union dissolved into its constituent republics.

Further Reading

Boyle, Peter G. *American-Soviet Relations: From the Russian Revolution to the Fall of Communism.* New York: Routledge, 1993. A scholarly monograph by a respected historian and specialist on international relations. Bibliography.

Garthoff, Raymond L. *The Great Transition: American-Soviet Relations and the End of the Cold War.* Washington, D.C.: Brookings Institution, 1994. A meticulous documented analysis by a diplomat and author of several important books on Soviet-American relations.

Gorbachev, Mikhail. *Perestroika and Soviet-American Relations.* Madison, Conn.: Sphinx Press, 1990. A collection of Gorbachev's speeches and interviews to Western audiences from late 1987 through 1989.

Halliday, Fred. *From Kabul to Managua: Soviet-American Relations in the 1980's.* New York: Pantheon Books, 1989. A critical analysis of the two superpowers by a controversial socialist professor from the London School of Economics.

Hill, Kenneth L. *Cold War Chronology: Soviet-American Relations, 1945-1991.* Washington, D.C.: Congressional Quarterly, 1993. An annotated chronology of the events from World War II until the end of the Soviet Union in 1991.

Ishaq, Mohammed. *The Politics of Trade Pressure: American-Soviet Relations, 1980-88.* Brookfield, Vt.: Ashgate, 1999. A monograph centering on economic issues between Moscow and Washington.

LaFeber, Walter. "The Two—or Three?—Phases of U.S.-Soviet Relations, 1981-1986." In *Crisis and Confrontation: Ronald Reagan's Foreign Policy,* edited by Morris H. Morley. Totowa, N.J.: Rowman & Littlefield, 1988. An examination of the policies and changes in Soviet-U.S. relations in the first half of the decade by one of America's most distinguished historians of the country's international affairs.

Nossal, Kim Richard. "The Politics of Circumspection: Canadian Policy Towards the USSR, 1985-1991." *International Journal of Canadian Studies* 9 (Spring, 1994). A scholarly examination of Canadian attitudes toward the Soviet Union after the advent of Gorbachev.

Stein, Janice Gross. *The Odd Couple: Analytical Perspectives on Canada's Relationship with the Soviet Union.* Toronto: Centre for Russian and East European Studies, University of Toronto, 1986. A short academic analysis prepared for a conference on Canadian-Soviet relations.

Trofimenko, G. A. *Lessons of Peaceful Coexistence: Fifty-Five Years of Soviet-American Diplomatic Relations.* Moscow: Novosti Press Agency, 1988. An analysis by a leading Russian academic specializing in American studies.

Frederick B. Chary

See also Berlin Wall; Cold War; Foreign policy of Canada; Foreign policy of the United States; Goodwill Games of 1986; Intermediate-Range Nuclear Forces (INF) Treaty; Miracle on Ice; Olympic boycotts; Olympic Games of 1980; Olympic Games of 1984; Reagan's "Evil Empire" speech; Reykjavik Summit; Smith, Samantha; Strategic Defense Initiative (SDI).

■ Space exploration

Definition Use of satellites and other spacecraft to gather scientific information about space and other planets

During the 1980's, U.S. space vehicles frequently exceeded all expectations, gathered a wealth of new information about planets and distant astronomical phenomena, and fulfilled the goal of visiting all the major planets in the solar system.

The 1980's witnessed a shift in emphasis in the U.S. space program. The National Aeronautics and Space Administration (NASA) turned away from human space flights of exploration, such as the moon voyages that had dominated attention in the 1970's, in favor of unpiloted probes and satellites. Crewed spaceflight, by contrast, was dedicated to delivery of cargo, maintenance of satellites, and performance of scientific experiments in low Earth orbit through the Space Transportation System. This program's inaugural flight was made by the space shuttle *Columbia* on April 12, 1981. However, the disastrous explosion of *Challenger* while launching on January 28, 1986, grounded the four-shuttle fleet for two years and resulted in even more emphasis being placed upon the use of uncrewed vehicles.

Satellite Observatories NASA put into Earth orbit four U.S.-produced astronomical observatories, two of which studied the Sun and two of which surveyed distant phenomena in the universe. Solar Maximum Mission was launched on February 14, 1980, and, after repair by a space shuttle crew in 1984, collected data on solar flares until 1989. Orbited on October 6, 1981, Solar Mesosphere Explorer monitored fluctuations in the Sun's production of ultraviolet light for five years. The Infrared Astronomical Satellite (IRAS), the first of its kind, reached orbit on January 26, 1983, in a joint project with the United Kingdom and the Netherlands. During its ten months of operations, IRAS examined more than 96 percent of the heavens, cataloging thousands of previously unknown galaxies and star-birthing gas clouds. It also discovered five new comets in the solar system. The Cosmic Background Explorer (COBE) entered orbit on November 18, 1989, and for four years mapped infrared background radiation to learn about the origin of the universe.

Landers and Deep Space Probes The decade opened with six of NASA's most renowned missions under way. Two landers were on Mars, taking photographs of the surface and gathering data on Martian soil and atmospheric conditions. Both had been launched in 1975; Viking 1 was operational until November 13, 1982, and Viking 2, until April 12, 1980. In addition, four probes were speeding deep into the solar system. Pioneer 10, launched in 1972, and Pioneer 11, launched in 1973, were far past their chief planetary objectives but continued transmitting to Earth valuable data about interplanetary magnetic fields, dust, and cosmic rays.

The most productive and far-ranging probes, however, were Voyager 1 and Voyager 2, both launched

The Voyager spacecraft undergoes vibration testing. (NASA-JPL)

in 1977 on a "Grand Tour" of the solar system's largest planets. From November 12 until December 15, 1980, Voyager 1 photographed the moons, rings, and atmosphere of Saturn and took magnetic and temperature readings. It revealed greater complexity in the rings than had previously been realized, found three new moonlets, and detected a thick, hydrocarbon-rich atmosphere on the moon Titan, a possible venue for life. Voyager 2 began collecting data on Saturn on June 5, 1981, and by the time it flew beyond instrument range three months later, it had taken high-resolution photographs of four moons and further studied Saturn's ring system.

Voyager 2 went on to Uranus, becoming the first craft to visit that planet. The flyby there, lasting from November 4, 1985, to February 25, 1986, produced photographs of the planet's thick clouds, showed that it rotated at 98 degrees from its orbital plane, examined its nine rings, and discovered ten new, small moons. The probe's next encounter (and another first) was with Neptune, making its closest approach to the planet on August 25, 1989. Voyager 2 discovered the Great Dark Spot, a hole in Neptune's cloud cover; spotted six new moonlets; and scrutinized its largest moon, Triton, detecting active volcanism.

Two additional highly successful probes were launched in 1989. Magellan was released into Earth orbit by a space shuttle on May 4 and then blasted off toward Venus, and on October 18, Galileo was also released from a space shuttle and sent on its way to Jupiter.

Impact   Once Voyager 2 passed Neptune in 1989, all of the solar system's major planets had been visited by U.S. probes, a triumph for NASA quite in addition to the wealth of photographs and data the Voyager probes returned. These successful programs encouraged the agency to focus on deep space probes through the next two decades. The COBE infrared observatory produced data that gave crucial support to a cosmological theory that the early universe experienced a spurt of "inflationary" growth. The theory later became accepted among cosmologists.

Subsequent Events   The Voyager probes soon passed Pioneer 10 to become the most distant human-made objects and throughout the decade continued returning data about the outermost reaches of the solar system. Magellan reached Venus on August 10, 1990, and began mapping its surface with radar. After photographing two asteroids en route, Galileo entered orbit around Jupiter on December 7, 1995, and was operational for eight years.

Further Reading

Evans, Ben, with David M. Harland. *NASA's Voyager Missions: Exploring the Outer Solar System and Beyond.* Chichester, England: Springer, 2004. Covers planetary discoveries of the two Voyager probes, and the historical background to them, in detail; describes the design, launch, and flights of the probes themselves. With an abundance of black-and-white and color photographs.

Godwin, Robert, and Steve Whitefield, eds. *Deep Space: The NASA Mission Reports.* Burlington, Ont.: Apogee Books, 2005. Contains original articles, overviews, and technical descriptions of the Pioneer and Voyager missions written during the programs, with many illustrations. A resource for space exploration enthusiasts and amateur historians.

Neal, Valerie, Cathleen S. Lewis, and Frank H. Winter. *Spaceflight: A Smithsonian Guide.* New York: Macmillan, 1995. This pleasantly written, nontechnical general history of American spaceflight includes a chapter on planetary probes and offers many dramatic photographs and graphics.

Tobias, Russell R., and David G. Fisher, eds. *USA in Space.* 3 vols. 3d ed. Pasadena, Calif.: Salem Press, 2006. Comprehensive collection of nontechnical articles that detail the history of American space programs and individual voyages. With black-and-white photographs and graphics.

Roger Smith

See also   Astronomy; *Challenger* disaster; Garneau, Marc; Ride, Sally; Science and technology; SETI Institute; Space shuttle program.

■ Space shuttle program

Definition   Program using reusable manned spacecraft

The space shuttle provided the National Aeronautics and Space Administration with the means to conduct varied missions for scientific, governmental, military, and commercial customers.

President Richard M. Nixon approved the space shuttle program in April, 1972. Capable of hauling cargo and personnel to low Earth orbit and returning to a runway landing, the Space Transportation System (STS) promised launch service cost reduction and reusability. In the realm of American crewed flight, after the Apollo program, only three Skylab missions and a joint U.S.-Soviet docking (Apollo-Soyuz Test Project) were conducted during the remainder of the 1970's. Shuttle development suffered budget constraints and technical problems. The first orbiter, *Columbia,* had been scheduled for a March, 1978, launch, but that date slipped repeatedly.

***Columbia*'s First Missions**   In 1981, the nation turned its attention toward Kennedy Space Center (KSC) for the first crewed National Aeronautics and Space Administration (NASA) spaceflight since 1975. Aboard *Columbia* on STS-1 were veteran astronaut John W. Young and rookie astronaut Robert L. Crippen, Jr. On April 10, a computer timing discrepancy scrubbed *Columbia*'s launch, but on April 12 the space shuttle was successfully launched. For thirty-six orbits, Young and Crippen evaluated systems, executed thruster firings, and held public affairs events. After two days, Young gently landed *Columbia* on Edwards Air Force Base's dry lake bed. *Columbia* launched again on November 12. STS-2 included testing of the Remote Manipulator System (RMS), a mechanical arm designed to manipulate cargo around *Columbia*'s payload bay Data were collected with an imaging radar system that filled up the bay. *Columbia* returned to Edwards Air Force Base after two days because of a fuel cell problem.

Columbia launched on March 22, 1982, for the seven-day STS-3 test flight, which included RMS arm operations and demonstrations of the shuttle middeck's utility to support research. The RMS arm grappled the Plasma Diagnostics Package, an instrument that recorded magnetohydrodynamic environments around *Columbia*. Unacceptable weather delayed *Columbia*'s reentry. *Columbia* was diverted to Northrup Strip at White Sands Missile Range, New Mexico.

Columbia's final test flight launched on June 27. Both solid rocket boosters (SRBs) were lost when parachutes failed to deploy properly. That had no effect on the shuttle's reaching orbit. Aboard was the classified military payload Cirris. STS-4 demonstrated that NASA could fly shuttles under Department of Defense (DOD) secrecy regulations. The mission ended after seven days, providing a patriotic setting for a Fourth of July celebration. President Ronald Reagan and shuttles *Enterprise* and *Challenger* were in place by Edwards Air Force Base's concrete runway to greet the returning astronauts. Reagan declared the STS fleet operational and signaled NASA's 747 carrier aircraft to taxi down the runway, beginning *Challenger*'s delivery flight to KSC.

Columbia's STS-5 mission launched on November 11 with the first four-person crew, and two communications satellites. Those satellites were housed within protective enclosures until deployment and

The space shuttle Columbia *lifts off on its first mission on April 12, 1981.* (NASA CORE/Lorain County JVS)

equipped with solid-fueled Payload Assist Modules (PAMs) to boost them to geosynchronous positions. An attempted space walk (or extravehicular activity, EVA) was thwarted by space suit problems. *Columbia* landed at Edwards Air Force Base after five days.

Challenger and Spacelab 1   *Challenger* first launched on April 4, 1983. Aboard was a four-person crew and a Tracking and Data-Relay Satellite (TDRS), the first component in NASA's network of geostationary communications satellites designed to establish continuous communications during shuttle missions. TDRS needed the more powerful Inertial Upper State (IUS) solid-fueled booster for its boost to geostationary altitude. STS-6's TDRS suffered an IUS motor failure. Over the course of many weeks, thrusters eventually nudged TDRS-A into operational position. Astronauts tested EVA translation methods within *Challenger*'s payload bay. The shuttle landed at Edwards Air Force Base after five days. *Challenger*'s STS-7 mission began on June 18. Among this initial five-person crew was the first American woman in space, Dr. Sally Ride. Two commercial satellites were deployed. Although scheduled to attempt the first landing at

Space Shuttle Missions in the 1980's

Mission Name	Dates	Astronauts
STS-1 *Columbia*	April 12-14, 1981	John W. Young and Robert L. Crippen, Jr.
STS-2 *Columbia*	November 12-14, 1981	Joseph H. Engle and Richard H. Truly
STS-3 *Columbia*	March 22-30, 1982	Jack R. Lousma and C. Gordon Fullerton
STS-4 *Columbia*	June 27-July 4, 1982	Thomas K. Mattingly II and Henry W. Hartsfield, Jr.
STS-5 *Columbia*	November 11-16, 1982	Vance D. Brand, Robert F. Overmyer, Joseph P. Allen, and William B. Lenoir
STS-6 *Challenger*	April 4-9, 1983	Paul J. Weitz, Karol J. Bobko, Donald H. Peterson, and F. Story Musgrave
STS-7 *Challenger*	June 18-24, 1983	Robert L. Crippen, Jr., Frederick H. Hauck, John M. Fabian, Sally Ride, and Norman E. Thagard.
STS-8 *Challenger*	August 30-September 5, 1983	Richard H. Truly, Daniel C. Brandenstein, Dale A. Gardner, Guion S. Bluford, Jr., and William E. Thornton
STS-9 *Columbia*	November 28-December 8, 1983	John W. Young, Brewster H. Shaw, Owen K. Garriott, Robert A. Parker, Byron K. Lichtenberg, and Ulf Merbold
STS 41-B *Challenger*	February 3-11, 1984	Vance D. Brand, Robert L. Gibson, Bruce McCandless II, Ronald E. McNair, and Robert L. Stewart
STS 41-C *Challenger*	April 6-13, 1984	Robert L. Crippen, Jr., Francis R. Scobee, George D. Nelson, James D. A. von Hoften, and Terry J. Hart
STS 41-D *Discovery*	August 30-September 5, 1984	Henry W. Hartsfield Jr., Michael L. Coats, Judith A. Resnik, Steven A. Hawley, Richard M. Mullane, and Charles D. Walker
STS 41-G *Challenger*	October 5-13, 1984	Robert L. Crippen, Jr., Jon A. McBride, Kathryn D. Sullivan, Sally Ride, David C. Leestma, Marc Garneau, and Paul D. Scully-Power
STS 51-A *Discovery*	November 8-16, 1984	Frederick H. Hauck, David M. Walker, Anna L. Fisher, Dale A. Gardner, and Joseph P. Allen
STS 51-C *Discovery*	January 24-27, 1985	Thomas K. Mattingly II, Loren J. Shriver, Ellison S. Onizuka, James F. Buchli, and Gary E. Payton
STS 51-D *Discovery*	April 12-19, 1985	Karol J. Bobko, Donald E. Williams, M. Rhea Seddon, Jeffrey A. Hoffman, S. David Griggs, Charles D. Walker, and Sen. E. Jake Garn
STS 51-B *Challenger*	April 29-May 6, 1985	Robert F. Overmyer, Frederick D. Gregory, Don L. Lind, Norman E. Thagard, William E. Thornton, Lodewijk van den Berg, and Taylor G. Wang
STS 51-G *Discovery*	June 17-14, 1985	Daniel C. Brandenstein, John O. Creighton, Shannon W. Lucid, John M. Fabian, Steven R. Nagel, Patrick Baudry, and Sultan Salman Al-Saud
STS 51-F *Challenger*	July 29-August 6, 1985	C. Gordon Fullerton, Roy D. Bridges, Jr., F. Story Musgrave, Anthony W. England, Karl G. Henize, Loren W. Acton, and John-David F. Bartoe
STS 51-I *Discovery*	August 27-September 3, 1985	Joseph H. Engle, Richard O. Covey, James D. A. van Hoften, John M. Lounge, and William F. Fisher

Mission Name	Dates	Astronauts
STS 51-J *Atlantis*	October 3-7, 1985	Joseph H. Engle, Richard O. Covey, James D. A. van Hoften, John M. Lounge, and William F. Fisher
STS 61-A *Challenger*	October 30-November 6, 1985	Henry W. Hartsfield, Jr., Steven R. Nagel, James F. Buchli, Guion S. Bluford, Bonnie J. Dunbar, Reinhard Furrer, Ernst Messerschmid, and Wubbo J. Ockels
STS 61-B *Atlantis*	November 26-December 3, 1985	Brewster H. Shaw, Jr., Bryan D. O'Connor, Mary L. Cleave, Sherwood C. Spring, Jerry L. Ross, Rodolfo Neri Vela, and Charles D. Walker
STS 61-C *Columbia*	January 12-18, 1986	Robert L. Gibson, F. Bolden, Jr., Franklin R. Chang-Diaz, Steven A. Hawley, George D. Nelson, Robert J. Cenker, and Congressman Bill Nelson.
STS 51-L *Challenger*	January 28, 1986	Francis R. Scobee, Michael J. Smith, Judith A. Resnik, Ellison S. Onizuka, Ronald E. McNair, Gregory B. Jarvis, and Christa McAuliffe
STS-26 *Discovery*	September 29-October 3, 1988	Frederick H. Hauck, Richard O. Covey, John M. Lounge, George D. Nelson, and David C. Hilmers
STS-27 *Atlantis*	December 2-6, 1988	Robert L. Gibson, Guy S. Gardner, Richard Mullane, Jerry L. Ross, and William M. Shepherd
STS-29 *Discovery*	March 13-18, 1989	Michael L. Coats, John E. Blaha, James P. Bagian, James F. Buchli, and Robert C. Springer
STS-30 *Atlantis*	May 4-8, 1989	David M. Walker, Ronald J. Grabe, Norman E. Thagard, Mary L. Cleave, and Mark C. Lee
STS-28 *Columbia*	August 8-13, 1989	Brewster H. Shaw, Richard N. Richards, James C. Adamson, David C. Leestma, and Mark N. Brown
STS-34 *Atlantis*	October 18-23, 1989	Donald E. Williams, Michael J. McCulley, Franklin R. Chang-Diaz, Shannon W. Lucid, and Ellen S. Baker
STS-33 *Discovery*	November 22-27, 1989	Frederick D. Gregory, John E. Blaha, F. Story Musgrave, Manley L. Carter Jr., and Kathryn C. Thornton

Source: National Aeronautics and Space Administration.

KSC, the *Challenger* was forced to divert to Edwards Air Force Base after six days.

STS-8 lifted off on August 30, performing the shuttle's first night launch. The crew included the first African American astronaut, Guion Stewart Bluford, Jr. A Payload Test Article was used to assess the RMS arm's ability to handle massive objects. An Indian communications satellite was dispatched to geosynchronous orbit. After six days, *Challenger* landed at night at Edwards Air Force Base.

On November 28, Spacelab 1 launched aboard *Columbia*. The European Space Agency (ESA) built and provided Spacelab to NASA in exchange for sending astronauts into space. The pressurized module housed inside *Columbia*'s payload bay allowed scientists to perform research programs. Ten days after launch, after seventy-two separate science projects concluded, *Columbia* landed at Edwards Air Force Base. STS-9 marked John Young's last command.

1984 Missions *Challenger*'s STS 41-B flight began on February 3, 1984, and included two satellite deployments and tests of a Manned Maneuvering Unit (MMU) that could independently take astronauts several hundred feet away from the shuttle. During two EVAs, the MMU was put through its paces. Astronaut Bruce McCandless II flew it nearly one hundred meters from the space shuttle. Each satellite's PAM failed, stranding these satellites in useless orbits. Engineers began devising rescue plans for these expensive communications satellites. *Challenger* achieved the first landing at KSC on February 11.

STS 41-C was the first satellite repair mission. The Solar Max observatory had malfunctioned, but its problems were understood. *Challenger* launched on April 6, and, after rendezvousing, astronaut George D. Nelson flew the MMU to Solar Max but could not dock. Commander Crippen then maneuvered *Challenger* within thirty-five feet of the observatory, and the RMS arm grappled it. Solar Max was secured to a work platform where astronauts repaired it. The observatory was released to continue its research. *Discovery*'s first flight (STS 41-D) occurred on August 30. The space shuttle carried three satellites and a large folded solar array designed for a space station. The latter contained no functional solar cells, as this was an array deployment dynamics test. *Discovery* landed at Edwards Air Force Base after six days. *Challenger* launched on October 5. STS 41-G included deployment of an Earth resources satellite, the first time that seven people were simultaneously launched into space, and the first space walk performed by an American woman, Kathryn D. Sullivan. Astronauts Sullivan and David Leetsma demonstrated satellite refueling methods. *Challenger* landed at KSC after eight days. *Discovery* launched on November 8. STS 51-A deployed two satellites like those on STS 41-B and captured the wayward STS 41-B satellites, Westar 6 and Palapa B-2. Astronauts Dale Gardner and Joseph P. Allen used the MMU to dock and capture the satellites, strapping them in *Discovery*'s payload bay for return to Earth at KSC after eight days.

1985 Missions The STS 51-C mission was the first fully classified DOD shuttle flight. Inside *Discovery* on January 24, 1985, was a classified electronic intelligence (ELINT) payload. After deployment, it suffered an IUS malfunction, but the ELINT satellite did collect reconnaissance data. After three days, *Discovery* returned to KSC.

Senator Jake Garn of Utah was an observer on STS 51-D, which launched on April 12. Two satellites were deployed from *Discovery*'s payload bay. However, the Syncom IV satellite failed to activate after deployment. Astronauts attached a makeshift device to the RMS arm's end effector during an unsched-

uled space walk. They dragged this device against a satellite lever designed to start a timer for solid-fueled rocket ignition; the attempt failed. *Discovery* landed at KSC after six days. *Challenger*'s STS 51-B/Spacelab 3 mission began with an April 29 liftoff and lasted seven days. Scientists inside Spacelab performed fifteen primary experiments in materials science, life sciences, fluid physics, atmospheric physics, and astronomy.

On July 17, *Discovery* flew its fifth mission, STS 51-G. NASA's crew hosted a Saudi prince, Sultan Salman Al-Saud, as Saudi Arabia had partially paid for the mission. During the mission, astronauts deployed three satellites, including an Arabsat communications satellite. *Challenger*'s STS 51-F/Spacelab 2 mission experienced an ascent mishap on July 29. One main engine shut down prematurely. The space shuttle executed an abort-to-orbit profile, entering a lower altitude than preferred. *Challenger*'s payload bay carried a sophisticated pointing system for a suite of four solar astrophysics telescopes. The shuttle's thrusters raised the orbit slightly, and research was carried out despite nagging pointing system problems. *Discovery* flew STS 51-I, launching on August 27. Three satellites were deployed during the seven-day mission. A spacewalking repair of the Syncom IV satellite succeeded, and the satellite's solid rocket motor fired to boost it into an operational position. *Discovery* landed at Edwards Air Force Base.

STS 51-J saw the first flight of *Atlantis*, launched on October 3. During the four-day classified DOD mission, a military communications satellite was deployed. *Atlantis* returned to Earth at Edwards Air Force Base.

The seven-day-long STS 61-A/Spacelab D-1 research mission was the first to involve control from an international (German) control center. Three ESA payload specialists flew among the first eight-person crew. *Challenger* returned to Earth at Edwards Air Force Base. *Atlantis*'s STS 61-B mission launched on November 26 . Three satellites were deployed, and astronauts tested orbital construction techniques. *Atlantis* landed at Edwards Air Force Base after seven days.

Robust 1985 space shuttle operations stretched program assets thin. Pressure existed to increase flight rates to make the shuttle financially self-sufficient, but problems surfaced during the early years of operations. One recurring, serious problem involved SRB joint O-ring erosion. Joint design required modification, which would have halted flight operations.

1986 Missions and the *Challenger* Disaster   *Columbia*'s six-day STS 61-C mission launched on January 12 with Congressman Bill Nelson of Florida aboard. This flight included investigations of Halley's comet. *Columbia* landed at Edwards Air Force Base.

STS 51-L was to deploy TDRS-B. President Reagan had directed NASA to search for a Teacher in Space participant, and Christa McAuliffe of New Hampshire was selected to join six other astronauts. *Challenger* experienced several weather delays and technical difficulties before its launch on January 28. Media and educational institutions focused on the historic Teacher in Space's journey. An SRB joint O-ring failed at ignition, leading to a catastrophic vehicle breakup seventy-three seconds after liftoff. All crew members onboard were killed.

A presidential commission issued a final report critical of how NASA left problems unaddressed while schedule pressures kept shuttles flying. A safer SRB joint design was developed and tested into the summer of 1988. Shuttle payload manifests had been severely disrupted, but NASA focused on safety; sadly, that lesson had not been learned until seven astronauts lost their lives and a $2 billion orbiter was destroyed.

Return to Flight   On September 29, 1988, NASA stood poised for *Discovery*'s STS-26 launch. *Discovery* carried another TDRS. Five astronauts deployed TDRS-C, paid tribute to *Challenger*'s crew, and landed at Edwards Air Force Base after four days. *Atlantis*'s classified STS-27 mission launched on December 2. *Discovery* lifted off on March 13, 1989, to begin the five-day STS-29 mission. After deploying TDRS-D and completing secondary experiments, the space shuttle landed at Edwards Air Force Base. Subsequent missions included STS-30, which carried the Magellan probe, sent to map Venus, and STS-34, which dispatched the Galileo probe to Jupiter. Classified DOD missions included *Columbia*'s STS-28 and *Discovery*'s STS-33.

Impact   Space shuttle operations commenced in 1981 and in four years ramped up to a flight per month. Fleet operations and the shuttle workforce experienced tremendous pressure. Vehicle problems were not addressed to better ensure safety, resulting in the *Challenger* launch accident of January, 1986.

After redesigns, the shuttle fleet resumed flight operations in September, 1988. Flight rates never again matched that of 1985, but the shuttle's function shifted from a commercial satellite delivery system to a research platform for Spacelab missions, a transport vehicle for Phase One astronauts going to Russia's Mir space station, and a workhorse for International Space Station (ISS) construction.

Subsequent Events   *Challenger, Discovery, Atlantis,* and *Endeavour* followed *Columbia* in turn. As a result of thermal protection system damage encountered during launch, *Columbia* and another seven-person crew were lost in February, 2003. After careful review, President George W. Bush directed NASA to complete the ISS by 2010 and then retire the shuttle fleet. Shuttles would be replaced by an Apollo-like Crew Exploration Vehicle, and astronauts would again leave low Earth orbit, where for thirty years the shuttle had been constrained to operate.

Further Reading

Harland, David M. *The Story of the Space Shuttle.* New York: Springer-Praxis, 2004. Covers shuttle origins through the post-*Columbia* accident period.

Jenkins, Dennis R. *Space Shuttle: The History of the National Transportation System—The First One Hundred Missions.* New York: D. R. Jenkins, 2001. A technical text details flight operations.

Reichhardt, Tony. *Space Shuttle: The First Twenty Years—The Astronauts' Experiences in Their Own Words.* London: Dorling Kindersley, 2002. As this title suggests, the text provides numerous first-person accounts of space shuttle experiences.

David G. Fisher

See also   *Challenger* disaster; Garneau, Marc; Reagan, Ronald; Ride, Sally; Science and technology; Space exploration.

■ Special effects

Definition   Images and sounds in motion pictures that are created or manipulated through means other than filming or recording the thing being represented

During the 1980's, both the film and special effects industries experienced a remarkable revival. The art and technology of special effects became increasingly sophisticated and

spectacular, resulting in large budgets and huge box-office blockbusters.

Beginning in the late 1890's, the father of special effects, Georges Méliès, used effects such as stop-action and double exposure, perspective tricks, and mirrors to create illusions in film. As filmmaking evolved during the 1900's, the art and science of special effects also grew to include techniques such as cel animation, prosthetic makeup, model making, claymation, matte painting, and finally computer technology.

Facing financial difficulties in the 1960's, major film studios eliminated special effects departments to reduce overhead costs. However, for Stanley Kubrick's 1968 movie *2001: A Space Odyssey*, artist Douglas Trumball invented the "slit scan" technique to create the famous "stargate" light sequence. The film's special effects helped make it a phenomenal box-office success. Partly as a result, in the 1970's a new generation of film directors began to revive special effects, setting the tone for the 1980's. Steven Spielberg's *Jaws* (1975) became the first blockbuster of the post-studio era, making over $100 million. His dazzling *Close Encounters of the Third Kind* (1977) employed some of the effects specialists who had worked on *2001*. George Lucas's *Star Wars* (1977) used the first computer-linked camera control system. The success of these movies helped guide the studios to change their business models. Over time, they ceased to focus on making a steady series of medium-budget, relatively successful films. Instead, they began to focus more of their energies on creating fewer but more lucrative films, blockbusters with massive budgets that sought to realize even more massive profits. Most such blockbusters were effects-driven, relying on spectacle rather than narrative as their primary draw.

During the 1980's, filmmakers met the public's growing expectation for impressive special effects and large-budget action and science-fiction films. In 1982, Disney produced *Tron*, an adventure film set largely in virtual reality that featured the first extensive use of computer-generated imaging (CGI). Other milestones in special effects history included *Blade Runner* (1982), which envisioned Los Angeles in 2015; *The Last Starfighter* (1984), the first film to use CGI instead of traditional, physical models of spaceships; and *Aliens* (1986), which used in-camera visuals.

In the 1980's, Lucas's Industrial Light and Magic (ILM) special effects studio worked on over fifty major films, became the world's most successful special effects company, and produced landmark effects, especially CGI. The company added impressive CGI effects in the climactic scene of Spielberg's *Raiders of the Lost Ark* (1981). In *Star Trek II: The Wrath of Khan* (1982) the "Genesis sequence" was the first completely computer-generated sequence in a major motion picture and the first use of a fractal-generated landscape. In two further collaborations with Spielberg, ILM produced the effects for *E.T.: The Extra-Terrestrial* (1982)—the most successful film of the decade—and *Young Sherlock Holmes* (1985), for which the company created the first fully computer generated character, the "stained-glass man."

Also in 1985, ILM created alien life-forms and a spaceship for *Cocoon. Labyrinth* (1986) opened with a digital owl, the first CGI animal. For the Metro-Goldwyn-Mayer and Lucasfilm coproduction *Willow* (1988), ILM performed the first digital morphing (the seamless evolution of one image or character into another). A Disney production, *Who Framed Roger Rabbit* (1988), combined hand-painted imagery with computer animation. *Back to the Future, Part II* (1989) used a computer-controlled camera to create stunning split-screen photography. In *The Abyss* (1989), ILM made the first computer-generated 3-dimensional (3-D) character, the alien pseudopod, which swam in the first digitally animated water. *Raiders of the Lost Ark, Cocoon, Who Framed Roger Rabbit*, and *The Abyss* won Academy Awards for Best Visual Effects.

In 1986, Lucas sold ILM's computer graphics department to Apple Computer founder Steve Jobs, and Pixar was born. Pixar produced *Luxo Jr.* (1986), a two-minute short film about a pair of desk lamps. This short was the first fully computer-animated film. *Tin Toy* (1988) was the first computer animation to win an Academy Award—for Best Animated Short Film—and was the inspiration for *Toy Story* (1995).

Impact Special effects in the 1980's had profound cultural, economic, and commercial impacts. The film and special effects industries were both revitalized, as audiences came to expect spectacular special effects and high-budget action films. During this decade, the average cost to produce a film rose from $10 million to $23 million, but movie theater revenues were higher than ever. In 1989, these revenues totaled $5.03 billion. The industry also reaped profits from movie-related merchandise, such as books, clothing, toys, and computer games. There was also a renaissance in the art and technology of special effects. Research and technological development intensified to meet increasing audience expectations. The leading studio, Industrial Light and Magic, continued to provide groundbreaking effects for films, music videos, television commercials, and theme-park attractions.

Further Reading

McCarthy, Robert. *Secrets of Hollywood Special Effects.* Boston: Focal Press, 1992. Comprehensive, in-depth source on special effects techniques, including case studies and over two hundred illustrations. Discussions of wire flying and levitation, rain and water, snow, steam, smoke, fire, and chemical effects.

Pinteau, Pascal. *Special Effects: An Oral History—Interviews with Thirty-Eight Masters Spanning One Hundred Years.* New York: Harry N. Abrams, 2004. Fascinating revelations about special effects techniques used in film, television, and theme parks. Includes over one thousand photographs and illustrations.

Rickitt, Richard. *Special Effects: The History and Technique.* New York: Billboard Books, 2000. A beautifully illustrated, comprehensive history, including interviews with hundreds of special effects masters, a helpful glossary, and a section on special effects landmarks.

Vaz, Mark Cota, and Patricia Duignan. *Industrial Light and Magic: Into the Digital Realm.* New York: Ballantine Books, 1996. Behind-the-scenes account of ILM's accomplishments from 1986 through the mid-1990's. Includes over six hundred illustrations and a foreword by Steven Spielberg.

Alice Myers

See also   Academy Awards; Action films; *Aliens*; *Back to the Future*; *Blade Runner*; *Empire Strikes Back, The*; *E.T.: The Extra-Terrestrial*; Film in the United States; Ford, Harrison; *Raiders of the Lost Ark*; Science-fiction films; Spielberg, Steven; *Tron*; *Who Framed Roger Rabbit.*

■ Spielberg, Steven

Identification   American film director and producer
Born   December 18, 1946: Cincinnati, Ohio

In many ways, the 1980's was cinematically Spielberg's decade. Not only did all three of his Indiana Jones movies appear during the decade, but also E.T.: The Extra-Terrestrial *became the decade's single most successful film, and* The Color Purple *relaunched Spielberg's career as a serious, albeit at times controversial, filmmaker.*

Steven Spielberg's *Jaws* (1975) began a transformation in Hollywood, as the blockbuster film changed the studios' expectations and strategies in producing and marketing motion pictures. It immediately defined Spielberg as a major force within the industry, although he ended the 1970's with one of his rare failures, *1941* (1979). In 1981, Spielberg's *Raiders of the Lost Ark*, the first film in the Indiana Jones series, introduced the daring, resourceful hero. *Indiana Jones and the Temple of Doom* (1984) and *Indiana Jones and the Last Crusade* (1989) also pitted the heroic individual American against the forces of darkness, a conflict in which the United States was triumphant.

These nostalgic films, set in the 1930's and deliberately designed to be stylistically reminiscent of old Saturday afternoon serials, capitalized on the 1980's nostalgia for earlier, idealized decades. They resonated with similar themes of nostalgia and of the role of the United States in the battle between good and evil that were central to Ronald Reagan's presidency. By most filmmakers' standards, all three Indiana Jones films were popular and financially successful, but the second failed to live up to the extremely high expectations that had attached to every Spielberg project by the time it was released.

Spielberg's reputation was furthered by the huge impact of his science-fiction film *E.T.: The Extra-Terrestrial* (1982), which gave American culture the phrase "E.T. phone home" and expanded the market for a chocolate-covered, peanut-butter candy. In the movie, Spielberg explored the impact of an alien on conventional, placid middle-class suburban life, a theme he had touched on previously in an earlier science-fiction movie, *Close Encounters of the Third Kind* (1976).

Spielberg's critical reputation increased considerably with the release of *The Color Purple* (1985), set in the segregated South and based on the celebrated novel by the African American author Alice Walker. The film traced the devastating effects of segregation and employed an almost entirely African American cast. He followed with *Empire of the Sun* (1987), based on the novel by J. G. Ballard and set in the late 1930's in Shanghai, during the Japanese military takeover. *Empire of the Sun* followed the adventures of a young boy in an internment camp during World War II and the emotional effects wrought on him by his imprisonment. Both films garnered critical attention not before received by Spielberg's films.

Steven Spielberg in 1985. (AP/Wide World Photos)

Impact Steven Spielberg helped reenergize American films of the 1980's with his technical skill, his reverence for the traditions of Hollywood, and his innovative reworking of standard themes of American cinema.

Further Reading

Brode, Douglas. *The Films of Steven Spielberg.* New York: Carol, 1995.

McBride, Joseph. *Steven Spielberg: A Biography.* New York: Simon & Schuster, 1997.

Perry, George. *Steven Spielberg.* New York: Thunder's Mouth Press, 1998.

Silet, Charles L. P., ed. *The Films of Steven Spielberg: Critical Essays.* Lanham, Md.: Scarecrow Press, 2002.

Charles L. P. Silet

See also Academy Awards; Action films; *Color Purple, The*; Epic films; *E.T.: The Extra-Terrestrial*; Ford, Harrison; Jewish Americans; *Raiders of the Lost Ark*; Science-fiction films; *Twilight Zone* accident.

■ Sports

Definition Athletic contests, both team and individual

In the final full decade before the cable and Internet revolutions, sports fans relied on "old" media (newspapers, radio, and television) to learn about the highlights from the sports world, and in the 1980's there were many.

In the 1980's, going to bed before a favorite team's game had ended often meant that discovering the final score was difficult. There was no Internet accessible from home computers. One likely could not turn on the television and check ESPN; cable at this point was only just fully integrating itself into most American homes. The 1980's were a time in which information about sports stars, games, and highlights had to be garnered from a printed newspaper or from the radio or a local television station. The Internet, the iPod, and other sources that allow for instantaneous tracking and relaying of information were not yet available.

Today, it is taken for granted that a game, regardless of how unimportant it is, can be found on cable television. It also is widely known that anytime an athlete or team approaches an important milestone that ESPN or some cable entity will be airing it live. Furthermore, information about teams, players, and events can now easily be gathered "in real time" from various news agencies. In short, immediate information is available. In such an environment, athletes can become instant stars and events can become instant classics. Whether the athlete or the game actually deserves such a label often is doubtful. While many people often did not learn about stars and classic moments as quickly or have the certainty of seeing them live as they do today, many events, people, and moments captivated the nation during the 1980's.

The Olympics and the Miracle on Ice   The brightest moment of the 1980's might very well have taken place just two months into the decade. In 1980, no professional athlete (as defined by the West) could take part in the Olympics. The absence of paid athletes allowed for the larger-than-life story that was the triumph of the U.S. men's hockey team, which won the gold medal in Lake Placid. Although the U.S. team had no professionals, many of its members would go on to play in the National Hockey League (NHL). Along the way, the Americans defeated the vaunted Soviets, a team considered the best in the world and that included, many in the West believed, professionals because of the subsidies provided to them by their government. The Soviet Union insisted that it was never in violation of Olympic rules.

Just six years later, the distinction between "amateur" and "professional" was a moot point; the terms had been deleted from the Olympic Charter, the document that outlines the rules and regulations of the Olympics. Among the first sports to benefit from the inclusion of professionals was tennis, which after a sixty-four-year hiatus returned to the Olympic program in 1988. In Seoul, one of the best tennis players in the world, Steffi Graf, won a gold medal.

Politics also overshadowed the Olympic movement during the 1980's. President Jimmy Carter led a boycott of the 1980 Moscow Olympics, in protest of the Soviet Union's military invasion of Afghanistan in December, 1979. Though widely criticized both at home and especially abroad, Carter's boycott call was endorsed by a number of Western nations. Soviet and East German athletes, in the absence of many of their Western colleagues, dominated the Games, winning a combined 321 medals. The image of the Olympics as a place for athletes to gather in friendly competition free of international politics had been shattered.

Four years later, the Soviets led a boycott of their own and refused to send their athletes to Los Angeles, the site of the 1984 Summer Games. Thirteen Eastern Bloc nations joined the Soviets, who said the boycott was necessary because the United States could not guarantee the safety of Soviet athletes while they were on American soil. American athletes, especially swimmers such as Mary T. Meagher, and track-and-field stars, most notably Carl Lewis, took advantage of the missing Eastern Bloc athletes to win numerous Olympic medals. The entire country seemed to revel in Olympic fever.

Although the Americans, the Soviets, and their allies were reunited at the 1988 Summer Olympics in Seoul, they actually had the chance to compete against each other two years earlier. In the mid-1980's, Ted Turner, founder of the Cable News Network (CNN), began what he called the Goodwill Games, which brought together athletes from the Eastern and Western Blocs in an athletics program that included multiple Olympic sports. The first Goodwill Games took place in 1986 and were hosted by Moscow. The games were broadcast in the United States on Turner Network Television (TNT), a network that was owned by Turner at the time. The location allowed American audiences a glance inside the Soviet Union, a somewhat rare opportunity during the Cold War. The Goodwill Games continued into the early twenty-first century, but their expressed purpose—to allow athletic competition to trump international politics—was never more important than in 1986.

Football   In the final seconds of the 1982 National Football Conference (NFC) championship game at Candlestick Park in San Francisco, Dwight Clark of the San Francisco 49ers ran to the back of the end zone and jumped as high as he could. When he came down, a football that had been thrown by quarterback Joe Montana was in his hands. "The Catch," as it has become known, not only allowed the 49ers to defeat the Dallas Cowboys and advance to the franchise's first Super Bowl but also ensured that the 49ers would become the NFC's glamour team for the remainder of the decade and beyond. Though the Cowboys were considered "America's Team," the 49ers would go on to win 159 regular-season games and five Super Bowls over the next fourteen years.

If the 49ers were the NFC's premier team during the 1980's, the closest equivalent in the American Football Conference (AFC) was the Denver Broncos. Although the Oakland/Los Angeles Raiders had a strong reputation and Super Bowl victories in 1981 and 1984, during the decade the Broncos won more regular-season games (ninety-three to eighty-nine) and appeared in more Super Bowls (three to two) than the Raiders. The Broncos lost those three championship games by a combined score of 136-40, highlighting an era in which NFC teams, including the 49ers, were simply better than their AFC counterparts. The Broncos (who went on to win two Super Bowls in the 1990's) built their team around one man—Hall of Fame quarterback John Elway, who in 1983 was drafted by the then Baltimore Colts, a team for which Elway refused to play. He was soon dealt to Denver.

In January, 1987, the legend of Elway fully developed. Though his team trailed 20-13 in the final six minutes of the AFC championship game in Cleveland, Elway led his team on an improbable fifteen-play, 98-yard touchdown drive that tied the score and forced overtime. In the extra period, he again drove the Broncos down the field, using nine plays to cover sixty yards. A short field goal followed, and the Broncos stunned the Cleveland Browns with a 23-20 victory.

Fans in three National Football League (NFL) cities were stunned—for a different reason—during the 1980's. They watched helplessly as their teams moved to new cities: the Oakland Raiders to Los Angeles in 1982, the Baltimore Colts to Indianapolis in 1984, and the St. Louis Cardinals to Phoenix, Arizona, in 1988. More franchises—including the Raiders, who returned to Oakland—would relocate in the 1990's.

Baseball In 1981, the Major League Baseball (MLB) season was damaged by a strike that lasted about two months and canceled more than seven hundred games. Many fans blamed the owners, although it was the players who decided to walk out. The strike also overshadowed the remarkable rookie season of Los Angeles Dodgers' pitcher Fernando Valenzuela. He began his first year in the majors with an 8-0 record and an earned run average (ERA) of 0.50. He finished the season with a 13-7 record, a 2.48 ERA, seven shutouts, and as the winner of the Rookie of the Year and Cy Young awards. The Dodgers also won their first world championship since 1965, defeating the New York Yankees in six games.

An even more improbable Dodgers team won the World Series in 1988, when it defeated the Oakland Athletics. Los Angeles pitcher Orel Hershiser completed an amazing season, which included setting a major-league record for consecutive shutout innings (fifty-nine), by being named the League Championship Series and World Series Most Valuable Player (MVP). Fittingly, he threw a complete game in the decisive game 5, which the Dodgers won 5-2.

In 1989, Nolan Ryan, baseball's all-time leader in career strikeouts with 5,714, recorded 301 strikeouts, marking the sixth and final time he reached the 300 plateau in a single year. Roger Clemens, who currently ranks second in all-time strikeouts, began his remarkable career in the 1980's. He went 24-4 in 1986, when the Boston Red Sox won their first division title in more than a decade. Two years later, he struck out 291 batters; only once has Clemens recorded more strikeouts in a single season. In fact, the top eight pitchers in all-time strikeouts played during some or all of the 1980's.

One of baseball's most historic records fell on September 11, 1985, when Cincinnati's Pete Rose hit a single to left field. It was career hit 4,192 for Rose, eclipsing Ty Cobb's record. Rose ended his playing career one year later, finishing with 4,256 hits, but he remained the Reds' manager through August, 1989. His Hall of Fame credentials seemed secure: He had won three World Series championships and an MVP award, and he was a seventeen-time All-Star. However, Rose's professional credentials were crushed by a looming controversy—did he bet on baseball games, including some involving the team he was managing? A damaging report, written by investigator John Dowd, left little doubt in the minds of the sport's executives that Rose was gambling (including on his Reds games) and therefore had to be banned from the game. Rose maintained that he did nothing wrong, but in late 1989 he agreed to be placed on baseball's ineligible list and resigned as manager.

Basketball Basketball during the 1980's was dominated by two men, although by the end of the decade a third man had come along to earn his spot among National Basketball Association (NBA) superstars. Earvin "Magic" Johnson proved that he was going to be something very special during his rookie year of 1979-1980, when he averaged more than eighteen points and seven rebounds per game for the Los Angeles Lakers. In the critical sixth game of the NBA finals, Johnson moved from guard to center, starting for the injured Kareem Abdul-Jabbar, and scored forty-two points and grabbed fifteen rebounds, as the Lakers held off the Philadelphia 76ers and won their first NBA championship in almost a decade. Johnson also won the first of his three NBA finals MVP awards that year.

Larry Bird entered the league in the same year Johnson did. Bird won the league's Rookie of the Year award, averaging more than twenty-one points and ten rebounds per game for the Boston Celtics. Bird's impact was felt much more in the standings: During the 1978-1979 season, the Celtics won twenty-nine games, but with Bird they won sixty-one games the following year. The team also advanced to the NBA's Eastern Conference finals, losing to Philadelphia.

Johnson's Lakers and Bird's Celtics took home many championships during the 1980's. Los Angeles won five NBA championships and played for three others. Boston won three titles and played for two others. The most intense period of this rivalry took place between the 1983-1984 and 1986-1987 seasons. Over that four-year stretch, the teams met three times in the NBA finals; the Lakers won twice.

Toward the end of the decade, basketball's man of the 1990's took center stage. Michael Jordan joined the NBA in 1984, a few months after helping the U.S. men's basketball team win an Olympic gold medal. He was an instant superstar, averaging more than 28 points per game for the Chicago Bulls. Jordan won multiple scoring titles over the remainder of the decade, but he and his teammates could not get past Boston in the middle of the decade, nor Detroit at the end of it, to advance to the NBA finals. Jordan and the Bulls would dominate the league in the 1990's.

Hockey   The Lakers and Celtics were basketball's dynasties in the 1980's. In hockey, the dynasty tag was owned by the New York Islanders at the beginning of the decade and by the Edmonton Oilers at the end of it. The Islanders won the Stanley Cup from 1980 through 1983. The Oilers lost the 1983 finals, but they quickly rebounded and were hockey's best team in 1984 (defeating the Islanders and denying New York a fifth consecutive title), 1985, 1987, 1988, and 1990.

The Oilers had all the makings of celebrity status: They were young, cocky, and brash, and they had perhaps the greatest player in the history of the sport—Wayne Gretzky. During the 1980's, he scored more than two hundred points in a single season four times, scored more than fifty goals in a season nine times, and won the league MVP award eight straight times (nine times overall).

The Oilers began to be dismantled in 1988, when owner Peter Pocklington agreed to trade Gretzky to the Los Angeles Kings. Although Gretzky never won another championship in his career, his superstar status ensured that hockey would survive on the West Coast. Sold-out crowds became the norm in Los Angeles.

Tennis and Golf   Women's tennis was the purview of Martina Navratilova during the 1980's. She won fifteen of her eighteen grand slam singles titles, including the most prestigious, Wimbledon, on six different occasions. She also won the singles title at the U.S. Open four times, in 1983, 1984, 1986, and 1987.

Two men repeatedly etched their names into the golf record books in the 1980's. Tom Watson won three of his five Open Championships, his only U.S. Open title, and the second of his two Masters championships during the decade. He also was named the PGA Golfer of the Year three times. The "Golden Bear," Jack Nicklaus, also proved he still had some bite left in him. The dominant golfer of the 1970's won three more majors in the 1980's, including the 1986 Masters. He rallied from a four-shot deficit on the final day to win the crown.

Impact   The 1980's saw professional and college football replace baseball as America's most popular spectator sport, while the superstars of the NBA helped to elevate the league to equal status with the NFL and MLB. The Olympics also experienced a significant change, as the 1988 Summer Games marked the first time that professional athletes were allowed to take part in the Games.

Further Reading

Craig, Roger, and Matt Maiocco. *Tales from the San Francisco 49ers Sideline.* New York: Sports Publishing, 2004. This is a somewhat typical but entertaining sports account.

Elway, John, Marc Serota, and Elise Glading. *Elway.* Media, Pa.: Benchmark Press, 1998. An easy-to-read book. Not the best choice for a scholarly project, but it provides a glimpse at Elway as a person and an athlete.

Feinstein, John. *A Season on the Brink: A Year with Bobby Knight and the Indiana Hoosiers.* New York: Simon & Schuster, 1987. This remains one of the most popular sports books of all time, chronicling the legendary basketball coach and his team. Ironically, this book covers the 1985-1986 Indiana season. One year later, the Hoosiers won the national championship.

Guttmann, Allen. *A History of the Olympic Games.* 2d ed. Champaign: University of Illinois Press, 2002.

One of the best books to help explain the growth of the Olympics, as well as the positive and negative elements that are now associated with this premier international event.

Podnieks, Andrew. *The Great One: The Life and Times of Wayne Gretzky.* New York: Triumph Books, 1999. A complete look at Gretzky and his impact on his sport.

Rose, Pete, and Rick Hill. *My Prison Without Bars.* New York: Rodale Books, 2004. Rose uses this book to make one case: that, despite his legal problems, he belongs in the Baseball Hall of Fame.

Senn, Alfred Erich. *Power, Politics, and the Olympic Games.* Champaign, Ill.: Human Kinetics Books, 1999. The writing is sometimes difficult to follow, but Senn nevertheless presents a well-researched book about the outside forces that weigh on the Olympic Games.

Anthony Moretti

See also Arena Football League; Baseball; Baseball strike of 1981; Basketball; Bird, Larry; Boitano, Brian; Boxing; Brett, George; Decker, Mary; Elway, John; Football; Gibson, Kirk; Golf; Goodwill Games of 1986; Gretzky, Wayne; Griffith-Joyner, Florence; Hershiser, Orel; Hockey; Holmes, Larry; Jackson, Bo; Johnson, Magic; Lemieux, Mario; LeMond, Greg; Leonard, Sugar Ray; Lewis, Carl; Louganis, Greg; McEnroe, John; Miracle on Ice; Montana, Joe; Navratilova, Martina; Olympic boycotts; Olympic Games of 1980; Olympic Games of 1984; Olympic Games of 1988; Play, the; Retton, Mary Lou; Rice, Jerry; Rose, Pete; Ryan, Nolan; SkyDome; Soccer; Taylor, Lawrence; Tennis; Thomas, Isiah; Tyson, Mike; Valenzuela, Fernando; Watson, Tom; Wave, the.

The northern spotted owl. (U.S. Fish and Wildlife Services)

■ Spotted owl controversy

Definition Debate over logging in the habitat of an arguably endangered species

The rarity of the spotted owl, a relative of the barred owl adapted to old-growth forests of the Pacific Northwest, led to prohibitions on logging in federal forests lying within its range.

Oregon and Washington are both the largest timber producers in the United States and home to some of the nation's most tenacious environmental groups. As a result, environmentalists fought timber and mining companies for decades in the Pacific Northwest. Logging is a traditional livelihood, generating thousands of jobs and hundreds of millions of dollars in the area every year. By the same token, the relatively unspoiled beauty of the region fuels a particularly strong environmental movement. The National Forest Service favored the timber industry in this battle. Thus, in the 1980's, logging increased until it reached a rate at which old-growth forests would disappear in ten to fifteen years if nothing was changed.

James G. Watt became secretary of the interior in 1981 and unapologetically promoted mining and lumbering on federal lands, with little thought of conservation. His tenure sparked a showdown between environmentalists and loggers. The forest service announced a record cut of trees in nineteen national forests in Washington and Oregon, with one in four of the resulting logs to be shipped overseas. The University of Oregon's Western Natural Resources Law Clinic (WNRLC), which specialized in environmental law, worked with nature organizations to develop a strategy to combat the government. The clinic's lawyers decided to argue that the northern spotted owl should be placed on the endangered species list. Because the owl lived in the threatened forests, its placement on the list would prevent the government from logging there under the Endangered Species Act (ESA).

Environmentalists had used the ESA in 1973 to stop the Tellico Dam in Tennessee from being built, because it would have encroached on the habitat of the snail darter. Using the same strategy, the WNRLC and activist groups argued that the northern spotted owl nested and reared its young only in old-growth forests, which were set to be cut by logging companies. Each pair of owls needed one thousand acres or more of uncut forest to rear their young. Without this unspoiled acreage, the spotted owl would disappear.

Of the nineteen forests targeted for cutting, thirteen held spotted owls. If the spotted owl were placed on the endangered species list, cutting in national forests would be reduced by 50 percent. The owl had been studied by the federal government for inclusion on the the list, but the government had demurred. When the WNRLC argued its case in federal district court in Seattle, the judge ruled that the government had acted illegally by not placing the owl on the list. Lawsuits against the government by activist groups tied the issue up in court, and no lumber was harvested.

Impact Eventually, Congress brokered a compromise that favored conservationists. Logging was reduced by 50 percent, and the federal government would not sell timber from areas identified as spotted owl habitats. At the same time, the timber industry was spared drawn-out lawsuits and court challenges. The controversy became important both for residents of the Pacific Northwest and for the Reagan administration, which was ideologically opposed to precisely the sort of federal interference with business interests represented by the ESA.

Further Reading

Chase, Alston. *In a Dark Wood: The Fight Over Forests and the Myths of Nature.* New Brunswick, N.J.: Transaction, 2001.

Yaffee, Steven Lewis. *The Wisdom of the Spotted Owl: Policy Lessons for a New Century.* Washington, D.C.: Island Press, 1994.

James Pauff

See also Environmental movement; *Exxon Valdez* oil spill; Reagan, Ronald; Watt, James G.

■ Springsteen, Bruce

Identification American singer-songwriter
Born September 23, 1949; Freehold, New Jersey

A critical and popular success as the decade began, Springsteen became in the 1980's a genuine cultural phenomenon, someone whose multiplatinum albums and extremely popular tours made him by 1985 one of the world's most talked-about entertainers.

Bruce Springsteen released five albums during the 1980's, *The River* (1980), *Nebraska* (1982), *Born in the U.S.A.* (1984), *Bruce Springsteen and the E Street Band Live, 1975-85* (1986), and *Tunnel of Love* (1987). Each album sold well: Four reached number one on the *Billboard* 200, and the other reached number three. *Born in the U.S.A.*, however, sold in such numbers (15 million copies in the United States alone) and for so long (eighty-five weeks in the top ten) that it warrants consideration alongside Michael Jackson's *Thriller* (1982) and Prince's *Purple Rain* (1984) as the most important album of the decade.

To understand the extraordinary popularity of *Born in the U.S.A.*, one must look at the cultural milieu into which the album was released. The year 1984 was both an Olympic year and an election year. Staged in Los Angeles, the 1984 Summer Olympic Games kindled in Americans a new and unabashed patriotism, as the nation celebrated not only its Olympic athletes but also the people (notably Peter Ueberroth) responsible for staging a globally admired Olympic Games. Sparked by the Olympics, American patriotism was stoked into flame by Ronald Reagan's reelection campaign, a campaign whose message, "It's morning in America," resonated powerfully with Americans feeling good—but wanting to feel better—about their country.

With patriotism in the air, *Born in the U.S.A.* (whose cover featured an American flag) seemed to represent another reason for Americans to feel good about themselves. The title song of the album told the story of an impoverished American forced to fight in the Vietnam War and beaten at every turn by an uncaring nation. However, the refrain, "I was born in the U.S.A." (meant to represent the character's protest against his treatment), was misunderstood by some to be a patriotic anthem. Other songs, also complaints about the economic woes of working-class Americans, similarly resonated with both those working-class individuals for whom they spoke and those others for whom the titles (such as "No Surrender" and "My Hometown") struck a patriotic chord.

The album was a worldwide hit. Springsteen looked heroic, and pundits and politicians—including President Ronald Reagan—soon seized on Springsteen as proof that America was the land of opportunity, much to the singer's chagrin. By October, 1984, Springsteen was more than just a chart-topping musician: He was a symbol of America itself. For politicians and patriots, the album's title seemed to support their agenda. For the working Americans left behind by the nation's economic growth, Springsteen was a powerful voice of protest and musical activism.

In a sense, Springsteen spent the second half of the 1980's living down the image he had acquired in 1984 and 1985. He struggled to correct misinterpretations of *Born in the U.S.A.*, advising listeners to pay closer attention to the lyrics. He connected audiences to charitable groups, arguing that too many Americans were neglected by government agencies. During this time, he also married model Julianne Phillips in an extremely high-profile wedding. Media scrutiny only increased when Springsteen, unhappy with the marriage, began an affair with his backup singer, Patti Scialfa. In the midst of these personal travails, Springsteen scaled down his music, releasing a low-key album (1987's *Tunnel of Love*) that was dominated by confessional love songs. In 1989, as if to draw a curtain on the turbulent 1980's, Springsteen dissolved the E Street Band and filed for divorce from Phillips.

Impact Bruce Springsteen's vision of America was enormously influential. Distancing himself from the flag-waving patriotism characteristic of the Reagan era, Springsteen in the 1980's espoused an alternate patriotism, one celebrating America not for its military prowess or economic might but for its compassion. He sought with his music to reactivate that compassion and put it to work, striving to counteract the tendencies that led his compatriots to be labeled the "Me generation."

Further Reading

Alterman, Eric. *It Ain't No Sin to Be Glad You're Alive: The Promise of Bruce Springsteen*. Boston: Little Brown, 1999.

George-Warren, Holly, ed. *Bruce Springsteen: The "Rolling Stone" Files*. New York: Hyperion, 1996.

Marsh, Dave. *Glory Days: Bruce Springsteen in the 1980's*. New York: Pantheon, 1987.

Matt Brillinger

Bruce Springsteen performs in Dallas, Texas, on September 14, 1985. (AP/Wide World Photos)

See also Elections in the United States, 1984; Jackson, Michael; MTV; Music; Music videos; Olympic Games of 1984; Pop music; Prince; Reagan, Ronald; USA for Africa.

■ Standards and accountability in education

Definition   Systems designed objectively to measurement success and failure in student instruction and to hold teachers responsible for their performance

The standards and accountability movement sought to import management practices from the business world to improve the nation's schools. It began as a grassroots movement early in the 1980's in response to the disappointment felt by many parents at their communities' educational systems. By the end of the decade, the movement had reached the national level, largely because of the publication of A Nation at Risk *in 1983.*

Americans had begun to question the quality of their educational system in the 1960's, when studies of segregated schools revealed that students were more likely to succeed when their schools had better resources. At that time, the reform movement sought more money for all public schools. In the 1970's, states began to be concerned about their budgets, so theorists and politicians began looking into applying business principles to school management. Rather than simply adding more money to school budgets, state administrators looked for ways to make education more cost-effective.

Respondents to a 1980 Gallup poll identified "low standards" as one of the top four problems in schools, and 79 percent of respondents favored teaching morality in public schools. The U.S. Department of Education had been founded by the Carter administration in 1979. President Ronald Reagan's initial intention had been to dissolve the department, until he realized he could use it to promote his agenda of a "new federalism." Reagan sought to use the department to strengthen state education departments and promote the idea of efficiency.

In 1982, Mortimer J. Adler, a classical philosopher and leader of the Great Books movement (which called for an education based upon certain texts considered to have universal importance and quality), published the *Paideia Proposal*, an argument for more rigorous standards in elementary education. Adler called on public schools to teach children the skills that would prepare them for a lifetime of self-motivated learning. Allan Bloom, another classical philosopher and Great Books theorist, published *The Closing of the American Mind* in 1987, arguing that

public schools were more interested in teaching moral and cultural relativism than in teaching basic cultural concepts and that students who grew up thinking of all truth as relative were incapable of learning anything.

In 1983, the National Commission on Excellence in Education issued *A Nation at Risk*, warning that American students were falling behind other nations' youth in math, science, and engineering. The main "front" of the Cold War with the Soviet Union was a competition over productivity and technological advancement. Both nations sought to be the world's leader in scientific advancement and economic growth. With the publication of *A Nation at Risk*, Americans feared that they were not only losing the Cold War but also falling behind other countries such as China and Japan. Reagan modified his attitude toward the Department of Education and tasked it with spearheading efforts to establish national standards and accountability mechanisms. In 1985, Reagan appointed William Bennett to be his new secretary of education, and Bennett became one of the main spokesmen for the standards movement.

The movement was criticized from all ends of the political spectrum. Advocates of classical educational theories, while supporting the establishment of higher educational standards, opposed using standardized tests to measure success. Adler, for example, argued in *Six Great Ideas* that a few minutes of conversation is a far better gauge of a student's learning than is any standardized test. Libertarians worried that the accountability movement would become an excuse to expand the federal bureaucracy, while many religious conservatives feared that educational standards would further marginalize religion in American culture. Social progressives, meanwhile, feared that standardization would stifle independent thought and student creativity and that accountability would compromise the integrity of the teaching profession. They argued that standardized tests unfairly penalized students who were academically gifted and successful but performed poorly on tests because of anxieties, learning disabilities, or confusion about procedures.

Nevertheless, the first federally funded testing program, the National Assessment of Education Progress (NAEP), began in 1988. The decade ended with President George H. W. Bush and the National Governors' Association meeting at the National Education Summit in Charlottesville, Virginia. There, they issued the first national standards for English, mathematics, science, history, and geography, as well as rules for standardized testing and enforcing teacher accountability. In the same year, the National Council of Teachers of Mathematics issued the *Curriculum and Evaluation Standards for School Mathematics*.

Impact The standards and accountability movement was relatively new in the 1980's but quickly gained national popularity and bipartisan political support. While Republicans Ronald Reagan and George H. W. Bush put school accountability on the national agenda, Democrat Bill Clinton was one of the pioneers of state-level accountability programs as governor of Arkansas, and he would continue to support the movement as president.

Further Reading

Adler, Mortimer. *Paideia Proposal.* New York: Touchstone, 1998. Argues that the flaw of the American educational system is that it does not teach children to think, but merely to memorize facts.

_____. *Six Great Ideas.* New York: Touchstone, 1997. Argues that specific core Western ideas should be part of every education. Critiques the use of standardized tests to evaluate student progress.

Gordon, David T. *A Nation Reformed: American Education Twenty Years After "A Nation at Risk."* Cambridge, Mass.: Harvard Educational, 2003. History of the standards and accountability movement, starting with *A Nation at Risk.*

Hayes, William. *Are We Still a Nation at Risk Two Decades Later?* Lanham, Md.: Scarecrow Education, 2004. Analyzes the impact of the reform movement that arose in response to the 1983 document.

McGuinn, Patrick J. *No Child Left Behind and the Transformation of Federal Education Policy, 1965-2005.* Lawrence: University Press of Kansas, 2006. History of federal education policies for the forty years prior to passage of George W. Bush's No Child Left Behind Act.

John C. Hathaway

See also Bennett, William; Bush, George H. W.; *Closing of the American Mind, The*; Cold War; Education in the United States; Magnet schools; Mainstreaming in education; Multiculturalism in education; *Nation at Risk, A*; National Education Summit of 1989; Reagan, Ronald; School vouchers debate.

■ Star Search

Identification Television talent and variety show
Date Aired from 1983 to 1995

Star Search was a nightly prime-time television talent competition, in which contestants competed against one another in six different categories for money and a chance at fame.

On September 17, 1983, *Star Search* premiered on the Columbia Broadcasting System (CBS) network and became a staple of 1980's television. The program was originally broadcast from the Earl Carroll Theater on Sunset Boulevard in Hollywood, California, and later from the Hollywood Center Studios on Las Palmas Boulevard in Hollywood. The show was hosted by the longtime cohost of *The Tonight Show*, Ed McMahon, and its announcer was Sam Riddle. *Star Search* was based on traditional talent competitions and variety shows: Contestants competed in various categories for a chance to remain on the program and ultimately to compete in the semifinal and final rounds. Before they could compete on the show, would-be contestants had to audition off-camera, and the competition was fierce. Once on the show, contestants sought to win nightly competitions against newcomers. The winner of each competition returned, and the loser was eliminated. *Star Search* competition was divided into six categories: Male Vocalist, Female Vocalist, Young Performer, Group, Fashion Model/Spokesperson, and Comedy. Each episode would pit a challenger against a returning champion, with the challenger having the advantage of performing first. After the brief performances, a panel of five celebrity judges voted on each contestant. Each judge could award a performance one to four stars. The scores were revealed after both performances, and the contestant with the highest average of votes would appear on the following program. In the event of a tie, the audience would cast the deciding vote, which would be revealed at the end of the show.

Originally, the contestant that remained on the show the longest in each category would win the grand prize in that category. Throughout the run of the series, however, the rules changed, and a rule was adopted that any contestant who managed to win three consecutive matches would be retired and invited to return the following week. For the semifinal and final rounds, the panel of judges was removed and replaced by audience voting. Winners of the Vocalist, Fashion Model/Spokesperson, and Comedy categories were awarded $100,000, and the winning youth performer was awarded $25,000.

Impact   Building on traditional variety- and talent-show platforms, *Star Search* created the foundation for reality talent shows such as *American Idol, So You Think You Can Dance, Dancing with the Stars,* and many more. *Star Search* also gave several notable celebrities their breaks in show business, including Drew Carey, Ray Romano, Dennis Miller, Rosie O'Donnell, and Sinbad.

Further Reading

Craig, Michael-Dante. *The Totally Awesome 80's TV Trivia Book.* Lincoln, Nebr.: Writers Club Press, 2001.

Mansour, David. *From Abba to Zoom: A Pop Culture Encyclopedia of the Late Twentieth Century.* Riverside, N.J.: Andrews McMeel, 2005.

Rettenmund, Matthew. *Totally Awesome 80's: A Lexicon of the Music, Videos, Movies, TV Shows, Stars, and Trends of That Decadent Decade.* New York: St. Martin's Griffin, 1996.

Sara Vidar

See also   *America's Most Wanted*; Cable television; Comedians; Infomercials; *People's Court, The*; Sitcoms; Soap operas; Talk shows; Television.

■ *Star Trek: The Next Generation*

Identification   Science-fiction television series
Creator   Gene Roddenberry (1921-1991)
Date   Aired from September 26, 1987, to May 21, 1994

A sequel series to the original Star Trek, Star Trek: The Next Generation *revitalized the franchise, creating a demand among American audiences for additional television series, movies, merchandise, and tie-in fiction set in Gene Roddenberry's idealized future.*

Set approximately eighty years after the events of the original *Star Trek* television series, *Star Trek: The Next Generation* (known to fans as *ST:TNG*) introduced viewers to a new crew and a new USS *Enterprise*. In an unusual step, Paramount produced *ST:TNG* in first-run syndication, selling the series to local television stations on an individual basis. This way, even if the

show failed after the initial thirteen episodes, the studio could recoup some expenses by bundling the episodes with the original series, which still did well in rerun syndication. *ST:TNG* did not fail, however. In spite of lukewarm early critical reception and initial resistance from some fans, it became highly successful, airing in over two hundred markets simultaneously.

Perhaps the biggest adjustment for *Star Trek* fans was the introduction of an entirely different style of captain. Instead of James T. Kirk, an action-oriented ladies' man, Captain Jean-Luc Picard was an older, balding Frenchman played by classically trained British actor Patrick Stewart. Other significant changes included a female security chief, a Klingon bridge officer, a blind crew member, and an android who aspired to become more human. Overall, *ST:TNG* encompassed a more sophisticated blend of optimism and realism than the original show had. It introduced the Borg, one of the *Star Trek* franchise's most interesting alien villains, as well as the Holodeck, a representation of a virtual reality system that was featured in many episodes and helped influence the public imagination of the possibilities of virtual reality during the decade. The show appealed not only to science-fiction fans but also to viewers who did not typically watch science fiction, in part because it placed increased emphasis on female and minority characters.

Impact   In 1994, stunning the show's fans, Paramount ended *ST:TNG* at the conclusion of the seventh season, citing several reasons: The studio had always planned on only seven seasons, a significant number for television programs hoping to be sold into perpetual syndication. Paramount also wanted the cast to begin making feature films based on the series. The studio did not want to price the series out of the rerun syndication market by having too many episodes, and it believed the show had reached its maximum profitability.

In spite of its cancellation, the overwhelming of success of *Star Trek: The Next Generation* led to an unprecedented revitalization of an old franchise into something relevant for both old and new generations of viewers. It showed that there was room in the *Star Trek* universe for countless new characters, alien species, and situations, and it paved the way for additional television series—*Star Trek: Deep Space Nine, Star Trek: Voyager,* and *Star Trek: Enterprise*—as well as

Patrick Stewart, left, star of Star Trek: The Next Generation, *poses with William Shatner, star of the original series, at an event in 1991.* (AP/Wide World Photos)

several successful movies starring the *Next Generation* cast members. It also led to a revival of *Star Trek* merchandise, such as action figures and other toys, and to the creation of a themed attraction in Las Vegas called *Star Trek: The Experience.*

Further Reading

Coit, Dawn G. "*Star Trek*: The Continuing Saga of a Sixties Sensation." *USA Today* 117 (January, 1989): 88-90.

Nemecek, Larry. *The "Star Trek: The Next Generation" Companion.* Rev. ed. New York: Pocket Books, 2003.

Reeves-Stevens, Judith, and Garfield Reeves-Stevens. *"Star Trek: The Next Generation": The Continuing Mission—A Tenth Anniversary Tribute.* New York: Pocket Books, 1997.

Amy Sisson

See also Science-fiction films; Sequels; Special effects; Television.

■ Starbucks

Identification Coffee franchise
Date Founded in 1971; incorporated in 1987

The Starbucks concept changed the way consumers viewed the coffee experience. Starbucks rapidly became a part of popular culture.

When Starbucks first opened in Seattle, Washington, in 1971, it was during a period of decline in coffee consumption. Large American coffee brands were adding cheaper beans to their blends, thus sacrificing flavor. In addition, consumers were concerned about the long-term health effects of caffeine. While a market study would therefore have indicated that the 1970's was a bad time to expand a coffee business, the situation did not deter the coffee store's owners. At the time, Starbuck's only sold coffee beans; it did not brew and sell coffee by the cup. The company's owners wanted their brand to stand for high-quality, dark-roasted coffee.

In 1982, Starbucks hired Howard Schultz as its director of retail operations and marketing. In the spring of 1983, the company sent Schultz to Milan, Italy, to attend an international housewares show. He was impressed with the popularity of espresso bars in Milan and saw the potential of building a similar coffee bar culture in the United States. He noted that Americans had increasing incomes, increased air travel, changing work patterns, and more time constraints. He believed that these were all factors that had the potential to change consumer priorities. His vision was to build a national brand around coffee and create a retail store that would become a third destination between home and work. In 1987, with the backing of local investors, Schultz purchased the company, which became known as the Starbucks Corporation.

By the late 1980's, Americans' desire for affordable luxuries had grown. More disposable income and European travel gave Americans a new interest in the cultures and products they sampled abroad. This interest fed the specialty coffee market, and sales soared. Starbucks was credited with changing people's expectations of how coffee should taste; changing the language of coffee drinks by introducing Italian terms such as *grande* (large) and *venti* (twenty ounces); changing the way coffee was ordered by offering customized options (for example, using skim milk instead of whole milk for a "nonfat" option or mixing regular and decaffeinated coffee to make a "half-caf"); changing how and where people met, as Starbucks became known as a safe place to socialize and conduct business; changing urban streetscapes, as a Starbucks located in a neighborhood became an indication that the area would be a desirable place to live and work; and raising social consciousness, as one aspect of the Starbucks mission statement encouraged employees to make a contribution to the community and the environment.

Impact From its humble beginnings, Starbucks grew to become the world's largest multinational chain of coffee shops. The initiatives and innovations that Starbucks developed to market specialty coffee became the standard for the industry. In addition, the company's popularity helped drive a broader explosion of coffee culture in the United States. Several other national and regional chains arose, such as Seattle's Best Coffee and Caribou Coffee, as did a great many individual coffee stores. Far from driving one another out of business, the sheer number of the stores seemed to encourage Americans to patronize coffee stores in general, as in some cities, multiple stores seemed able to thrive on the same block.

Further Reading

Koehn, Nancy. "Howard Schultz and Starbucks Coffee Company." In *How Entrepreneurs Earned Consumers' Trust: From Wedgewood to Dell.* Boston: Harvard Business School Press, 2001.

Michelli, Joseph. *The Starbucks Experience: Five Principles for Turning Ordinary into Extraordinary.* New York: McGraw-Hill, 2007.

Schultz, Howard, and Dori Jones Yang. *Pour Your Heart Into It: How Starbucks Built a Company One Cup at a Time.* New York: Hyperion, 1997.

Sharon M. LeMaster

See also Business and the economy in the United States; Fads; Food trends.

■ Statue of Liberty restoration and centennial

The Event Full-scale restoration effort and centennial celebration for the Statue of Liberty

Date Restoration took place from 1984 to 1986; centennial celebration held July 4-6, 1986

Place Statue of Liberty National Monument, Ellis Island, New York City

The much-needed restoration of the Statue of Liberty and subsequent centennial celebration provided Americans with an opportunity to reflect upon their nation's history and the heritage of the immigrants that passed through Ellis Island.

The Statue of Liberty National Monument, one of the United States' most recognizable national symbols, turned one hundred years old on October 28, 1986. France had given the statue, designed by Frédéric-Auguste Bartholdi, to the United States in 1886, in recognition of a friendship that had begun during the American Revolution. Erecting the statue had been a joint effort between the two countries, with France responsible for designing the statue and assembling it in the United States and the United States responsible for building its pedestal. In May of 1982, President Ronald Reagan appointed former Chrysler executive Lee Iacocca to head a private-sector effort to raise funds to restore the Statue of Liberty. A partnership formed between the government, represented by the National Park Service, and the newly formed, private Statue of Liberty-Ellis Island Foundation. The foundation also sought resources to beautify the surroundings of the statue and to rehabilitate the crumbling ruins of Ellis Island.

The Statue   A combination of weather, pollution, time, and the high volume of sightseers visiting the island had left the Statue of Liberty in serious need of attention. In 1984, therefore, the statue was closed for renovation, and scaffolding was erected around it, obscuring it from view until its rededication. At this point, the United Nations designated the Statue of Liberty National Monument as a World Heritage Site.

Various procedures were performed on the monument's interior and exterior. Liquid nitrogen was used to strip away seven layers of paint from the interior, and other techniques were employed to remove the layers of tar that originally been applied to plug leaks and prevent corrosion. Large holes in the copper skin were smoothed out and patched with new copper. Each of the over one thousand supporting iron ribs of the statue had to be removed and replaced, because the iron had corroded to such an extent that it had lost a great deal of its original density. Teflon film was inserted between the new bars and the skin to provide insulation and reduce friction. Chemicals were applied to sections of the copper skin to ensure that the statue was strengthened. The support structure of the right arm was updated and reinforced to make the arm structurally sound. The crown's seven rays were also reinforced. Thousands

During the Statue of Liberty centennial celebration, traditional sailing vessels are welcomed into New York Harbor, under the watchful eyes of the statue (background) and the aircraft carrier USS John F. Kennedy *(foreground). (U.S. Department of Defense)*

of rivets were replaced, and any seams or open holes were sealed.

A significant feature of the restoration was the replacement of the torch. The original torch, which had been modified extensively in 1916, was considered beyond repair. The new torch included features designed to enhance its visibility, such as gold plating on the exterior of the flame and external lamps on the surrounding balcony platform. Other renovations to the statue included upgraded climate-control systems and the addition of two elevators, one to the top of the pedestal and a second emergency elevator reaching the crown. Improvements were also made to the administration and concession buildings on Liberty Island. New walkways were added, along with landscaping to prepare the island for the centennial celebration. Restoration work on Ellis Island was limited to the main building and the power station.

The Centennial   On July 5, 1986, the Statue of Liberty reopened to the public during a centennial celebration known as Liberty Weekend. Acclaimed producer David Wolper was selected to orchestrate the $32-million gala. The event began on July 4 with over three thousand restoration sponsors and members of the media from more than forty nations joining President Reagan for the grand unveiling. Numerous celebrities such as Frank Sinatra and Elizabeth Taylor joined in the salute to the statue. The president kicked off the ceremonies by pressing a button that activated the floodlights on the statue. The event included the presentation of a special medal, created solely for the centennial, called the Medal of Liberty. The medal was given to twelve naturalized American citizens, including Irving Berlin, Bob Hope, Henry Kissinger, Albert Sabin, and Itzhak Perlman. Thirty-three naval vessels from fourteen nations passed the statue and fired twenty-one gun salutes. From Ellis Island, Chief Justice Warren Burger administered the citizenship oath to thirteen thousand people via satellite television broadcast. The evening was concluded with a dramatic fireworks display.

The following day, First Lady Nancy Reagan led French and American schoolchildren on the first tour through the renovated statue, and a conference on the meaning of liberty began in New York City. On July 6, an event was held featuring sports legends Muhammad Ali, Billie Jean King, and Hank Aaron.

It included a skating exhibition by Dorothy Hamill, Peggy Fleming, and others. The closing ceremonies of the centennial included a cast of over twelve thousand, including notables Charlton Heston, Willie Nelson, Gene Kelly, the Four Tops, and the Pointer Sisters, as well as two hundred Elvis impersonators, gospel choirs, drill teams, dancers, and the Statue of Liberty All-American Marching Band.

Impact   The restoration of the Statue of Liberty National Monument and its subsequent centennial celebration provided Americans with a chance to celebrate their diverse heritage by recalling the immigrants who passed through Ellis Island and whose first image of America was the welcoming sight of the Statue of Liberty. The festivities portrayed the renewal of the statue as a renewal of the United States itself. Some believed that the restoration of the Statue of Liberty served as a metaphor for the restoration of the American Dream that, according to Reagan and his supporters, occurred during the 1980's.

Further Reading

Bell, James B., and Richard I. Abrams. *In Search of Liberty*. New York: Doubleday, 1984. Comprehensive treatment of the story of the Statue of Liberty and Ellis Island. Printed for the Centennial Commission as a souvenir. Contains excellent images.

Moreno, Barry. *The Statue of Liberty Encyclopedia*. New York: Simon & Schuster, 2000. Thorough history of the Statue of Liberty and the restoration. Quick reference source.

Smith, V. Elaine. "Engineering Miss Liberty's Rescue." *Popular Science* 228, no. 6 (June, 1986): 68-73. Cover story on the restoration process that focuses on the techniques and products used to renovate the structure.

United States General Accounting Office. *National Parks: Restoration of the Statue of Liberty Monument—Report to the Chairman, Subcommittee on National Parks and Recreation, Committee on Interior and Insular Affairs, House of Representatives*. Washington, D.C.: Author, 1986. Complete history of the project, including detailed budget, organizational chart, and numerous engineering blueprints and reports.

Amanda Bahr-Evola

See also   Iacocca, Lee; Immigration to the United States; Reagan, Ronald; Reagan Revolution.

■ Stealth fighter

Definition   Innovative military aircraft
Manufacturer   Lockheed Advanced Development
   Projects Unit of Lockheed Martin
Date   First flight in 1982; revealed in 1988

The F-117 Nighthawk was a classified aircraft of the United States Air Force that was developed during the 1980's. Initially kept secret from the public, it was declassified during the latter part of the decade.

Throughout the 1980's, the Lockheed Advanced Development Projects Unit, nicknamed the "Skunk Works," developed and constructed a fleet of stealth aircraft. The director of this project was Ben Rich. Rich took over the Skunk Works from Kelly Johnson, who had founded it. The F-117 Nighthawk was the first aircraft designed around stealth technology. Lockheed Martin was originally awarded the contract in 1973, but the first operational aircraft was not completed until 1982. By the end of the decade,

Lockheed Martin had fulfilled its contractual obligation to build a fleet of Nighthawks.

The Skunk Works was a well-kept secret. Even the invoices for construction materials were designed to keep the project secret, as all such materials were listed as spare parts for other Lockheed Martin aircraft, such as the F-16 Fighting Falcon. Lockheed Martin also began working on a stealth fighter known as the F-22 Raptor, while Northrup developed a stealth bomber known as the B-2 Spirit. The F-117, although a fighter in design, was capable only of delivering bombs.

The stealth technology employed by the F-117 makes the aircraft nearly invisible to radar. It is not completely invisible, however. The paint of the aircraft is an important part of its stealth capabilities, because it is made from radar-absorbent material (RAM). As a result, it absorbs rather than reflects radar signals, making the vehicle less detectable. Other aspects of the plane's stealth technology include its engines and overall shape, both of which

The F-117 Nighthawk. (Catalan/cc-by-sa-2.0)

are modified to make it less visible to enemies in the air and on the ground.

Impact   The F-117 Nighthawk was kept secret from the public until 1988. When it and the B-2 were revealed that year, such demonstrably next-generation technology seemed like science fiction come to life. Had it been developed earlier, such an invisible aircraft would have represented a major strategic imbalance in the Cold War between the United States and the Soviet Union. Because the Cold War was winding down, however, the new strategic capabilities made possible by stealth technology were less significant to the nuclear arms race than they would have been just a few years earlier.

The aircraft flew its first military mission in 1989, during the U.S. invasion of Panama. Two Nighthawks dropped two bombs on Rio Hato airfield. Later, the Nighthawks would gain fame during the first Persian Gulf War of the early 1990's.

Further Reading

Jenkins, Dennis R. *Lockheed Secret Projects: Inside the Skunk Works.* St. Paul, Minn.: MBI, 2001. Useful monograph on the Skunk Works unit of Lockheed Martin.

Pace, Steve. *Lockheed Skunk Works.* Osceola, Wis.: Motorbooks International, 1992. Comprehensive history of the program that developed the F-117 Nighthawk and other U.S. military aircraft.

Rich, Ben R., and Leo Janos. *Skunk Works: A Personal Memoir of My Years at Lockheed.* Boston: Little, Brown, 1994. Ben Rich was the director of the Skunk Works, and in this memoir of the project, he discusses the development of the F-117.

Timothy C. Hemmis

See also   Cold War; Foreign policy of the United States; Military spending; Panama invasion; Science and technology.

■ Steel, Danielle

Identification   Best-selling author of romantic fiction
Born   August 14, 1947; New York, New York

In the 1980's, Steel's consistently staggering popularity made her an unrivaled benchmark of trends in the rapidly changing romance genre.

Danielle Steel was one of the first authors to move romantic fiction into a new phase in which the heroines were strong, independent women determined to find themselves and solve their own problems. The lives of Steel's heroines mirrored many of her own personal experiences, such as divorce, battling cancer, and difficulties with her children. In an interview, Steel once stated that she liked to create worlds in which her heroines' struggles were rewarded with something she herself had missed out on—a happy ending.

Steel's fifth book, *The Ring* (1980), was her first hardcover publication. It boasted a more sophisticated look than had her paperbacks, featuring a glamorous black-and-white photograph of the author on the back cover. This was a great accomplishment for Steel, who had to push hard to achieve it. Her publisher, Delacorte (an imprint of Dell), had felt that the kind of readers who bought Steel's books would not pay hardcover prices. Dell finally agreed to publish *The Ring* in hardcover, however, and Steel's readers purchased it eagerly.

With millions of books in print and a fan club and as the subject of numerous interviews, Steel moved into the next phase of her career. In 1983, she fired her longtime agent and hired Mort Janklow, one of the most powerful literary "superagents" in the country. Janklow was adept at negotiating television and movie deals for his clients. He also helped Steel make the transition from romance fiction to contemporary fiction. In addition to adult fiction, Steel also wrote the Max and Martha series of children's books, which sought to help young readers face problems such as attending a new school or losing a grandparent. She was also one of seven women authors who contributed to *Having a Baby* (1984), in which she described her experience of suffering through a miscarriage. Extremely organized and focused, Steel created an elaborate filing system for keeping her writing on track. She prioritized her time, often writing well into the night so she could be available for her children during the day.

Impact   One of the three best-selling authors of the decade, Steel left her mark on the publishing industry. Her novels appealed to millions of readers and opened up the field of romance fiction for many other women writers. In 1989, Steel held the *Guinness Book of World Records* record for the longest run on the *New York Times* best seller list: 381 consecutive weeks.

Further Reading

Bane, Vickie, and Lorenzo Benet. *The Lives of Danielle Steel.* New York: St. Martin's Press, 1994.

Hoyt, Nicole. *Danielle Steel: The Glamour, the Myth, the Woman.* New York: Windsor, 1994.

Maryanne Barsotti

See also   Book publishing; King, Stephen; Literature in the United States.

■ Sting

Identification   British musician, songwriter, and actor

Born   October 2, 1951; Wallsend, Northumberland, England

During the first half of the 1980's, Sting was the lead singer, bass player, and primary songwriter for the New Wave band the Police, one of the most popular musical groups of the decade. When the band's members went their separate ways, Sting concentrated on his solo career, achieving great success.

In early 1977, Gordon Sumner, who was nicknamed "Sting" after wearing a black and yellow jersey early in his career, formed the Police with drum player Stewart Copeland and lead guitarist Henry Padovani (who was soon replaced by Andy Summers). Embracing eclecticism, the Police merged reggae and ska with punk and even jazz, produced several successful albums, and won six Grammy Awards in the early 1980's. Their final album, *Synchronicity* (1983), included their most successful song, "Every Breath You Take."

Even before the Police disbanded, Sting began to make solo appearances. In 1982, he released a solo single, "Spread a Little Happiness," from the sound track to the television play *Brimstone and Treacle*, in which he also appeared. The single became a hit in the United Kingdom. His first solo album, *The Dream of the Blue Turtles* (1985), blended rock, reggae, jazz, and pop and featured many important jazz and fusion musicians, including Kenny Kirkland, Darryl Jones, Omar Hakim, and Branford Marsalis. Later albums continued to blend various musical styles and always featured intelligent, literate lyrics. In 1987, Sting again worked with jazz artists, such as Marsalis and veteran jazz arranger Gil Evans, releasing . . . *Nothing Like the Sun*, which included the hit songs "We'll Be Together," "Fragile," "Englishman in New York," and "Be Still My Beating Heart." In February, 1988, he released *Nada Como el Sol*, a selection of five songs from . . . *Nothing Like the Sun* sung in Spanish and Portuguese. Later that year, he performed an arrangement of "Murder by Numbers" (a song from *Synchronicity*) on Frank Zappa's album *Broadway the Hard Way.*

Active in support of various humanitarian and environmental causes, Sting performed on all four nights of the fourth Amnesty International benefit, *The Secret Policeman's Other Ball*, in 1981, and he led an all-star band that included Eric Clapton, Phil Collins, and Bob Geldof in the Live Aid concert in 1985. In 1988, Sting joined a group of major artists, such as Peter Gabriel and Bruce Springsteen, for Amnesty International's *Human Rights Now!* world tour and also released a single, "They Dance Alone," which chronicled the plight of women under the Augusto Pinochet Ugarte regime in Chile. Sting also founded the Rainforest Foundation.

Sting, center, with fellow Police members Andy Summers, right, and Stewart Copeland. (PA Photos/Landov)

Sting pursued a minor acting career during the decade, appearing in such films as *Dune* (1984), *Plenty* (1985), *The Bride* (1985), *Bring on the Night* (1985), *The Adventures of Baron Munchausen* (1988), and *Stormy Monday* (1988). In 1989, he starred as Macheath in a failed Broadway revival of *Die Dreigroschenoper* (pr. 1928, pb. 1929; *The Threepenny Opera*, 1949).

Impact   During the 1980's, Sting was involved in numerous musical projects that testified to his eclectic tastes. His intelligent lyrics and jazz-pop-world music fusion expanded the boundaries of popular music and led to a richness and expressiveness that were rare in rock. His work on behalf of charitable causes became legendary.

Further Reading

Berryman, James. *Sting and I.* London: John Blake, 2005.

Sandford, Christopher. *Sting: Demolition Man.* New York: Little, Brown, 1998.

Sumner, Gordon. *Broken Music.* New York: Simon & Schuster, 2003.

Mary A. Wischusen

See also   Film in the United States; Jazz; Live Aid; Music; New Wave music; Pop music; World music.

■ Stockton massacre

The Event   Patrick Edward Purdy kills five children and wounds thirty others when he opens fire on his former elementary school

Date   January 17, 1989

Place   Cleveland Elementary School in Stockton, California

The Stockton massacre sparked significant controversy and debate over possible restrictions on the manufacture and sale of assault weapons.

On January 17, 1989, a twenty-six-year-old drifter, Patrick Edward Purdy, drove to his former elementary school in Stockton, California. After getting out of his car, Purdy poured gasoline on it and set it ablaze. Afterward, he walked toward the schoolyard of Cleveland Elementary School, where the children were enjoying lunch recess. There, Purdy opened fire on the schoolchildren, mostly children enrolled in kindergarten through third grade. Within minutes, he had fired 106 rounds from his personally engraved AK-47 assault rifle, killing five Asian immigrants ranging in age from six to nine years old. Another thirty individuals were injured, including one teacher. Once the assault was over, Purdy used a nine-millimeter handgun to kill himself. This tragic event, known as the Stockton massacre, was actually the second shooting to take place at the same school in a ten-year span.

Almost immediately, there was a public uproar. People questioned how an individual with Purdy's criminal history, which included convictions for attempted robbery and unlawful weapons sales, could readily purchase an automatic rifle such as an AK-47. There was a call for tightened legislation to restrict the availability of all weapons with large ammunition capacities, including domestic and foreign assault weapons. Finally, a growing number of school systems banned all weapons on school grounds. Some of the controversy also stemmed from the apparent racially motivated nature of the crime.

Impact   The Stockton massacre led to statewide and national debates over proposed legislation to restrict assault weapons. As a result of the murders, California became the first state to ban certain types of assault weapons that same year.

Subsequent Events   On September 13, 1994, the Crime Control Act of 1994 was enacted. It banned the production, distribution, and possession of certain types of firearms, including assault weapons.

Further Reading

"Death on the Playground." *Newsweek* 113, no. 5 (January 30, 1989): 35.

Holmes, Ronald, and Stephen Holmes, eds. *Murder in America.* 2d ed. Thousand Oaks, Calif.: Sage, 2001.

"Slaughter in a School Yard." *Time*, January 30, 1989, 29.

Jocelyn M. Brineman and Richard D. McAnulty

See also   Asian Americans; Education in the United States; Post office shootings; San Ysidro McDonald's massacre.

■ Stone, Oliver

Identification American film director and
screenwriter
Born September 15, 1946; New York, New York

*The 1980's marked for Stone the end of his apprenticeship
as a writer of scripts for other directors and the beginning of
his own career as a filmmaker.*

Oliver Stone began the 1980's writing and directing
his first feature, a horror film called *The Hand* (1981).
Afterward, he spent the next five years writing screen-
plays for other filmmakers, including *Conan the Bar-
barian* (1982) for John Milius, *Scarface* (1983) for
Brian de Palma, *Year of the Dragon* (1985) for Michael
Cimino, and *Eight Million Ways to Die* (1986) for Hal
Ashby. Writing for such talented directors prepared
him to craft better screenplays for his own films.
Stone had served in the U.S. Army for fifteen months
along the Cambodian boarder in the Vietnam War.
He was wounded twice and was awarded a Purple
Heart with an oak leaf cluster, as well as a Bronze Star
for valor. He returned home a changed man. It was
not surprising, then, that as a film director he eventually turned to the war for material.

In 1986, Stone released his third fea-
ture-length directorial effort, *Platoon*,
the first of what would become a trilogy
dealing with the Vietnam War and its
effects on those who fought in Southeast Asia. *Platoon* focused on the day-to-
day combat experience of infantry soldiers, and *Born on the Fourth of July*
(1989) dealt with the experiences of
returning vets as they worked to reinte-
grate themselves into American society.
Heaven and Earth (1993) would complete the trilogy. The three movies provided perhaps one of the most devastating critiques of the war on film. The two
films released in the 1980's helped fuel
a larger reassessment of the Vietnam
experience and its aftermath that became one of the hallmarks of American
cinema in the 1980's. This reassessment
led to an increasing number of films
critical of U.S. overseas engagements
generally, especially when they inter-
fered with the domestic social and political environment of another country.

Stone's social criticism did not stop with the Vietnam War, however. In *Salvador* (1986), released before *Platoon*, he explored the involvement of the
United States in Central America and provided a
vivid portrayal of a foreign policy both devastating
and dangerous in its execution. *Wall Street* (1987),
dedicated to his stockbroker father, exposed the financial excesses of the stock market during a period
of widespread corruption and insider trading, practices his father deplored. The line "Greed is good,"
delivered by Michael Douglas portraying Gordon
Gekko, the principal offender in the film, could
have become a mantra for the period.

Impact Oliver Stone became the most famous
American director of politically focused films of the
1980's. His films were often brash, angry, violent,
and confrontational, and they usually dealt with controversial subject matter. As a result, Stone simultaneously became one of the most admired and the
most reviled filmmakers in international cinema.
He won two Academy Awards for Best Director during the decade, honoring his work on *Platoon* and
Born on the Fourth of July.

Oliver Stone, left, celebrates with Ron Kovic, the subject of the director's Born on
the Fourth of July, *after the film swept most of the top drama awards at the 1990
Golden Globe Awards ceremony.* (AP/Wide World Photos)

Further Reading

Beaver, Frank. *Oliver Stone: Wakeup Cinema.* New York: Twayne, 1994.

Kagan, Norman. *The Cinema of Oliver Stone.* New York: Continuum, 2000.

Salewicz, Chris. *Oliver Stone.* London: Orion Media, 1997.

Silet, Charles L. P., ed. *Oliver Stone: Interviews.* Jackson: University Press of Mississippi, 2001.

Charles L. P. Silet

See also   Academy Awards; Action films; Cruise, Tom; Douglas, Michael; Film in the United States; *Platoon; Wall Street.*

■ Strategic Defense Initiative (SDI)

Identification   Plan to establish an antiballistic missile defense

In an effort to protect the United States from a possible nuclear attack by the Soviet Union, President Ronald Reagan proposed a high-tech defense shield capable of shooting down incoming Soviet missiles. The plan generated much criticism, both of its technical infeasibility and of its political ramifications.

In the 1970's, the United States followed a nuclear deterrence strategy known as mutually assured destruction (MAD), which depended on a situation in which the United States and the Soviet Union each possessed enough nuclear weapons to survive an attack by the other and still launch a devastating counterstrike. The certainty of utter annihilation in a nuclear war thus prevented one from happening. When Ronald Reagan became president, however, he considered MAD a risky strategy, especially as the number of Soviet nuclear warheads increased. After consultations with scientific advisers, Reagan gave a nationally televised speech on March 23, 1983, in which he announced plans to establish the Strategic Defense Initiative (SDI), which was tasked with creating a defensive shield to protect the United States from nuclear attack. Reagan's televised proposal envisioned a space-based front line of satellite defenses that could destroy Soviet missiles at the early-launch stage, a space-based second line to destroy individual warheads released by Soviet missiles that got through the front line, and a ground-based third line

to destroy any warheads in their terminal phase that avoided the other defensive lines.

Pushing the Technical Boundaries   Shooting down Soviet missiles represented a huge technical challenge. The project started with ground-based missile technology, such as the Extended Range Interceptor (ERINT), originally developed for the Safeguard Anti-Ballistic Missile system devised in the 1970's. The Strategic Defense Initiative Organization (SDIO), established at the Pentagon in 1984, funded a number of innovative approaches based on the ERINT technology that sought to detect, target, and destroy Soviet missiles. On the relatively low-tech end of development were projects like the Homing Overlay Experiment, a missile-launched projectile with four-meter-diameter fans to increase the size of the projectile and ensure a hit, and Brilliant Pebbles, watermelon-sized satellites that would destroy Soviet missiles by purposely colliding with them.

On the high-tech end of the research spectrum were a number of directed-energy weapons programs that used energy to destroy missiles, rather than physical collisions between missiles and targeting projectiles. These high-tech projects, centered on beam-projecting weaponry, earned SDI its skeptical nickname, "Star Wars." The first research centered on an X-ray laser powered by a nuclear explosion, with first tests carried out in 1983. In 1985, the SDIO began tests with a deuterium fluoride laser, which successfully destroyed a Titan missile booster and several low-flying target drones. Another promising project was the Hypervelocity Rail Gun, a space-based platform that destroyed satellites with "bullets" fired at fourteen hundred miles per hour. The main drawback of the fluoride laser and the Rail Gun was the massive electricity requirement of the systems. Experiments on sensors designed to detect and target incoming Soviet warheads, such as the Boost Surveillance and Tracking System, proved much more successful, as they proved capable of tracking Soviet missiles from their initial launches through their entire flight path. The total of SDI funding amounted to approximately $30 billion between 1983 and 1989.

Criticism of SDI   While many Americans supported SDI, the plan attracted a considerable amount of criticism. Some critics believed the system to be so far beyond the technical capability of current science that it would remain unfeasible for the foresee-

A Vision of the Future

Excerpts from Ronald Reagan's televised speech regarding the Strategic Defense Initiative, delivered March 23, 1983:

Let me share with you a vision of the future which offers hope. It is that we embark on a program to counter the awesome Soviet missile threat with measures that are defensive. Let us turn to the very strengths in technology that spawned our great industrial base and that have given us the quality of life we enjoy today.

What if free people could live secure in the knowledge that their security did not rest upon the threat of instant U.S. retaliation to deter a Soviet attack, that we could intercept and destroy strategic ballistic missiles before they reached our own soil or that of our allies?

I know this is a formidable, technical task, one that may not be accomplished before the end of the century. Yet, current technology has attained a level of sophistication where it's reasonable for us to begin this effort. It will take years, probably decades of efforts on many fronts. There will be failures and setbacks, just as there will be successes and breakthroughs. And as we proceed, we must remain constant in preserving the nuclear deterrent and maintaining a solid capability for flexible response. But isn't it worth every investment necessary to free the world from the threat of nuclear war? We know it is. . . .

I call upon the scientific community in our country, those who gave us nuclear weapons, to turn their great talents now to the cause of mankind and world peace, to give us the means of rendering these nuclear weapons impotent and obsolete.

Tonight, . . . I am directing a comprehensive and intensive effort to define a long-term research and development program to begin to achieve our ultimate goal of eliminating the threat posed by strategic nuclear missiles. This could pave the way for arms control measures to eliminate the weapons themselves. We seek neither military superiority nor political advantage. Our only purpose—one all people share—is to search for ways to reduce the danger of nuclear war.

My fellow Americans, tonight we're launching an effort which holds the promise of changing the course of human history. There will be risks, and results take time. But I believe we can do it.

that should receive a higher priority. Some foreign-policy critics saw SDI as an open provocation to the Soviets that might trigger a new arms race.

Antiwar advocates postulated that SDI actually increased the chance of a nuclear war. They feared that the United States, safe behind its SDI shield, might be more inclined to launch a nuclear attack on the Soviet Union, because the Soviets would not be able to inflict similar damage in a counterstrike. It also seemed possible that the Soviet Union might consider launching a preemptive attack against the United States before SDI became operational and Soviet nuclear weapons became useless. Another major criticism of SDI was its potential violation of the 1972 Anti-Ballistic Missile (ABM) Treaty, which placed limitations on American and Soviet missile defense systems. Supporters of SDI claimed that the ABM Treaty applied only to ground-based systems and not to the space-based systems envisioned by President Reagan.

Impact Research continued on SDI throughout the 1980's. With the fall of the Soviet Union, however, the project lost much of its purpose. Many pro-Reagan analysts claim that SDI helped bankrupt the communist system, as the Soviets were forced to spend money they could not afford on technology designed to match or overcome the initiative.

Subsequent Events Later presidents continued antiballistic missile research, but for regional defense against missiles launched by terrorist groups or rouge nations. In 1993, President Bill Clinton renamed SDIO the Ballistic Missile Defense Organization (MBDO), reflecting its reduced mission from global to regional defense. Even this more modest program remained controversial, however, because it continued to violate the ABM Treaty and was ac-

able future. They therefore argued that it represented a massive waste of resources. Others saw SDI as a waste of resources even if it worked, because it diverted funds from other government programs

cused by critics of potentially provoking a new Cold War-style arms race.

Further Reading

Guertner, Gary L., and Donald M. Snow. *The Last Frontier: An Analysis of the Strategic Defense Initiative.* Lexington, Mass.: Lexington Books, 1986. Examination of the scientific and political ramifications of the project.

Linenthal, Edward. *Symbolic Defense: The Cultural Significance of the Strategic Defense Initiative.* Urbana: University of Illinois Press, 1989. Discussion of how America and the rest of the world perceived SDI and reacted to the project's expectations and implications.

Reiss, Edward. *The Strategic Defense Initiative.* Cambridge, England: Cambridge University Press, 2003. Well-documented history of SDI and its impact, with analysis of subsequent projects beyond the 1980's.

Steven J. Ramold

See also Cold War; Foreign policy of the United States; Intermediate-Range Nuclear Forces (INF) Treaty; Military spending; Reagan, Ronald; Reagan Doctrine; Soviet Union and North America; Weinberger, Caspar.

■ Streep, Meryl

Identification American actor
Born June 22, 1949; Summit, New Jersey

By the mid-1980's, Streep had become the most admired film actor of her generation.

Building on a broad general education; expert training in theater at Vassar, Darmouth, and the Yale Drama School; and commercial work that ranged from Off-Broadway to Broadway to made-for-television movies, Meryl Streep entered film acting in the late 1970's. She immediately made her presence known, most memorably as a young working-class woman loved by two friends in *The Deer Hunter* (1978). Soon after, Streep advanced to leading roles and became recognized for her meticulous preparation and her ability to handle a wide range of accents and behaviors. Although adept at musical performance and comedy, Streep was celebrated in the 1980's for her success in a string of powerful dramatic roles,

At the April 14, 1980, Academy Awards ceremony, Meryl Streep holds her Oscar for Best Supporting Actress, awarded for her work in Kramer vs. Kramer. *(AP/Wide World Photos)*

usually playing strong-willed women. Off screen, Streep was an active proponent of women's rights and equity within the Screen Actors Guild.

In 1981, Streep appeared in the dual roles in the aggressively self-reflexive *The French Lieutenant's Woman*, portraying the nineteenth century title character as well as the contemporary actor who plays the part in a film version of the novel. For both the film's characters, independence becomes a central issue. This theme of independence would resonate across Streep's film roles and in many of her interviews and published statements. She played a factory worker who finds the strength to confront corrupt plutonium-plant owners in the biopic *Silkwood* (1983), adventuresome writer Isak Dinesen in *Out of Africa* (1985), and a former French Resistance patriot unwilling to be satisfied with a domesticated British life in *Plenty* (1985). In *Heartburn* (1986), Streep portrayed an embittered betrayed wife and writer. In *A*

Cry in the Dark (1988; also known as *Evil Angels*), she depicted an Australian mother unjustly accused of killing her child. In these roles, Streep brought to the screen women of courage, intelligence, and determination. Even when playing a destitute drunk in *Ironweed* (1987) or the tragic Holocaust survivor in *Sophie's Choice* (1982), Streep conveyed a core of personal integrity in the most humiliating of circumstances.

Streep won an Academy Award for her performance in *Sophie's Choice* and was nominated for another five during the decade, an unprecedented achievement. Her acting was honored at Cannes, by the New York Film Critics Council, and at the Golden Globe Awards. Additionally, she won the People's Choice award for Favorite Dramatic Motion Picture Actress five years out of six between 1984 and 1989.

Impact   Meryl Streep raised the bar of expectation for American film performance with her technical skill, careful preparation, and creativity. Despite winning only one of the six Academy Awards for which she was nominated in the 1980's, Streep became synonymous with Oscar-caliber dramatic performances during the decade.

Further Reading

Cardullo, Bert, et al., eds. *Playing to the Camera: Film Actors Discuss Their Craft.* New York: Yale University Press, 1998.

Maychick, Diana. *Meryl Streep: The Reluctant Superstar.* New York: St. Martin's Press, 1984.

Carolyn Anderson

See also   Academy Awards; Film in the United States; Feminism; Theater; Women in the workforce.

■ Sununu, John H.

Identification   Governor of New Hampshire from 1983 to 1989 and White House chief of staff from 1989 to 1991
Born   July 2, 1939; Havana, Cuba

Sununu's political success in New Hampshire and his work for George H. W. Bush in the 1988 presidential campaign resulted in his appointment as White House chief of staff, a position he used to advance the causes of the Republican right wing.

Although John H. Sununu was a successful businessman and the president of JHS Engineering Company and Thermal Research (1963-1983), it was his political rather than financial career that was most important during the 1980's. In 1980, he ran unsuccessfully for a U.S. Senate seat from New Hampshire, losing the primary election to Warren Rudman. After his defeat, he became Rudman's campaign manager in the general election. Two years later, Sununu bested Hugh Gladden in a gubernatorial election and went on to serve three terms as governor of New Hampshire.

While governor, Sununu opposed raising taxes, brought new businesses to New Hampshire, and supported the controversial Seabrook nuclear power plant. He gained national prominence by serving as the chair of the Coalition of Northeastern Governors, chair of the Republican Governors Association, and chair of the National Governors Association. He was a member of the Council for National Policy from 1984 to 1985 and again in 1988. During the 1988 presidential campaign, he was a key player, helping George H. W. Bush win the key early New Hampshire primary to become the Republican nominee. Sununu also lead attacks on Michael Dukakis, the Democratic presidential nominee.

President George H. W. Bush rewarded Sununu for his help by naming him White House chief of staff in 1989, a post that he held until 1991. When Robert Teeter was considered for an appointment as counselor to the president, a position that would have rivaled Sununu's in importance, Sununu squelched the appointment and became the president's closest political adviser. He spent about 40 percent of his working day with the president and also served as the president's legislative liaison with Congress. A staunch ally of the more conservative wing of the Republican Party, Sununu used his influence with the moderate Republican Bush to downplay the importance of the environment, deny access to the disabled, oppose the Clean Air Act, and stop funding for abortions.

Impact   Sununu was described by detractors as the president's lightning rod; others described him as the president's "pit bull" and the "bad cop" to the president's "good cop." Possessed of a sizable ego, an extremely high IQ, and an abrasive personality, he enjoyed taking on the media. That behavior did not make him popular with more moderate Republicans, however, nor did it endear him to the press. In 1991, Sununu was accused of misusing government aircraft for personal use. The resulting scandal ended with his resignation on December 3, 1991.

Further Reading

Burke, John P. *The Institutional Presidency: Organizing and Managing the White House from FDR to Clinton.* 2d ed. Baltimore: Johns Hopkins University Press, 2000.

Kessel, John H. *Presidents, the Presidency, and the Political Environment.* Washington, D.C.: Congressional Quarterly, 2001.

O'Neil, John. *The Paradox of Success.* New York: Tarcher, 1994.

Thomas L. Erskine

See also   Abortion; Bush, George H. W.; Conservatism in U.S. politics; Dukakis, Michael; Elections in the United States, 1988; Environmental movement.

■ Superconductors

Definition   Elements, alloys, and ceramic compounds through which electric current flows without resistance

The discovery of high-temperature superconductors in the late 1980's by European and American researchers was quickly recognized as extremely important by both scientists and journalists, who emphasized such potential applications as magnetically levitated trains.

The discovery and development of superconductors, as well as their theoretical explanation and practical applications, were due to the collective efforts of many Europeans and Americans throughout the twentieth century. In 1911, the Dutch physicist Heiki Kamerlingh Onnes made the surprising discovery that mercury, when cooled in liquid helium to near absolute zero (about 4 Kelvins), permitted electricity to flow through it without resistance. A few decades later, German researchers found that superconductors repelled magnetic fields, a phenomenon later called the Meissner effect, after one of its discoverers. In the late 1950's, three American physicists, John Bardeen, Leon Cooper, and John Schrieffer, explained superconductivity in a mathematical theory based on the movement of electron pairs. This theory became known as the BCS theory,

from the first letter of each physicist's last name. Impressive as these early developments were, the 1980's became a nonpareil period of momentous discoveries in superconductivity.

High-Temperature Superconductivity   Before the 1980's, all superconductivity research took place at temperatures close to absolute zero, but in 1986, the Swiss physicist Karl Alexander Müller and his younger German colleague, Johannes Georg Bednorz, working at the International Business Machines (IBM) research laboratory in Switzerland, made a ceramic compound composed of the elements lanthanum, barium, copper, and oxygen. To their surprise, this compound superconducted at the highest temperature then known for any substance, 35 Kelvins. When the researchers published this discovery, it stimulated the search for substances that superconducted at even higher temperatures, and it also led to their winning the 1987 Nobel Prize in Physics.

Two researchers who built on the work of Bednorz and Müller were Maw-Kuen Wu at the University of Alabama in Huntsville and Paul (Ching-Wu) Chu at the University of Houston. Early in 1987, Wu and his students made a new ceramic material composed of yttrium, barium, copper, and oxygen (YBCO) that appeared to superconduct at a temperature much higher than any previous material. Paul Chu, Wu's doctoral dissertation adviser, used his sophisticated equipment to observe a transition in the magnetic susceptibility of the YBCO ceramic material at the astonishing temperature of 92 Kelvins. The relatively high temperature of YBCO and other materials' superconductivity made it possible to conduct research at temperatures above 77 Kelvins, using the safer and more economical liquid nitrogen rather than liquid helium.

Many scientists called high-temperature superconductors the "discovery of the decade," and research in the field exploded throughout the rest of the 1980's. Within six months of the initial discoveries, more than eight hundred papers were published. These papers reported on the physical and chemical properties of the new materials, as well as on their detailed atomic arrangements. A variety of new ceramic superconductors were made that challenged the tenets of the BCS theory. This theory had successfully explained superconductivity in the range of 4 to 40 Kelvins, but it had predicted a limit of about 40 Kelvins for superconductive materials. Many scientists quickly saw that the BCS theory was inadequate to make sense of the new ceramic superconductors.

Impact The race to commercialize the epochal 1986 and 1987 discoveries of high-temperature superconductors accelerated through the remaining years of the 1980's and beyond. The first company to take advantage of these discoveries was the firm later known as ISCO International, which introduced a sensor for medical equipment. Researchers around the world wrestled with the formidable problems of fabricating wires from brittle ceramic substances. If such wires could be made, energy efficiencies in various electrical devices would be dramatically improved. Major corporations around the world invested heavily in the research and development of superconductors because of their potential to render more efficient computers, magnetically levitated (maglev) trains, and many other machines. Physi-

cists did make progress in creating materials that superconducted at 125 Kelvins and 138 Kelvins. However, because basic questions about the structure and behavior of these new materials needed to be answered and because many manufacturing and marketing problems needed to be solved, it turned out that the road from discovery through research and development to successful application was more tortuous than early enthusiasts had initially envisioned.

Further Reading

Hazen, Robert M. *The Breakthrough: The Race for the Superconductor.* New York: Summit Books, 1988. Hazen, who was involved in Wu and Chu's discovery of the yttrium superconductor, provides a vivid, behind-the-scenes account of the scientists and the research of this great breakthrough.

Mayo, Jonathan L. *Superconductivity: The Threshold of a New Technology.* Blue Ridge Summit, Pa.: TAB Books, 1988. After introducing readers to the ba-

Karl Alexander Müller, left, and Johannes Georg Bednorz won the 1987 Nobel Prize in Physics for synthesizing a new ceramic substance capable of superconductivity at 35 degrees Kelvin. (IBM Corporation, AIP Emilio Segrè Visual Archives)

sics of superconductivity, Mayo emphasizes the possible applications of high-temperature superconductors for computers, medicine, and transportation. Helpful glossary.

Schechter, Bruce. *The Path of No Resistance: The Story of the Revolution in Superconductivity*. New York: Simon & Schuster, 1989. After a survey of early work on superconductivity, Schechter concentrates on the pivotal discoveries of Bednorz and Müller, as well as Wu and Chu. Emphasis is on superconductor theory, applications, and possible commercialization.

Simon, Randy, and Andrew Smith. *Superconductors: Conquering Technology's New Frontier*. New York: Plenum Press, 1988. Intended for readers with no background in physics. Analyzes the nature, history, and theories of superconductivity, as well as the possible influence of discoveries in high-temperature superconductivity on future technologies.

Tinkham, Michael. *Introduction to Superconductivity*. 2d ed. New York: Dover Books, 2004. Accessible to science students with some knowledge of physics and mathematics, this book contains a historical overview and an analysis of the principal experiments and theories in the field, including high-temperature superconductors.

Robert J. Paradowski

See also Computers; Inventions; Nobel Prizes; Science and technology.

■ Superfund program

Identification Program setting up a general fund to pay for cleanup of hazardous waste sites

The Superfund was a joint public and private program designed to facilitate cleanup of the worst American toxic waste sites. However, it was underfunded and litigation intensive, and it did not represent a permanent total solution to the nation's hazardous waste problem.

The Superfund program, started in 1980, was the United States' primary answer to the growing problem of toxic waste dumps in the 1980's. That problem burst into the national consciousness in the 1970's, when an entire neighborhood in upstate New York was declared unlivable as a result of toxic

waste: At Love Canal, near Niagara Falls, a subdivision had been built over a former toxic waste dump. After many protests, eight hundred families living there were relocated. Even after the national scope of the toxic waste problem was acknowledged, however, President Jimmy Carter was unable to convince Congress to pay for a long-term nationwide cleanup program. The compromise reached was the Superfund, created by the Comprehensive Environmental Response, Compensation, and Liability Act (1980).

The Superfund was promoted as a way to clean up the various toxic waste dumps around the country without massive federal aid. The Superfund's moneys come from taxes on petroleum products and chemicals. To be eligible for cleanup using Superfund money, a contaminated site must be placed on an official list of Superfund sites. It must first be nominated for inclusion and then inspected and certified. Sites on the Superfund list are ranked by priority, which is important, because the Superfund has never collected nearly enough revenue to clean up most of the sites on the list. Thus, only those near the top have a chance of receiving government-funded attention.

When it was recognized that the Superfund's federal revenues were inadequate, the government sought to force polluting companies to clean up the contamination they had produced. Such companies could be fined tens of thousands of dollars per day if they refused to comply. These companies often then sued other responsible parties, either to recoup the costs of cleanup or to recover the money spent to pay fines.

While the Love Canal disaster was the main incident that helped lead to the Superfund legislation, it was not the only environmental disaster of the 1970's and 1980's. During the mid-1980's, a wide variety of environmental issues surfaced. In Missouri, the entire town of Times Beach was closed and relocated because of dioxin contamination. The town had hired a contractor to pour oil on its dirt roads to contain dust, and the contractor used oil that had two thousand times the level of dioxin present in many herbicides. In New Jersey, huge quantities of medical waste washed up on the state's shores in 1987 and 1988, forcing the closing of many beaches. The medical waste came from a New York City landfill.

Impact The Superfund attempted to create a government-private partnership to clean up hazard-

Superfund workers conduct drilling operations for soil sampling at Bruin Lagoon in Bruin, Pennsylvania. (U.S. Army Corps of Engineers)

ous waste dumps in the United States. However, the government's funding was inadequate, and the private companies failed to contribute funds of their own until they were forced to do so. As a result, much litigation ensued and only a small percentage of the sites were cleaned up.

Further Reading

Colten, Craig E., and Peter N. Skinner. *The Road to Love Canal: Managing Industrial Waste Before EPA.* Austin: University of Texas Press, 1996. Examines how industrial waste was handled before 1970, when the Environmental Protection Agency was established.

Dixon, Lloyd S. *The Financial Implications of Releasing Small Firms and Small-Volume Contributors from Superfund Liability.* Santa Monica, Calif.: RAND Institute for Civil Justice, 2000. This short work examines the implications of a proposal to ex-

empt small businesses from Superfund regulations.

Mazur, Allan. *A Hazardous Inquiry: The Rashomon Effect at Love Canal.* Cambridge, Mass.: Harvard University Press, 1998. Studies the Love Canal environmental disaster from a wide variety of perspectives, including those of the school board, the industry, and the public.

Stephenson, John B. *Superfund Program: Updated Appropriation and Expenditure Data.* Washington, D.C.: U.S. General Accounting Office, 2004. Updates information about how much Superfund money has been gathered and spent since passage of the law creating the fund.

Scott A. Merriman

See also Environmental movement; *Ocean Ranger* oil rig disaster; Times Beach dioxin scare; Water pollution.

■ Supreme Court decisions

Definition   Rulings made by the highest court in
the United States

*A number of U.S. Supreme Court decisions had an impact
during the 1980's and future decades.*

Chief Justice Warren E. Burger headed the Supreme
Court from 1969 until his retirement in 1986, when
President Ronald Reagan appointed conservative
federalist William H. Rehnquist as chief justice. The
Supreme Court handed down a wide range of decisions during the 1980's that affected abortion, affirmative action, women's and gay rights, education,
and freedom of speech and religion.

Abortion   After the Supreme Court's landmark *Roe
v. Wade* (1973) decision legalizing abortion, state
and local governments immediately started passing
complex laws aimed at weakening the impact of *Roe*.
As a result, the Court spent much of the 1980's hearing challenges to these state laws, and antiabortion
groups hoped that the Court's rulings in these cases
would ultimately lead to the overturning of *Roe*.
After *Roe*, the federal government's Medicaid program began covering the costs of abortions for low-
income women. In 1976, Congress passed the Hyde
Amendment, which barred the use of Medicaid funds
for abortions except when the mother's life was in
danger and in cases of rape or incest. A group of indigent women sued the federal government, challenging the constitutionality of the amendment. In
the first of many abortion decisions during this decade, *Harris v. McRae* (1980) upheld the constitutionality of the Hyde Amendment. The Court ruled
that a woman's right to terminate a pregnancy did
not entitle her to receive government funding for
that choice.

In three 1983 decisions, *City of Akron v. Akron Center for Reproductive Health, Planned Parenthood Association of Kansas City v. Ashcroft,* and *Simopoulos v. Virginia,* the Court struck down state and local laws that,
among other things, imposed a twenty-four-hour
waiting period between the signing of a consent
form and having an abortion and required minors
to receive parental consent before having an abortion. Citing its 1983 abortion decisions, the Court in
*Thornburgh v. American College of Obstetricians and Gy-
necologists* (1986) overturned portions of a Pennsylvania antiabortion law because it infringed on a

woman's right to an abortion. The Court said that
states could not require doctors to inform women
seeking abortions about potential risks and about
available benefits for prenatal care and childbirth.
Webster v. Reproductive Health Services (1989) was the
Court's last abortion decision that pro-choice advocates believed weakened *Roe v. Wade.* The 5-4 decision upheld a Missouri law that barred state employees and facilities from performing abortions. The
Webster ruling was narrow in that it did not affect private doctors' offices or clinics where most abortions
were performed. However, *Webster* did give state legislatures new authority to limit a woman's right to an
abortion without reversing *Roe v. Wade.*

Affirmative Action and Discrimination   During the
1980's, the federal government had various laws and
affirmative action programs in place in an effort to
encourage more minorities and women to earn college degrees or to own their own businesses.

*Chief Justice Warren E. Burger presided over the Court during the
first half of the 1980's.* (Library of Congress)

During the decade, the Internal Revenue Service (IRS) stopped providing tax-exempt status to private schools that discriminated against African Americans, and two religious institutions that had race-based admission policies sued the government to regain their tax-exempt status. In *Bob Jones University v. United States* (1983), the Supreme Court upheld the IRS's authority to deny tax-exempt status for private religious schools that practiced racial discrimination. The Court ruled that the government's interest in the eradication of racial discrimination outweighed a school's need for tax-exempt status when that school discriminated based on race.

In *Fullilove v. Klutznick* (1980), nonminority contractors challenged Congress's decision to set aside 10 percent of federal public works funding for minority contractors. A deeply divided Court held that the minority set-aside program was a legitimate exercise of congressional power to remedy past discrimination. This decision reaffirmed Congress's right to set racial quotas to combat discrimination.

The Court handed down various decisions during the decade that centered on racial discrimination in the criminal justice system. In *Batson v. Kentucky* (1986), the Court ruled that an African American man had not received a fair trial because the prosecuting attorney had deliberately disqualified all the potential African American jurors during the selection process, resulting in him being convicted by an all-white jury. The Court ruled that attorneys who rejected qualified prospective jurors solely on the basis of their race violated the Sixth Amendment. In its *Vasquez v. Hillery* (1986) decision, the Court ruled that the conviction of any defendant indicted by a grand jury from which members of his or her race had been illegally excluded must be reversed. In *Turner v. Murray* (1986), the Court held that an African American defendant facing a possible death penalty for the murder of a white victim was entitled to have prospective jurors questioned about racial bias.

Women's and Gay Rights Title IX of the Education Amendments of 1972 banned sex discrimination at colleges and universities that received federal funding. The federal government would cut off government grants and student loans to schools that discriminated against women. In *Grove City College v. Bell* (1984), the Supreme Court upheld the federal requirement and ruled that in order for colleges and

universities to continue to receive federal funding, they must comply with Title IX.

In *Rostker v. Goldberg* (1981), the Court refined the limits of sexual equality by ruling that women may be excluded from the military draft. Unlike other areas in which the judicial body had struck down male-female distinctions, the Court ruled that Congress may discriminate between men and women when it came to the draft because it was based on the need for combat troops and not equity. While the Court refused to allow women to become part of the military draft, it did give women access to private men's clubs. In *Roberts v. United States Jaycees* (1984) and *Rotary International v. Rotary Club of Duarte* (1987), the Court ruled that private, men-only clubs could not exclude women from their membership.

The Court handed down two decisions during the 1980's that dealt with gay rights issues. In a case involving a homosexual man arrested in his own bedroom, the Court decided for the first time whether states could be allowed to regulate private sexual activities between consenting adults. In *Bowers v. Hardwick* (1986), the Court upheld a Georgia antisodomy law that made it a crime to engage in homosexual acts even in the privacy of one's home. In *Webster v. Doe* (1988), the Court allowed a former Central Intelligence Agency (CIA) employee to sue the government agency for firing him because the agency considered him to be a threat to national security because he was a homosexual.

Education The Supreme Court was asked to decide if states could allow taxpayers to deduct from their state income taxes tuition and other expenses for their children's religious elementary or secondary school education. Minnesota law permitted such deductions, and some taxpayers sued the state, arguing that the law violated the establishment clause separating church and state. In its *Mueller v. Allen* (1983) decision, the Court ruled that a state tax deduction for education expenses was constitutional because the law had the secular purpose of ensuring that children were well educated and did not "excessively entangle" the state in religion.

The clash over the teaching of creationism and evolution in the public schools reached the Supreme Court in 1987. In *Edwards v. Aguillard*, the Court ruled that Louisiana public schools that taught evolution could not be required to teach creationism as "creation science" if such a requirement was intended to promote a religious belief. The Court said that the state law had no secular purpose and endorsed religion in violation of the Constitution's establishment clause of the First Amendment.

In *Wallace v. Jaffree* (1985), the Supreme Court struck down an Alabama law that allowed public school teachers to hold a one-minute period of silence for "meditation or voluntary prayer" each day. The Court did not rule that the moment of silence was itself unconstitutional. Rather, it held that Alabama lawmakers had passed the law solely to advance religion, thereby violating the First Amendment.

How much freedom of speech minors should have at school was the issue before the Court in two First Amendment cases during the 1980's. In *Bethel School District v. Fraser* (1986), the Court upheld a school district's suspension of a high school student for delivering a speech that contained "elaborate, graphic, and explicit sexual" metaphors. The Court ruled that the First Amendment did not prevent school officials from prohibiting vulgar and lewd speech that would undermine the school's basic educational mission. Two years later, the Court handed down a similar decision that First Amendment advocates considered to be a major setback in protecting students' rights to freedom of expression. The Court held in *Hazelwood School District v. Kuhlmeier* (1988) that a school principal could censor the content of a student newspaper if that newspaper was part of a class assignment and not a forum for public discussion.

However, students did win an important Supreme Court victory during the 1980's in the area of school censorship. Steven Pico was one of five students who challenged their school board's decision to remove books from their high school library because they were "anti-American, anti-Christian, anti-Semitic, and just plain filthy." The Court ruled in *Island Trees School District v. Pico* (1982) that school officials could not remove books from school library shelves simply because they disliked the ideas contained in those books.

Freedom of Speech   During the 1980's, the Supreme Court heard a variety of First Amendment cases ranging from copyright issues to the public's access to court trials. By the 1980's, many Americans were using videocassette recorders (VCRs) to record their favorite television programs while they were away from home. Movie producers believed that this use of the VCR was a violation of copyright law and sued the VCR manufacturer. However, the Court ruled in *Sony Corp. of America v. Universal City Studios, Inc.* (1984) that the home use of VCRs to tape television programs for later viewing ("time shifting") did not violate federal copyright law.

Evangelist Jerry Falwell believed that the First Amendment did not give pornography publisher Larry Flynt the right to publish a fake ad poking fun at him and his deceased mother. However, in its 1988 *Hustler Magazine v. Falwell* decision, the Court decided in favor of Flynt and *Hustler,* ruling that satire and parody were protected forms of free speech.

The American flag is a symbol associated with freedom, nationalism, patriotism, and sometimes militarism. Protesters sometimes burn the flag to demonstrate their opposition to a government policy. Outside the 1984 Republican National Convention in Dallas, Texas, Gregory Lee Johnson burned a flag in protest against President Ronald Reagan's policies. Johnson was arrested under the state's flag desecration statute. In its 5-4 ruling in *Texas v. Johnson* (1989), the Court struck down the Texas flag desecration law as well as similar laws in forty-eight states by ruling that flag burning was a constitutionally protected form of symbolic speech.

The Court reaffirmed that the public's right to have access to the courts could outweigh a defendant's desire to keep the public out of the courtroom. In *Richmond Newspapers v. Virginia* (1980), the Court ruled that a trial judge's order to close the courtroom to the public and media during a murder trial was unconstitutional. The Court ruled that the arbitrary closing of a courtroom to avoid unwanted publicity violated the First Amendment and that the closure of court hearings was permissible only under unusual circumstances.

Public broadcasting, unlike commercial broadcasting with its advertisers, is dependent on the government for much of its funding. In the 1980's, the government tried to prevent public radio and television stations from voicing opinion through editorials. In its 1984 *FCC v. League of Women Voters of California* decision, the Court struck down the federal regulation that prohibited any noncommercial educational station receiving government funding from engaging in editorializing. The Court ruled that this

U.S. Supreme Court Justices During the 1980's

Justices are nominated to the Supreme Court by the president and approved by the U.S. Senate. The table below lists the justices who served during the 1980's. The names are placed in the order in which they took the judicial oath of office and thereby started their tenure on the court. Asterisks (*) indicate the terms of chief justices.

Justice	Term
William J. Brennan	1956-1990
Potter Stewart	1958-1981
Byron White	1962-1993
Thurgood Marshall	1967-1991
Warren E. Burger	1969-1986*
Harry A. Blackmun	1970-1994
Lewis F. Powell, Jr.	1972-1987
William H. Rehnquist	1972-1986
	1986-2005*
John Paul Stevens	1975-
Sandra Day O'Connor	1981-2006
Antonin Scalia	1986-
Anthony Kennedy	1988-

regulation violated the free speech rights of public broadcasters because it curtailed the expression of editorial opinion that was at "the heart of First Amendment protection."

Freedom of Religion The establishment clause of the First Amendment bars the government from preferring one religion over another. During the 1980's, the Supreme Court handed down a number of decisions that challenged the separation of church and state. The constitutionality of including religious symbols in public holiday displays came before the Court in *Lynch v. Donnelly* (1984) and again in *Allegheny County v. Greater Pittsburgh ACLU* (1989). In *Lynch*, the Court ruled that an annual city park Christmas display that included a nativity scene was constitutional because the scene was displayed with

other Christmas symbols and was used to promote retail sales and goodwill, not to endorse a particular religion. In *Allegheny County*, however, the Court ruled that a nativity scene placed inside the Allegheny County Courthouse with the words "Gloria in Excelsis Deo," referring to the words sung by the angels at the Nativity (Luke 2:14), did endorse religion and violated the Constitution. At the same time, the Court upheld the display of a nearby menorah, which appeared along with a Christmas tree and a sign saluting liberty, reasoning that the combined display of the tree, the sign, and the menorah did not endorse one particular religion but instead recognized that both Christmas and Hanukkah were part of the same winter-holiday season, which had a secular status in society.

Members of the religious movement International Society for Krishna Consciousness wanted to walk among the crowd, distribute flyers, and solicit donations during the Minnesota State Fair. However, state fair organizers required the group to distribute its literature in a fixed location along with the other fair vendors. The Court ruled in *Heffron v. International Society for Krishna Consciousness* (1981) that the Krishna members had not been discriminated against, because fair organizers had treated all groups the same, regardless of their religious or political affiliations. The Court also ruled that the fair organizers had legitimate interest in confining vendors to a designated space because of the need to avoid congestion with the large amounts of pedestrian traffic at the fair.

During the 1980's, some states passed "blue" laws requiring businesses and sporting events to be closed on Sundays and "Sabbath" laws that required employers to give employees the day off on their chosen day of worship. However, in *Thornton v. Caldor* (1985), the Court ruled that state laws that endorsed a specific religious practice, like observing a Sabbath, were unconstitutional.

In *Goldman v. Weinberger* (1986), S. Simcha Goldman, an Orthodox Jew and ordained rabbi serving as an officer in the U.S. Air Force, sued the military after being punished for wearing his yarmulke (skullcap) indoors while in uniform, in violation of military regulations. The Court upheld the Air Force penalties against Goldman, ruling that the military's interest in enforcing its dress code outweighed the officer's religious obligation to keep his head covered.

Pornography   During the 1980's, antipornography groups and some feminists convinced some state and local governments that pornography should be banned because it violated women's civil rights by portraying them as sex objects and could be linked to violence against women. Cities and states began passing antismut laws that allowed women to sue porn producers and distributors if the women could prove that they had been harmed by the pornographic material. In *American Booksellers Association v. Hudnut* (1985), the Court struck down an Indianapolis antipornography ordinance, ruling that the law and others like it were unconstitutional.

The selling of pornography moved to the telephone lines when pornographers began providing sexually oriented telephone services known as "dial-a-porn." Congress immediately passed a law making dial-a-porn illegal. In *Sable Communications of California, Inc. v. FCC* (1989), a unanimous Court overturned the federal law, ruling that it violated the free speech rights of pornographers. The Court said that the dial-a-porn industry should be regulated to protect minors, but it could not be outlawed altogether because banning dial-a-porn would deny adults access to this sexually oriented telephone service.

Throughout the 1980's, the Court reaffirmed that pornography deserved some First Amendment protection, but not at the same level as political speech. Despite the legal victories pornographers won during the 1980's, the Court reminded them that there were still limits to how much free speech protection pornographers possessed. Some cities regulated pornography by moving X-rated movie theaters away from churches, schools, homes, or parks. Despite arguments that such zoning laws were a form of censorship and violated free speech, the Court in *Renton v. Playtime Theatres* (1986) ruled that state and local governments could use zoning laws to restrict the location of theaters that showed sexually explicit films without violating pornographers' First Amendment rights.

Impact   Through the rulings handed down by the Supreme Court during the 1980's, women no longer could be forced to sign a consent form or wait twenty-four hours before having an abortion. However, the Court did give state governments more authority in restricting a woman's ability to have an abortion. Women were excluded from the military draft, but African Americans could not be excluded from jury duty solely because of their race. Colleges and universities could still lose federal funding or their tax-exempt status for gender or race discrimination. Cities could not ban pornography on the basis that it discriminated against women, but they could zone X-rated movie theaters away from neighborhoods and children. State and local governments had to make sure that any public displays of religious objects were in a secular context and did not promote a particular religion. School officials had more authority in controlling the inappropriate speech of their students but less authority in imposing religious-based regulations such as school prayer disguised as a "moment of silence" and the teaching of creationism. Parents could deduct from their state income taxes expenses related to sending their children to religious schools, but they could not force school officials to censor books from the school libraries. Protesters could burn the American flag as a form of protected symbolic speech. The government could not refuse federal funding to public radio and television stations that aired editorials. Consumers could use their VCRs to record their favorite programs without fear of violating federal copyright law. The impact of these Supreme Court decisions continued to resonate throughout U.S. politics and culture long after the decade was over.

Further Reading

Harrison, Maureen, and Steve Gilbert, eds. *Abortion Decisions of the United States Supreme Court: The 1980's.* Beverly Hills, Calif.: Excellent Books, 1993. For the general reader, a discussion of all the abortion cases decided by the Supreme Court from *Harris v. McRae* through *Webster v. Reproductive Health Services.*

Irons, Peter. *A People's History of the Supreme Court.* New York: Viking Press, 1999. A general history of the Supreme Court and its most significant decisions placed in their cultural and political context.

McCloskey, Robert G. *The American Supreme Court.* 4th ed. Chicago: University of Chicago Press, 2005. A classic work offering a concise introduction into the workings of the Supreme Court and its role in constructing the U.S. Constitution and its role in U.S. politics.

Eddith A. Dashiell

See also   Abortion; Affirmative action; *Bowers v. Hardwick*; Education in the United States; Feminism;

Flag burning; Homosexuality and gay rights; *Hustler Magazine v. Falwell*; *Meritor Savings Bank v. Vinson*; O'Connor, Sandra Day; Pornography; Racial discrimination; Rehnquist, William H.; *Roberts v. United States Jaycees*; *Thompson v. Oklahoma*; *Webster v. Reproductive Health Services*; Women's rights.

■ Swaggart, Jimmy

Identification Pentecostal minister and
   televangelist
Born March 15, 1935; Ferriday, Louisiana

A popular televangelist known for his dramatic, "spirit-filled" preaching style, Swaggart left public ministry during the late 1980's in the wake of news of his reported involvement with a prostitute. Swaggart tearfully confessed his sins to his followers in a memorable videotaped sermon.

A scandal-ridden Jimmy Swaggart addresses the press in April, 1988. (AP/Wide World Photos)

Jimmy Swaggart began building his Assemblies of God ministry in the 1960's after refusing a gospel music recording deal from Sun Records, the home label of Swaggart's cousin Jerry Lee Lewis. Instead of pursuing a recording career, Swaggart chose to use his musical talents to inspire conversions to Christianity. Over the next several years, he built an empire that eventually included television and radio ministries and the Jimmy Swaggart Bible College near his church in Baton Rouge. At the height of Swaggart's career in the mid-1980's, the Jimmy Swaggart Ministries posted incomes of $140 million per year. However, in 1988—just a year after Jim Bakker, another Assemblies of God minister, confessed to his own financial and sexual indiscretions—it was revealed that Swaggart had solicited the services of prostitutes, and that the trysts featured sexual practices that many of his followers thought to be depraved. Rumors persisted that it was Swaggart's preaching rival, Marvin Gorman of New Orleans, who had tracked and recorded his liaisons and then used his surveillance to undo the more popular Swaggart.

After his sexual practices were made public, Swaggart on February 21, 1988, preached a tearful sermon to his loyal followers—a group that was dwindling every day. The sermon was broadcast, excerpted, and analyzed nationwide. Swaggart retained his standing as an ordained minister under the General Presbytery of the Assemblies of God until May of 1988, when he was expelled for violating that group's injunction on public preaching during a term of suspension. Though he lost his media empire, Swaggart continued to preach at what became the Family Workshop Center in Baton Rouge.

Impact More than any other figure, Jimmy Swaggart became associated with the ups and downs of televangelism in the 1980's. At the height of his career, he attracted an extremely large following—and equally sizable donation revenues—with his emotional and passionate preaching style. His downfall, with its related tales of ministry rivalry and sexual escapades, was a public blow to an industry always in search of greater credibility and respect.

Further Reading

Balmer, Randall. "Still Wrestling with the Devil: A Visit with Jimmy Swaggart Ten Years After His Fall." *Christianity Today*, March 2, 1998, 31.
Seaman, Ann Rowe. *Swaggart: The Unauthorized Biog-*

raphy of an American Evangelist. New York: Continuum, 1999.

Jennifer Heller

See also   Bakker, Jim and Tammy Faye; Falwell, Jerry; Heritage USA; Religion and spirituality in the United States; Robertson, Pat; Scandals; Televangelism; Television.

■ Synthesizers

Definition   Electronic devices for producing and manipulating sound, especially music

Synthesizers became common in popular music during the 1980's in genres ranging from rock to country, as well as classical, stage, and sound track music.

Analog synthesizers had existed since the early 1960's. While their sound was not realistic, it created unique musical effects that opened up new avenues of experimentation for composers and performers. Nevertheless, analog synthesizers were able to produce only one note at a time. Technologies developed in the 1970's made synthesizers capable of polyphony and of more realistic sounds, but the initial versions were expensive. The 1980's saw these technologies become practical and affordable.

Companies such as Casio, Yamaha, Roland, Kurzweil, and Korg pioneered the decade's new synthesizer technologies, dominating the industry. Casio and Yamaha broke into the retail-priced keyboard market in 1980. Korg introduced the first mid-level polyphonic synthesizer in 1981. Yamaha took its place in the music industry by licensing the technology for frequency-modulated (FM) synthesis from Stanford University, achieving more realistic sounds by combining waveforms.

Another breakthrough of the decade was digital music sampling. The same digital technology that recorded compact discs was used to record "samples" of real instrument sounds. Kurzweil introduced the first sampling keyboard in 1983, but Roland's version, released in 1985, was both more affordable and more nuanced, closely mimicking the sound of a real piano. Casio released a low-end sampling keyboard in 1986.

As digital music evolved, interconnectivity became a concern. In 1983, the industry-wide Musical Instrument Digital Interface (MIDI) standardized interfaces and data formats, so users could connect synthesizers, keyboards, computers, and other devices to one another. MIDI would be updated to deal with newer problems and technologies.

Impact   Gradually, these new technologies removed the stigma once attached to electronic instruments. New genres, such as synthpop and New Age music, specialized in the use of synthesizers. In 1981, composer Vangelis produced the entire sound track to the film *Chariots of Fire* with a synthesizer. After his success with *Cats* (pr. 1982), theatrical composer Andrew Lloyd Webber continued to use synthesizers in his shows and adopted a digital piano as his instrument of choice for composing. Sampling also became a crucial technology, as artists learned to manipulate sampled sounds, especially voices and snippets of other musicians' work, to create new musical effects.

During the 1980's, synthesizers became commonly accessible and used by average people. Churches began purchasing them in place of organs. Where musical instruments had previously been relegated to specialty stores, department stores and electronics stores began dedicating shelf space to synthesizers. More affordable, portable, and space-saving than pianos, the instruments were frequently found in homes. Many products were marketed encouraging people to teach themselves how to play keyboard instruments with computerized assistance.

Further Reading

Friedman, Dean. *Complete Guide to Synthesizers, Sequencers, and Drum Machines.* London: Music Sales, 1985.

Jenkins, Mark. *Analog Synthesizers: Understanding, Performing, Buying—From the Legacy of Moog to Software Synthesis.* St. Louis: Focus Press, 2007.

Russ, Martin. *Sound Synthesis and Sampling.* 2d ed. St. Louis: Focal Press, 2004.

John C. Hathaway

See also   Compact discs (CDs); Computers; Consumerism; Inventions; MTV; Music; New Wave music; Pop music; Science and technology; Vangelis.

T

■ Tabloid television

Definition Sensationalistic television newsmagazine programs modeled after print tabloids

Meant to be the televised equivalent of tabloid newspapers, tabloid television shows established a foothold in both daytime and prime time during the 1980's. Their proliferation blurred the line between entertainment and mainstream traditional news, the public accepted this shift, and network news programs modified their formats in response to their tabloid competition.

Tabloid television in the 1980's encompassed a range of programming that used provocative titles, an exaggerated style, and content related to crime, sex, celebrity gossip, and other outlandish or sensational subjects. The television landscape was changing during the decade as a result of the proliferation of cable channels, as well as an increase in the number of independent broadcast television stations and the establishment of FOX as a viable fourth network. The explosion in the number of channels entailed a demand for content and created a thriving marketplace for syndicated programming—inexpensive alternative programming that was sold to individual stations or groups of stations, rather than entire networks. Unscripted, nonfiction programming, moreover, was the among the least expensive such programming to produce.

Rupert Murdoch had already built an international tabloid newspaper empire when he bought FOX. He programmed the fourth network with such "reality" and tabloid shows as *COPS, A Current Affair,* and *America's Most Wanted.* The latter series was the first FOX show to break into the Nielsen ratings' top fifty. As a man who had been the subject of tabloid attention because of his son's kidnapping and murder, John Walsh was a perfect host of *America's Most Wanted.*

Tabloid Television Genres Three formats or genres of nonfiction programming became the basis for tabloid television. The first format, a type of "reality" television, used minicams to capture documentary footage of law enforcement or rescue personnel performing their duties. Extraordinary amounts of footage were shot and carefully edited to heighten the drama, and staged reenactments sometimes substituted for actual footage. FOX built early primetime success on *COPS,* a show in which viewers were offered the experience of riding along in police patrol cars in different cities around the country.

The second format, the tabloid newscast or documentary, copied the appearance of a nighttime news-

Tabloid talk show host Geraldo Rivera's nose was broken in a brawl with white supremacists that broke out during a taping of his show on November 3, 1988. (AP/Wide World Photos)

cast or documentary but defied accepted journalistic standards. Examples of the format included *A Current Affair* (also a FOX creation), *Hard Copy*, *America's Most Wanted*, and *Unsolved Mysteries*, which relied heavily on reenactment. *America's Most Wanted* and *Unsolved Mysteries* added audience participation to the tabloid format.

The third format or genre of tabloid television was the tabloid talk show. Usually, such a show's host posed a question in each episode or segment, and guests represented various sides of the featured issue. Phil Donohue and Oprah Winfrey began as Chicago favorites before their talk shows became nationally syndicated. Winfrey was credited with legitimizing the daytime talk show by bringing a level of sincerity to controversial subjects. Morton Downey, Jr., was far more provocative. He did not interview guests so much as scream at and belittle them. He treated members of his audience in the same fashion. Downey aired only in late-night time slots.

Few people personified tabloid television more than did Geraldo Rivera, an Emmy and Peabody award-winning reporter. Rivera's career turned to the sensational when he hosted a special titled *Secrets of Al Capone's Vault* in 1986. It was revealed on live television that there were in fact no secrets inside the vault, but the program was highly rated for a syndicated special. Within a year, Rivera had his own talk show and covered everything from crossdressers to neo-Nazis. In one show featuring neo-Nazis, a skinhead broke a chair over Rivera's head and broke his nose.

Impact   Tabloid television brought changes in local and national news, forcing journalists to compete for stories that they once would have ignored. To the distress of many longtime journalists, by the end of the 1980's, network news departments were examining successful tabloid programs to see what aspects they could incorporate in their own newscasts and news specials.

Further Reading

Glynn, Kevin. *Tabloid Culture: Trash Taste, Popular Power, and the Transformation of American Television.* Durham, N.C.: Duke University Press, 2000. Analyzes tabloid television's effect on television in general.

Kearns, Burt. *Tabloid Baby.* New York: Celebrity Books, 1999. Kearns—the producer of *A Current Affair* who had worked in print media for Rupert Murdoch—discusses his career in both print and television tabloids.

Kimmel, Daniel M. *The Fourth Network: How Fox Broke the Rules and Reinvented Television.* Chicago: Ivan R. Dee, 2004. History of the FOX Network through 2000, with accounts by insiders.

Krajicek, David J. *Scooped! Media Miss Real Story on Crime While Chasing Sex, Sleaze, and Celebrities.* New York: Columbia University Press, 1998. Print journalist examines taboidization and its negative effects on legitimate news coverage.

Povich, Maury, and Ken Gross. *Current Affairs: A Life on the Edge.* New York: Putnam's, 1998. Talk show host Maury Povich's account of *A Current Affair.*

Nancy Meyer

See also   *America's Most Wanted*; Cable television; Crime; FOX Network; Journalism; Network anchors; Rivera, Geraldo; Talk shows; Television; Winfrey, Oprah.

■ Talk shows

Definition   Television programs in which the host, guests, and audience engage in topical conversations

Talk shows of the 1980's reflected changing demographics in society and offered television viewers opportunities for self-improvement through relevant topics and "infotainment."

Since the beginning of television, talk shows have been a popular programming choice of both producers and viewers. With appealing hosts, interesting guests, and timely topics, talk shows have consistently attracted large and loyal audiences. During the 1980's, however, talk shows not only maintained their popularity but also saw an increase in viewership, resulting in an explosion of talk show formats, increased competition, diverse hosts, and groundbreaking subject matter.

Sociological Changes   Prior to the 1980's, talk shows and news programs generally were hosted by white males such as Johnny Carson, Phil Donahue, and Dick Cavett. On the heels of the civil rights movements of the 1960's and 1970's, the 1980's witnessed great shifts in traditional demographics. Minorities became recognized and sought-after consumers, and television producers had to adjust the face of talk shows and their personalities to attract and accommodate this growing and diverse new demographic. Women and minorities such as Oprah Winfrey, Sally Jessy Raphael, Arsenio Hall, and Geraldo Rivera began dominating the talk show circuit, ushering in changes in topics, guests, and audience members. The 1980's redefined what was acceptable to discuss on television, expanding talk show topics to include traditionally taboo subjects such as teen pregnancies, alternative lifestyles, and eating disorders.

With the 1980's obsession with self-improvement, talk shows adopted the term "infotainment" and offered information about health, news events, and trends affecting Americans. Talk shows began to include ordinary people as guests, not just celebrities or experts, to discuss issues that were relevant to viewers' lives. In doing so, the average person was elevated to celebrity status, and viewers received televised therapy in the security of their own homes. Hosts acted as surrogates for the audience at home, asking personal questions and supporting their guests as they responded.

The queen of therapeutic and informative talk was Winfrey, whose debut show aired in September, 1986. Winfrey comforted guests as they opened up, and she shared her own stories of abuse and neglect, relationships, and weight problems, frequently crying with her audience. Although Donahue had discussed controversial topics since the 1970's, his approach was more intellectual than emotional.

Industry and Technological Changes Technological advances in hardware and syndication distribution methods, along with changes within the broadcast and cable industries, also contributed to the talk show revolution of the 1980's. Cable television and its new networks offered viewers more entertainment choices, and videocassette recorders (VCRs) and remote controls offered viewers more ways to pick and choose their entertainment. These advancements created new challenges for producers to overcome in order to retain their sponsors.

Cable and satellite networks, along with the emerging television networks, found themselves with numerous hours to program. Talk shows provided needed "filler" programming at a low cost, since they required no writers or actors and minimal sets. Also, the prevalence of syndication and the ease of distributing programming over satellites made it affordable for small stations to receive new talk shows, free from network constraints.

During the 1980's, Americans had more consumer choices because of deregulation policies, more disposable income as a result of a soaring stock market and a sense of prosperity, and more entertainment choices because of technological advances and broadcasting distribution methods. Viewers' ability to "channel surf" (and their diminishing attention spans) meant that producers had seconds to capture and retain viewers. In order to do this, talk shows transformed into quick, over-the-top programming based on attention-grabbing sound bites.

Impact During the fast-paced decade, Americans turned to talk shows for both emotional security and entertaining escape. Shows became ethnically diverse to meet societal expectations and to compete in the changing media landscape, and they became more prevalent through syndication advancements and an abundance of cable and network channels.

Further Reading

Day, Nancy. *Sensational TV: Trash or Journalism?* Springfield, N.J.: Enslow, 1996. Explores the motives and practices of television talk and news shows.

Grindstaff, Laura. *The Money Shot: Trash, Class, and the Making of Talk Shows.* Chicago: University of Chicago Press, 2002. Examines ambush and emotional tactics employed by talk shows.

Kurtz, Howard. *Hot Air: All Talk All the Time.* New York: Basic Books, 1997. An in-depth look into the biggest names in talk shows.

Manga, Julie Engel. *Talking Trash: The Cultural Politics of Daytime TV Talk Shows.* New York: New York University Press, 2003. Investigates sociological factors contributing to talk shows' popularity.

Parish, James Robert. *Let's Talk: America's Favorite Talk Show Hosts.* Las Vegas: Pioneer Books, 1993. Includes biographies of television talk show hosts.

Scott, Gini Graham. *Can We Talk? The Power and Influence of Talk Shows.* New York: Insight Books, 1996. A history of the rise in popularity of talk shows.

Shattuc, Jane M. *The Talking Cure: TV Talk Shows and Women.* New York: Routledge, 1997. Analysis of the interaction between women's issues and talk shows.

Sara Vidar

See also Cable television; Demographics of Canada; Demographics of the United States; FOX network; Journalism; Pauley, Jane; Rivera, Geraldo; Soap operas; Tabloid television; Television; Winfrey, Oprah.

■ Talking Heads

Identification American New Wave rock band
Date 1974-1991

A rock band that combined an art-school sensibility with pop and punk influences, Talking Heads profoundly influenced the sound of popular music in the 1980's.

Talking Heads was formed in the mid-1970's at the Rhode Island School of Design (RISD) in Providence by classmates Tina Weymouth (bass and vocals), David Byrne (guitar and vocals), and Chris Frantz (drums). The band released its debut album, *Talking Heads: 77* in 1977, a pivotal year for both punk and New Wave music. By then, it had added Jerry Harrison as a fourth member, playing guitar and keyboards.

By the time Talking Heads' fourth album, *Remain in Light* (1980), came out, the band had become a fixture on the New York City punk scene, playing frequent gigs at important music clubs CBGB and the Mudd Club. The group had its first top ten hit with the single "Burning Down the House" from 1983's album *Speaking in Tongues.* Talking Heads took advantage of the new music video format to impress their unique style on the new MTV generation, producing striking videos for both "Burning Down the House" and an earlier single, "Once in a Lifetime." Both became popular standards in the MTV rotation.

Talking Heads followed up their first top ten single with a major U.S. tour. The film director Jonathan Demme documented the tour in what became the 1984 concert film, *Stop Making Sense.* A live album of the same name followed. *Little Creatures* came out in 1985, and Byrne directed a musical comedy in 1986 called *True Stories.* The accompanying album and a follow-up in 1988,

Naked, were the last original studio albums recorded by the band. Issues of control and increasing interest in pursuing separate projects made it difficult for the band members to work together. After a long hiatus, they announced in 1991 that Talking Heads had officially broken up.

Impact Talking Heads drew from a vast pool of sources that grew and altered from one album to the next. During the 1980's, they incorporated into their music African, Caribbean, and South American rhythms, as well as funk and abstract sounds more often associated with avant-garde composers such as Philip Glass. In the mid-1980's, they introduced both electronic and hip-hop elements into their songs, confirming and transforming the influence of those genres on popular music. Although the group was closely associated with other New York City bands of the time, such as the Ramones and Blondie, it brought a distinctive and revolutionary type of music to the popular music scene, becoming one of the most influential bands of the 1980's.

Further Reading

Bowman, David. *This Must Be the Place: The Adventures of Talking Heads in the Twentieth Century.* New York: HarperEntertainment, 2001.

Gittins, Ian. *Talking Heads: Once in a Lifetime—The Stories Behind Every Song.* Milwaukee: Hal Leonard, 2004.

Talking Heads in 1983. From left: David Byrne, Jerry Harrison, Tina Weymouth, and Chris Frantz. (Deborah Feingold/Archive Photos)

McNeil, Legs, and Gillian McCain, eds. *Please Kill Me: The Uncensored Oral History of Punk.* New York: Penguin Books, 1997.

Lacy Schutz

See also Blondie; Boy George and Culture Club; Glass, Philip; MTV; Music; Music videos; New Wave music; Performance art; Pop music; Synthesizers; World music.

■ Tamper-proof packaging

Definition Product packaging designed to frustrate attempts to alter its contents

After the Tylenol murders, consumer fears about the safety of over-the-counter medications were partly allayed by the development of protective packaging.

Prior to the 1980's, medicines such as aspirin were routinely placed on open shelves with nothing more than screw-on caps and a wad of cotton inside. Some medicines might be sold in boxes, but their flaps generally slid in and out with ease. The first kind of protective packaging used by pharmaceutical companies, the familiar "push down and turn" lid, came only after wide publicity focused on the accidental poisonings of small children. However, child-proof caps were primarily intended to protect the innocent from their own curiosity, and they often frustrated adults seeking to take their medications. As a result, packages without child-proof lids were made available for the elderly and other people living in households without small children.

Tylenol Murders This casual approach to pharmaceutical safety changed after the 1982 Tylenol murders in Chicago. The murders made plain in the most shocking way possible the vulnerability of over-the-counter medicines to being made vehicles for poisoners' malice. Not only were all Tylenol products swept from store shelves while investigators tried to determine how extensive the contamination was, but also many other non-prescription drugs were withdrawn because of fears of copycat criminals seeking further media attention at the expense of human life.

Immediately after the Tylenol killings, there was real concern that the murders might end the sale of over-the-counter medications, making it necessary to reinstitute policies requiring pharmacists to keep even non-prescription medications behind their counters. However, consumer advocates called upon pharmaceutical corporations to cooperate with the Food and Drug Administration to develop alternative means of protecting the public from future tainting of common drugs. The solution they developed was to create barriers that would make it difficult or impossible for future poisoners to imitate the Tylenol murders.

The most obvious security solution was to seal the flaps of boxes containing retail drugs. In order to open the sealed boxes, it became necessary to tear the flap loose, leaving visible damage. However, there was concern that a sufficiently skilled poisoner might develop a means to loosen such flaps without leaving tell-tale damage. As a result, it was decided to add additional layers of protection, such as a plastic sleeve around the neck of a bottle, or a paper under the lid that sealed the bottle's neck altogether.

In addition, it was noted that the Extra-Strength Tylenol capsules that had been the primary vehicle for the Tylenol murders had been adulterated by carefully pulling apart the two halves of each capsule, dripping in a droplet of cyanide, and reassembling the capsule. As a result, it was decided that rigid plastic capsules would henceforth be restricted to prescription medicines, which were considered less vulnerable to tampering because access to them was restricted. All over-the-counter medicines that could not be administered in tablet form would henceforth use a softer gelatin-based capsule that would crush or disintegrate if disassembled.

Impact The development of tamper-proof packaging enabled the public to regain confidence in the safety of over-the-counter medicines. Within a matter of months, the sale of Tylenol products returned to levels comparable to those prior to the Tylenol murders. However, security came at a price. Protective packaging was often difficult and frustrating for legitimate users to remove, particularly if they were elderly or disabled. Furthermore, all the additional packaging had to be discarded, adding to the burden on the nation's landfills. However, it was generally agreed that these downsides were an acceptable price to pay for safety.

More subtly, the growing ubiquity of tamper-proof packaging marked a loss of innocence by the American people. Every protective sleeve and inner lid that had to be peeled off a bottle of over-the-counter medicine was a reminder that there were people out there who could not be trusted—who, if given a chance, would be happy to do others harm through devious means. Although the immediate fear of product tampering soon receded, the sense that the world was a fundamentally dangerous place became an artifact of American culture.

In time, the use of tamper-proof and tamper-evident packaging moved beyond the pharmaceutical industry to include many other products that were susceptible to malicious tampering or even inadvertent contamination by careless shoppers. Many prepared foods—particularly baby foods, which were seen as particularly vulnerable because of the helplessness and innocence of their intended consumers—soon received various forms of protective packaging. Cosmetics formed another group of consumer products that began to be enclosed in various forms of shrink-wrap or protective bands, rather than simply being marketed in loose-lidded boxes, as it became obvious that careless "sampling" of such products could pass infections. By the end of the 1980's, it had become unthinkable to purchase many of these items from open shelves if their protective packaging was not firmly in place.

Further Reading

Dean, D. A. *Pharmaceutical Packaging Technology.* Oxford, England: Taylor and Francis, 2000. Detailed explanation of how tamper-proof and tamper-evident packaging is produced. Somewhat technical, but a good source of in-depth information.

Jenkins, Philip. *Decade of Nightmares: The End of the Sixties and the Making of Eighties America.* New York: Oxford University Press, 2006. Helps place the development of tamper-proof packaging within a larger cultural context that goes beyond the obvious impetus of product tampering.

Useem, Michael. *The Leadership Moment: Nine True Stories of Triumph and Disaster and Their Lessons for Us All.* New York: Three Rivers Press, 1998. Includes among its nine studies that of the Tylenol murders and how Johnson & Johnson restored the reputation of its brand by aggressively promoting tamper-proof packaging to prevent similar incidents.

Leigh Husband Kimmel

See also   Business and the economy in the United States; Medicine; Tylenol murders.

■ *Tanner '88*

Identification   Cable television political satire series

Date   Aired from February 15 to August 22, 1988

Tanner '88 accelerated the blurring of presidential campaigns with television entertainment, as it highlighted the performance aspects of political life.

Although the practice of fake documentary is as old as filmmaking itself, with *Tanner '88*, two of America's best satirists, Garry Trudeau, the creator of the comic strip *Doonesbury*, and Robert Altman, the director of *M*A*S*H* (1970) and *Nashville* (1975), joined forces with Home Box Office (HBO) to produce a truly original project. In the eleven-part series, an imaginary candidate, Jack Tanner (played by Michael Murphy), ran for the Democratic nomination for president of the United States. Tanner and his fictional staff and family appeared in narratives scripted by Trudeau set in real political environments, from New Hampshire to the floor of the Democratic National Convention in Atlanta.

Along the primary route, actual candidates—Pat Robertson, Bob Dole, and Gary Hart—interacted briefly with Tanner, whom they may or may not have recognized. In one lengthy conversation, Governor Bruce Babbit, who had dropped out of the running, counseled Tanner to oppose the "silver screen of unreality" and "take a risk," advice both ludicrous and heartfelt. Ironies multiplied as the show progressed, as Tanner—whose campaign slogan was "for real"—struggled with his pragmatic staff and idealistic daughter to find his voice in the artificial world of campaign politics. This world was populated by pretentious ad makers, confused pollsters, vacuous speech coaches, and gossip-hungry journalists. The most jarring sequence in the series occurred when Tanner visited an actual inner-city meeting of Detroit parents whose children had been murdered; their expressions of authentic grief and frustration momentarily cut through the satire.

Mid-campaign, HBO reran the six previously aired episodes of *Tanner '88* in one block, introduced by real television journalist Linda Ellerbe. Viewers were urged to "choose from a group of presidential candidates, one or more of whom is not a real person." Tanner won the straw poll, receiving 38 percent of the approximately forty-one thousand votes cast, followed by George H. W. Bush (with 22 percent), Jesse

Jackson (with 21 percent), and Michael Dukakis (with 19 percent).

Impact   *Tanner '88* influenced the growth of the "mockumentary" style, solidified HBO's reputation for innovative productions, and extended the reputations of Robert Altman (who won an Emmy for his direction) and Gary Trudeau as brilliant critics of American culture.

Further Reading

Goff, Michael J. *The Money Primary: The New Politics of the Early Presidential Politics.* Lanham, Md.: Rowman & Littlefield, 2004.

Juhasz, Alexandra, and Jesse Lerner, eds. *F is for Phony: Fake Documentary and Truth's Undoing.* Minneapolis: University of Minnesota Press, 2006.

Keyssar, Helene. *Robert Altman's America.* New York: Oxford University Press, 1991.

Trudeau, G. B. *Flashbacks: Twenty-Five Years of "Doonesbury."* Kansas City: Andrews and McMeel, 1995.

Carolyn Anderson

See also   Atwater, Lee; Bush, George H. W.; Cable television; Comic strips; Dukakis, Michael; Elections in the United States, 1988; Hart, Gary; Jackson, Jesse; Liberalism in U.S. politics; Television.

■ Tax Reform Act of 1986

Identification   U.S. federal legislation
Date   Became law on October 22, 1986

The Tax Reform Act of 1986 made major changes in how income was taxed in the United States by simplifying the tax code, reducing the top marginal income tax rate, and eliminating many tax shelters and other preferences.

Though it was officially deemed revenue neutral because it did not increase overall tax levels, the Tax Reform Act of 1986 significantly altered the distribution of federal taxes. The top tax rate was lowered from 50 percent to 28 percent, and the bottom rate was raised from 11 percent to 15 percent, the only time in history that the top rate was reduced and the bottom rate was simultaneously increased. Other reforms of the act included reducing the capital gains tax to the same tax rate as that for ordinary income and increasing incentives favoring investment in owner-occupied housing relative to rental housing by increasing the home mortgage interest deduction. Because the measure was seen as revenue neutral, the act passed by a large bipartisan majority in Congress.

The bill originated in a Democratic tax reform proposal first advanced in August, 1982, by Senator Bill Bradley and Representative Dick Gephardt, as well as in President Ronald Reagan's call for tax reform in his January, 1984, state of the union address. As enacted, the legislation cut individual tax rates more than had originally been anticipated, but it cut corporate taxes less than originally proposed. The law shifted tax liability from individuals to corporations, reversing a long trend of corporate taxes supplying a decreasing share of federal revenues.

Enactment of the measure was accomplished through the perseverance of its chief backers in Congress over the objections of many special interests that would lose the favored status they enjoyed under the current tax code. Although the law was originally envisioned as a way of eliminating all tax loopholes, the tax reform debate almost immediately focused on which tax loopholes would be preserved or added under the new law. Despite the nation being mired in a period of large budget deficits, Reagan refused to support any tax increases, and as a result, the bill neither raised nor reduced total federal tax collections over a five-year period after its enactment. Ultimately, that principle allowed the bill's adherents to turn back costly amendments to restore tax breaks, because the sponsors of those amendments were not able to produce offsetting revenues.

Impact   The Tax Reform Act of 1986 was a considerable change from the previous tax code. The fact that Congress passed serious tax reform at all was remarkable, considering all the obstacles it faced. Of all post-World War II-era domestic goals, tax reform was among the most politically difficult to bring about. After the 1986 tax reforms were enacted, however, Congress would go on to make at least fourteen thousand further changes to the tax code, very few of which could be considered reform. Many of the loopholes and exceptions that were excised by the Tax Reform Act of 1986 were later essentially restored.

Further Reading

Birnbaum, Jeffrey, and Alan Murray. *Showdown at Gucci Gulch.* New York: Random House, 1987.

Fisher, Patrick. *Congressional Budgeting: A Representational Perspective. Lanham, Md.: University Press of America, 2005.

Peters, B. Guy. *The Politics of Taxation.* Cambridge, England: Blackwell, 1991.

Patrick Fisher

See also Congress, U.S.; Economic Recovery Tax Act of 1981; Reagan, Ronald.

■ Taylor, Lawrence

Identification NFL Hall of Fame linebacker
Born February 4, 1959; Williamsburg, Virginia

Taylor, better known as LT, was perhaps the NFL's best defensive player during the 1980's.

Lawrence Taylor played for only one team, the New York Giants, during his career in the National Football League (NFL). He was an outside linebacker and was best known for sacking quarterbacks. Taylor recorded a total of 132.5 sacks, and at the time of his retirement, only one other player had more. One of Taylor's sacks is best remembered because its impact ended the career of a rival player. During a *Monday Night Football* game in 1985, Taylor raced past a Washington Redskins offensive lineman, turned, and jumped, in an effort to tackle quarterback Joe Theismann. Once he made the tackle, he immediately got up and frantically waved to the Redskins' bench, indicating that Theismann was hurt. The quarterback's right leg was badly broken, and he never played again. The image of Taylor—his intensity known to everyone—desperate to get help for an injured player was a lasting one for those who remembered the play.

Taylor's successes on the field were sadly matched by terrible mistakes off it. He later admitted that by his second year in the NFL he was already addicted to cocaine. In 1988, he was suspended for thirty days

New York Giants Lawrence Taylor, right, and George Martin smash into Tampa Bay Buccaneer Steve DeBerg, forcing him to fumble, during a Giants home game in September, 1984. (AP/Wide World Photos)

by the league after his second positive drug test. Many more problems off the field would dog him well into the 1990's. Ironically, it was also in 1988 that Taylor played what many observers called his most memorable game. Taylor took the field against the New Orleans Saints, even though he had a torn pectoral muscle. The injury was severe enough that he needed a harness to keep his shoulder in place. He nevertheless recorded multiple sacks and tackles, leading the Giants to an important win.

Impact   Experts have argued that it was Taylor who made all NFL teams realize how critical it was to have a powerful outside linebacker capable of disrupting the opposition's offense. Taylor was named the NFL Defensive Player of the Year three times (including following his rookie season), he was an All-Pro nine times, and he earned ten Pro Bowl berths. He was also selected as the league's most valuable player following the 1986 season, when he led the Giants to their first Super Bowl championship, which was also the first Super Bowl loss for Denver Bronco quarterback John Elway.

Further Reading

Taylor, Lawrence, and David Falkner. *LT: Living on the Edge.* New York: Random House, 1987.

Taylor, Lawrence, and Steve Serby. *LT: Over the Edge—Tackling Quarterbacks, Drugs, and a World Beyond Football.* New York: HarperCollins, 2004.

Anthony Moretti

See also   Elway, John; Football; Sports.

■ Teen films

Definition   Popular films portraying the lives and struggles of suburban American teenagers

Teen films ruled the box office in the 1980's, portraying characters and situations to which American teenagers could easily relate and launching the careers of several stars.

The teen film genre can be traced to the James Dean (*Rebel Without a Cause,* 1955) and beach films of the 1950's and 1960's. The 1980's proved to be the golden age of the teen film. Movies like *Sixteen Candles* (1984) and *The Breakfast Club* (1985) demonstrated that teen films could be fun, meaningful, and profitable, dealing with issues that teenagers and

young adults found most important while still bringing in a significant profit for Hollywood.

Most teen films are set in high schools or deal with characters that are of high school age. Films such as *Fast Times at Ridgemont High* (1982) combined humor with serious coming-of-age topics such as popularity, sex, dating, and abortion. Often, teen film plots focus on the so-called nerd lusting after a dream girl, as in *Weird Science* (1985), in which two teen boys successfully create their "perfect woman" through a freak computer accident. Although *Weird Science* was purely comedic, movies such as *Pretty in Pink* (1986) dealt with drama and struck a chord with teen girls. In this film, the lead character, played by Molly Ringwald, goes from being an overlooked, average girl to winning the heart of the most popular boy in school.

The Brat Pack and John Hughes   In the 1980's, writer and director John Hughes quickly became known as the king of teen films. He wrote and/or directed some of the most popular films at the time, including *Sixteen Candles, Pretty in Pink, The Breakfast Club, Ferris Bueller's Day Off* (1986), and *Weird Science.* Each of his movies centers on middle-class teenagers from the midwestern United States who are trying to find their place in the world. As in other teen films, Hughes's characters often represent teen stereotypes: the nerd, the jock, the popular cheerleader, the troublemaker, and the girl struggling to fit in. Hughes often cast the same group of actors to play these parts, and they became known as the Brat Pack: Molly Ringwald, Anthony Michael Hall, Judd Nelson, Ally Sheedy, Emilio Estevez, Demi Moore, Andrew McCarthy, and Rob Lowe built great careers in the 1980's thanks to Hughes's films.

Impact   Teen films were designed to tap into the psyche of young people by using a mix of comedy and drama that dealt with issues such as sex, drugs, high school, relationships, and the pressure to live up to society's standards. Although the demand for the types of teen films made in the 1980's tapered off in favor of more lighthearted fantasy films of the 1990's and 2000's (for example, *The Princess Diaries,* 2000; *What a Girl Wants,* 2003), the teen film genre left a lasting impression on Hollywood. While some stars of the 1980's had a hard time shaking their teen film pasts and struggled to find roles later in their careers, films like *Risky Business* (1983) launched the career of superstar Tom Cruise, *About Last Night . . .*

(continued on page 948)

Selected 1980's Teen Films

Year	Title	Director	Young Actors
1980	The Hollywood Knights	Floyd Mutrux	Robert Wuhl, Tony Danza, Fran Drescher, Michelle Pfeiffer
1982	Fast Times at Ridgemont High	Amy Heckerling	Sean Penn, Jennifer Jason Leigh, Judge Reinhold, Phoebe Cates
	Zapped!	Robert J. Rosenthal	Scott Baio, Willie Aames
1983	Risky Business	Paul Brickman	Tom Cruise
	Class	Lewis John Carlino	Rob Lowe, Andrew McCarthy, John Cusack, Alan Ruck
	The Outsiders	Francis Ford Coppola	Matt Dillon, Ralph Macchio, C. Thomas Howell, Patrick Swayze, Rob Lowe, Emilio Estevez, Tom Cruise
1984	Sixteen Candles	John Hughes	Molly Ringwald, Justin Henry, Anthony Michael Hall, John Cusack
	Making the Grade	Dorian Walker	Judd Nelson, Dana Olson
1985	The Breakfast Club	John Hughes	Emilio Estevez, Anthony Michael Hall, Judd Nelson, Molly Ringwald, Ally Sheedy
	Weird Science	John Hughes	Anthony Michael Hall, Ilan Mitchell-Smith, Robert Downey, Jr.
	Girls Just Want to Have Fun	Alan Metter	Sarah Jessica Parker, Helen Hunt, Jonathan Silverman, Shannen Doherty
	St. Elmo's Fire	Joel Schumacher	Emilio Estevez, Rob Lowe, Andrew McCarthy, Demi Moore, Judd Nelson, Ally Sheedy, Mare Winningham
	Private Resort	George Bowers	Rob Morrow, Johnny Depp
	Teen Wolf	Rob Daniel	Michael J. Fox
	Real Genius	Martha Coolidge	Val Kilmer, Gabriel Jarret
1986	Pretty in Pink	Howard Deutch	Molly Ringwald, Jon Cryer, James Spader, Andrew McCarthy
	Ferris Bueller's Day Off	John Hughes	Matthew Broderick, Alan Ruck, Jennifer Grey, Charlie Sheen
	Lucas	David Seltzer	Corey Haim, Charlie Sheen, Winona Ryder, Courtney Thorne-Smith
1987	Some Kind of Wonderful	Howard Deutch	Eric Stoltz, Mary Stuart Masterson, Lea Thompson
	Can't Buy Me Love	Steve Rash	Patrick Dempsey, Amanda Peterson, Seth Green
	Adventures in Babysitting	Chris Columbus	Elisabeth Shue, Anthony Rapp
	Square Dance	Daniel Petrie	Winona Ryder, Rob Lowe
	The Lost Boys	Joel Schumacher	Jason Patric, Corey Haim, Kiefer Sutherland, Jami Gertz, Corey Feldman
1988	A Night in the Life of Jimmy Reardon	William Richert	River Phoenix, Ione Skye, Matthew Perry
1989	Say Anthing	Cameron Crowe	John Cusack, Ione Skye, Lili Taylor

(1986) catapulted Demi Moore to stardom, *Ferris Bueller's Day Off* cemented Matthew Broderick's career, and former teen geek Anthony Michael Hall found great success on *The Dead Zone* television series, which aired in 2002. The fact that 1980's teen films such as *The Breakfast Club* remained popular in the early twenty-first century shows that the issues presented in these films are perennially pertinent.

Further Reading

Bernstein, Jonathan. *Pretty in Pink: The Golden Age of Teenage Movies.* New York: St. Martin's Griffin, 1997. A filmography for fans of the 1980's teen films, the book provides funny and lighthearted facts about some of the decade's most popular films.

Clark, Jaime, ed. *Don't You Forget About Me: Contemporary Writers on the Films of John Hughes.* New York: Simon Spotlight Entertainment, 2007. Offers a variety of perspectives on Hughes's teen films. Foreword by Ally Sheedy.

Deziel, Shanda. "The Man Who Understood Teenagers." *Maclean's* 119, no. 45 (November, 2006): 7. Discusses a documentary about the impact of teen films in the 1980's. Addresses the importance of teen films, especially those directed by Hughes.

Neale, Steve. "Major Genres." In *Genre and Hollywood.* New York: Routledge, 2000. The text is helpful to the study of Hollywood films and genre theory. The chapter titled "Major Genres" addresses teen films and their impact.

Prince, Stephen. *History of the American Cinema: A New Pot of Gold—Hollywood Under the Electronic Rainbow, 1980-1989.* New York: Charles Scribner's Sons, 2000. The tenth volume in a set of books dedicated to laying out the history of American film one decade at a time. This volume is a great resource for the teen films of the 1980's.

Jennifer L. Titanski

See also Brat Pack in acting; *Breakfast Club, The;* Fads; Fashions and clothing; *Fast Times at Ridgemont High;* Film in the United States; Hughes, John; MTV; New Wave music; PG-13 rating; Pop music; Preppies; Slang and slogans.

■ Teen singers

Definition   Young singers whose music is marketed to teen or preteen audiences

While Music Television provided exposure for teen artists such as New Kids on the Block and Debbie Gibson, another method of teen music marketing—mall tours—helped propel singers such as Tiffany to the top of the charts. The success of these teen artists renewed the record industry's interest in teen acts and led to the boy band craze of the 1990's.

The 1970's had seen television give teen singers such as David and Shaun Cassidy a ready-made audience. With the advent of MTV in 1981, the market expanded to include teenage singers and groups. Additionally, the singer Tiffany cultivated her success through reaching out to teens where they congregated—the mall.

New Edition and New Kids on the Block   Boston-based songwriter and producer Maurice Starr formed the boy band New Edition in 1980. Made of up five black teenage boys, the group had top ten hits with "Cool It Now" and "Candy Girl." Starr noted that he modeled the group after the Jackson 5. Eventually, New Edition fired Starr, and in 1984 he created a new band, New Kids on the Block, which he decided to model after the family pop group the Osmonds, but with "soul and good material—good black material." New Kids on the Block dominated the teenybopper market in the late 1980's, with songs written by Starr and music videos that made use of synchronized dance moves, which became part of the standard template for boy bands of the 1990's.

Teen Queens   In 1987, two young teenage girls, each with a different hook, conquered the pop market. Long Island native Debbie Gibson began writing songs as a child and began producing them shortly thereafter. At the age of sixteen, she was signed to Atlantic Records and released her first single, "Only in My Dreams," which made the top ten. She followed this up with two number one singles, "Foolish Beat" and "Lost in Your Eyes" (the latter from her second album). Unlike the other teen artists mentioned, Gibson wrote all her songs, and her record label made the effort not to promote her through teen magazines. Gibson's manager, Doug Breitbart, told the *Los Angeles Times,* "It's a major stigma, and I hadn't spent four years working with Debbie . . . to get discarded as a teen act."

Tiffany (full name Tiffany Renee Darwish) had been singing in public since she was nine years old. In 1987, she recorded her first album, which initially was not successful. Tiffany's manager, George Tobin, recounted that he was told by industry executives that "teen stars went out with Donny and Marie [Osmond]." Tobin and the record label eventually hit on the idea of a mall tour to sell her to her targeted audience. At each mall stop, she would play several shows. The tour was successful, and by 1988 Tiffany had two number one hits. New Kids on the Block would also do the mall tour circuit early in their career.

Following the success of Gibson and Tiffany, record labels began releasing songs by more teen singers, including Glenn Medeiros, Shanice Wilson, and Tracie Spencer. As with Tiffany and New Kids on the Block, these artists were promoted through MTV and especially teen magazines. A number of these singers became "one-hit wonders," known for only one successful hit. Another one-hit wonder teen singer who did not fit either the pop singer or Maurice Starr boy band mold was Charlie Sexton, the rock guitarist who had a top twenty hit at age seventeen with "Beat's So Lonely" in 1985. While he remained a successful musician, the 1985 single was his only hit on the pop charts.

Teen singing group New Kids on the Block at the American Music Awards on January 22, 1990. (AP/Wide World Photos)

Impact   Teen singers in the 1980's had a new medium that teen idols of the past did not—music videos. The success of bands such as New Edition and New Kids on the Block was a precursor to the boy band phenomenon of the 1990's, and the success of Tiffany's mall tours is a reminder of the importance of marketing in music for teenagers.

Further Reading

Cooper, Kim, and David Smay, eds. *Bubblegum Music Is the Naked Truth*. Los Angeles: Feral House, 2001. Though focused on the "tween" music of the late 1960's and 1970's, the book does include a helpful section on Starr's two bands of the 1980's, New Edition and New Kids on the Block, as well as many photos of great 1980's merchandise.

Grein, Paul. "Teen-Agers Making Their Voices Heard: Tiffany, 16, Is Not 'Alone Now' on Pop Scene as Recording Industry Capitalizes on Young Artists." *Los Angeles Times*, December 1, 1987, p. 1. Excellent article concisely summarizes paths Tiffany and Gibson took to their careers and includes the prediction that as many baby boomers were having kids later, the teen artists explosion would actually occur in the 1990's.

Hunt, Dennis. "Stardom's Not Only in Her Dreams." *Los Angeles Times*, August 23, 1987, p. 88. Provides background on Gibson's early songwriting and signing to Atlantic Records.

_____. "Young, Gifted, and Sounding Black: New Kids on the Block Are the Osmonds with Soul, Sings Their Creator." *Los Angeles Times*, June 4, 1989, p. 8. Discusses the creation of New Kids on the Block and how Starr modeled the boy band off of his earlier group, New Edition.

Julie Elliott

See also   MTV; Music videos; Pop music; Women in rock music.

■ Televangelism

Definition The use of television as a medium to communicate Christianity

Scandals caused the rapid downfall of some of the most famous televangelists in the 1980's. Many Americans saw these events as confirmation of their suspicions that televangelists were corrupt and out of touch with mainstream religious views.

The technology of television, which became a popular form of news and entertainment in American homes in the 1950's, had long been ignored by religious groups. While some saw the television as a symbol of modernism and secularism, most simply did not develop the tools and technology necessary to transfer their message to television until the late 1970's and early 1980's. Partly because of a new responsiveness by religious groups to the potential power of television and partly because of a broader engagement by many Christians in the realm of American popular culture, many enthusiastic preachers moved their ministries to the television airwaves during the 1980's. Still others launched their careers with local, regional, and even national programming plans that grew into vast media communications networks and broadcast empires.

The Rise of Televangelism American Christianity has a long history of utilizing the most efficient and effective communications strategies of each generation in order to carry out the "Great Commission," Jesus Christ's instruction to his disciples to spread the gospel teachings throughout the world. Evangelist Aimee Semple McPherson, founder of the International Church of the Foursquare Gospel, was criticized in the early twentieth century for her use of the relatively new medium of radio as a tool for "winning souls for Christ." In subsequent years, however, ministers embraced not only radio but also television as a viable method of communicating their message.

One of the earliest to do this was Pat Robertson, who founded the Christian Broadcasting Network (CBN) in 1961. Its flagship show, *The 700 Club*, began broadcasts in the mid-1960's. Part news reporting and part talk show, *The 700 Club* continued to broadcast into the early twenty-first century, featuring popular hosts and guests from a variety of backgrounds. Though Robertson became known for his controversial and outspoken views, he remained a strong voice for followers of Judeo-Christian traditional values.

Another controversial televangelist was Oral Roberts, the son of a midwestern preacher and an evangelist and faith healer in the charismatic tradition. Roberts began his ministry in the 1950's and launched a series of television specials during the 1970's. His Oral Roberts Ministries continued to broadcast into the early twenty-first century. In the 1980's, however, Roberts became the target of jokes and criticism when he claimed to have had visions of God about raising money for his ministries, including the City of Faith Medical and Research Center, which was open from 1981 to 1989.

Like Pat Robertson, Jerry Falwell became well known for his television ministries in the 1980's. Though he had established the Thomas Road Baptist Church in Lynchburg, Virginia, and the *Old Time Gospel Hour* radio program in 1956, he became a mobilizing force when his Moral Majority coalition (founded in 1979) endorsed Ronald Reagan in his 1980 election bid.

The Decline of Televangelism Roberts and Falwell spent the 1980's building ministries that continued to play a role in national religious and political life in later decades. However, in many ways, their careers—at least during the 1980's—were eclipsed by two other figures.

In 1987, Assemblies of God minister Jim Bakker resigned from his position as head of the PTL television network and as host of its popular television show of the same name. Bakker's resignation came in the wake of scandals involving a sexual encounter with a church secretary named Jessica Hahn and allegations of massive fraud. During their heyday, Jim and his wife, Tammy Faye, lived an excessive lifestyle, even while asking viewers to maximize their financial contributions to their ministry. After serving five years in prison for charges related to fraud and tax evasion, Bakker continued to minister, though on a much smaller scale.

The year after Bakker's resignation, Jimmy Swaggart, another Assemblies of God preacher, was forced to resign as head of Jimmy Swaggart Ministries (then worth more than $100 million) when allegations surfaced that he had met with prostitutes. Swaggart became another target of critics and skeptics, in part because of his tearful videotaped apology to his followers.

Impact The rising stars of American televangelism during the late 1970's and 1980's helped lay the groundwork for the development of the Christian media empires that continued to thrive in the early twenty-first century. The Trinity Broadcasting Network, which calls itself the "world's largest Christian television network," began in 1973 but expanded its reach during the 1980's, thanks in part to early work by Jim and Tammy Faye Bakker, whose *PTL Club* actually debuted there. Pioneers in the field contributed to both the legitimization of television as a potential medium for spreading Christianity and the increase in skepticism from those who questioned televangelists and their motives as well as from fellow evangelists and other Christian leaders who believed that the industry lent itself easily to corruption and greed, even in the hands of otherwise good people.

Further Reading

Jorstad, Erling. *The New Christian Right, 1981-1988: Prospects for the Post-Reagan Decade.* Studies in American Religion 25. Lewiston, N.Y.: Edwin Mellen Press, 1987. Investigates the social and cultural influences behind the rise and fall of the Religious Right.

Schmidt, Rosemarie, and Joseph F. Kess. *Television Advertising and Televangelism: Discourse Analysis of Persuasive Language.* Philadelphia: J. Benjamins, 1986. As the title suggests, this book analyzes televangelism from a sociolinguistic standpoint.

Schultze, Quentin J. *Televangelism and American Culture: The Business of Popular Religion.* Grand Rapids, Mich.: Baker Book House, 1991. Analyzes how televangelist ministries have been corrupted by power and wealth.

Jennifer Heller

See also Bakker, Jim and Tammy Faye; Falwell, Jerry; Heritage USA; Moral Majority; Religion and spirituality in the United States; Robertson, Pat; Swaggart, Jimmy; Television.

■ Television

Definition Programs and series, both fictional and nonfictional, produced for or broadcast on U.S. television

A transformation in television took place during the 1980's as a result of the advent of home video recording devices and the deregulation of the industry during the Reagan administration. Cable and satellite systems soon represented the demise of free television.

Three major networks—the American Broadcasting Company (ABC), the Columbia Broadcasting System (CBS), and the National Broadcasting Company (NBC)—controlled the programming offered on television from 1940 to 1980. With the introduction of cable, satellite delivery systems, and home video, executives began to target shows that captured smaller niche audiences, often referred to as narrowcasting. The television industry became a global business headed by mass conglomerates, and by the end of the decade pressures to streamline expenses led to fewer programming options. Programmers depended on the stability of the economy, and because cable was based on subscriber services, they had to offer shows that pleased the majority of the viewing public. The problem was that such systems were highly dependent on syndication, airing old movies, and programs that usually lacked originality and creativity.

Cable systems could deliver "superstations" such as WTBS (Atlanta), WGN-TV (Chicago), and WWOR-TV (New York City) that became widely available throughout the United States. The three mainstream networks could no longer maintain a monopoly on what the American public viewed in their living rooms. By 1986, 82 percent of the American adults watched television on an average of seven hours per day while 88 percent of all households had subscribed to pay cable television networks such as Home Box Office (HBO), MTV (Music Television), Nickelodeon, and the Disney Channel. These new channels were not part of cable systems but satellite-distributed choices that allowed local cable companies to offer the channels in programming packages. This resulted in pricing arrangements in which subscribers paid more for "premium channels" with no commercial interruptions, such as HBO, while Nickelodeon was supported through advertisers; thus, viewers could get this channel free or for a nominal fee.

Deregulation and Mergers The decade saw not only unprecedented technological growth but also changes that were taking place as conglomerates began seeking wider diversification. The Federal Communications Commission (FCC) abided by the antimonopolistic charter clauses that limited the number of stations that could be owned by a single person. However, when President Ronald Reagan appointed Mark S. Fowler and Dennis R. Patrick as FCC chairmen, the situation drastically changed for the television industry. Both men rejected the idea that broadcasters were trustees using the medium as a way to serve the public good. They believed in Reagan's conservative economic policies that reinforced consumerism and market forces. The general public should be the ultimate consumer, unfettered by government rules for viewing choices. Thus, deregulation of the communications industry began to take place in the early 1980's.

Shareholders now considered television as a commodity, a profitable endeavor that could be bought and sold at will. Major corporations began to buy the floundering networks—Capital Cities took over ABC, and General Electric took over CBS and NBC. Entrepreneurs flocked to the airwaves as profits soured and emerged as media moguls. In 1980, Ted Turner unveiled the Cable News Network (CNN), and he spearheaded the movement with several satellite services (WTBS, CNN, and TNT). Eventually, Turner bought the television rights to the MGM library of motion pictures for rebroadcasting on his channels. Native Australian Rupert Murdoch first bought Metromedia television stations that served New York and Washington. Murdoch then acquired Twentieth Century-Fox and formed the FOX network to compete with the three mainstream networks.

New Technologies and Piracy Issues New technologies—including the videocassette recorder (VCR), video games, and remote control devices—caused a significant revolution in home recordings of programs. Warner-Amex in Columbus, Ohio, introduced interactive two-way technology television with Qube in 1980. Subscribers could respond with a handheld device to answer multiple choice questions or order merchandise, and the system was even used by local universities to offer classes. However, by 1984, with mounting costs and rising subscriber concerns over privacy issues about what information was being stored in the company's databases, Qube was discontinued. The camcorder, a video and recorder, enabled people to watch home movies on their television sets. The remote control changed the way viewers watched television, allowing them to flip channels and see snippets of several shows at one time. Videocassette tape replaced bulky reel-to-reel machines; the tape could be reused and recorded over, and soon companies developed handheld video cameras that enabled faster production in the field in television journalism.

Consumers could now record their favorite television programs, avoiding network schedules to accommodate their own lifestyles. In 1982, only 4 percent of households owned a VCR, but by 1988, with the costs of production going down, the number rose to 60 percent. Viewers became their own independent programmers, but the downside was that the VCR caused a boom in film piracy by some foreign countries and violations of copyright. In a 1984 lawsuit brought by Disney and Universal against Sony, the leading manufacturer of VHS recorders, the U.S. Supreme Court ruled that taping a copyrighted program off the air for one's own personal viewing was not an illegal act. The decision caused the movie and television industry to move into marketing home video releases once the program was in syndication so that viewers would buy or rent the video before taping it directly off the air. By the mid-1980's, HBO began to scramble transmissions to stop nonpaying viewers who had satellite dishes but did not receive regular cable service. In order to receive clear reception, viewers had to pay for the service and get decoders for their television sets. The Cable Communications Policy Act of 1984 also banned the illegal sharing or wiring of cable television and telephone systems.

Programs and Reaganism Mergers, deregulation, and new technologies would have a dramatic effect on the type of shows the American public would watch on their television screens. During this decade, the decline of musical variety shows and Westerns occurred because of a lack of viewer interest. Innovation did not appear as hoped; instead, by the mid-1980's, the cable networks relied on the reruns of classic programs such as *Bewitched, Rifleman, Father Knows Best, Lassie,* and *Dragnet.* Prime-time programmers increasingly used segmented scheduling to target specific demographic groups. For example, the first hour of prime time was devoted to family shows such as the *Head of the Class, The Cosby Show, The Facts of Life,* and *Growing Pains.* There was an attempt to appeal to older Americans in such series as *The Golden Girls,* in which three self-confident, mature women deal with retirement in Florida, while *Mur-*

der, She Wrote starred Angela Lansbury as an amateur sleuth in a small New England town.

Many programs featured movie stars from the 1940's and 1950's in guest appearances to generate nostalgic reactions from viewers. Feminist positions also began to have a greater influence on television series such as *Cagney and Lacey,* since there were more female producers and writers with liberal political positions during the 1980's. Also, women traditionally watched more television than men. On the other hand, programs such as *thirtysomething* and *Moonlighting* appealed to the yuppie crowd, young and upcoming professionals who mixed professional careers with raising families. The yuppies were part of the baby-boom generation that stressed work, especially with women rising into the managerial class. Career choices were meant to be meaningful to one's personal life.

Programming was also influenced by the Reagan administration's renewed Cold War rhetoric against the Soviet Union as the "Evil Empire," and network executives took note. In 1983, ABC broadcast a two-hour movie, *The Day After,* showing the United States in the aftermath of a nuclear war with the Soviet Union. In 1988, the same network broadcast a fourteen-hour miniseries, *Amerika,* depicting the United States after an extended period of Soviet occupation. Reagan's conservatism shaped the political landscape of television journalism as panelists with right-wing viewpoints appeared with more frequency on news reports, commentary programs, and talk shows.

Television journalism addressing controversial topics in documentaries dwindled, and ratings for these programs declined, so much so that reporters often lamented that television news was becoming an entertainment medium. By the end of the decade, the evening news broadcasts on the three major networks went from an hour to thirty minutes in length. With video and satellite systems, fundamentalist religious leaders invested in these technologies, and televangelists such as Jimmy Swaggart, Pat Robertson, Jerry Falwell, and Jim and Tammy Faye Bakker emerged. They used the new medium to speak out against various issues that they found too prevalent—abortion, homosexuality, the Equal Rights Amendment, pornography, and sex education in schools.

The decade certainly represented the golden age for prime-time soap operas—*Dallas, Dynasty, Falcon*

Crest, and *Knots Landing*—that reflected Reagan-era federalism and an emphasis on glamour. Such shows epitomized the Reagan era with its concern over image and the fiscal conservatism found in supply-side economics. Materialism was expressed in lavish home design, decor, and gourmet food culture. The American public could not get enough of the ultrarich Carringtons on *Dynasty* and the Ewings, the larger-than-life Texans on *Dallas,* as these families grew in their obsessive need for wealth. Featured on location, *Miami Vice* was a television show that was focused on high style, lush cinematography, and couture fashions that revolutionized the look of detective dramas. The show's portrayal of drugs, smuggling activities, and prostitution was set to music with hypnotic synthesizer beats that appealed to the MTV generation.

However, the baby-boom generation, despite its materialistic tendencies, remained liberal on social issues. Dramas often held a gritty realism in shows such as *Hills Street Blues* and *St. Elsewhere,* in which "good" and "bad" were not always easily defined. One of the major themes in many of the crime dramas was that good cops were halted from doing their jobs by inept courts, bureaucratic red tape, and department policies that allowed criminals to be released because of legal technicalities. Justice was not always enforced or easily found; the police had to make deals with informants and bargain with the assistant district attorney. Officers often had to confront their own personal demons with alcoholism, sexual harassment, and racism. Another successful series was *L.A. Law,* which focused on attorneys and their relationships in a law firm. The action took place outside the courtroom and centered on their personal or professional lives. The series was true to form in depicting the blurred line between justice and the law; for example, plea bargaining may reveal the truth or obstruct justice. Vigilantes or freelance enforcers included those found on such popular series as *The A-Team, Knight Rider,* and *The Equalizer,* in which modern avengers went after evildoers in covert operations. These individuals defended the weak and innocent against violent criminals.

The situation comedy, or sitcom, began a rebirth with *The Cosby Show, Cheers,* and *Family Ties.* Television network executives began to look at demographic information that indicated that African American households watched more television than other groups. In 1988, it was found that black viewers watched television 10.6 hours daily while other groups watched an average of 7.3 hours per day. *The Cosby Show* was the first series in which the majority of the creative team and cast were black. The series premiered in 1984 and was a smash success from the very first episode. Both parents were professionals, a doctor and a lawyer, who offered an upbeat portrait of a black family in which the parents respected one another and nurtured their five children. The show often characterized the joys and tribulations of raising a large family and was subtle in its approach to improving race relations. By the late 1980's, irreverent comedies such as *Roseanne, Married . . . with Children,* and the animated series *The Simpsons* began to rule the airwaves. These sitcoms maintained a satirical edge to current issues and social problems in environments where the families were decidedly dysfunctional.

Another genre that started to emerge was reality show programming, which ran the gamut in regards to content. Some shows genuinely addressed adult topics on sensitive cultural issues that were informative to viewers, while other programs reverted to salacious Hollywood gossip found in the tabloids. Ratings for these programs proved extremely high and profitable to the cable networks. The daytime television talk show, with hosts such as Phil Donahue and Oprah Winfrey, began to replace documentaries. Some hosts, such as Geraldo Rivera and Morton Downey, Jr., used sensationalized scenarios, called trash TV, to boost ratings. The producers of these shows wanted to provoke their guests by goading them into argumentative confrontations that sometimes escalated into brawls or fistfights. The negativity that pervaded tabloid talk shows began to affect advertising in commercials, in which companies would malign a rival product using a cleverly disguised name. In presidential political campaigns, ads showed opponents veering away from discussing the issues in favor of personal attacks.

Impact In 1979, the average television viewing time was 29 hours per week. As the local number of cable systems began to grow in the early 1980's, new outlets for the television industry took center stage. Pay television altered the viewing habits of the American public. These technological innovations allowed network and cable executives to export American programs abroad as television truly became international in scope throughout the decade. The "Big

Three" networks that had supervised shows for more than forty years were finding it very difficult to compete with the interests of major corporations.

The deregulation that occurred during the Reagan years caused critics to take sides. Some argued that television had been democratized, that the public was able to take control and choose its own programming, while others contested that the quality of shows had declined because companies were concerned only with ratings and profit margins. These reviewers contended that the packaging of shows to audiences led to a rise in syndication rather than the development of creative shows. As a result, quality programming, such as programs geared toward children, news commentaries, documentaries, and fine arts, declined during the decade.

Further Reading

Abramson, Albert. *The History of Television, 1942 to 2000.* Jefferson, N.C.: McFarland, 2003. A retired network television engineer traces the technological innovations in the industry over sixty years. Focuses on the rise of the camcorder and digital prototypes for audio/video during the 1980's.

Barnouw, Erik. *Tube of Plenty: The Evolution of American Television.* 2d rev. ed. New York: Oxford University Press, 1990. Barnouw, professor emeritus of dramatic arts at Columbia University, addresses the development and impact of the communications revolution in radio and television from 1920 to 1990.

Comstock, George. *Television in America.* 2d ed. Newbury Park, Calif.: Sage Publications, 1991. Analyzes the social, political, and behavioral forces that shaped the programming habits of the American public. Discusses emerging technologies such as cable, satellites, and VCRs. Meant to be a text for courses in communication, journalism, and popular culture.

Doyle, Marc. *The Future of Television: A Global Overview of Programming, Advertising, Technology, and Growth.* Lincolnwood, Ill.: NTC Business Books, 1993. Focuses on the future of television programs, marketing, and policy in an era of mass globalization. Chapter 1 is an overview of the 1980's.

Feuer, Jane. *Seeing Through the Eighties: Television and Reaganism.* Durham, N.C.: Duke University Press, 1995. Delves into the relationship between politics, television programming, and viewing behavior during the Reagan administration.

Lichter, S. Robert, Linda S. Lichter, and Stanley Rothman. *Prime Time: How TV Portrays American Culture.* Washington, D.C.: Regnery, 1994. A comprehensive study on prime-time entertainment from 1950 to 1990, focusing on how Hollywood depicts changes in American society, with chapters on private lives, crime and punishment, the working class, and controversial issues.

MacDonald, J. Fred. *One Nation Under Television: The Rise and Decline of Network TV.* New York: Pantheon Books, 1990. Historical study of how the major networks rose to power and shaped viewer ratings until the introduction of cable television and home video substantially weakened their power in the 1980's.

Montgomery, Kathryn C. *Target, Prime Time: Advocacy Groups and the Struggle over Entertainment Television.* New York: Oxford University Press, 1989. Montgomery demonstrates how various advocacy groups shaped the messages and values found in prime-time television from the early 1970's to the mid-1980's.

Moorfoot, Rex. *Television in the Eighties: The Total Equation.* London: BBC, 1982. Examines the technological advancements occurring in the television industry in the early 1980's.

Gayla Koerting

■ Tennis

Definition Racket sport played in singles or pairs

Tennis experienced tremendous growth in the 1980's because of the influence of television coverage and the most successful players, including Martina Navratilova and John McEnroe. The professionals fueled the amateur popularity of the sport, and there was a significant rise in sales of tennis products.

The popularity of viewing top professional sports players on television gave a significant boost to the tennis industry in the 1980's. Television networks such as CBS, ESPN, HBO, NBC, and ABC provided year-round coverage of the major professional tournaments, adding to the fame and wealth of champion players. Amateur tennis players were influenced to purchase tennis rackets, shoes, and clothing that the champions used. In the early 1980's, the tennis racket itself underwent a transformation, as graphite, boron, aluminum, and titanium were introduced to make the rackets lighter and stronger than their wood and steel predecessors. The two most popular rackets were the Dunlop Max 200G, introduced in 1980, and the wide-body Wilson Profile, introduced in 1987.

During the decade, advances in nutrition and notions about physical conditioning influenced the

In 1981, tennis greats (from left) John McEnroe, Björn Borg, and Vitas Gerulaitis particpate in Gerulaitis's annual youth tennis clinic in New York City. (AP/Wide World Photos)

sport. Amateur and professional tennis players trained according to these research concepts to maximize their performance. One notable player, Martina Navratilova, literally transformed herself with diet and physical conditioning into the greatest female tennis player of the 1980's.

Players The four major professional tennis tournaments of the world (known as the grand slam tournaments) include the French, Australian, and U.S. Opens and Wimbledon. The best of the men's players of the early 1980's included Jimmy Connors, Björn Borg, and John McEnroe. Two of the greatest matches in the history of Wimbledon occurred in 1980 and 1981. In 1980, Borg defeated McEnroe in five sets to win Wimbledon, which included a thrilling fourth-set tiebreaker won by McEnroe eighteen points to sixteen. Two months later, McEnroe defeated Borg, again in five sets, to win the U.S. Open. In 1981, the two men met again in the finals at Wimbledon and the U.S. Open, with McEnroe winning both tournaments. The physical skills and psychological will exhibited by both players made these matches memorable, but McEnroe's anger and disrespectful behavior in those tournaments made headlines all over the world as well. McEnroe won Wimbledon in 1981, 1983, and 1984, and the U.S. Open in 1980 and 1981. Connors won Wimbledon in 1982 and the U.S. Open in 1982 and 1983. Later in the decade, the best of the male professionals included Ivan Lendl, Mats Wilander, Stefan Edberg, and Boris Becker. During the 1980's, Lendl won seven grand slam singles tournaments and finished second ten times. Wilander won seven grand slam singles tournaments and finished second four times. Edberg and Becker each won four grand slam singles titles. Becker was only seventeen years old when he won Wimbledon in 1985.

Among the women's competition, the 1980's is best known for the number of tournaments won by and the rivalry between Navratilova and Chris Evert (Evert-Lloyd). Evert won nine grand slam singles tournaments, was second ten times, and clearly was the public favorite. However, in terms of grand slam victories in singles, doubles, and mixed doubles, Navratilova was the greatest player, male or female, of the 1980's. She won fifteen grand slam singles titles, came in second ten times, and was ranked number one longer than Evert. Pam Shriver and Navratilova won twenty-one grand slam doubles tour-

naments during the 1980's, and Navratilova also won four mixed doubles grand slam tournaments. In 1985-1987, Navratilova was in the singles final in all eleven of the grand slam tournaments that she entered. A very rare achievement occurred in 1987, when she won the singles, doubles, and mixed doubles, all the available events, at the U.S. Open. Away from the tennis court, she received a lot of media attention for her public declaration of her lesbian identity. As a world-famous athlete and public figure, she handled the media attention with pride and poise and added awareness and public sensitivity to issues concerning equal rights and women's rights.

Another great female professional of the late 1980's was Steffi Graf of Germany, who won eight grand slam singles titles between 1987 and 1989. In 1988, she had one of the greatest years in the history of tennis, winning all four grand slam singles tournaments and even the gold medal at the 1988 Olympic Games. Historians refer to this accomplishment as the "golden slam."

Hall of Famers Many great players were inducted into the International Tennis Hall of Fame during the 1980's, including Ken Rosewall and Lew Hoad in 1980, Rod Laver in 1981, Charlotte Dod in 1983, Arthur Ashe in 1985, John Newcombe in 1986, and Billie Jean King and Björn Borg in 1987. Ashe, a three-time grand slam singles champion, is a special figure in sports history, as he is the greatest male African American tennis player of all time and was a leader of the world civil rights movement. He was especially active in was the antiapartheid movement in South Africa. He made world news headlines in 1988 when he announced that he had contracted human immunodeficiency virus (HIV) through blood transfusions during two major heart surgeries. The heterosexual Ashe's personal battle with acquired immunodeficiency syndrome (AIDS) increased world awareness about the disease and brought attention to the fact that it was not one to affect only homosexuals. Ashe also emphasized the importance of developing valid testing methods of donated blood.

Impact Tennis in the 1980's saw great performances by a number of stars, from the fiery John McEnroe to the greatest player of the decade, Martina Navratilova. Increased sports coverage by television networks as well as notable competition, such as that between Navratilova and Evert, and Borg and McEnroe, increased the popularity of the sport.

Further Reading

Collins, Bud. *Total Tennis, Revised: The Ultimate Tennis Encyclopedia.* Toronto: Sport Classic Books, 2003. Provides year-by-year (1919-2002) comprehensive statistics of the top professional players and the grand slam tournaments. Includes a biographical section of the best players.

McEnroe, John, and James Kaplan. *You Cannot Be Serious.* New York: Penguin Books, 2003. The tennis great reflects on his colorful professional career and personal life.

Parsons, John. *The Ultimate Encyclopedia of Tennis: The Definitive Illustrated Guide to World Tennis.* London: Carlton Books, 2007. Provides a history of the sport, its players, tournaments, and controversies.

Alan Prescott Peterson

See also McEnroe, John; Navratilova, Martina; Sports.

■ *Terminator, The*

Identification American science-fiction film
Director James Cameron (1954-   )
Date Released October 26, 1984

Representing a pessimistic view of technology, The Terminator *contrasted with the positive view of technology in the films of the original* Star Wars *trilogy and the* Star Trek: The Next Generation *television series. Coupling nuclear war and computerized defense systems with the emergence of intelligent computers, the film reflected the technological and political situation of the mid-1980's—the increasing presence of computers and President Ronald Reagan's Strategic Defense Initiative at the height of the Cold War.*

The story line of *The Terminator* (1984) focuses on a cyborg assassin (Arnold Schwarzenegger) created by Skynet, an artificially intelligent computer defense network that developed self-awareness and attempted to annihilate humanity by starting World War III. Skynet built cyborgs to infiltrate the few surviving camps of humans. The film's title character is sent back in time from the postapocalyptic world of 2029 to kill Sarah Connor (Linda Hamilton), who is to become the mother of the leader of the human rebellion. From the future, her son John sends Kyle Reese (Michael Biehn) to protect her from the human-like assassin.

Machine imagery pervades the film. Appearing frequently are machines such as household devices, including an answering machine that exhorts callers to be nice to it, motorcycles and trailer trucks, and an automated factory where Sarah manages to crush the terminator in a press. In a larger sense, this story reflects contemporary concerns about the progression from human dependence on machines to being dominated by them. The extreme masculine physique of the terminator represents military technology gone awry.

The film uses common science-fiction themes, notably artificial intelligence. The terminator acts in a conscious, purposive manner, yet its alien nature is reflected by the images of internal, decision-making screens. Furthermore, the terminator has no emotions and cannot be reasoned with. Another theme is time travel, including a variation of the grandfather paradox, as John Connor sends Reese back in time to impregnate Sarah and thus to become John's father. *The Terminator* garnered generally favorable reviews and became an unexpected sleeper hit. Shot on the relatively small budget of $6.5 million, it had collected $38.4 million by the end of its first run. During 1985, it was one of the most popular rental videos.

Impact *The Terminator* was the first major directing effort by James Cameron, who went on to direct other highly successful films (notably, 1997's *Titanic*). The film solidified the acting career of Schwarzenegger and also led to major roles for Hamilton and Biehn. Furthermore, it inspired a number of other science-fiction films, including *RoboCop* (1987).

Further Reading

Hollinger, Veronica, and Joan Gordon, eds. *Edging into the Future: Science Fiction and Contemporary Cultural Transformation.* Philadelphia: University of Pennsylvania Press, 2002.

Kozlovic, Anton Karl. "Technophobic Themes in Pre-1990 Computer Films." *Science as Culture* 12, no. 3 (2003): 3341-3372.

Telotte, J. P. *Replications: A Robotic History of the Science Fiction Film.* Urbana: University of Illinois Press, 1995.

Kristen L. Zacharias

See also *Blade Runner;* Computers; Cyberpunk literature; *Empire Strikes Back, The;* Film in the United

States; *RoboCop*; Robots; Schwarzenegger, Arnold; Science-fiction films; *Star Trek: The Next Generation*; Strategic Defense Initiative (SDI); *Tron*.

■ Terms of Endearment

Identification   American film
Director   James L. Brooks (1940-   )
Date   Released November 23, 1983

Successfully mixing sentiment and humor, the film provided a showcase for the principal actors and a mirror reflecting many of the preoccupations of the decade.

Terms of Endearment traces the life of a single mother, Aurora Greenway (Shirley MacLaine), as she raises her daughter Emma (Debra Winger), fights with her over her marriage (she hates her future son-in-law Flap Horton, played by Jeff Daniels) and her pregnancies (she has to face up to aging when she becomes a grandmother), and finally rec-

onciles with her as Emma succumbs to cancer (she must assume the responsibility for raising her three grandchildren). It is a relationship that does not gloss over the tensions of a single-parent household.

Living next door is womanizer Garrett Breedlove (Jack Nicholson), a former astronaut who gradually has to face his own aging and develops a relationship with Aurora despite her age and the fact that she becomes a grandmother—twice. American movies had been reluctant to portray romantic situations involving older actresses, and MacLaine established the first of her feisty older women roles in this film, a trademark she continued to exploit.

The emotional centerpiece of the film is the series of scenes showing the gradual deterioration of Emma as she fights her cancer. It is a sequence that culminates in the farewell scene between Emma and her two young sons and little daughter. Winger was nominated for an Academy Award for Best Actress, and although she did not win, her performance in these scenes was undoubtedly the reason the film

From left: James L. Brooks, Shirley MacLaine, and Jack Nicholson celebrate their Oscar victories for Terms of Endearment *at the April 9, 1984, Academy Awards ceremony.* (AP/Wide World Photos)

did so well at the Academy Awards. *Terms of Endearment* was something of a surprise hit in 1983 when it won a significant number of Oscars. The film beat out *The Big Chill, The Dresser, The Right Stuff,* and *Tender Mercies* for Best Picture and James L. Brooks, directing his first picture, won Best Director, beating out a formidable lineup of veterans: Bruce Beresford, Mike Nichols, Peter Yates, and even Ingmar Bergman. MacLaine won Best Actress and Nicholson won Best Supporting Actor. Brooks also won for Best Adapted Screenplay from Larry McMurtry's novel. A sequel, *The Evening Star* (1996), allowed MacLaine to reprise her eccentric character Aurora Greenway as she raises her grandchildren left behind when their mother died.

Impact *Terms of Endearment* struck a chord with movie audiences in the early 1980's with its depiction of romance between older characters Aurora Greenway and Garrett Breedlove, its exploration of a single-parent family, and its heartfelt rendering of the death of a young mother who must leave her children.

Further Reading

Evans, Peter William, and Celestion Deleyto, eds. *Terms of Endearment: Hollywood Romantic Comedy in the 1980's and 1990's.* Edinburgh: Edinburgh University Press, 1998.

McMurtry, Larry. *Terms of Endearment.* New York: Simon & Schuster, 1975.

Speidel, Constance. "Whose Terms of Endearment?" *Literature/Film Quarterly* 12, no. 4 (1984): 271-273.

Charles L. P. Silet

See also Abortion; Academy Awards; *Big Chill, The;* Feminism; Film in the United States; Nicholson, Jack.

■ Terrorism

Definition Acts of violence committed by individuals or groups seeking to influence public opinion or public policy

Although incidents of terrorism within the United States and Canada during the 1980's were fewer in number and overall effect than the two previous decades, several notable incidents occurred.

According to the Federal Bureau of Investigation (FBI), there were at least two hundred terrorist incidents in the United States during the 1980's; the largest single type of incident involved bombing, which made up seventy-eight of the incidents. Other types of incidents included armed robbery, a rocket attack, sniper attacks, arson and other property destruction, and assassinations. While some terrorist groups involved in these attacks had been active since the 1960's and 1970's, a few new organizations grabbed headlines with their armed activities, including the white supremacist Christian Identity and the neo-Nazi movement. In addition, certain leftist groups re-formed under different names and with different personnel.

Canadian Incidents Canada experienced fourteen acts of terrorism during the 1980's. Three were attributed to groups pushing for a Sikh nation separate from India. Three others were attributed to Armenian nationalists targeting Turkish government representatives. One incident was committed by a former U.S. Air Force officer protesting the visit of Pope John Paul II. The officer's bombing attack resulted in the deaths of three people in Montreal's Victoria Station. Another incident involved a man from the Canadian Armed Forces who was opposed to the Parti Québécois's desire for Quebec to secede from Canada. The man attacked the Quebec parliament building, killing three individuals. The anti-Castro group Omega 7 bombed the Cuban embassy in Montreal in 1980.

On October 14, 1982, the left-wing anarchist group Direct Action bombed a Toronto Litton factory that manufactured triggers for U.S. military cruise missiles. Direct Action was also responsible for the bombings of three Vancouver pornographic bookstores and a hydroelectric substation on Vancouver Island, British Columbia.

Although Canada was the site of far fewer incidents than the United States, the bombing of an airplane departing from Montreal Airport was one of the deadliest incidents of the decade. On June 23, 1985, Air India Flight 182 was flying over the Atlantic Ocean when a bomb exploded, killing all 329 people on board. Canadian police believed that the leader of the terrorist attack was Talwinder Singh Parmar, head of the militant Sikh separatist group Babbar Khalsa.

Domestic Organizations Foremost among terrorist organizations in terms of numbers of attacks were a number of groups fighting for the independence of Puerto Rico from the United States. The best known of these groups were the Fuerzas Armadas de Liberación Nacional (FALN), the Macheteros, and the Organization of Volunteers for the Puerto Rican Revolution. Although usually leftist in their politics, the groups' overriding concern was Puerto Rican independence. According to the FBI, these groups were responsible for eighty-eight of the known terrorist incidents in the United States during the 1980's. Their primary modus operandi was bombings and armed robberies. Other leftist groups involved in terrorism in the United States during this period included the May 19 Communist Organization; the Black Liberation Army (BLA), an offshoot of the defunct Black Panther Party; the United Freedom Front (UFF); the Armed Resistance Unit (ARU); and the Red Guerrilla Resistance. The UFF and ARU shared some members, and most observers believe that the Red Guerrilla Resistance was made up of members of the May 19 Communist Organization.

The militant Zionist group the Jewish Defense League (JDL) and its offshoot, the Jewish Underground, were also involved in terrorism during the 1980's. At least twenty acts of terrorism in the United States were attributed to the JDL. Many of these acts targeted Soviet diplomatic facilities and businesses because of Moscow's alleged mistreatment of its Jewish citizens. Other nations whose facilities were targeted by the JDL included Syria, Iran, and other Middle Eastern nations opposed to Israel. The actions were primarily bombings, including two bombs detonated at the Washington, D.C., office of the Soviet airline Aeroflot on February 21, 1982.

Offshoots of the left-wing Weather Underground were linked to one of the most newsworthy terrorist crimes in the early part of the decade. The incident involved an armored truck robbery that the May 19 Communist Organization carried out with the BLA on October 20, 1981, outside Nyack, New York. Two policemen and one BLA member died in the robbery and manhunt. Former Weather Underground members were also among the membership of the UFF and the ARU.

Right-wing groups involved in terror incidents included the Cuban exile group Omega 7. Most of the actions of the Omega 7 were bombings of diplomatic buildings owned by governments that had official relations with Cuba and businesses owned by Cubans unsympathetic to the anti-Castro exiles. At least thirty acts of terrorism committed in the United States during the decade were attributed to groups that the FBI labels as "anti-Castro Cuban." Most of the acts were carried out by this group. Omega 7 has an unusual past, as some of its members have links to the U.S. Central Intelligence Agency (CIA) that date back to the failed attempt by the U.S. government to overthrow the revolutionary government of Cuba in 1961.

The Order was a neo-Nazi organization dedicated to what members called the "preservation of the Caucasian race" and was active in 1983 and 1984. Members of the organization were involved in burning down a synagogue and a church, whose minister opposed them, and bombing a pornography shop. In addition, Order members were convicted of murdering Alan Berg, a Denver disc jockey opposed to the neo-Nazi doctrine; a policeman; and a fellow member whom they suspected of disclosing their activities. The most spectacular of the group's actions was the $3.7 million robbery of a Brink's armored truck.

Two other right-wing terrorist organizations were The Covenant, the Sword and the Arm of the Lord (CSA) and the Order II. CSA is known to have committed two acts of arson in 1983, setting fire to a Jewish community center and to a church that supported gay rights. In addition, the group set off an explosive near a natural gas pipeline in an attempt to disrupt natural gas distribution throughout the Midwest.

The Order II was organized after Order leader Robert Jay Mathews was killed in a shootout with FBI agents on Whidbey Island, Washington. Based in Idaho near Richard Butler's Aryan Nations church compound, this group was responsible for seven bombings. All seven members of the group were arrested during an attempt to rob three banks simultaneously.

Organizations with Foreign Links In the United States, several terrorist acts were committed by groups with grievances tangentially related to the U.S. government, including the Armenian Revolutionary Army and Justice Commandos for the Armenian Genocide. These two groups, believed by most authorities to be composed of the same members, supported Armenian independence and sought justice for the early twentieth century Armenian genocide carried out by Turkey. Acts of terrorism by the

Police at the scene of the notorious Brinks armored truck robbery of 1981. The robbery, carried out by left-wing extremists, resulted in the deaths of two police officers and one member of the Black Liberation Army. (AP/Wide World Photos)

two groups included the August 27, 1982, assassination of the Turkish military attaché to Canada in Ottawa. This murder was preceded by the assassinations of the Turkish consul general in Los Angeles, California, on January 28, and the honorary Turkish consul general of New England in Somerville, Massachusetts, on May 4. Other incidents claimed by these organizations were bombing attacks on shops owned by Turkish government officials and Turkish diplomatic facilities.

A Croatian separatist organization known as the Croatian Freedom Fighters was responsible for four bombings in 1980 and 1981, including a pipe bombing of the New York State Supreme Court building in Manhattan on January 23, 1981, two attacks on businesses owned by Yugoslavian officials, and a car bomb targeting the Washington, D.C., home of Yugoslavia's chargé d'affaires.

An unusual terrorist incident occurred in Washington, D.C., on August 7, 1981, when twenty-four members of the People's Mujahideen of Iran invaded the Iranian interests section of the Algerian embassy and took six people hostage. The siege lasted one hour. An individual act of terrorism occurred in Richmond, Virginia, on September 14, 1988, when a young armed Lebanese man frustrated with the civil war in his country took over a military recruiting office and demanded that a statement about the Lebanese situation be read over two local radio stations. He surrendered peacefully after six hours.

Impact   On November 7, 1983, the U.S. Senate was bombed by the ARU. Though no one was injured in the attack, the reaction by officials in Washington was quick. Security was heightened around government buildings, and federal funding increased for agencies involved in security and the surveillance of political activists of all persuasions. Much of the government reaction was related to recent terrorist incidents overseas (in particular the October 23 bombing of Marine barracks in Beirut that killed 241 American servicemen), especially those committed by or attributed to Palestinian and Islamic groups, some of whom were believed to be sponsored by the governments of Libya and Iran. Security enhancements included the erection of concrete barriers around government buildings, the curtailing of parking around potential targets, and enhanced identification requirements for entrance to government buildings, airports, and other locations that might attract terrorists. Federal law enforcement agencies increased efforts to pass tougher legislation that would focus on prosecuting terrorists and their supporters. The primary change in Canadian governmental responses to terrorism was the creation of the Canadian Security Intelligence Service (CSIS), an agency involved in gathering intelligence on perceived threats to Canadian security.

Further Reading

Burns, Vincent, and Kate Dempsey Peterson, eds. *Terrorism: A Documentary and Reference Guide.* Westport, Conn.: Greenwood Press, 2005. An easy-to-use account of the past forty years of terrorism in the United States, with particular emphasis on the rise of terrorism related to the Middle East. The text contains more than seventy essays and documents discussing and detailing the issue of terrorism and the United States.

Hansen, Ann. *Direct Action: Memoirs of an Urban Guerrilla.* Oakland, Calif.: AK Press, 2002. A first-person account by one of the members of the Canadian leftist anarchist group convicted of bombing the Litton Systems factory in Toronto.

Woodger, Elin, and David F. Burg. *The 1980's.* New York: Facts On File, 2006. An encyclopedic survey of the events of the 1980's written for a high school audience.

Ron Jacobs

See also Air India Flight 182 bombing; Anderson, Terry; Beirut bombings; Berg, Alan; Canadian caper; Crime; Iranian hostage crisis; Klinghoffer, Leon; Libya bombing; Pan Am Flight 103 bombing; Skinheads and neo-Nazis; Tylenol murders; U.S. Senate bombing; West Berlin discotheque bombing.

■ Theater

Definition   Significant stage presentations on Broadway and across the United States

Major trends in theater, such as issues concerning women's rights and gay and lesbian rights, came to fruition in the 1980's. Professional theater strengthened its position across the United States, and there emerged new playwrights, actors, directors, and designers who included women, African Americans, and Asian Americans.

The 1980's saw the maturation and realization of trends in American theater that had been developing in the past two decades. Among the most important of these were the emergence of significant female, Asian American, and African American theatrical artists and the recognition of the issues surrounding gay and lesbian individuals in American society. Most important, perhaps, was the strengthening of professional theater across the United States, so that American theater was no longer simply Broadway theater.

Theaters Across the United States   Until the 1960's, theater in the United States meant almost exclusively theater on Broadway, but a movement away from Broadway commenced in that decade and reached maturation in the 1980's. Off-Broadway theaters not only were located away from Times Square playhouses but also were smaller in seating capacity. Thus, the Actors' Equity Association allowed the performers to be paid less than their Broadway counterparts. In Off-Broadway houses, such as the Roundabout Theatre and the Manhattan Theatre Club, new and experimental works were performed, as were presentations by the Pan Asian Repertory Theatre and the Negro Ensemble Company.

Soon, playhouses seating one hundred or less were applying for even lower Actors' Equity Association rates, and these theaters took the designation Off-Off-Broadway. Among the interesting Off-Off-Broadway theaters was Ellen Stewart's La MaMa Experimental Theatre Club, which in the 1980's presented new experimental comedy and performance art. By the 1980's, there were important nonprofit professional repertory theaters across the United States, such as the Yale Repertory Theatre, the American Repertory Theatre at Harvard, the Mark Taper Forum in Los Angeles, the Actors Theatre of Louisville, Kentucky, and even two repertory theaters in

Atlanta, Georgia: the Alliance Theatre and Theatre in the Square. At the end of the decade, more than two hundred such theaters existed, and many of the playwrights who would become known as leaders in their field began in regional or Off-Broadway and Off-Off Broadway theaters. For example, Beth Henley's *Crimes of the Heart* (pr. 1979), winner of the 1981 Pulitzer Prize for Drama, premiered at the Actors Theatre of Louisville before moving to Broadway.

Women Playwrights and Feminist Theater Chief among those who commenced their careers outside Broadway were a number of important female playwrights in addition to Henley—such as Marsha Norman, Tina Howe, and Wendy Wasserstein—two of whom won the Pulitzer Prize for Drama during the 1980's: Norman, for *'night Mother* (pr. 1983), and Wasserstein, for *The Heidi Chronicles* (pr. 1988). In 1983, Howe won a collective Obie Award, the Off-Broadway award, for her overall contribution to dramatic literature. In various ways, these playwrights and other women playwrights of the decade, such as two-time Obie Award-winner Corinne Jacker, took up issues involved in the lives of women and in the emerging women's rights movement.

María Irene Fornés's *The Conduct of Life* (pr. 1985) examined Chicano experiences as women attempted to deal with male dominance. To explore the ongoing interest in women's rights, the Women's Experimental Theatre presented plays investigating the role pf women in Western patriarchal families. In 1980, Lois Weaver and Peggy Shaw introduced *Split Britches*, based on the lives of Weaver's aunts in the Virginia mountains, at the Women's One World Festival of feminist theater held in New York City. In 1982, the Split Britches Company founded the Women's One World (WOW) Café in New York City, dedicated to producing works by and for women. Along with collaborator Deb Margolin, the Split Britches Company presented several important feminist plays at WOW Café during the 1980's. Women also claimed leadership in other ways. In 1982, Ellen Burstyn was elected the first female president of the Actors' Equity Association, followed by Colleen Dewhurst in 1985. In the same year, Heidi Landesman became the first female designer to win a Tony Award, for her scenery for *Big River* (pr. 1985).

African Americans and Asian Americans In addition to the emerging women playwrights, the 1980's saw the rise of two important Asian American playwrights: Philip Kan Gotanda, author of such works as *Yankee Dawg You Die* (pr. 1989), and David Henry Hwang, who won the 1988 Tony Award for the Broadway hit *M. Butterfly*. African American dramatists were led into the 1980's by Ntozake Shange, August Wilson, and Charles Fuller, winner of the 1982 Pulitzer Prize for Drama for *A Soldier's Play* (pr. 1981). It is August Wilson, whose work was first produced by Yale Repertory Theatre under the direction of Lloyd Richards, whom many consider to be the most significant playwright of contemporary theater. In 1987, he won the Pulitzer Prize for Drama for *Fences* (pr. 1985), starring Tony Award-winner James Earl Jones. Wilson's other plays of the 1980's include *Ma Rainey's Black Bottom* (pr. 1982), *The Piano Lesson* (pr. 1987), and *Joe Turner's Come and Gone* (pr. 1988), all of which continue to be produced throughout the United States.

Gay and Lesbian Issues Feminist theater groups such as Split Britches and WOW Café considered issues of lesbianism, as in the WOW Café 1985 productions of Alice Forrester's *Heart of the Scorpion* (pr. 1984) and Holly Hughes' *The Well of Horniness* (pr. 1985). In 1983, Harvey Fierstein would win the Pulitzer Prize for Drama for *Torch Song Trilogy* (pr. 1982), three one-act plays examining homosexual issues through the evolving life of a Jewish drag queen. That year also saw the hit drag musical *La Cage aux Folles*, based on the 1973 French play by Jean Poiret. Ultimately, however, more serious presentations of gay men would be made, as in Langford Wilson's *Burn This* (pr. 1987). The gay experience turned extremely dark in the 1980's with the advance of the AIDS epidemic, which is treated seriously in 1985 in William F. Hoffman's drama *As Is* and Larry Kramer's *The Normal Heart*.

Musical Theater The most interesting phenomenon in musical theater of the 1980's was the maturation of a type of artist developed in the 1970's: the director-choreographer. It was this individual who created both the dance and the overall artistic statement of the musical, often including the story line as well. When the latter was the case, the work was referred to as a "concept musical," perhaps best exemplified by *A Chorus Line*, created by Michael Bennett in 1975, which ran throughout the 1980's and was revived in the early twenty-first century. Bennett created *Dreamgirls* (pr. 1981) and *The Tap Dance Kid* (pr. 1983). He was preceded as a director-choreographer by the famous Bob Fosse, creator of *Chicago* (pr. 1975), whose concept musical *Big Deal* opened in 1986.

Another such artist was Tommy Tune, who achieved top rank as a director-choreographer with *Nine* (pr. 1982) and followed with the hit *Grand Hotel* (pr. 1989). Not known as a choreographer but as a frontline director of musical theater was Hal Prince. Prince became well known with his work on concept musicals he produced in the 1970's with the composer-lyricist Stephen Sondheim. *Sweeney Todd*, perhaps their best-known work, starring Angela Lansbury, opened in 1979 and ran throughout the 1980's. Their last joint production was *Merrily We Roll Along* (pr. 1981). In the 1980's, Prince devoted himself to importing and staging English musicals such as Andrew Lloyd Webber's *The Phantom of the Opera* (pr. 1986).

Indeed, it was the English import that came to dominate the American musical theater scene in the late 1980's. In addition to *The Phantom of the Opera*, which became the longest-running musical in Broadway history, was Lloyd Webber's *Cats*, inspired by T. S. Eliot's *Old Possum's Book of Practical Cats* (1939), which opened in the United States in 1982 and became the second-longest-running musical in Broadway history.

New and Established Theater Artists   David Mamet, who continues to be an important dramatist in the early twenty-first century, was introduced in the 1980's. Mamet's powerful work on the lack of ethics of some businessmen, *Glengarry Glen Ross*, won the 1984 Pulitzer Prize for Drama. He followed in 1988 with *Speed-the-Plow*. Mamet was joined by emerging playwrights Langford Wilson and A. R. Gurney. Gurney contributed five plays during the 1980's, his two most successful being *The Dining Room* (pr. 1981) and *Love Letters* (pr. 1988). Wilson opened the 1980's with the Pulitzer Prize for Drama for *Talley's Folly* (pr. 1979). In addition to *Angel's Fall* (pr. 1983) and *Burn This*, his *Hot L Baltimore* (pr. 1973) ran throughout the decade.

Sam Shepard, Edward Albee, and Neil Simon were a trio of established playwrights who found success in the 1980's. Shepard had two important 1980's plays, *True West* (pr. 1980) and *A Lie of the Mind* (pr. 1985). Albee contributed *Marriage Play* (pr. 1987), and Simon had successes with *They're Playing Our Song* (pr. 1979), *Brighton Beach Memoirs* (pr. 1983),

Biloxi Blues (pr. 1985), and *Broadway Bound* (pr. 1986). In speaking of established playwrights, it should be noted that one of the twentieth century's most prominent American dramatists, Tennessee Williams, died in 1983.

The number of talented new actors on Broadway in the 1980's was impressive. They included Kevin Kline, Bernadette Peters, Mandy Patinkin, Glenn Close, Stockard Channing, and Swoosie Kurtz, many of whom went on to distinguished film careers. Joining these stars were three impressive talents who returned from filmmaking to grace Broadway productions: Meryl Streep, Kathleen Turner, and Dustin Hoffman. In addition to performers, there emerged new designers to join the ranks of established artists. Freddy Wittop, famed for his costume designs for *Hello, Dolly!* (pr. 1964), made his last contribution to Broadway in 1986's *The Three Musketeers*. His reins were taken up by William Ivey Long, who received the 1982 Tony Award for his costume designs for *Nine*. Long was joined by scene designer John Lee Beatty, who, by the mid-1980's, had designs for six shows running simultaneously. Broadway designers were not all men, however. Scenery and costume designer Heidi Landesman contributed designs for four Broadway productions.

Alternative Theater   In addition to professional productions in New York City and across the United States, interesting forms of alternative theater matured during the 1980's. The best-known director creating alternative theater is Robert Wilson, who mixes various forms of media and live theater. In 1985, he moved his work *CIVIL warS* from Europe to the United States. Wilson's works do not have plots, and they take place in slow-motion so that the sense of time is altered and the audience is assaulted with nonstop images and sound effects. Another aspect of alternative theater involves performers who spend an entire evening presenting autobiographical information. Such artists include Laurie Anderson, Spalding Gray, Lily Tomlin, and Whoopi Goldberg. Some performance artists went beyond autobiography and included the audience in their work. This technique might range from chatting to traditional song and dance to dangerous activity such as cutting the artist with a knife or sticking him or her with pins. An important alternative theater, the Mabou Mimes, presented *Dead End Kids: A History of Nuclear Power* in 1980. The production intermixes text, such as scientists' diaries, with government films and excerpts from opera and night club acts to present a surrealistic image of atomic nightmares. Another such group presenting surrealistic productions was Richard Foreman's Ontological-Hysteric Theatre, which offered four productions in the 1980's.

Impact The 1980's signaled a coming of age of the theater in the United States. Gay and lesbian issues and the matter of women's rights were thoroughly and openly explored. Female playwrights and designers made considerable impact, as did African and Asian American artists. New writers, performers, and other theater artists appeared who would lead the theater into the twenty-first century. Moreover, successful professional theaters were located not only Off-Broadway but also in most major U.S. cities.

Further Reading

Brockett, Oscar G., and Franklin J. Hildy. *History of the Theatre.* 9th ed. Boston: Allyn & Bacon, 2002. An excellent history of the theater from its beginnings, with a general section on theater in the United States since 1968.

Wilmeth, Don B., and Christopher Bigsby, eds. *Post-World War II to the 1990's.* Vol. 3 in *The Cambridge History of American Theatre.* New York: Cambridge University Press, 2000. A collection of essays by recognized experts detailing every aspect of American theater since the 1940's.

Wilmeth, Don B., and Tice L. Miller, eds. *The Cambridge Guide to American Theatre.* New York: Cambridge University Press, 1993. Contains more than two thousand entries covering people, places, venues, and subject matter from the beginnings of American theater to the early 1990's.

August W. Staub

See also African Americans; AIDS epidemic; Art movements; Asian Americans; Broadway musicals; *Heidi Chronicles, The*; Close, Glenn; Feminism; Henley, Beth; Hoffman, Dustin; Homosexuality and gay rights; Hwang, David Henry; Literature in Canada; Literature in the United States; Mamet, David; Performance art; *Phantom of the Opera, The*; Shepard, Sam; Streep, Meryl; *Torch Song Trilogy*; Turner, Kathleen; Wilson, August.

■ Third Wave, The

Identification The second book in a trilogy on the process, directions, and control of technological and social changes
Author Alvin Toffler (1928-   )
Date Published in 1980

At a time of bewildering changes and societal upheavals, Toffler argued that industrialized countries were in the birth throes of a new knowledge-based civilization.

In 1970, Alvin Toffler published *Future Shock*, whose depiction of individuals and organizations overwhelmed by accelerating technological and societal changes helped to define the 1970's, and in 1990 he published *Powershift*, in which he foretold a future in which companies as well as countries would split into opposing power centers based on different "wealth creation systems." Sandwiched between these two books was *The Third Wave*, in which he expanded and deepened ideas he had introduced in *Future Shock*, and in which he prepared the ground for the changes in power structures that he analyzed in *Powershift*. The primary focus of *The Third Wave* is on a new civilization that he foresaw emerging out of industrial civilization. In *Future Shock*, he called this new civilization "super-industrial society," but in his new book he eschewed this term for the "Third Wave." He was not the first to use the metaphor of a wave for radical societal change, but he claimed that he was the first to apply it to the civilizational shift occurring in the 1980's.

According to Toffler's framework, the "First Wave" began about ten thousand years ago when societies based on domesticated plants and animals replaced hunter-gatherer cultures. The "Second Wave" is Toffler's term for what traditional historians have called the Industrial Revolution, associated with the mass production, mass distribution, and mass consumption of goods. It took thousands of years for the First Wave to decline, whereas the Second Wave played itself out in about three hundred years (1650 to 1950). Toffler believes that the Third Wave will grow, crest, and decline in several decades rather than centuries or millenniums. Humans in the 1980's had difficulty perceiving this Third Wave because they were not yet in it but in a transition between the Second and Third Waves. Consequently, Toffler's description of the Third Wave is more foretelling than observing, though he does extrapolate from his knowledge of contemporary cultures at the dawn of the 1980's.

What will the world look like after this global revolution is complete? New ways of life will exist, fueled by diversified, renewable energy sources. The customized production and distribution of goods and services will replace assembly lines and corporate control of marketing. Communications will be "demassified" and replaced by person-to-person contacts via computers. The nuclear family will be enhanced by a kaleidoscopic variety of new and different interpersonal relationships. Even human identity will change, for Third Wave societies will be more heterogeneous than Second Wave societies, with many varying racial, ethnic, and religious subgroupings. People who readily adapt to changes will prosper in Third Wave economies. New forms of political organization will arise that transcend the traditional nation-state. Finally, monetary wealth will be superseded by knowledge as the determinant of power, and this theme would be extensively developed in the last book of Toffler's trilogy.

Impact Unlike many social critics and science-fiction writers, Toffler was optimistic that accelerating scientific, technological, economic, and cultural changes would, on the whole, be liberating and beneficial for humanity, and he was prescient about the role that knowledge would play in a future information age. Like *Future Shock*, *The Third Wave* was a worldwide best seller and influenced many people and organizations. For example, the book had a direct influence on such American politicians as Newt Gingrich and on American military leaders who embraced such Third Wave doctrines as flexibility and decentralization. The book also influenced liberation movements in Poland and China. Toffler's book also affected analysts who were hypothesizing a "Fourth Wave" associated either with "ecoglobalism" or the human conquest of outer space, but he himself stated that his trilogy was complete, with no Fourth Wave analysis to come.

Further Reading

Toffler, Alvin. *Future Shock*. New York: Random House, 1970.

_____. *Powershift: Knowledge, Wealth, and Violence at the Edge of the Twenty-First Century*. New York: Bantam Books, 1990.

Toffler, Alvin, and Heidi Toffler. *Creating a New Civilization: The Politics of the Third Wave*. Atlanta: Turner, 1995.

Robert J. Paradowski

See also Agriculture in the United States; Alternative medicine; Business and the economy in the United States; Computers; Education in the United States; Europe and North America; Genetics research; Information age; Inventions; Science and technology.

■ *thirtysomething*

Identification   American television drama
Date   Aired from 1987 to 1991

With its sensitive writing and introspective performances, thirtysomething *focused on a group of baby boomers as they dealt with issues intrinsic to growing up. Considered overindulgent by some and groundbreakingly honest by others, the show was the first television drama of its kind.*

Married actors Ken Olin and Patricia Wettig, whose characters are married to other characters on thirtysomething, *arrive at the 1988 Emmy Awards, where Wettig won an Emmy as Best Supporting Actress in a drama series for her work on the show.* (AP/ Wide World Photos)

Creators Edward Zwick and Marshall Herskovitz peopled their fictional Philadelphia with seven main characters: Michael Steadman (played by Ken Olin), the sensitive Jewish advertising executive always trying to make sense of his world and become a better man; Hope Murdoch Steadman (Mel Harris), his Protestant wife, struggling with first-time child rearing; Elliot Weston (Timothy Busfield), Michael's business partner whose perpetual selfishness nearly destroys his marriage and forces him to change his life; Nancy Krieger Weston (Patricia Wettig), Elliot's wife, who discovers, through their separation, her new career as an artist and ultimately her cancer and her identity separate from her family; Melissa Steadman (Melanie Mayron), Michael's photographer cousin who is continually in and out of therapy, trying to work out her issues with men; Ellyn Warren (Polly Draper), Hope's best friend from high school who has chosen her career over a family life; and Gary Shepherd (Peter Horton), Michael's hippie college friend, now a college English professor, who criticizes the bourgeois lives of his friends while refusing to grow up.

The lives and loves of these seven characters formed the plot of the show for the four seasons it aired on the American Broadcasting Company (ABC). The writing on the show, touted by some critics as some of the best writing ever seen on television nd criticized by others for being either too sophisticated or too "whiny," earned the show Emmy nominations for each year it was on the air, two of which it won. The show also garnered numerous nominations and wins in acting, directing, and technical categories. *Thirtysomething* tackled several serious topical issues not previously featured on network television, including homosexuality, AIDS, second-wave feminism, divorce, and a long and detailed look at cancer. It also treated religion, sex, parenting, and friendship as the most important parts of a person's life, things that require profound and constant attention.

Impact Though it aired only for four seasons, *thirtysomething* had a lasting impact on television and culture. The show focused on average people dealing with normal life events, a turn in television culture viewed by some as overindulgent and by others as the first move into making television a more serious and profound medium.

Further Reading

Heide, Margaret J. *Television Culture and Women's Lives: "Thirtysomething" and the Contradictions of Gender.* Philadelphia: University of Pennsylvania Press, 1995.

Thompson, Richard. *Television's Second Golden Age.* Syracuse, N.Y.: Syracuse University Press, 1997.

Lily Neilan Corwin

See also AIDS epidemic; *Big Chill, The*; Feminism; Homosexuality and gay rights; Jewish Americans; Marriage and divorce; Religion and spirituality in the United States; Television; Yuppies.

■ This Is Spiñal Tap

Identification American comedy film
Director Rob Reiner (1945-   )
Date Released March 2, 1984

Reiner's debut independent film was one of the first "mockumentaries," a deadpan, right-on-target satire on the excesses and outright silliness of the heavy metal rock-and-roll scene of the 1980's.

In the mock documentary *This Is Spiñal Tap*, Rob Reiner plays director Marty DiBergi, who is making a documentary concert film on the heavy metal group Spiñal Tap, distinguished as "one of England's loudest bands." The band was supposedly formed in 1976 and is making a comeback tour across the United States in 1982. The film pretends to be a rock documentary (like Martin Scorsese's 1978 *The Last Waltz*, about the last concert of the Band, or Michael Lindsay-Hogg's 1970 *Let It Be*, about the impending breakup of the Beatles) but portrays the stupidity, hedonism, and blind following of rock bands of this era, combining the satiric targets of early heavy metal bands such as Led Zeppelin and Black Sabbath and later 1980's glam rock and theatrical metal bands such as Kiss, Megadeth, W.A.S.P., and Mötley Crüe.

The film's three lead actors, Christopher Guest, Michael McKean, and Harry Shearer, helped Reiner script and improvise the scenes, and the three also helped compose the music they played in the film. The first half of the film accurately pokes fun at the musical styles the band goes through, the television media spots, the difficulty of finding hotel accommodations on the road (or top billing at gigs), and the small-minded and self-important record industry people. Though the second half of the film recounts the tour's crash and the band's disintegration, it also warmly tells a story of friendship, change, soul searching, and final reunion. The always-in-character acting style, something like "the method" mixed with deadpan comic improvisation, derives from Peter Sellers's style of acting in *Dr. Strangelove* (1964) or *Being There* (1979) and Andy Kaufman's television spots on the comedy variety show *Saturday Night Live* and foreshadows Sacha Baron Cohen in the film *Borat* (2006).

Impact Although Reiner later directed other successful comedies such as *The Princess Bride* (1987) and *When Harry Met Sally . . .* (1989), *This Is SpiñalTap* spawned a series of "reality" docucomedies, including a *Return of Spiñal Tap* reunion concert film in 1992. In fact, the three lead actors, Guest, McKean, and Shearer, along with comedians Eugene Levy and Fred Willard, later starred in other mockumentaries directed by Guest: *Waiting for Guffman* (1996), about a local theater group; *Best in Show* (2000), about dog shows; *A Mighty Wind* (2003), about nearly forgotten folk singers; and *For Your Consideration* (2006), about Hollywood actors and awards.

Further Reading

French, Karl, ed. *This Is Spiñal Tap: Official Companion.* New York: Bloomsbury, 2000.

Maslin, Janet. "Film: *This Is Spiñal Tap,* a Mock Documentary." *The New York Times,* March 2, 1984.

Occhiogrosso, Peter. *Inside SpiñalTap.* New York: Arbor House, 1985.

Joseph Francavilla

See also Comedians; Film in the United States; Heavy metal; Mötley Crüe; *When Harry Met Sally . . . .*

From left: Michael McKean, Harry Shearer, and Christopher Guest as Spiñal Tap. (Hulton Archive/Getty Images)

■ Thomas, Isiah

Identification Hall of Fame professional basketball player
Born April 30, 1961; Chicago, Illinois

Thomas became a superstar NBA player during the 1980's, leading the Detroit Pistons to become one of the league's top teams and finally winning a national championship near the end of the decade.

After leading Indiana University to the National Collegiate Athletic Association (NCAA) Championship in 1981, Isiah Thomas signed a contract to play in the National Basketball Association (NBA) for the Detroit Pistons. In his first season with Detroit, Thomas was a member of the Eastern All-Stars and was also named to the NBA All-Rookie Team. In the 1983-1984 season, Thomas led the Pistons into the NBA playoffs, where they were eliminated by the New York Knicks. Thomas then helped the Pistons reach the Eastern Conference semifinals against the Boston Celtics in 1985, where they lost in six games.

During the 1986-1987 NBA campaign, Thomas led the Pistons to the Eastern Conference finals, where they were again eliminated by Larry Bird and the Celtics. In 1988, Detroit made it to the NBA finals for the first time in franchise history. Although Thomas played well, defeat came at the hands of Magic Johnson and the Los Angeles Lakers. In the 1988-1989 season, Thomas guided the Pistons to a 63-19 regular season record and again into the NBA finals. Led by Thomas, the Pistons became NBA champions, prevailing over the Lakers. During the 1989-1990 campaign, Thomas again led the Pistons to the NBA championship by defeating the Lakers in four straight games. Thomas was named the NBA Finals Most Valuable Player (MVP).

During his illustrious NBA career from 1981 to 1994, Thomas averaged 19.2 points per game; re-

Detroit Piston Isiah Thomas shoots over the head of Chicago Bull Ronnie Lester during a regular-season game on January 12, 1982. (AP/Wide World Photos)

corded a .452 field goal percentage, a .759 free throw percentage, 9,061 assists, and 1,861 steals; and shot .290 from beyond the three-point line. He was named an NBA All-Star twelve times, a member of the All-NBA First Team three times, and a member of the All-NBA Second Team twice. Thomas was named the NBA All-Star Game MVP in 1984 and again in 1986.

Impact   Thomas was one of the best smaller men to play in the NBA. He was known for his superior dribbling ability, his accurate passing, his uncanny ability to score on drives to the basket, and his scrappy, aggressive play. Considered to be one of the greatest players to ever play for the Pistons, his jersey number, 11, was retired by the Detroit franchise when Thomas retired from the NBA. In 1987, Thomas was awarded the J. Walter Kennedy Citizenship Award.

Further Reading

Challen, Paul. *The Book of Isiah: The Rise of a Basketball Legend.* Toronto: ECW Press, 2004.

Kramer, Sydelle A. *Basketball's Greatest Players.* New York: Random House, 1997.

Thomas, Isiah. *The Fundamentals: Eight Plays for Winning the Games of Business and Life.* New York: Collins, 2002.

Alvin K. Benson

See also   Basketball; Bird, Larry; Johnson, Magic; Sports.

■ *Thompson v. Oklahoma*

Identification   U.S. Supreme Court decision
Date   Decided on June 29, 1988

The Court's ruling in Thompson v. Oklahoma *abolished the death penalty for convicts who were aged fifteen or younger at the time they committed their crimes. Capital punishment remained legal for minors older than fifteen.*

When he was only fifteen years old, William W. Thompson participated in a brutal murder and was consequently sentenced to death by the State of Oklahoma. The Oklahoma Court of Criminal Appeals supported the trial court's decision, and the case was appealed to the U.S. Supreme Court. In a 5-3 decision (including a four-justice plurality and a separate concurring opinion), Thompson was spared the death penalty. The plurality opinion, written by John Paul Stevens, based its reasoning upon the "evolving standards of decency of society." The dissent, written by Antonin Scalia, could not dismiss the notion of a minor potentially being mature and responsible enough for a crime to warrant state execution. Sandra Day O'Connor cast the deciding vote: She wrote in her concurring opinion that Thompson could not be executed, because the Oklahoma law establishing the death penalty for murder did not specify a minimum age of eligibility for receiving that penalty.

The legal significance of the case was that capital punishment could no longer be applied to those criminals who were aged fifteen or younger during the commission of their crime. Opponents of the death penalty have historically pursued so-called death penalty exception cases. These are controversial cases in which a characteristic of the accused murderer could potentially negate the prosecution's attempt to seek death on behalf of the state. For instance, the 2002 *Atkins v. Virginia* case established that mentally retarded offenders could not be executed. Typically these "exception" arguments are supported by the Eighth Amendment's ban on "cruel and unusual punishment." As in the *Atkins* case, *Thompson* was argued on Eighth Amendment grounds and Fourteenth Amendment grounds. Executing a fifteen-year-old was found to be cruel and unusual, and the Fourteenth Amendment applied this clause of the Eighth Amendment to the states.

Impact The larger societal issue that the *Thompson* case raised was the appropriateness of the state-sanctioned execution of minors. Under the legal concept of *parens patriae*, juveniles have traditionally been treated with different rights and obligations than adults. Though this concept has been variously interpreted, it was not unusual for the American justice system to treat children as adults in cases of perpetrating murder. This practice met with both international disdain, as the United States was one of the few countries to permit the practice, and ire among the country's voters. The *Thompson* case was the first to limit the practice, hence saving minors fifteen years and younger from the death penalty. This finding was not only popular but also supported by contemporary psychiatric evidence on the reduced culpability of minors resulting from the incomplete maturation of the adolescent brain. However, the execution of sixteen- and seventeen-year-olds continued after *Thompson*.

Further Reading

Fagan, Jeffrey. "Atkins, Adolescences, and the Maturity Heuristic: Rationales for a Categorical Exemption for Juveniles from Capital Punishment." *New Mexico Law Review* 33 (Spring, 2003): 207-254.

Skovron, Sandra Evans, Joseph E. Scott, and Francis T. Cullen. "The Death Penalty for Juveniles: An Assessment of Public Support." *Crime and Delinquency* 35, no. 4 (1989): 546-561.

R. Matthew Beverlin

See also Crime; Supreme Court decisions.

■ Times Beach dioxin scare

The Event Pollution incident destroys a town
Date 1982-1997
Place Times Beach, Missouri

Dioxin spraying of Times Beach, population 2,240, made it one of the most toxic areas in the United States. The town was so polluted that the U.S. government purchased the entire town and evacuated its residents.

During the late 1960's and early 1970's, Russell Bliss, a waste hauler, was hired to oil the dusty roads and horse arenas of Times Beach, Missouri, twenty-five miles southwest of St. Louis, near Interstate 44. Not knowing it was toxic, on May 26, 1971, Bliss mixed carcinogenic dioxin-contaminated waste with two thousand gallons of oil. He sprayed the contaminated oil on the town's roads.

During 1982, more than ten years later, the Environmental Protection Agency (EPA) took soil samples at various sites in Missouri to test for dioxin levels and found extremely high levels in the soil at Times Beach. The 2,240 citizens of Times Beach discovered that they were sitting on one of the most toxic patches of earth in the United States. In February, 1983, the EPA announced plans to purchase the entire town for almost $33 million in Superfund moneys and sealed it off. The deserted town was listed as a Superfund site and awaited cleanup. The cleanup would occur in the next decade, during which dioxin-contaminated materials would be incinerated, spreading the dioxin into the atmosphere and dispersing it across the planet.

Impact The Times Beach dioxin scare brought further attention to the toxic substances contaminating portions of the country and the planet. It provided some impetus to environmental activists, and it increased the growing sense during the 1980's that the world was a dangerous place, largely as a result of human activity.

Within two months after Times Beach shut down its incinerator, dioxin was discovered in soil of the west St. Louis County suburb of Ellisville. Officials with the EPA said that a private driveway in Ellisville had dioxin levels as high as 195 parts per billion, many times the level it considered safe. In dry soil, a concentration of 50 parts per billion is considered hazardous waste; 3 parts per billion is the standard for edible food.

Authorities began burning the dioxin-contaminated material in Times Beach, Missouri, in the 1990's. Here, project manager Robert M. Kain is seen near an incinerator used to burn hundreds of thousands of tons of contaminated material. (AP/Wide World Photos)

Further Reading

Johansen, Bruce E. *The Dirty Dozen: Toxic Chemicals and the Earth's Future.* Greenwood, Conn.: Praeger, 2003.

Mansur, Michael. "After Fifteen Years, Dioxin Incineration at Times Beach, Mo., Is Finished." *Kansas City Star,* June 18, 1997.

Bruce E. Johansen

See also   Air pollution; Environmental movement; Superfund program; Water pollution.

■ *Titanic* wreck discovery

The Event   Marine geologists locate an ocean liner that sank in 1912

Date   September 1, 1985

Place   Northwest Atlantic Ocean

The glamour and tragedy associated with the Titanic *fostered public interest in its discovery; technologies used to find and photograph the ship broke new ground in undersea exploration.*

In September, 1985, an expedition led by marine geologist Robert Ballard of Massachusetts' Woods Hole Oceanographic Institution found the wreckage of the luxury liner *Titanic* resting on the bottom of the northwest Atlantic Ocean. The *Titanic* had collided with an iceberg four days into its maiden voyage, on the evening of April 14, 1912, and sank shortly after 2:00 A.M. on April 15. Although state-of-the-art for its time and considered unsinkable, the *Titanic* was easily compromised, and it had enough lifeboats to hold fewer than half its passengers. The sinking claimed over fifteen hundred victims, including several famous and wealthy Americans to whom the *Titanic* had offered luxurious first-class accommodations.

Ballard used the *Titanic*'s popular appeal to raise funds for an expedition to find it. His Woods Hole team was developing submarines, remote-controlled robots, and cameras to investigate deep-sea environments inhospitable to humans. In the summer of 1985, Woods Hole and the French National Institute of Oceanography (IFREMER) launched a joint search for the *Titanic*. The French scanned the ocean bottom with sonar (sound waves), seeking large, metallic objects; the Americans investigated further with two vehicles used to take video and still photographs underwater: *Argo* and the Acoustically Navigated Geological Underwater Survey (ANGUS). IFREMER's goal was to find the *Titanic*, while Ballard, partially funded by the United States Navy, was officially testing *Argo* and ANGUS.

The French ship *Le Suroit* searched from July 5 to August 6 without success. The American ship *Knorr* resumed the search on August 25, towing *Argo* and its cameras 12,500 feet beneath the surface. French and American scientists worked in shifts to operate *Argo* and watch the video. Just before 1:00 A.M. on September 1, *Argo* began relaying pictures of human-made objects; the crew identified the *Titanic* when the outline of her circular boilers became visible. Further passes with *Argo* and twelve thousand color photographs taken by ANGUS would reveal that, although *Titanic*'s bow and stern were separated by about two thousand feet, they remained upright, and much of the ship was intact. Thousands of objects, including the *Titanic*'s once-elegant furnishings and its passengers' personal effects, lay strewn around the wreck.

Impact International media outlets immediately sought news and photos of the *Titanic*. Ballard and IFREMER fell into a dispute over releasing the expedition's photographs, and the French declined to participate when Ballard returned to the *Titanic* in July, 1986, with *J.J.* (*Jason Jr.*), a smaller camera-equipped robot that could move independently while tethered to a submarine.

Subsequent expeditions, including a 1987 effort by IFREMER in partnership with an American company unconnected to Ballard, recovered many artifacts from the site. Two of the ship's safes were opened on live television on October 28, 1987, in a syndicated special hosted by Telly Savalas; the show was modeled after a similar special featuring Al Capone's vault hosted by Geraldo Rivera. Although in 1985 Ballard supported salvage efforts, he later campaigned

to leave the *Titanic* undisturbed as a memorial to the dead.

Further Reading

Ballard, Robert D., with Rick Archbold. *The Discovery of the Titanic*. Rev. ed. Toronto: Madison Press Books, 1995.

Ballard, Robert D., with Michael S. Sweeney. *Return to Titanic: A New Look at the World's Most Famous Lost Ship*. Washington, D.C.: National Geographic, 2004.

Maureen Puffer-Rothenberg

See also Archaeology; Robots; Science and technology.

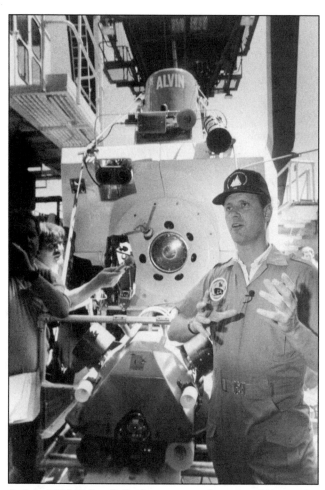

In July, 1986, Robert Ballard answers questions about his upcoming return voyage to excavate the wreck of the Titanic. *Behind him is the* ALVIN, *a submersible capable of diving more than one mile below the ocean's surface.* (AP/Wide World Photos)

■ *Torch Song Trilogy*

Identification Play and film
Author Harvey Fierstein (1954-   )
Date Play opened June 10, 1982; film released on
    December 14, 1988

*A Tony Award-winning play turned into a feature film,
Fierstein's* Torch Song Trilogy *addressed gay themes in a
way that had previously been taboo—in terms of love. It
brought to the general population a representation of same-
gendered relationships that looked very much like the heterosexual ones the world better understood.*

Torch Song Trilogy is a collection of three short plays—
The International Stud, Fugue in the Nursery, and *Widows
and Children First!*—that are produced together to
form three stories from the life of Arnold Beckoff, a
Jewish drag queen who lives in New York and favors
singing torch songs. The play received much acclaim when it opened in 1982, including winning
the Tony Award for Best Play in 1983. Much of the

*Playwright Harvey Fierstein in 1982. (AP/Wide World
Photos)*

play's recognition resulted from the way Fierstein
handled topics such as gay-bashing, drag, bisexual-
ity, infidelity, adoption, and family dysfunction. Moreover, in addressing these issues, the play placed its
central focus on homosexual characters, who were
treated not as abnormal but rather as strong, fully realized protagonists dealing with many issues that
were also acutely familiar to heterosexual audiences.
That Fierstein himself was an openly gay writer and
actor who unabashedly wrote with such open candor
and then played in the starring role was of no small
significance either.

Following the show's successful Broadway run,
New Line Cinema asked Fierstein to adapt the four-
hour play into a two-hour film script. Making extensive cuts, Fierstein created a film that still preserved
the three distinct vignettes and met studio criteria.
However, there was one hurdle to overcome; New
Line would not support setting the story in its original time frame of the early 1980's, indicating that
with the rise of acquired immunodeficiency syndrome (AIDS) in the gay community, the story was
not plausible if it did not address that subject.
Fierstein wanted to focus on other themes, so the setting of the film was changed to the 1970's, prior to
the AIDS crisis. This change highlights another significant shift in gay representation of the 1980's, as
Fierstein made a move that many others within the
gay community would not make for another decade:
He saw AIDS as a world crisis and not as something
that was only a gay issue or that had to dominate all
gay discussions to the exclusion of other topics or
other sexualities.

Impact *Torch Song Trilogy* brought gay themes to the
forefront of mainstream culture in a way that differed from other attempts; it did so by casting a positive light on the gay characters within the story. This
shift created a larger discussion of equity within media representations of gay, lesbian, bisexual, and
transgender characters and issues.

Further Reading

Busch, Charles. "Torch Song Trilogy." *Advocate* 876
    (November, 2002): 103-104.
Duralde, Alonso. "This Torch Still Burns." *Advocate*
    917 (June, 2004): 194-195.
Guernsey, Otis L., ed. *The Best Plays of 1981-1982.*
    New York: Dodd, Mead, 1983.

Needham Yancey Gulley

See also ACT UP; AIDS epidemic; Broderick, Matthew; Film in the United States; Homosexuality and gay rights; *Kiss of the Spider Woman*; Theater.

■ Toronto bathhouse raids of 1981

The Event Toronto police raid four gay bathhouses, arresting hundreds of gay men
Date February 5, 1981
Place Toronto, Ontario

The Toronto bathhouse raids galvanized the city's community into action, marking a point after which they would no longer endure ill treatment by police or the wider community. The protests that followed came to be known as "Canada's Stonewall."

At 11:00 P.M. on February 5, 1981, 150 Toronto police officers conducted simultaneous raids, code-named Operation Soap, on four Toronto bathhouses: the Club Baths, the Romans II Spa, the Richmond Street Health Emporium, and the Barracks. Police broke down doors and smashed windows to gain entry. Once inside, they heavily damaged each establishment; the Richmond Street Health Emporium never reopened. They terrorized and verbally abused the men found inside. The officers had removed their badge numbers prior to the raid, so individual officers could not be identified. In all, 253 gay men were arrested and charged as "found-ins," 14 were charged with minor drug possession, and 20 additional men were charged with "keeping a common bawdy house." The violence of the raid was unprecedented, and it represented the largest Canadian mass arrest since the invocation of the War Measures Act during the FLQ Crisis of October, 1970.

The following night, more than three thousand gay men and lesbians filled the streets of downtown Toronto in a protest that lasted late into the night. In an angry and sometimes violent protest, the community demanded action. With the rallying cry of "No More Shit," they made it clear police violence could no longer be used to intimidate the community. On February 20, over four thousand gay men and lesbians marched on the provincial legislature and then to Police Division 52, whose officers had led the raid. Demanding a public inquiry from the government, they also demanded that the Ontario Human Rights Code be amended to protect gay men and lesbians.

Impact In the aftermath of the raids, 249 of those arrested were found not guilty. The police rationale for the raids, namely that the baths were actually bawdy houses and provided on-site prostitution, was found to be baseless. The raids capped a long period of police harassment of the gay community. Officers repeatedly engaged in entrapment and arrested gay men in cruising areas, raided the *Body Politic* gay newspaper in December, 1977, and raided the Barracks bathhouse in December, 1978, when twenty-eight men were arrested. After years of police attempts to enforce their view of morality on Toronto's growing gay community, the police raids of 1981 pushed relations between that community and the police to a breaking point. As a result, the community came together and organized in a manner never previously achieved, establishing a base from which it would go on to respond to an even greater crisis: the looming HIV/AIDS pandemic.

Further Reading

The Canadian Gay and Lesbian Archives. http:// www.clga.ca/.
Kinsman, Gary. *The Regulation of Desire: Homo and Hetero Sexualities.* 2d ed. Montreal: Black Rose Books, 1996.
McCaskell, Tim. "The Bath Raids and Gay Politics." In *Social Movements/Social Change*, edited by Frank Cunningham. Toronto: Between the Lines, 1988.

Michael E. Graydon

See also ACT UP; AIDS epidemic; Homosexuality and gay rights.

■ Tort reform movement

Definition Legislation passed by the majority of the states in order to alleviate the tort and insurance crises
Date Mid- to late 1980's

The majority of the states enacted legislation that included caps on "pain and suffering" awards, limits on punitive damages, and modification of joint and several liability rules.

Among the reasons cited for the tort reform movement was the increased size and number of tort awards in personal injury, medical malpractice, and product liability cases, causing insurance companies to raise premiums to cover increased awards. The so-called insurance cycle began at the end of the 1960's, when the insurance industry's profitability was declining and when the doctrine of strict liability was expanded to include personal liability cases. (The doctrine originally applied solely to businesses conducting abnormally dangerous activities.) With that expansion, a plaintiff no longer had to prove negligence but merely had to prove that the plaintiff was injured while using the product in the manner intended.

In the mid-1970's, the slump in insurance industry activity brought insurance premium increases. In 1976, President Gerald R. Ford convened a White House conference on product liability, and in 1979, during President Jimmy Carter's administration, a special task force produced a model uniform product liability act for the states. The early 1980's saw the insurance industry booming again because of good investment income and high interest rates. Policies were underpriced to generate premiums for investments. By 1984, interest rates fell, as did insurance investment income and profits. Pressure to increase premiums came about because of higher tort damage awards. The jury awards were so high that companies as well as individuals who could not pay their premiums went bankrupt. Others "went bare"; that is, they operated without insurance, knowing that a large verdict against them could annihilate them. The Tort Policy Working Group, formed during the administration of President Ronald Reagan, released a report advocating tort reforms, including the elimination of joint and several liability, limits on contingent fees, and a $100,000 cap on noneconomic damages.

Some Reforms Numerous states passed legislation that aimed at reducing huge jury awards, limiting the areas for which suits may be brought, and imposing caps on punitive damage awards (damages granted beyond compensatory damage awards assessed as punishment for aggravated, wanton, reckless, or oppressive conduct and as a deterrence to others to prevent them from engaging in like conduct) either through a specific numerical cap or through limiting the circumstances under which punitive damage claims can be awarded. It had not been uncommon for juries to award actual damages of a few thousand dollars yet award millions of dollars in punitive damages. Additionally, amounts

assessed by juries to compensate for lost wages, medical payments, and the like (called "special damages") made up a small part of many liability awards. Juries were likely to add on larger amounts for noneconomic damages, such as pain and suffering and loss of the ability to enjoy life (called "general damages").

In an effort to quell this trend, new legislation was sought. Tort reform involved putting limits on damage awards in malpractice, negligence, and personal injury cases. The legislation passed by the states was not uniform; not every reform was enacted in each state.

In addition to imposing caps on punitive damage awards, limits were imposed for pain and suffering awards, and strict standards were adopted for proving liability for an accident or injury. In order to accomplish this, the joint and several liability principle was revised or abolished. Under the joint and several liability doctrine, two or more defendants are jointly (together) held financially responsible for a plaintiff's injury, and each defendant severally (individually) may be held financially responsible for the full value of the harm. The most common form of joint and several liability reform was to limit its application when awarding general or noneconomic damages. Under this reform, defendants could be severally liable for economic damages but not for noneconomic damages.

The intent of the reform was to provide assurance that injured plaintiffs are paid for their out-of-pocket expenses even if some defendants are insolvent. At the same time, this reform limited the "deep pocket" approach to awarding damages for noneconomic losses. Another pattern limited joint and several liability when the defendants are together less than 50 percent at fault or less at fault than the plaintiff. This reform aimed at "fairness": limiting the number of situations in which a defendant who is only slightly at fault will have to pay for the entire amount or a large portion of damages. Generally, tort reform in this area was focused on financial responsibility in proportion to fault rather than on one's ability to pay. Few, if any, of the reforms completely abolished joint and several liability. Of the thirty-three states that passed joint and several liability reform, only four completely eliminated the use of that doctrine.

Some states enacted restrictions limiting frivolous lawsuits (in which there is no foundation for a liability claim); others instituted fines against attorneys who filed frivolous suits. Contingent fee arrangements were also limited so that attorneys would have less incentive to seek unusually large damages for clients.

Impact   Some of the measures passed, such as caps on damage awards, both compensatory and punitive, have modestly reduced lawsuits, damage awards, and liability insurance premiums. Most of the reforms, however, have had little or no effect. Research has indicated that publicity about the "litigation explosion" may be changing the attitudes of juries and judges toward plaintiffs in personal injury cases. Juries have become increasingly suspicious of plaintiffs in tort cases, and judges in product liability cases have curtailed some of the litigious policies of the 1960's, 1970's, or 1980's, perhaps in reaction to publicity generated by tort reformers. Consequently, numbers of claims have dropped and plaintiffs' awards have become more difficult to obtain.

Further Reading

Burke, Thomas F. *Lawyers, Lawsuits, and Legal Rights: The Battle over Litigation in American Society.* Berkeley: University of California Press, 2002. Describes the policies that promote the use of litigation in resolving disputes and implementing public policy. Contains detailed endnotes and numerous scholarly references.

Church, George J. "Sorry, Your Insurance Has Been Cancelled." *Time* 127, no. 12 (March 24, 1986): 16-26. An overview of the scenarios leading to tort reform and several of the proposals for reform.

Daniels, Stephen, and Joanne Martin. *Civil Juries and the Politics of Reform.* Evanston, Ill.: Northwestern University Press, 1995. Analysis of patterns of jury verdicts in areas such as medical malpractice, product liability, and punitive damages within the context of the larger political and academic debate over tort reform.

Depperschmidt, Thomas O. "State Tort and Insurance Reform: The Net Result of Two Years Effort." *Journal of Forensic Economics* 2, no. 1 (1989): 23-46. A well-researched scholarly article on tort reform, with numerous references.

Lee, Han-Duck, Mark J. Browne, and Joan T. Schmit. "How Does Joint and Several Tort Reform Affect the Rate of Tort Filings? Evidence from the State Courts." *The Journal of Risk and Insurance* 61, no. 2 (1994): 295-316. A scholarly article emphasizing the doctrine of joint and several liability in tort reform.

Marcia J. Weiss

See also   Business and the economy in the United States; Crime.

■ Tower Commission

Identification   The board appointed by U.S. president Ronald Reagan to investigate the Iran-Contra affair

As the first official inquiry into the Iran-Contra affair, the Tower Commission uncovered the basic facts of the arms sales to Iran and the diversion of proceeds to the Nicaraguan Contras and reported these facts candidly to Reagan and the American public.

U.S. foreign policy in the 1980's faced twin threats from civil wars in Central America and growing terrorism in the Middle East. In June, 1986, media reports began to appear about allegations of U.S. aid to the right-wing Contra guerrillas operating in Nicaragua against the left-wing Sandinista government. In October, 1986, attention focused in particular on an American crew member who was captured by the Sandinistas after his plane was shot down during a supply mission to the Contras. This incident in turn touched off a crisis for the Ronald Reagan administration because of the possibility that the U.S. government had been providing aid to the Contras in contravention of the Boland Amendment passed by Congress to ban such assistance. Aides of Attorney General Edwin Meese III visited the offices of the National Security Council (NSC) and discovered a memorandum that confirmed that there had been arms sales to Iran and that some of the proceeds had been diverted to the Contras.

On October 26, 1986, Meese informed President Reagan of the diversion. Not knowing the full extent of the actions taken by his NSC staff, and under pressure to furnish answers to Congress and the media, Reagan appointed on November 26, 1986, a three-member commission chaired by former senator John Tower and including former secretary of state Edmund Muskie and retired Air Force lieutenant general Brent Scowcroft. Initially given a mandate to complete its work in just sixty days, the commission assembled a staff of twenty-three employees and began searching for evidence.

In addition to investigating the Iran-Contra affair, the commission recruited outside experts to conduct twelve studies of how the NSC had performed in crises dating back to the presidency of Harry S. Truman. With the notable exceptions of the president's national security adviser, Navy vice admiral John Poindexter, and his assistant, Marine lieutenant colonel Oliver North, both of whom faced possible prosecution, the commission completed interviews of more than fifty individuals, including principals in the Iran-Contra operation, the three living former presidents, various past presidential advisers, President Reagan, and Vice President George H. W. Bush. Two weeks before its mandate was to expire, the commission made the important discovery that hundreds of backup copies of deleted electronic messages remained in the NSC's computer system, and these "PROF notes" allowed the

commission to solidify and add credibility to its conclusions. After receiving two time extensions, the commission presented its report to Reagan and the public on February 26, 1987.

The Commission's Findings   The Tower Commission's report presented a detailed account of the six arms deliveries that the United States made to Iran, for which Iran paid $48 million, and traced how some of the proceeds, along with money raised from donors in the United States and foreign countries, was used to fund and supply the Contras in Nicaragua. The commission drew the conclusion that the structure of the NSC was sound but that members of its staff had been allowed to function too independently and to usurp the role normally served by the Central Intelligence Agency in conducting covert operations. Finding that the motive for arms sales to Iran was to gain release of several Americans being held hostage in Lebanon, the commission con-

Members of the Tower Commission take questions from the press on February 26, 1987. From left: Edmund Muskie, John Tower, and Brent Scowcroft. (AP/Wide World Photos)

cluded that a strategic opening to Iran was a worthwhile objective, but that the U.S. government should not have engaged in an arms-for-hostages deal when it ran against its own policy of refusing to deal with terrorists and because its actions might serve as an incentive for further kidnappings.

Concerning aid to the Contras, the commission was undecided as to whether the congressional ban applied to the NSC staff, but it questioned the aid on the grounds that, if disclosed, it could jeopardize the Reagan administration's pro-Contra position. The commission criticized the NSC staff members responsible for the Iran-Contra affair for running a highly unprofessional operation and also cast an unfavorable light on Reagan, who, while he had not been involved in any effort to cover up the facts, had failed to exercise sufficient care in overseeing the implementation of U.S. foreign policy.

Impact   The Iran-Contra affair was the crowning government scandal of the 1980's and, for a time, appeared to threaten Reagan's political future. Had he been forced from the presidency, or even remained under a lingering cloud of suspicion, especially just a decade after President Richard M. Nixon's resignation in the wake of the Watergate scandal, the American political scene could have faced a very uncertain future. The Tower Commission accomplished the difficult feat of conducting both a speedy and evenhanded investigation that, while shedding an unflattering light on Reagan's administrative style, pinpointed the principals behind the Iran-Contra affair at the staff level of the National Security Council. The commission built a solid foundation for the lengthier congressional and criminal investigations that followed it and that produced a fuller and more detailed picture of the Iran-Contra affair.

Further Reading

Draper, Theodore. *A Very Thin Line: The Iran-Contra Affairs.* New York: Hill & Wang, 1991. One of the

---

The Tower Report

In its report on the Iran-Contra affair, the Tower Commission cited a "failure of responsibility" on the part of the principal members of the National Security Council (NSC), as well as of President Ronald Reagan, as set forth in this excerpt:

The NSC system will not work unless the President makes it work. . . .

By his own account, as evidenced in his diary notes, and as conveyed to the Board [Tower Commission] by his principal advisors, President Reagan was deeply committed to securing the release of the hostages. It was this intense compassion for the hostages that appeared to motivate his steadfast support of the Iran initiative, even in the face of opposition from his Secretaries of State and Defense.

In his obvious commitment, the President appears to have proceeded with a concept of the initiative that was not accurately reflected in the reality of the operation. The President did not seem to be aware of the way in which the operation was implemented and the full consequences of U.S. participation. . . .

The President's management style is to put the principal responsibility for policy review and implementation on the shoulders of his advisors. Nevertheless, with such a complex, high-risk operation and so much at stake, the President should have insured that the NSC system did not fail him. He did not force his policy to undergo the most critical review of which the NSC participants and the process were capable. At no time did he insist upon accountability and performance review. Had the President chosen to drive the NSC. system, the outcome could well have been different.

---

most detailed and comprehensive histories of the Iran-Contra affair.

Tower, John. *Consequences: A Personal and Political Memoir.* Boston: Little, Brown, 1991. Includes a chapter on the author's experiences as chair of the Tower Commission.

Tower, John G., Edmund S. Muskie, and Brent Scowcroft. *The Tower Commission Report: The Full Text of the President's Special Review Board.* New York: Bantam Books, 1987. The report of the Tower Commission as released to the public.

Walsh, Lawrence. *Firewall: The Iran-Contra Conspiracy and Cover-Up.* New York: W. W. Norton, 1997. The story of Iran-Contra from the point of view of the independent counsel who conducted the criminal investigation from 1986 to 1993.

Larry Haapanen

See also Foreign policy of the United States; Iran-Contra affair; North, Oliver; Poindexter, John; Reagan, Ronald; Reagan Doctrine.

■ Toys and games

Definition Recreational products, introduced in the 1980's, that had major economic and/or cultural significance

The 1980's saw a series of new toy and game brands that had unprecedented popularity, many becoming cultural icons.

Several factors contributed to the toy industry of the 1980's. New technologies allowed for the development of a wide range of electronic toys. The oil crisis of the late 1970's caused an increase in the cost of plastic, which, in turn, inspired toy manufacturers to pursue less expensive ways of making plastic toys as well as to increase the use of other materials, such as die-cast metal. These experimentations with new technologies and materials led to new product designs and gimmicks.

Meanwhile, many companies tried to imitate the success that Kenner had with its toys based on the *Star Wars* films from 1977 to 1983, using elements of the company's formula: action figures with vehicles and play sets, figures that were based on "good versus evil" archetypes, and cross-merchandising. This trend was compounded when the Federal Communications Commission (FCC) lifted its restrictions on tie-ins between children's programs and toys.

The rise of national retailers such as Toys "R" Us and Wal-Mart created opportunities to sell toys year round, not just on holidays and birthdays. Cable television broadened opportunities for advertising, allowing fads to spread more quickly than before. This led to the creation of an annual tradition: the "must have" toy that parents were expected to buy for Christmas, leading to long lines and waiting lists at department stores.

Games The first fad toy to hit America in the 1980's was the Rubik's Cube, a puzzle that had been invented in 1974. The puzzle was a cube with nine colored squares on each side, in six different colors. The objective of the puzzle was to get all the same color on each side. Consumers of all ages spent hours trying to solve the puzzle. At the height of the fad, there were books being published about how to solve the cube as well as similar puzzles and replacement stickers to put on an unsolved cube.

The other craze in 1980's games was trivia. While television game shows were on decline in general, syndicated evening versions of *Jeopardy!* and *Wheel of Fortune* became national phenomena, spinning off various board game and electronic versions. Trivial Pursuit was released in 1982 and had become a fad by 1984, spinning off dozens of sequels and variations. It was an easy game for large groups of people to play at parties, and similar kinds of "guessing games" came to be released by the end of the decade, such as Pictionary (and its television game show spin-off *Win, Lose or Draw*), Scattergories, and Outburst.

Electronics The early 1980's saw the rise of popular video games, such as *Pac-Man* and *Donkey Kong*, a new medium that changed the cultural landscape. Children, teenagers, and adults alike would gather around home computers and home video game consoles. Stand-alone arcade machines became fixtures at restaurants and other gathering places. Video games would increase in popularity and technology throughout the 1980's and beyond, eventually overwhelming the market share of traditional toys.

Advances in electronics created more than video games. Electronic games such as Simon were released in the late 1970's, but their popularity and proliferation grew in the 1980's. While remote-controlled and radio-controlled toy vehicles had been around for decades, refined technologies led to a new wave of popularity in the 1980's, and many other toy lines began incorporating motorized components. Meanwhile, some companies began to produce dolls, action figures, and vehicles with built-in voice recordings.

Other toy lines capitalized on advances in laser and infrared technology to make a new kind of toy gun: Lazer Tag and Photon lines were games in which players used special light guns and "body armor" to shoot at each other and score points based on hits recorded by the armor. A similar idea was attempted, unsuccessfully, in Captain Power, an action

The Masters of the Universe were featured in their own half-hour-long children's cartoon show, which drove sales of the action figures. (Hulton Archive/Getty Images)

figure line in which the toy guns and vehicles could be used by children to interact with the television series.

In 1982, Hasbro's Playskool division released Glo Worm, a plush doll that glowed when squeezed, providing young children with a combined comfort toy and night light. In 1985, Hasbro released the My Buddy and Kid Sister dolls, which were partially motorized to serve as imaginary friends. While the line was not successful, its aggressive advertising campaign created a popular jingle. Far more successful was Teddy Ruxpin, an animatronic teddy bear with a built-in tape player that "told stories" by moving its mouth and eyes. Teddy Ruxpin pioneered a whole new area for toys and novelties in the following decades.

Action Figures Mattel and Hasbro both found huge success with their attempts to jump on the *Star Wars* bandwagon. Novels and films in the "sword and sorcery" subgenre had been popular at the time.

While the film *Conan the Barbarian* was not released until 1982, Mattel released a toy line in 1981 that was loosely based on characters and concepts from the novel. Masters of the Universe, first marketed in a comic book by DC Comics, featured the war between the warrior He-Man and the evil sorcerer Skeletor. The franchise's first few action figures were released in 1981, and the line came out in full force in 1982, but the concepts would be tweaked several times before the line finally became a huge hit.

In 1983, the FCC lifted a long-standing rule forbidding connections between cartoons and toy lines. As a result, toy manufacturers began producing cartoons based on their latest lines. When Mattel went to Filmation, one of the leading animation companies of the time, to make Masters of the Universe into a cartoon, Filmation took the unprecedented route of putting the cartoon in first-run syndication and airing the new episodes on weekday afternoons, rather than on Saturdays. The move paid off. The toys became a top-selling brand for several years and inspired a spin-off line for girls, She-Ra: Princess of Power, featuring He-Man's sister. An ill-fated live-action movie released in 1987 signaled the decline of the brand, and an attempted revival and repositioning in 1989 failed. However, Masters of the Universe would continue to enjoy international popularity and a strong fan base.

Similarly, in 1982, Hasbro reinvented its G.I. Joe brand, which had been out of production for several years as a direct competitor to *Star Wars*. Reducing the 12-inch action figures to the same size as the 3.75-inch *Star Wars* figures, Hasbro introduced a similar line of vehicles and play sets, an "evil empire" enemy, and personalities (previously, the G.I. Joe toys had been anonymous soldiers). The line was designed in conjunction with Marvel Comics and with an animated advertising campaign by Sunbow Productions. The toy line and the comic book were issued on the same day in September, 1982. Both sold out within a few days, and the comic became one of the most successful titles of the 1980's. An animated series, produced by Sunbow, premiered in 1983, setting G.I. Joe: A Real American Hero as a perennial brand for Hasbro.

A major trend in American toys was imported from Japan. Several Japanese toy companies had produced toy lines featuring robots that changed into other forms. These toy lines coincided with the popularity of anime in Japan and were imported to the United States in the mid-1980's. Many of the lines introduced in the United States were pastiches of Japanese toys and cartoons licensed and then rebranded by American companies. Lines included such brands as Voltron, Gobots, and Robotech, but by far the most successful of the "transforming robots" brands, in fact the brand that gave the category its name, was Hasbro's Transformers, introduced in 1984.

Hasbro licensed the designs for various robot-themed toys from Takara, a Japanese company that had originally licensed the G.I. Joe brand from Hasbro in the 1960's. Using the same formula that had succeeded with the new G.I. Joe toys, Hasbro cross-promoted its Transformers line with Marvel Comics comic books and a Sunbow cartoon. Eager for new products, Hasbro also licensed robot toys from other Japanese manufacturers, but those designs led to copyright issues when those companies' brands came to the United States. The Transformers line was so successful that Takara canceled its original lines and bought the Transformers concept from Hasbro. The line was an international hit, and, even when one of the companies put the line on hiatus, Transformers was continually produced by either Takara or Hasbro for more than two decades. The line would see a renewal in 2007 with a major motion picture that become one of the highest-grossing films of all time.

As the *Star Wars* line faded with the release of *Return of the Jedi* (1983) and as the new brands from Hasbro and Mattel featured various action gimmicks, Kenner needed a new brand to regain its market share. In 1984, Kenner licensed the rights to make action figures based on DC Comics's superheroes and had great success with the Super Powers Team line. Another success for Kenner was M.A.S.K., a series about a team of heroes, similar to G. I. Joe, that drove shape-changing vehicles and battled an evil organization. However, neither line quite captured the market the way Hasbro and Mattel had done.

The *Ghostbusters* (1984) movie was spun off into both a successful toy line and cartoon named *The Real Ghostbusters* (to distinguish from the similarly named television series *Ghost Busters*, a Filmation copyright that predated the film and was made into a competing toy line by Mattel). Other movies and television series turned into action figures included *The A-Team*, *Knight Rider*, and the World Wrestling Federation.

In 1987, Playmates issued a line of toys based on the *Teenage Mutant Ninja Turtles* comic book and cartoon series. The franchise would be hugely successful, sparking various movies, cartoon series, and revival toy lines. The final big toy line of the decade was Galoob's Micro Machines, a line of toy cars introduced in 1989. The toy cars were smaller than the traditional Hot Wheels and Matchbox cars and featured elaborate play sets.

Dolls Perhaps the biggest toy craze of the 1980's was none of the various action figure lines but rather a line of dolls marketed to girls. The Cabbage Patch Kids were a line of unusual dolls designed by Xavier Roberts and first mass-marketed by Coleco in 1982. The gimmick was that each particular doll was not just a toy; rather, it was an adopted child, complete with an imaginary adoption certificate and the conceit that it was as unique as a child. The Cabbage Patch Kids became the first "must have" Christmas toy. Parents waited in long lines to try to obtain the dolls, inspiring marketers and toy companies to focus on creating the next big "craze." The dolls generated more than $2 billion in the year 1984 alone.

Also in 1982, Hasbro introduced My Little Pony, a line of cute, somewhat anthropomorphic and multicolored toy ponies that ranked with Transformers and G.I. Joe in success and, for a time, overtook Mattel's Barbie as the top girls' toy brand. Hasbro also enjoyed great success with Jem, a line of dolls released in 1985 with an accompanying Sunbow cartoon, featuring the adventures of an all-girl rock band.

In the early 1980's, Kenner had success in the girls' and young children's markets with toys based on characters from American Greetings's juvenile cards, including the Care Bears and Strawberry Shortcake. Mattel and Hallmark responded with Rainbow Brite, a billion-dollar franchise at its peak. Tonka's Pound Puppies, released in 1985, applied the Cabbage Patch Kids concept to stuffed animals, presenting its characters as rescue dogs with supplies and adoption certificates.

Impact Many of the toy franchises introduced in the 1980's became cultural icons. As children who grew up in the 1980's became the teenagers and young adults of the Internet revolution in the late 1990's, they reached out to one another online, starting Web sites and online discussion groups to share their continued love for their favorite childhood toys and entertainment franchises. This led to many of these toys being revived in the early twenty-first century as part of a nostalgia movement. While some lines were revived only briefly and mostly unsuccessfully, certain brands from the 1980's, such as the Transformers, Cabbage Patch Kids, Trivial Pursuit, and My Little Pony, have demonstrated perennial, cross-generational, and international appeal, making them indelible landmarks of American culture.

Further Reading

Miller, G. Wayne. *Toy Wars: The Epic Struggle Between G. I. Joe, Barbie, and the Companies That Make Them.* New York: Crown, 1998. The story of how Mattel and Hasbro dominated the toy industry and then bought up most of its competition throughout the 1980's and 1990's.

Santelmo, Vincent. *The Complete Encyclopedia to G. I. Joe.* 3d. ed. Iola, Wis.: Krause, 2001. Covers the G.I. Joe brand from 1964 to 2000.

Sweet, Roger. *Mastering the Universe: He-Man and the Rise and Fall of a Billion-Dollar Idea.* Cincinnati: Emmis Books, 2005. The man who originally designed He-Man for Mattel chronicles the history of the toy line, its success, and its failure.

Walsh, Tim. *Timeless Toys: Classic Toys and the Playmakers Who Created Them.* Kansas City, Mo.: Andrews McMeel, 2005. A history of various "classic" toys, from Slinky to Trivial Pursuit.

John C. Hathaway

See also Advertising; Cabbage Patch Kids; Consumerism; *Ghostbusters*; Hobbies and recreation; *Pac-Man*; Trivial Pursuit; Video games and arcades.

■ Transplantation

Definition Transferring tissues or organs from one person to another

The 1970's had represented a period of significant change in procurement of organs for transplantation. For instance, the concept of "brain death" allowed for a larger source of tissues and organs, rather than using cadavers as the sole source. In the 1980's, a series of acts were passed by Congress that established a network for procuring organs and further refined the procedures begun in the previous decades. The necessity for genetic matching had likewise been a problem, one which invariably resulted in rejection if the donor and recipient were genetically distinct. The approval of cyclosporine, the first of the major antirejection drugs, allowed for greater leeway in addressing the problem of matching.

Serious attempts at successful organ transplantation date as far back as the early 1900's, but it was only with the development of immunogenetics and the discovery of tissue-associated proteins known as histocompatibility antigens in the 1930's that it became possible to understand the science of rejection. In the 1950's, the first attempts to transplant tissues was carried out between identical twins. In the following decade, transplantation of other organs was attempted, including the heart and lungs, but with only limited success.

Antirejection Drugs One of the greatest problems associated with transplantation between donors and recipients was the likelihood of rapid rejection if the individuals did not genetically match. The earlier generation of antirejection drugs had been initially developed for use in cancer chemotherapy and were too toxic for more than limited application. In 1983, cyclosporine was approved for use by the Food and Drug Administration (FDA). Discovered in the 1970's, cyclosporine represented the first antirejection drug with wide application for the transplantation field because of its specificity and limited toxicity. The success rate for kidney transplantation as well as other organs showed an immediate increase.

The maintaining of organs once they had been removed from the donor but prior to their actual implantation in a recipient was also a problem. Cold saline solutions had been helpful. Researchers at the University of Wisconsin developed an improved isotonic solution, known as UW solution, that was shown to be more effective than other solutions in maintaining organs in a viable state. Marketed as Viaspan, the solution received FDA approval in 1988 for preservation of donated livers. Viaspan subsequently was found to be equally effective for preservation of other organs and tissues.

Establishment of Transplant Networks   In 1968, the Uniform Anatomical Gift Act was passed by Congress, establishing the use of a "donor card" as a means to allow a person or family to request organ donation upon death; the definition of "death" was later more firmly clarified to mean "brain death" (1978). However, a legitimate concern was whether this law would result in a "market" for organs, one producing both a "seller" and a recipient, or "buyer." In 1984, Congress passed the National Organ Transplant Act, which prohibited the sale of organs for use in transplantation. The result was the Organ Procurement and Transplantation Network, which two years later was placed under the auspices of the United Network for Organ Sharing (UNOS). Among the duties of the UNOS was the maintenance of a national registry of potential recipients, the number of which subsequently grew to nearly 100,000 persons within two decades. No cost for the organ was to be passed to the recipient. In 1986, a "routine request" law required hospitals to discuss organ transplantation with families under appropriate circumstances.

Impact   During the 1980's, a number of developments in organ transplantation allowed for not only a greater increase in such procedures but also (coupled with improvements in medical technology) a much wider range in the types of surgeries that could be safely carried out. The first cornea transplant, one of the first types of transplant surgery, was successfully carried out in 1905; kidney transplantations, first between twins and then between unrelated individuals, had been carried out since the 1950's. Nobel Prizes in Physiology or Medicine were awarded in 1990 to two of the pioneers in this area, Joseph Murray and E. Donnall Thomas. The 1980's saw the transplantation of organs previously thought to be too complex for such procedures, such as the lungs or liver. Even heart transplants became more common, though hardly yet routine.

Further Reading

Brent, Leslie. *A History of Transplantation Immunology.* San Diego, Calif.: Academic Press, 1997. Focuses on the early (pre-1980) history of the subject. The impact of immunosuppressive drugs such as cyclosporine is described.

Murphy, Kenneth. *Janeway's Immunobiology.* 7th ed. New York: Garland Science, 2007. Classical textbook on the subject of immunology. An extensive portion addresses transplantation genetics and immunity.

Roitt, Ivan, et al. *Roitt's Essential Immunology.* 11th ed. Malden, Mass.: Blackwell Science, 2006. Several chapters in this textbook address the subject of immunology. Includes a large number of photographs.

Veatch, Robert. *Transplantation Ethics.* Washington, D.C.: Georgetown University Press, 2000. Addresses issues such as the definition of death, sources of organ procurement, and questions related to organ allocation.

Richard Adler

See also   Cancer research; Fetal medicine; Genetics research; Medicine.

■ Trivial Pursuit

Definition   Trivia board game

A serious fad among baby boomers in the early 1980's, Trivial Pursuit helped revive sales of adult-oriented board games and was a good example of the use of word-of-mouth advertising.

Created by two Canadian reporters in the 1970's, Trivial Pursuit was first made available for sale in the

United States in 1982. The company that purchased the game, Selchow and Righter, employed a word-of-mouth advertising strategy, sending copies of the game to people in the entertainment industry, radio personalities, and toy buyers at the 1983 New York Toy Fair. This promotion strategy led to 1.3 million copies of the game being sold in 1983; the company's goal had been to sell 300,000 copies. By 1984, Trivial Pursuit had become a fad similar to the Cabbage Patch Kids, with copies of the game selling out as quickly as they hit the shelves. It was estimated that about 20 million copies of the game were sold in 1984. *The New York Times* that year published several stories of Trivial Pursuit parties that lasted well into the night, and confessions from "Trivial Pursuit addicts." In 1984, thanks to the popularity of the game, sales of the adult board games reached $777 million. In 1986, it was estimated that 1 in 5 families in the United States owned the game.

Impact Numerous articles were written speculating about Trivial Pursuit's popularity, with popular cul-

ture critic Jack Santino suggesting in 1985 that the game's devotion among baby boomers was a result of their generation "developing a nostalgia for a shared era." Strong sales continued throughout the decade, as new versions of the game, such as Silver Screen, Junior, Genus II, and Baby Boomer were introduced. Similar games were produced by other board-game companies in an attempt to cash in on the fad, and there was an increase in the number of adult board games being introduced to the market overall.

Further Reading

Dougherty, Philip. "Trivial Pursuit Campaign." *The New York Times*, July 17, 1984, p. D19.

Santino, Jack. "From Jogging to Trivia Games, Fads Create Status." *U.S. News and World Report*, February 11, 1985.

"Seeking Board Game Bonanza." *The New York Times*, December 30, 1986. p. D1.

Wulffson, Don. L. *Toys! Amazing Stories Behind Some Great Inventions.* New York: Henry Holt, 2000.

Julie Elliott

Students at St. Vincent College in Latrobe, Pennsylvania, play Trivial Pursuit on an auditorium-sized version of the game on October 17, 1984. (AP/Wide World Photos)

The Pursuit of Trivia

In the original Genus edition of Trivial Pursuit, players had to correctly answer questions in six categories: geography, entertainment, history, arts and literature, science and nature, and sports and leisure. The questions were written on a set of cards, with the questions on one side of the card and the answers on the other side. Below are the questions and answers on one of the game's cards.

Category	Question	Answer
Geography	What Rocky Mountain ridge separates North America's eastward and westward-flowing rivers?	The Continental Divide
Entertainment	What was Stanley Kubrick's first film after *2001: A Space Odyssey*?	*A Clockwork Orange*
History	What was the nineteenth-century term used by the United States to justify expansion?	Manifest Destiny
Arts and Literature	What Samuel Taylor Coleridge poem tells of sailor who kills an albatross?	*The Rime of the Ancient Mariner*
Science and Nature	How many grams make up a dekagram?	Ten
Sports and Leisure	What do you call the playing pieces in dominoes?	Bones

See also   Advertising; Cabbage Patch Kids; Fads; Hobbies and recreation; Toys and games.

■ *Tron*

Identification   Science-fiction film
Director   Steven Lisberger (1951-   )
Date   Released July 9, 1982

One of the first feature films extensively to utilize computer-generated imagery, Tron *also combined an innovate technique called backlight compositing with footage of live actors, creating a visually exciting virtual computer environment for the big screen.*

Released in 1982 by the Walt Disney Company, *Tron* stars Jeff Bridges as Kevin Flynn, a talented programmer whose video game inventions have been stolen by an unscrupulous corporate executive named Dillinger (David Warner). Flynn asks Alan (Bruce Boxleitner) and Lora (Cindy Morgan), who both work at Dillinger's company Encom, for help in proving the theft, but the sinister Master Control Program (MCP) "digitizes" Flynn and transports him into the virtual computer environment over which it rules.

Disoriented, Flynn is shocked to find that computer programs are not just lines of code, but rather individual alter-egos of the users who create them. Tron, for instance, is Alan's counterpart, a heroic program who defies the MCP in its efforts to wipe out programs' belief in the users. The MCP forces programs to play games to the death in a gladiator-like environment (represented as the "reality" behind computer video games) and intends to make Flynn play on the grid until he dies, but Flynn, Tron, and another program named Ram escape the grid and mount an assault on the MCP with the help of Yori, Lora's alter-ego program. Ultimately, the good guys destroy the MCP, restoring open communication between programs and their users. *Tron* represents one of the earliest attempts visually to portray cyberspace, an inhabitable "virtual reality" somehow located inside and between computers. Written by its director, Steven Lisberger, *Tron*'s plot grew out of the visuals that Lisberger hoped to create, rather than the other way around. Several computer and special-effects companies contributed to the film, and part of the shooting took place at the Lawrence Livermore National Laboratory in California, lending authenticity to many of the film's "real world" sequences.

Although *Tron*'s story line is somewhat simplistic, the idea of individuals battling against a multinational corporation for free and open access to computer information was popular among audiences. A Tron video arcade game, which included four subgames based on sequences in the film, was introduced in the same year and became quite profitable. Later, computer-game film tie-ins would become de rigeur for almost any action or science-fiction film.

Impact Although many critics felt that *Tron* embraced visual style over substance, the film quickly gained a cult following among viewers of the video-game generation. In addition, *Tron*'s relatively extensive use of computer-generated imaging (CGI) hinted at the vast potential for computer technology to be used in filmmaking and helped pave the way for future breakthroughs in this area. In 2002, a twentieth anniversary collector's edition DVD was released that included extensive features about the making of the movie.

Further Reading

Bankston, Douglas. "Wrap Shot." *American Cinematographer* 84 (June, 2003): 136.

Bonifer, Michael. *The Art of Tron.* New York: Simon & Schuster, 1982.

Glass, Fred. "Sign of the Times: The Computer as Character in *Tron, War Games,* and *Superman III.*" *Film Quarterly* 38 (Winter, 1984/1985): 16-27.

Amy Sisson

See also *Blade Runner;* Computers; Cyberpunk literature; Film in the United States; Gibson, William; Science-fiction films; Special effects; Video games and arcades; Virtual reality.

■ Trudeau, Pierre

Identification Canadian prime minister, 1968-1979, 1980-1984
Born October 18, 1919; Montreal, Quebec, Canada
Died September 28, 2000; Montreal, Quebec, Canada

The final part of Trudeau's political career was particularly significant, as his administration dealt with a major economic downturn, a separatist movement in the province of Quebec, increasing alienation among the western provinces, and major constitutional reform. Trudeau's impact, however, extended to the international scene as he initiated an ultimately unsuccessful peace effort in the months before his retirement.

Prime Minister Pierre Trudeau, around 1980. (Library and Archives Canada)

Pierre Trudeau's political career appeared to end in 1979 when he and his government were voted out of office. He even announced his retirement, although he had not followed through on this when the Progressive Conservative government of Prime Minister Joe Clark called an election for February, 1980. Trudeau led the Liberal campaign to victory and a majority government.

The Domestic Agenda Once back in office, Trudeau and his government quickly had to face a referendum in the province of Quebec, as its sovereignist government under the leadership of Premier René Lévesque sought a mandate to begin the process that would ultimately lead to a form of independence for the province. Trudeau, a strong federalist, had long opposed Quebec nationalism, and he and his government made a concerted effort at defeating the referendum, which they did decisively. Part of Trudeau's campaign involved the promise of constitutional reform. He followed through on this in 1982, when the Canadian constitution was brought back to Canada from the United Kingdom and, in the process, amended. The major amendment involved the creation of a Canadian Charter of Rights and Freedoms that guaranteed individual rights for Canadians, a strong Trudeau principle. The reform did not occur without opposition. Several provincial governments, most notably that of Quebec, strongly opposed the change. In the end, Trudeau won them all over, with the exception of Quebec, which remained opposed to the new constitution.

Other domestic issues bedeviled Trudeau. His government appeared incapable of addressing a major economic recession that saw high levels of unemployment, inflation, and interest rates. Energy was another major issue, and Trudeau's government, in an effort to assert federal control over the sector, introduced the National Energy Program (NEP). The program proved unpopular both in the province of Alberta, Canada's leading oil producer, and with the U.S. presidential administration of Ronald Reagan. A decline in the price of oil that followed the NEP led some in Alberta to put the blame for the setback on the NEP and the Trudeau government. Trudeau became widely despised in parts of western Canada, a region that he later admitted to never having fully understood.

The Peace Mission and Retirement   Suffering unpopularity at home and facing the prospect of another election or retirement, Trudeau turned to international policy in the seeming pursuit of a legacy for him. The first half of the 1980's was a period of heightened Cold War tensions between the Soviet Union and the United States. Trudeau was personally concerned by the apparent hard-line stance taken by the Reagan administration toward the Soviets. At a G7 summit in March, 1983, he repeatedly clashed with Reagan and British prime minister Margaret Thatcher. Trudeau also found himself at odds with Washington over the reaction to the Soviet downing of a Korean Air Lines passenger plane in September, 1983.

Seeking his own path, in October, 1983, Trudeau initiated a peace mission to improve relations between the two superpowers. He began traveling the globe and conducting a series of meetings with world leaders, including Chinese leader Deng Xiaoping. His effort was greeted with cynicism back in Canada, and the Reagan administration was adamantly opposed to his mission. In the end, nothing came of his travels. By February, 1984, he had had enough. After a long walk in the midst of a snowstorm, he announced his retirement. Before leaving office, however, he would reward several of his loyal supporters with patronage appointments. These arrangements, combined with a poor record at handling the economy over the previous four years, left his Liberal Party in a weak position when it sought reelection under a new leader, John Turner, in September, 1984. The Progressive Conservatives, led by Brian Mulroney, crushed the Liberals, and Trudeau quickly disappeared from public life. Occasionally, he would reemerge in subsequent years to make public comments, most notably in 1990 when he successfully opposed the Meech Lake Accord, an ultimately failed effort by the Mulroney government to amend the Canadian constitution and, in the process, bring the province of Quebec back into the constitutional fold.

Impact   Always a colorful character, Trudeau in the 1980's had a decidedly mixed record as Canadian prime minister. The high point of his time in office was the repatriation of the Canadian constitution and the creation of the Charter of Rights and Freedoms, Trudeau's ultimate legacy. On the other hand, his government presided over the increasing alienation of Quebec and western Canada while appearing to be unable to cope with and fully understand the economic malaise that gripped Canada in these years.

Further Reading

Bliss, Michael. *Right Honourable Men: The Descent of Canadian Politics from Macdonald to Chrétien.* Toronto: HarperCollins Canada, 2004. A collection of short biographies of Canadian prime ministers, including Trudeau.

Clarkson, Stephen, and Christina McCall. *Trudeau and Our Times.* Vol. 2. Toronto: McClelland & Stewart, 1997. A detailed study of the political career of Trudeau, with particular attention to the 1980's.

Martin, Lawrence. *The Presidents and the Prime Ministers: Washington and Ottawa Face to Face—The Myth of Bilateral Bliss, 1867-1982.* Toronto: Doubleday Canada, 1982. A history of relations between prime ministers and presidents, including a brief section about Trudeau and Reagan.

Simpson, Jeffrey. *Discipline of Power.* Toronto: University of Toronto Press, 1976. An award-winning study of the short-lived government of Clark and

Trudeau's return to power in February, 1980.

Thompson, John Herd, and Stephen J. Randall. *Canada and the United States: Ambivalent Allies.* Montreal: McGill-Queen's University Press, 2002. A strong history of relations between Canada and the United States, including during the tenure of Trudeau.

Steve Hewitt

See also Business and the economy in Canada; Canada Act of 1982; Canada and the United States; Canadian Charter of Rights and Freedoms; Elections in Canada; Foreign policy of Canada; Inflation in Canada; Lévesque, René; National Energy Program (NEP); Quebec referendum of 1980; Reagan, Ronald; Soviet Union and North America; Strategic Defense Initiative (SDI); Turner, John; Unemployment in Canada.

■ Turner, John

Identification Prime minister of Canada in 1984
Born June 7, 1929; Richmond, Surrey, England

The Liberal Turner was seen as a more moderate and business-friendly successor to Prime Minister Pierre Trudeau, but his party was swept from power less than three months after he became prime minister, and Conservative Brian Mulroney assumed the ministry.

Long-serving Liberal Canadian prime minister Pierre Trudeau had announced his retirement from politics in 1979, after his party was defeated at the polls by the Conservative Party. He returned, however, in February, 1980, to lead his party in defeating the Conservatives, headed by Prime Minister Joe Clark, and to reassume the ministry. In 1984, though, Trudeau felt ready to retire for good at age sixty-five, so the Liberals had to elect a new leader.

The two main contenders for the post were John Turner, a former finance minister who had spent the last nine years working on Bay Street—the Canadian equivalent of Wall Street—in Toronto, and Jean Chrétien, a working-class Quebecer who ran a more populist campaign. Turner won the support of his party and accordingly became prime minister early in July, 1984. Turner was widely seen as being more pragmatic than was the idealistic Trudeau, bringing the atmosphere of the business world into Parliament. One Canadian radio commentator christened

Turner's government "Boys Town on the Rideau." (The Rideau is the canal that runs through Ottawa, right by Parliament Hill.)

Turner faced fundamental problems, however. The Liberal Party was unpopular, and he had little time to renovate it before the next election. Furthermore, Trudeau had made large-scale patronage appointments before leaving office, and Turner, in turn, made even more such appointments once he assumed power. Turner seemed unable to decide whether to assume Trudeau's mantle or to jettison it. This perceived vacillation hurt Turner, especially in Quebec, the traditional stronghold of the Liberals. Despite his distinguished appearance, Turner came across as stiff and conventional on the campaign trial. Unusually, Conservative leader Brian Mulroney was himself a Quebecer who spoke French with near fluency, and Mulroney's party swept Quebec on the way to comprehensively defeating the Liberals. It was all Turner could do to win his own seat in the British Columbia riding of Vancouver Castro.

Despite the Liberal defeat, Turner retained leadership of the party, defeating another challenge by Chrétien in 1986. In the next few years, Liberals assumed the premiership of Ontario, and the Conservatives began to look vulnerable again, as constitutional tension over Quebec's role in the nation mounted. Mulroney had also alienated many vocal Canadian constituencies through his perceived alignment with the United States, especially his advocacy of a free trade agreement with that nation. Leading the Liberals into the 1988 campaign, Turner swerved sharply from his previous pro-business stance, advocating a platform of economic protectionism that would preserve Canada's distinct economic and cultural identities. Though Turner won significantly more seats for the Liberals in 1988 than in 1984, however, the Liberals still lost badly, prompting many to assert that Canada had chosen an irreversible path toward absorption into the American economic sphere.

Impact Turner inherited the leadership of a party in decline, and he was unable to retain his party's majority in the 1984 elections. His changing tactics in the late 1980's responded to the changing national perception of its proper cultural and economic relationship to the United States, but that issue alone proved insufficient to bring the Liberals back to power.

Further Reading

Cahill, Jack. *John Turner: The Long Run*. Toronto: McClelland and Stewart, 1984.

Weston, Greg. *Reign of Error: The Inside Story of John Turner's Troubled Leadership*. Toronto: McGraw-Hill Ryerson, 1988.

Nicholas Birns

See also Canada and the United States; Canada-United States Free Trade Agreement; Elections in Canada; Meech Lake Accord; Mulroney, Brian; Trudeau, Pierre.

■ Turner, Kathleen

Identification American actor
Born June 19, 1954; Springfield, Missouri

A throwback to the stars of earlier eras, Turner was one of the leading film stars of the decade.

During the 1980's, it was relatively rare for television actors to transition successfully to playing leading film roles. However, Kathleen Turner was able to do so. A featured performer in the daytime television soap opera *The Doctors*, she achieved film stardom with her first cinematic role, in Lawrence Kasdan's *Body Heat* (1981). In this film noir reminiscent of *Double Indemnity* (1944), Turner played a sultry woman who manipulates a lawyer (William Hurt) into murdering her rich husband (Richard Crenna). Turner's breathy delivery of such lines as "You're not too smart, are you? I like that in a man" earned her comparisons with such 1940's stars as Lauren Bacall and Lizabeth Scott, and *Double Indemnity* star Barbara Stanwyck sent Turner a fan letter.

Turner showed her versatility by playing a gold digger in Carl Reiner's *The Man with Two Brains* (1983), a farce costarring Steve Martin. The film showcased Turner's comedic skills, which she would display several more times during the decade. She followed with one of her biggest hits, Robert Zemeckis's *Romancing the Stone* (1984), playing a meek romance writer who discovers her more adventurous side while trying to rescue her kidnapped sister in Colombia with the help of a soldier of fortune played by Michael Douglas. *The Jewel of the Nile* (1985) was a less successful sequel.

Next came the most overtly sexual of Turner's many smoldering roles during the decade: In Ken Russell's *Crimes of Passion* (1984), she played a bored fashion designer who spends her nights as a flamboyant prostitute. As with *Romancing the Stone*, the film could be interpreted as a commentary on the failure of some successful women to find fulfillment in their jobs. One of Turner's most unusual roles was in John Huston's *Prizzi's Honor* (1985), in which she played an assassin who marries hit man Jack Nicholson only for the two to be assigned to kill each other. *Prizzi's Honor* reinforced Turner's femme fatale skills, though her performance was more tongue-in-cheek than it had been in *Body Heat*.

Turner's other notable 1980's roles include an unhappily married woman transported to her high school days in Francis Ford Coppola's time-travel comedy *Peggy Sue Got Married* (1986); another unhappy wife in *The Accidental Tourist* (1988), in which she reunited with Kasdan and Hurt; and her unhappiest wife yet, opposite Douglas, in Danny DeVito's darkly comic look at divorce, *The War of the Roses* (1989). The number of Turner films with disintegrating, complicated marriages may be seen to reflect the decade's unease with this social institution.

Turner also provided the voice for Jessica Rabbit in the combined live action-animated film noir spoof *Who Framed Roger Rabbit* (1988). As the title character's sexy wife, Turner huskily purred, in the manner of Bacall and Scott, her most famous line: "I'm not bad. I'm just drawn that way."

Impact Turner specialized in playing strong, resourceful women who controlled their destinies. Because many of her films had strong sexual content, she acquired a reputation as the decade's most sensual star.

Further Reading

D'Agostino, Annette M. *From Soap Stars to Superstars.* New York: St. Martin's Press, 1999.

Fuller, Graham. "Kathleen Turner." *Interview* 25 (August, 1995): 66-69.

Segrave, Kerry, and Linda Martin. *The Post-feminist Hollywood Actress: Biographies and Filmographies of Stars Born After 1939.* Jefferson, N.C.: McFarland, 1990.

Michael Adams

See also Film in the United States; Hurt, William; Martin, Steve; Nicholson, Jack; *Who Framed Roger Rabbit*.

■ Turner, Ted

Identification American media mogul
Born November 19, 1938; Cincinnati, Ohio

In 1980, Turner founded the first major cable television news network, CNN. His media empire eclipsed the three broadcast television networks and established twenty-four-hour news networks as a powerful factor in journalism.

Ted Turner grew up in Savannah, Georgia, and proved to be an indifferent student who was fascinated by visionary leaders. He took over his father's billboard business, then purchased a struggling Atlanta television station in 1970, WJRJ, changing the station's call letters to WTCG. Turner became fascinated with the potential of satellite broadcasts in the 1970's, and in 1976, WTCG became one of the nation's first so-called superstations, that is, local stations that broadcast via satellite to more than one market. As the broadcasts were picked up by cable television providers across the country, the station (which again changed its name, to WTBS, in 1979)

Ted Turner. (George Bennett)

became a fixture on basic cable. It broadcast primarily old movies, basketball, and baseball.

Interested in further exploiting the possibilities of satellite broadcasts, Turner assembled a team to launch the Cable News Network (CNN). The project faced daunting hurdles, as start-up costs were steep, and investors and advertisers were skeptical that viewers would tune in. In 1979, the satellite Turner had hired to eventually carry the network malfunctioned, and it took a lawsuit to acquire another one. The Federal Communications Commission (FCC) fought Turner's application for a broadcasting license for CNN and relented less than ninety days before the network launch. Once CNN hit the air in June, 1980, viewer share was only half of what Turner had projected, and the network lost $30 million during its first year.

CNN lacked a sound financial foundation, but it filled a major void that had developed in American broadcast journalism. For years, network newsrooms had cut back on international coverage. Turner and CNN covered world events at a fraction of the cost the broadcast networks spent. The result was a steadily growing viewership, although the quality in the first years was decidedly uneven and earned CNN the nickname "Chicken Noodle Network." However, the network's mix of news veterans and eager neophytes created a powerful synergy that baffled the legions of skeptics.

Turner was resolute in his support of the network through its lean years. Salaries for journalists were extremely low, but Turner reminded them that he was risking his own fortune on the network. Turner became a global gadfly and went to meet Fidel Castro in Cuba to try to convince him of the merits of cable news. Castro watched fascinated as CNN became the only network to show footage of the search-and-salvage operation at a Titan missile silo in Arkansas. CNN also provided extended coverage of the trial of the Gang of Four in China, an event that offered valuable insights into the political situation in post-Mao Zedong China. In its first ten years, the network's viewership grew from under two million to sixty million.

Despite the impact of CNN, not all of Turner's endeavors in the 1980's proved successful. His first Goodwill Games, an attempt to hurdle the political issues that had crippled the Olympics, lost $26 million. In 1987, his failed bid to purchase the Columbia Broadcasting System (CBS) showed that his thirst for expansion was coming to an end. A $40 million divorce payout was another setback for Turner.

Impact Turner transformed cable television from a media sideshow into a powerful factor in news and entertainment. Of all his endeavors, CNN revolutionized the way people get their news. In the wake of the network's success, a continuing controversy arose over the pros and cons of twenty-four-hour news. One highlight was CNN's coverage of the space shuttle *Challenger* explosion in January, 1986. Broadcast networks no longer covered shuttle launches, but CNN was there, providing an anguished nation with all the tragic details. A network dedicated solely to news was better equipped to cover breaking stories.

However, twenty-four-hour news was criticized, because, in the rush to cover such breaking news, rumor and speculation could taint the quality of journalism. Moreover, because twenty-four-hour news networks require far more content than do traditional network news programs, they were more likely to cover sensational and other marginally newsworthy events in order to fill airtime. They were also more likely to overdramatize minor developments in ongoing stories, in order to keep those stories fresh. For better or for worse, however, the model first popularized by CNN became common, and the nature of television journalism was permanently changed.

Further Reading

Evans, Harold. *They Made America.* New York: Little, Brown, 2004.

Hack, Richard. *Clash of the Titans.* Beverly Hills, Calif.: New Millennium Press, 2003.

Michael Polley

See also Business and the economy in the United States; CNN; Goodwill Games of 1986; Journalism; Sports; Television.

■ Turner, Tina

Identification American rock-and-roll singer
Born November 26, 1939; Nutbush, Tennessee

The phenomenal success of her musical career at age forty-five and beyond made Turner a legend and changed public perceptions of middle-aged women.

Tina Turner performs in 1988. (Hulton Archive/Getty Images)

By 1980 and age forty, Tina had divorced Ike Turner, ending nearly two decades of violent abuse. The divorce settlement left Tina with no money, but it allowed her to keep the name given to her by her ex-husband to form the Ike and Tina Turner Revue. Once enjoying moderate fame and relative wealth as part of this duo, Tina Turner entered the 1980's nearly broke and struggling to regain credibility.

Acquiring a new manager and updating her wardrobe and hairstyle, Turner toured Europe to welcoming crowds. In the summer of 1981, she was invited to entertain at New York City's Ritz nightclub. Turner's new persona and natural talent were a surprising success. Her startling and unusual appearance, a legacy of mixed African and Native American ancestry, combined with a modern, high-voltage vitality and spirituality, made Turner unique in contemporary American popular music. In 1983, she was again invited to perform at the Ritz. Her show was extremely well attended by celebrities and the general public and was hailed by the music press as Turner's "comeback performance." In England, also in 1983, Turner recorded and released the song "Let's Stay Together"; it reached number six on the United Kingdom singles chart. Later, in the United States, it reached number twenty-six on the *Billboard* Hot 100 and number three on the *Billboard* Hot R&B/Hip-Hop Singles and Tracks chart.

With the 1984 release of the album *Private Dancer*, Turner became an acknowledged international superstar. The album reached number three on the *Billboard* 200, and a single from the album, "What's Love Got to Do with It," reached number one on the *Billboard* Hot 100, a first for one of Turner's recordings. With the best available musicians, song material, and stage settings, Turner performed to sold-out crowds. She won the American Music Award in 1985 for Favorite Female Vocalist and Favorite Video Artist. Later that year, she also won a Grammy award. In 1988, Turner was named in the *Guinness Book of World Records* for having the largest audience for a single performer (in Rio de Janeiro, Brazil). In 1989, she was fifty years old and still enjoying the status of an international superstar.

Impact Tina Turner overcame domestic violence to serve as a role model for women of the 1980's and beyond. Her personal experiences, outlined in an autobiography, gave insight into the restorative powers of determination, self-respect, religious faith, and health-promoting practices. Turner's on-stage persona and style, complete with leather mini-skirts, tangled blond hair, and high-energy sexuality, shattered age stereotypes for female entertainers of the era.

Further Reading

Carby, Hazel V. *Cultures in Babylon: Black Britain and African America.* New York: Verso, 1999.

Lyman, Darryl, and Michael Russel. *Great African-American Women.* New York: J. David, 2005.

Turner, Tina, with Kurt Loder. *I, Tina.* New York: Morrow 1986.

Twyla R. Wells

See also Adams, Bryan; African Americans; Hairstyles; Music; Music videos; Pop music; USA for Africa; Women in rock music.

■ *Twilight Zone* accident

The Event Vic Morrow and two Vietnamese juvenile extras are killed filming a movie
Date July 23, 1982
Place Indian Dunes Park, near Los Angeles, California

The Twilight Zone *accident raised public awareness of the risks assumed by film actors, stunt performers, and crew members to meet directors' demands for realism. The ensuing court case marked the first trial of a Hollywood film director for crimes related to an on-set accident.*

At 2:30 A.M. on July 23, 1982, the final day of shooting on the first of four planned segments of *Twilight Zone: The Movie*, actor Vic Morrow, seven-year-old Myca Dinh Lee, and six-year-old Renee Shinn Chen were killed when detonated explosives hit the tail rotor of a low-flying helicopter. The three performers were struck by the main rotor; Morrow and Lee were beheaded. The actors were shooting a scene in which Morrow's character, an American bigot transported into the past and transformed from oppressor to oppressed, had become a Vietnamese citizen being attacked by American soldiers. His character was rescuing two children from a bomb-besieged village.

An inquiry by the National Transportation Safety Board was followed by a Los Angeles County grand jury investigation in 1983 and a preliminary hearing in 1984. The investigations culminated with five production crew members being charged with involuntary manslaughter. The most famous defendant was director John Landis, who was also one of the movie's producers (with Steven Spielberg). Landis had directed *The Blues Brothers* (1980) and *An American Werewolf in London* (1981) in the previous two years.

When the trial opened on July 23, 1986, prosecutor Lea Purwin D'Agostino described the defendants as "careless and negligent"; Landis's attorney, James Neal, countered by characterizing the deaths as an "unforeseeable accident." Over sixty-nine days, seventy-one witnesses were called, many offering potentially damaging testimony regarding Landis's conduct and demeanor on the set. When Neal called his client to testify on February 19, 1987, Landis admitted breaking California child labor laws by hiring Lee and Chen to work after 6:30 P.M. However, he maintained that he was never warned of any potential peril in shooting the scene. After closing arguments on May 19, 1987, the jury deliberated for nine days and returned not guilty verdicts for all defendants. The acquittal was based on the prosecution's failure to prove that the accident was foreseeable. When the film was released in 1983, it included the work of Vic Morrow.

Impact The *Twilight Zone* accident inspired increased oversight on film sets. Studios and production companies became both more careful and more carefully regulated in their use of children; their efforts to achieve bigger, more dramatic mechanical and physical effects; and their safety precautions to protect actors and stunt doubles. The tragedy also marked the end of the era of silence and secrecy regarding potentially dangerous film scenes; workers in the industry felt freer to express safety concerns without fear of losing their jobs.

Further Reading

Farber, Stephen, and Marc Green. *Outrageous Conduct: Art, Ego, and the "Twilight Zone" Case.* New York: Arbor House, 1988.

Labrecque, Ron. *Special Effects: Disaster at "Twilight Zone"—The Tragedy and the Trial.* New York: Scribner, 1988.

McBride, Joseph. *Steven Spielberg: A Biography.* New York: Simon & Schuster, 1997.

Cecilia Donohue

See also Action films; Epic films; Film in the United States; Horror films; Science-fiction films; Special effects; Spielberg, Steven.

■ Tylenol murders

The Event Tylenol capsules are poisoned with cyanide, resulting in seven deaths

Date September, 1982

Place Chicago, Illinois

The Tylenol murders pressured Congress and the Food and Drug Administration to enact federal laws regulat-

Chicago City Health Department employees test Extra Strength Tylenol capsules for cyanide in October, 1982, in the wake of the September murders in the city. (AP/Wide World Photos)

ing over-the-counter medications and requiring tamper-resistant packaging.

On September 29, 1982, four people in Chicago were hospitalized for similar symptoms that ultimately led to their deaths. Analysis of blood samples indicated that all four deaths were the result of cyanide poisoning. Investigation determined that all four deaths also resulted from the use of Extra Strength Tylenol capsules. Further lab analysis revealed that the capsules contained approximately sixty-five milligrams of cyanide poison, more than ten thousand times the amount needed kill a single individual.

In an attempt to save the reputation of Tylenol, as well as their own, the companies that produced the product, McNeil Consumer Products and Johnson & Johnson, issued a recall. Questions remained, however, concerning whether the poison was added before or after the product was sold. Prior to the re-call, three more citizens in the Chicago area were found dead as a result of poisoned Tylenol capsules. These well-publicized deaths produced a nation-wide fear that overwhelmed hospitals and medical providers, who provided care for many patients with suspected cyanide poisoning symptoms. Federal investigations concluded the deaths were most likely the result of a lone individual who implanted cyanide poison into the bottles and then returned them back to store shelves to be sold.

Investigators had two primary suspects. The first suspect was an employee at a Tylenol warehouse from which two of the poisoned bottles were shipped. He was an amateur chemist, and searches of his residence found research on the methods of killing people with poisoned capsules. The evidence was inconclusive, however, and the suspect was not charged. The second suspect, James W. Lewis, was pursued after he mailed a handwritten letter to Johnson & Johnson claiming that the murders would continue until the company paid him one million dollars. Further investigation concluded that Lewis was not the murderer, but only a con artist. No further leads presented themselves, and the Tylenol murderer was never identified.

Impact Congress responded to the Tylenol murders by passing the Federal Anti-Tampering Act, which President Ronald Reagan signed into law in October, 1983. This law made tampering with consumer products a federal offense. In February of 1989, the Food and Drug Administration increased the tamper-resistant requirements for over-the-counter human drug products. All hard gelatin products were required to have two forms of tamper-resistant packaging. The publicity surrounding the Tylenol murders influenced copycat killers throughout the United States.

Further Reading

Beck, Melinda, and Susan Agrest. "Again, a Tylenol Killer." *Newsweek*, February 24, 1986, 25.

Beck, Melinda, Sylvester Monroe, and Jerry Buckley. "Tylenol: Many Leads, No Arrests." *Newsweek*, October 25, 1982, 30.

Wolnik, K. A., et al. "The Tylenol Tampering Incident: Tracing the Source." *Analytical Chemistry* 56 (1984): 466.

Nicholas D. ten Bensel

See also Business and the economy in the United States; Crime; Medicine; Night Stalker case; Post office shootings; San Ysidro McDonald's massacre; Stockton massacre; Tamper-proof packaging; Terrorism.

■ Tyler, Anne

Identification American novelist
Born October 25, 1941; Minneapolis, Minnesota

The novels published by Tyler during the 1980's firmly cemented her status as a major figure in contemporary American literature. Two of these titles received major writing awards.

Although Anne Tyler had published seven novels between 1964 and 1977, it was her work during the 1980's that established her reputation as an influential twentieth century fiction writer. The decade began for Tyler with the publication of *Morgan's Passing* (1980), a novel featuring a type of lead character

Anne Tyler. (© Diana Walker)

that would become the signature Tyler protagonist: an ordinary Baltimore-area resident (in this case, Morgan Gower) who addresses middle-age malaise with random acts of interpersonal connection laced, more often than not, with an extraordinarily quirky dimension.

Morgan's Passing was followed by *Dinner at the Homesick Restaurant* (1982), which received extensive critical acclaim from both scholarly and casual readers. This novel, a narrative told in flashback of Pearl Tull's problematic relationships with her three children, is arguably Anne Tyler's richest in terms of plot and character, and it stands as the work that placed her name on the list of must-read writers of the era. Her next two novels enjoyed equal popularity, and both were honored with prestigious literary awards. *The Accidental Tourist* (1985), winner of the National Book Critics Circle Award, introduced readers to Macon Leary, a travel writer who overcomes family tragedy and obsession with control to experience another Tyler trademark plot point: the opportunity to reinvent one's life.

Three years later, Tyler's novel *Breathing Lessons* (1988) received the Pulitzer Prize. In this work, the family foibles of the Moran clan unfold against the backdrop of a drive from Baltimore to Pennsylvania to attend a funeral. *Breathing Lessons* features several plot devices that Tyler employed in the two novels immediately preceding it. For example, both Macon Leary and Ira Moran are male lead characters who crave control. Impulsive marriages following an abrupt jilting play a role in *Dinner at the Homesick Restaurant* as well as in *Breathing Lessons*, and both novels include scenes of unpleasant family dinners. Despite recurring motifs and situations, Tyler's consistently careful crafting of characters makes each family ensemble unique and memorable.

Impact Anne Tyler's treatment of subject matter previously considered too mundane for the novel—life events randomly experienced by average, uncelebrated families—paved the way for other writers of the 1980's and beyond to address similar topics. In addition, her concentration on the Baltimore, Maryland, region of the United States was influential in the growth and popularity of American Southern regional fiction.

Further Reading

Bail, Paul. *Anne Tyler: A Critical Companion*. Westport, Conn.: Greenwood Press, 1998.

Salwak, Dale, ed. *Anne Tyler as Novelist*. Iowa City: University of Iowa Press, 1994.

Cecilia Donohue

See also Beattie, Ann; Erdrich, Louise; Literature in the United States; Miller, Sue; Naylor, Gloria.

■ Tyson, Mike

Identification World heavyweight boxing champion
Born June 30, 1966; Brooklyn, New York

Tyson exploded onto the heavyweight boxing scene in the middle of the 1980's and remained a dominant figure in the sports world generally for the remainder of the decade.

After experiencing a troubled, inner-city childhood, Mike Tyson was discovered in the early 1980's by well-known boxing manager and trainer Cus D'Amato, who guided him into a professional boxing career. Although relatively short for a modern-era heavyweight fighter at five feet, eleven inches, Tyson's physique was heavily muscled and compact, and he punched with a ferocious, animal intensity. On November 11, 1986, after winning his first twenty-seven bouts—twenty-five of them by knockout—and less than two years after the start of his professional career, Tyson defeated Trevor Berbick in a dramatic second-round technical knockout (TKO) to win the World Boxing Council's heavyweight title. At the age of twenty years and four months, he was the youngest man ever to win the heavyweight title, and his dramatic ascent in the sport captivated the nation in a manner reminiscent of the emergence of Muhammad Ali two decades earlier.

Trained by D'Amato protégé Kevin Rooney following D'Amato's death in November of 1985, Tyson quickly fought the leading heavyweights of the period, and in the process unified the splintered heavyweight division. He won the World Boxing Association title by decision from James "Bonecrusher" Smith in March of 1987, defeated highly ranked heavyweight Pinklon Thomas by a sixth-round knockout in May, and won the International Boxing Federation title by decision from Tony Tucker in August. After defending the title once more in December, he took on former champion Larry Holmes in January of 1988, inflicting the only knockout scored against Holmes in his seventy-five-fight career.

Tyson continued to score dramatic victories during the remainder of 1988, defeating Tony Tubbs by a second-round TKO in Tokyo in March and knocking out Michael Spinks, the man who had taken the title from Larry Holmes earlier in the decade, in the first round in June. By 1989, however, problems had surfaced in both Tyson's career and his personal life. Late in 1988, he fired Rooney and without his guidance became increasingly reckless and undisciplined in the ring. He looked sloppy in defeating British heavyweight Frank Bruno in February of 1989, although he managed to defeat Carl Williams with a first-round knockout in July. During this time, he also came under the control of controversial boxing promoter Don King, whose role in Tyson's career seemed more exploitative than attuned to the boxer's best interests. Finally, Tyson's brief (1988-1989) marriage to actress Robin Givens ended in a highly publicized divorce, amid accusations of physical abuse and marital infidelity.

Impact In the years that followed, Tyson's personal life would continue its decline, including a three-year prison term for rape in the early 1990's, and his invincibility in the ring would fade, but during the second half of the 1980's, he was unquestionably one of the best-known and most dynamic figures in the world of professional sports.

Further Reading

Heller, Peter. *Bad Intentions: The Mike Tyson Story.* New York: New American Library, 1989.

O'Connor, Daniel, ed. *Iron Mike: A Mike Tyson Reader.* New York: Thunder's Mouth Press, 2002.

Scott Wright

See also African Americans; Boxing; Holmes, Larry; Sports.

U

■ Ueberroth, Peter

Identification   President of the 1984 Summer
Olympics and commissioner of Major League
Baseball, 1984-1989
Born   September 2, 1937; Evanston, Illinois

*Ueberroth brought an entrepreneurial spirit to his position
as the president of the 1984 Los Angeles Summer Olympics,
which resulted in a major financial windfall for the Olympics. Later, as commissioner of Major League Baseball,
Ueberroth instituted a zero tolerance drug policy for baseball
players and resolved other labor issues.*

Peter Ueberroth, a multimillionaire and travel industry executive, served as the president of the 1984
Los Angeles Summer Olympic Games. As an entrepreneur, Ueberroth brought business acumen to the
Games. His negotiations with the American Broadcasting Company (ABC) television network to air
the Summer Olympics resulted in
revenue of $225 million. He raised
$150 million from foreign television corporations, and he increased
the number of corporate sponsorships to the Olympics Games. Ueberroth accomplished all this despite a boycott led by the Soviet
Union. As a result of his hard-nosed
managerial approach, he turned a
multimillion-dollar profit for the
Olympics, the first time the Games
made a profit in over fifty years.

Ueberroth also lent his time and
expertise to public affairs. He
served on several of President Ronald Reagan's presidential committees to address some national social
issues, and he was tapped by Lee
Iacocca, president of Chrysler Corporation, to join the commission
for the restoration of the Statue of
Liberty.

After his tenure as president of the 1984 Summer
Olympics, Ueberroth took office as the sixth commissioner of Major League Baseball (MLB) on October 1, 1984. He approached baseball with the same
passion and problem-solving skills with which he
had approached the Olympics Games. At that time,
MLB faced several challenges and controversies.
Ueberroth resolved these issues and returned baseball to its prominent position as America's favorite
sport. In March, 1985, he reinstated baseball Hall of
Famers Willie Mays and Mickey Mantle, who had
been banned from the sport because of their association with Atlantic City casinos.

In 1985, Ueberroth arbitrated a labor dispute between team owners and the Major League Baseball
Players Association union regarding the issue of free
agents; however, the players later filed charges of
collusion (which Ueberroth had facilitated) against
the team owners and won. In February, 1986, show-

*Peter Ueberroth, right, leads International Olympic Committee president Juan Antonio
Samaranch through the Los Angeles Memorial Coliseum before the opening ceremonies
of the 1984 Summer Olympics. (AP/Wide World Photos)*

ing little patience for baseball players who tested positive for drug use, he suspended and fined several players, continuing this zero tolerance policy over the next few years. In one of his last major actions as commissioner, in February, 1989, Ueberroth met with incoming baseball commissioner Bart Giamatti to discuss alleged gambling in baseball. Ueberroth left his commissionership prior to the start of the 1989 baseball season and returned to the private sector to work as a corporate turnaround specialist.

Impact   Through his actions, Ueberroth set a new standard for the Olympic Games. His take-charge leadership style and his no-nonsense policies lifted Major League Baseball from a dark period and brought a new appreciation for the country's national pastime.

Further Reading

Ajemian, Robert. "Peter Ueberroth, Man of the Year." *Time* 125, no. 1 (January 7, 1985).

Ueberroth, Peter, with Richard Levin and Amy Quinn. *Made in America: His Own Story.* New York: William Morrow, 1985.

Joseph C. Santora

See also   Baseball; Business and the economy in the United States; Olympic boycotts; Olympic Games of 1984; Rose, Pete; Sports; Statue of Liberty restoration and centennial.

■ Unemployment in Canada

Definition   The proportion of the Canadian labor force that is without work and seeking work

The rate of unemployment in the United States and Canada was virtually the same from 1948 to 1980. Beginning in 1981, however, the Canadian unemployment rate averaged more than two percentage points higher, and it rose throughout the decade.

The year 1981 marked the beginning of a deep recession in Canada caused by inflationary pressures from the energy crisis of the 1970's. Although increased capital investment created more jobs, with employment growing by an annual rate of 2.5 percent, consumer spending reflected economic insecurity. Interest rates rose significantly in the 1980's, and the monetary policy pursued by the Bank of

Canada widened the gap between Canadian and U.S. interest rates.

The first Canadian industries to reflect the recession were those most responsive to interest rates: home construction, durable consumer goods, and export goods. Regional differences in unemployment increased substantially, with British Columbia, the Atlantic provinces, and Quebec suffering most.

Unemployment was also unevenly distributed among segments of the population. Although older workers (those aged fifty-five to sixty-four) had always had higher-than-average unemployment rates compared to other workers, the 1980's saw a two-percentage-point rise in unemployment for that segment of the population. Female unemployment was always higher than the male rate, but the actual spread between the rates did not change. The most considerable rise in unemployment occurred among the low-skilled or undereducated segment (those with eight or fewer years of schooling). This group's unemployment rate rose to more than 11 percent, an increase of 2.5 percentage points from 1981 to 1989. Finally, the percentage of long-term unemployment (defined as twelve months or more) rose from 3.6 percent to a peak of 9.5 percent in 1984-1987, then fell to 6.9 percent by the end of the decade. Older workers were especially likely to suffer longer periods of joblessness.

Impact   Because the economic performance of the United States and Canada was similar during the 1980's, the difference in the countries' unemployment rates requires explanation. Some researchers believe that the disparity between U.S. and Canadian unemployment rates is partly accounted for by statistical issues; for example, "passive" job searchers, whose only effort to find employment involves searching want ads, were classified as unemployed by Canada, but not by the United States. A case can also be made that the more generous coverage of unemployment insurance in Canada raised labor force participation and made longer-term unemployment more bearable than in the United States.

Further Reading

Card, David, and W. Craig Ridell. "Unemployment in Canada and the United States: A Further Analysis." In *Trade, Technology, and Economics: Essays in Honour of Richard G. Lipsey,* edited by B. Curtis Eaton and Richard G. Harris. Cheltenham, England: Edward Elgar Press, 1997.

Sharpe, Andrew. "The Canada-U.S. Unemployment Rate Gap: An Assessment of Possible Causes." Research Paper R-96-15E.a. Ottawa: Human Resources Development Canada, Strategic Policy, Applied Research Branch, 1996.

Jan Hall

See also   Business and the economy in Canada; Business and the economy in the United States; Canada and the United States; Demographics of Canada; Demographics of the United States; Inflation in Canada; Inflation in the United States; Recessions; Unemployment in the United States.

■ Unemployment in the United States

Definition   The proportion of the U.S. labor force that is both without work and seeking work

Persistently high and growing unemployment in the early 1980's created anxiety regarding the health of the U.S. economy.

As an economic indicator, the unemployment rate is used to gauge the state of the economy and to guide economic policy. When the unemployment rate during the early part of the 1980's reached its highest level since the 1930's (the years that included the Great Depression), many saw this high unemployment as evidence that the economy was in decline. Viewed from a longer perspective, though, the high unemployment rate in the early 1980's, followed by its steady decline to much lower levels at the end of the decade, seems to indicate that the national economy was adjusting to globalization.

The official U.S. unemployment rate is compiled monthly by the Bureau of Labor Statistics, which is part of the U.S. Department of Labor. Based on a random sample of households, the unemployment rate estimates the percentage of individuals in the labor force without a job. To be considered part of the labor force, an individual must be sixteen years old or older and either have a job or be actively seek-ing one. Those without a job who are not looking for one are not considered to be unemployed, because they are not part of the labor force.

Types of Unemployment   In order to understand what caused changes in the unemployment rate during the 1980's, it is useful to divide unemployment into three categories. Frictional unemployment results when people who are qualified for available jobs have not yet secured a position. Structural unemployment results when people are unqualified for the jobs available. Cyclical unemployment results when too few jobs are available because the economy is not strong enough to support its entire labor force. The unemployment rate will change if there is a change in any one of these three type of unemployment.

Changes in the unemployment rate during the 1980's resulted from changes in both structural and

President Ronald Reagan's son, Ronald Reagan, Jr., stands in line to collect unemployment benefits on October 14, 1982. (AP/Wide World Photos)

U.S. Unemployment Rates, 1980-1989

Year	Unemployment %
1980	7.1
1981	7.6
1982	9.7
1983	9.6
1984	7.5
1985	7.1
1986	7.0
1987	6.2
1988	5.5
1989	5.3

Source: Department of Labor, Bureau of Labor Statistics, Local Area Unemployment Statistics, March, 2005.

cyclical unemployment. Early in the decade, the Federal Reserve attempted to slow the growth of the money supply in order to reduce the rate of inflation. This decision caused a decline in economic activity and resulted in two recessions spanning the period from 1980 to 1982. As a result, the number of available jobs decreased, increasing cyclical unemployment.

The early 1980's also witnessed an increase in the value of the dollar relative to the currencies of other countries. Economic policies implemented under the Ronald Reagan administration, often referred to as "Reaganomics," included tax cuts and increased defense spending. These policies led to increased borrowing by the federal government, which, combined with the slowing growth of the money supply, raised interest rates and, in the process, the value of the dollar. The increased value of the dollar made it more difficult for U.S. producers to sell their products in other countries, while the relatively low value of foreign currency made it easier for foreign producers to sell their producets in the United States. Not only did this contribute to a rise in cyclical unemployment, but it also increased structural unemployment, as many manufacturing jobs permanently moved to other countries, eliminating the need in the United States for those skills possessed by many manufacturing workers.

As the economy emerged from the recession that ended in 1982, inflation came under control and the Federal Reserve allowed the money supply to grow at a faster rate. As a result, the unemployment rate began to fall from its high of 11.4 percent in January, 1983, and by 1988 it had settled at 5 to 6 percent. Many economists see that range as being within the range of the "natural" rate of unemployment, that is, the rate at which only frictional and structural unemployment exist. As the value of the dollar began to fall relative to other currencies over the latter part of the decade, U.S. firms became more competitive relative to the rest of the world. The expansion in economic activity eliminated cyclical unemployment.

Impact High unemployment imposes a burden on both individuals and society. Individuals lose a major source of income, and society loses the output that could have been produced. In addition, the high unemployment of the early 1980's, coupled with shrinking union membership accompanying the decline of manufacturing jobs, reduced the bargaining power of labor. Although policies were implemented that cut the unemployment rate through the remaining part of the decade, the fear of unemployment tended to keep wage demands relatively modest. As cyclical unemployment decreased, moreover, structural unemployment (which results largely from inadequate education and training) became a greater source of worry. When a federal commission published *A Nation at Risk* in 1983, Americans' attention was focused on the importance of education to sustain the long-term health of the economy.

Further Reading

Brenner, Robert. *The Boom and the Bubble: The U.S. in the World Economy.* London: Verso, 2002. Wonderful analysis of the impact of globalization on the U.S. economy since the early 1970's and its effect on unemployment in the 1980's.

French, Michael. *U.S. Economic History Since 1945.* Manchester, England: Manchester University Press, 1997. Concise overview of American socioeconomic history since World War II; puts the events of the 1980's into a larger context.

Heilbroner, Robert, and Lester Thurow. *Economics Explained.* New York: Touchstone, 1998. Useful overview of key economic concepts such as unemployment, inflation, and globalization and how those phenomena have affected society.

Randall Hannum

See also Business and the economy in the United States; Demographics of the United States; Economic Recovery Tax Act of 1981; Globalization; Income and wages in the United States; Inflation in the United States; *Nation at Risk, A*; Reaganomics; Recessions; Tax Reform Act of 1986; Unemployment in Canada; Unions; Welfare.

■ Unions

Definition Organizations of workers who join together to protect their common interests and improve their wages and working conditions

From the 1930's to the 1970's, organized labor was a potent economic and political force; by 1980, one-quarter of American workers belonged to a union. During the 1980's, however, union membership fell rapidly as a result of economic changes, outsourcing of jobs overseas, and an increasingly hostile legal and political climate.

The 1980's was a devastating decade for American workers and their unions. Approximately eighty national unions existed in the United States during the 1980's; roughly 84 percent were affiliated with the AFL-CIO, and 16 percent were independent unions. Overall union membership declined from 25 percent of workers in 1980 to 16 percent in 1990. Some of the largest and most powerful unions were particularly hard hit: Between 1978 and 1981 alone, the steelworkers lost 827,000 members, autoworkers lost 659,000, and building trades unions lost more than 1 million. Only public-sector unionism held relatively strong, averaging 37 percent of eligible workers (not all public employees had the right to join unions). By contrast, private-sector unionism plummeted to 11 percent in 1990, by far the lowest rate of any Western industrialized country. In neighboring Canada, 36 percent of the total workforce remained unionized.

The causes of this decline are multifaceted. As the 1980's began, the nation was still in the midst of the worst economic downturn (1979-1981) since the Great Depression of the 1930's. Since the mid-1970's, U.S. corporations had faced increasing competition from abroad. They sought to reduce costs by cutting wages and moving their plants to nonunion areas within the United States (primarily the South and the West) or overseas. Industrial America, once the heartland of blue-collar unionism, was decimated by plant closings. Meanwhile, many employers adopted aggressive antiunion policies, hiring new "union-busting" firms at the first hint of union organizing in their plants. Others sought to break unions with which they had bargained for years, resulting in some of the most bitterly fought strikes of the decade. At the same time, unions faced a far chillier political, legal, and social climate. The National Labor Relations Board (NLRB), the courts, the media, and the executive branch all endorsed policies that increasingly restricted the rights of American workers to organize, bargain collectively, and strike.

Reagan and PATCO The policies of the Ronald Reagan administration were pivotal in helping to establish this antiunion climate. On August 3, 1981, nearly 13,000 federal air traffic controllers walked off their jobs after months of unsuccessful negotiations. For years, they had complained about obsolete equipment, chronic understaffing, mandatory overtime, rotating shift schedules, safety problems, and stress.

Within four hours, President Reagan declared on national television that controllers who did not return to work within forty-eight hours would lose their jobs. Two days later, Reagan fired approximately 11,300 controllers. After breaking the strike, he announced that the strikers would never be rehired for their former positions and the Professional Air Traffic Controllers Organization (PATCO) would be decertified (essentially destroyed). PATCO's demise represented the most stunning defeat for unions in many decades. The president's actions foreshadowed the increasingly harsh political climate facing union organizers and heralded a decade of dramatic defeats that reversed many of the gains of the previous fifty years. Ironically, the politically conservative PATCO had been one of the few unions to support Reagan. To many observers, Reagan's defeat of PATCO appeared to put a presidential seal of approval on hard-line antiunion strategies.

Concessions and Givebacks Unions were on the defensive throughout the decade. In almost every strike and contract negotiation, union leaders conceded to demands for ever larger givebacks and concessions. During the first half of the 1980's, workers lost an estimated $500 billion to cuts in wages and benefits. In 1982 alone, the seven largest steel companies demanded $6 billion in concessions in that

Garment workers in Scranton, Pennsylvania, march with picket signs in 1984. (AP/Wide World Photos)

year's Master Steel Agreement negotiations. By 1986, less than 33 percent of major union contracts still had cost-of-living adjustments (COLAs, which are indexed to inflation), compared with 60 percent in 1979. Annual raises were replaced by bonuses that were not included in a worker's base pay. "Two-tiered" systems were established in which new hires received significantly lower pay and benefits. Unions also relinquished some paid holidays and personal days, acceded to cuts in medical and retirement plans, and agreed to work out changes that gave employers more control. Nationally, average wages declined. By 1990, unions no longer set the wage standards in any major industry, as they had done for decades in auto, steel, rubber, mining, and transportation.

The nation's dramatic shift from a manufacturing to a service economy compounded the problem. Between 1979 and 1989, the number of manufacturing jobs declined from 21 million to 19.4 million, while the number of service-sector jobs (in fast-food restaurants, retail and discount stores, hotels, nursing homes, and offices) mushroomed from 32 million to 45 million. These new jobs tended to be poorly paid, insecure, devoid of benefits, and non-unionized.

Strike Breaking and Replacement Workers Employers seized upon an obscure loophole in a 1938 Supreme Court decision, in the case of *National Labor Relations Board v. Mackay Radio*, that allowed them to continue operations by "permanently replacing" rather than firing striking workers. Between 1985 and 1989, employers hired permanent replacement workers in nearly 20 percent of strikes. In theory, a striking worker lost only his or her particular job; the employer was legally obligated to offer such an employee the first new position that opened. However, in an era of downsizing, few striking workers were recalled. Before 1981, the *Mackay Radio* decision was little known and rarely used. However, it quickly became the bane of the labor movement, as a growing number of major corporations began using it.

Replacement workers were recruited during strikes at Maytag and Greyhound Lines in 1983; Phelps Dodge and Continental Airlines in 1984;

Hormel and the *Chicago Tribune* in 1985; Colt and Trans World Airlines in 1986; International Paper in 1987; and Eastern Airlines, Pittston Coal Company, and Greyhound Lines in 1989. These strikes were among the bitterest and most violent of the post-World War II period. During the 1980's, thousands of strikers lost their jobs to permanent replacement hires, sending a profound chill through union ranks. Strike activity declined sharply. The number of major walkouts (defined as involving 1,000 or more workers) plummeted from an average of 290 per year in the 1970's to 35 per year in the early 1990's.

Firings for Legally Protected Activities In 1984, pro-union workers were fired at a rate four times greater than in 1960. Legally, workers had the right to form unions, and an employer could not fire a worker for union activity. However, because the penalties were modest (illegally fired workers received no punitive damages), employers increasingly resorted to firing union supporters, leaving it up to the workers to seek redress.

In the 1950's, the NLRB ruled that workers were illegally fired in only 4 percent of union-organizing drives; by the early 1980's, that percentage had soared to 32 percent. In 1985, an average of one of every thirty-eight workers who voted for a union was illegally fired (and later reinstated by NLRB order), compared to one worker in six hundred during the 1950's. However, a far greater number of illegally fired workers simply gave up and failed to request reinstatement. According to a 1990 Government Accounting Office (GAO) study, it took three years for the average worker to complete the prolonged NLRB appeals process. When illegally fired workers were finally rehired, they returned to a very different workplace: The union organizing drive they had been fired for supporting had typically collapsed.

Hostile Legal and Judicial Climate From 1981 to 1983, the Reagan administration failed to fill two seats on the NLRB, creating a backlog of cases. When appointments were made, openly probusiness candidates were selected. Under the chairmanship of corporate lawyer Donald Dotson, the NLRB issued a string of antiunion decisions. For example, in *Meyers Industries, Inc.,* the NLRB overturned a 1975 decision by upholding the firing of a truck driver who had complained about an unsafe truck. In *Rossmore House,* the NLRB overturned previous precedents by ruling that an employer could inter-

rogate workers about a union organizing drive. In a series of decisions on plant closings and runaway shops, the board removed barriers to employer relocation to nonunion, low-wage areas.

Meanwhile, since the 1940's the Supreme Court had been redefining labor law. Nearly all of the tactics used by unions during the great upsurge of the 1930's—including sit-down strikes, factory occupations, mass picketing, secondary boycotts, wildcats (strikes without formal union authorization), and strikes over grievances—had been declared unconstitutional. Whereas corporations faced no punitive damages for illegally firing workers for their union activity, during the 1980's unions faced severe penalties and hefty fines if they engaged in any of these activities. Meanwhile, employers hired antiunion consulting firms in more than half of organizing drives.

Unions Adopt a Cautious Approach For the most part, union leaders adopted a conciliatory stance. Many unions responded to their declining numbers by either merging with other unions or competing to win over independent employee associations, neglecting the critical yet time-consuming task of organizing and recruiting new members. Although coalitions against plant closings sprang up across the nation, such as the "Save Our Valley" coalition in Youngstown, Ohio (which saw the closing of three steel mills and loss of ten thousand union jobs by 1980), few enjoyed any significant success.

Lane Kirkland's presidency of the AFL-CIO (1979-1995) began with high hopes that were quickly dashed. Although he appeared more open-minded and exuded a more professional persona than his burly, cigar-chomping predecessor, George Meany (AFL-CIO president, 1955-1979), as the 1980's wore on it became apparent that little had changed. Kirkland devoted few resources to recruiting and new outreach initiatives until 1989, when an AFL-CIO "Organizing Institute" was created.

While Kirkland played a major financial role in supporting the Polish trade union Solidarity, he also embraced the movement against communism and lent labor's support to various right-wing groups and institutes abroad, further alienating the federation from other progressive movements. The AFL-CIO continued to hold itself aloof from potential new constituencies and social movements. Although Kirkland did expand the executive council to include its first woman and more minorities, in 1989 there were only two women and two minorities on the thirty-five-member board.

Increasingly, union leaders were perceived as a clique of mostly middle-aged white men, even though women and minorities represented the fastest-growing sectors of the labor movement. Grassroots discontent mounted and was channeled into the formation of groups such as Teamsters for a Democratic Union, the autoworkers' New Directions Caucus, Black Workers for Justice, Asian Pacific American Labor Alliance, Jobs with Justice, and the Gay and Lesbian Labor Activist Network. Throughout the 1980's, insurgents challenged union bureaucrats on issues relating to foreign policy, concessions, corruption, lack of internal democracy, failure to organize new members, racism, and sexism. These reform efforts culminated in 1995 with the election of John Sweeney as president of the AFL-CIO on a "new voice" slate that defeated all of the federation's top officers. Sweeney's victory represented the first successful challenge to an AFL-CIO president in more than one hundred years.

Successes and Failures Although successful campaigns were few and far between during the 1980's, they were significant in pointing the way toward new strategies and forms of organizing. In many cases, "rank-and-file" or local union activists came into bitter conflict with their more conservative national union leadership. The most successful struggles utilized creative tactics and welcomed broad community support. Victories (full and partial) included the 1984 United Mine Workers strike; the 1985-1987 strike of Watsonville cannery workers in Salinas Valley, California; the Justice for Janitors campaign that began in Los Angeles in 1985; and successful union organizing drives among clerical and technical staff at Yale and Harvard Universities. Both university campaigns lasted three years and involved civil disobedience, community rallies, student and faculty support, and office shutdowns. During the 1989 United Mine Workers strike against the Pittston Coal Company, workers established a "camp solidarity" program whereby the "Daughters of Mother Jones" trained thousands in civil disobedience. In eleven states, forty thousand miners staged wildcat solidarity strikes while others occupied a plant. Unions also lobbied successfully for legislation to provide some severance pay and retraining programs for workers laid off as a result of plant closings.

Among the most significant union defeats were the 1983 Phelps Dodge Mining Company copper miners' strike and the 1985 Hormel meatpackers' strike. Both involved the use of National Guard troops. Equally representative of the decade's struggles was the stunning defeat of the United Auto Workers' effort to unionize a Nissan plant in Tennessee in 1989. When the election results were announced, antiunion workers cheered and danced in the street, carrying banners that read "Union Free and Proud."

Impact During the 1980's, the rights of American workers to organize, bargain collectively, and strike were seriously eroded. The NLRB's conservative rulings created enduring legal precedents. Likewise, employers' use of permanent replacement workers and other union-busting tactics continued long after the decade's end.

Nearly all studies reveal that unionized workers receive higher wages and better benefits than their nonunionized peers. The loss of union jobs contributed to the shrinking of the American middle class. After 1980, a declining number of workers enjoyed benefits such as full medical coverage, guaranteed retirement plans, and vacation and sick pay. Between 1980 and 1990, more than 10 million new jobs were created that paid less than thirteen thousand dollars per year, while only 1.6 million new jobs were created that paid more than twenty-seven thousand dollars (in year 2000 dollars). Whereas between 1947 and 1978, real hourly wages grew 80 percent (adjusted for inflation) and workers saw their standard of living steadily improve, during the 1980's real hourly wages declined. Family income did rise slightly after 1986, but only because more wives were working outside the home and both men and women were working longer hours. Under attack from all sides, American unions, which had once enjoyed great power, influence, and prestige, lost the leading role they had played in the nation's economy and, at the same time, lost their ability to lift a significant portion of America's blue-collar and industrial workers into the ranks of the middle class.

Further Reading

Babson, Steve. *The Unfinished Struggle: Turning Points in American Labor, 1877-Present.* Lanham, Md.: Rowman & Littlefield, 1999. Chapter 5, "At the Crossroads," offers a thoughtful examination of the crisis of unions in the 1980's. Extremely concise yet comprehensive.

Brisbin, Richard A. *A Strike Like No Other Strike: Law and Resistance During the Pittston Coal Strike of 1989-1990.* Baltimore: The Johns Hopkins University Press, 2003. Brisbin recounts one of the decade's few successful union victories. Theoretical, for more advanced students.

Dubofsky, Melvyn, and Foster Rhea Dulles. *Labor in America: A History.* 7th ed. Wheeling, Ill.: Harlan Davidson Press, 2004. Written by two of the leading scholars of U.S. labor history, this classic, vividly written overview has an excellent chapter on the 1980's, aptly titled "Hard Times."

Goldfield, Michael. *The Decline of Organized Labor in the United States.* Chicago: University of Chicago Press, 1989. An incisive analysis of the causes of union decline in the 1980's. Uses statistical and historical data to puncture many popular myths.

Moody, Kim. *U.S. Labor in Trouble and Transition: The Failure of Reform from Above, the Promise of Revival from Below.* New York: Verso Press, 2007. A leading labor scholar and activist, Moody offers a penetrating analysis of the failure of unions in the 1980's. Concludes with a survey of the new leadership, strategies, and initiatives that have emerged since then.

Murolo, Priscilla, and A. B. Chitty. *From the Folks Who Brought You the Weekend: A Short, Illustrated History of Labor in the United States.* New York: The New Press, 2001. Easily accessible and written for a popular audience, this comprehensive survey devotes a lengthy chapter to the 1980's, titled "Hard Times." The section "Fighting Back" chronicles a number of innovative union campaigns.

Perusek, Glenn, and Kent Worcester, eds. *Trade Union Politics: American Unions and Economic Change, 1960's-1990's.* Atlantic Highlands, N.J.: Humanities Press, 1995. A sophisticated analysis for advanced students, this provocative volume offers competing theories and perspectives on unions' responses to globalization and corporate offenses.

Rachleff, Peter. *Hard-Pressed in the Heartland: The Hormel Strike and the Future of the Labor Movement.* Boston: South End Press, 1992. A brief and engaging account of one of the most important strikes of the decade. The conflict pitted local union activists against their national affiliate and AFL-CIO leadership.

Rosenblum, Jonathan D. *Copper Crucible: How the Arizona Miners Strike of 1983 Recast Labor-Management Relations in America.* Ithaca, N.Y.: Cornell University Press, 1995. Sympathetic but not uncritical examination of the 1983-1986 strike against the Phelps Dodge copper company. The use of the National Guard and permanent replacement workers made this a pivotal event in 1980's labor history.

L. Mara Dodge

See also Air traffic controllers' strike; Business and the economy in the United States; Chrysler Corporation federal rescue; De Lorean, John; Globalization; Iacocca, Lee; Income and wages in the United States; Reagan Revolution; Reaganomics; Recessions; Unemployment in Canada; Unemployment in the United States; Women in the workforce.

■ United Nations

Identification   International organization
Date   Established in 1945
Place   Headquartered in New York City

During the 1980's, the United Nations faced a wide array of global problems but managed to maintain global peace and continue its work addressing the worldwide problems of hunger, poverty, and disease.

The 1980's proved to be a tenuous decade, as the Soviet Union and the United States intensified efforts to undermine each other during the Cold War. Many violent conflicts that drew the support of one superpower immediately attracted the opposing support of the other, escalating the level of death and destruction. As the leading members of the United Nations, including the superpowers, often limited the organization's decision-making abilities, it had to assume a rather awkward position—or one of ambivalence—in many of the decade's conflicts, despite its best efforts to bring about peace.

Some of the most controversial conflicts of the decade included the Soviet invasion and occupation of Afghanistan, the Iran-Iraq War, and the impasse over apartheid in South Africa. The Islamic revolution in Iran that was attended by 444 days of a U.S. hostage standoff, the 1982 Israeli invasion of Lebanon, the escalating tensions between Pakistan and India, and the intensification of terrorist acts in the Middle East combined to create a deadly scenario for the United Nations during the decade.

As the levels of interest in many of the conflicts created a kaleidoscope of alliances and blocs of protest among nations, it was often difficult if not impossible for the United Nations to take a decisive and unambiguous position on many of these issues. The Soviet invasion of Afghanistan in December, 1979, was a case in point. At its meeting in Islamabad in January, 1980, the Organization of the Islamic Conference deplored the Soviet invasion and demanded its withdrawal. In the same vein, the U.N. General Assembly voted overwhelmingly for a resolution that "strongly deplored" the "recent armed intervention" in Afghanistan and called for the "total withdrawal of foreign troops" from the country. The resolution was considered illegal, however, because the invasion was favored by the "legitimate" government of Afghanistan; therefore, the resolution was a violation of its sovereign rights. Ironically, many nonaligned countries such as India, Algeria, Iraq, Syria, Libya, and Finland considered the U.N. resolution illegal and failed to grant their support.

The U.N. Security Council found it impossible to act, because the Soviets had veto power. The General Assembly was therefore limited to passing various resolutions opposing the Soviet occupation. Informal negotiations for a Soviet withdrawal from Afghanistan that started in 1982 came to fruition in 1988 as the governments of Pakistan and Afghanistan signed an agreement settling their major differences during the Geneva Accords. The United Nations set up a special mission to oversee the process, and the withdrawal of Soviet troops was announced on July 20, 1987.

Fighting Poverty, Hunger, and Disease

The United Nations was confronted with two major problems in its efforts to combat disease, hunger, and poverty in most developing parts of the world during the 1980's: the massive debt crisis that had crippled the economies of developing nations and the acquired immunodeficiency syndrome (AIDS) pandemic caused by human immunodeficiency virus (HIV).

The International Monetary Fund (IMF) and the World Bank, subsidiaries of the United Nations, were blamed directly for the exacerbating poverty that spread throughout most of the developing world following countries' compliance with Structural Adjustment Programs (SAP). The programs had,

among other things, insisted on the removal of government subsidies on essential services such as education, health, and transport, which in turn led to a drastic reduction of jobs, real income, and purchasing power.

As most of the developing world, especially Africa, stood in the throes of the HIV/AIDS pandemic, the United Nations was forced to redouble its efforts to address this urgent problem threatening millions of lives during the decade. The United Nations, working through the World Health Organization (WHO) and nongovernmental organizations (NGOs), collaborated with various governments to provide both education and medicine in highly affected regions.

Impact   In the 1980's, the United Nations demonstrated that it could withstand turbulent global events that threatened its existence. The League of Nations, the precursor to the United Nations, proved to be less resilient at the outbreak of World War II. Although the United Nations was not threatened by a conflict of that magnitude, there were many close calls, especially the festering ideological conflict of the Cold War between the East and West, that set the tone for many proxy conflicts around the world.

During the 1980's, the leadership of the United Nations managed to maintain its commitment to dealing with issues of conflict and peace as well as those of hunger, poverty, and disease affecting many of the developing countries of the world. As expected, there were many high and low points for the administration.

Further Reading

Bennett, LeRoy, and James K. Oliver. *International Organizations: Principles and Issues.* 7th ed. Upper Saddle River, N.J.: Prentice Hall, 2002. Describes the organization, structure, and operations of the United Nations.

O'Sullivan, Christopher D. *The United Nations: A Concise History.* Huntington, N.Y.: Krieger, 2005. Covers the first sixty years of the United Nations.

Peterson, M. J. *The General Assembly in World Politics.* Boston: Unwin Hyman, 1986. Provides an in-depth look at the structure and function of the U.N. General Assembly during the 1980's.

United Nations. www.un.org. The organization's official Web site. Contains a search feature allowing users to research U.N. actions.

Austin Ogunsuyi

See also   Africa and the United States; China and the United States; Cold War; Europe and North America; Foreign policy of Canada; Foreign policy of the United States; Iranian hostage crisis; Israel and the United States; Japan and North America; Latin America; Mexico and the United States; Middle East and North America; Soviet Union and North America.

■ US Festivals

The Event   Two popular music festivals take place in Southern California

Date   September 3-5, 1982; May 28-30 and June 4, 1983

Place   Glen Helen Regional Park, near Devore, California

The US Festivals were the largest multiday music events in North America during the 1980's.

The US Festivals were the first major multiday rock music festivals produced in the United States since the mid-1970's. They were the brainchild of Apple Computer executive Steve Wozniak, who invested over $12 million in the festivals. Both festivals took place near the small town of Devore, California. Wozniak paid concert promoter Bill Graham's agency to hire the performers. Approximately 400,000 people attended the 1982 concerts. Tickets cost $37.50 for all three days. Friday's performers included the Ramones, Gang of Four, the Police, Talking Heads, the B-52s, and Oingo Boingo. Saturday's show featured Santana, Tom Petty and the Heartbreakers, Pat Benatar, Eddie Money, the Cars, and The Kinks. Sunday's show began at 9:30 A.M. with the Grateful Dead, followed by Jackson Browne, Jerry Jeff Walker, Jimmy Buffett, and Fleetwood Mac. The 1982 festival lost $4 million, yet the organizers considered the festival a success in artistic and entertainment terms. The festival featured several air-conditioned tents filled with then-new personal computers.

Members of Gang of Four perform at the beginning of the first US Festival on September 3, 1982. More than eighty thousand people were in attendance. (AP/Wide World Photos)

The US Festivals

Performers at the US Festivals, in order of appearance:

Friday, September 3, 1982
Gang of Four
The Ramones
The English Beat
Oingo Boingo
The B52s
Talking Heads
The Police

Saturday, September 4, 1982
The Joe Sharino Band
Dave Edmunds
Eddie Money
Santana
The Cars
The Kinks
Pat Benatar
Tom Petty and the
    Heartbreakers

Sunday, September 5, 1982
Grateful Dead
Jerry Jeff Walker

Jimmy Buffett
Jackson Browne
Fleetwood Mac

Saturday, May 28, 1983
Divinyls
INXS
Wall of Voodoo
Oingo Boingo
The English Beat
Flock of Seagulls
Stray Cats
Men at Work
The Clash

Sunday, May 29, 1983
Quiet Riot
Mötley Crüe
Ozzy Osbourne
Judas Priest
Triumph
Scorpions
Van Halen

Monday, May 30, 1983
Little Steven and the
    Disciples of Soul
Berlin
Quarterflash
U2
Missing Persons
Pretenders
Joe Walsh
Stevie Nicks
David Bowie

Saturday, June 4, 1983—
    Country Day
Riders in the Sky
Thrasher Brothers
Ricky Skaggs
Hank Williams, Jr.
Emmylou Harris and the
    Hot Band
Waylon Jennings
Alabama
Willie Nelson

The 1983 US Festival took place over two weekends. One-day tickets cost twenty dollars. The concert began on Memorial Day weekend, 1983. The opening day acts were the Divinyls, INXS, Wall of Voodoo, Oingo Boingo, the English Beat, Flock of Seagulls, Stray Cats, Men at Work, and the Clash. Saturday's show was titled Heavy Metal Day and was attended by over 400,000 fans. The day was marred by several incidents, including a fatal beating and a fatal overdose. The bands that played were Quiet Riot, Mötley Crüe, Ozzy Osbourne, Judas Priest, Triumph, the Scorpions, and Van Halen. Monday featured David Bowie, Stevie Nicks, Little Steven and the Disciples of Soul, Berlin, Quarterflash, U2, Missing Persons, the Pretenders, and Joe Walsh. There was a country music day the following Saturday. Over 100,000 fans showed up to see and hear country music groups Riders in the Sky, Thrasher Brothers, Ricky Skaggs, Hank Williams, Jr., Emmylou Harris and the Hot Band, Waylon Jennings, Alabama, and Willie Nelson.

Impact The US Festivals represented one of the first attempts to combine a music-oriented demographic with personal computers. The strategy would ultimately pay incredible dividends in future decades, as the relationship between popular music and computer technology grew.

Further Reading

Hunter, David. "Steve Wozniak Throws a Party." *Soft-Talk Magazine* 3, no. 10 (October, 1982): 128-140.

Kirk, Cynthia. "Fun and Violence Mingle at US Festival: Break-Even Point Is Still Elusive." *Variety* 311 (June 1, 1983): 55.

_____. "US Festival in Cal. Deemed a Success, Attendance Is Good." *Variety* 308 (September 8, 1982): 1.

Ron Jacobs

See also Apple Computer; Country music; Farm Aid; Heavy metal; Live Aid; Mötley Crüe; Music; New Wave music; Osbourne, Ozzy; Pop music; Talking Heads; U2; Van Halen.

■ U.S. Senate bombing

The Event A leftist group calling itself the Armed Resistance Unit sets off a bomb in the Senate Wing of the U.S. Capitol
Date November 7, 1983
Place Washington, D.C.

The U.S. Senate bombing resulted in tightened security measures in and around the U.S. Capitol. The Senate Chamber was closed to the public, and a system of staff identification cards was instituted.

At 10:58 P.M. on November 7, 1983, a small, powerful bomb composed of six or seven sticks of dynamite exploded near the Senate Chamber of the U.S. Capitol. The bomb had been placed underneath a bench at the eastern end of a corridor outside the chamber several hours earlier; it used a pocket watch for its timing device. The explosion ripped the door off the office of Senator Robert Byrd of West Virginia, tore a hole in a wall, and shattered several mirrors and paintings opposite the Republican cloakroom. Officials estimated the cost of the damage at around $250,000.

A group calling itself the Armed Resistance Unit claimed responsibility for the bombing in a call to the Capitol switchboard minutes before the explosion. The group also sent a letter to National Public Radio that claimed responsibility for the bombing. Both claims stated that the bombing was in response to the October 25, 1983, U.S. military invasion of Grenada and the U.S. military intervention in Lebanon that autumn. The Senate was originally scheduled to be in session until at least 11:00 that evening but adjourned early, potentially preventing injuries and even deaths.

Police and Federal Bureau of Investigation (FBI) officials publicly considered that the bombing was tied to other similar attacks on a number of other government installations, including the National War College building in Washington, D.C.; the Staten Island, New York, Federal Building; and several Navy and Army Reserve centers in the Washington, D.C., area and around New York City. In May, 1988, federal agents arrested six U.S. citizens in connection with the Capitol bombing and several other attacks on U.S. government buildings. The defendants included Linda Evans and Susan Whitehorn, two former members of the Weather Underground, and Marilyn Buck, a member of the May 19 Communist Organization. Buck had recently been convicted for her participation in the 1981 robbery of a Brink's truck outside Nyack, New York, that resulted in the deaths of three people. Buck, Whitehorn, and Evans were sentenced to long prison terms for conspiracy and malicious destruction of government property. Charges against the other three defendants were dropped.

Impact In the wake of the bombing, security in and around the U.S. Capitol building was tightened. Areas once open to the public were closed off, a series of staff identification badges was instituted, several entrances were closed, and metal detectors were set up at all the remaining entrances.

Further Reading

Berger, Dan. *Outlaws of America: The Weather Underground and the Politics of Solidarity.* Oakland, Calif.: AK Press, 2006.
Memorial Institute for the Prevention of Terrorism. MIPT Terrorism Knowledge Base. http://www .tkb.org/Home.jsp

Ron Jacobs

See also Beirut bombings; Foreign policy of the United States; Grenada invasion; Terrorism.

■ USA for Africa

Identification Popular music benefit project to fund African famine relief
Date "We Are the World" recorded on January 28, 1985
Place A & M Studios, Hollywood, California

On the heels of a widely publicized famine in East Africa, a star-studded group of forty-five popular music artists recorded a song and produced an accompanying music video to raise money to help victims of the famine. The project earned millions of dollars and served as inspiration for thousands of additional efforts across America in support of the cause.

A Stellar Ensemble

The following performers participated in USA for Africa, recording the song "We Are the World":

Dan Ackroyd
Harry Belafonte
Lindsey Buckingham
Kim Carnes
Ray Charles
Bob Dylan
Sheila E.
Bob Geldof
Daryl Hall
James Ingram
Jackie Jackson
LaToya Jackson
Marlon Jackson
Michael Jackson
Randy Jackson
Tito Jackson
Al Jarreau
Waylon Jennings
Billy Joel

Cyndi Lauper
Huey Lewis and the News
Kenny Loggins
Bette Midler
Willie Nelson
John Oates
Jeffrey Osborne
Steve Perry
The Pointer Sisters
Lionel Richie
Smokey Robinson
Kenny Rogers
Diana Ross
Paul Simon
Bruce Springsteen
Tina Turner
Dionne Warwick
Stevie Wonder

When a devastating famine struck Ethiopia in the fall of 1984, Americans began exploring ways to contribute to the relief efforts. Singer Harry Belafonte, known for his hit songs and movies from the 1950's and early 1960's and his civil rights activism, approached his manager, music producer Ken Kragen, about organizing a benefit concert. In November of 1984, a group of Britain's most famous pop musicians had assembled under the name Band Aid and recorded a song, "Do They Know It's Christmas?" that had raced to the top of the music charts and earned millions for African relief. As a result, Belafonte and Kragen, along with Lionel Richie (another of Kragen's clients) and Michael Jackson, two of pop music's most successful artists and composers, began to organize a similar effort with American musicians.

The group recruited Quincy Jones, a successful producer whose work with Jackson had helped resurrect the singer's career, to produce the effort, and Jackson and Ritchie composed a new song for the occasion. Instrumental tracks were recorded and mailed to a broad spectrum of artists, and on January 28, 1985, a group of forty-five performers gathered at A & M Studios in Hollywood following the American Music Awards to record "We Are the World." Among the forty-five singers assembled in the studios were Belafonte, comedian Dan Ackroyd, Band Aid producer Bob Geldof, and band members and family members of the twenty-one artists for whose brief solo performances the song came to be known. These included many who were among pop music's biggest stars of the 1980's—Richie, Stevie Wonder, Paul Simon, Kenny Rogers, James Ingram, Tina Turner, Billy Joel, Michael Jackson, Diana Ross, Dionne Warwick, Willie Nelson, Al Jarreau, Bruce Springsteen, Kenny Loggins, Steve Perry, Daryl Hall, Huey Lewis, Cyndi Lauper, Kim Carnes, Bob Dylan, and Ray Charles. When the record was released in March of 1985, the group was identified on the label as USA for Africa.

Impact The song became an immediate hit, reaching number one on the music charts in just three weeks, and it eventually sold more than seven million copies over the next seven years. It won the 1985 Grammy awards for Song of the Year, Record of the Year, and Best Pop Performance by a Duo or Group. The foundation created by Kragen to administer and distribute the sixty-four million dollars raised in the effort, United Support of Artists for Africa, continued to operate and sponsored later efforts on behalf of America's music industry to address emergency and long-term development needs in Africa.

Further Reading

Berger, Gilda. *USA for Africa: Rock Aid in the Eighties.* London: Franklin Watts, 1987.

Garofalo, Reebee, ed. *Rockin' the Boat: Mass Music and Mass Movements.* Cambridge, Mass.: South End Press, 1991.

Devon Boan

See also Africa and the United States; Comic Relief; Farm Aid; Jackson, Michael; Journey; Lauper, Cyndi; Live Aid; Music; Music videos; Pop music; Richie, Lionel; Springsteen, Bruce.

■ *USA Today*

Identification First general-interest national daily
newspaper
Publisher Gannett Company
Date Launched on September 15, 1982

Founded by Gannett Company CEO Al Neuharth, USA
Today *was designed to represent a completely novel alternative to the traditional newspapers of the 1980's.*

In style, content, and physical appearance, the new
national newspaper *USA Today* was designed for the
television generation, and it rejected established
rules about what a newspaper should be. It focused
on celebrity news written in short, attention-getting
articles with simplistic prose that could be read easily
and quickly by busy people. It included many sentence fragments that began with typographical
bullets, instead of complete, grammatically correct
sentences. *USA Today* also featured bold color photographs, charts, and graphics, along with a huge, colorful national weather map. The color ink used to
publish *USA Today* did not rub off on readers' hands
the way traditional gray newsprint could. Gannett
Company chief executive officer (CEO) Al Neuharth founded the magazine in the belief that *USA
Today's* new type of journalism and design would be
an effective way to communicate to readers a greater
number of discrete news items.

When the first issue of *USA Today* hit the stands in
1982, it sold out. By the end of its first year, *USA Today's* circulation reached almost 400,000, and seven
months later the newspaper had more than one million readers. By 1985, *USA Today* was publishing internationally, printing via satellite in Singapore and
Switzerland. The success of *USA Today* was not without its challenges, however. The newspaper was an
expensive, high-risk venture, and it had a difficult
time securing advertising. It took five years before
USA Today began to make a profit.

Newspaper traditionalists did not welcome the
entry of *USA Today* and disapproved of its departure
from the rules of traditional journalism. Critics compared *USA Today's* content to the offerings at a fast-food restaurant, earning the newspaper the nickname "McPaper, the junk food of journalism." While
critics coined this nickname to show their contempt
of the newspaper, Neuharth, confident about its success, used the "McPaper" image to his advantage.
One columnist would later describe *USA Today* as the

"Big Mac of journalism," and over time traditional
newspapers began adapting *USA Today's* "McNuggets" style of journalism in their own publications.

Impact *USA Today* changed the world of journalism. Its enterprising approach to journalism, using
colorful layout and short, easy-to-read articles,
would later be copied by its competitors, who had to
reinvent themselves to keep newspapers relevant in
the digital age. *USA Today* would later publish more
serious news stories and would one day be ranked
with *The Wall Street Journal* and *The New York Times*
as one of the top-selling newspapers in the United
States.

Further Reading

Mogal, Leonard. "The Three Titans: *USA Today, The
Wall Street Journal,* and *The New York Times.*" In *The
Newspaper: Everything You Need to Know to Make It
in the Newspaper Business.* Pittsburgh: GATFPress,
2000.

Neuharth, Al. *Confessions of an S.O.B.* New York:
Doubleday, 1989.

Pritchard, Peter S. *The Making of McPaper: The Inside
Story of "USA Today."* Kansas City, Mo.: Andrews,
McMeel & Parker, 1987.

Eddith A. Dashiell

See also CNN; FOX network; Journalism; Tabloid
television; Television; Turner, Ted.

■ USS *Stark* incident

The Event An Iraqi fighter jet launches two
missiles into a U.S. Navy vessel
Date May 17, 1987
Place The Persian Gulf

The USS Stark *incident was at the time the worst peacetime naval disaster in American history. It was surpassed
only by the explosion of a gun turret on the USS* Iowa *in
1989.*

During the Iran-Iraq War (1980-1988), an Iraqi
Dassault Mirage F1EQ fighter launched two Exocet
missiles, hitting the American Oliver Hazard Perry-class guided-missile frigate USS *Stark* and severely
damaging the vessel. The *Stark* was in international
waters in the Persian Gulf at the time of the attack.
President Ronald Reagan had ordered a U.S. naval
fleet to the Persian Gulf to monitor the area.

The USS Stark *lists to port after being struck by two Iraqi missiles on May 18, 1987.* (U.S. Department of Defense)

The *Stark*'s crew was unaware of the firing of the first missile, which failed to detonate when it hit the port side of the hull. The fuel from the rocket caught fire, however, increasing the damage caused by its impact. Now aware that they were under attack, the crew was nevertheless helpless to stop the second missile from being fired: It impacted at roughly the same part of the ship as the first, penetrated to the crew's quarters, and exploded. The casualty list included thirty-seven sailors killed and twenty-one injured.

After the attack, the *Stark* was listing and on fire. The crew struggled to gain control of the ship, finally succeeding during the night. The *Stark* made its way to the tiny kingdom of Bahrain, near Qatar, where it was met by the USS *Acadia*. The *Stark* was returned to seaworthiness with temporary repairs made by the crew of the *Acadia*. Under its own power, the *Stark* made it back home to the United States. The ship returned to Mayport, Florida, its home

port. In 1988, the ship traveled to Mississippi for permanent repairs conducted by Ingalls Shipbuilding at a cost of $142 million. After the repairs were made, the *Stark* returned to active service.

Impact The attack on the USS *Stark* was not provoked; Iraq and the United States were at peace at the time. It is unknown if the Iraqi pilot who launched the missiles was ever punished for the accident, because the Saddam Hussein regime was in control of Iraq at the time. American officials have speculated that the pilot was executed.

Further Reading

Levinson, Jeffrey L., and Randy L. Edwards. *Missile Inbound: The Attack on the Stark in the Persian Gulf.* Annapolis: Naval Institute Press, 1997.

Wise, Harold Lee. *Inside the Danger Zone: The U.S. Military in the Persian Gulf, 1987-88.* Annapolis: Naval Institute Press, 2007.

Timothy C. Hemmis

See also   Beirut bombings; Iranian hostage crisis; Libya bombing; Middle East and North America; USS *Vincennes* incident; West Berlin discotheque bombing.

■ USS *Vincennes* incident

The Event   An American warship accidentally shoots down an Iranian passenger airliner
Date   July 3, 1988
Place   Strait of Hormuz

The Vincennes *shot down Iran Air Flight 655, killing all 290 people on board. Besides being a tragedy for those on the airplane and their families, the incident further poisoned relations between the United States and Iran.*

In 1980, Iraq—under the leadership of President Saddam Hussein—invaded the Islamic Republic of Iran, beginning the Iran-Iraq War (1980-1988). The bloody war eventually devolved into stalemate and led to the deaths of hundreds of thousands of people. One of the war's battlefields was the Persian Gulf, specifically the Strait of Hormuz, where Iran began to attack tankers carrying oil as a means of damaging Iraq's economy. The presidential administration of Ronald Reagan deployed warships from the U.S. Navy to the region to protect the oil tankers, if necessary through the use of force.

One of the ships sent to the region in 1988 was the USS *Vincennes*, a Ticonderoga-class guided-missile cruiser under the command of Captain William C. Rogers III. On July 3, 1988, the ship pursued Iranian gunboats operating in the area. Afterward, the bridge of the *Vincennes* picked up a single airplane flying over Iranian territory that seemed to be preparing for a possible attack on the *Vincennes*. In fact, it was Iran Air Flight 655, an Airbus A300B2 on a regularly scheduled flight from Bandar Abbas, Iran, to Dubai, United Arab Emirates. The ship's bridge radioed the plane to warn it off, but the Airbus A300 was unable to receive military communications. As the airliner flew closer to the American cruiser, the order was given to fire on the airplane. A missile was launched, destroying the airplane and killing all on board, including dozens of children.

Impact   The USS *Vincennes* incident was met with outrage in Iran and a denial of responsibility on the part of the U.S. Navy and the Reagan administration. Vice President George H. W. Bush later made it clear that the United States had no intention to apologize for the tragic mistake, and the commander of the *Vincennes* later received a medal from President Reagan for his service in the region. It would later emerge that the airliner had been ascending, not descending, as the U.S. Navy claimed in the immediate aftermath of the attack, and that other American naval commanders in the area had been concerned about the behavior of the *Vincennes*'s captain. Although the U.S. government would never admit responsibility for shooting down the airliner, it did in the 1990's propose compensation to the families of the dead.

Further Reading
Ansari, Ali M. *Confronting Iran: The Failure of American Foreign Policy and the Next Great Crisis in the Middle East.* New York: Basic Books, 2006.

The USS Vincennes *launches a missile during exercises in July, 1987, one year before it shot down Iran Air Flight 655.* (U.S. Navy)

Rajaee, Farhang, ed. *The Iran-Iraq War: The Politics of Aggression.* Gainesville: University Press of Florida, 1993.

Rogers, Will, Sharon Rogers, and Gene Gregston. *Storm Center: The USS Vincennes and Iran Air Flight 655—A Personal Account of Tragedy and Terrorism.* Annapolis: Naval Institute Press, 1992.

Steve Hewitt

See also Air India Flight 182 bombing; Bush, George H. W.; Foreign policy of the United States; Iran-Contra affair; Iranian hostage crisis; Middle East and North America; Pan Am Flight 103 bombing; Reagan, Ronald; USS *Stark* incident.

■ U2

Identification Irish rock band
Date Formed in 1976

During the 1980's, U2 became one of the most popular musical acts in the world. The band had a substantial impact on pop culture, particularly in the United States.

U2 formed in 1976 in Dublin, Ireland. With a lineup of Larry Mullen, Jr., on drums, Adam Clayton on bass, Dave "the Edge" Evans on guitar and keyboards, and Paul "Bono" Hewson as lead singer, U2's live performances had already attracted a solid fan base in the United Kingdom before it signed with Island Records in March, 1980. Later that year, the band released its first album, *Boy*, and the single "I Will Follow" gave U2 its first radio airplay in North America. Its second album, *October* (1981), featured spiritual and religious themes, influenced by U2's involvement with the charismatic Shalom religious movement.

By 1983, U2 was on the verge of stardom, and the group's increasingly sophisticated songwriting and politically charged lyrics propelled the album *War*, featuring the radio hits "New Year's Day" and "Sunday Bloody Sunday," into the top twenty in the United States and Canada. U2's members donned combat boots and proclaimed themselves "Militants for Peace" as they headlined a North American tour in the summer of 1983. Their concert at Red Rocks Amphitheatre, near Denver, spawned a live album, *U2 Live: Under a Blood Red Sky*, and a video in heavy rotation on MTV.

In 1984, U2 retreated to Slane Castle in Ireland to record *The Unforgettable Fire*. Produced by the legendary Brian Eno, this more experimental album sold fewer copies than *War* had, but its track "Pride (In the Name of Love)" became the group's first Top 40 single on the U.S. pop charts, as it reached number thirty-three on the *Billboard* Hot 100 chart. "Pride (In the Name of Love)" was inspired by the life of Martin Luther King, Jr., and reflected the band's growing fascination with America. U2 performed at the Live Aid festival in 1985, and Bono's unscripted leap into the crowd turned him into a celebrity. In a cover feature, *Rolling Stone* magazine proclaimed U2 to be the "Band of the Eighties."

U2's commitment to social and political issues continued to evolve. Bono and his wife, Ali, volunteered in Ethiopia and toured war-torn Central America, and the band participated in the Artists Against Apartheid campaign. This activism, along with band members' growing interest in American roots music, influenced their most successful album, *The Joshua Tree*, released in March, 1987. Musically and lyrically, *The Joshua Tree* showcased U2's simultaneous love of American culture and frustration with American foreign policy. The album topped the charts in twenty-two countries around the world and featured two number one hits on the *Billboard* Hot 100 chart: "With or Without You" and "I Still Haven't Found What I'm Looking For." U2 closed out the decade with a tour that filled stadiums around the world, chronicled in the documentary film *Rattle and Hum* (1988). An album with the same name featured live performances and several new songs, including a duet with B. B. King.

Impact U2 was a cultural phenomenon in the 1980's, selling over 20 million albums in the United States alone and raising awareness of political issues and social causes among the MTV generation. In addition to strongly influencing the popular music of the decade, U2 played a major role in Live Aid and other high-profile humanitarian events.

Further Reading

Scrimgeour, Diana. *U2 Show.* New York: Riverhead Books, 2004.

U2 and Neil McCormick. *U2 by U2.* London: HarperCollins, 2006.

Caroline Small and Andrew J. LaFollette

See also Live Aid; Music; Music videos; MTV; Pop music; Rock and Roll Hall of Fame.

V

■ Valenzuela, Fernando

Identification   Mexican American baseball player
Born   November 1, 1960; Etchohuaquila, Mexico

A Mexican-born, left-handed pitcher for the Los Angeles Dodgers, Valenzuela became a star among both Spanish- and English-speaking baseball fans across the United States.

Both in their original home in Brooklyn and, since 1958, in Los Angeles, the Dodgers had been a baseball organization known for developing young play-

Los Angeles Dodger Fernando Valenzuela pitches in the 1986 All Star game. Valenzuela struck out five consecutive batters, tying an All Star game record. (AP/Wide World Photos)

ers. At times during the twentieth century, the Rookie of the Year award seemed virtually a Dodger preserve. Thus, it was no surprise to seasoned observers of baseball when Fernando Valenzuela—a young left-hander who had been signed with the Dodgers organization by scout Mike Brito two years earlier—was promoted to the major leagues in 1980 and quickly dazzled fans as a relief pitcher.

A truly startling phenomenon emerged the following year, however, when Valenzuela was inserted into the Dodgers' starting rotation. He threw three shutouts in his first four games, an unprecedented feat. Valenzuela's pudgy physique, his youth, and his inability to speak English contributed to his aura. Despite striking out many batters, he was not a traditional hard thrower. His most effective pitch was a screwball (a pitch that uses a reverse motion from those of curveballs and sliders); it spun away from batters, leaving them swinging at air. His mastery of this unusual pitch made Valenzuela particularly entertaining to watch.

Valenzuela, a Mexican pitcher, was performing in Los Angeles, which was home to the second-largest urban population of Mexicans in the world, after Mexico City. He excited Latino fans to come to the ballpark as never before. The socioeconomic gap between Valenzuela's home state of Sonora, in northern Mexico, and the bucolic, well-manicured Dodger Stadium was far greater than the physical distance of several hundred miles between them. The pitcher's ability to bridge this gap made him a hero to Latinos across America.

Valenzuela became a huge star among the English-speaking population of the United States as well, even though his postgame comments had to be translated for the media by Dodgers coach Manny Mota. When, in Valenzuela's fifth start of 1981, he shut out the San Francisco Giants in a Monday evening game, his status as a legitimate sensation was confirmed, and the era of "Fernandomania" began. Two starts later, Valenzuela made his debut in America's largest city, as the Dodgers faced the New York

Mets. Mets manager Joe Torre, hoping to succeed where other managers had failed against Valenzuela's devastating screwball, started a number of left-handed batters, unusual in facing a left-handed pitcher. Although this strategy proved to be to no immediate avail—Valenzuela shut out the Mets, striking out eleven batters—it did demonstrate a potential avenue by which teams could approach Valenzuela. The pitcher did not continue to dominate to the extent he had in the early months of his first season. He did lead the Dodgers to the World Championship in 1981, however, providing the principal highlight in a strike-marred season.

Impact Valenzuela continued as a premier pitcher until the late 1980's, when injuries slowed him down. He ended up winning 173 games in the major leagues from 1980 to 1997, achieving the record for victories by a Mexican-born pitcher. His career inspired many Latino children, who dreamed of the success their hero had achieved playing baseball.

Further Reading

Delsohn, Steve. *True Blue: The Dramatic History of the Los Angeles Dodgers.* New York: Harper, 2002.

Regalado, Samuel. *Viva Baseball! Latin Major Leaguers and Their Special Hunger.* Urbana: University of Illinois Press, 1998.

Stout, Glenn, and Richard A, Johnson. *The Dodgers: 120 Years of Dodgers Baseball.* Boston: Houghton Mifflin, 2004.

Nicholas Birns

See also Baseball; Baseball strike of 1981; Immigration to the United States; Latinos; Mexico and the United States; Sports.

■ Valley girls

Definition Pop-culture female icons representing self-centered, spoiled, wealthy, sexually promiscuous teenage girls

The 1980's gave rise to the Valley girl icon of the dim-witted, sexy, spoiled teenage girl, which in time gained in popularity and remains a twenty-first century icon.

Although the Valley girl does not exist in reality, the image of her was established during the 1980's as a caricature of spoiled, wealthy, usually privileged white teenage girls. Although the expression "Valley girl" originated in the 1980's San Fernando Valley of Los Angeles, the Valley girl figure, strongly resembling a walking and talking Barbie doll, remains a cultural icon, generally depicted as a young woman with bleached-blond hair who is skinny, sexy, enormously rich, entirely self-centered, and brainless.

In 1980's magazines, the ever-evolving Valley girl image sold cosmetics and fashions to an enormous teenage market and became a popular trope in film that would last into the twenty-first century. In 1982, Frank Zappa released "Valley Girl," a song containing typical Valley girl expressions, in an effort to satirize the trend and illustrate how the image had come to represent the dumbing down of America. His attempt backfired: The Valley girl image became even more popular. The following year, the movie *Valley Girl* (1983), featuring Nicolas Cage and Deborah Foreman, was well received; it portrayed the relationship of a punk teenage boy and a Valley girl in the setting of a high school prom. The stereotype resonated with audiences and established the icon.

The Stereotypical Valley Girl First on the Valley girl's checklist of characteristics is her wealth, or rather her parents' wealth, which is conspicuously displayed upon her, and around her. With her clique of other Valley girls in tow, she flits around the local shopping mall from store to store. The mall is her natural habitat, where she spends most of her time paying no attention to the price tags of fashionable clothes and accessories while flashing a variety of platinum credit cards.

For the Valley girl, fashion is foremost; she must own and wear the latest styles and trends. "Vals," as they came to be known, are also characterized by their desire to be the center of attention. In addition to looking good, they must display the assets that set them apart from the everyday teenage girl. Although they are notoriously poor drivers, older Valley girls have driver's licenses and must have the proper luxury car to project the correct high-class image as they gad about geographically spread out Los Angeles.

In addition, the Valley girl generally has a good-looking boyfriend, typically a sports star. Getting male attention is almost as important to the Valley girl as is jealous female attention. The Valley girl does not understand the concept of "no," or any form of self-denial. Often she is considered to be sexually "easy." In the 1980's, Valley girls had fancy phones and unlisted phone numbers; today's Valley girls carry the latest cell phones.

Beyond her striking physical appearance and material possessions, the next most noticeable characteristic of the Valley girl is her lack of intelligence. Not only is she a blond; she is a dumb blond. Her attendance at school and sports events is admirable, but she doesn't grasp the concept of homework and may manipulate other more nerdy types to do it for her.

Valspeak   Beginning in the 1980's, Valley girls developed a form of dialect known as Valspeak that spread quickly around the country. It serves to emphasize her minimum intelligence. Utilizing a variety of mid-sentence qualifiers such as "like" and "duh," Valspeak is characterized by inflections that convey exaggerated emotions, from enthusiasm to disdain, such as the raising of the voice at the end of every sentence—as if each statement were a question. The vocabulary and inflections of Valspeak contributed to the idea that Valley girls were not very intelligent, suggesting that they could not articulate their limited thoughts. Similarly, short statements that stood in for sentences—"As *if*," "Whatever," "Totally," "I'm sure," and "Gag me with a spoon"—added to the stereotype of the Valley girl as inherently stupid.

Impact   The 1980's Los Angeles Valley girl icon spread throughout the country and became enormously popular in advertising and film. Films of the 1980's and post-1980's featuring the Valley girl include *Fast Times at Ridgemont High* (1982), *Buffy the Vampire Slayer* (1992), *Clueless* (1995), *Romy and Michele's High School Reunion* (1997), *She's All That* (1999), *Jawbreaker* (1999), *Bring It On* (2000), and *Legally Blonde* (2001). Valley girls have also become a trope in such horror films as *Scream* (1996), *Scream 2* (1997), *I Know What You Did Last Summer* (1997), and *Scream 3* (2000). The enormously popular *Buffy the Vampire Slayer* television series featuring blond Valley girl Buffy Summers aired between 1997 and 2003.

In turn, the image infiltrated everyday Americans' lives, affecting mannerisms, attitudes, fashion, and the way Americans speak. Valspeak slang and expressions survived into the twenty-first century, transforming mainstream American English, particularly among teens. Calling someone a Valley girl today is to denigrate a young woman as superficial, self-centered, and overspending.

Further Reading

Bernstein, Jonathan. *Pretty in Pink: The Golden Age of Teenage Movies.* New York: St. Martin's Griffin, 1997. Bernstein examines the 1980's, the Golden Age of Teenage Movies, particularly middle- and upper-middle-class teenagers, whose great concern with personal appearance and popularity gave rise to the Valley girl image.

Blyth, Carl, Sigrid Recktenwald, and Jenny Wang. "I'm Like, 'Say What?!' A New Quotative in American Oral Narrative." *American Speech* 65 (Autumn, 1990): 215-227. Scholarly but approachable article that discusses how Valley girl speech patterns, especially "like," have entered popular American speech.

Clover, Carol J. *Men, Women, and Chainsaws: Gender in the Modern Horror Film.* Princeton, N.J.: Princeton University Press, 1992. Illustrates how the image of the 1980's Valley girl has become a lasting trope in American horror film.

Douglas, Susan. "Valley Girl Feminism: New Feminist Magazine *Jane* Does Not Compare to *Ms.* Magazine." *The Progressive* 61 (November, 1997): 17. Douglas recalls her first issue of *Ms.* magazine and considers how times have changed in her quest to find the premier issue of the latest feminist magazine for "uppity" Valley-girl women.

M. Casey Diana

See also   Advertising; Cell phones; *Closing of the American Mind, The*; Consumerism; Fads; Fashions and clothing; *Fast Times at Ridgemont High*; Feminism; Film in the United States; Horror films; Preppies; Slang and slogans; Teen films.

■ Van Halen

Identification   American hard rock band
Date   Formed in 1974

One of the most popular bands of the 1980's, Van Halen brought fresh energy to the rock genre and influenced several bands of the decade.

Van Halen is a hard rock band from Pasadena, California. Its original members were Eddie Van Halen (lead guitarist), David Lee Roth (lead vocalist), Michael Anthony (bass guitarist), and Alex Van Halen (drummer). After forming in 1974, the band created its unique style of rock music, marked by Eddie

Van Halen in 1986. From left: Michael Anthony, Sammy Hagar, Eddie Van Halen, and Alex Van Halen. (Paul Natkin)

dicate the band's willingness to follow a trend in popular music by utilizing more keyboards. This change, however, caused tension within the group. Following the tour for this album, Roth left the band.

Van Halen ushered in a new era by acquiring Sammy Hagar as its new lead vocalist in 1986. Hagar had already established a solo career in music, playing guitar and singing lead vocals. The band's first release with Hagar was *5150* (1986), produced by Mick Jones of the rock band Foreigner. Despite the change in membership, the album sold numerous copies and continued the style of *1984*. The band's final album of the decade was *OU812* (1988), which included the hit song "Finish What You Started."

Van Halen's virtuoso guitar playing. The group's live shows featured long guitar solos by Eddie, along with wild stage antics by the flamboyant Roth.

In 1978, the group released its debut album, *Van Halen*, to immediate popular and critical success. Notable songs on that album included "Ain't Talkin' 'Bout Love"; "Eruption," which included a popular and highly influential guitar solo; and "Runnin' with the Devil." *Van Halen II* was released the following year and included the hit song "Dance the Night Away." The band's third album, *Women and Children First*, released in 1980, continued the band's established pattern of high-energy rock, with Eddie Van Halen's guitar providing much of the sound, and included the single "And the Cradle Will Rock." The band's fourth album, *Fair Warning* (1981), also sold numerous copies, but its songs did not receive as much airplay as had others by Van Halen. The group's 1982 album, *Diver Down*, is best known for two cover songs: "Dancing in the Street," first recorded by Martha and the Vandellas, and "Oh, Pretty Woman," cowritten by Roy Orbison.

On December 31, 1983, the band released *1984*. This album revealed a slight change in the band's musical style: The hit single "Jump" included substantial use of synthesizers. Though most of the songs on the album still featured guitar, they did in-

Impact Van Halen created a unique sound within the rock world that influenced the popular "hair bands" of the late 1980's. The band succeeded in matching the high-energy sound on its studio works with its stage performances and helped to reinvigorate the rock genre.

Further Reading

Bogdanov, Vladimir, et al., eds. *All Music Guide to Rock: The Definitive Guide to Rock, Pop, and Soul.* 3d ed. San Francisco: Backbeat Books, 2002.

Levy, Joe, et al., eds. *The 500 Greatest Albums of All Time.* New York: Wenner Books, 2005.

Kevin L. Brennan

See also Bon Jovi; Guns n' Roses; Heavy metal; Music; Osbourne, Ozzy; Pop music.

■ Vancouver Expo '86

The Event International exposition
Date May 2 to October 13, 1986
Place Vancouver, British Columbia

Vancouver Expo '86 coincided with the city's centennial and the arrival on the Pacific coast of the first passenger train. It was the second time that Canada had held a

world's fair in the period after World War II, and the fair benefited from a terrorism scare in Europe that kept many potential travelers within North America's borders.

The 1986 World Exposition on Transportation and Communications (known as Vancouver Expo '86) was a world's fair sanctioned by the Bureau of International Expositions (BIE) and held in Vancouver, British Columbia, from May 2 through October 13, 1986. The fair, whose theme was "Transportation and Communication: World in Motion, World in Touch," was the first Canadian world's fair since Expo '67. The latter fair, held in Montreal during the Canadian centennial, was one of the most successful world's fairs in history, attracting some 50 million people at a time when Canada's population was only 20 million. Expo '86 was categorized by the BIE as a "class 2, special category fair," reflecting its specific emphases on transportation and communications. The government of Canada contributed $9.8 million to the exposition's cultural projects, including $5.8 million for the program at the Canada Pavilion, $2 million to enable Canadian artists to tour other centers en route to or from the exposition, $1.5 million for Canadian participation in the World Festival, and $500,000 to fund cultural projects for Vancouver's centennial celebrations.

The exposition was opened by England's Prince Charles and Princess Diana and Canadian prime minister Brian Mulroney on May 2, 1986. It featured pavilions from fifty-four nations and numerous corporations. Expo '86's participants were given the opportunity to design their own pavilions or to opt for less expensive standardized modules. Each module was approximately two and one-half stories high and had floor space equal to one-third of a city block. The design was such that any number of the square modules could be placed together in a variety of shapes. The roof design allowed the interior exhibit space to be uninterrupted by pillars.

Expo '86 was held on the north shore of False Creek, along Vancouver's inner-city waterway. The seventy-hectare site featured over eighty pavilions and many indoor and outdoor performance venues. Canada's pavilion was located on a pier not contiguous with the rest of the site. To reach the pavilion, visitors would take Vancouver's newly opened SkyTrain rapid rail system. After the exposition, the pier became Canada Place, one of Vancouver's most recognizable landmarks. Other Canadian host pavilions included Canadian provincial and territorial pavilions for Alberta, British Columbia, Nova Scotia, Ontario, Prince Edward Island, Quebec, Saskatchewan, Yukon, and the Northwest Territories. Canadian Pacific's main feature was a film, *Rainbow War,* while Telecom Canada presented a Circle-Vision 360 movie, *Portraits of Canada-Images du Canada.*

A geodesic dome, known as Expo Centre, represented a style of architecture first seen in the U.S. pavilion at Montreal in 1967. At Expo '86, the U.S. pavilion was devoted to space exploration in the wake of the *Challenger* space shuttle disaster, and the displays from the Soviet Union were colored by the Chernobyl nuclear power plant explosion. These dueling pavilions represented one of the last face-offs between the two superpowers before the end of the Cold War only three years later. Corporate and nongovernmental-organization (NGO) pavilions included those representing Air Canada, the local BCTV television station, Canadian National, and General Motors—which had one of the more popular exhibits, "Spirit Lodge," a live show augmented with holographic and other special effects.

Impact   In all, 22 million people attended Expo '86, and, despite a deficit of 311 million Canadian dollars, it was considered a tremendous success. The event was later viewed as a transitional moment for Vancouver, which transformed from a sleepy provincial backwater to a city with some global clout. In particular, the exposition marked a strong boost to tourism for the province. It was also the last twentieth century world's fair to take place in North America.

Further Reading
Anderson, Robert, and Eleanor Wachtel, eds. *The Expo Story.* Madeira Park, B.C.: Harbour, 1986.
Findling, John E., and Kimberly Pelle, eds. *Historical Dictionary of World's Fairs and Expositions, 1851-1988.* New York: Greenwood Press, 1990.
Kahn, E. J. "Letter from Vancouver." *The New Yorker,* July 14, 1986, 73-81.

Martin J. Manning

See also   Canada and the British Commonwealth; Canada and the United States; *Challenger* disaster; Knoxville World's Fair; Louisiana World Exposition; Mulroney, Brian.

■ Vangelis

Identification   Greek composer and keyboardist
Born   March 29, 1943; Volos, Greece

A prolific, accomplished keyboard composer in both classical and electronic jazz, Vangelis brought to film scores in the 1980's an opulent feel that lent emotional weight to the theatrical experience. Recordings of his scores also stood on their own, enjoying wide commercial success.

Vangelis was born Evangelos Odysseas Papathanassiou in Greece. As a composer, he spent more than twenty years compiling a distinguished repertoire of distinctive keyboard works that reflected his era's experimentation with lush electronic sounds and the studio construction of massive sonic effects around a single, often plaintive melody line, participating in a movement that would be dubbed New Age music. He first achieved international success with his score for Hugh Hudson's 1981 film *Chariots of Fire*, the inspirational story of two British runners at the 1924 Paris Olympics. Forsaking the traditional expectation that the score of a period film should reflect the musical tastes and styles of its setting, Vangelis crafted a pulsing, electronic score that itself contained a kind of heroic narrative, swelling to emotional, even inspirational peaks. The film's main theme, released as a single in 1982, enjoyed rare international commercial success for an instrumental composition, including a week as the number one single on the *Billboard* Hot 100 chart. It went on to become a staple among sports anthems—as well as the subject of countless parodies. The film's full score won an Academy Award.

That same year, Vangelis was approached to provide the score for Ridley Scott's dystopian futuristic film *Blade Runner* (1982). The score captured the anxious, isolated feel of the stylish science-fiction thriller. Artistic differences between director and composer led to entangling legal actions that prevented the music as Vangelis scored it from accompanying the film's initial release. However, when the film was later re-released in a "director's cut," it included Vangelis's original score. In the interim, the score was distributed in bootleg recordings, gaining a cult following similar to that of *Blade Runner* itself.

The reclusive Vangelis continued his prodigious output, composing dozens of New Age recordings, as well as pieces for the stage (particularly ballet), and scoring films, especially epics. Ironically, for a composer who conceived of music as a purely aesthetic form unto itself, his soaring and hummable musical themes were most often recognized because they had been appropriated by successful marketing campaigns for commodities, events, and television programs.

Impact   Vangelis's work demonstrated a deliberate disregard for the conventions of film scoring that dominated the 1980's. Those conventions were driven by the rise in tandem of music videos and aggressive cross-marketing campaigns by film studios attempting to exploit a plurality of merchandising opportunities for each film. Thus, film scores of the 1980's were often little more than catalogs of commercial hits with Top 40 potential linked by nondescript background music, as directors received mandates to include montage sequences in their films that could enable hit singles to be played in their entirety. Vangelis, however, brought to his film scores a sense of classical elevation and unity. Aided by his uncanny ear for unforgettable themes delivered by the stirring vibrato of his signature synthesizer, his music provided a rich emotional underscoring to the events within a film's narrative and thus became an integral part of the film's aesthetic impact.

Further Reading

Boundas, Constantin. *Film's Musical Moments.* Edinburgh: Edinburgh University Press, 2006.

Calotychos, Vangelis. *Modern Greece: A Cultural Poetics.* Oxford, England: Berg, 2003.

Summer, Lisa, and Joseph Summer. *Music: The New Age Elixir.* Amherst, N.Y.: Prometheus, 1996.

Joseph Dewey

See also   Academy Awards; Advertising; *Blade Runner*; Classical music; Jazz; Music; Music videos; Pop music; Synthesizers.

■ Video games and arcades

Definition   Electronic games played by manipulating images on a video display and public centers devoted to playing them

Video games began to become a significant aspect of popular culture during the 1980's, as they were mass marketed in both home and coin-operated versions. By the end of the decade, video game characters such as Pac-Man and Mario

were as well known to children as were cartoon characters, and indeed, several such characters made the transition from games to cartoon series.

In video games, a player is usually rewarded for continued success at the game through such mechanisms as points, additional lives, and level advancements. Video games of the 1980's could be played on a variety of platforms, including consoles (which were attached to televisions), handheld devices, personal computers, and dedicated, coin-operated game machines. Home computing technology during the decade was not yet sophisticated enough to emulate the graphics of coin-operated machines, however, so the most graphically advanced games were generally those available in arcades.

History   In 1980, Atari released its home version of the arcade video game *Space Invaders* as a cartridge for the Atari 2600 game console. The cartridge allowed fans of the game to play it for a one-time fee and in the privacy of their own homes. The same year, Mattel released its competing Intellivision game console. Consumers flocked to buy these and similar systems. Coin-operated arcade game technology did not cease in the meantime—*Pac-Man*, the most popular arcade game of all time, was released in 1980 as well. Advances in video game technology would continue at a rapid pace with the release of *Donkey Kong* and *Tempest* in 1981. In 1982, Coleco released the Colecovision game console, which—with forty-eight kilobytes of random-access memory (RAM) and an eight-bit processor—was the most powerful home system available. Manufacturers flocked increasingly to the thriving home video game market, with predictable results.

The American market for home game systems became oversupplied, and it crashed in 1983. The crash drove out of business many of the third-party game manufacturers (that is, independent manufacturers of game cartridges to be played on other companies' consoles). The newly burgeoning video game industry collapsed and was stagnant for the next several years, with manufacturers afraid that any attempts to innovate would be met with further losses. In 1985, Nintendo gingerly test-marketed its Nintendo Entertainment System (NES) in the United States and found that its limited release was a rousing success.

In the same year, Russian game writer Alex Pajitnov released one of the most popular puzzle games of all time, *Tetris*, leading more and more people to the world of casual video games. Within the next few years, demand for console systems grew, and newly emboldened Nintendo, Sega, and Atari emerged as video game industry leaders, vying for market position. Nintendo was responsible for such games as *Super Mario Brothers* and *The Legend of Zelda*, as well as the translation to its console platform of many coin-operated games by the popular and innovative company Namco, such as *Dig Dug* and *Galaga*. In 1989, Nintendo released the Game Boy, a handheld video game console.

Impact   The video game industry began to come into its own during the 1980's, first as a source of

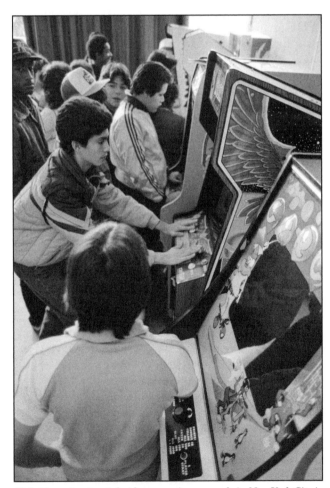

Kids play coin-operated video games in an arcade in New York City in December, 1981. (AP/Wide World Photos)

coin-operated arcade games and then as a source of home computing technology—both general and dedicated solely to gaming. By the end of the decade, console games were a common platform, and almost every personal computer in the world had at least one game on it. Movies such as *War Games* and *Tron* reflected some of the fears and hopes for these games in the 1980's, from nuclear war to the ability of an artificial intelligence to intervene in such a scenario. At the same time, games drove many advances in technology, particularly in the areas of video capability and processor speed. Much of the drive to improve home computers and bring them down in price was driven by the consumer demands of gamers and the possibilities glimpsed by game developers. Demand for Internet connectivity was also later shaped by its implications for gaming. As video games became more sophisticated, they began to participate in popular culture as a source of both entertainment and narrative equal to film and television. Indeed, by the early twenty-first century, the game industry would earn more revenue annually than the film industry in the United States.

Further Reading

Beck, John C. *Got Game: How the Gamer Generation Is Reshaping Business Forever.* Boston: Harvard Business School Press, 2004. Discusses video game-facilitated knowledge acquisition and argues that such knowledge exerts a transformative force on the workplace.

Chaplin, Heather, and Aaron Ruby. *Smartbomb: The Quest for Art, Entertainment, and Big Bucks in the Videogame Revolution.* New York: Algonquin Books, 2005. Discusses the corporations behind the various games, as well as the more prominent players, looking at tournaments and expositions for much of the narrative.

Gee, James Paul. *What Video Games Have to Teach Us About Learning and Literacy.* New York: Palgrave Macmillan, 2004. Demonstrates the intersections of video game theory and educational theory without oversimplifying either field.

Johnson, Steve. *Everything Bad Is Good for You.* New York: Riverhead Books, 2005. Tests the theory that influences such as video games are bad for the mind and argues that such games require more cognitive work than watching television.

Kent, Steven L. *The Ultimate History of Video Games: From "Pong" to "Pokemon"—The Story Behind the Craze That Touched Our Lives and Changed the World.* New York: Three Rivers Press, 2001. Provides a thorough and interesting overview of the history of video games, including interviews with many of the industry's most important figures.

Poole, Steven. *Trigger Happy: Video Games and the Entertainment Revolution.* New York: Arcade, 2004. Includes an exhaustive history of the game industry, along with an analysis of types of games and their varying appeals.

Prensky, Mark. *Don't Bother Me Mom—I'm Learning! How Computer and Video Games Are Preparing Your Kids for Twenty-First Century Success and How You Can Help!* St. Paul, Minn.: Paragon House, 2006. Discusses the multitude of skills that children can acquire through playing video games.

Takahashi, Dean. *Opening the Xbox.* San Francisco: Prima Lifestyles, 2002. Provides insightful analysis of the video game industry, focusing on Microsoft and the company's entrance into the industry with the Xbox console.

Cat Rambo

See also Apple Computer; Computers; Hobbies and recreation; Information age; Inventions; *Pac-Man*; Science and technology; Toys and games; Virtual reality.

■ Vietnam Veterans Memorial

Identification U.S. war monument
Creators Envisioned by Jan Scruggs and designed by Maya Ying Lin
Date Built in 1982
Place National Mall, Washington, D.C.

Millions of people from around the globe would visit the black granite memorial etched with the names of more than fifty-eight thousand American military personnel who lost their lives in the Vietnam War.

The painful wounds inflicted on the United States by its longest war were still fresh in 1979, when Vietnam veteran Jan Scruggs and his wife, after viewing the movie *The Deer Hunter* (1979), decided to launch an effort to honor Scruggs's fallen comrades. Only four years had passed since the collapse of South Vietnam and the fall of Saigon. Scruggs once said of his own service in that divisive conflict:

The Vietnam Veterans Memorial in Washington, D.C.

The bitterness I feel when I remember carrying the lifeless bodies of close friends through the mire of Vietnam will probably never subside. I still wonder if anything can be found to bring any purpose to all the suffering and death.

The Memorial   The Vietnam Veterans Memorial was conceived by Scruggs and fellow veterans to serve as a permanent tribute to the U.S. dead and as a means for the country to reflect on the war in all its dimensions. Scruggs founded an organization, the Vietnam Veterans Memorial Fund, but it got off to a shaky start, initially raising only $144.50 and becoming a subject of ridicule, even from mainstream media. Undeterred, Scruggs enlisted the support of national leaders such as U.S. senator John Warner of Virginia, who donated $5,000 of his own money and helped raise $50,000 more. Donations, large and

small, began to pour in from 275,000 people, and the memorial fund ballooned to $8.4 million. Private money would fulfill Scruggs's dream of explaining the conflict to many who were not personally involved in Southeast Asia.

Scruggs lobbied Congress for a suitably prominent location on the National Mall for a memorial that would serve as a site of healing and reflection, as well as become a tangible tribute to all who were touched by the conflict. Two acres near the Lincoln Memorial were reserved for the monument, and on July 1, 1980, President Jimmy Carter signed legislation authorizing that location for the construction of the Vietnam Veterans Memorial. For the next two years, Scruggs and his organization monitored the design and construction of the memorial.

A national design competition, judged by a panel of architects and artists, commenced after the project received its presidential approval. Bob Doubek, Scruggs's fellow Vietnam veteran and a member of the founding organization, explained, "The hope is that the creation of the memorial will begin a healing process." Some 1,421 entries were submitted, and the competition had four criteria: The design must be reflective and contemplative, it must be harmonious with the site, it must be inscribed with the names of the dead and the missing, and it must make no political statement about war. The panel of experts reviewed the submissions and, after four days of careful deliberations, unanimously chose the design offered by a Chinese American Yale University undergraduate architecture student, Maya Ying Lin.

Lin was only twenty-one years of age and had led a life untouched by death. Her entry had been submitted as a course requirement. She saw her challenge as enormous, but she methodically set out to create a memorial that was faithful to the competition's original guidelines. Visiting the site, Lin commented,

> I thought about what death is, what a loss is. A sharp pain that lessens with time, but can never quite heal over. The idea occurred to me there on the site. I had an impulse to cut open the earth. The grass would grow back, but the cut would remain.

Inspired, Lin returned to Yale and placed the finishing touches on the design, completing it in only three weeks.

Public reaction to Lin's design was mixed. Race interjected itself into the discussion because of Lin's ethnicity. Some veterans likened the black granite memorial to an ugly scar. Others, however, applauded the memorial, with its simple listing of the dead and missing, row after row.

The wall's construction phase continued from 1981 to 1982. The memorial was built into the earth, below ground level, with two panels arranged as giant arms pointing to either the Washington Monument or the Lincoln Memorial. On these black granite panels were etched the names of more than fifty-eight thousand men and women, some of whom remained missing. The first casualty had occurred in 1956 and the last had taken place in 1975. The names were ordered chronologically, so at first—in the section corresponding to the war's early years—only a few appeared. As a visitor walked farther into the memorial, longer and longer lists of the dead would accumulate. Such visitors, as Lin envisioned, would walk toward the monument's vortex, the cen-

ter where the two arms meet in a warm embrace. There, they would search for the names of friends, relatives, and unknown heroes of America's longest war. From the first day, the memorial drew people bearing gifts for the dead and paper upon which to trace names of the fallen.

Impact   The memorial, dedicated on Veteran's Day in 1982 by President Ronald Reagan, put a human face on a conflict that brought pain to so many people. The inscription on the memorial's plaque proudly honors "the courage, sacrifice and devotion to duty and country of its Vietnam veterans."

Further Reading

Karnow, Stanley. *Vietnam: A History.* New York: Harper & Row, 1983. History of the war that includes mention of the memorial and its function in postwar healing.

Lee, J. Edward, and H. C. "Toby" Haynsworth. *Nixon, Ford, and the Abandonment of South Vietnam.* Jefferson, N.C.: McFarland, 2002. History that focuses on the failure of civilian leadership to bring the war to a successful conclusion.

Library of Congress, U.S. American Treasures of the Library of Congress: Vietnam Veterans Memorial. http://www.loc.gov/exhibits/treasures/trm022.html. Official government Web site that documents the monument's construction and meaning.

Palmer, Laura. *Shrapnel in the Heart: Letters and Remembrances from the Vietnam Veterans Memorial.* New York: Vintage Books, 1987. Combines transcripts of messages left at the site of the memorial with interviews with those who left them there.

Vietnam Veterans Memorial: Official Park Guide. Washington, D.C.: National Park Service, U.S. Department of the Interior, 1995. The official guide of the National Park Service, whose job it is to oversee the Vietnam Veterans Memorial.

Wagner-Pacifici, Robin, and Barry Schwartz. "The Vietnam Veterans Memorial: Commemorating a Difficult Past." *The American Journal of Sociology* 97 (1991): 376-420. Examines they pyschological and sociological effects and implications of the memorial.

Joseph Edward Lee

See also   Architecture; Asian Americans; Boat people; Cold War; Foreign policy of the United States; *Platoon*; Reagan, Ronald.

■ Virtual reality

Definition   Computer-generated simulation of experience designed to mimic actual experience

In the late 1980's, the term "virtual reality" was popularized by Jaron Lanier, founder of VPL Research, which built many of the early virtual reality goggles and gloves.

Virtual reality, also known as artificial reality, is a technology designed to enable users to interact with fabricated environments in ways that resemble the ways in which they interact with real environments. This interaction may be limited to one dimension, such as movement, or it may seek to replicate the entire experience of being in the world. In the 1980's, nascent virtual reality technologies appeared, and users interacted with these three-dimensional, computer-simulated environments by means of special goggles or gloves that provided the experience of directly manipulating the computer world. While the worlds were usually depicted only visually, some environments went so far as to have auditory or tactile components.

While virtual reality technology was fairly primitive and quite rare during the decade, fictional representations of virtual reality were more common. The concept of virtual reality captured the imaginations of many, as it seemed to be the ideal form of representation, a form that would eventually replace film, literature, and most other media. However, it was generally the dangers of simulated reality, rather than its benefits, that most fascinated science-fiction authors and filmmakers.

Impact   Virtual reality became a mainstay of science fiction, where it was quickly juxtaposed with the related concept of cyberspace. Cyberpunk authors thus led the vanguard of portrayals of the possibilities and hazards of the nascent technology, as did the television program *Star Trek: The Next Generation*, which featured a virtual reality system called a "holodeck" in several of its episodes. Later, as technology progressed, more real-world applications for virtual reality technology would emerge, including military, medical, therapeutic, and architectural uses.

Further Reading

Burdea, Grigore C., and P. Coffet. *Virtual Reality Technology.* Hoboken, N.J.: John Wiley & Sons, 2003.

Kalwasky, R. S. *The Science of Virtual Reality and Virtual Environments: A Technical, Scientific, and Engineering Reference on Virtual Environments.* New York: Addison-Wesley, 1993.

Krueger, Myron W. *Artificial Reality.* New York: Addison-Wesley, 1991.

Markley, Robert. *Virtual Realities and Their Discontents.* Baltimore: Johns Hopkins University Press, 1996.

Sherman, William C., and Alan Craig. *Understanding Virtual Reality: Interface, Application, and Design.* San Francisco: Morgan Kaufmann, 2003.

Teixeira, Kevin, and Ken Pimentel. *Virtual Reality: Through the New Looking Glass.* 2d ed. New York: Intel/McGraw-Hill, 1995.

Cat Rambo

See also   CAD/CAM technology; Computers; Cyberpunk literature; Gibson, William; Inventions; Science and technology; *Star Trek: The Next Generation*; *Tron*; Video games and arcades.

■ Voicemail

Definition   Centralized telecommunications technology in which spoken messages are recorded for later retrieval by the recipient

The popularity of voicemail in the 1980's sped up business and family life.

Prior to the invention of voicemail, phone users employed answering machines, which were cumbersome. Voicemail originated in 1975 with Steven J. Boies of International Business Machines (IBM), and the concept caught on in the early 1980's when it was commercialized by Octel Communications. In the late 1980's, after the American Telephone and Telegraph (AT&T) breakup, Scott Jones of Boston Technology found it possible to make the system more accessible to everyone.

Voicemail added a large number of features that answering machine systems lacked. In the corporate realm, it allowed each member of a business to have a separate storage for incoming messages. Eventually, companies were able to centralize their voicemail work on one system. Voicemail was easy to use: Messages could be left even if the recipient was on another call, and users could hear instructions on the phone about how to use it. Each employee was assigned a mailbox, and a person could record a personal greeting for callers.

With the introduction of voicemail, business people could make many more calls without having to rely on other staff members, thereby saving companies money as well as lost time and messages. Educators could reach students' parents without getting a busy signal. The recipient could store messages, play them back remotely and at any time, or forward them to another location.

The downside to voicemail was that the recipient might have to spend a lot of time listening to calls. At home, people received unwanted sales calls on their voicemail. For people who wanted to speak with each other live, a lot of time might be spent playing "phone tag" with each other before they actually connected. People who called businesses often were automatically redirected without being able to speak to a customer service representative.

Impact By the early twenty-first century, voicemail had become a ubiquitous feature for cell phone users and many businesses. People found voicemail to be both a blessing and a hindrance. While it liberated them from many of the hassles associated with earlier phone systems, it required people to be always "on call"—always able to be contacted.

Further Reading

Bates, Regis J., with Donald W. Gregory. *Voice and Data Communications Handbook*. New York: McGraw-Hill, 2006.

LeBon, Paul. *Escape from Voicemail Hell: Boost Your Productivity by Making Voicemail Work for You*. Highland Village, Tex.: Parleau, 1999.

Jan Hall

See also AT&T breakup; Cell phones; Computers; Fax machines; Globalization; Inventions; Science and technology.

■ *Voyager* global flight

The Event An airplane circles the earth in nonstop flight

Date December 14-23, 1986

Place Left from and returned to Edwards Air Force Base, Mojave Desert, California

Two U.S. pilots circumnavigated the world in an innovative composite-material aircraft that transported sufficient fuel to enable them to complete the trip without stopping or refueling in transit. Their achievement inspired aerospace design.

During the early twentieth century, several airplane pilots successfully circumnavigated the earth, setting various records, as advancements in aviation technology lengthened the possible distance and duration of flight. Aviators were inspired by a 1962 B-52 Stratofortress nonstop flight covering 12,519 miles between Okinawa, Japan, and Madrid, Spain, without refueling. Their next goal was a nonstop circumnavigation of the globe requiring no supplementary fueling. In 1981, brothers Burt Rutan, an aircraft designer, and Richard Rutan, a former U.S. Air Force pilot, and their colleague Jeana Yeager envisioned an airplane capable of transporting sufficient fuel to sustain an Earth-circling nonstop flight.

The trio established Voyager Aircraft and utilized Burt Rutan's experiences with composites and canard wings to design a light aircraft capable of lifting large amounts of fuel. For approximately eighteen months, they assembled the *Voyager* from layers of carbon fibers, polymers, and epoxy molded into various components and heated to strengthen the aircraft, which resembled the letter "W" with a 110-foot bendable wing bisecting it. The *Voyager*'s small cabin, seventeen fuel tanks, canard, and wing totaled 939 pounds. Two engines powered *Voyager*. A Federal Aviation Administration (FAA) inspector approved *Voyager* for flight.

The *Voyager* team pushed to attain the record before rival aviators achieved that goal. Starting on June 22, 1984, Richard Rutan and Yeager began test flights in the *Voyager*, discovering technical issues needing repair, as well as optimal flying strategies to respond to various flight conditions. Inside the narrow *Voyager*'s cabin, one pilot sat, while the other reclined. During sixty-seven flight tests, they achieved records, including a 11,857-mile flight in July, 1986, between San Luis Obispo, California, and San Francisco, California, with no refueling. This flight resulted in the *Voyager* project receiving some funds, but corporate financial support—which they had hoped to secure—remained an elusive goal. The Rutans and Yeager invested an estimated two million dollars in *Voyager*.

Around the World Rutan and Yeager prepared to fly in early December, 1986, but rain disrupted their plan. After skies cleared, they transferred the *Voyager* to Edwards Air Force Base on December 13. The

The Voyager *aircraft returns from its record-breaking nonstop trip around the world in 1986.* (NASA)

next morning, National Aeronautics Association representative Richard Hansen placed seals and other devices on the *Voyager* to detect any refueling or stops. Piloting the *Voyager* first, Rutan departed at 8:01 A.M. and flew west, attaining an altitude of fifty-eight hundred feet. Burt Rutan initially followed in another plane to monitor the *Voyager,* and ground support personnel maintained radio contact.

Flying over the Pacific Ocean, Rutan and Yeager navigated with radar and a Global Positioning System (GPS) to maneuver between storms and turbulent areas. They passed Hawaii and reached the South Pacific on the second day of flight. Rutan avoided flying into Typhoon Marge but benefited from its winds to speed toward the Philippine Islands. On the third day, exhausted after flying since the beginning of the voyage, Rutan slept while Yeager piloted the *Voyager* through Southeast Asia.

On the fourth day, the pilots stayed near the Inter-

tropical Convergence Zone (ITCZ), risking storms to benefit from winds to push *Voyager* along its flight path over the Indian Ocean. As it neared Africa the next day, the *Voyager* set the record for the greatest flight distance reached without refueling. The pilots crossed mountainous hazards by using the front engine to lift over tall peaks.

During day six, the *Voyager* pilots turned off the front engine after clearing African mountains and reaching coastal landmarks. On the following day, they completed crossing the Atlantic Ocean to Brazil. Yeager resumed piloting while Rutan slept, guiding *Voyager* toward the Pacific Ocean. By day eight, the pilots headed north. They experienced fuel pump problems, and the rear engine stopped. As the *Voyager* began to descend over the ocean, the pilots attempted to turn the front engine on. It started when the aircraft was only thirty-five hundred feet above ground. The *Voyager*'s movement caused fuel to reach the rear engine, which also started, and the pilots decided to continue toward Edwards Air Force Base with both engines operating.

On December 23, 1986, the *Voyager* reached Edwards at around 7:30 A.M. A crowd of approximately twenty-three thousand people watched as Rutan flew around the airfield while Yeager lowered the landing gear. The *Voyager* landed at 8:05 A.M. Hansen verified that his seals were still in place and confirmed the world record flight, which had covered 25,012 miles during nine days, three minutes, and forty-four seconds aloft.

Impact International news reporters covered the *Voyager*'s global flight, emphasizing the Rutans' and Yeager's achievement as an aviation milestone. On December 29, 1986, Yeager and both Rutan brothers accepted the Presidential Citizens Medal from President Ronald Reagan. They also received aviation's prestigious Robert Collier Trophy. Pilots Rutan and Yeager discussed their flight at a February 3, 1987, hearing of the U.S. House of Representatives Committee on Science, Space, and Technology, encouraging expanded research and application of composites to military and commercial aircraft. During the summer of 1987, the *Voyager* was transported for inclusion in the National Air and Space Museum at Washington, D.C.

The *Voyager* represented the emerging field of aerospace development without government support, foreshadowing later private space exploration that would not be controlled by governmental bureaucracy and restrictions. The Rutans and Yeager retained interest in designing experimental composite aircraft for the remainder of the 1980's. Their *Voyager* experiences influenced designs by Burt Rutan's company, Scaled Composites.

Further Reading

Fink, Donald E. "Salute to *Voyager*." *Aviation Week and Space Technology* 126, no. 1 (January 5, 1987): 13. Editorial examines the *Voyager*'s possible influence on governmental and civilian aerospace in this issue, which provides thorough coverage.

Marbach, William D., and Peter McAlevey. "Up, Up, and Around." *Newsweek* 108, no. 26 (December 29, 1986): 34-36, 41-44. Account supplemented with maps, diagrams, and information profiling significant aviation records.

Mordoff, Keith F. "*Voyager* Crew Faces Turbulence, Fatigue on World Flight Attempt." *Aviation Week and Space Technology* 125, no. 25 (December 22, 1986): 18-21. Describes *Voyager*'s original flight plan, preparations, and conditions en route.

Schatzberg, Eric. *Wings of Wood, Wings of Metal: Culture and Technical Choice in Airplane Materials, 1914-1945*. Princeton, N.J.: Princeton University Press, 1999. Considers the *Voyager*'s composite materials in context with predecessors using similar strategies.

Yeager, Jeana, and Dick Rutan, with Phil Patton. *Voyager*. New York: Alfred A. Knopf, 1987. Comprehensive pilots' account discussing all aspects of *Voyager*. Includes unique photographs.

Elizabeth D. Schafer

See also Gimli Glider; Inventions; Science and technology.

W

■ *Wall Street*

Identification American film
Director Oliver Stone (1946-   )
Date Released December 11, 1987

Considered by some to be a study, or revelation, of social Darwinism at its worst, Wall Street *offered a compelling portrait of a man, Gordon Gekko, for whom financial profit is the ultimate aim of human endeavor and the pursuit of financial success the only religion worthy of the name. The film creates such a vivid portrait of a man for whom greed is both aphrodisiac and consummation that the movie's moral seems to pale by comparison.*

Wall Street attracted attention from movie critics because of its character Gordon Gekko's unapologetic defense of greed as a positive motivating force in American life. Michael Douglas (who won an Academy Award for his performance) created such a powerful portrait of the financial wizard that it was difficult for viewers not to be taken in by his argument that winning is the only goal worth pursuing and that obeying the law is only for the timid. Gekko is ultimately undone in the film by his protégé, Bud Fox, but the film provides no assurance that the free market system will change as a result. Other Gekkos may easily arise to fill the vacuum left by his downfall.

Director Oliver Stone used Gekko to give voice to what he saw as the collective values corrupting American culture in the 1980's. Gekko's famous statement "Greed is good" would at many times in history have been taken as simply wrong if not insane. During the decade that gave rise to the nickname the Me generation, however, "Greed is good" resonated with a great many Americans, either as a slogan to embrace or as a distillation of the mistake at the heart of the nation's values.

Impact *Wall Street* paints a startling portrait of an unprincipled man who manipulates people and uses illegal means to gain money and power. One implication of the film was that a free economy is vulnerable to the abuses of people like Gordon Gekko and

that only the goodness of people like the ambitious Bud Fox and his father can protect it. This implication seemed to apply particularly well to the 1980's, a decade during which extreme wealth was being created on Wall Street, but real wages did not increase. *Wall Street* was taken, both at the time and later, as distilling the economic culture of the decade and giving it a villainous but frighteningly compelling face.

Further Reading

Boozer, Jack, Jr. "*Wall Street*: The Commodification of Perception." *The Journal of Popular Film and Television* 17, no. 3 (Fall, 1989): 90-99.

Kunz, Don. *The Films of Oliver Stone*. Lanham, Md.: Scarecrow Press, 1997.

Simon, John. "*Wall Street*." *National Review* 40, no. 1 (January 22, 1988): 65.

Bernard E. Morris

See also Academy Awards; Black Monday stock market crash; Business and the economy in the United States; Crime; Douglas, Michael; Film in the United States; Hannah, Daryl; Power dressing; Reaganomics; Stone, Oliver; Yuppies.

■ Washington, Harold

Identification Mayor of Chicago, 1983-1987
Born April 22, 1922; Chicago, Illinois
Died November 25, 1987; Chicago, Illinois

Washington made local and national history as Chicago's first African American mayor. His victory demonstrated the power of unified African American voters and challenged decades of white domination of Democratic Party politics in Chicago.

Harold Washington was a thirty-year veteran of Chicago politics when he entered the city's 1983 mayoral race. An attorney by profession, Washington served in the Illinois statehouse from 1964 to 1976 and the state senate from 1976 to 1980. He ran unsuccessfully for mayor of Chicago in 1977 following the death of Richard J. Daley, whose political machine controlled the city for decades. Washington was committed to Daley early in his career but later earned a reputation for independence. The socioeconomic interests of African Americans were central to Washington's agenda, and he built a power base among voters neglected by Chicago's political establishment.

As a U.S. representative from the first congressional district from 1980 to 1983, Washington opposed President Ronald Reagan's policies before leaving Congress reluctantly to mount a second mayoral bid. Despite his achievements and experience, Washington was an underdog in the Democratic primary against incumbent Jane Byrne and Richard M. Daley, the late mayor's son. Washington's opponents raised ethical questions about his law practice and a short jail term that he had served for income tax evasion in 1971. Washington was a charismatic campaigner, however, and benefited from high African American voter registration and dissatisfaction with Byrne. After a difficult primary victory, Washington endured a general election filled with attacks on him and his supporters. White voters who had been lifelong Democrats rejected Washington and bluntly expressed racial motivations for voting for Republican Bernard Epton.

Washington took office in April, 1983, after receiving almost 100 percent of Chicago's African American votes and barely 12 percent of its white votes. His agenda met fierce resistance from members of Washington's own party. The "Council Wars" of 1983-1986 pitted Washington against a mostly white group of Democrats who held the majority of seats on Chicago's city council and created a virtual stalemate until late in his first term. Washington's progress in bringing diversity to his city's government and improving public transportation and conditions in urban neighborhoods carried him to a second term in 1987, but he died after serving just seven months.

Impact Harold Washington's struggles and successes in Chicago's tough political climate made him the most important African American elected official of the 1980's. The racial divisions of Washington's campaigns and terms in office highlighted similar events in national politics as large numbers of white Democrats defected to the Republican Party in the 1980's.

Further Reading

Rivlin, Gary. *Fire on the Prairie: Chicago's Harold Washington and the Politics of Race.* New York: Henry Holt, 1992.
Young, Henry J. *The Black Church and the Harold Washington Story: The Man, the Message, the Movement.* Bristol, Ind.: Wyndham Hall, 1988.

Ray Pence

See also African Americans; Jackson, Jesse; Racial discrimination; Reagan, Ronald; Reagan Democrats.

■ Water pollution

Definition Decline in water quality resulting from biological, chemical, or thermal agents

Although the United States made progress in dealing with water pollution during the 1980's, the issue was not a high priority for the Reagan administration. In addition to concern with surface water, some Americans began to register increasing concern for the quality and quantity of water available from underground aquifers during the decade.

Congress had set standards for water quality in 1972 with amendments to the Federal Water Pollution Control Act (FWPCA), a 1948 law. This legislation set water quality standards for a variety of chemical, biological, and thermal pollutants and prescribed standards for the treatment and pretreatment of industrial and municipal wastes. The Federal Water Pollution Control Act Amendments (FWPCAA) also indicated that by 1985 the country should achieve a zero discharge standard of wastes into water sources. By 1977, however, it had already become evident that this standard was unachievable, and so the standard was modified to the best level possible.

The construction during the 1970's of new municipal wastewater treatment plants, often with federal assistance, led to improvements in water quality by the early 1980's. Discharge from municipal sewage treatment plants or industrial sites is referred to as point pollution, as it is emitted at a specific point and the discharge can be monitored. Another form of point pollution occurs when water is drawn from a body of water, used for cooling, and then returned to the body of water. Thermal pollution, such as that occurring when water is used for cooling in nuclear reactors, can produce "hot" spots in rivers or lakes when the water is returned. The application of federal standards reduced the temperature of returned water, although it generally did not return it to the original level. During the 1980's, several states developed water quality standards for point pollution to supplement the federal rules, and there continued to be improvements in stream quality, although at a slower rate than during the previous decade.

Nonpoint Pollution   In spite of continuing gains in dealing with point pollution during the decade, a major source of water pollution remained more difficult to handle. Runoff from farms, parking lots, construction sites, or industrial sites is not concentrated in any one location and is more difficult to monitor than is point pollution. Nonetheless, such nonpoint pollution was a major contributor to the pollution of streams and lakes before, during, and after the 1980's. Fertilizers such as nitrogen, used to enhance agricultural production, are a major source of nutrient material that becomes available to organisms in water when some of the fertilizer runs off from agricultural land. The growth of these oxygen-requiring microorganisms in water reduces the amount of oxygen available to satisfy the biochemical oxygen demand (BOD) of fish or useful aquatic life, leading to fish kills.

Agriculture became an increasingly important source of this form of pollution during the decade. For example, approximately 16 percent of all nitrogen fertilizer applied in the Mississippi River basin was washed into the Mississippi. Some advocates urged the Environmental Protection Agency (EPA) to act to regulate nonpoint pollution, but the Reagan administration was disinclined to regulate the environment further.

Nonpoint pollution could be chemical as well as biological in nature. Runoff from roads or parking lots added minute amounts of chemicals or heavy metals of various sorts to nearby water sources. In this case, the remedy often caused additional problems. Many cities piped storm water into the sewer system. Large rainstorms at times caused sewer systems to bypass water treatment plants because of the excess capacity. Although road runoff was contained

A polluted lakefront beach in Hammond, Indiana, poses a health hazard to swimmers. (Library of Congress)

in this case, the bypassing of waste treatment facilities led to raw sewage being dumped into streams. Some cities acknowledged the problem but did not have the money to construct larger treatment facilities to deal with the issue.

One form of nonpoint pollution did begin to be addressed during the 1980's. Several states and local governments required that construction sites control runoff from the sites. This simple measure reduced the flow of dirt, organics, and chemicals into water courses.

Underground Water   Initial efforts at dealing with water pollution had focused on surface water, but efforts would also focus on underground water. Underground aquifers provide sources of water for drinking, irrigation, and industrial use in many parts of the country.

Tests of the wells of individuals and some cities began to reveal that pollution was also a problem for this water source. Chemicals from underground gasoline storage tanks, hazardous waste sites, or even municipal landfills was found to migrate gradually through the soil at the site into nearby wells and aquifers.

Awareness of this problem dated to the 1970's, but it became an increasing concern in some regions during the 1980's that was coupled, in some cases, to fears about overuse of aquifers. The misuse and overuse of aquifers reduced water supplies that were not replaceable, leading to worries about the sustainability of water supplies in areas such as the Great Plains.

Impact   The United States continued to make some improvements in achieving cleaner water during the 1980's. A lax regulatory climate as well as increasingly costly methods for securing improvement slowed the progress in managing water pollution. People became more aware of the impact of nonpoint water pollution during the decade, although little was done to deal with the issue. In addition, little monitoring of water quality was done, so it was difficult to measure progress accurately. Water pollution remained an often ignored issue at the end of the decade.

Further Reading

Freedman, Barry D. *Regulation in the Reagan-Bush Era: The Eruption of Presidential Influence.* Pittsburgh: University of Pittsburgh Press, 1995.

An analysis of the Reagan-Bush environmental record.

Peirce, J. Jeffrey, Ruth F. Weiner, and P. Aarne Vesilind. *Environmental Pollution and Control.* 4th ed. Boston: Butterworth-Heinemann, 1998. Several chapters deal with the nature and treatment of water pollution.

Rogers, Peter. *America's Water: Federal Role and Responsibilities.* Cambridge, Mass.: MIT Press, 1999. A good analysis of the role of the federal government in ensuring water quality.

Rosenbaum, Walter A. *Environmental Politics and Policy.* 7th ed. Washington, D.C.: CQ Press, 2008. Provides a broad political context for an analysis of water pollution issues.

John M. Theilmann

See also   Air pollution; Environmental movement; Reagan, Ronald; Watt, James G.

■ Watson, Tom

Identification   American professional golfer
Born   September 4, 1949; Kansas City, Missouri

Watson was the best golf professional in the world from 1980 to 1983, winning five major championships.

Tom Watson is recognized by golf historians as one of the great champions of the modern era, having won eight of golf's major championships from 1975 to 1982. From 1980 through 1983, he won five major championships, including the British Open (1980, 1982, and 1983), the Masters (1981), and the United States Open (1982). Watson's victory in the 1982 United States Open at Pebble Beach is symbolic of his golf legacy. He battled champion Jack Nicklaus throughout the final round and made an unexpected birdie, holing a chip shot from heavy rough just off the seventeenth green. He also defeated Nicklaus in one-on-one competition at the 1977 British Open and the 1977 Masters. Therefore, Watson became recognized both for his eight major championships and as the man who beat Jack Nicklaus more dramatically than anyone else.

The year 1980 was notable for Watson, because he became the professional tour's first player to win over one-half million dollars in one season, winning seven total tournaments. At the 1980 British Open, he finished four shots ahead of his nearest competi-

Tom Watson. (Ralph W. Miller Golf Library)

tor, Hall of Fame golfer Lee Trevino. His victory at the Masters in 1981 was by two shots over two great champions, Jack Nicklaus and Johnny Miller. In 1983, Watson almost won consecutive U.S. Open titles, finishing second by one shot to Larry Nelson at Oakmont. Watson again finished second at the U.S. Open in 1987, behind Scott Simpson. Also in 1987, Watson won the first-ever season-ending tour championship, his first tournament win in three years.

Impact   Tom Watson was voted six times as the United States Professional Golfers' Association (PGA) Player of the Year, including in 1980, 1982, and 1984. He was a member of the United States' Ryder Cup team in 1981, 1983, and 1989. In 1987, he received the Bob Jones Award, the United States Golf Association's highest honor for distinguished sportsmanship in golf. In 1988, Watson was inducted into the World Golf Hall of Fame.

Further Reading

Campbell, Malcolm. *The Encyclopedia of Golf.* 3d ed. New York: DK, 2001.

Watson, Tom. "The Thinker Tom Watson." Interview by Lisa Taddeo. *Golf Magazine*, October, 2006, 80-87.

_____. *Tom Watson's Strategic Golf.* New York: Pocket Books, 1992.

Alan Prescott Peterson

See also   Golf; Sports.

■ Watt, James G.

Identification   Secretary of the interior from January, 1981, to November, 1983
Born   January 31, 1938; Lusk, Wyoming

Watt's business background and the perception that he was pro-development made him a lightning rod for criticism during his brief tenure as head of the Department of the Interior.

James G. Watt served as secretary of the interior under President Ronald Reagan from January, 1981, until November, 1983. Born in Lusk, Wyoming, he graduated from the University of Wyoming in 1960 and from that university's law school in 1962. In 1962, he became the deputy assistant secretary of water and power in the Department of the Interior, and in 1975, he was made vice chairman of the Federal Power Commission. Before being appointed to Reagan's cabinet, Watt was the founding president of the Mountain States Legal Foundation, a conservative organization that sought to protect and advance the interests of businesses involved in oil, timber, mining, and other natural resource development fields.

With his pro-business and pro-development background, Watt was immediately controversial as the choice to head the Department of the Interior, although he was quickly confirmed by the U.S. Senate. As secretary, Watt led the way in implementing President Reagan's environmental policies. Reagan sought to apply cost-benefit analysis to environmental regulations, to determine whether the cost and the impact on jobs and the economy outweighed the value of the regulations. Reagan also promoted "environmental federalism," which involved transferring the responsibility for many decisions on environmental matters back to the states. Many of Watt's appointees within the Department of the Interior were recruited from the business community, often from the very industries that the department was charged with regulating. Watt cut funding and personnel for some regulatory programs and sought to open some coastal lands and wilderness areas to exploration for resource development.

Impact   Within four months of his appointment, activist environmental groups such as the Sierra Club were calling for Watt's removal. By the summer of 1981, even the more moderate National Wildlife Federation was calling for Watt to step down. By October, 1981, the Sierra Club's "Dump Watt" petition drive had delivered to Congress over one million signatures calling for Watt's firing. Despite the heavy criticism of Watt's policies, the immediate cause of his resignation was the furor over a remark he made in a speech in September, 1983, in which he described the personnel of a Senate oversight committee with which he worked. He referred to the gender, ethnic backgrounds, and physical disability of committee members in a way that was perceived as bigoted. The Senate began considering a resolution calling for Watt's removal, but he resigned before being forced out. Watt announced his resignation on October 9, 1983, and left the Interior Department on November 8, 1983.

Further Reading

Kraft, Michael E., and Norman J. Vig. "Environmental Policy in the Reagan Presidency." *Political Science Quarterly* 99, no. 3 (Fall, 1984): 415-439.

Watt, James G., with Doug Wead. *The Courage of a Conservative.* New York: Simon & Schuster, 1985.

Mark S. Joy

See also   Conservatism in U.S. politics; Environmental movement; Reagan, Ronald; Scandals.

■ Wave, the

Definition   Mass gesture involving spontaneous coordinated movement by an audience, usually at a sporting event, mimicking the appearance of a large wave

The wave became popular at sporting events across North America and eventually across the world during the 1980's.

"The wave," also known as the "audience wave" or "Mexican wave," involves large numbers of participants standing and raising their arms in succession to create a wave of movement through an assembled crowd. The origins of the wave are unclear, having been traced to various possible sources, including a hockey game in Alberta, Canada, in 1980; an American League baseball playoff game in October, 1981; and a football game at the University of Washington later that month. Having no apparent connection with a single sport or team, the wave was less a cheer than a mass communal gesture akin to the popular act of bouncing a beach ball through the crowd at a concert or sporting event. Although generally considered innocuous, the wave has been criticized for its meaningless nature and for causing food, beverages, and other objects to be thrown or spilled into the participating crowd.

Although sometimes performed by specific groups of spectators, the wave was more often a nonpartisan action in which spectators were compelled by peer pressure to participate. Waves often traveled around a stadium or arena or back and forth across a section of grandstands numerous times before dying out as spontaneously as they had begun when the crowd became weary of them. Variations on the standard wave, including the simultaneous creation of two oppositely rotating waves and successive waves performed at various predetermined speeds, were sometimes performed in settings conducive to preplanning and crowd discipline, such as student sections at collegiate sporting events.

The wave grew rapidly in popularity during the early 1980's, partly as a result of mass media coverage of sporting events, and it was a standard feature of American and Canadian sporting events by the mid-1980's. The 1984 Olympic Games in Los Angeles, California, exposed an international audience to the wave, which subsequently achieved global prominence during the 1986 World Cup soccer tournament in Monterrey, Mexico. As a result, the cheer became known in many parts of the world as the "Mexican wave."

Impact   Although a fixture of sporting events by the end of the 1980's, the wave was essentially an act devoid of meaning or context, and as such exerted little discernible cultural influence. It became the subject of research by scholars studying crowd psychology and social phenomena and, despite its eventual international popularity, has been cited as an example of cultural conformity in 1980's America. The wave waned in popularity after the 1980's but continued to appear sporadically at sporting events into the twenty-first century.

Further Reading

Free, Marcus. *The Uses of Sport: A Critical Study.* London: Routledge, 2004.

Wann, Daniel L. *Sport Fans: The Psychology and Social Impact of Spectators.* London: Routledge, 2001.

Michael H. Burchett

See also Fads; Olympic Games of 1984; Sports.

■ Weaver, Sigourney

Identification American actor
Born October 8, 1949; New York, New York

During the 1980's, Weaver established herself as an actor capable of playing strong, aggressive women willing to take on impossible odds.

At the beginning of the 1980's, Sigourney Weaver had just played Ellen Ripley, an independent woman who takes on the alien in *Alien* (1979), a moderate box-office hit. This role set the tone for her film performances of the decade, especially her reprisal of the role in the 1986 sequel, *Aliens* (1986), another successful film for which she received an Academy Award nomination. Weaver also starred as Dian Fossey in *Gorillas in the Mist* (1988), a film based on the life of a conservationist and activist who was eventually killed by poachers.

Weaver was affected by the film's material and became an ardent environmentalist, as well as the honorary chairperson of the Dian Fossey Gorilla Fund, which is devoted to the preservation of that endangered species. She received an Academy Award nomination for Best Actress for her role as Fossey and in the same year was also nominated as Best Supporting Actress for playing Katherine Parker, the conniving, ruthless career woman who finally gets her comeuppance in *Working Girl* (1988). She thus became one of very few actresses ever to receive two Oscar nominations in one year. Although she failed to win an Oscar, she did receive Golden Globe awards for both films.

In addition to the films of the 1980's for which she was best known, Weaver starred in other films in which she remained true to type. She was an intrepid reporter in the thriller *Eyewitness* (1981), and she

Sigourney Weaver as Ripley in Alien, *the role for which she was best known at the beginning of the 1980's.* (Hulton Archive/ Getty Images)

played opposite Mel Gibson in Peter Weir's *The Year of Living Dangerously* (1982), an underappreciated Australian film in which she portrayed a British attaché in revolutionary Indonesia. Although she is less known for her comedic talents, Weaver held her own in *Ghostbusters* (1984), a hugely popular comedy featuring Bill Murray and Dan Ackroyd; she repeated her role in the sequel, *Ghostbusters 2* (1989).

Impact Standing almost six feet tall, Weaver embodied the strong, powerful, imposing woman of the 1980's, a role model for women to emulate. Whether confronting aliens or poachers, she was a force to be reckoned with, but she also represented the aggressive woman many men were encountering at the office and at home. Thus, she came to stand for some men as a figure to be feared. The fine line in film portrayals between strong woman and threat to men was approached and at times crossed by several of the most famous 1980's actresses, including Weaver and Glenn Close, and it represented on screen tensions being experienced in American society, as more households began to require two incomes to remain financially secure.

Further Reading

Maguffe, T. D. *Sigourney Weaver.* New York: St. Martin's Press, 1989.

Sellers, Robert. *Sigourney Weaver.* London: Robert Hale, 1992.

Thomas L. Erskine

See also   Action films; *Aliens*; Business and the economy in the United States; Close, Glenn; Environmental movement; Feminism; Film in the United States; *Ghostbusters*; Gibson, Mel; Murray, Bill; Women in the workforce.

■ Webster v. Reproductive Health Services

Identification   U.S. Supreme Court decision
Date   Decided on July 2, 1989

In Webster v. Reproductive Health Services, *the Court upheld a Missouri state law regulating abortion, thereby signaling to other states that abortion regulation was constitutionally permissible.*

Webster v. Reproductive Health Services began in 1986, when Missouri health care professionals involved in providing abortion services challenged a state law regulating abortion. The Missouri law barred the use of public funds or resources for the purposes of abortion counseling or to perform abortions except to save a mother's life. It also required health care professionals to perform tests, such as assessments of fetal weight and lung maturity, to determine the viability of a fetus after twenty weeks gestational age. The law's preamble declared that life begins at conception, so a fetus should enjoy constitutional rights and protections. The district court found the law's restrictions on abortion unconstitutional and in violation of the precedents established in the Supreme Court's decision in *Roe v. Wade* (1973) protecting women's abortion rights. Missouri attorney general William Webster appealed the case to the Supreme Court.

Norma McCorvey, left, better known as the Jane Roe of Roe v. Wade *(1973) stands with attorney Gloria Allred outside the U.S. Supreme Court Building in April, 1989, after attending the oral arguments in* Webster v. Reproductive Health Services. *(AP/Wide World Photos)*

Supreme Court Action   The Court upheld the Missouri law's abortion provisions. The decision was complex, in that a portion of it was unanimous, while other portions were contested. Chief Justice William H. Rehnquist wrote the majority opinion, which stated that the Missouri law did not contradict *Roe v. Wade,* because it allowed pregnant women to terminate their pregnancies so long as neither public funds nor public facilities were used during such abortion procedures. The Court did not explicitly rule on the law's preamble proclaiming life to begin at conception. Instead, the Court interpreted the preamble statement as a "value judgment" favoring childbirth over abortion. According to the Court,

Roe did not prohibit states from issuing such value judgments.

Justice Antonin Scalia wrote a separate concurrence in favor of overturning *Roe*. Scalia argued that abortion was a political issue that should be under the domain of state legislatures. Justice Sandra Day O'Connor, also a part of the majority, also wrote a separate concurrence. She agreed with the majority that the trimester system of *Roe* was problematic but indicated that there was no need to modify it in *Webster*. Instead, she argued that the performance of tests to determine the viability of a fetus after twenty weeks gestational age did not impose an "undue burden" on a pregnant woman's abortion decision.

Justice Harry A. Blackmun, who had written the Court's decision in *Roe*, concurred in part and dissented in part. He was joined in his partial dissent by William Brennan and Thurgood Marshall, while John Paul Stevens wrote a separate opinion, also concurring in part and dissenting in part. Blackmun argued that the majority's decision challenged *Roe* and other legal precedents that established the notion of an individual's right to privacy. He indicated that the Missouri law and other state laws restricting abortion services would lead to an increase in unsafe, illegal abortions.

Impact Following the Supreme Court's *Webster* decision, advocates on both sides of the abortion debate disputed state regulatory measures concerning when and under what conditions a woman could seek an abortion in the light of *Roe*. The *Webster* case signaled to states that abortion regulation was constitutionally permissible, laying the foundation for later decisions permitting further regulation.

Further Reading

Craig, Barbara Hinkson, and David M. O'Brien. *Abortion and American Politics*. Chatham, N.J.: Chatham House, 1993.

Kerber, Linda K., and Jane Sherron De Hart, eds. *Women's America: Refocusing the Past*. New York: Oxford University Press, 2003.

O'Connor, Karen. *No Neutral Ground? Abortion Politics in an Age of Absolutes*. Boulder, Colo.: Westview Press, 1996.

Segers, Mary C., and Timothy A. Byrnes, eds. *Abortion Politics in American States*. New York: M. E. Sharpe, 1995.

Brooke Speer Orr

See also Abortion; Feminism; Supreme Court decisions; Women's rights.

■ Weinberger, Caspar

Identification U.S. secretary of defense from 1981 to 1987
Born August 18, 1917; San Francisco, California
Died March 8, 2006; Bangor, Maine

As secretary of defense under President Ronald Reagan, Weinberger oversaw expenditures of more than $3 trillion to develop the U.S. military. This development of personnel and technology provided the basis for an aggressive foreign policy that was directed at victory in the Cold War; it also contributed to the collapse of the Soviet Union early in the next decade.

After graduating from Harvard Law School (1941) and serving in the U.S. Army in the Pacific theater

U.S. secretary of defense Caspar Weinberger. (U.S. Deparment of Defense)

during World War II, Caspar Weinberger worked in a San Francisco law firm before entering California Republican politics in 1952, when he won a seat in the California Assembly (1952-1958). While he did not gain any higher elected office, Weinberger became powerful in the California Republican Party. With the election of President Richard M. Nixon in 1968, Weinberger was appointed chair of the Federal Trade Commission (1969), then director of the Office of Management and the Budget (1970); in both of these positions, he developed a reputation for being careful with the public's funds. In 1973, Weinberger reached cabinet rank, when he was appointed Secretary of Health, Education, and Welfare (1973-1975). Weinberger worked in the private sector between 1975 and 1980. During that time, he supported Ronald Reagan's candidacy for president.

With Reagan's election, Weinberger became his secretary of defense. In that capacity, Weinberger was charged with restoring the U.S. armed forces both quantitatively and qualitatively. The impact of the Vietnam War and the administration of President Jimmy Carter had both contributed to a decline in the capacity, reputation, and morale of the U.S. military. Weinberger was provided a blank check by Reagan and moved rapidly to expand the size of the military, develop and deploy new weapons systems, support technical innovations, and rebuild the Air Force and the Navy. His tenure became particularly associated with the development of new military technologies, a more professional and highly paid cadre of soldiers, a six-hundred-ship navy, and the Strategic Defense Initiative (SDI).

Weinberger also became involved in the case of Israeli spy Jonathan Pollard, when he argued that Pollard should be punished harshly for compromising American security. More seriously, Weinberger was associated with the Iran-Contra affair, which led to his resignation and indictment on charges that he deceived investigators looking into the sale of missiles to Iran and the use of those funds to support the pro-U.S. forces in Nicaragua. Weinberger was never tried on these charges; President George H. W. Bush pardoned Weinberger and others on December 24, 1992.

Impact Weinberger's major achievement was overseeing the buildup of the U.S. military during the first six years of the Reagan administration. He also

became embroiled in a constitutional crisis, the Iran-Contra affair, that involved the illegal use of government funds to support the anticommunist forces in Nicaragua. Weinberger remained a power in American conservative circles until his death in 2006.

Further Reading

Baker, James A. *The Politics of Diplomacy*. New York: Putnam, 1995.

Weinberger, Caspar W., with Gretchen Roberts. *In the Arena: A Memoir of the Twentieth Century*. Washington, D.C.: Regnery, 2003.

_____. *The Next War*. Washington, D.C.: Regnery, 1996.

William T. Walker

See also Cold War; Conservatism in U.S. politics; Elections in the United States, 1980; Europe and North America; Foreign policy of the United States; Grenada invasion; Iran-Contra affair; Israel and the United States; Reagan, Ronald; Reagan Doctrine; Reagan's "Evil Empire" speech; Stealth fighter; Strategic Defense Initiative (SDI).

■ Welfare

Definition   Public provision of cash, goods, or services to those in need

During the 1980's, the link between welfare and work was strengthened, culminating in passage of the Family Support Act of 1988. Welfare-to-work demonstration programs were encouraged, and the nation's child support enforcement system was also strengthened.

The election of Ronald Reagan in 1980 provided a political wedge for antiwelfare punditry about the values and behavior of poor persons, particularly unmarried mothers and noncustodial fathers who failed to pay child support. Martin Anderson's *Welfare* (1978), Irwin Garfinkel and Sara McLanahan's *Single Mothers and Their Children* (1986), George Gilder's *Wealth and Poverty* (1981), Charles Murray's *Losing Ground* (1984), Lawrence Mead's *Beyond Entitlement* (1986), and David Ellwood's *Poor Support* (1988) provided much of the theoretical and empirical underpinnings of the welfare debates throughout the 1980's. Antiwelfare scholars such as Murray and Mead, for example, respectively argued that welfare was a moral hazard, encouraging sloth and illegitimacy, and that welfare programs, to the extent they were to be retained, should have stronger work requirements. Even sympathetic welfare reformers such as Ellwood sought to turn the Aid to Families with Dependent Children program (AFDC, a federal financial assistance program started in 1935 to provide cash assistance to those whose household income fell below official federal poverty thresholds, depending on family size) into a transitional support program designed to promote short-term financial, educational, and social support, such that AFDC would be more like a stepping-stone into the labor market.

Workfare over Welfare   The Omnibus Budget Reconciliation Act of 1981 provided for community work experience programs (CWEP), making it possible for the first time for states to choose to make workfare, or job-training and community-service activities, mandatory for AFDC recipients. It authorized states to fund on-the-job training programs by using (diverting) a recipient's welfare grant as a wage subsidy for private employers. States were also permitted to develop their own work incentive (WIN) demonstration programs. According to the U.S. General Accounting Office 1987 study *Work and Welfare*, roughly 22 percent (714,448) of all AFDC recipients participated in these programs nationwide.

The 1980's also witnessed increased federal and state efforts to obtain child support payments from noncustodial parents, particularly from fathers of AFDC mothers, in the light of enactment of the Child Support Enforcement (CSE) program in 1975 and in the light of a high profile the Reagan administration gave to promoting family values. In 1980, only 5.2 percent of AFDC payments were recovered through child support collections, and this percentage increased to 8.6 in 1986 when Reagan called for more extensive welfare reform in his state of the union address. On September 2, 1987, Reagan issued Executive Order 12606 requiring government agencies to assess all measures that might have a significant impact on family formation, maintenance, and general well-being in the light of how an action by government strengthens or erodes the stability of the family and particularly the marital commitment.

Between 1986 and 1988, a congressional consensus emerged regarding welfare reform. The one hundredth session of Congress focused on three major bills: the Family Security Act of 1987, introduced by Democratic senator Daniel Patrick Moynihan; the Family Welfare Reform Act of 1987, introduced by Democratic representative Harold Ford; and the Welfare Independence Act of 1987, the Republican alternative for welfare reform, introduced by Republican senator Bob Dole and by Republican representative Robert Michel. Despite differences in some specifics, each bill linked welfare reform to work.

Despite political consensus over workfare, there was some public opposition. Writing in the November, 1987, issue of *Ms.*, political essayist and social critic Barbara Ehrenreich, for example, viewed the consensus for workfare as a throwback to the seventeenth century workhouse or worse, slavery. Writing in the September 26, 1988, issue of *The Nation*, social welfare policy scholar and activist Mimi Abramovitz called such welfare reform efforts a sham, whose work requirements would cheapen the costs of women's labor force participation and weaken the basic principles on which modern welfare states rested.

The Family Support Act of 1988   As welfare expenses approached $16.7 billion in 1988, Reagan signed the Family Support Act (FSA) on October 13. Titles I and II of the FSA specifically addressed child support enforcement and welfare-to-work programs.

Title I amended part D of Title IV of the Social Security Act of 1935 to require withholding of child support payments from noncustodial parents' wages upon issuance or modification of a child support order for families receiving part D services. It required immediate wage withholding for all new child support orders issued on or after January 1, 1994. Parties in a contested paternity case had to submit to genetic tests upon the request of a party in such cases. States that did not have automated data processing and information retrieval systems in effect had to have such systems operational by October 1, 1995.

Title II required states to establish a job opportunities and basic skills training program (JOBS). It also authorized states to institute a work supplementation program under which state reserves sums that would otherwise be payable to JOBS participants as AFDC benefits would be used instead to subsidize jobs for such participation. Title II authorized any state to establish CWEPs.

Other provisions of the FSA directed states to guarantee child-care services to AFDC families to the extent that such services were necessary for a family member's employment or participation in an education and training activity of which the state approved. The law also required a state to continue a family's Medicaid eligibility for six months after the family loses AFDC eligibility because of specified circumstances; retained the entitlement nature of AFDC; and authorized appropriations for fiscal year 1990 through 1992 for grants to states. These grants were to fund demonstration projects testing the efficacy of early childhood development programs on families receiving AFDC benefits and participating in JOBS and of JOBS on reducing school dropouts, encouraging skill development, and avoiding sole reliance on AFDC payments.

Impact One impact of welfare activities over the decade was to reduce the rate of increase in expenditures and the numbers of beneficiaries. According to the House Committee on Ways and Means' *1994 Green Book*, total costs for AFDC in 1980 had nearly tripled in a decade, reaching $11.5 billion from $4.1 billion in 1970 after adjusting for inflation. The number of families receiving AFDC benefits had increased from 1.9 million to 3.6 million; the number of recipients had grown from 7.4 million to 10.6 million. By 1989, total AFDC expenditures had reached $17.2 billion, a 48 percent increase, while the average number of families increased by 3.5 percent to 3.8 million and the total number of recipients lingered around 11 million annually throughout the decade.

The Manpower Demonstration Research Corporation (MDRC) was hired to evaluate these programs using experimental and control groups at various sites throughout the United States. Summarizing the results, Judith Gueron concluded that the programs did lead to consistent and measurable increases in employment and earnings and also led to some welfare savings. Women with no work experience showed the most significant gains, while long-term welfare recipients with no recent employment did not show consistent gains. However, Gueron cautioned that work programs did not offer an immediate cure for poverty or dependence on government for cash assistance. The impact of the programs that MDRC evaluated was modest, with many participants remaining dependent and many of those who moved off welfare remaining poor. In addition, the rates of individual and family poverty during

the Reagan administration were several percentage points higher than those on average throughout the 1970's.

Poor women also benefited from the increased efforts to obtain child support throughout the 1980's. Of the 2.6 million women below poverty with their own children twenty-one years of age or younger present from an absent father in 1981, 39.7 percent were awarded child support, but only 19.3 percent actually received any payments. In 1987, of 3.2 million such mothers, 27.7 percent received payments.

Although the immediate impact of Title I of the FSA on poor persons was deemed negligible, with 25.4 percent of poor eligible mothers receiving payment in 1989, the child support provisions applied to everyone, regardless of income level. These provisions enhanced the role of the federal government in family matters traditionally left to the states. In particular, by requiring states to establish automated information systems, the federal government increased the capacity of government in general to identify and track noncustodial parents who change jobs, cross state lines, and the like, for purposes of garnishing wages if necessary to secure child support payments due custodial parents.

Further Reading

Caputo, Richard K. "The Limits of Welfare Reform." *Social Casework: The Journal of Contemporary Social Work* 70 (February, 1989): 85-95. Argues for shifting public debate and intervention programs for poor persons from welfare reform to poverty reduction.

_____. "Presidents, Profits, Productivity, and Poverty: A Great Divide Between the Pre- and Post-Reagan U.S. Economy." *Journal of Sociology and Social Welfare* 31 (September, 2004): 5-30. Shows the persistence of high rates of poverty despite an improved economy and welfare reform efforts in the decade.

Ellwood, David T. *Poor Support: Poverty and the American Family.* New York: Basic Books, 1988. Documents the nature and effects of income support programs for poor persons on families in the United States.

Garfinkel, Irwin, and Sara S. McLanahan. *Single Mothers and Their Children: A New American Dilemma.* Washington, D.C.: Urban Institute Press, 1986. Describes the nature and extent of single motherhood in the United States.

Gueron, Judith M. "Work and Welfare: Lessons on Employment Programs." *Journal of Economic Perspectives* 4 (Winter, 1990): 79-98. Analyzes results of work-related welfare programs at eight sites and is cautious about the effectiveness of such programs on poverty reduction.

Handler, Joel F., and Yeheskel Hasenfeld. *The Moral Construction of Poverty: Welfare Reform in America.* Newbury Park, Calif.: Sage, 1991. Traces the history of welfare policy through the Family Support Act. Highlights the importance of symbols in defining and redefining different moral categories of poor persons and in framing responses to them.

_____. *We the Poor People: Work, Poverty, and Welfare.* New Haven, Conn.: Yale University Press, 1997. Argues that welfare reform efforts signify symbolic politics rather than address the spread of poverty among working persons.

Mink, Gwendolyn, and Rickie Solinger, eds. *Welfare: A Documentary History of U.S. Policy and Politics.* New York: New York University Press, 2003. A collection of excerpts from key documents marking the development of U.S. welfare policy in the twentieth century. Uses original sources that provide a historical record of how our understanding of poverty and interventions to deal with it has or has not changed over time.

Richard K. Caputo

See also African Americans; Conservatism in U.S. politics; Economic Recovery Tax Act of 1981; Elections in the United States, 1980; Elections in the United States, 1984; Elections in the United States, 1988; Homelessness; Income and wages in the United States; Liberalism in U.S. politics; Marriage and divorce; Moral Majority; Reagan, Ronald; Reagan Revolution; Reaganomics; Social Security reform; Unemployment in the United States; Women in the workforce.

■ West Berlin discotheque bombing

The Event A terrorist bomb explodes in a nightclub frequented by American servicemen

Date April 5, 1986

Place La Belle nightclub, West Berlin

Media-orchestrated outrage at this event generated support for the Reagan administration's increasingly aggressive stance toward alleged foci of terrorism in the Middle East.

At 1:40 A.M. on April 5, 1986, a terrorist bomb exploded in the crowded La Belle nightclub in West Berlin, an establishment frequented by U.S. servicemen. One American soldier and a Turkish woman were killed outright, and more than two hundred people were injured, some seriously. A second American later died of injuries.

Firefighters search the debris after the bombing of the La Belle discotheque in West Berlin on April 5, 1986. (AP/Wide World Photos)

No organization claimed responsibility for the bombing. German investigators pursued several leads, including neo-Nazi German nationalists, the Palestine Liberation Organization (PLO), and Libyan agents seeking revenge for an American naval attack in the Gulf of Sidra in late March. Seizing upon the Libyan connection and citing two coded messages emanating from the Libyan embassy in Berlin, the United States used the La Belle nightclub bombing as justification for an aerial attack on Tripoli and Benghazi on April 15.

That attack occurred as the Cold War threat of the Soviet Union was on the wane, and the Ronald Reagan administration sought to replace it with the threat of international terrorism. Libyan leader Muammar al-Qaddafi, who actively supported the PLO and the Irish Republican Army (IRA), was an obvious target. A majority of Americans approved of the action, but international reaction was mainly negative.

In 1990, after the fall of the Berlin Wall, examination of East German Stasi (secret police) files led German and American investigators to Libyan Musbar Eter, who implicated Palestinian Yasser Chraidi, a driver at the Libyan embassy in East Berlin in 1986; Ali Chanaa, a Lebanese-born German citizen who worked for the Stasi; and Verena Chanaa, his German wife. Arraigned in 1996, the four were convicted in November, 2001, of murder and attempted murder after a lengthy trial described by commentators as murky. A 1998 documentary for German ZDF television claimed that Eter worked for both the Central Intelligence Agency (CIA) and Israeli intelligence, that Chraidi was not the mastermind and possibly was innocent, and that evidence pointed to several people who were never prosecuted. Following the verdict, Qaddafi agreed to pay compensation to German victims of the bombing as part of a German-Libyan commercial treaty, but he denied direct Libyan responsibility for the attack. American victims have yet to be compensated.

Impact The bombing provided justification for a military attack on Libya. After having faded from the public consciousness, the incident assumed fresh immediacy following the 1998 bombings of American embassies in Kenya and Tanzania, which prompted American missile strikes against alleged terrorist facilities in Afghanistan and the Sudan. The La Belle bombing and its aftermath established a pattern of immediate and massive American retaliation against targets whose connection to the terrorist attack was never subsequently proven.

Further Reading

Chomsky, Noam. *Pirates and Emperors: International Terrorism in the Real World.* New York: Black Rose Books, 1987.

Davis, Briant. *Qaddafi, Terrorism, and the Origins of the U.S. Attack on Libya.* New York: Praeger, 1996.

Kaldor, Mary, and Paul Anderson. *Mad Dogs: The U.S. Raids on Libya.* London: Pluto Press, 1986.

St. John, Ronald Bruce. *Libya and the United States: Two Centuries of Strife.* Philadelphia: University of Philadelphia Press, 2002.

Martha A. Sherwood

See also Foreign policy of the United States; Libya bombing; Middle East and North America; Pan Am Flight 103 bombing; Reagan, Ronald; Terrorism; USS *Vincennes* incident.

■ *When Harry Met Sally . . .*

Identification Romantic comedy film
Director Rob Reiner (1945-)
Date Released July 12, 1989

When Harry Met Sally . . . was one of the most critically and popularly successful romantic comedies of the 1980's. Clever scripting, memorable performances, and a sound track made up of vocal standards drove the film's popularity, and many of its lines and ideas entered the cultural vocabulary of 1980's America.

Nora Ephron, the accomplished screenwriter and director, wrote the Oscar-nominated script for *When Harry Met Sally . . .*, directed by Rob Reiner. It tells a story about college classmates Harry Burns and Sally Albright, who after graduation periodically run into each other during their early adulthood. The neurotic, depressed, Jewish Burns, played by comic actor Billy Crystal, and the optimistic, sweet, Protestant Albright, played by Meg Ryan, first meet through a friend on a shared drive from college to New York, where both are moving. They dislike each other and decide not to keep in touch once they arrive at their destination. They meet again five years later on an airplane and then again five years after that, this time in a bookstore. After this meeting they become friends. Harry is going through a divorce and Sally through a breakup, and they find comfort in what is, for both of them, their first honest friendship with a member of the opposite sex. Ultimately, however, they sleep together, after which they fight bitterly. It is not until some months pass that Harry realizes that he is in love with Sally, and they become a couple.

When Harry Met Sally . . . raises the question of whether men and women can ever really be platonic friends—a question that particularly preoccupied young adults during the 1980's. Harry argues "no" from the beginning, then agrees with Sally that it is possible, only to discover that sex and love replace the friendship, proving his original theory correct: Men and women cannot be friends. The supporting actors, Bruno Kirby and Carrie Fisher, also play important roles both in creating the comedy of the film and in providing an example of a successful marriage.

Impact   Many of the scenes in the picture have become iconic, including one in which Sally pretends to be having an orgasm loudly in a diner, only to have a nearby patron say to her waiter, "I'll have what she's having." The film featured vocal standards, such as "It Had to Be You" and "Our Love Is Here to Stay," performed by various artists, but the sound track album was recorded entirely by Harry Connick, Jr., and rose high on the *Billboard* charts.

Further Reading

Krutnik, Frank. "Love Lies: Romantic Fabrication in Contemporary Romantic Comedy." In *Fatal Attractions: Rescripting Romance in Contemporary Literature and Film*, edited by Lynne Pearse and Gina Wisker. London: Pluto Press, 1998.

Pio, Ramón. "Gender and Genre Conventions in *When Harry Met Sally . . .* " In *Gender, I-Deology: Essays on Theory, Fiction, and Film*, edited by Chantal Cornut-Gentille D'Arcy and José Angel García Landa. Atlanta: Rodopi, 1996.

Lily Neilan Corwin

See also   Academy Awards; Comedians; Film in the United States; Jewish Americans; Music.

■ White, Ryan

Identification   AIDS patient and activist
Born   December 6, 1971; Kokomo, Indiana
Died   April 8, 1990; Indianapolis, Indiana

White, a teenage hemophiliac infected with HIV through a tainted blood transfusion, drew international attention to the treatment of AIDS patients at the height of widespread alarm over the new disease.

On December 17, 1984, Ryan White, then thirteen, was notified by doctors that he had contracted human immunodeficiency virus (HIV) through transfusion of a contaminated blood-clotting agent, Factor VIII, administered during a partial lung removal procedure as part of a treatment for his pneumonia. He was told that he had six months to live. At the time, acquired immunodeficiency syndrome (AIDS) was widely associated with careless habits of so-called

Ryan White prepares for a televised interview in Rome, Italy, in February, 1986. (AP/Wide World Photos)

alternative lifestyles, including intravenous drug use, promiscuous sex, and homosexuality. Indeed, misconceptions about the disease's transmission stirred community resistance to White's continued attendance at school in his rural Indiana hometown. When the family resisted the school's initial decision essentially to quarantine him by providing him separate bathroom facilities and disposable silverware and its subsequent decision that White be home-schooled, White was expelled. White found his case the center of a national outcry, led by AIDS activists who saw in this case manifest evidence of public ignorance. White himself became a leading advocate, appearing before congressional panels, in national magazines, and on network television, tirelessly explaining that casual contact did not transmit the disease and that its patients should be treated with compassion rather than ostracism.

When a district court ordered White reinstated, fear of violence against the boy led the family to relocate to nearby Cicero, Indiana, where White attended public school without incident. Although he often asserted that he wanted only to be healthy and go to school, he accepted the importance of his fame to educate people about the disease and the dangers of stigmatizing AIDS patients. Celebrities such as Michael Jackson (who bought the Whites their home in Cicero) and Elton John (who was at the hospital bedside when White died) and politicians such as President Ronald Reagan, who had consistently resisted AIDS funding, all rallied about the boy's quiet determination and easy charisma. White's celebrity, however, was not without controversy, as gay activists pointed out that opprobrium was still accorded those patients whose lifestyle suggested that they somehow "deserved" the virus.

Impact In 1990, White, at age eighteen, died from complications of pneumonia. He had changed perceptions about AIDS by arguing that with common-sense precautions, patients could be treated with respect. The year he died, Congress voted to fund the Ryan White Comprehensive AIDS Resources Emergency Act, an unprecedented government support of AIDS research, after stalling for years in the face of public unease fueled by ultraconservative activists. White's heroic poise in the face of community prejudice and then ultimately in the face of death at a young age raised awareness about the disease at a critical moment in the epidemic, giving health agencies an unparalleled example of grace under pressure.

Further Reading

Berridge, Virginia, and Philip Strong, eds. *AIDS and Contemporary History*. New York: Cambridge University Press, 2002.

Cochrane, Michel. *When AIDS Began*. London: Routledge, 2003.

Shilts, Randy. *And the Band Played On: Politics, People, and the AIDS Epidemic*. New York: St. Martin's Press, 1987.

White, Ryan, with Ann Marie Cunningham and Jeanne White. *My Own Story*. New York: Signet, 1997.

Joseph Dewey

See also ACT UP; AIDS epidemic; AIDS Memorial Quilt; Homosexuality and gay rights; Hudson, Rock; Jackson, Michael; Johnson, Magic; Louganis, Greg; Medicine; Reagan, Ronald.

■ *White Noise*

Identification Postmodern novel
Author Don DeLillo (1936-   )
Date Published in 1985

The novel brought DeLillo's works to a wider audience and defined the postmodern experience in America.

White Noise (1985) opens in a mildly comic fashion as professor Jack Gladney, chair of the Hitler Studies department, looks out his office window and watches families arrive in their vans and unpack hordes of possessions for arriving students. Gladney is obsessed with death, his own and his wife's, and his life is constructed around attempts to evade the inevitable. His obsession reaches its apex when he and his family attempt to escape after a chemical spill labeled as an "Airborne Toxic Event." Gladney learns that he has been contaminated and that the dosage is likely fatal, but the doctors cannot predict when his death will occur.

The incident exacerbates Gladney's rampant insecurities, which he masks with repeated spending sprees, believing that possessions will confer security and fulfillment. Thus he and his family are the ultimate consumers—of food, clothes, and TV news and shows. The irony, of course, is that goods and a large

Don DeLillo. (Thomas Victor)

physical stature (Gladney admires heavy people, believing that bulk staves off death) cannot insulate him from the inevitable.

Television is yet another of Gladney's evasions; the set is constantly on, and the house is awash in commercial jingles, lines from comedies and various talking heads, and volumes of misinformation. Much of the novel's abundant comedy emerges from family debates in which one erroneous "fact" is traded for another with smug assurance by each of the conversants. The family especially enjoys watching news coverage of catastrophes, gaining a false sense of power because of their seeming immunity from such perils. However, once Gladney is exposed to toxins, the sense of dread has a definable identity.

The novel's title emphasizes that the characters are surrounded by unseen or unrecognized forces, the most obvious of which are the waves of radio transmission and the radiation from television and other sources. Even the toxic event is "airborne," a cloud that is perceptible but the contamination and effects of which are hidden. Just as the characters are surrounded by noise and one another, they are surrounded by the inevitability of death, which Gladney grudgingly comes to terms with at the novel's close

when he witnesses his infant son's miraculous escape from an auto accident. Gladney lacks the comfort of religion but struggles to find some replacement for faith in order to face his mortality.

Impact   *White Noise*, Don DeLillo's eighth novel, became an instant popular and critical success and won the National Book Award in 1985. Since its publication, the novel has been a mainstay in university literature courses and the subject of considerable scholarly research. Reassessments of DeLillo's oeuvre now rank him as one of America's foremost novelists.

Further Reading

Bloom, Harold, ed. *Don DeLillo*. Philadelphia: Chelsea House, 2003.

Kavadlo, Jesse. *Don DeLillo: Balance at the Edge of Belief.* New York: Peter Lang, 2004.

Lentricchia, Frank, ed. *Introducing Don DeLillo.* Durham, N.C.: Duke University Press, 1991.

David W. Madden

See also   Air pollution; Book publishing; Consumerism; Literature in the United States.

■ *Who Framed Roger Rabbit*

Identification   American film
Director   Robert Zemeckis (1952-   )
Date   Released June 24, 1988

The first full-length movie to feature live actors and animated characters throughout, this Disney production also featured cartoon characters from a variety of competing studios.

Who Framed Roger Rabbit was the most expensive motion picture ever made when it was released. It also was the first full-length film effectively to combine animation and live action for its entire length, the first partnership of Disney and Warner Bros., and the first teaming of familiar cartoon characters from different studios. One example was the first and only teaming of Donald Duck and Daffy Duck, seen performing a wild piano duet.

The 103-minute film earned considerable critical praise, and a sizable box office, in its original theatrical release, more than doubling its reported cost of $70 million. "Where else in the Eighties can you do this?" asked director Robert Zemeckis in *Rolling*

Stone magazine. Hollywood had attempted similar combinations of live and cartoon characters, such as a dance scene featuring Gene Kelly and Jerry the Mouse (of the *Tom and Jerry* animated series) in *Anchors Aweigh* (1945), as well as a nine-minute Looney Tunes cartoon, 1940's black-and-white *You Ought to Be in Pictures*, starring Porky Pig, Daffy Duck, and real-life Warner Bros. producer Leon Schlesinger. To create believable visuals for *Who Framed Roger Rabbit*, more than eighty-five thousand hand-painted cels were created after plotting each shot. Legendary animator Chuck Jones himself storyboarded the Daffy-Donald scene (although he later criticized the film for giving live actors more sympathy than cartoon characters).

Besides a fine display of new technology, *Who Framed Roger Rabbit* was also a good movie. Coproduced by Steven Spielberg and Disney, it was written by Peter S. Seaman and Jeffrey Price, who based their screenplay on Gary K. Wolf's 1981 novel *Who Censored Roger Rabbit?* Inspired by the film *Chinatown* (1974) and the actual conspiracy to destroy California's streetcar systems to sell more cars, tires, and gasoline, *Who Framed Roger Rabbit* was an allegory for capitalism run amok versus an ideal, pastoral, Jeffersonian innocence, and it targeted adults as well as younger audiences.

Set in 1947 in a world inhabited by both humans and cartoon characters ("Toons"), the movie is a strange, funny blend of cartoon high jinks and film noir. Roger is the nephew of *Bambi* (1942) costar Thumper and is distracted from his acting jobs by jealousy over his wife Jessica. Roger's boss hires hard-boiled (and Toon-hating) detective Eddie Valiant (Bob Hoskins) to look into it, but things get complicated when Roger is suspected of murdering Jessica's possible patty-cake partner.

Helping Hoskins juggle all kinds of detective and cartoon devices—plus crime-drama starkness and cartoon sunniness—are Christopher Lloyd (as Judge Doom), Kathleen Turner (as Jessica Rabbit), Stubby Kaye (as Marvin Acme), Joanna Cassidy (as Dolores), and Charles Fleischer (as Roger). Before casting Hoskins, filmmakers reportedly considered approaching several high-profile actors for the detective role, including Jack Nicholson, Eddie Murphy, and Bill Murray.

Distributed by Disney's Touchstone subsidiary, the film was codirected by Richard Williams, who handled the animated segments. Those moments featured many other famous cartoon characters from several studios, including Goofy, Porky Pig, Woody Woodpecker, Betty Boop, Droopy, and both Bugs Bunny and Mickey Mouse.

Behind the scenes, the film featured notable voice actors, including Mel Blanc (Daffy Duck, Bugs Bunny, and others), Wayne Allwine (Mickey Mouse), Tony Anselmo (Donald Duck), and Mae Questel (Betty Boop).

Impact *Who Framed Roger Rabbit* earned $150 million in its original theatrical release, won three Academy Awards, and was nominated for four others. It is credited with reviving Hollywood animation, paving the way for Dreamworks, Pixar, Fox, and other companies producing animated features.

Further Reading

Corliss, Richard. "Creatures of a Subhuman Species." *Time*, June 27, 1988, 52.

Powers, John. "Tooned Out." *Rolling Stone*, August 11, 1988, 37-38.

Wolf, Gary. *Who Censored Roger Rabbit?* New York: St. Martin's Press, 1981.

Bill Knight

See also Academy Awards; Computers; Film in the United States; Special effects; Turner, Kathleen.

■ Williams, Robin

Identification American actor and comedian
Born July 21, 1951; Chicago, Illinois

Williams is best known for the unique, high-intensity, stream-of-consciousness comedy that has earned him the reputation as one of the best improvisational comedians of all time.

Robin Williams overcame his childhood shyness by becoming involved in drama during high school and pursued this interest at Claremont Men's College. In 1973, he was accepted into the highly selective advanced program at Juilliard, along with Christopher Reeve, where the two classmates studied under John Houseman and established a lifelong friendship. At Houseman's advice, Williams returned to San Francisco to pursue a career in stand-up comedy. In February, 1978, he was cast in a guest role as the space alien Mork on the *Happy Days* television series, which led to a starring role in the spin-off series *Mork and*

Mindy, which ran from 1978 to 1982. The American public was captivated by the manic, free-associating character of Mork, who was featured on lunchboxes and posters and added several catchphrases to the lexicon, including his trademark greeting, "nanoo nanoo." Williams had become an overnight sensation.

In 1980, Williams graduated from television to film with his debut in Robert Altman's version of *Popeye*, a critical and box-office disappointment. His next movie, *The World According to Garp* (1982), was a critical success, and *Moscow on the Hudson* (1984) was also well received, but it was *Good Morning, Vietnam* (1987) that not only secured Williams's reputation as a serious actor but also garnered him a Best Actor Oscar nomination. In 1989, he received a second Best Actor nomination for his work in *Dead Poets Society.*

During the 1980's, Williams continued his stand-up career with Home Box Office (HBO) comedy specials in 1982 and 1986 and was named number thirteen on Comedy Central's list of 100 Greatest Stand-Ups of All Time.

Impact In addition to his reputation as a comedian, Robin Williams established himself as a well-regarded and versatile actor after the mid-1980's, able to move effortlessly from comedy to serious drama with *The Fisher King* (1991), *Good Will Hunting,* (1997), and *One Hour Photo* (2002). He also became well known for his charitable work, particularly the Comic Relief specials on HBO with Whoopi Goldberg and Billy Crystal, which raised funds for the homeless. Williams, a tireless supporter of U.S. troops in Iraq and Afghanistan during the early twenty-first century, appeared in several United Service Organizations shows over the course of the Iraq War.

Further Reading

Dougan, Andy. *Robin Williams*. New York: Thunder's Mouth Press, 1999.

Givens, Ron. *Robin Williams*. New York: Time, 1998.

Jay, David. *The Life and Humor of Robin Williams: A Biography*. New York: HarperPerennial, 1999.

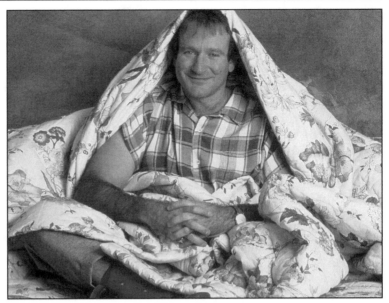

Robin Williams around 1987. (Hulton Archive/Getty Images)

Spignesi, Stephen J. *The Robin Williams Scrapbook.* New York: Citadel Press, 1997.

Mary Virginia Davis

See also Academy Awards; Comedians; Comic Relief; Film in the United States; Television.

■ Williams, Vanessa

Identification Miss America, singer, and actor
Born March 18, 1963; Tarrytown, New York

Williams was the first African American to be crowned Miss America.

Until 1984, the Miss America pageant had not been noted for cultural or racial diversity. Though a Jewish woman, Bess Myerson, had won the Miss America crown, that victory had occurred decades earlier and not without substantial controversy. Vanessa Williams attended the School of Performing Arts in New York City (made famous by the movie and television series *Fame*). She also began winning beauty contests in the early 1980's, including the Miss New York contest, thereby qualifying to enter the Miss America contest. Williams won the crown in 1984. Thrilled to win and undeniably performing outstandingly well in her new role, Williams seemed to be an ideal choice. Halfway through her tenure, however, a scandal erupted when it was revealed that she had posed for nude photos a few years before entering the contest.

As a result of the highly publicized scandal, Williams received death threats and hateful letters from disgruntled devotees of the pageant. She tried to redeem her reputation, insisting that the photos were artistic rather than pornographic, but finally resigned the crown amid growing controversy and opposition to her reign as Miss America. Williams's nude photos were published in an issue of *Penthouse* magazine that grossed fourteen million dollars.

After Williams resigned the Miss America crown, her runner-up, Suzette Charles, became the new Miss America. Though Charles was also African American, there were still claims that the forced resignation of Williams was due to racism. Williams went on to establish a singing career, performing backup vocals for George Clinton on a 1986 record album. Her first solo album, *The Right Stuff*, was released in 1988. A ballad from the album eventually reached number one on the *Billboard* Hot Black Singles chart. The album subsequently was very successful and was certified gold, spawning a successful singing career for Williams. Williams was also interested in being an actor. Her first film was *Under the Gun* (1986). She developed very successful singing and acting careers, garnering public praise, as well as financial freedom.

Impact Williams was the first woman to overcome the race barrier that seemed to prevent African American women from winning the Miss America pageant. Although she was devastated by her forced resignation of the crown, she went on to achieve great success as a singer and actress, becoming a role model for young African American girls in the process.

Further Reading

Boulais, Sue. *Vanessa Williams: Real Life Reader Biography.* Childs, Md.: Mitchell Lane, 1998.

Freedman, Suzanne. *Vanessa Williams.* New York: Chelsea House, 1999.

Twyla R. Wells

See also African Americans; Feminism; Film in the United States; Music; Pop music; Pornography; Racial discrimination; Scandals.

Vanessa Williams announces her resignation as Miss America at a press conference on July 23, 1984. (AP/Wide World Photos)

■ Wilson, August

Identification African American playwright
Born April 27, 1945; Pittsburgh, Pennsylvania
Died October 2, 2005; Seattle, Washington

Wilson gained prominence as an American playwright in the 1980's. It was during this decade that Wilson's vision of writing a cycle of ten plays, each set in a specific decade of the twentieth century, began to take shape.

Born Frederick August Kittel and having grown up in the predominantly African American Hill District of Pittsburgh, August Wilson often returned in his imagination to his native soil, mining its richness for artistic purposes. His plays explore themes ranging from African American identity and the impact of history on his many memorable characters to the challenges confronting family, especially fathers and sons.

Of the five plays Wilson wrote and produced during the 1980's, four received multiple awards. *Ma*

Rainey's Black Bottom (pr. 1984) received a Tony Award and the New York Drama Critics Circle Award for the best new play of 1984-1985. *Fences* (pr. 1985), which grossed over $11 million in its first year on Broadway, won a handful of awards, including the Pulitzer Prize in drama in 1987. *Joe Turner's Come and Gone* (pr. 1986) garnered a Tony Award and the New York Drama Critics Circle Best Play Award for 1988. Wilson received a second Pulitzer Prize in drama in 1990 for *The Piano Lesson* (pr. 1987). These plays served as testimony to Wilson's versatility and success as a playwright.

Set in the musical world of 1920's Chicago, *Ma Rainey's Black Bottom* utilizes the blues as a means of exploring this important decade in African American history. *Fences* brings to life the trials and tribulations of a family in an unnamed northern industrial city during the 1950's. *Joe Turner's Come and Gone* revisits Pittsburgh during the first decade of the twentieth century and dramatizes the legacy of slavery on characters living in a boardinghouse after coming north during the Great Migration. *The Piano Lesson*, set in Pittsburgh during the 1930's, again bridges characters' lives in the South and in the North. Similar to Wilson's literal and figurative use of fences in *Fences*, a piano is used in *The Piano Lesson* to show characters in conflict over the past and the present in relation to what the future holds.

Impact Wilson's plays place him securely within both mainstream and African American literary traditions. *Fences* has been favorably compared to Arthur Miller's *Death of a Salesman* (1949) in its pathos and moving depiction of protagonist Troy Maxson, feared, loved, and ultimately forgiven by a family he berates and betrays. Wilson enriched the way American theater depicted race, while he encouraged younger African American artists to write plays. Not since Lorraine Hansberry in the 1950's and Amiri Baraka in the 1960's had an African American artist had such an impact on American drama.

Further Reading

Elkins, Marilyn, ed. *August Wilson: A Casebook.* New York: Garland, 1994.

Shannon, Sandra G. *The Dramatic Vision of August Wilson.* Washington, D.C.: Howard University Press, 1995.

Wolfe, Peter. *August Wilson.* New York: Twayne, 1999.

Kevin Eyster

See also African Americans; Broadway musicals; Literature in the United States; Mamet, David; Racial discrimination; Shepard, Sam; Theater.

■ Winfrey, Oprah

Identification Talk-show host
Born January 29, 1954; Kosciusko, Mississippi

Winfrey's direct approach to interviewing her guests, coupled with her ability to make them feel at ease, made her show the nation's top-rated talk show in the 1980's.

On January 2, 1984, Oprah Winfrey hosted her first talk show on *AM Chicago*. She chose discussion topics to which everyone in her audience could relate. In many cases, she had experienced the same pain or circumstances as her guests. Winfrey's popularity grew as she dealt with issues honestly and enthusiastically. By 1985, the show was changed from a half hour to an hour-long show and was renamed *The Oprah Winfrey Show.*

Winfrey experienced a life-changing event when director Steven Spielberg cast her as Sofia in the film *The Color Purple* (1985). Many of the struggles of African Americans in the Deep South represented in the film were struggles that Winfrey had faced during her own life. Her role in the film revealed her talent as an actor and earned her an Academy Award nomination and a Golden Globe nomination for Best Supporting Actress.

On September 8, 1986, *The Oprah Winfrey Show* became nationally syndicated. Winfrey formed her own production company, Harpo Productions, and served as its chief executive officer. The program increased in popularity and continued to get top ratings, garnering both Winfrey and the show several awards. She eventually bought the rights to *The Oprah Winfrey Show* and built Harpo Studios, making her the first African American woman to own a studio and production company. Winfrey was then able to produce the show in her own way. One change she made was to air taped shows as opposed to live broadcasts. Another change was no longer to use cue cards. Because she believed that prepared questions would compromise the show's and her own authenticity, she conducted her show using only a few note cards and her own instincts. She asked her guests about issues that interested her audience, and her easy interaction with ordinary people softened

Oprah Winfrey relaxes in her office in December, 1985, after a morning broadcast of her local Chicago, Illinois, show. The show was syndicated nationally the following year. (AP/Wide World Photos)

the gap between societal norms for public and private expression. While talking to her guests was important, listening to them was crucial, and Winfrey demonstrated through her questions, exchanges, tone of voice, and body language that she was clearly able to do that.

Impact Viewers became like Winfrey's extended family. Her influence—not only on women and African Americans but on Americans of all other races and cultures as well—was profound. Her strong message that the power to change comes from within was reflected in her phenomenal success.

Further Reading

Adler, Bill, ed. *The Uncommon Wisdom of Oprah Winfrey.* Secaucus, N.J.: Carol, 1997.

Bly, Nellie. *Oprah! Up Close and Down Home.* New York: Kensington, 1993.

Garson, Helen S. *Oprah Winfrey: A Biography.* Westport, Conn.: Greenwood Press, 2004.

King, Norman. *Everybody Loves Oprah!* New York: William Morrow, 1987.

Krohn, Catherine. *Oprah Winfrey.* Minneapolis: Lerner, 2002.

Mair, George. *Oprah Winfrey.* New York: Carol, 1994.

Waldron, Robert. *Oprah!* New York: St. Martin's Press, 1988.

Elizabeth B. Graham

See also Academy Awards; African Americans; *Color Purple, The*; Film in the United States; Spielberg, Steven; Talk shows; Television; Women in the workforce.

■ Women in rock music

Definition Female singers and musicians in several genres of popular music

In the 1980's, the most obvious accomplishment made by women in rock music pertained to sheer quantity, with female singers and instrumentalists making their presence known in greater numbers than ever before. More subtly, the

emergence of women in rock during the 1980's represented an age-old pattern of how women often achieve gender equity in popular culture. In doing so, they also influenced the demographics of rock in regard to age.

Two women from the 1960's, one a holdover and one a crossover, provided two of the biggest surprises of the decade. Grace Slick, vocalist for the band Jefferson Airplane, continued to write songs and sing with that group's descendant, Jefferson Starship, through most of the 1980's; in 1985, for example, she issued the massive hit "We Built This City," a paean to San Francisco pop music. Tina Turner, a veteran of her husband Ike's rhythm-and-blues revues for twenty years, embarked on a solo career by reinventing herself as a full-throated rock "belter," beginning with her 1984 hit, "What's Love Got to Do with It." Three newcomers during the 1980's who reflected the back-to-basics approach to rock music

Madonna performs at an AIDS benefit concert in New York's Madison Square Garden in 1987. (AP/Wide World Photos)

led by Turner were Laura Branigan, Pat Benatar, and Chrissie Hynde.

Expanding the Audience of Rock   Some of the new women in rock expedited their success by appealing to an audience hitherto unexploited by music promoters: girls in their preteens and early teens. The early 1980's saw the simultaneous appearance of two of the most talented performers of the decade, Cyndi Lauper and Madonna. Although they projected highly sexualized images, both women's playful, extravagant fashion styles caught on with young girls across North America, inspiring millions of them to parade through schoolyards and shopping malls costumed as their idols. Almost overnight, rock, which for thirty years had been largely the provenance of high school and college students, enlisted legions of fans of elementary and middle-school age. This trend was cannily imitated by two other young women toward the end of the decade, Debbie Gibson and Tiffany, who formed fan bases by performing in malls frequented by young girls.

More Women, More Rock   The sheer number of bands that included female members or were all-female in the 1980's is staggering, as is the breadth of styles these women reflected. Two California bands solely comprising women, the Bangles and the Go-Go's, specialized in cheery pop music suggestive of the Beach Boys and the early Beatles. The Pixies, from Boston, with bassist Kim Deal, performed serious, sophisticated music of the sort that came to be called college rock. Throwing Muses and 'Til Tuesday, led by Kristin Hersh and Aimee Mann, respectively, were characterized by straightforward, "no-frills" rock, while Siouxsie and the Banshees, led by Susan Dallion, helped pioneer gothic rock, a somber subgenre employing gothic imagery. Edie Brickell and the New Bohemians, from Texas, performed gentle folk/jazz tunes, while the Plasmatics was a violent punk band whose lead singer, Wendy O. Williams, sometimes demolished cars on stage with a blowtorch.

What did female artists do with their expanding presence in rock? Benatar's work exemplifies the themes that women explored in the 1980's. Like Turner, she established that women could have a tough-minded approach to romance (as expressed in songs such as "Love Is a Battlefield" and "Sex as a Weapon"), and she also expressed female assertive-

Selected Women in Rock Music in the 1980's

Artist/Group	Notable 1980's Songs
Paula Abdul	"Forever Your Girl," "Opposites Attract," Straight Up"
Bananarama	"Cruel Summer," "I Heard a Rumor," "Venus"
The Bangles	"If She Knew What She Wants," "Manic Monday," "Walk Like an Egyptian"
Pat Benatar	"Hit Me with Your Best Shot," "Love Is a Battlefield," "We Belong"
Laura Branigan	"Gloria," "Imagination," "Self Control"
Edie Brickell and the New Bohemians	"Little Miss S," "What I Am"
Belinda Carlisle	"Heaven Is a Place on Earth," "I Get Weak," "Mad About You"
Cher	"If I Could Turn Back Time," "Just Like Jesse James," "We All Sleep Alone"
Gloria Estefan & Miami Sound Machine	"Anything for You," "1-2-3," "Falling in Love (Uh-Oh)"
Aretha Franklin	"Freeway of Love," "I Knew You Were Waiting (for Me)," "Sisters Are Doin' It for Themselves"
Debbie Gibson	"Foolish Beat," "Lost in Your Eyes," "Only in My Dreams"
The Go-Go's	"Our Lips Are Sealed," "Vacation," "We Got the Beat"
Heart	"All I Wanna Do Is Make Love to You," "Never," "These Dreams"
Whitney Houston	"How Will I Know," "I Wanna Dance with Somebody (Who Loves Me)," "Saving All My Love for You"
Janet Jackson	"Control," "Miss You Much," "Nasty"
Joan Jett and the Blackhearts	"Crimson and Clover," "I Hate Myself for Loving You," "I Love Rock 'n Roll"
Cyndi Lauper	"Girls Just Want to Have Fun," "Time After Time," "True Colors"
Madonna	"Borderline," "Everybody," "Holiday," "Into the Groove," "Like a Prayer," "Live to Tell," "Papa Don't Preach"
Olivia Newton-John	"Heart Attack," "Physical," "Suddenly"
Stevie Nicks	"Edge of Seventeen (Just Like a White Winged Dove)," "Leather and Lace," "Stop Draggin' My Heart Around"
The Pointer Sisters	"I'm So Excited," "Jump," "Neutron Dance"
Sade	"Never as Good as the First Time," "Smooth Operator," "The Sweetest Taboo"
Siouxsie and the Banshees	"Belladonna," "Cities in the Dust," "Dazzle"
Donna Summer	"Cold Love," "She Works Hard for the Money," "The Wanderer"
Tiffany	"Should've Been Me," "I Think We're Alone Now," "Could've Been"
Tina Turner	"Break Every Rule," "Private Dancer," "What's Love Got to Do with It"

ness in relationships ("Treat Me Right"). More important, she dealt with subjects usually neglected by male rock singers, such as child abuse ("Hell Is for Children"). However, two songs by Lauper and Madonna best illustrate how female artists of the decade achieved thematic redress by tackling subjects that males ignored or by taking a feminist tack on those issues. In "Papa Don't Preach," Madonna sings of teenage pregnancy without bathos or moralizing: An unwed mother tells her father that she is pregnant, takes responsibility for her situation, and asserts her right to make her own decision on the matter. In the most famous song of the decade on gender issues, Lauper's "Girls Just Want to Have Fun," the singer equates "fun" not with giddiness and good times alone but with freedom and self-expression. When she insists that, rather than be isolated by male possessiveness, she wants "to be the one to walk in the sun," this anthemic song accomplishes what good pop lyrics of any genre do—it states with simple eloquence a truth or feeling often obfuscated by verbosity and cant in more sophisticated texts.

Impact   The strides made by female rock musicians in the 1980's illustrate a technique women in Western culture have often used to gain access to previously male-dominated venues. For example, in the late 1700's women in large numbers began to write novels, a new genre lacking a tradition of sexism. Likewise, in the 1800's many women embraced Spiritualism as a means of claiming leading roles denied them in mainstream religion, as the new movement had no patriarchal tradition. In the 1980's, women similarly used two trends in rock that emerged in the late 1970's and early 1980's: punk and synthpop (a New Wave form of soft rock depending primarily on electronic synthesizers for instrumentation). The punk ethos questioned everything remotely traditional, even the young traditions of rock itself, including sexism. Therefore, a woman becoming a punk rock musician was not contradicting that ethos; she was embodying it. Furthermore, both punk and synthpop downplayed guitar pyrotechnics of the sort practiced by Jimi Hendrix and instead foregrounded lyrics, melody, and vocals. This is not to say that women were poor guitarists: Many of the female rock musicians of the 1980's were excellent guitarists or bassists. However, synthpop provided an avenue into rock for women not interested in emulating male idols of the past.

Further Reading

DeCurtis, Anthony, et al., eds. *The Rolling Stone Album Guide.* New York: Random House, 1992. Of the various editions of this very useful guide, this one from the early 1990's is best for research on artists of the 1980's.

Gaar, Gillian G. *She's a Rebel: The History of Women in Rock and Roll.* Seattle: Seal Press, 1992. Excellent history of women in pop music, with good coverage of the 1980's.

Lewis, Lisa. *Gender Politics and MTV: Voicing the Difference.* Philadelphia: Temple University Press, 1990. Thoughtful examination of the role of music videos and their effect on women in rock.

O'Dair, Barbara, ed. *Trouble Girls: The Rolling Stone Book of Women in Rock.* New York: Random House, 1997. Another good review of the role of women in rock.

Reddington, Helen. *The Lost Women of Rock Music: Female Musicians of the Punk Era.* Brookfield, Vt.: Ashgate, 2007. Though focusing on British rockers, this insightful account also reveals how women found ingress to the rock world through punk.

Thomas Du Bose

See also   Blondie; Cher; Go-Go's, The; Heavy metal; Lauper, Cyndi; Madonna; MTV; Music; Music videos; New Wave music; Pop music; Turner, Tina.

■ Women in the workforce

Definition   Women employed or seeking employment during a specific period

Changes in the gender of the workforce had a significant impact on the culture of the later twentieth century, creating new work ethics and new demands for goods and services. During the 1980's, women left their traditional roles as full-time housewives and mothers to join the workforce in unprecedented numbers.

The 1980's began with the inauguration of newly elected president Ronald Reagan and his lavish display of wealth in the attendant ceremonies. College graduates were entering the workplace to fill prestigious office professions that offered high salaries. These factors led to a demand for trendy and luxurious goods and a more affluent lifestyle, which in a single household often depended on the earning power of both the man and the woman. Fresh from the feminist movement of the 1970's, which emphasized gender equality, women sought both more education and more jobs in the 1980's.

The demographics of gender in the workforce shifted for reasons that went beyond the women's movement, however: As a result of the spread of no-fault divorce laws in many states, divorce rates rose, and divorce became widely acceptable in the United States. Growing numbers of illegitimate children and single-parent families also played a role in women entering the workforce, as well as a trend toward delayed marriage. Many of the women who entered the workforce in the 1980's did so because they had to work to support themselves and their children. The policies of the Reagan administration increased women's need to work. The Reagan administration curtailed the growth of social welfare programs and limited benefits to those whom Reagan called the "truly needy." Between 1981 and 1984, spending on the federal financial assistance program Aid to Families with Dependent Children (AFDC) was cut by 13 percent, food stamps by 13 percent, and federal support for child nutrition in the schools by 28 percent.

The changing nature of work itself also increased the number of working women. The United States was in transition from an industrial age to an information age, and the 1980's saw an expansion of technology that eventually defined the modern world of work. Not only did more jobs require technological knowledge rather than physical strength, but also some new technologies, such as commercially available handheld mobile phones and personal computers, made it easier for women to supervise their families from the workplace or even to telecommute from home.

Child Care Reagan's Republican presidential campaign emphasized "family values," a strategy that contributed significantly to his election in 1980. Subsequently, the Democrats began to emphasize family issues, calling for concrete programs to help working mothers, such as flexible work hours, maternity and paternity leave, uniform standards for child care, and federal enforcement of child-support payments. In the 1984 elections, the Democrats unsuccessfully tried to take the family issue away from the Republicans, leading to angry controversies that surrounded child care and family concerns in the 1980's. The result was a stalemate on family issues.

While the government was deadlocked, child-care problems continued to grow and cause anxiety for both parents and society as a whole. Child care was the most difficult issue for young families to face. By the end of the 1980's, nearly half of all marriages were ending in divorce, and the plight of single-parent families (usually headed by the mother) was often one of severe economic hardship. Single parents had to make the difficult choice between caring for children at home and finding employment to help support their families. By the end of the 1980's, the number of children five years old or younger whose mothers worked had increased to ten million. The number of affordable child-care programs was never enough to meet the demand.

Research has typically found few significant differences between children whose mothers are employed and those whose mothers are not. However, the effects of a mother's employment on her child often differ depending on the characteristics of the child, conditions at the mother's workplace, and the type and quality of child care the mother is able to secure. The social class, age, and gender of children also may influence the effects of child care. Group care of children is improved when the ratio of children to caregivers is low, allowing the caregiver to be responsive to each child; when caregivers are trained; and when the caregiving environment is stimulating.

Studies in the 1980's found that infants and preschool children with employed mothers were not significantly different from those with nonemployed mothers in respect to language development, motor development, and intelligence. These studies showed that, as role models, working mothers had a positive effect on adolescent daughters; these daughters tended to be outgoing, active, and high achievers with educational aspirations. Children with mothers in the workforce viewed women and women's employment more positively than children of full-time homemakers, and they had less traditional views of marriage and gender roles.

Professional Work Prior to the 1970's, the professions of medicine and law were generally closed to women, and the (male) practitioners of these professions controlled the membership. However, as the feminist movement provided women with a vision of equality, women advocated for new laws to ensure their access to education, jobs, and equal pay.

Women in the Workforce

During the 1980's, the number of women workers increased, and each year women accounted for a larger percentage of the total workforce, rising from 41.8 percent in 1980 to 44.9 percent in 1989, according to the Bureau of Labor Statistics.

Year	Civilian Labor Force (in thousands)	Female Employees (in thousands)	% of Total	Male Employees (in thousands)	% of Total
1980	78,010	32,593	41.8	45,417	58.2
1981	80,273	33,910	42.2	46,363	57.7
1982	82,014	34,870	42.6	47,144	57.4
1983	83,615	35,712	42.7	47,903	57.2
1984	86,001	37,234	43.3	48,767	56.7
1985	88,426	38,779	43.9	49,647	56.1
1986	90,500	39,767	44.0	50,733	56.0
1987	92,965	41,105	44.2	51,860	55.8
1988	94,870	42,254	44.6	52,616	55.4
1989	97,318	43,650	44.9	53,668	55.1

Source: Department of Labor, Bureau of Labor Statistics.

Once these laws were in place, women entered professional schools in vast numbers, and opportunities began to open in typically male professions.

Between 1970 and 1985, the proportion of female physicians almost doubled, and between 1983 and 1984 half of all applications to medical schools were from women. Women earned one-third of all U.S. law degrees being granted by the mid-1980's, and their status in the legal profession improved. Former Supreme Court justice Sandra Day O'Connor's experience is typical of the obstacles professional women faced. When she graduated from Stanford Law School in the top 10 percent of her class in 1952, she received only one job offer—for the position of legal secretary for a San Francisco law firm. On July 7, 1981, Reagan, who had pledged in his presidential campaign to appoint the first woman to the Supreme Court, appointed O'Connor associate justice to that prestigious body. She served in the Supreme Court from 1981 until her retirement in 2006.

The formerly male-dominated field in which women found the greatest opportunities during the 1980's was academia. Although women tended to teach in less prestigious institutions than men, to teach more courses, to have less access to research resources, and to be concentrated in the lower-status disciplines of the humanities, education, and social work, they nevertheless grew to occupy a quarter of the full-time college and university faculty membership.

Until the 1980's, few women were able to pursue careers in science. If a woman did manage to acquire the necessary education, subtle barriers excluded her from scientific networks and encouraged her to remain in a marginal position, with little or no support from colleagues. Because women were discouraged from studying mathematics and because various specialties were still considered "male," women were underrepresented in engineering, physics, chemistry, mathematics, and the earth sciences.

In the traditionally female profession of nursing, many nurses concerned themselves with providing psychosocial services to patients, while others specialized in technical services, such as radiology. New knowledge and technologies in the 1980's demanded that almost all nurses acquire sophisticated technological expertise for their practices. Nurses also sought more responsibilities as nurse practitioners, midwives, and anesthetists. Several problems were common to nursing, in addition to restricted opportunities for advancement. Lack of autonomy and respect, low pay, often difficult working conditions, and lack of unity among nurses led to strategies to improve their status. In the late 1980's, it was found that nurses' working conditions presented serious physical, chemical, and biological hazards. Nurses were often exposed to infectious diseases and suffered high rates of hepatitis B and staphylococcus infections. In addition, nurses were exposed to toxic chemical agents and to carcinogens and radiation hazards.

Teaching, another traditionally female profession, was, unlike nursing, highly organized. In 1985-1986, 630,000 teachers were members of the American Federation of Teachers, and 1,537,967 (about 70 percent of public school teachers) were members of the National Education Association (NEA). During the 1980's, teacher shortages began to emerge in such fields as mathematics, the sciences, data processing, and computer programming. Teachers began to lose their enthusiasm for the profession for some of the same reasons nurses had lost enthusiasm for theirs: lack of autonomy and respect, low pay, and often difficult working conditions.

Women in Blue-Collar Occupations   Blue collars symbolize men and women who work at manual labor: semiskilled operatives, skilled craft workers, and unskilled laborers. Blue-collar workers are generally involved in some type of production process: making and repairing goods and equipment. Traditionally, women were excluded from such jobs or were limited to a small number of low-wage, semiskilled jobs in the textile, apparel, and electronics industries. During the 1980's, some changes occurred, and the work of women became divided into traditional and nontraditional categories.

Patience, dexterity, and speed are the main requirements for the operative jobs within the traditional textile and apparel industries. These jobs do not require formal experience or training and can be learned within a few days or weeks, making them good opportunities for women with little education, little training, or limited English fluency. Nontraditional occupations for women as carpenters, machinists, coal miners, and transportation operatives proved more satisfying and better-paying than traditional jobs, as well as more challenging and rewarding. When women started to enter these jobs in significant numbers in the 1980's, studies showed that

these women had secured these jobs through great initiative. On the job, they were not averse to filing union grievances and reporting sex discrimination to state and federal agencies when the occasion demanded.

Impact   The great influx of women into the workforce during the 1970's and 1980's changed the ways people think about work. Young women began to realize that any occupation they dreamed of was possible for them to achieve. Girls began to think about future careers in a more challenging way, often dreaming of a career in law or medicine instead of a more traditional field. Men, especially married men, slowly revised their views of women in the workplace. Husbands and wives grew to respect each other's achievements. In response to the rising numbers of employed and employable women, new employment opportunities arose. While society debated the role of government in providing child care, private and corporate facilities for preschools and infant care arose. Demand for nannies continued to grow. The food industry also felt the impact, as the need for take-out food and home delivery grew. Women's apparel also changed during the decade, as designers competed to provide suitable office attire for women. These changes had lasting effects on society in the United States, the repercussions of which are still being felt and studied.

Further Reading

Acker, Joan. *Doing Comparable Worth: Gender, Class, and Pay Equity.* Philadelphia: Temple University Press, 1989. Reveals inconsistencies and inadequacies in pay structures of the 1970's and 1980's.

Ferber, Marianne, Brigid O'Farrell, and La Rue Allen, eds. *Work and Family: Policies for a Changing Work Force.* Washington, D.C.: National Academy Press, 1991. Describes and advocates many policy changes to help double-income families.

Hochschild, Arlie Russell. *The Time Bind: When Work Becomes Home and Home Becomes Work.* New York: Henry Holt, 1997. A fascinating study of a husband and wife employed by a family-friendly company and the challenges they meet as they try to achieve a balanced life.

Stromberg, Ann Helton, and Shirley Harkness, eds. *Women Working: Theories and Facts in Perspective.* 2d ed. Palo Alto, Calif.: Mayfield, 1988. An important, comprehensive collection of essays that covers such topics as "Contributions of Marxism and Feminism to the Sociology of Women and Work" and "The Data on Women's Labor Force Participation."

Sheila Golburgh Johnson

See also Affirmative action; Consumerism; Feminism; Marriage and divorce; O'Connor, Sandra Day; Power dressing; Unemployment in Canada; Unemployment in the United States; Unions; Women's rights.

■ Women's rights

Definition The movement to attain equal rights for women in Canada and the United States

During the 1980's, women's rights in the United States and Canada changed significantly, primarily in terms of reproductive and workplace rights.

Changes in the rights of women affected both genders throughout the 1980's and helped to shape gender attitudes as well as produce a backlash against these changes that would shape American politics and facilitate the rise of the conservative right.

Third-Wave Feminism In both the United States and Canada, the 1980's saw the advent of third-wave feminism, which would shape feminist approaches to politics and rights. Whereas first-wave feminism of the early twentieth century focused on correcting legal inequalities, such as gaining the right to vote, and second-wave feminism of the 1960's and 1970's focused on unofficial inequalities, such as discrimination, third-wave feminism focused on production and work, reproduction and sexuality, and gender and the state. This third wave was heavily influenced by postmodern discourse and its evaluation of the politics of representation. Rather than viewing all women as a homogeneous group, as second-wave feminists had, third-wave feminists looked at other important characteristics that complicated attempts to categorize women, such as race, ethnicity, socioeconomic status, religion, and class. The underlying motive of this philosophy was an acknowledgment that women did not universally share their needs and experiences, which differed according to other characteristics. The needs and experiences of

a middle-class, well-educated black woman, for example, differed from those of her white, lower-class counterpart.

These questions of race, class, and sexuality were central to third-wave feminism, as were a multitude of issues concerning women in the workplace, such as the glass ceiling, inequities in pay, sexual harassment, and maternity leave. Other areas of concern for third-wave feminists included representations of women in the media that may lead to eating disorders or unrealistic body standards, the lack of role models for girls, the presentation of women solely as sexualized objects, and antifeminism.

The third wave relied on the second wave to produce women accustomed to thinking about feminist issues and questioning gender norms, and women for whom the workplace had been made accessible. Throughout the 1980's, these attitudes would shape feminist political thought and expectations—as well as fuel conservative backlash that would end up negating many of the advances made by women in earlier decades by removing legal acts and agencies designed to promote equity in education and the workplace.

One extreme and tragic example of the hatred inspired by changes in the rights of women would take place in an engineering classroom at the École Polytechnique, University of Montreal, on December 6, 1989, when fourteen female students were gunned down by Marc Lépine, a fellow student who claimed that feminists had ruined his life.

The Equal Rights Amendment The Equal Rights Amendment (ERA) proved to be a major legal battleground for proponents of women's rights throughout the early 1980's. Originally proposed in 1923 as the "Lucretia Mott Amendment" by suffragist leader Alice Paul, the ERA was intended to bar legal discrimination against women. It had been introduced in every session of Congress from 1923 to 1970, and it finally was presented for ratification in 1972, with a seven-year deadline, which was later extended by another thirty-nine months. By 1979, thirty-five of the required thirty-eight states had ratified the amendment, but five of the states had withdrawn their ratification. In 1981, a federal court ruled that the extension had been unconstitutional and that the rescindment of ratification had been valid (*Idaho v. Freeman*, 1981). The National Organization for Women (NOW), formed by Betty Friedan in 1966,

Significant Events Affecting Women in the 1980's

1980

Medicaid cannot be used to pay for abortions, according to the U.S. Supreme Court decision *Harris v. McRae.*

The United Nations Second World Conference on Women is held in Copenhagen, Denmark.

1981

In *County of Washington v. Gunther,* the U.S. Supreme Court rules that women can seek remedies for sex-based wage discrimination under the provisions of Title VII of the Civil Rights Act of 1964.

Sandra Day O'Connor becomes the first woman appointed to the U.S. Supreme Court.

The Equal Rights Amendment (ERA) fails to meet the deadline for state ratification.

The Congresswomen's Caucus reorganizes as the Congressional Caucus for Women's Issues and admits male members.

The Reagan administration closes down the Office of Domestic Violence.

1982

Hysterectomy Educational Resources and Services (HERS) is founded to provide information about alternatives to this frequently performed surgical procedure.

The ERA dies after failing to attain the necessary thirty-eighth state ratification; the amendment is reintroduced annually in Congress thereafter.

1983

In *City of Akron v. Akron Center for Reproductive Health,* the U.S. Supreme Court strikes down a state law requiring a twenty-four-hour waiting period before abortion and mandating that the physician must tell the patient that a fetus is a "human life from moment of conception."

The Coalition Against Media Pornography is founded in Canada to protest the airing of soft-core pornography on cable television.

1984

Congress passes the Child Support Enforcement Amendments to give women means of collecting late child support payments.

Jeanne Sauvé becomes the first female governor-general of Canada; she serves until 1990.

Antiabortion women in Canada create Real, Equal, Active for Life (REAL) and claim to speak for "real" women of the nation.

Congress passes the Retirement Equality Act.

In *Grove City v. Bell,* the U.S. Supreme Court rules that Title IX of the Education Amendments of 1972 applies only to college programs receiving direct federal support; nonfederally funded programs, such as women's athletics, are required to comply.

The Democratic Party nominates Geraldine Ferraro for vice president, making her the first female candidate of a major party in the United States. Despite the appeal of her candidacy and the gender gap in voting, President Ronald Reagan defeats her running mate, Walter Mondale.

The Reagan administration ends U.S. financial contributions to international birth control programs.

1985

EMILY's List is established to raise funds for Democratic women's campaigns; the acronym EMILY stands for Early Money Is Like Yeast—it makes the dough rise.

1985 *(continued)*

Feminists Andrea Dworkin and Catharine A. MacKinnon draft an antipornography ordinance for Indianapolis, Indiana, that calls works of pornography an infringement on women's rights; the Feminist Anti-Censorship Task Force (FACT) is founded to oppose the ordinance.

1986

In *Meritor Savings Bank v. Vinson*, the U.S. Supreme Court unanimously recognizes that sexual harassment in the workplace represents a violation of Title VII of the Civil Rights Act of 1964.

The U.S. Supreme Court strikes down an antipornography ordinance as a violation of the First Amendment in *American Booksellers Association v. Hudnut*.

Randall Terry creates Operation Rescue to close down abortion clinics.

1987

Canada passes the Pay Equity Act.

Fund for the Feminist Majority (FFM) is launched to place women in positions of leadership in business, education, government, law, and other fields.

1988

Congress passes the Civil Rights Restoration Act, restoring the ability to enforce provisions of Title IX of the Education Amendments of 1972.

The Canadian Supreme Court strikes down a federal law regulating abortion as unconstitutional.

Congress passes the Women's Business Ownership Act.

Congress passes the Family Support Act, which is designed to enforce child support orders and to promote self-sufficiency among large numbers of female welfare recipients.

1989

In *Wards Cove Packing Company v. Atonio*, the U.S. Supreme Court shifts the burden of proof in Title VII employment discrimination cases to the plaintiffs, requiring them to show that the employment practices they challenge actually cause the discrimination they claim to have suffered.

The U.S. Supreme Court in *Lorance v. AT&T Technologies* rules that an employee filing a complaint about unfair employment practices must do so within 180 days of the alleged violation. The opinion is regarded as a setback for female employees who cannot anticipate the deadlines that they confront in filing charges.

Antonia Novello is appointed U.S. surgeon general, the first woman and first Latino to fill that position.

The U.S. Supreme Court rules in *Webster v. Reproductive Health Services* that states have the authority to limit a woman's ability to obtain an abortion.

attempted to appeal the U.S. district court decision, but in 1982 the Supreme Court declared the ERA dead and any attempts to resuscitate it invalid.

Opposition to the ERA was at times an exercise in irony. For example, one of the ERA's most vocal opponents, conservative spokeswoman Phyllis Schlafly, declared that the ERA would "take away the marvelous legal rights of a woman to be a full-time wife and mother in the house supported by her husband."

Schlafly was herself a Harvard-educated lawyer and a two-time congressional candidate.

The fate of the ERA reflected a shift in political attitudes and a rise in the power of conservative Republicans such as Schlafly and Paul Weyrich. Critics of the ERA declared that the amendment would have granted too much power to Congress and the federal courts. Campaigns played on public fears, declaring that the ERA would mean that women would be drafted into military service or have to perform heavy labors or that the government would be forced to recognize same-sex marriage. One highly successful campaign posited the rise of mandatory mixed-sex sports teams and bathrooms.

The possible impact of the ERA on abortion laws, however, was the fear that opponents of the ERA repeatedly played on the most. On November 15, 1983, the Democratic majority in the House of Representatives tried to pass the ERA again, starting the ratification process from scratch, under a procedure that prevented the consideration of any amendments. Fourteen cosponsors proceeded to vote against the bill, insisting on an amendment proposed by Congressman James Sensenbrenner that read, "Nothing in this Article shall be construed to grant, secure, or deny any right relating to abortion or the funding thereof."

Reproductive Rights The focus on reproductive rights by ERA opponents highlighted many fears about the changing status of women and the ERA's potential impact on antiabortion laws. This focus was in part fueled by the practice of states using ERAs to challenge antiabortion policies, efforts that succeeded in Connecticut and New Mexico.

Reproductive rights continued to be a major area of contention throughout the 1980's. In 1986, antiabortion activist Randall Terry founded Operation Rescue, whose mission was to block access to family-planning clinics. Antiabortion leaders not only pointed to the rights of the fetus but also asserted that legal abortion challenged the potential father's right to control the family. That same year, George Gilder wrote in his book *Men and Marriage* that making abortion and birth control available to women reduced the penis to "an empty plaything." Multiple cases were brought to court defending the rights of fathers, usually against women who would not comply with male demands or who had recently filed for divorce. Many doctors stopped offering the abortion procedure; by 1987, 85 percent of the counties in the United States had no abortion services.

The 1980's also saw the implementation of fetal protection policies by numerous companies, including fifteen major corporations, such as Dow and General Motors. These policies barred women from jobs that had been traditionally male and that paid high wages but that involved exposure to harmful chemicals or radiation that might harm a fetus.

Around that time, the Reagan administration barred investigation into the harmful effects of video display terminals (VDTs), machines employed in traditionally female occupations. When the National Institute for Occupational Safety and Health attempted to investigate higher rates of reproductive problems among women working with VDTs, the Office of Management and Budget demanded that questions dealing with fertility and stress be dropped from a survey administered to the workers, saying that such questions had no practical utility. Although evidence existed that industrial toxins affected both men and women in producing birth defects, no laws were passed protecting them. Reducing the level of toxins in the workplace was also not considered.

In 1984, the case *Oil, Chemical, and Atomic Workers International Union v. American Cyanamid Co.*, brought by a group of women who had undergone sterilization in order to keep their jobs, reached a federal court. Federal appellate judge Robert H. Bork ruled in favor of the company, saying that the fetal protection policy was valid and that the company had been sued only because "it offered the women a choice." The company's settlement of $200,000 was divided among the eleven plaintiffs.

The Conservative Backlash to Feminism The few victories for women's rights made in earlier decades did not go unchallenged in the 1980's. Conservative leaders such as Weyrich and Howard Phillips proclaimed that women's equality led only to unhappiness for women. Conservatives criticized the women's movement for destroying moral values and dismantling the traditional family, while evangelist and Moral Majority cofounder Jerry Falwell declared that "the Equal Rights Amendment strikes at the foundation of our very social structure" in his 1981 book *Listen, America!* In 1981, the Heritage Foundation, a conservative think tank, produced *Mandate for Leadership*, which warned against "the increasing leverage of feminist interests" and claimed that feminists had infiltrated government agencies.

That same year, the Heritage Foundation drafted its first legislative effort: the Family Protection Bill, which sought to dismantle legal achievements of the women's movement. Its proposals included the elimination of federal laws supporting equal education, the forbidding of "intermingling of the sexes in any sport or other school-related activities," the requirement that marriage and motherhood be emphasized as a career for girls, the revocation of federal funding from any school using textbooks that portrayed women in nontraditional roles, the repeal of all federal laws regarding domestic violence, and the banning of any federally funded legal aid for women seeking abortion counseling or a divorce. The bill provided tax incentives designed to discourage women from working, such as allowing a husband to establish a tax-deductible retirement fund only if his wife had earned no money the previous year.

Perhaps as a result of such efforts, new female judicial appointments fell from 15 percent of appointments to 8 percent during Reagan's first term, and the proportion fell even lower during the second term. Despite federal regulations requiring the Justice Department to set hiring goals aimed at increasing the number of women within its ranks, by 1986 Attorney General Edwin Meese III had yet to hire a woman as a senior policy maker. The Federal Women's Program, which had been established in 1967 to increase the number of women in government agencies, was dismantled by removing its recruitment coordinators and its budget. As a result of the Paperwork Reduction Act, the federal government ceased collecting recruitment statistics on women. The highest female post on the Reagan staff was held by Faith Whittlesey, assistant to the president for public liaison, covering women's and children's issues.

A central target for the Heritage Foundation was the Women's Educational Equity Act (WEEA) program and its director, Leslie Wolfe. The only federal program to promote equal education for girls, the WEEA program had been called one of the most cost-effective programs in the government. After taking office in 1981, Reagan removed 25 percent of the program's already-approved budget and declared his intention to completely remove its funding the following year. The program's supporters succeeded in winning a reprieve for the program, although not without some casualties: 40 percent of the program's budget was cut. Its field reader staff, which evaluated grant proposals, was replaced with women from Schlafly's Eagle Forum who were unfamiliar with the program's policies and methods and who did such things as repeatedly reject proposals to study sexual discrimination on the basis that such discrimination did not exist. A year later, Wolfe was fired along with every other woman on staff, and the office was demoted to the lowest level of bureaucracy.

Women and the Workplace Unlike their American counterparts, Canadian women were achieving some significant legal victories. As a result of the Royal Commission, led by Judge Rosalie Abella in 1984, the Employment Equity Act was passed in 1986, requiring employers to identify and remove unnecessary barriers to the employment of women and minorities. The same year, the Federal Contractors Employment Equity Program was implemented, requiring contractors with at least one hundred employees who were providing goods or services for the Canadian government to implement employee equity.

In 1988, the Family and Medical Leave Act was introduced in the U.S. Congress and failed to pass, having been tied to the ABC Childcare bill and an antipornography bill that proved too contentious. It entitled employees to family leave in certain cases involving birth, adoption, or serious medical conditions and protected the employment and benefit rights of employees taking such leave. Such a bill would not pass until 1993.

In 1983, a thirty-nine-year-old newscaster, Christine Craft, filed suit against her former employer, Metromedia, a Kansas City affiliate of the American Broadcasting Company (ABC), on charges of sex discrimination related to dismissal from her position. Among the reasons Metromedia allegedly cited for dismissing her were that she was "too old, too unattractive, and not deferential to men." Other women working for the company confirmed that she was not alone in her treatment; they quoted Metromedia's "fanatical obsession" with their appearance and had also felt pressured to quit as a result of failing to meet the company's appearance standards for women. No men reported similar treatment.

In August, 1983, the case was tried at the federal district court in Kansas City, Missouri. The jury returned a unanimous verdict in Craft's favor, awarding her $500,000 in damages. U.S. district court judge Joseph E. Stevens threw out the verdict and called for a second trial in Joplin, Missouri. Stevens justified Craft's dismissal on the grounds that it was not based on sex discrimination but on an application of market logic. In the second trial, which took place in 1984, the jury again decided in Craft's favor. Metromedia appealed the decision, and this time the verdict was dismissed by the U.S. Court of Appeals for the Eighth Circuit. The Supreme Court refused to hear the case, ending the legal struggle in Metromedia's favor.

While the concept of sexual harassment became more visible in the 1980's, such cases were usually dismissed or determined in the defendant's favor in the United States. In 1986, Mechelle Vinson filed suit against her employer, the Meritor Savings Bank, on the grounds of sexual harassment, arguing that her employer had subjected her to fondling, exposure, and rape. The district court ruled that her attractive appearance could be held against her and that testimony regarding whether or not her clothing could be considered provocative could determine whether or not she had encouraged the rape on her employer's part.

Across the border in Canada, some legal victories occurred. In 1987, systemic discrimination in the hiring of women was found to be illegal in the case *C.N.R. v. Canada*, and in 1989 the Canadian Supreme Court ruled that sexual harassment was a form of discrimination in *Janzen v. Platy Enterprises*.

In academia, the case of Nancy Shaw led to increased awareness of women's studies. Shaw, a lesbian and women's studies professor at the University of California, Santa Cruz, brought suit against the university when she was denied tenure in 1982 on the basis that her work on women's health in prison was not sufficiently scholarly. Shaw's legal battle ran for five years; in 1987, she was granted tenure and allowed to return to teaching.

Impact   Events of the 1980's would shape women's political experience throughout the following decades and force politicians to consider their positions on women's rights and to make a conscious effort to include or exclude those issues from their campaigns. Workplace legislation passed in the 1980's would shape the experience of both Canadian and American women in the labor force and eventually open up new professions while removing some barriers and implementing others.

Further Reading

Brownmiller, Susan. *In Our Time: Memoir of a Revolution.* Boston: Dial Press, 1999. Provides an insider's view of the Meese Commission's investigation of pornography and the feminists on either side of the pornography debate.

Craft, Christine. *Too Old, Too Ugly, Not Deferential to Men.* Rocklin, Calif.: Prima, 1986. Craft's book details her legal struggles with Metromedia and media coverage of the case, which included accusations that she was lesbian as well as charges that she had been fired because she "wasn't worth the money."

Critchlow, Donald T. *Phyllis Schlafly and Grassroots Conservatism: A Woman's Crusade.* Princeton, N.J.: Princeton University Press, 2005. Describes Schlafly's political career, including her battle against the ERA and her far-right stance on reproductive issues and feminism.

Faludi, Susan. *Backlash: The Undeclared War Against America's Women.* New York: Crown, 1991. Describes the conservative backlash evoked by legal victories for women in the 1980's and points to media representations of women showcasing this reaction.

Kauffman, Linda S. *American Feminist Thought at Century's End: A Reader.* Cambridge, Mass.: Blackwell, 1993. This anthology contains a diverse selection of essays showcasing some of the major strands of feminist thought in the 1980's and 1990's.

MacKinnon, Catharine A. *Feminism Unmodified: Discourses on Life and Law.* Cambridge, Mass.: Harvard University Press, 1988. Collection of insightful lectures given by feminist legal scholar MacKinnon that discusses the legal and social subjugation of women.

Wolf, Naomi. *The Beauty Myth: How Images of Beauty Are Used Against Women.* New York: William Morrow, 1991. Describes media backlash against gains in women's rights and how it shapes women's work experience.

Cat Rambo

See also   Abortion; Affirmative action; Bork, Robert H.; Conservatism in U.S. politics; Craft, Christine; Domestic violence; Dworkin, Andrea; École Polytechnique massacre; Environmental movement; Feminism; Ferraro, Geraldine; Gender gap in voting; Liberalism in U.S. politics; Marriage and divorce; *Meritor Savings Bank v. Vinson*; Pornography; Reagan, Ronald; Sexual harassment; Supreme Court decisions; *Webster v. Reproductive Health Services*; Women in the workforce.

■ *Wonder Years, The*

Identification   Television series
Date   Aired from March 15, 1988, to May 12, 1993

Unlike other family sitcoms of the 1980's, The Wonder Years *was a coming-of-age mixture of comedy and drama. The show's complex tone came in part from its setting in the turbulent 1960's.*

The Wonder Years was primarily a show about the anxieties of teenage life, but because of its context, it uniquely appealed to both children growing up in the suburbs in the 1980's and their parents, who had grown up twenty years earlier, during the era portrayed by the show. Although sitcoms like *Cheers* and *The Cosby Show* dominated the ratings in the 1980's, *The Wonder Years* earned a place in the Nielsen top ten for two of its seasons, and it won the Emmy Award for best comedy in 1988.

The series followed the daily life of adolescent Kevin Arnold (played by Fred Savage) in American suburbia during the 1960's, a time of extreme turmoil and change in the United States. Kevin struggled with many of the typical complications of teenage life: acne, dating, conflicts with authority, fighting with siblings, and trying to negotiate the difficult transition from boyhood to manhood. Kevin represented the average American kid growing up in an average suburb, and the show illuminated his relationships with his mother (played by Alley Mills), father (played by Dan Lauria), brother Wayne (played by Jason Hervey), hippie sister Karen (played by Olivia d'Abo), best friend Paul (played by Josh Saviano), and heartthrob Winnie (played by Danica McKellar). Episodes were narrated in voice-over by an adult Kevin (voiced by Daniel Stern), who reflected in the present about the past events portrayed in each episode. *The Wonder Years* differed from such other 1980's sitcoms as *The Cosby Show, Married . . . with Children,* and *Family Ties* in that Kevin struggled through his adolescence against the backdrop of large-scale social events such as the Vietnam

Cast members of The Wonder Years *celebrate their Emmy Award for Best Comedy Series at the 1988 ceremony. From left: Alley Mills, Jason Hervey, producer Jeff Silver, Josh Saviano, Olivia D'Abo, and Dan Lauria.* (AP/Wide World Photos)

War, the counterculture, the early stages of space exploration, and changes in gender roles in American society. The show appealed to and navigated the nostalgia for earlier decades so central to 1980's culture, as well as a lingering cultural need to understand the social upheaval of the 1960's from the vantage point of the 1980's.

Impact *The Wonder Years* had a widely varied viewership. As a result, the show sold air time to a broader than average range of advertisers, seeking to reach the show's wider than average demographic. This marketing strategy was partially responsible for the show's success. The series also offered a retrospective look at the turmoil of the 1960's and allowed viewers to gain some historical, as well as personal, understanding from each episode.

Further Reading

Gross, Edward A. *The Wonder Years.* Las Vegas: Pioneer Books, 1990.

Lasswell, Mark. *TV Guide: Fifty Years of Television.* New York: Crown, 2002.

Roman, James. *Love, Light, and a Dream: Television's Past, Present, and Future.* Westport, Conn.: Praeger, 1996.

Jennifer L. Amel

See also *Back to the Future*; *Cheers*; *Cosby Show, The*; *Family Ties*; *Married . . . with Children*; Sitcoms; Television.

■ World music

Definition A marketing category for music originating from, influenced by, or blending or incorporating elements of non-Western musical traditions

Large concerts and recordings with famous popular musicians in the 1980's gave traditional musicians a chance to be heard by a greatly expanded audience. The music industry began to market traditional musicians by using a more blended or universalist approach.

Until the 1980's, most published recordings of traditional music (with the notable exception of productions controlled by academics) were marketed as a kind of tourist experience, with appeal to the exoticism and adventure of hearing something "different." In contrast to this, scholars in the field of ethnomusicology had developed methods for the formal study of music on a global scale, and a few Western classical composers had already utilized non-Western rhythmic and melodic elements in their works. Starting in the 1950's, jazz musicians embraced Latin music, followed by pianist Dave Brubeck with meters from Eastern Europe, saxophonist John Coltrane with African and East Indian musical concepts, and other musicians who were interested in expanding their horizons. The term "world music" was used in academic circles during the 1960's as a way of identifying the breadth of global traditions and to express cross-cultural identification. Interest in global traditions accelerated in the late 1960's when members of the popular British rock group the Beatles began using Indian music and instruments in some of their pieces.

New Age and World Music Later, some musicians began exploring the possibilities of music, especially world music, for holistic therapy and meditation, in a related movement known as New Age music. This term is credited to guitarist William Ackerman, founder of the Windham Hill recording label. Jazz flutist Paul Horn became known for incorporating the actual acoustic environments of various famous sacred spaces around the world. Similarly, jazz saxophonist Paul Winter, who also tended to blur the distinction between New Age and world music, became interested in environmental sounds, especially finding affinities with animal sounds. Another important exponent of New Age music was R. Carlos Nakai, a flutist and composer of Native American (Navajo and Ute) ancestry who began using a traditional cedar flute in compositions that blended native melodies with ideas inspired by his own cultural experiences, including a deep reverence for nature.

By the 1980's, music fans had become accustomed to hearing elements of global traditions blended with jazz and popular music. Indian tabla virtuoso Zakir Hussain, who started the Diga Rhythm Band with drummer Mickey Hart of the Grateful Dead in the 1970's, was active in experimenting with combining world percussion instruments and styles. Hart also collaborated with Nigerian drummer Babatunde Olatunji during the 1980's. Jazz guitarist John McLaughlin, who played in Shakti (a quartet with Hussain and two South Indian musicians) during the 1970's, continued to include Indian elements in his music during the 1980's, when he formed a trio that included Indian percussionist Trilok Gurtu, who played with Oregon, a world music fusion group that started in the 1970's. A new interest in European folk traditions, including Celtic and klezmer music among others, also emerged in the 1980's. The Klezmer Conservatory Band was established in the early 1980's, and McLaughlin supplemented his Indian music and jazz activities by collaborating with flamenco guitarist Paco De Lucía.

Global Influences on WOMAD and Minimalism One of the most noticeable world music phenomena that emerged during the 1980's was the World of Music, Arts and Dance festival (WOMAD), initially sponsored by Peter Gabriel, a famous rock musician whose political identification with the struggle against racial segregation in South Africa had inspired him to explore that country's music. The first festival—which included Gabriel, drummers from Burundi, and other musicians—was held in 1982 and attracted more than fifteen thousand people. The festival expanded in subsequent years, being held in many different countries, as often as ten times per year, and has featured thousands of musicians. In 1986, world music got another important boost when American musician Paul Simon recorded *Graceland*, which included the South African choral group Ladysmith Black Mambazo.

Although more publicity was generated by the activities of popular musicians, intercultural influence was expanding in elite circles as well. A movement known as minimalism, which also represented a break with the extreme complexity of many twentieth century compositions, incorporated aesthetic concepts as well as musical elements from Asian, African, and other sources. Philip Glass, who had supplemented his graduate work in composition with lessons from Indian sitar virtuoso Ravi Shankar; Terry Riley, who was also influenced by Indian music; and Steve Reich, who was interested in rhythms from Indonesia and Africa, were just a few of the composers who successfully incorporated global elements.

Impact Criticisms have been raised that the world music trend aspires to breadth but sacrifices depth. Even the breadth has been called into question, because the less easily understood, less danceable genres have been underrepresented. The technological ability to "sample" or electronically capture fragments of sound and then use them in other contexts is also problematic. There is concern that globalization might obscure or even destroy some unique aspects of musical traditions and the identities they reflect. On the other hand, many musicians benefited artistically from the stimulating and challenging collaborations and benefited financially from the increased exposure resulting from the explosion of interest in world music during the 1980's. Most of the musicians involved in these activities have continued them into the twenty-first century, and their audiences are still listening.

Further Reading

Feld, Steven. "A Sweet Lullaby for World Music." *Public Culture* 12, no. 1 (Winter, 2000): 145-171. This critical essay provides an overview of the history of the term "world music," with attention to the 1980's, and explores the moral, technical, and legal implications of musical appropriation.

Fletcher, Peter. *World Musics in Context: A Comprehensive Survey of the World's Major Musical Cultures.* New York: Oxford University Press, 2004. A comprehensive study that includes a historical overview, focusing on connections among the world's peoples.

Nidel, Richard. *World Music: The Basics.* New York: Routledge, 2004. This accessible book is primarily descriptive of the most popular genres, but still fairly broad, with 130 countries represented.

Witzleben, Lawrence. "Whose Ethnomusicology? Western Ethnomusicology and the Study of Asian Music." *Ethnomusicology* 41, no. 2 (1997): 220-242. Explores fundamental issues and possibilities in the cross-cultural academic study of the musics of the world.

John Myers

See also Classical music; Glass, Philip; Jazz; Music; Native Americans; Pop music.

■ World Wrestling Federation

Identification Professional sports entertainment organization

The forerunner of the World Wrestling Entertainment empire, the World Wrestling Federation in the 1980's changed the face of professional wrestling. The company transformed the industry from a fractured regional structure with loose alliances into a cohesive national organization

and emphasized professional wrestling as a form of entertainment rather than an authentically competitive sport.

During the early years of professional wrestling, a variety of regional organizations dominated the industry, and despite monikers that denoted global competition, most activities focused on personalities and events in the northeastern United States. In 1980, however, a young Vincent McMahon founded Titan Sports, parent company to the World Wrestling Federation (WWF). McMahon, a third-generation wrestling entrepreneur, set out to build a national organization; throughout the 1980's, he purchased regional organizations and developed national promotional strategies that ran counter to the industry's traditional territory system. The WWF's biggest rivals during this period were the National Wrestling Alliance (NWA), a group of northeastern independent wrestling promotions, and the American Wrestling Alliance (AWA), a Minneapolis-based territorial organization that held to the tenet that wrestling was to be presented as a traditional sport. The AWA's matches were aired weekly on the Entertainment and Sports Programming Network (ESPN) on cable television.

WWF Goes Nationwide In the early 1980's, McMahon infuriated rival promoters by syndicating his wrestling events to television stations nationwide and by selling videotapes of matches via his Coliseum Video distribution company. He used the revenues generated by televised and videotaped matches, as well as by advertising, to lure major-name wrestlers from other organizations.

The WWF's most significant talent acquisition of the 1980's was wrestling superstar Hulk Hogan (Terrence Gene Bollea), who had gained national recognition with his appearance in the film *Rocky III* (1982). Hogan was frequently pitted against another WWF employee poached from a rival promoter, the Scottish kilt-wearing bodybuilder Roddy Piper (Roderick George Toombs). This pairing created a sense of ongoing, bitter rivalry that rapidly beame a mainstay of professional wrestling.

A host of memorable names and personalities followed, including ultrapatriot Sgt. Slaughter (Robert Remus) and his Iranian nemesis the Iron Sheik (Hossein Khosrow Ali Vaziri). Additional WWF acquisitions during the 1980's included future Minnesota governor Jesse "The Body" Ventura, typically acting as a commentator rather than competitor because of health problems; Don Muraco (Don Morrow), a huge Hawaiian wrestler with an arrogant and intimidating persona; and the nearly seven-foot-tall André the Giant (André René Roussimoff). Roussimoff, the product of a rare pituitary disorder, also appeared both on television series and in film; he may be best known for his role in the 1987 classic *The Princess Bride*.

Among other significant changes during this period was the introduction in 1985 of a nationwide pay-per-view championship event, *WrestleMania*, billed by WWF promoter McMahon as the Super Bowl of professional wrestling. Unlike other national wrestling events, which generally attracted only dedicated wrestling fans, *WrestleMania* targeted a wider, more mainstream audience by involving celebrities outside wrestling, such as Mr. T and Cyndi Lauper. McMahon later identified the introduction of *WrestleMania* as a major turning point in the identification of professional wrestling as "sports entertainment." MTV also helped promote professional wrestling during the 1980's, in what was termed the "Rock 'n' Wrestling Connection," by featuring significant WWF coverage and programming.

Throughout the remainder of the 1980's, the WWF's business continued to boom, thanks to its blossoming empire and the popularity of Hulk Hogan, who remained the federation's golden boy through the early 1990's. However, toward the end of the 1980's, it appeared that Hogan's popularity had begun to decline, in part because it seemed that he was virtually unbeatable.

Impact The 1980's became known in the industry as the Second Golden Age of Wrestling for revitalizing the sport by wedding it with showmanship. Wrestlers wore their hair long, reminiscent of the biblical strongman Sampson, and donned elaborate, glittering costumes. Intricate, soap-opera-like plotlines enhanced the wrestling matches, luring viewers from all over the world by the millions. This focus on entertainment also de-emphasized fair play in favor of dramatic elements such as cheating, extremely violent acts both inside and outside the ring, shouting matches, and sexual, financial, and relational intrigue, raising the ire of many social critics. Equally important, this period marked the establishment of the WWF as the primary player in the professional wrestling industry, bringing the sport and its questionable social effects to a truly global audience.

Further Reading

Ball, Michael R. *Professional Wrestling as Ritual Drama in American Popular Culture.* Lewiston, N.Y.: Edwin Mellen Press, 1990. Investigates professional wrestling from a sociological perspective as a reflection of working-class values.

Beekman, Scott M. *Ringside: A History of Professional Wrestling in America.* Westport, Conn.: Praeger, 2006. Examines the disreputable reputation of professional wrestling compared to other sports.

Guttman, James. *World Wrestling Insanity: The Decline and Fall of a Family Empire.* Toronto: ECW Press, 2006. Provides an exposé of the McMahon monopoly on professional wrestling and examines issues such as racism, creativity, and manipulation of the industry.

Hackett, Thomas. *Slaphappy: Pride, Prejudice, and Professional Wrestling.* New York: HarperCollins, 2006. Uses interviews with wrestlers, promoters, and fans to investigate a range of issues surrounding professional wrestling, including fame, masculinity, violence, performance, and play.

Mazer, Sharon. *Professional Wrestling: Sport and Spectacle.* Jackson: University Press of Mississippi, 1998. Examines how professional wrestling performances are constructed and promoted and how fans deal with the artificial nature of the sport.

Soulliere, Dannelle M. "Wrestling with Masculinity: Wrestling with Images of Manhood in the WWE." *Sex Roles* 55 (July, 2006): 1-11. Study examining messages about manhood presented in professional wrestling.

Tamborini, Ron, et al. "The Raw Nature of Televised Professional Wrestling: Is the Violence a Cause for Concern?" *Journal of Broadcasting and Electronic Media* 49, no. 2 (2005): 202-220. Study linking physical violence portrayed on professional wrestling with harm to viewers.

Cheryl Pawlowski

See also   Action films; Advertising; Cable television; Children's television; Lauper, Cyndi; Martial arts; Mr. T; MTV; Sports; Television.

■ Wright, Jim

Identification   Speaker of the U.S. House of Representatives, 1987-1989
Born   December 22, 1922; Fort Worth, Texas

Wright's rise and fall from power reflected the battles taking place between liberals and conservatives in American politics during the Reagan years.

As the 1980's began, Democrat Jim Wright of Texas was one of the most powerful members of the U.S. House of Representatives. First elected in 1954, he had attained the position of House majority leader by 1976. His ascent to power continued as the decade progressed, and in January of 1987 he was elected House Speaker following the retirement of Democrat Tip O'Neill.

Wright's political philosophy was shaped by the New Deal and Great Society eras and thus stood in direct opposition to President Ronald Reagan's philosophy of lower taxes and smaller government. As Speaker, Wright sought to expand the position's role and to give it a stronger voice in the creation of national policy as a means of offering opposition to the president. When Reagan blocked Wright's domestic policy efforts by refusing to raise taxes and by blaming soaring budget deficits on the Democrats, Wright attempted to challenge the president in the area of foreign policy, notably the Iran-Contra affair. Wright justified this foray into foreign policy on the grounds that he, as Speaker of the House, represented the American people as much as the president did. In addition to his battles with the president and House Republicans, Wright ruled his own party with an iron hand, insisting on absolute loyalty and exercising strict discipline among his fellow Democrats.

To counter Wright's growing power, and reflecting the growing conflict between liberal and conservative forces within U.S. politics at the time, Republican congressman Newt Gingrich of Georgia set out on a personal mission to remove Wright from office. Following in the pattern of Democratic attacks on prominent Republican appointees and officeholders such as Robert H. Bork and Attorney General Edwin Meese III, Gingrich sought to expose questionable financial dealings and ethics violations by Wright. The most prominent of these violations involved sales to lobbyists of a self-published autobiography, *Reflections of a Public Man*, and a job and other perquisites received by his wife. In the end, none of

House Speaker Jim Wright, left, talks with Senator Alan Cranston and Representative Nancy Pelosi on Capitol Hill in June, 1987. (AP/ Wide World Photos)

these activities proved to be technically illegal, being based on various loopholes in the ethics rules, and they were not inconsistent with the practices of other House members at the time. Still, the appearance of misconduct, combined with the persistence of Gingrich's attacks, eventually forced Wright to resign as Speaker on May 31, 1989, and to give up his House seat shortly thereafter.

Impact Wright's political success during the early 1980's and his fall from power at the end of the decade were key events in the battle taking shape between liberal and conservative elements in government during the Reagan years. His story is also a study in the personal quest for power and the hubris that can be associated with it.

Further Reading

Barry, John M. *The Ambition and the Power.* New York: Viking Press, 1989.

Taylor, Stuart, Jr. "Wright's Deeds Pale Next to Systemic Corruption." *The New Jersey Law Journal* 123, no. 23 (June 8, 1989): 12.

Wright, Jim. *Reflections of a Public Man.* Fort Worth, Tex.: Madison, 1984.

Scott Wright

See also Bork, Robert H.; Congress, U.S.; Conservatism in U.S. politics; Iran-Contra affair; Liberalism in U.S. politics; Meese, Edwin, III; O'Neill, Tip; Reagan, Ronald; Reagan Revolution; Reaganomics; Scandals.

X

■ Xanadu Houses

Definition Experimental homes designed to showcase new architectural methods and home technology

Place Wisconsin Dells, Wisconsin; Kissimmee, Florida; and Gatlinburg, Tennessee

The three Xanadu Houses built in the United States in the 1980's were meant to showcase and promote new architectural methods and home automation systems, though in reality the houses were merely tourist attractions, and their methods and ideologies were never widely adopted.

The Xanadu House project was born in 1979, the brainchild of Bob Masters, who envisioned a future of ergonomically designed houses built with novel materials and featuring advanced computer technology. The first Xanadu House was designed by architect Stewart Gordon and built in Wisconsin Dells, Wisconsin. The second, and by far the best known of the houses, was designed by Roy Mason and built in 1983 in Kissimmee, Florida, to take advantage of the tourist population drawn to the area by Disney's Experimental Prototype Community of Tomorrow (EPCOT) Center. The final house was located in Gatlinburg, Tennessee.

The houses were designed to be energy efficient and very quickly built by spraying polyurethane insulating foam over inflatable balloon forms. The resulting structures were bright white and had gently curving lines, both inside and out, which, visitors often thought, resembled something from a science-fiction film. An integrated computer system controlled virtually every aspect of the homes' functioning, from watering plants in the greenhouses to suggesting nutritious menus and helping to prepare meals. The designers intended for such labor-saving devices to leave more time for families to come together around the "electronic hearth"—a high-technology entertainment center featuring multiple televisions, video games, stereo equipment, and, in at least one of the homes, a video screen showing an image of a cozy fire.

Impact Though they were meant to showcase serious architectural possibilities for the future and to change the way people interacted with their shelters, in truth the Xanadu Houses never quite rose above the status of curiosity or tourist attraction. The Kissimmee Xanadu House, by far the most popular of the three, attracted more than one thousand visitors per day during its peak of popularity in the mid-1980's. Despite their grand vision, however, the architects never really reckoned with the tastes and preferences of ordinary home buyers. No one, in fact, ever lived in any of the Xanadu Houses.

The rooms in the houses were small, and the curved walls could make them feel cramped and cavelike; the building materials were not well suited to stand up over the long term to the ravages of weather; and many people found the designs, reminiscent of science fiction, strange and even ugly. Perhaps most important, rapid developments in technology made many of the homes' "futuristic" features quickly obsolete. The Wisconsin and Tennessee houses were demolished in the 1990's, and even the once-popular Florida house closed in 1996 and was demolished in 2005.

Further Reading

Mason, Roy, et al. "A Day at Xanadu." *Futurist* 18 (February, 1984): 17-24.

Mason, Roy, Lane Jennings, and Robert Evans. *Xanadu: The Computerized Home of Tomorrow and How It Can Be Yours Today!* New York: Acropolis Books, 1983.

Janet E. Gardner

See also Architecture; CAD/CAM technology; Computers; Deconstructivist architecture.

Y

■ Yankovic, Weird Al

Identification American comedy songwriter and
performer
Born October 23, 1959; Downey, California

*Yankovic's humorous songs portrayed and sometimes paro-
died popular culture and music of the 1980's.*

Born Alfred Matthew Yankovic, "Weird Al" received
his nickname as a deejay at his university's radio
station. After some minor successes, the singer-

*Weird Al Yankovic poses for the press at the 1987 MTV Video
Music Awards in Universal City, California.* (Hulton Archive/
Getty Images)

songwriter became known through the help of deejay Dr. Demento, whose syndicated weekly radio
show popularized novelty songs of the past and
showcased new talent such as Yankovic.

Yankovic's first album, *"Weird Al" Yankovic*, appeared in 1983, followed by *"Weird Al" Yankovic in 3-D*
(1984), *Dare to Be Stupid* (1985), *Polka Party!* (1986),
and *Even Worse* (1988). Most of his work uses the music of popular songs whose lyrics he playfully alters,
sometimes putting an ironic twist to the original.
"Fat," on the 1988 album, for example, mimics Michael Jackson's 1987 "Bad" but substitutes bragging
about girth.

Many of Yankovic's songs praise food, including
"I Love Rocky Road," based on the 1982 cover version of "I Love Rock 'n Roll" by Joan Jett and the
Blackhearts, and "Addicted to Spuds," based on
Robert Palmer's 1985 song "Addicted to Love." Other
songs comment on television and film, especially science fiction: "Yoda," to the tune of the Kinks' 1970
hit "Lola," was also popular with fans. His lyrics also
refer to mundane aspects of life, from sales jobs to
having a hernia to paying alimony. Yankovic generally avoids political commentary, although his original song "Christmas at Ground Zero" (1986) reflects
Cold War fears of nuclear war. Some of his best songs
satirize the originals: "Dare to Be Stupid" does not
parody any particular single song by New Wave band
Devo but captures and exaggerates the group's tone,
while "(This Song's Just) Six Words Long" summarizes "Got My Mind Set on You," recorded by George
Harrison in 1987.

Many of Yankovic's songs became excellent music
videos, including "Eat It," which parodied the video
for Jackson's 1982 hit single "Beat It," as well as "Like
a Surgeon," based on "Like a Virgin" and featuring
Madonna-like gyrations, and "I Lost on Jeopardy,"
based on the 1983 song "Jeopardy" by the Greg Kihn
Band. In 1989, Yankovic cowrote and starred in
the film *UHF,* which satirized television and movies.
Home Box Office (HBO) aired a "mockumentary"
of Weird Al's life, issued in 1991 as *The Compleat Al.*

A bomber drops liquid fire retardant in Yellowstone National Park to combat the 1988 forest fires. (NPS photo by Jeff Henry)

Impact A number of Yankovic's albums reached gold or platinum status in the United States and Canada in the 1980's and later decades. Yankovic continued to produce successful albums, including 1992's *Off the Deep End*, which parodied Nirvana's *Nevermind* (1991) album cover and the rock band's hit "Smells Like Teen Spirit," and 2003's *Poodle Hat*, which went gold and earned the Grammy Award for Best Comedy Album. Yankovic's satire is accurate but good-humored; he does not anticipate trends but identifies current, major aspects of culture.

Further Reading

http://www.weirdal.com.

Insana, Tino, and Weird Al Yankovic, *The Authorized Al.* Chicago: Contemporary Books, 1985.

Bernadette Lynn Bosky

See also Comedians; Dance, popular; Devo; Jackson, Michael; Madonna; Music; Music videos; Pop music; *This Is Spiñal Tap*.

■ Yellowstone National Park fires

The Event A devastating series of fires driven by drought and high winds burns thousands of acres

Date June 22-September 11, 1988

Place Yellowstone National Park in Wyoming, Montana, and Idaho

Causing $120 million in damages, the Yellowstone fires were the most costly in U.S. history. Media attention from the fires and a policy allowing natural fires to burn sparked intense public debate.

In 1972, the U.S. National Park Service adopted the "natural-burn" policy allowing lightning-ignited fires to burn when there was no threat to human life or property. Between 1972 and the 1987, 235 naturally caused fires burned 33,759 acres within Yellowstone National Park. These fires were credited with reducing surplus fuel that accumulated following years of fire suppression and with restoring the natural role of fire in improving forest growth and wildlife habitat.

In a normal year, rainfall contains fires. However, in 1988 Yellowstone experienced its driest season on record, with 32 percent of normal annual precipitation. The park's fire season began with a lightning strike on June 22 that ignited a stand of lodgepole pine. Buildups of dry fuel combined with high winds spread the flames rapidly, and by the end of July almost 99,000 acres had burned. Reacting to increased media attention, park managers elected to suppress all fires in the park. The single worst day of the 1988 fire season was August 20, called "Black Saturday," when 40-mile-per-hour winds pushed a firestorm across 150,000 acres. Flames reached two hundred feet in the air. As a result of danger associated with the fires, many of the park's roads and facilities were closed to visitors. On September 6, fire swept through the Old Faithful area, destroying sixteen cabins but sparing the Old Faithful Inn. The first snowfall on September 11 helped contain the fires.

Of fifty fires that burned within Yellowstone in 1988, forty-one were caused by lightning and nine by human activities. The total area burned within the park was 793,000 acres, amounting to about 36 percent of the park's 2,221,800 acres. More than twenty-five thousand firefighters participated in efforts to save human life and property. Destruction was limited to sixty-seven structures worth more than $3 million. Remarkably, none of Yellowstone's famous attractions or historic lodges was damaged by fire. Impacts on wildlife were also relatively low, given the magnitude of acreage burned. Field surveys revealed that the number of animals killed included 9 bison, 12 moose, 6 black bears, and 345 elk (out of an estimated elk population of 40,000). Ample precipitation during the years immediately following the fires led to rapid regeneration of trees in most burned areas.

Impact   Nearly twenty years after the 1988 fires in Yellowstone, many burned areas remained visible. The Yellowstone fires of that year created a national debate concerning the natural-burn policy. In the years immediately following the fires, public land managers across the United States revised fire management plans with strict guidelines for circumstances under which naturally occurring fires would be allowed to burn.

Further Reading

Patent, Dorothy H. *Yellowstone Fires: Flames and Rebirth.* New York: Holiday House, 1990.

Wallace, Linda. *After the Fires: The Ecology of Change in Yellowstone National Park.* New Haven, Conn.: Yale University Press, 2004.

Thomas A. Wikle

See also   Environmental movement; Natural disasters.

■ Yuppies

Definition   Young, well-educated, well-paid urban professionals who live an affluent lifestyle

This group emerged as a growing middle class in the United States during the 1980's. Yuppies became a dominant political and cultural force in society, focusing on successful careers, economic privilege, and materialism.

American journalist Bob Greene of the *Chicago Tribune* is recognized as first individual to use the term "yuppies" (coined from "young urban professionals" and later associated with "young upwardly mobile professionals" as well) in his syndicated column in March, 1983. Yuppies were an ambitious, competitive, self-reliant, and upwardly mobile class between the ages of twenty-five and thirty-nine that earned salaries of more than $40,000 per year. *Newsweek* declared 1984 as the "Year of the Yuppie," especially after Democratic senator Gary Hart ran his presidential campaign espousing yuppie values.

The Yuppie Lifestyle   Throughout the decade, an economic boom occurred in the United States. Careers in business administration, law, and medicine became the fastest ways to achieve a good salary and advancement. Universities and colleges that offered these programs experienced a dramatic increase in enrollment. Yuppies held high-paying white-collar jobs in metropolitan areas. As overachievers, they brought work home at night and on the weekends if necessary, living by schedules and appointment books. Because they spent so much time working, they needed to live in close proximity to their jobs. New housing markets sprang up in the inner cities, and developers began to renovate buildings, turning them into sleek condominiums or studio apartments designed with postmodern elements.

Yuppies were part of the "new rich" generation that lavished in extravagance by purchasing luxury items. Conspicuous consumption was typical for this segment of American society. Marketing campaigns and advertisements targeted this demographic group, raised on popular culture and rock music. Yuppies "dressed for success" by wearing the latest designer fashions; men wore suits from Brooks Brothers and shirts by Perry Ellis, purchased expensive Rolex watches, and drove BMW cars. Casual style was achieved by wearing clothes from Banana Republic and L.L.Bean, while women would often wear Nike running shoes while scurrying from one place to another, even if they were dressed in a tweed skirt and jacket. Yuppies, because of their hectic schedules, ate out at trendy ethnic restaurants while sipping the best house wine. However, despite their expensive tastes, these professionals remained health-conscious with low-fat diets, all-natural fruit drinks, and bottled water. For exercise, they were often found jogging. Self-help books became best sellers, and a New Age guru, the Reverend Terry Cole-Whittaker, spread the yuppie-inspired message, "You can have it all—now!" Yuppies were obsessed with technological gadgets that would make their hectic lives more efficient. They were voracious consumers of videocassette recorders (VCRs), personal computers, cordless phones, answering machines, microwave ovens, food processors, and fax machines.

Television shows such as *Dynasty* and *Dallas*, which depicted powerful families who continued to amass wealth by any means, appealed to the yuppie generation. On the other hand, *Hill Street Blues* was popular among yuppies because the show centered on their liberal political ideology concerning social justice. Movies portrayed yuppies and their relationships in *The Big Chill* (1983), *Baby Boom* (1987), and *When Harry Met Sally . . .* (1989). Personal relationships were often secondary to career goals, and this dichotomy was portrayed as "Yuppie angst" in the television program *thirtysomething*. Yuppies had decided to defer marriage and children until they were firmly established in their professional positions. Those who married but decided not to have children were referred to as "dinks" (double income, no kids), while couples who did have children often hired nannies to care for them.

Impact Radical antiwar activists who epitomized the counterculture movement in previous decades started to work for corporate America as the 1970's drew to an end. The idealism of the late 1960's began to be replaced as the baby-boom generation became older. The yuppies agreed with President Ronald Reagan's supply-side economics and its promotion of free market capitalism, rejecting the socioeconomic liberalism of the New Deal. They favored cuts in social spending and rejected high taxes and government regulation, but, despite their fiscal conservatism, yuppies remained liberal on positions that involved personal freedom and lifestyle choices. Many yuppies were in favor of the Equal Rights Amendment (ERA), were pro-choice regarding abortion, and opposed discrimination in the workplace.

The superficial and selfish nature of yuppiedom created fodder for parody by journalists and comedians. However, economic prosperity came to an abrupt halt when a stock market crash (Black Monday) occurred on October 19, 1987. The fast money that yuppies had accumulated in Wall Street investments suddenly disappeared, and by the early 1990's businesses began to suffer financially as globalization, massive layoffs, and downsizing in the marketplace occurred. In 1991, *Time* magazine officially proclaimed the death of the yuppie.

Further Reading

Adler, Jerry, et al. "The Year of the Yuppies." *Newsweek* 104, no. 31 (December, 1984): 14-24. The popular magazine proclaimed 1984 as the year in which the yuppie generation dominated in politics, advertising, and business.

Bondi, Victor, ed. "Baby Boomers Become Yuppies." In *American Decades: 1980-1989.* Detroit: Gale Research, 1995. The entry provides good background information and a general overview of yuppies.

Burnett, John, and Alan Bush. "Profiling the Yuppies." *Journal of Advertising Research* 26 (April/May, 1986): 27-35. Authors study the lifestyle differences, purchasing behavior, and media habits of yuppies in order to formulate strategies for advertising to this segment of the American population.

Ehrenreich, Barbara. *Fear of Falling: The Inner Life of the Middle Class.* New York: HarperPerennial, 1989. Ehrenreich provides a social analysis of the insecurities and anxieties that plagued the middle class from 1970 to 1990.

Hammond, John L. "Yuppies." *The Public Opinion*

Quarterly 50 (Winter, 1986): 487-501. Hammond analyzes the political persuasion of the yuppie population, noting the group's liberal stance on personal life choices, but he also contends that the group is not always as conservative on social welfare issues as portrayed by the media.

Hertzberg, Hendrik. "The Short Happy Life of the American Yuppie." In *Culture in an Age of Money: The Legacy of the 1980's in America*, edited by Nicolaus Mills. Chicago: Ivan R. Dee, 1990. A sa-tirical essay about the moral and political decline of yuppiedom.

Gayla Koerting

See also Advertising; *Big Chill, The*; Business and the economy in the United States; Consumerism; Demographics of the United States; *Dynasty*; Fads; Food trends; *Hill Street Blues*; *L.A. Law*; Power dressing; Reaganomics; *thirtysomething*; *When Harry Met Sally . . .*

The one hundred titles listed here are a representative sampling of 1980's films that are regarded as significant because of their box-office success, their Academy Award honors, or their critical reputations. Entries that include "*See also* main entry" have a full essay in *The Eighties in America*. All references to awards refer to the Academy Awards given by the Academy of Motion Picture Arts and Sciences.

1980

Airplane! (Howard W. Koch/Paramount; dir. Jim Abrahams, David Zucker, Jerry Zucker) This hugely popular satire of disaster films inspired numerous other spoofs of film genres. Features deadpan performances by veteran actors Lloyd Bridges, Peter Graves, and Robert Stack, sparking a second career for Leslie Nielsen as a comic actor. *See also* main entry.

Caddyshack (Orion/Warner Bros.; dir. Harold Ramis) Slapstick golf farce pokes fun at rich people played by Rodney Dangerfield and Chevy Chase. Bill Murray dominates the hilarity as psychotic groundskeeper trying, at all costs, to rid his course of gophers.

Coal Miner's Daughter (Universal; dir. Michael Apted) Sissy Spacek won an Oscar for her portrayal of country singer Loretta Lynn. The film traces Lynn's rise from Kentucky poverty to fame and focuses on her happy marriage to Mooney Lynn (Tommy Lee Jones) and her friendship with ill-fated singer Patsy Cline (Beverly D'Angelo).

The Elephant Man (Brooks Films/Paramount; dir. David Lynch) The true story of the hideously deformed John Merrick (John Hurt), a sideshow freak in Victorian London until rescued by Dr. Frederick Treves (Anthony Hopkins).

The Empire Strikes Back (Lucasfilm/Twentieth Century-Fox; dir. Irvin Kershner) Considered by many fans to be the best of the *Star Wars* series, this sequel to the original finds Luke Skywalker (Mark Hamill) absorbing wisdom from Yoda (voice of Frank Oz) and discovering a secret about Darth Vader (voice of James Earl Jones, body of David Prowse). The film won Oscars for sound and special effects. *See also* main entry.

Fame (MGM/United Artists; dir. Alan Parker) A singer (Irene Cara), a dancer (Gene Anthony Ray), and an actor (Paul McCrane) are among the students at New York's High School for the Performing Arts. The film won Oscars for Michael Gore's score and the title song by Gore and Dean Pitchford. Some of the actors continued their roles in the 1982-1987 television series.

Friday the 13th (Sean S. Cunningham/Paramount; dir. Sean S. Cunningham) A summer camp cook (Betsy Palmer) seeks revenge for the accidental death of her son, Jason (Ari Lehman), twenty-five years earlier. Followed by several sequels, this grisly horror film helped popularize the decapitation-of-vacuous-teenagers genre. A young Kevin Bacon plays one victim.

Ordinary People (Wildwood/Paramount; dir. Robert Redford) A teenager (Timothy Hutton) feels guilty for the drowning death of his brother and is not helped by his harsh parents (Mary Tyler Moore and Donald Sutherland). The adaptation of Judith Guest's novel won Oscars for Best Picture, Best Director, and Best Supporting Actor (Hutton) and for Alvin Sargent's screenplay. *See also* main entry.

Raging Bull (United Artists; dir. Martin Scorsese) Scorsese's portrait of brutal middleweight boxer Jake La Motta (Robert De Niro) is one of the director's most acclaimed films. Some critics' polls have named it the best film of the decade. De Niro and editor Thelma Schoonmaker won Oscars. *See also* main entry.

The Shining (Stanley Kubrick/Warner Bros.; dir. Stanley Kubrick) Accompanied by his wife (Shelley Duvall) and young son (Danny Lloyd), a writer (Jack Nicholson) becomes winter caretaker of a remote mountain hotel and slowly sinks into madness. Kubrick's adaptation of a Stephen King novel was critically lambasted but has slowly attained cult status.

1981

Arthur (Orion/Warner Bros.; dir. Steve Gordon) Arthur (Dudley Moore), an alcoholic millionaire, resists an arranged marriage to a socialite (Jill Eikenberry) and falls for a shoplifter (Liza Minnelli). The film was a hit despite its anachronistic 1930's premise. As Arthur's butler and father figure, John Gielgud won an Oscar, as did the theme song.

Atlantic City (Cine Neighbor/France 3 Cinema/ Planfilm/SDICC/Selta Films/Paramount; dir. Louis Malle) An aging mobster (Burt Lancaster) who fears he has lost his touch falls for a casino croupier (Susan Sarandon). Inspired by Malle's direction and John Guare's script, Lancaster gives one of his best performances.

Body Heat (Ladd Company/Warner Bros.; dir. Lawrence Kasdan) A mediocre lawyer (William Hurt) in a small Florida town is manipulated by a femme fatale (Kathleen Turner) into murdering her rich, older husband (Richard Crenna). Screenwriter Kasdan's first directorial effort was one of the most satisfying tributes to film noir, made a star of Turner in her first film, and featured a moody score by John Barry.

Chariots of Fire (Allied Stars/Enigma Productions/ Twentieth Century-Fox; dir. Hugh Hudson) The conflicting personalities of a devout Christian runner (Ian Charleson) and a Jewish sprinter (Ben Cross) are examined at the 1924 Olympics in Paris. With an outstanding performance by Ian Holm as a coach, the film won four Oscars, including Best Picture and Colin Welland's original screenplay.

Heaven's Gate (United Artists; dir. Michael Cimino) The decade's most notorious box-office failure depicts a range war between immigrant settlers and cattle barons. The film was blamed for ending the creative freedom given directors during the previous decade and for crippling United Artists. *See also* main entry.

Modern Romance (Columbia; dir. Albert Brooks) A neurotic film editor (Brooks) breaks up with his girlfriend (Kathryn Harold) and does whatever he can to try to forget his troubles. An additional problem is his attempt to salvage a weakly conceived science-fiction film. One of Brooks's most satisfying comedies, *Modern Romance* shows the influence of Woody Allen.

On Golden Pond (Associated Film Distribution/ IPC Films/ITC Films/Universal; dir. Mark Rydell) A daughter (Jane Fonda) and her crusty father (Henry Fonda) come to an understanding during a summer at their New England cottage. Henry Fonda won an Oscar for his final film, and Katharine Hepburn, as the mother, won her fourth and last. Ernest Thompson also won for his adaptation of his play. *See also* main entry.

Prince of the City (Orion/Warner Bros.; dir. Sidney Lumet) As with *Serpico* (1973), Lumet bases his examination of corruption in the New York Police Department on an actual case. A Manhattan detective (Treat Williams) becomes an outcast for breaking his department's so-called code of silence.

Raiders of the Lost Ark (Lucasfilm/Paramount; dir. Steven Spielberg) The first film about archaeologist/adventurer Indiana Jones (Harrison Ford) is a large-scale version of the low-budget movie serials of the 1930's and 1940's. It won four Oscars. *See also* main entry.

Reds (Paramount; dir. Warren Beatty) Beatty's long-time dream project about John Reed, the only American buried in the Kremlin, focuses equally on his radical political activism during the Russian Revolution and his turbulent romance with fellow journalist Louise Bryant (Diane Keaton), involving a love triangle with playwright Eugene O'Neill (Jack Nicholson). Interspersed throughout the film are interviews with those who knew the couple and the period. The epic film won Oscars for Best Director, Best Supporting Actress (Maureen Stapleton as Emma Goldman), and Best Cinematography (Vittorio Storaro).

1982

Blade Runner (Ladd Company/Warner Bros.; dir. Ridley Scott) A cop (Harrison Ford) in 2019 Los Angeles deals with runaway androids. Scott's visionary blend of science fiction and film noir has been highly influential, gaining considerably in reputation since its release. *See also* main entry.

Diner (MGM/United Artists; dir. Barry Levinson) Levinson's first nostalgic look back at the Baltimore of his youth finds six young men in 1959 taking their first awkward steps into adulthood. The impressive cast includes Mickey Rourke, Daniel Stern, Kevin Bacon, Steve Guttenberg, Tim Daly, Paul Reiser, and Ellen Barkin, in her first film.

E.T.: The Extra-Terrestrial (Universal; dir. Steven Spielberg) Spielberg's distinctive blend of science fiction, fairy tale, family drama, and coming-of-age tale was one of the most popular and beloved films of the decade and won four Oscars. *See also* main entry.

Fast Times at Ridgemont High (Universal; dir. Amy Heckerling) The decade's most popular and influential teen sex comedy is notable for its cast:

Jennifer Jason Leigh, Phoebe Cates, Judge Reinhold, and Sean Penn as the stoned surfer. Nicolas Cage, Eric Stoltz, and Forest Whitaker also have small roles. *See also* main entry.

Gandhi (Goldcrest Films International/Indo-British Films/International Film Investors/National Film Development Corporation of India/Columbia; dir. Richard Attenborough) Attenborough's biography of the Indian independence leader (Ben Kingsley) won eight Oscars, including Best Picture, Best Director, and Best Actor.

Shoot the Moon (MGM/United Artists; dir. Alan Parker) Influenced by the considerations of marriage and adultery in the films of Ingmar Bergman, Bo Goldman's perceptive screenplay examines middle-class mores. Albert Finney and Diane Keaton give outstanding performances as the unhappy Marin County, California, couple.

Sophie's Choice (Associated Film Distribution/ITC Entertainment/Keith Barish Productions/Universal; dir. Alan J. Pakula) Meryl Streep won her second Oscar as a Polish refugee with a shocking secret in 1947 Brooklyn. The moody cinematography of Néstor Almendros highlights Pakula's adaptation of William Styron's 1979 novel.

Tootsie (Mirage/Punch Productions/Columbia; dir. Sydney Pollack) Dustin Hoffman plays a character loosely based on his experiences as a hard-luck New York actor. Unlike the real Hoffman, his character dresses as a woman to win a role on a television soap opera. One of the decade's most popular comedies features several outstanding performances, including Bill Murray as the actor's playwright roommate and director Pollack as his frustrated agent. The film was nominated for ten Oscars but won only one, for Jessica Lange's supporting performance as the confused object of the actor's affections.

Tron (Buena Vista/Walt Disney; dir. Steven Lisberger) A computer programmer (Jeff Bridges) becomes trapped in a video game in the first major film to deal with this new medium. *See also* main entry.

The Verdict (Zanuck Company/Twentieth Century-Fox; dir. Sidney Lumet) Paul Newman gives one of his finest performances as an aging, failed Boston lawyer given a chance to redeem himself in a complicated malpractice case. James Mason is his adversary and Charlotte Rampling a woman with a secret. David Mamet adapted Barry Reed's novel.

1983

The Big Chill (Carson Production Group/Delphi Productions/Columbia; dir. Lawrence Kasdan) Kasdan followed *Body Heat* with an even bigger commercial success about a group of baby boomers, including Glenn Close, William Hurt, and Kevin Kline, who examine their dissatisfaction with their lives. *See also* main entry.

Flashdance (Polygram/Paramount; dir. Adrian Lyne) The story of a Pittsburgh welder (Jennifer Beals) who performs erotic dances in a bar after work won an Oscar for the title song. *See also* main entry.

Local Hero (Enigma Productions/Goldcrest Films International/Warner Bros.; dir. Bill Forsyth) Houston oilmen Peter Riegert and Burt Lancaster visit a small Scottish fishing village planning to exploit it and find themselves unexpectedly changed by their experiences. Forsyth's delightful film may be the decade's most charming.

El Norte (Independent Productions/Island Alive; Cinecom Pictures; dir. Gregory Nava) Two Guatemalans (Zaide Silvia Gutiérrez and David Villalpando) flee the oppression of their government and travel through Mexico into California to begin new lives. Nava's film, cowritten with Anna Thomas, is one of the most notable treatments of the hardships faced by illegal immigrants.

Return of the Jedi (Lucasfilm/Twentieth Century-Fox; dir. Richard Marquand) Jabba the Hutt and the child-friendly Ewoks make their first appearances as Luke Skywalker (Mark Hamill) and friends continue the *Star Wars* saga and their battle against the Empire. Its special effects received an Oscar.

The Right Stuff (Ladd Company/Warner Bros.; dir. Philip Kaufman) Kaufman's adaptation of Tom Wolfe's book about the first astronauts may be the decade's best fact-based film. Stealing the film from Scott Glenn as Alan Shepard, Ed Harris as John Glenn, Fred Ward as Gus Grissom, and Dennis Quaid as Gordon Cooper is Sam Shepard as Chuck Yeager, the pilot considered to be too reckless for space travel. It won four Oscars.

Risky Business (Geffen Pictures/Warner Bros.; dir. Paul Brickman) Tom Cruise became a star playing a Chicago high school senior involved with a prostitute (Rebecca De Mornay) while his parents are out of town. The decade's best look at sexual awakening and the mores of upper-middle-class teenagers is also memorable for its use of one of the most popular songs of the 1980's, Phil Collins's "In the Air Tonight," in an unusual romantic scene.

Scarface (Universal; dir. Brian De Palma) Director Howard Hawks's groundbreaking 1932 gangster drama is updated for the 1980's by screenwriter Oliver Stone as the tale of a ruthless Cuban immigrant (Al Pacino) who becomes a Miami crime lord. Featuring graphic violence, including a famous buzz saw scene, the film has become one of the most quoted of all time for such lines as "Say hello to my little friend." Its reputation has increased since its release, and the film has become a particular favorite in the hip-hop culture.

Silkwood (ABC/Twentieth Century-Fox; dir. Mike Nichols) An Oklahoma factory worker (Meryl Streep) becomes outraged at her employer's indifference to radiation contamination. She dies in a mysterious accident en route to give evidence to a *New York Times* reporter.

Terms of Endearment (Paramount; dir. James L. Brooks) This look at the relationship between a mother (Shirley MacLaine) and daughter (Debra Winger) won Oscars for Best Picture, Best Director, Best Actress (MacLaine), and Best Supporting Actor (Jack Nicholson as one of MacLaine's suitors) and for Brooks's adaptation of the 1975 Larry McMurtry novel. *See also* main entry.

1984

Amadeus (Saul Zaentz Company/Orion; dir. Milos Forman) Based on Peter Shaffer's play, *Amadeus* examines the jealousy of composer Antonio Salieri (F. Murray Abraham) over the success of the young Wolfgang Amadeus Mozart (Tom Hulce). It won eight Oscars, including Best Film, Best Director, and Best Actor (Abraham).

Beverly Hills Cop (Paramount; dir. Martin Brest) Eddie Murphy became a superstar as a Detroit cop on the trail of a gangster (Steven Berkoff) in Beverly Hills. Murphy is at his most self-assured in one of the decade's biggest commercial hits.

Blood Simple (River Road Productions/Circle Releasing; dir. Joel Coen) Joel and Ethan Coen launched their careers with this black comedy. An unfaithful wife (Frances McDormand) and her lover (John Getz) plot to murder her bar-owner husband (Dan Hedaya), who has hired a private eye (M. Emmett Walsh) to kill her in this

affectionate send-up of film noir conventions.

Ghostbusters (Black Rhino/Delphi Productions/Columbia; dir. Ivan Reitman) Bill Murray and Dan Ackroyd look for spirits in Manhattan. This special-effects-laden hit was the most expensive comedy made to this point. *See also* main entry.

A Nightmare on Elm Street (Smart Egg Pictures/Media Home Entertainment/New Line Cinema; dir. Wes Craven) A horror franchise was launched as murder victim Freddy Krueger (Robert Englund) seeks revenge through dreams.

Once upon a Time in America (Ladd Company/PSO International/Warner Bros.; dir. Sergio Leone) Leone's epic gangster yarn was drastically reedited by its producers, yet the story of betrayal starring Robert De Niro and James Woods still retained considerable power in its truncated form.

Places in the Heart (TriStar; dir. Robert Benton) A Texas woman (Sally Field) struggles to maintain her family farm during the Depression. It won Oscars for Best Actress and Benton's original screenplay and introduced actor John Malkovich.

Stranger than Paradise (Samuel Goldwyn; dir. Jim Jarmusch) In this deadpan comedy, one of the decade's most significant independent films, three aimless friends (John Lurie, Richard Edson, and Eszter Balint) drift from New York to Cleveland to Miami. A comic highlight is Lurie's explanation of the significance of TV dinners.

The Terminator (Hemdale/Pacific Western/Orion; dir. James Cameron) Cameron established himself as a major director and made Arnold Schwarzenegger a superstar in this science-fiction thriller. *See also* main entry.

This Is Spïnal Tap (Embassy; dir. Rob Reiner) The mockumentary genre began with this account of the American tour of a has-been hard-rock group (Christopher Guest, Michael McKean, and Harry Shearer). *See also* main entry.

1985

Back to the Future (Amblin Entertainment/Universal; dir. Robert Zemeckis) A high school student (Michael J. Fox) is accidentally transported, in the time machine of an eccentric scientist (Christopher Lloyd), back to the 1950's and into the romance of his parents (Lea Thompson and Crispin Glover). *See also* main entry.

The Breakfast Club (A&M Films/Universal; dir. John Hughes) The most enduringly popular of the decade's many films about teenagers finds five students (Emilio Estevez, Anthony Michael Hall, Judd Nelson, Molly Ringwald, and Ally Sheedy) suffering Saturday detention in their school library. *See also* main entry.

Dreamchild (PHF Limited/Thorn EMI/Universal; dir. Gavin Millar) Dennis Potter's imaginative screenplay has the inspiration for *Alice's Adventures in Wonderland* (1865) traveling to 1932 New York to celebrate the centenary of the birth of Lewis Carroll (Ian Holm). The film cuts between the present, the past, and events from the novel. Coral Browne plays the older Alice and Amelia Shankley the younger, and Jim Henson designed the Wonderland creatures.

Kiss of the Spider Woman (HB Filmes/Island Alive/Sugarloaf Films; dir. Hector Babenco) A political prisoner (Raul Julia) and a homosexual (William Hurt) share a prison cell in this adaptation of Manuel Puig's 1976 novel. Hurt won an Oscar for his sensitive performance. *See also* main entry.

Lost in America (Geffen Pictures/Warner Bros.; dir. Albert Brooks) Los Angeles yuppies David (Brooks) and Linda (Julie Hagerty) sell everything they own and hit the road to see America, only to lose all their savings and find themselves stranded in a small Arizona town. Brooks satirizes the decade's obsession with money and the continuing adolescence of baby boomers.

Out of Africa (Universal; dir. Sydney Pollack) Karen Blixen (Meryl Streep) marries Baron Bor Blixen (Klaus Maria Brandauer) for convenience in 1914 and moves to Kenya, only to fall in love with hunter Denys Finch Hatton (Robert Redford). This lush romantic drama, inspired by the writings of Isak Dinesen (Karen's pseudonym), won seven Oscars, including Best Picture, Best Director, and Best Score (John Barry).

Prizzi's Honor (ABC/Twentieth Century-Fox; dir. John Huston) Veteran director Huston rebounded from a lengthy slump to make one of his best and most entertaining films. Mafia hit man Charlie Partanna (Jack Nicholson) falls for Irene Walker (Kathleen Turner), not knowing she is also an assassin. Nominated for eight Oscars, it won only for the star-making turn of the director's daughter, Anjelica Huston, as Partanna's spurned lover.

The Purple Rose of Cairo (Orion; dir. Woody Allen) Allen's tender fantasy finds a frustrated woman (Mia Farrow) escaping from her dismal 1930's life by going to films. One day, a character in a film she has seen several times leaves the screen to romance her.

Rambo: First Blood Part II (TriStar; dir. George Pan Cosmatos) The pulpy sequel to *First Blood* (1982) was a much bigger commercial success than the more realistic original. John Rambo (Sylvester Stallone) is released from prison and dispatched to Vietnam to rescue American prisoners of war.

Witness (Paramount; dir. Peter Weir) An Amish boy (Lukas Haas) witnesses a murder in the restroom of a Philadelphia train station, and police detective John Book (Harrison Ford) links the crime to a conspiracy within his department. Fleeing to the Amish community, Book falls in love with the boy's widowed mother (Kelly McGillis). One of the decade's best thrillers won Oscars for the original screenplay by William Kelley, Earl W. Wallace, and Pamela Wallace and for Thom Noble's editing.

1986

Aliens (Brandywine/Twentieth Century-Fox; dir. James Cameron) The first sequel to Ridley Scott's *Alien* (1979) was an even bigger hit, with Ripley (Sigourney Weaver) becoming a surrogate mother to an orphan (Carrie Henn). Its special effects won an Oscar. *See also* main entry.

Blue Velvet (De Laurentiis; dir. David Lynch) The corrupt underbelly of suburbia is exposed as all-American boy Kyle MacLachlan tries to protect innocent Laura Dern and unstable Isabella Rosselini from an especially vicious Dennis Hopper, in the best performance of his long career. *See also* main entry.

Children of a Lesser God (Paramount; dir. Randa Haines) A speech teacher (William Hurt) falls for a difficult student (Marlee Matlin) in this adaptation of Mark Medoff's play. Matlin won an Oscar as Best Actress.

The Color of Money (Buena Vista/Touchstone; dir. Martin Scorsese) Paul Newman finally won an Oscar in this sequel to *The Hustler* (1961), which recounts how Fast Eddie Felson becomes a reluctant mentor to an arrogant young pool shark (Tom Cruise).

Crocodile Dundee (Rimfire Productions; dir. Peter Faiman) Australian television personality Paul Hogan, who also cowrote the screenplay, became a star as the legendary crocodile hunter who finds a different set of dangers while visiting New York City.

Ferris Bueller's Day Off (Paramount; dir. John Hughes) A teenager (Matthew Broderick), famous for cutting class, stages one final, elaborate day off before graduation. One of Hughes's biggest hits blends slapstick with social commentary.

Hannah and Her Sisters (Orion; dir. Woody Allen) The prolific Allen's best film of the decade presents the tangled personal lives of three quite different sisters (Mia Farrow, Dianne Wiest, and Barbara Hershey). Wiest and Michael Caine, as Farrow's husband in love with Hershey, won their first Oscars for their supporting roles, and Allen won for his original screenplay.

Platoon (Hemdale/Orion; dir. Oliver Stone) Stone's first film about his Vietnam War experiences finds innocent Charlie Sheen affected by the contrasting personalities of his sergeants: the corrupt Tom Berenger and the saintly Willem Dafoe. It won four Oscars, including Best Picture and Best Director. *See also* main entry.

She's Gotta Have It (Forty Acres and a Mule Filmworks/Island Pictures; dir. Spike Lee) Groundbreaking for both independent and African American filmmakers, Lee's comedy finds a young Brooklyn woman (Tracy Camila Johns) trying to maintain her personal freedom while juggling relationships with three men (Tommy Redmond Hicks, John Canada Terrell, and Lee himself).

Top Gun (Paramount; dir. Tony Scott) Military clichés were reborn in the year's box-office champion as navy pilot Tom Cruise carries on a romance with civilian consultant Kelly McGillis while conducting a rivalry with fellow pilot Val Kilmer. "Take My Breath Away" won the best-song Oscar.

1987

Broadcast News (Twentieth Century-Fox; dir. James L. Brooks) Television news producer Jane Craig (Holly Hunter) is good at her job but not her personal life. Reporter Aaron Altman (Albert Brooks) secretly yearns for her, while Jane falls for a dumb anchorman (William Hurt) against her better judgment. Jack Nicholson offers a delightful cameo as the smarmy lead anchor. The film was nominated for seven Oscars but did not win any.

Dirty Dancing (Vestron; dir. Emile Ardolino) One

of the most popular teen films in a decade dominated by the genre finds Baby Houseman (Jennifer Grey) spending the summer of 1963 in the Catskills and learning sexy dance moves from Patrick Swayze. "The Time of My Life" won the best-song Oscar.

Fatal Attraction (Jaffe-Lansing Productions/Paramount; dir. Adrian Lyne) The one-night stand of a married man (Michael Douglas) and an unbalanced woman (Glenn Close) leads to terror. *See also* main entry.

Full Metal Jacket (Warner Bros.; dir. Stanley Kubrick) Kubrick's Vietnam drama focuses first on the training of Marine recruits and then on their combat experiences. Vincent D'Onofrio famously gained seventy pounds to play a Marine who cracks under pressure. *See also* main entry.

Lethal Weapon (Warner Bros.; dir. Richard Donner) A reckless Los Angeles police detective (Mel Gibson) becomes partners with a family man (Danny Glover) whose goal is to stay alive. The film was one of the first to be even more popular on video than in theaters, leading to sequels.

Moonstruck (MGM/United Artists; dir. Norman Jewison) Loretta (Cher), a widowed Brooklyn bookkeeper on the verge of marrying a man (Danny Aiello) she does not love, finds herself falling for his younger brother (Nicolas Cage). It won Oscars for Best Actress, Best Supporting Actress (Olympia Dukakis as Loretta's mother), and Best Original Screenplay by John Patrick Shanley.

The Princess Bride (Act III/Twentieth Century-Fox; dir. Rob Reiner) A pirate (Cary Elwes) strives to rescue his true love (Robin Wright) from an evil prince (Chris Sarandon). William Goldman's adaptation of his tongue-in-cheek fairy tale did modest business in 1987 but has developed cult status.

RoboCop (Orion; dir. Paul Verhoeven) A dead policeman (Peter Weller) is resurrected as a half-human, half-robot fighting force. *See also* main entry.

The Untouchables (Paramount; dir. Brian De Palma) De Palma and screenwriter David Mamet transformed the popular 1959-1963 television series into a crime epic as Federal Bureau of Investigation (FBI) agent Eliot Ness (Kevin Costner) goes up against the powerful gangster Al Capone (Robert De Niro). The film's set piece is a stairway shootout patterned after a scene in Sergei

Eisenstein's *The Battleship Potemkin* (1925). Sean Connery's role as an honest cop earned him an Oscar.

Wall Street (American Entertainment Partners/Twentieth Century-Fox; dir. Oliver Stone) Michael Douglas won an Oscar as an unprincipled corporate raider in Stone's evisceration of 1980's greed. *See also* main entry.

1988

Beetlejuice (Warner Bros.; dir. Tim Burton) The highly imaginative Burton's first big hit presents dead newlyweds (Alec Baldwin and Geena Davis) who enlist the aid of rambunctious spirit Beetlejuice (Michael Keaton) to rid their house of an obnoxious couple (Catherine O'Hara and Jeffrey Jones), only for Beetlejuice to fall for the yuppies' gloomy daughter (Winona Ryder). Beetlejuice's distinctive makeup received an Oscar.

Big (Twentieth Century-Fox; dir. Penny Marshall) Tom Hanks became a star playing a thirteen-year-old granted his wish to be "big," becoming an adult overnight, getting a job with a toy company, and falling for a fellow employee (Elizabeth Perkins), only to discover that adulthood is not so wonderful.

Bull Durham (Mount Company/Orion; dir. Ron Shelton) One of the decade's sexiest romantic comedies, as well as one of the best baseball films ever, presents career minor-leaguer Crash Davis (Kevin Costner) and his romance with a baseball groupie (Susan Sarandon). Tim Robbins gives a star-making performance as Crash's goofy rival, Nuke LaLoosh.

Die Hard (Gordon Company/Silver Pictures/Twentieth Century-Fox; dir. John McTiernan) A New York cop (Bruce Willis) visits his estranged wife (Bonnie Bedelia) in her Los Angeles office building just as a ruthless criminal (Alan Rickman) and his gang take everyone in the skyscraper hostage. This huge hit spawned sequels and imitations.

A Fish Called Wanda (MGM/United Artists; dir. Charles Crichton) A con artist (Jamie Lee Curtis) plots to obtain jewels stolen by her gangster lover (Tom Georgeson) and falls in love with his stuffy lawyer (John Cleese, who also wrote the screenplay). Kevin Kline won an Oscar for portraying her dim-witted henchman.

The Last Temptation of Christ (Cineplex Odeon Films/Universal; dir. Martin Scorsese) The decade's most controversial film offers a look at the human side of Jesus (Willem Dafoe). *See also* main entry.

Rain Man (Guber-Peters Company/MGM/United Artists; dir. Barry Levinson) A selfish young man (Tom Cruise) learns he has an autistic older brother (Dustin Hoffman) and discovers his humanity as they travel across the country together. It won Oscars for Best Picture, Best Director, Best Actor (Hoffman), and Best Original Screenplay.

The Thin Blue Line (American Playhouse/Third Floor/Miramax; dir. Errol Morris) Randall Dale Adams was released from prison in 1988 after Morris's documentary proved he was innocent of a 1976 Texas murder. The failure of the film to earn an Oscar nomination called into question the Academy's procedure for considering documentaries.

The Unbearable Lightness of Being (Saul Zaentz Company/Orion; dir. Philip Kaufman) Adapted from Milan Kundera's 1984 novel, the decade's most erotic drama presents a womanizing Prague surgeon (Daniel Day-Lewis) and his relations with his wife (Juliette Binoche) and his mistress (Lena Olin) against the backdrop of the 1968 Soviet invasion of Czechoslovakia.

Who Framed Roger Rabbit (Amblin Entertainment/Buena Vista/Silver Screen Partners III/Touchstone; dir. Robert Zemeckis) Cooperation between Disney and Warner Bros. allowed most of the 1940's cartoon characters to appear in this live-action and animation tribute to film noir. Its technical virtuosity earned four Oscars. *See also* main entry.

1989

Batman (Guber-Peters Company/Warner Bros.; dir. Tim Burton) The year's box-office champion finds Burton creating a darker view of the superhero than previously seen in serial and television versions. The affection of Batman/Bruce Wayne (Michael Keaton) for reporter Vicki Vale (Kim Basinger) makes him vulnerable to the evil Joker (Jack Nicholson). Its art direction won an Oscar.

Dead Poets Society (Buena Vista/Silver Screen Partners IV/Touchstone; dir. Peter Weir) Robin Williams subdues his manic style as an unconventional teacher at a 1959 prep school, though the teacher's unorthodox approach to education has tragic consequences. Tom Shulman's original screenplay won an Oscar.

Do the Right Thing (Forty Acres and a Mule Filmworks/Universal; dir. Spike Lee) Lee's look at racial tensions in his native Brooklyn earned him acclaim as a major American filmmaker. *See also* main entry.

Driving Miss Daisy (Zanuck Company/Warner Bros.; dir. Bruce Beresford) A wealthy Jewish woman (Jessica Tandy) and her black chauffeur (Morgan Freeman) struggle to understand changes in the South during the civil rights era. Alfred Uhry's adaptation of his Pulitzer Prize-winning play earned four Oscars, including Best Picture, Best Actress, and Best Screenplay.

Drugstore Cowboy (Avenue Entertainment; dir. Gus Van Sant) Matt Dillon leads a gang of misfits who rob pharmacies to feed their drug habits in independent filmmaker Van Sant's breakthrough film.

Field of Dreams (Gordon Company/Universal; dir. Phil Alden Robinson) W. P. Kinsella's 1982 novel *Shoeless Joe* is the basis of one of the most popular baseball films ever. An Iowa farmer (Kevin Costner) recruits a reclusive writer (James Earl Jones) and a doctor (Burt Lancaster) who played one game in the major leagues to witness a miracle in his cornfield.

Indiana Jones and the Last Crusade (Lucasfilm/Paramount; dir. Steven Spielberg) Spielberg's third Indiana Jones film finds Indy (Harrison Ford) joining his father (Sean Connery) on a quest for the Holy Grail in 1938. The film, which won a sound-effects Oscar, set a record by grossing fifty million dollars during its first week of American release.

The Little Mermaid (Buena Vista/Silver Screen Partners IV/Walt Disney; dir. Ron Clements) Disney began recovering its reputation for quality animation with this box-office hit about a teenager whose father is king of the sea. Alan Menken won Oscars for best song and score. *See also* main entry.

sex, lies, and videotape (Outlaw Productions/Miramax; dir. Steven Soderbergh) The decade's most acclaimed independent film launched Soderbergh's career and boosted those of stars Andie MacDowell, James Spader, Laura San Giacomo, and Peter Gallagher. *See also* main entry.

When Harry Met Sally . . . (Castle Rock Entertainment/Nelson Entertainment/Columbia; dir. Rob Reiner) The most popular romantic comedy of the 1980's shows how longtime friends (Meg Ryan and Billy Crystal) slowly fall in love. *See also* main entry.

Further Reading

Biskind, Peter. *Down and Dirty Pictures: Miramax, Sundance, and the Rise of Independent Film.* New York: Simon & Schuster, 2004. Entertaining, informative look at the birth of independent American films.

Brode, Douglas. *The Films of the Eighties.* Secaucus, N.J.: Carol, 1990. Heavily illustrated overview of the decade's films.

Diawara, Manthia, ed. *Black American Cinema.* New York: Routledge, 1993. Includes essays on the decade's biracial buddy films and the rise of black independent films.

Haines, Richard W. *The Moviegoing Experience: 1968-2001.* Jefferson, N.C.: McFarland, 2003. Explains how distribution changes, multiplexes, and home video affected the film industry.

Nowlan, Robert A., and Gwendolyn Wright Nolan. *The Films of the Eighties.* Jefferson, N.C.: McFarland, 1991. Encyclopedic look at 3,400 films.

Palmer, William J. *The Films of the Eighties: A Social History.* Carbondale: Southern Illinois University Press, 1993. Analysis of how the decade's films reflected American society.

Toplin, Robert Brent, ed. *Oliver Stone's USA: Film, History, and Controversy.* Lawrence: University of Kansas Press, 2000. Essays provide a detailed examination of Stone's work as a director and screenwriter.

Michael Adams

■ Entertainment: Academy Awards

A title or name followed by an asterisk (*) indicates the presence of a full-length essay within *The Eighties in America.*

1980

Best Picture: *Ordinary People**
Best Actor: Robert De Niro, *Raging Bull**
Best Actress: Sissy Spacek, *Coal Miner's Daughter*
Best Supporting Actor: Timothy Hutton, *Ordinary People**
Best Supporting Actress: Mary Steenburgen, *Melvin and Howard*
Best Director: Robert Redford, *Ordinary People**
Best Original Screenplay: Bo Goldman, *Melvin and Howard*
Best Adapted Screenplay: Alvin Sargent, *Ordinary People**
Best Cinematography: Geoffrey Unsworth and Ghislain Cloquet, *Tess*

1981

Best Picture: *Chariots of Fire*
Best Actor: Henry Fonda, *On Golden Pond**
Best Actress: Katharine Hepburn, *On Golden Pond**
Best Supporting Actor: John Gielgud, *Arthur*
Best Supporting Actress: Maureen Stapleton, *Reds*
Best Director: Warren Beatty, *Reds*
Best Original Screenplay: Colin Welland, *Chariots of Fire*
Best Adapted Screenplay: Ernest Thompson, *On Golden Pond**
Best Cinematography: Vittorio Storaro, *Reds*

1982

Best Picture: *Gandhi*
Best Actor: Ben Kingsley, *Gandhi*
Best Actress: Meryl Streep*, *Sophie's Choice*
Best Supporting Actor: Louis Gossett, Jr., *An Officer and a Gentleman*
Best Supporting Actress: Jessica Lange, *Tootsie*
Best Director: Richard Attenborough, *Gandhi*
Best Original Screenplay: John Briley, *Gandhi*
Best Adapted Screenplay: Costa-Gavras and Donald Stewart, *Missing*
Best Cinematography: Billy Williams and Ronny Taylor, *Gandhi*

1983

Best Picture: *Terms of Endearment**
Best Actor: Robert Duvall, *Tender Mercies*

Best Actress: Shirley MacLaine, *Terms of Endearment**
Best Supporting Actor: Jack Nicholson*, *Terms of Endearment**
Best Supporting Actress: Linda Hunt, *The Year of Living Dangerously*
Best Director: James L. Brooks, *Terms of Endearment**
Best Original Screenplay: Horton Foote, *Tender Mercies*
Best Adapted Screenplay: James L. Brooks, *Terms of Endearment**
Best Cinematography: Sven Nykvist, *Fanny and Alexander*

1984

Best Picture: *Amadeus*
Best Actor: F. Murray Abraham, *Amadeus*
Best Actress: Sally Field, *Places in the Heart*
Best Supporting Actor: Haing S. Ngor, *The Killing Fields*
Best Supporting Actress: Peggy Ashcroft, *A Passage to India*
Best Director: Milos Forman, *Amadeus*
Best Original Screenplay: Robert Benton, *Places in the Heart*
Best Adapted Screenplay: Peter Shaffer, *Amadeus*
Best Cinematography: Chris Menges, *The Killing Fields*

1985

Best Picture: *Out of Africa*
Best Actor: William Hurt*, *Kiss of the Spider Woman**
Best Actress: Geraldine Page, *The Trip to Bountiful*
Best Supporting Actor: Don Ameche, *Cocoon*
Best Supporting Actress: Anjelica Huston, *Prizzi's Honor*
Best Director: Sydney Pollack, *Out of Africa*
Best Original Screenplay: Earl W. Wallace, William Kelley, and Pamela Wallace, *Witness*
Best Adapted Screenplay: Kurt Luedtke, *Out of Africa*
Best Cinematography: David Watkin, *Out of Africa*

1986

Best Picture: *Platoon**
Best Actor: Paul Newman, *The Color of Money*
Best Actress: Marlee Matlin, *Children of a Lesser God*
Best Supporting Actor: Michael Caine, *Hannah and Her Sisters*
Best Supporting Actress: Dianne Wiest, *Hannah and Her Sisters*
Best Director: Oliver Stone, *Platoon**
Best Original Screenplay: Woody Allen, *Hannah and Her Sisters*
Best Adapted Screenplay: Ruth Prawer Jhabvala, *A Room with a View*
Best Cinematography: Chris Menges, *The Mission*

1987

Best Picture: *The Last Emperor*
Best Actor: Michael Douglas, *Wall Street**
Best Actress: Cher*, *Moonstruck*
Best Supporting Actor: Sean Connery, *The Untouchables*
Best Supporting Actress: Olympia Dukakis, *Moonstruck*
Best Director: Bernardo Bertolucci, *The Last Emperor*
Best Original Screenplay: John Patrick Shanley, *Moonstruck*
Best Adapted Screenplay: Mark Peploe and Bernardo Bertolucci, *The Last Emperor*
Best Cinematography: Vittorio Storaro, *The Last Emperor*

1988

Best Picture: *Rain Man*
Best Actor: Dustin Hoffman*, *Rain Man*
Best Actress: Jodie Foster, *The Accused*
Best Supporting Actor: Kevin Kline, *A Fish Called Wanda*
Best Supporting Actress: Geena Davis, *The Accidental Tourist*
Best Director: Barry Levinson, *Rain Man*
Best Original Screenplay: Ronald Bass and Barry Morrow; *Rain Man*
Best Adapted Screenplay: Christopher Hampton, *Dangerous Liaisons*
Best Cinematography: Peter Biziou, *Mississippi Burning*

1989

Best Picture: *Driving Miss Daisy*
Best Actor: Daniel Day-Lewis, *My Left Foot*
Best Actress: Jessica Tandy, *Driving Miss Daisy*
Best Supporting Actor: Denzel Washington, *Glory*
Best Supporting Actress: Brenda Fricker, *My Left Foot*
Best Director: Oliver Stone, *Born on the Fourth of July*
Best Original Screenplay: Tom Schulman, *Dead Poets Society*
Best Adapted Screenplay: Alfred Uhry, *Driving Miss Daisy*
Best Cinematography: Freddie Francis, *Glory*

■ Entertainment: Major Broadway Plays and Awards

This list contains all Broadway plays that ran for at least one full month between January 1, 1980, and December 31, 1989, and which had total runs of at least two hundred performances. It also includes plays with shorter runs that received major awards. An asterisk (*) next to a title or personage indicates that a full essay exists on the topic within *The Eighties in America*.

Plays Opening in 1979

Evita (opened September 25, 1979) 1,567 performances
  1980 Tony Awards: Best Musical, Robert Stigwood (producer); Best Book of a Musical, Tim Rice; Best Original Score, Andrew Lloyd Webber and Tim Rice; Best Actress in a Musical, Patti LuPone; Best Featured Actor in a Musical, Mandy Patinkin; Best Direction of a Musical, Harold Prince
  1980 New York Drama Critics Circle Award: Best Musical, Andrew Lloyd Webber and Tim Rice

Sugar Babies (opened October 8, 1979) 1,208 performances

Romantic Comedy (opened November 8, 1979) 396 performances

Strider (opened November 14, 1979) 214 performances

Bent (opened December 2, 1979) 241 performances

Oklahoma! (opened December 13, 1979) 293 performances (revival)

Plays Opening in 1980

Betrayal (opened January 5, 1980) 170 performances
  1980 New York Drama Critics Circle Award: Best Foreign Play, Harold Pinter (playwright)

West Side Story (opened February 14, 1980) 333 performances (revival)

Talley's Folly (opened February 20, 1980) 286 performances
  1980 Pulitzer Prize: Lanford Wilson (playwright)
  1980 New York Drama Critics Circle Award: Best Play, Lanford Wilson

Children of a Lesser God (opened March 30, 1980) 887 performances
  1980 Tony Awards: Best Play, Emanuel Azenberg, The Shubert Organization, Dasha Epstein, and Ron Dante (producers); Best Actor in a Play, John Rubinstein; Best Actress in a Play, Phyllis Frelich

I Ought to Be in Pictures (opened April 3, 1980) 324 performances
  1980 Tony Awards: Best Featured Actress in a Play, Dinah Manoff

Morning's at Seven (opened April 10, 1980) 564 performances (revival)
  1980 Tony Awards: Best Featured Actor in a Play, David Rounds; Best Direction of a Play, Vivian Matalon; Best Reproduction of a Play or Musical, Elizabeth I. McCann, Nelle Nugent, and Ray Larson (producers)

Barnum (opened April 30, 1980) 854 performances
  1980 Tony Awards: Best Actor in a Musical, Jim Dale

A Day in Hollywood/A Night in the Ukraine (opened May 1, 1980) 588 performances
  1980 Tony Awards: Best Featured Actress in a Musical, Priscilla Lopez; Best Choreography, Tommy Tune and Thommie Walsh

Home (opened May 7, 1980) 278 performances

42nd Street (opened August 25, 1980) 3,486 performances
  1981 Tony Awards: Best Musical, David Merrick (producer); Best Choreography, Gower Champion

Fifth of July (opened November 5, 1980) 511 performances
  1981 Tony Awards: Best Featured Actress in a Play, Swoosie Kurtz

Lunch Hour (opened November 12, 1980) 262 performances

A Lesson from Aloes (opened November 17, 1980) 96 performances
1981 New York Drama Critics Circle Award: Best Play, Athol Fugard (playwright)

Amadeus (opened December 17, 1980) 1,181 performances
1981 Tony Awards: Best Play, Peter Shaffer (playwright) and The Shubert Organization, Elizabeth I. McCann, Nelle Nugent, and Roger S. Berlind (producers); Best Actor in a Play, Ian McKellen; Best Direction of a Play, Peter Hall
1981 New York Drama Critics Circle Award: Best Play Runner-Up, Peter Shaffer

Plays Opening in 1981

The Pirates of Penzance (opened January 8, 1981) 787 performances (revival)
1981 Tony Awards: Best Actor in a Musical, Kevin Kline; Best Direction of a Musical, Wilford Leach; Best Reproduction of a Play or Musical, Joseph Papp (producer)
1981 New York Drama Critics Circle Award: Special Citation

Piaf (opened February 5, 1981) 165 performances
1981 Tony Awards: Best Actress in a Play, Jane Lapotaire

Sophisticated Ladies (opened March 1, 1981) 767 performances
1981 Tony Awards: Best Featured Actor in a Musical, Hinton Battle

Woman of the Year (opened March 29, 1981) 770 performances
1981 Tony Awards: Best Book of a Musical, Peter Stone; Best Original Score, John Kander and Fred Ebb; Best Actress in a Musical, Lauren Bacall; Best Featured Actress in a Musical, Marilyn Cooper

The Floating Light Bulb (opened April 27, 1981) 62 performances
1981 Tony Awards: Best Featured Actor in a Play, Brian Backer

Lena Horne: "The Lady and Her Music" (opened May 12, 1981) 333 performances
1981 New York Drama Critics Circle Award: Special Citation

The Life and Adventures of Nicholas Nickleby (October 4, 1981) 49 performances
1982 Tony Awards: Best Play, David Edgar (adapter) and James M. Nederlander, The Shubert Organization, Elizabeth I. McCann, and Nelle Nugent (producers); Best Actor in a Play, Roger Rees; Best Direction of a Play, Trevor Nunn 1982 New York Drama Critics Circle Award: Best Play, David Edgar

Crimes of the Heart (opened November 4, 1981) 535 performances
1981 Pulitzer Prize: Beth Henley* (playwright)
1981 New York Drama Critics Circle Award: Best American Play, Beth Henley*

Mass Appeal (opened November 12, 1981) 212 performances

The Dresser (opened November 19, 1981) 200 performances

Dreamgirls (opened December 20, 1981) 1,521 performances
1982 Tony Awards: Best Book of a Musical, Tom Eyen; Best Actor in a Musical, Ben Harney; Best Actress in a Musical, Jennifer Holliday; Best Featured Actor in a Musical, Cleavant Derricks; Best Choreography, Michael Bennett and Michael Peters

Plays Opening in 1982

Joseph and the Amazing Technicolor Dreamcoat (opened January 27, 1982) 747 performances

Pump Boys and Dinettes (opened February 4, 1982) 573 performances

Agnes of God (March 30, 1982) 599 performances
1982 Tony Awards: Best Featured Actress in a Play, Amanda Plummer

Medea (opened May 2, 1982) 65 performances
1982 Tony Awards: Best Actress in a Play, Zoe Caldwell

"MASTER HAROLD" . . . and the Boys (opened May 4, 1982) 344 performances
1982 Tony Awards: Best Featured Actor in a Play, Zakes Mokae

1982 New York Drama Critics Circle Award: Best Play Runner-Up, Athol Fugard (playwright)

Nine (opened May 9, 1982) 729 performances
1982 Tony Awards: Best Musical, Michel Stuart, Harvey J. Klaris, Roger S. Berlind, James M. Nederlander, Francie LeFrak, and Kenneth D. Greenblatt (producers); Best Original Score, Maury Yeston; Best Featured Actress in a Musical, Lillane Montevecchi; Best Direction of a Musical, Tommy Tune

*Torch Song Trilogy** (opened June 10, 1982) 1,222 performances
1983 Tony Awards: Best Play, Harvey Fierstein (playwright) and Kenneth Waissman, Martin Markinson, Lawrence Lane, John Glines, BetMar, and Donald Tick (producers); Best Actor in a Play, Harvey Fierstein
1982 New York Drama Critics Circle Award: Best American Play Runner-Up, Harvey Fierstein

Little Shop of Horrors (opened July 27, 1982) 2,209 performances
1983 New York Drama Critics Circle Award: Best Musical, Alan Menken (music) and Howard Ashman (book and lyrics)

*Cats** (opened October 7, 1982) 7,485 performances
1983 Tony Awards: Best Musical, Cameron Mackintosh, The Really Useful Theatre Company, David Geffen, and the Shubert Organization (producers); Best Book of a Musical, T. S. Eliot; Best Original Score, Andrew Lloyd Webber and T. S. Eliot; Best Featured Actress in a Musical, Betty Buckley; Best Direction of a Musical, Trevor Nunn

Foxfire (opened November 11, 1982) 213 performances
1983 Tony Awards: Best Actress in a Play, Jessica Tandy

Steaming (December 12, 1982) 65 performances
1983 Tony Awards: Best Featured Actress in a Play, Judith Ivey

Plays Opening in 1983

Plenty (opened January 6, 1983) 92 performances
1983 New York Drama Critics Circle Award: Best Foreign Play, David Hare (playwright)

On Your Toes (March 6, 1983) 505 performances (revival)
1983 Tony Awards: Best Actress in a Musical, Natalia Makarova; Best Reproduction of a Play or Musical, Alfred de Liagre, Jr., Roger L. Stevens, John Mauceri, Donald R. Seawall, and André Pastoria (producers)

Brighton Beach Memoirs (opened March 27, 1983) 1,299 performances
1983 Tony Awards: Best Featured Actor in a Play, Matthew Broderick*; Best Direction of a Play, Gene Saks
1983 New York Drama Critics Circle Award: Best Play, Neil Simon (playwright)

'night, Mother (opened March 31, 1983) 380 performances
1983 Pulitzer Prize: Marsha Norman (playwright)
1983 New York Drama Critics Circle Award: Best Play Runner-Up, Marsha Norman

You Can't Take It With You (opened April 4, 1983) 312 performances (revival)

My One and Only (opened May 1, 1983) 767 performances
1983 Tony Awards: Best Actor in a Musical, Tommy Tune; Best Featured Actor in a Musical, Charles Honi Coles; Best Choreography, Tommy Tune and Thommie Walsh

The Caine Mutiny Court-Martial (opened May 5, 1983) 216 performances (revival)

La Cage aux Folles (opened August 21, 1983) 1,761 performances
1984 Tony Awards: Best Musical, Allan Carr, Kenneth D. Greenblatt, Marvin A. Krauss, Stewart F. Lane, James M. Nederlander, Martin Richards, Barry Brown, and Fritz Holt (producers); Best Book of a Musical, Harvey Fierstein; Best Original Score, Jerry Herman; Best Actor in a Musical, George Hearn; Best Direction of a Musical, Arthur Laurents

Zorba (opened October 16, 1983) 362 performances (revival)
1984 Tony Awards: Best Featured Actress in a Musical, Lila Kedrova

Baby (opened December 4, 1983) 241 performances

Noises Off (opened December 11, 1983) 553 performances

The Tap Dance Kid (opened December 21, 1983) 669 performances
1984 Tony Awards: Best Featured Actor in a Musical, Hinton Battle; Best Choreography, Danny Daniels

Plays Opening in 1984

The Real Thing (opened January 5, 1984) 566 performances
1984 Tony Awards: Best Play, Tom Stoppard (playwright) and Emanuel Azenberg, The Shubert Organization, Icarus Productions, Byron Goldman, Ivan Bloch, Roger S. Berlind, and Michael Codron (producers); Best Actor in a Play, Jeremy Irons; Best Actress in a Play, Glenn Close*; Best Featured Actress in a Play, Christine Baranski; Best Direction of a Play, Mike Nichols
1984 New York Drama Critics Circle Award: Best Play, Tom Stoppard

The Rink (opened February 9, 1984) 204 performances
1984 Tony Awards: Best Actress in a Musical, Chita Rivera

Glengarry Glen Ross (opened March 25, 1984) 378 performances
1984 Tony Awards: Best Featured Actor in a Play, Joe Mantegna
1984 Pulitzer Prize: David Mamet* (playwright)
1984 New York Drama Critics Circle Award: Best American Play, David Mamet*

Sunday in the Park with George (opened May 2, 1984) 604 performances
1985 Pulitzer Prize: Stephen Sondheim and James Lapine
1984 New York Drama Critics Circle Award: Best Musical, Stephen Sondheim (music and lyrics) and James Lapine (book)

Design for Living (opened June 20, 1984) 245 performances (revival)

Hurlyburly (opened August 7, 1984) 343 performances
1985 Tony Awards: Best Featured Actress in a Play, Judith Ivey

Ma Rainey's Black Bottom (opened October 11, 1984) 276 performances
1985 New York Drama Critics Circle Award: Best Play, August Wilson* (playwright)

Much Ado About Nothing (opened October 14, 1984) 53 performances (revival)
1985 Tony Awards: Best Actor in a Play, Derek Jacobi

Plays Opening in 1985

The Odd Couple (opened January 11, 1985) 295 performances (revival)

Joe Egg (opened March 27, 1985) 93 performances (revival)
1985 Tony Awards: Best Actress in a Play, Stockard Channing; Best Reproduction of a Play or Musical, The Shubert Organization, Emanuel Azenberg, Roger S. Berlind, Ivan Bloch, and MTM Enterprises, Inc. (producers)

Biloxi Blues (opened March 28, 1985) 524 performances
1985 Tony Awards: Best Play, Neil Simon (playwright) and Emanuel Azenberg and the Center Theater Group/Ahmanson Theater (producers); Best Featured Actor in a Play, Barry Miller; Best Direction of a Play, Gene Saks
1985: New York Drama Critics Circle Award: Best Play Runner-Up, Neil Simon

Grind (opened April 16, 1985) 71 performances
1985 Tony Awards: Best Featured Actress in a Musical, Leilani Jones

Big River (opened April 25, 1985) 1,005 performances
1985 Tony Awards: Best Musical, Rocco Landesman, Heidi Landesman, Rick Steiner, M. Anthony Fisher, and Dodger Theatricals (producers); Best Book of a Musical, William Hauptman; Best Original Score, Roger Miller; Best Featured Actor in a Musical, Ron Richardson; Best Direction of a Musical, Des McAnuff

As Is (opened May 1, 1985) 285 performances

Doubles (opened May 8, 1985) 277 performances

Singin' in the Rain (opened July 2, 1985) 367 performances

Song and Dance (opened September 18, 1985) 474 performances
1986 Tony Awards: Best Actress in a Musical, Bernadette Peters

The Search for Signs of Intelligent Life in the Universe (opened September 26, 1985) 391 performances
1986 Tony Awards: Best Actress in a Play, Lily Tomlin
1986 New York Drama Critics Circle Award: Special Citation, Lily Tomlin and Jane Wagner

I'm Not Rappaport (opened November 19, 1985) 891 performances
1986 Tony Awards: Best Play, Herb Gardner (playwright) and James Walsh, Lewis Allen, and Martin Heinfling (producers); Best Actor in a Play, Judd Hirsch

The Mystery of Edwin Drood (opened December 2, 1985) 608 performances
1986 Tony Awards: Best Musical, Joseph Papp (producer); Best Book of a Musical, Rupert Holmes; Best Original Score, Rupert Holmes; Best Actor in a Musical, George Rose; Best Direction of a Musical, Wilford Leach

Benefactors (opened December 22, 1985) 217 performances
1986 New York Drama Critics Circle Award: Best Foreign Play, Michael Frayn (playwright)

Plays Opening in 1986
Big Deal (opened April 10, 1986) 69 performances
1986 Tony Awards: Best Choreography, Bob Fosse

Social Security (opened April 17, 1986) 388 performances

Sweet Charity (opened April 27, 1986) 369 performances (revival)
1986 Tony Awards: Best Featured Actor in a Musical, Michael Rupert; Best Featured Actress in a

Musical, Bebe Neuwirth; Best Reproduction of a Play or a Musical, Jerry Minskoff, James M. Nederlander, Arthur Rubin, and Joseph Harris (producers)

The House of Blue Leaves (opened April 29, 1986) 398 performances
1986 Tony Awards: Best Featured Actor in a Play, John Mahoney; Best Featured Actress in a Play, Swoosie Kurtz; Best Direction of a Play, Jerry Zaks

Arsenic and Old Lace (opened June 26, 1986) 221 performances (revival)

Me and My Girl (opened August 10, 1986) 1,420 performances
1987 Tony Awards: Best Actor in a Musical, Robert Lindsay; Best Actress in a Musical, Maryann Plunkett; Best Choreography, Gillian Gregory
1987 New York Drama Critics Circle Award: Best Musical Runner-Up, Noel Gay (music), Douglas Furber (book and lyrics), and L. Arthur Rose (book and lyrics)

Broadway Bound (opened December 4, 1986) 756 performances
1987 Tony Awards: Best Actress in a Play, Linda Lavin; Best Featured Actor in a Play, John Randolph

Jackie Mason's The World According to Me! (opened December 22, 1986) 367 performances
1987 Tony Awards: Special Award, Jackie Mason

Plays Opening in 1987
The Nerd (opened March 2, 1987) 441 performances

Coastal Disturbances (opened March 4, 1987) 350 performances

Les Misérables (opened March 12, 1987) 6,680 performances
1987 Tony Awards: Best Musical, Cameron Mackintosh (producer); Best Book of a Musical, Alain Boublil and Claude-Michel Schönberg; Best Original Score, Claude-Michel Schönberg, Herbert Kretzmer, and Alain Boublil; Best Featured Actor in a Musical, Michael Maguire; Best Featured Actress in a Musical, Frances Ruffelle; Best

Direction of a Musical, Trevor Nunn and John Caird

1987 New York Drama Critics Circle Award: Best Musical, Claude-Michel Schönberg, Alain Boublil, and Herbert Kretzmer

Starlight Express (opened March 15, 1987) 761 performances

Fences (opened March 26, 1987) 525 performances
1987 Tony Awards: Best Play, August Wilson* (playwright) and Carole Shorenstein Hays and Yale Repertory Theatre (producers); Best Actor in a Play, James Earl Jones; Best Featured Actress in a Play, Mary Alice: Best Direction of a Play, Lloyd Richards
1987 Pulitzer Prize: August Wilson*
1987 New York Drama Critics Circle Award: Best Play, August Wilson*

Les Liaisons Dangereuses (opened April 30, 1987) 149 performances
1987 New York Drama Critics Circle Award: Best Foreign Play, Christopher Hampton (playwright)

Burn This (opened October 14, 1987) 437 performances
1988 Tony Awards: Best Actress in a Play, Joan Allen

Anything Goes (opened October 19, 1987) 784 performances (revival)
1988 Tony Awards: Best Featured Actor in a Musical, Bill McCutcheon; Best Choreography, Michael Smuin; Best Revival, Lincoln Center Theater (producer)

Cabaret (opened October 22, 1987) 261 performances (revival)

Into the Woods (opened November 5, 1987) 765 performances
1988 Tony Awards: Best Book of a Musical, James Lapine; Best Original Score, Stephen Sondheim; Best Actress in a Musical, Joanna Gleason
1988 New York Drama Critics Circle Award: Best Musical, Stephen Sondheim and James Lapine

Plays Opening in 1988

*The Phantom of the Opera** (opened January 26, 1988)
8,213 performances as of October 7, 2007
1988 Tony Awards: Best Musical, Cameron Mackintosh and the Really Useful Theatre Company (producers); Best Actor in a Musical, Michael Crawford; Best Featured Actress in a Musical, Judy Kaye; Best Direction of a Musical, Harold Prince
1988 New York Drama Critics Circle Award: Best Musical Runner-Up, Andrew Lloyd Webber, Charles Hart, and Richard Stilgoe

Sarafina! (opened January 28, 1988) 597 performances

M. Butterfly (opened March 20, 1988) 777 performances
1988 Tony Awards: Best Play, David Henry Hwang* (playwright) and Stuart Ostrow and David Geffen (producers); Best Featured Actor in a Play, B. D. Wong; Best Direction of a Play, John Dexter
1988 New York Drama Critics Circle Award: Best Play Runner-Up, David Henry Hwang*

Joe Turner's Come and Gone (opened March 27, 1988) 105 performances
1988 Tony Awards: Best Featured Actress in a Play, L. Scott Caldwell
1988 New York Drama Critics Circle Award: Best Play, August Wilson* (playwright)

Romance, Romance (opened May 1, 1988) 297 performances

Jackie Mason's The World According to Me! (opened May 2, 1988) 206 performances (return engagement)

Speed-the-Plow (opened May 3, 1988) 279 performances
1988 Tony Awards: Best Actor in a Play, Ron Silver

Rumors (opened November 17, 1988) 535 performances
1989 Tony Awards: Best Featured Actress in a Play, Christine Baranski

Plays Opening in 1989

Black and Blue (opened January 26, 1989) 829 performances
   1989 Tony Awards: Best Actress in a Musical, Ruth Brown; Best Choreography, Cholly Atkins, Henry LeTang, Frankie Manning, and Fayard Nicholas

Shirley Valentine (opened February 16, 1989) 324 performances
   1989 Tony Awards: Best Actress in a Play, Pauline Collins

Jerome Robbins' Broadway (opened February 26, 1989) 633 performances
   1989 Tony Awards: Best Musical, The Shubert Organization, Roger S. Berlind, Suntory International Corporation, Byron Goldman, and Emanuel Azenberg (producers); Best Actor in a Musical, Jason Alexander; Best Featured Actor in a Musical, Scott Wise; Best Featured Actress in a Musical, Debbie Shapiro; Best Direction of a Musical, Jerome Robbins

Lend Me a Tenor (opened March 2, 1989) 476 performances
   1989 Tony Awards: Best Actor in a Play, Philip Bosco; Best Direction of a Play, Jerry Zaks

The Heidi Chronicles* (opened March 9, 1989) 622 performances
   1989 Tony Awards: Best Play, Wendy Wasserstein (playwright) and The Shubert Organization and Playwrights Horizons (producers); Best Featured Actor in a Play, Boyd Gaines

   1989 Pulitzer Prize: Wendy Wasserstein
   1989 New York Drama Critics Circle Award: Best Play, Wendy Wasserstein

Aristocrats (opened April 11, 1989) 189 performances
   1989 New York Drama Critics Circle Award: Best Foreign Play, Brian Friel (playwright)

Largely New York (opened May 1, 1989) 144 performances
   1989 New York Drama Critics Circle Award: Special Citation, Bill Irwin

Meet Me in St. Louis (opened November 2, 1989) 253 performances

Grand Hotel (opened November 12, 1989) 1,018 performances

A Few Good Men (opened November 15, 1989) 497 performances

Gypsy (opened November 16, 1989) 476 performances (revival)

The Circle (opened November 20, 1989) 208 performances (revival)

City of Angels (opened December 12, 1989) 878 performances

Tru (opened December 19, 1989) 295 performances (revival)

■ Entertainment: Most-Watched U.S. Television Shows

This list shows the top-ten U.S. television programs of each September-April season, as ranked by the Nielsen Media Company. The ratings in the right column indicate the average percentage of American homes with televisions watching each show. For example, during the 1980-1981 season, 34.5 percent of all American homes with a television watched *Dallas* on the evenings that it was broadcast. Titles followed by an asterisk (*) indicate that the program has its own full-length essay within *The Eighties in America*.

1980-1981
1. *Dallas**	CBS	34.5
2. *The Dukes of Hazzard*	CBS	27.3
3. *60 Minutes*	CBS	27.0
4. *M*A*S*H*	CBS	25.7
5. *The Love Boat*	ABC	24.3
6. *The Jeffersons*	CBS	23.5
7. *Alice*	CBS	22.9
8. *House Calls*	CBS	22.4
Three's Company	ABC	22.4
10. *Little House on the Prairie*	NBC	22.1

1981-1982
1. *Dallas**	CBS	28.4
2. *60 Minutes*	CBS	27.4
3. *The Jeffersons*	CBS	23.4
4. *Three's Company*	ABC	23.3
5. *Alice*	CBS	22.7
6. *The Dukes of Hazzard*	CBS	22.6
Too Close for Comfort	ABC	22.6
8. *ABC Monday Night Movie*	ABC	22.5
9. *M*A*S*H*	CBS	22.3
10. *One Day at a Time*	CBS	22.0

1982-1983
1. *60 Minutes*	CBS	25.5
2. *Dallas**	CBS	24.6
3. *M*A*S*H*	CBS	22.6
*Magnum, P.I.**	CBS	22.6
5. *Dynasty**	ABC	22.4
6. *Three's Company*	ABC	21.2
7. *Simon and Simon*	CBS	21.0
8. *Falcon Crest*	CBS	20.7
9. *The Love Boat*	ABC	20.3
10. *The A-Team*	NBC	20.1
Monday Night Football	ABC	20.1

1983-1984
1. *Dallas**	CBS	25.7
2. *60 Minutes*	CBS	24.2
3. *Dynasty**	ABC	24.1
4. *The A-Team*	NBC	24.0
5. *Simon and Simon*	CBS	23.8
6. *Magnum, P.I.**	CBS	22.4
7. *Falcon Crest*	CBS	22.0
8. *Kate and Allie*	CBS	21.9
9. *Hotel*	ABC	21.1
10. *Cagney and Lacey**	CBS	20.9

1984-1985
1. *Dynasty**	ABC	25.0
2. *Dallas**	CBS	24.7
3. *The Cosby Show**	NBC	24.2
4. *60 Minutes*	CBS	22.2
5. *Family Ties**	NBC	22.1
6. *The A-Team*	NBC	21.9
7. *Simon and Simon*	CBS	21.8
8. *Murder, She Wrote*	CBS	20.1
9. *Knot's Landing*	CBS	20.0
10. *Falcon Crest*	CBS	19.9
Crazy Like a Fox	CBS	19.9

1985-1986
1. *The Cosby Show**	NBC	33.7
2. *Family Ties**	NBC	30.0
3. *Murder, She Wrote*	CBS	25.3
4. *60 Minutes*	CBS	23.9
5. *Cheers**	NBC	23.7
6. *Dallas**	CBS	21.9
7. *Dynasty**	ABC	21.8
*The Golden Girls**	NBC	21.8
9. *Miami Vice**	NBC	21.3
10. *Who's the Boss?*	ABC	21.1

1986-1987
1. *The Cosby Show**	NBC	34.9
2. *Family Ties**	NBC	32.7
3. *Cheers**	CBS	27.2
4. *Murder, She Wrote*	CBS	25.4
5. *The Golden Girls**	NBC	24.5
6. *60 Minutes*	CBS	23.3
7. *Night Court*	NBC	23.2

8. *Growing Pains*	ABC	22.7
9. *Moonlighting**	ABC	22.4
10. *Who's the Boss?*	ABC	22.0

1987-1988

1. *The Cosby Show**	NBC	27.8
2. *A Different World*	NBC	25.0
3. *Cheers**	NBC	23.4
4. *The Golden Girls**	NBC	21.8
5. *Growing Pains*	ABC	21.3
6. *Who's the Boss?*	ABC	21.2
7. *Night Court*	NBC	20.8
8. *60 Minutes*	CBS	20.6
9. *Murder, She Wrote*	CBS	20.2
10. *Alf*	NBC	18.8
*The Wonder Years**	ABC	18.8

1988-1989

1. *The Cosby Show**	NBC	25.6
2. *Roseanne*	ABC	23.8

3. *A Different World*	NBC	23.0
4. *Cheers**	NBC	22.3
5. *60 Minutes*	CBS	21.7
6. *The Golden Girls**	NBC	21.4
7. *Who's the Boss?*	ABC	20.8
8. *Murder, She Wrote*	CBS	19.9
9. *Empty Nest*	NBC	19.2
10. *Anything but Love*	ABC	19.0

1989-1990

1. *The Cosby Show**	NBC	23.1
Roseanne	ABC	23.1
3. *Cheers**	NBC	22.7
4. *A Different World*	NBC	21.1
5. *America's Funniest Home Videos*	ABC	20.9
6. *The Golden Girls**	NBC	20.1
7. *60 Minutes*	CBS	19.7
8. *The Wonder Years**	ABC	19.2
9. *Empty Nest*	NBC	18.9
10. *Monday Night Football*	ABC	18.1

■ Entertainment: Emmy Awards

The categories and titles of the Emmy Awards changed almost every year. This list contains a selection of the television awards generally considered to be the most important. Programs followed by an asterisk (*) are the subject of their own full-length essay within *The Eighties in America*.

1980-1981

Outstanding Drama Series: *Hill Street Blues** (NBC)
Outstanding Comedy Series: *Taxi* (ABC)
Outstanding Limited Series: *Shogun* (NBC)
Outstanding Drama Special: *Playing for Time* (CBS)
Outstanding Variety, Music, or Comedy Program: *Lily: Sold Out* (CBS)
Outstanding Lead Actor in a Drama Series: Daniel J. Travanti, *Hill Street Blues** (NBC)
Outstanding Lead Actress in a Drama Series: Barbara Babcock, *Hill Street Blues** (NBC)
Outstanding Lead Actor in a Comedy Series: Judd Hirsch, *Taxi* (ABC)
Outstanding Lead Actress in a Comedy Series: Isabel Sanford, *The Jeffersons* (CBS)
Outstanding Supporting Actor in a Drama Series: Michael Conrad, *Hill Street Blues** (NBC)
Outstanding Supporting Actress in a Drama Series: Nancy Marchand, *Lou Grant* (CBS)
Outstanding Supporting Actor in a Comedy or Variety or Music Series: Danny De Vito, *Taxi* (ABC)
Outstanding Supporting Actress in a Comedy or Variety or Music Series: Eileen Brennan, *Private Benjamin* (CBS)
Outstanding Directing in a Drama Series: Robert Butler, *Hill Street Blues** (NBC)
Outstanding Directing in a Comedy Series: James Burrows, *Taxi* (ABC)
Outstanding Directing in Variety, Music, or Comedy Program: Don Mischer, *The Kennedy Center Honors: A National Celebration* (CBS)

1981-1982

Outstanding Drama Series: *Hill Street Blues** (NBC)
Outstanding Comedy Series: *Barney Miller* (ABC)
Outstanding Limited Series: *Marco Polo* (NBC)
Outstanding Drama Special: *A Woman Called Golda* (syndicated)
Outstanding Variety, Music, or Comedy Program: *Night of 100 Stars* (ABC)
Outstanding Lead Actor in a Drama Series: Daniel J. Travanti, *Hill Street Blues** (NBC)

Outstanding Lead Actress in a Drama Series: Michael Learned, *Nurse* (CBS)
Outstanding Lead Actor in a Comedy Series: Alan Alda, *M*A*S*H* (CBS)
Outstanding Lead Actress in a Comedy Series: Carol Kane, *Taxi* (ABC)
Outstanding Supporting Actor in a Drama Series: Michael Conrad, *Hill Street Blues** (NBC)
Outstanding Supporting Actress in a Drama Series: Nancy Marchand, *Lou Grant* (CBS)
Outstanding Supporting Actor in a Comedy or Variety or Music Series: Christopher Lloyd, *Taxi* (ABC)
Outstanding Supporting Actress in a Comedy or Variety or Music Series: Loretta Swit, *M*A*S*H* (CBS)
Outstanding Directing in a Drama Series: Harry Harris, *Fame* (NBC)
Outstanding Directing in a Comedy Series: Alan Rafkin, *One Day at a Time* (CBS)
Outstanding Directing in a Variety or Music Program: Dwight Hemion, *Goldie and Kids . . . Listen to Us* (ABC)

1982-1983

Outstanding Drama Series: *Hill Street Blues** (NBC)
Outstanding Comedy Series: *Cheers** (NBC)
Outstanding Limited Series: *Nicholas Nickleby* (syndicated)
Outstanding Drama Special: *Special Bulletin* (NBC)
Outstanding Variety, Music, or Comedy Program: *Motown 25: Yesterday, Today, Forever* (NBC)
Outstanding Lead Actor in a Drama Series: Ed Flanders, *St. Elsewhere** (NBC)
Outstanding Lead Actress in a Drama Series: Tyne Daley, *Cagney and Lacey** (CBS)
Outstanding Lead Actor in a Comedy Series: Judd Hirsch, *Taxi* (ABC)
Outstanding Lead Actress in a Comedy Series: Shelley Long, *Cheers** (NBC)
Outstanding Supporting Actor in a Drama Series: James Coco, *St. Elsewhere** (NBC)
Outstanding Supporting Actress in a Drama Series: Doris Roberts, *St. Elsewhere** (NBC)

Outstanding Supporting Actor in a Comedy, Variety, or Music Series: Christopher Lloyd, *Taxi* (ABC)

Outstanding Supporting Actress in a Comedy, Variety, or Music Series: Carol Kane, *Taxi* (ABC)

Outstanding Directing in a Drama Series: Jeff Bleckner, *Hill Street Blues** (NBC)

Outstanding Directing in a Comedy Series: James Burrows, *Cheers** (NBC)

Outstanding Directing in a Variety or Music Program: Dwight Hemion, *Sheena Easton . . . Act One* (NBC)

1983-1984

Outstanding Drama Series: *Hill Street Blues** (NBC)

Outstanding Comedy Series: *Cheers** (NBC)

Outstanding Limited Series: *Concealed Enemies: American Playhouse* (PBS)

Outstanding Drama/Comedy Special: *Something About Amelia: An ABC Theatre Presentation* (ABC)

Outstanding Variety, Music, or Comedy Program: *The Sixth Annual Kennedy Center Honors: A Celebration of the Performing Arts* (CBS)

Outstanding Lead Actor in a Drama Series: Tom Selleck, *Magnum, P.I.** (CBS)

Lead Actress in a Drama Series: Tyne Daley, *Cagney and Lacey** (CBS)

Outstanding Lead Actor in a Comedy Series: John Ritter, *Three's Company* (ABC)

Outstanding Lead Actress in a Comedy Series: Jane Curtin, *Kate and Allie* (CBS)

Outstanding Supporting Actor in a Drama Series: Bruce Weitz, *Hill Street Blues** (NBC)

Outstanding Supporting Actress in a Drama Series: Alfre Woodard, *Hill Street Blues** (NBC)

Outstanding Supporting Actor in a Comedy Series: Pat Harrington, *One Day at a Time* (CBS)

Outstanding Supporting Actress in a Comedy Series: Rhea Perlman, *Cheers** (NBC)

Outstanding Directing in a Drama Series: Corey Allen, *Hill Street Blues** (NBC)

Outstanding Directing in a Comedy Series: Bill Persky, *Kate and Allie* (CBS)

Outstanding Directing in a Variety or Music Program: Dwight Hemion, *Here's Television Entertainment* (NBC)

1984-1985

Outstanding Drama Series: *Cagney and Lacey** (CBS)

Outstanding Comedy Series: *The Cosby Show** (NBC)

Outstanding Limited Series: *The Jewel in the Crown: Masterpiece Theatre* (PBS)

Outstanding Drama/Comedy Special: *Do You Remember Love* (CBS)

Outstanding Variety, Music, or Comedy Program: *Motown Returns to the Apollo* (NBC)

Outstanding Lead Actor in a Drama Series: William Daniels, *St. Elsewhere** (NBC)

Outstanding Lead Actress in a Drama Series: Tyne Daly, *Cagney and Lacey** (CBS)

Outstanding Lead Actor in a Comedy Series: Robert Guillaume, *Benson* (ABC)

Outstanding Lead Actress in a Comedy Series: Jane Curtin, *Kate and Allie* (CBS)

Outstanding Supporting Actor in a Drama Series: Edward James Olmos, *Miami Vice** (NBC)

Outstanding Supporting Actress in a Drama Series: Betty Thomas, *Hill Street Blues** (NBC)

Outstanding Supporting Actor in a Comedy Series: John Larroquette, *Night Court* (NBC)

Outstanding Supporting Actress in a Comedy Series: Rhea Perlman, *Cheers** (NBC)

Outstanding Directing in a Drama Series: Karen Arthur, *Cagney and Lacey** (CBS)

Outstanding Directing in a Comedy Series: Jay Sandrich, *The Cosby Show** (NBC)

Outstanding Directing in a Variety or Music Program: Terry Hughes, *Sweeney Todd: Great Performances* (PBS)

1985-1986

Outstanding Drama Series: *Cagney and Lacey** (CBS)

Outstanding Comedy Series: *The Golden Girls** (NBC)

Outstanding Miniseries: *Peter the Great* (NBC)

Outstanding Drama/Comedy Special: *Love Is Never Silent: Hallmark Hall of Fame* (NBC)

Outstanding Variety, Music, or Comedy Program: *The Kennedy Center Honors: A Celebration of the Performing Arts* (CBS)

Outstanding Lead Actor in a Drama Series: William Daniels, *St. Elsewhere** (NBC)

Outstanding Lead Actress in a Drama Series: Sharon Gless, *Cagney and Lacey** (CBS)

Outstanding Lead Actor in a Comedy Series: Michael J. Fox, *Family Ties** (NBC)

Outstanding Lead Actress in a Comedy Series: Betty White, *The Golden Girls** (NBC)

Outstanding Supporting Actor in a Drama Series: John Karlen, *Cagney and Lacey** (CBS)

Outstanding Supporting Actress in a Drama Series: Bonnie Bartlett, *St. Elsewhere* * (NBC)

Outstanding Supporting Actor in a Comedy Series: John Larroquette, *Night Court* (NBC)

Outstanding Supporting Actress in a Comedy Series: Rhea Perlman, *Cheers* * (NBC)

Outstanding Directing in a Drama Series: Georg Stanford Brown, *Cagney and Lacey* * (CBS)

Outstanding Directing in a Comedy Series: Jay Sandrich, *The Cosby Show* * (NBC)

Outstanding Directing in a Variety or Music Program: Warris Hussein, *Copacabana* (CBS)

1986-1987

Outstanding Drama Series: *L.A. Law* * (NBC)

Outstanding Comedy Series: *The Golden Girls* * (NBC)

Outstanding Miniseries: *A Year in the Life* (NBC)

Outstanding Drama/Comedy Special: *Promise: Hallmark Hall of Fame* (CBS)

Outstanding Variety, Music, or Comedy Program: *The 1987 Tony Awards* (CBS)

Outstanding Lead Actor in a Drama Series: Bruce Willis, *Moonlighting* * (ABC)

Outstanding Lead Actress in a Drama Series: Sharon Gless, *Cagney and Lacey* * (CBS)

Outstanding Lead Actor in a Comedy Series: Michael J. Fox, *Family Ties* * (NBC)

Outstanding Lead Actress in a Comedy Series: Rue McClanahan, *The Golden Girls* * (NBC)

Outstanding Supporting Actor in a Drama Series: John Hillerman, *Magnum, P.I.* * (CBS)

Outstanding Supporting Actress in a Drama Series: Bonnie Bartlett, *St. Elsewhere* * (NBC)

Outstanding Supporting Actor in a Comedy Series: John Larroquette, *Night Court* (NBC)

Outstanding Supporting Actress in a Comedy Series: Jackee Harry, *227* (NBC)

Outstanding Directing in a Drama Series: Gregory Hoblit, *L.A. Law* * (NBC)

Outstanding Directing in a Comedy Series: Terry Hughes, *The Golden Girls* * (NBC)

Outstanding Directing in a Variety or Music Program: Don Mischer, *The Kennedy Honors: A Celebration of the Performing Arts* (CBS)

1987-1988

Outstanding Drama Series: *thirtysomething* * (ABC)

Outstanding Comedy Series: *The Wonder Years* * (ABC)

Outstanding Miniseries: *The Murder of Mary Phagan* (NBC)

Outstanding Drama/Comedy Special: *Inherit the Wind* (NBC)

Outstanding Variety, Music, or Comedy Program: *Irving Berlin's 100th Birthday Celebration* (CBS)

Outstanding Lead Actor in a Drama Series: Richard Kiley, *A Year in the Life* (NBC)

Outstanding Lead Actress in a Drama Series: Tyne Daly, *Cagney and Lacey* * (CBS)

Outstanding Lead Actor in a Comedy Series: Michael J. Fox, *Family Ties* * (NBC)

Outstanding Lead Actress in a Comedy Series: Beatrice Arthur, *The Golden Girls* * (NBC)

Outstanding Supporting Actor in a Drama Series: Larry Drake, *L.A. Law* * (NBC)

Outstanding Supporting Actress in a Drama Series: Patricia Wettig, *thirtysomething* * (ABC)

Outstanding Supporting Actor in a Comedy Series: John Larroquette, *Night Court* (NBC)

Outstanding Supporting Actress in a Comedy Series: Estelle Getty, *The Golden Girls* * (NBC)

Outstanding Directing in a Drama Series: Mark Tinker, *St. Elsewhere* * (NBC)

Outstanding Lead Actress in a Drama Series: Tyne Daly, *Cagney and Lacey*

Outstanding Directing in a Comedy Series: Gregory Hoblit, *Hooperman* (ABC)

Outstanding Directing in a Variety or Music Program: Patricia Birch and Humphrey Burton, *Celebrating Gershwin: Great Performances* (PBS)

1988-1989

Outstanding Drama Series: *L.A. Law* * (NBC)

Outstanding Comedy Series: *Cheers* * (NBC)

Outstanding Miniseries: *War and Remembrance* (ABC)

Outstanding Drama/Comedy Special: *Day One: AT&T Presents* (CBS)

Outstanding Variety, Music, or Comedy Program: *The Tracey Ullman Show* (FOX)

Outstanding Lead Actor in a Drama Series: Carroll O'Connor, *In the Heat of the Night* (NBC)

Outstanding Lead Actress in a Drama Series: Dana Delany, *China Beach* (ABC)

Outstanding Lead Actor in a Comedy Series: Richard Mulligan, *Empty Nest* (NBC)

Outstanding Lead Actress in a Comedy Series: Candice Bergen, *Murphy Brown* (CBS)

Outstanding Supporting Actor in a Drama Series: Larry Drake, *L.A. Law** (NBC)

Outstanding Supporting Actress in a Drama Series: Melanie Mayron, *thirtysomething** (ABC)

Outstanding Supporting Actor in a Comedy Series: Woody Harrelson, *Cheers** (NBC)

Outstanding Supporting Actress in a Comedy Series: Rhea Perlman, *Cheers** (NBC)

Outstanding Directing in a Drama Series: Robert Altman, *Tanner '88** (HBO)

Outstanding Directing in a Comedy Series: Peter Baldwin, *The Wonder Years** (ABC)

Outstanding Directing in a Variety or Music Program: Jim Henson, *The Jim Henson Hour* (NBC)

1989-1990

Outstanding Drama Series: *L.A. Law** (NBC)

Outstanding Comedy Series: *Murphy Brown* (CBS)

Outstanding Miniseries: *Drug Wars: The Camarena Story* (NBC)

Outstanding Drama/Comedy Special (tie): *Caroline? Hallmark Hall of Fame* (CBS); *The Incident: AT&T Presents* (CBS)

Outstanding Variety, Music, or Comedy Series: *In Living Color* (FOX)

Outstanding Lead Actor in a Drama Series: Peter Falk, *Columbo* (ABC)

Outstanding Lead Actress in a Drama Series: Patricia Wettig, *thirtysomething** (ABC)

Outstanding Lead Actor in a Comedy Series: Ted Danson, *Cheers** (NBC)

Outstanding Lead Actress in a Comedy Series: Candice Bergen, *Murphy Brown* (CBS)

Outstanding Supporting Actor in a Drama Series: Jimmy Smits, *L.A. Law** (NBC)

Outstanding Supporting Actress in a Drama Series: Marg Helgenberger, *China Beach* (ABC)

Outstanding Supporting Actor in a Comedy Series: Alex Rocco, *The Famous Teddy Z* (CBS)

Outstanding Supporting Actress in a Comedy Series: Bebe Neuwirth, *Cheers** (NBC)

Outstanding Directing in a Drama Series (tie): Thomas Carter, *Equal Justice* (ABC); Scott Winant, *thirtysomething** (ABC)

Outstanding Directing in a Comedy Series: Michael Dinner, *The Wonder Years** (ABC)

Outstanding Directing in a Variety or Music Program: Dwight Hemion, *The Kennedy Center Honors* (CBS)

■ Legislation: Major U.S. Legislation

Year	Legislation	Significance
1980	Paperwork Reduction Act	Established the Office of Information and Regulatory Affairs within the Office of Management and Budget to oversee new paperwork requirements and to create means to reduce paperwork.
1980	Staggers Rail Act	Lessened restrictions on mergers and abandonment of rail lines; established policy to reduce regulation of railroads and permit the market to set rates; repealed antitrust immunity for collectively manipulated rates.
1980	Judicial Conduct and Disability Act	Allowed chief judge and governing council of each federal judicial circuit to investigate allegations of wrongdoing and to impose sanctions against judges or magistrates in that circuit.
1980	Refugee Act	Created the Office of U.S. Coordinator of Refugee Affairs within the Department of Health and Human Services; revised policies for admitting and resettling refugees in the United States.
1980	Superfund Act	Authorized the federal government to establish procedures for cleaning up toxic waste sites; earmarked $1.6 billion for an emergency fund to assist cleanup of targeted toxic waste sites.
1980	Debt Limit Law	Permitted the public debt limit to extend beyond June 30; eliminated the oil import fee imposed by the Carter administration; became law pursuant to override of President Jimmy Carter's veto.
1980	Veterans Affairs Personnel Act	Promoted recruitment and retention of health care personnel in the Veterans Administration; became law pursuant to override of President Jimmy Carter's veto.
1980	Motor Carrier Act	Loosened the procedures enabling truck firms to acquire operating authority from the Interstate Commerce Commission; eased restrictions on certain truck carriers; made it federal policy to ensure competition in the trucking industry; paved the way for deregulation.
1980	Chrysler Loan Guarantee Act	Specified how the federal government would approve and administer a $1.5 billion loan to the Chrysler Corporation; required a series of concessions by Chrysler, including development of an energy plan.
1980	Privacy Protection Act	Prohibited all law enforcement officers from using warrants to search the offices of legitimate news organizations; required the attorney general to draft new guidelines for federal searches of certain individuals.
1981	Economic Recovery Tax Act	Authorized universal cuts in tax rates; reduced or eliminated taxes on various forms of income.
1981	Social Security Amendments	Restored previously canceled minimum benefits for recipients of Social Security; allowed borrowing among trust funds to ensure payments.
1981	Veterans Health Care, Training, and Small Business Loan Act	Approved nursing home or hospital care for veterans who were exposed to Agent Orange or other herbicides; extended the period for Vietnam veterans to request readjustment counseling; permitted small businesses owned by disabled or Vietnam-era veterans to obtain loans from the Veterans Administration.

Year	Legislation	Significance
1981	International Security and Development Cooperation Act	Authorized two-year appropriations, including credits and loans, for security and development assistance programs; directed the president to review items on the U.S. Munitions List in order to eliminate unnecessary export controls.
1981	Uniformed Services Pay Act	Increased pay, allowances, and benefits to members of the armed services and their dependents; added three occupations to the list of hazardous-duty positions.
1981	Education Consolidation and Improvement Act	Consolidated programs, creating a single block grant to states for elementary and secondary schools; continued programs for some disadvantaged children.
1981	Municipal Wastewater Treatment Construction Grant Amendments	Reauthorized the federal sewer construction grant program though fiscal year 1985; directed states to conduct a review of water quality standards.
1981	National Tourism Policy Act	Created the U.S. Travel and Tourism Administration within the Department of Commerce; augmented the federal government's role in promoting foreign travel in the United States.
1981	Steel Industry Compliance Extension Act	Enacted procedures to permit the steel industry to extend Clear Air Act compliance deadlines.
1982	Voting Rights Act Amendments	Renewed selected provisions of the 1965 Voting Rights Act for another twenty-five years; established guidelines for eliminating preclearance requirement; approved funding for bilingual election materials for specified groups.
1982	Boland Amendments	Prohibited the United States' assistance to paramilitary groups trying to overthrow the government of Nicaragua or to provoke hostilities between Nicaragua and Honduras.
1982	Bus Regulatory Reform Act	Deregulated certain aspects of the passenger bus industry; mandated cooperation between the Interstate Commerce Commission and the states to monitor intrastate compliance with the act.
1982	Small Business Innovation Development Act	Reserved a specified portion of federal agency research and development budgets for small businesses; required participating agencies to establish small business innovation programs.
1982	Fiscal Year 1983 Supplemental Appropriations	Provided $14.2 billion in new budget authority; enacted after an override of President Ronald Reagan's veto.
1982	Federal Courts Improvement Act	Created the Court of Appeals for the Federal Circuit (CAFC); granted CAFC jurisdiction over appeals of patent cases and of Merit Systems Protection Board decisions.
1982	Prompt Payment Act	Required federal agencies to pay an interest penalty on overdue payments for rental property or services.
1982	Intelligence Identities Protection Act	Designed to protect the identity of undercover intelligence agents; added a new provision to the National Security Act of 1947 specifying penalties for identifying secret agents.

Year	Legislation	Significance
1982	Export Trading Company Act	Established the Office of Export Trade in the Department of Commerce; promoted increased export of American goods and services; authorized Export-Import Bank to furnish loans to export trading companies.
1982	Copyright Law Amendment	Extended until 1986 the manufacturing clause of the U.S. Copyright Law; enacted pursuant to override of President's Ronald Reagan's veto.
1982	Garn-St. Germain Depository Institutions Act	Created a three-year program to enable failing federally insured financial institutions to receive government notes; expanded powers of the Federal Deposit Insurance Corporation and Federal Savings and Loan Insurance Corporation to arrange mergers of banks and savings and loan organizations.
1983	Surface Transportation Assistance Act	Authorized $53.6 billion for highway construction and repair and $17.8 billion for mass transit systems during fiscal years 1983-1986.
1983	Nuclear Waste Policy Act of 1982	Required the president to recommend two sites to be permanent federal repositories for nuclear waste; exempted nuclear waste produced by defense programs from most of the law's features.
1983	Martin Luther King Day	Established the third Monday in January as a federal holiday honoring the legacy of civil rights leader Martin Luther King, Jr.
1983	Social Security Amendments	Raised retirement age of Social Security recipients from sixty-three to sixty-seven by 2027; made future cost-of-living adjustments payable in January; increased payroll taxes for employers and employees.
1983	Lebanon Emergency Assistance Act	Authorized supplemental assistance to Lebanon to promote stability and sovereignty; required the president to obtain statutory permission from Congress before expanding American armed forces in Lebanon.
1983	Dairy and Tobacco Adjustment Act	Initiated a program to halt milk production over a fifteen-month period; froze tobacco price support levels; permitted the secretary of agriculture to sell poor-quality feed corn at reduced rates to farmers and ranchers in drought areas.
1983	U.S. Commission on Civil Rights Act	Restructured the Commission on Civil Rights and renewed the commission through October 31, 1989.
1983	Federal Anti-Tampering Act	Imposed federal penalties for persons found guilty of tampering with consumer products, labels, or containers that affect interstate or foreign commerce.
1983	Extension of Trade Adjustment Act	Two-year extension of the Trade Adjustment Assistance program under the Trade Act of 1974, which furnished financial assistance and training to workers and businesses hurt by competition from imports.
1983	Fiscal Year 1984 Department of Defense Authorization	Authorized $187 billion for most Department of Defense activities, including $2.1 billion for production of MX missiles.
1984	Water Resources Research Act	Released funds for research and development to protect water resources; authorized states to establish water resource centers at land grant institutions; enacted pursuant to override of President Ronald Reagan's veto.
1984	Insider Trading Sanctions Act	Amended the Securities and Exchange Act of 1934 to increase penalties for buying stocks with nonpublic information.

Year	Legislation	Significance
1984	Cable Communications Policy Act	Forbade local television and telephone companies from owning local cable interests unless approved by the Federal Communications Commission; limited the authority of cities to regulate basic cable television rates to two years.
1984	National Organ Transplant Act	Earmarked funds for a national computerized network to match organ donors and recipients; prohibited the purchase or sale of human organs for transplantation.
1984	Retirement Equity Act	Lowered the age for employees to participate in private pension plans to twenty-one; permitted workers to retain pension rights after leaving and returning to a job.
1984	Child Abuse Amendments	Approved funds for child abuse prevention programs, to encourage adoption of disabled children, and for matching grants to assist states in providing domestic violence treatment and prevention programs.
1984	Hazardous and Solid Waste Amendments	Reauthorized the Solid Waste Disposal Act for four years; required the Environmental Protection Agency to enact regulations for certain generators of hazardous waste by March 31, 1986; prohibited disposal of hazardous waste close to underground drinking water sources.
1984	Deficit Reduction Act	Increased tax revenues by deferring certain tax reductions; amended several federal programs to reduce spending.
1984	Drug Price Competition and Patent Term Restoration Act	Loosened the Food and Drug Administration's drug application procedures in order to expedite approval of generic drugs; specified patent protection provisions.
1984	Veterans Health Care Act	Authorized the Veterans Administration to establish treatment programs for Vietnam veterans suffering from post-traumatic stress disorder.
1985	Public Health Service Act Amendment	Revised and extended provisions under the Public Health Services Act relating to the National Institutes of Health and the National Research Institutes; enacted pursuant to override of President Ronald Reagan's veto.
1985	Food Security Act	Reduced federal price supports and direct income subsidies to farmers for the 1986-1990 fiscal years; exempted certain Department of Agriculture export financing programs from federal shipment requirements.
1985	Gramm-Rudman-Hollings Act	Amended the 1974 Budget Control and Impoundment Act; required that the federal government meet annual targets to eliminate deficit within five years; specified procedures for cuts if annual deficit reduction targets were not met. The Supreme Court in 1986 ruled portions of this law unconstitutional.
1985	Clark Amendment Repeal	Repealed a section of the International Security and Development Act of 1980, which prohibited assistance for military operations in Angola.
1985	U.S.-China Nuclear Cooperation Agreement	Established a process for implementation of a nuclear cooperation agreement between the United States and China; mandated that a report be sent to Congress detailing China's nonproliferation policies; cleared the way for sale of nonmilitary nuclear technology to China.

Year	Legislation	Significance
1986	Tax Reform Act	Simplified the federal tax system by replacing the existing fourteen tax brackets with two; revised the tax code by curtailing or eliminating dozens of tax breaks.
1986	Comprehensive Anti-Apartheid Act	Prohibited loans to and investments in South Africa; imposed a series of economic sanctions against South Africa; enacted pursuant to override of a veto by President Ronald Reagan.
1986	Age Discrimination in Employment Amendments	Forbade most employers from setting mandatory retirement ages.
1986	Anti-Drug Abuse Act	Increased penalties for drug-related crime; created new offenses; expanded enforcement in the United States and in drug-producing countries.
1986	Immigration Reform and Control Act	Required that employers verify the status of all workers; made it a crime for employers to knowingly recruit or hire illegal immigrants.
1986	Superfund Amendments and Reauthorization Act	Established a $8.5 billion fund to clean up the most dangerous hazardous waste sites; formulated a five-year schedule for the Environmental Protection Agency to start cleaning up the 375 worst hazardous waste sites; created new taxes on petroleum and raw chemicals.
1986	Safe Drinking Water Act Amendments	Renewed the Safe Drinking Water Act of 1974 for five years; directed the Environmental Protection Agency to set maximum containment standards for water supplies; created a schedule for regulating certain toxic pollutants within three years.
1986	Electronic Communications Privacy Act	Extended privacy protection to electronic mail, cellular phones, computer transmissions, paging devices, and private satellite transmissions.
1986	Firearms Owners Protection Act	Removed the ban on interstate sale of rifles and shotguns; barred the establishment of a firearms registration ban; restricted conditions under which federal officials could seize firearms or ammunition.
1986	Goldwater-Nixon Act	Reorganized the Department of Defense by designating the chairman of the joint chiefs of staff as chief military adviser to the president and the secretary of defense; authorized the chairman to assume strategic planning and budgeting responsibilities; consolidated duplicate functions.
1987	Water Quality Act	Renewed the Federal Water Pollution Control Amendments of 1972 for ten years; furnished construction grants for state and local sewage treatment facilities; enacted pursuant to override of presidential veto.
1987	Balanced Budget and Emergency Deficit Control Reaffirmation Act	Increased the public debt authority from $2.1 trillion to $2.8 trillion; established new federal budget deficit targets for 1988-1993 fiscal years.
1987	Airport and Airway Safety and Capacity Extension Act	Provided $20.1 billion for a airport renewal measures; set a target for hiring air traffic controllers; extended taxes and fees to finance the Airport and Airway Trust Fund.
1987	McKinney Homeless Assistance Act	Established the Interagency Council on the Homeless to coordinate homeless assistance; authorized funding for two years for a broad range of programs to help homeless persons.

Year	Legislation	Significance
1987	New G.I. Bill Continuation Act	Created a permanent educational benefits program for persons who began military service after June 30, 1985; specified active duty requirements to qualify for the program.
1987	Surface Transportation Act	Authorized funds for construction of highways; approved mass transit funds; expanded and improved the relocation assistance program; enacted pursuant to override of presidential veto.
1988	Trademark Law Revision Act	Permitted American companies to file a trademark application with the U.S. Patent and Trademark Office, with certain deadlines noted.
1988	Veterans Judicial Review Act	Created a new review procedure for veterans' claim cases; authorized the Board of Veterans Appeals to make initial decisions in these cases; established the U.S. Court of Appeals for Veterans Claims to review the board's decisions; specified membership requirements for the Board of Veterans Appeals.
1988	Civil Rights Restoration Act	Renewed the broad scope of coverage under Title IX of the Educational Amendments of 1972, Rehabilitative Act of 1973, Age Discrimination Act of 1975, and Title VI of the Civil Rights Act of 1964; enacted pursuant to override of veto by President Ronald Reagan.
1988	Fair Housing Amendments	Authorized the Department of Housing and Urban Development to penalize those who discriminated in the sale or rental of housing; barred discriminatory housing practices against the handicapped and families with young children.
1988	Women's Business Ownership Act	Created a Small Business Administration program to provide bank loans to small businesses owned by women; established a Women's Business Council to monitor government assistance to women-owned businesses.
1988	Family Support Act	Started a Job Opportunities and Basic Skills Program for recipients of Aid to Families with Dependent Children; strengthened child support enforcement procedures; approved projects to examine how to lessen welfare dependence.
1988	Berne Convention Implementation Act	Permitted the United States to participate in the Berne Convention for the Protection of Literary and Artistic Works; revised certain American copyright laws to conform with the convention.
1988	Video Privacy Act	Prohibited the disclosure of names, addresses, and other information about patrons who rented or purchased videotapes from video stores, with limited exceptions.
1988	Department of Veterans Affairs	Elevated the Veterans Administration to a cabinet department; specified an appointment process for a secretary of veterans affairs and certain department officials.
1988	Japanese American Reparations Act	Approved a payment of $20,000 to each surviving Japanese American who had been interned in a relocation camp during World War II; permitted payment to some internees' descendants; offered a government apology for internment.
1989	Whistleblower Protection Act	Established the Office of Special Counsel as an independent federal agency to investigate allegations of retaliation against government employees who expose waste or fraud; permitted complaints to be filed with the Merits Systems Protection Board.

Year	Legislation	Significance
1989	Ethics Reform Act	Began an annual automatic pay adjustment procedure for members of Congress based on private sector pay; specified reduction or elimination of speaking fees and honoraria; eliminated a provision which allowed members of the House of Representatives who had been in office since 1980 to convert campaign funds for personal use.
1989	Financial Institutions Reform, Recovery, and Enforcement Act	Approved allotment of $50 billion over three years to sell or close insolvent savings and loan institutions; created the Resolution Trust Corporation to take over failed thrift organizations and sell their assets; abolished the Federal Home Loan Bank Board and Federal Savings and Loan Corporation; established the Office of Thrift Supervision within the Department of the Treasury to supervise thrifts.
1989	Bipartisan Accord on Central America Act of 1989	Authorized the president to transfer funds to the Agency for International Development to provide humanitarian assistance to Nicaraguan resistance forces.
1989	Omnibus Budget Reconciliation Act	Approved $14.7 billion for deficit reduction; removed the U.S. Postal Service from deficit reduction act requirements.
1989	Department of Housing and Urban Development Reform Act	Required the Department of Housing and Urban Development (HUD) to distribute housing program funds according to a revised formula; mandated certain personnel who dealt with HUD to report their earnings, based on their salaries; permitted civil fines for violations of HUD mortgage programs.

Samuel B. Hoff

■ Legislation: U.S. Supreme Court Decisions

Year	Case	Significance
1980	*Fullilove v. Klutznick*	Chief Justice Warren Burger wrote the majority opinion, which upheld Congress's right to set aside 10 percent of federal public works funding for minority contractors. This decision reaffirmed Congress's right to set racial quotas to combat discrimination.
1980	*Harris v. McRae*	In what would become the first of a series of decisions on abortion during the 1980's, the justices upheld a federal law barring the use of Medicaid funds for abortions, except when the mother's life was in danger and in cases of rape or incest. The 5-4 decision held that a woman's right to terminate a pregnancy did not entitle her to receive government funding for that choice.
1980	*Lewis v. United States*	In a 6-3 decision, the justices upheld Congress's authority to prohibit convicted felons from owning firearms. The Court ruled that Congress could rationally conclude that any felony conviction is sufficient basis on which to prohibit the possession of a firearm.
1980	*Richmond Newspapers v. Virginia*	By a ruling of 7-1, the Court determined that a trial judge's order to close the courtroom to the public and media during a murder trial was unconstitutional. The opinion maintained that the arbitrary closing of a courtroom to avoid unwanted publicity violated the First Amendment, and the closure of court hearings was permissible only under unusual circumstances.
1981	*Heffron v. International Society for Krishna Consciousness*	Chief Justice Burger's majority opinion held that state fair organizers did not violate a religious organization's First Amendment rights when it required the group to distribute its literature at a fixed location. Members of the Krishna religion argued that the rule suppressed their practice of distributing religious literature and soliciting donations in public places. The Court maintained that the religious and free speech rights of the Krishna members were not violated because fair organizers treated all groups the same, regardless of their religious or political affiliations.
1981	*Metromedia v. City of San Diego*	In his majority opinion, Justice Byron White ruled that an ordinance banning billboards within San Diego city limits violated the First Amendment. The Court determined that the city's need for public safety and appearance was insufficient to justify a ban on outdoor advertising that was used by politicians and businesses.
1981	*Rostker v. Goldberg*	This case was a challenge to a federal law that required men—but not women—to register for possible military service. The majority opinion, written by Justice William Rehnquist, held that the law did not violate the Constitution or discriminate against women because the draft was based on the need for combat troops and not on equity.
1981	*United States Postal Service v. Council of Greenburgh Civic Associations*	The Court found that a federal law prohibiting the delivery of unstamped material to private mailboxes was constitutional and did not violate the First Amendment rights of groups seeking to deposit messages at private homes without paying postage.

Year	Case	Significance
1982	*Island Trees School District v. Pico*	In his majority opinion, Justice William Brennan ruled that a local school board violated the First Amendment when it ordered the removal of books from school libraries because the board found the books to be "anti-American, anti-Christian, anti-Semitic, and just plain filthy." The justices determined that school officials could not remove books from school libraries simply because they disliked the ideas contained in those books.
1982	*New York v. Ferber*	In a unanimous opinion, the Court upheld a state law that made it a crime to own or sell child pornography. The justices defined child pornography as the visual depiction of sexual conduct by children without serious literary, artistic, political, or scientific value, and they ruled that child pornography—like obscenity—was not protected by the First Amendment.
1983	*Akron v. Akron Center for Reproductive Health*	One of three abortion decisions handed down on June 15, 1983. This 6-3 opinion overturned portions of an Akron, Ohio, ordinance that required the parents of unmarried minors under the age of fifteen to be notified and to give their consent before the minors could have an abortion. The decision also maintained it was unconstitutional to require a woman to sign a consent form and wait twenty-four hours before she could have an abortion.
1983	*Planned Parenthood Association of Kansas City v. Ashcroft*	Decided on the same day as *Akron v. Akron Center for Reproductive Health*, this 5-4 opinion upheld a Missouri state law requiring minors under the age of eighteen to obtain parental consent for their abortions. While it ruled that the Akron, Ohio, parental consent ordinance was unconstitutional, the Court upheld the Missouri parental consent law because it met the standard the Court had specified in a 1979 decision.
1983	*Simopoulos v. Virginia*	In the third abortion decision delivered on June 15, 1983, the Court upheld the criminal conviction of a physician for violating a Virginia law that required all post-first-trimester abortions to be performed in hospitals. By an 8-1 ruling, the justices determined the law was constitutional because it allowed for the licensing of clinics as well as full-care hospitals, which made the law less restrictive than the laws struck down in *Akron v. Akron Center for Reproductive Health* and *Planned Parenthood v. Ashcroft*. The doctor would have avoided criminal prosecution if his clinic had been licensed.
1983	*Bob Jones University v. United States*	Eight of the nine justices upheld the Internal Revenue Service's (IRS) authority to deny tax-exempt status for private religious schools that practiced racial discrimination. The Court determined that the IRS did not violate Bob Jones University's First Amendment rights because the government's interest in the eradication of racial discrimination outweighed a school's need for tax-exempt status when that school discriminated on the basis on race.
1983	*Bolger v. Young Drug Products*	Considered a major decision in the First Amendment protection of commercial speech, this ruling overturned a federal law that made it a crime to send unsolicited advertisements for contraceptives through the U.S. mail.
1983	*Equal Employment Opportunity Commission v. Wyoming*	This decision extended the federal law prohibiting discrimination on the basis of age to apply to employees of state government agencies.

Year	Case	Significance
1983	*Metropolitan Edison v. People Against Nuclear Energy and Nuclear Regulatory Commission*	The Court ruled that the Nuclear Regulatory Commission was not required to consider the psychological health and well-being of a community when deciding where to locate a nuclear power plant.
1983	*Pacific Gas & Electric Co. v. State Energy Resources Conservation and Development Commission*	This case challenged California's authority to place a moratorium on the construction of nuclear power plants. The Court ruled that states were free to ban future nuclear power plants as long as the ban was motivated by economic reasons and not by considerations of safety, which were the responsibility of the federal government.
1983	*Mueller v. Allen*	The majority opinion, written by Chief Justice Burger, upheld a Minnesota law allowing parents of children in public or private schools to obtain a tuition tax reduction when paying their state income tax. This 5-4 decision held that a state tax deduction for education expenses was constitutional, even though parochial schools would reap most of the benefits.
1984	*Federal Communications Commission v. League of Women Voters of California*	In a 5-4 opinion, the Court struck down a federal regulation prohibiting any noncommercial educational station that received government funding from engaging in editorializing. The justices ruled that this regulation violated the free speech rights of public broadcasters because it curtailed the expression of editorial opinion that was at "the heart of First Amendment protection."
1984	*Grove City College v. Bell*	The Court upheld a federal requirement that colleges and universities receiving federal funding must comply with a federal law prohibiting sex discrimination in "any education program or activity receiving federal financial assistance." The justices ruled that this requirement did not violate the First Amendment rights of colleges and their students.
1984	*Lynch v. Donnelly*	By a 5-4 ruling, the Court held that an annual city park Christmas display featuring a nativity scene was constitutional because the scene was displayed with other Christmas symbols and was used to promote retail sales and goodwill—not to endorse a particular religion. The case arose because Daniel Donnelly, a resident of Pawtucket, Rhode Island, objected to the city's display and sued Pawtucket's mayor, Dennis Lynch.
1984	*Regan v. Time, Inc.*	Writing for a majority of the justices, Chief Justice Burger overturned as unconstitutional part of a federal law designed to curb counterfeiting. The Court ruled that a *Time* magazine could publish illustrations of United States' currency as long as the illustrations were not in color and not shown in actual size.
1984	*Roberts v. United States Jaycees*	A unanimous Court upheld a Minnesota law barring private clubs from discriminating against women. The justices ruled that the United States Jaycees was not a private club, and, therefore, could not exclude women from its membership. The Court would reach the same conclusion in *Rotary International v. Rotary Club of Duarte* (1987).
1984	*Sony Corp. of America v. Universal City Studios, Inc.*	Justice John Paul Stevens delivered the 5-4 opinion in a case addressing entertainment corporations' concerns about video piracy. The Court ruled that home use of videocassette recorders (VCRs) to tape television programs for later viewing did not violate federal copyright law. Justices maintained that a VCR manufacturer's sale of home VCRs that were later used to record television programs did not violate the copyrights of these programs' producers.

Year	Case	Significance
1985	*New Jersey v. T.L.O.*	This 6-3 opinion concluded that, in general, the Fourth Amendment ban on unreasonable searches applied to searches by public school officials, as well as by law enforcement personnel. However, the Court determined that in this case the search of a student's purse by public school officials did not violate the student's civil rights.
1985	*Wallace v. Jaffree*	This decision struck down an Alabama law that allowed public school teachers to hold a one-minute period of silence for "meditation or voluntary prayer" each day. The Court determined that the law had no secular purpose and endorsed religion in violation of the First Amendment's establishment clause separating church and state.
1985	*Thornton v. Caldor*	This case challenged the constitutionality of Connecticut's Sabbath laws, which prevented private companies from forcing employees to work on Sunday or any day that would be the employees' Sabbath. The Court declared the law unconstitutional and ruled that private companies are free to fire any employees who refused to work on any day they considered to be their Sabbath because the First Amendment's guarantee of freedom of religion applied only to the government and not to private employers.
1985	*American Booksellers Association v. Hudnut*	The Court struck down as unconstitutional a city ordinance that banned pornography on the grounds that pornography violated women's civil rights by portraying them as sex objects.
1986	*Batson v. Kentucky*	In his majority opinion, Justice Lewis Powell ruled that attorneys who rejected prospective jurors solely on the basis of their race violated the Sixth Amendment. The Court concluded that racial discrimination in jury selection damaged the community by "undermining public confidence" in the justice system.
1986	*Bethel School District v. Fraser*	In a 7-2 decision, the Court upheld a school district's suspension of a high school student for delivering a speech containing "elaborate, graphic, and explicit sexual" metaphors. The opinion determined that the First Amendment did not prevent school officials from prohibiting vulgar and lewd speech that would undermine the school's basic educational mission.
1986	*Bowers v. Hardwick*	This controversial decision upheld a Georgia sodomy law that made it a crime to engage in homosexual acts, even in the privacy of the home. The case involved a homosexual man arrested in his bedroom. Gay rights groups referred to this case as their "Dred Scott decision," comparing it to *Dred Scott v. Sandford* (1857), in which the Court ruled that African Americans were not "citizens" entitled to constitutional protection.
1986	*Goldman v. Weinberger*	Ruling 5-4, the justices upheld U.S. Air Force penalties against a Jewish chaplain who wore a yarmulke (skull cap) while on duty in defiance of the military's uniform regulations. The Court ruled that the military's interest in uniformity outweighed an individual's religious beliefs.

Year	Case	Significance
1986	*Renton v. Playtime Theatres*	In this pornography case, the Court held that communities could restrict the location of X-rated movie theaters to sites away from homes, schools, churches, and parks. This ruling was consistent with its 1986 ruling in *American Booksellers Association v. Hudnut,* because in both decisions the justices reaffirmed that sexually explicit materials—unlike obscenity—deserved some First Amendment protection but less protection than other kinds of speech, especially political speech.
1986	*Thornburgh v. American College of Obstetricians and Gynecologists*	Citing its 1983 decisions in *Akron v. Akron Center for Reproductive Health* and *Planned Parenthood v. Ashcroft,* the Court overturned portions of the Pennsylvania Abortion Control Act of 1982, finding that these provisions infringed on a woman's fundamental right to an abortion. The majority opinion by Justice Harry A. Blackmun stated that it was unconstitutional to give a woman information designed to dissuade her from having an abortion; the decision maintained it also was unconstitutional to invade a woman's privacy by making information about her abortion available to the public.
1987	*Edwards v. Aguillard*	In a 7-2 opinion, the Court ruled that Louisiana could not require public schools that taught evolution to also teach creationism as "Creation Science." The opinion concluded the law had no secular purpose and endorsed religion in violation of the Constitution's establishment clause separating church and state.
1987	*Rotary International v. Rotary Club of Duarte*	The justices upheld a California law that required Rotary Clubs to admit women. The Court found that the state's compelling interest in ending sexual discrimination outweighed the group's right of association.
1987	*South Dakota v. Dole*	Chief Justice William Rehnquist wrote the majority opinion, in which he ruled as constitutional a federal law that withheld 5 percent of a state's highway funds if that state did not raise its minimum drinking age to 21. The law was upheld because it was passed in the interest of the "general good" and by "reasonable means."
1988	*Hazelwood School District. v. Kuhlmeier*	In a decision that First Amendment advocates considered a major setback in protecting students' free speech rights, the Court concluded that a school principal could censor the contents of a student newspaper if that newspaper was part of a class assignment and not a forum for public discussion.
1988	*Lyng v. Northwest Indian Cemetery Protective Association*	Justice Sandra Day O'Connor's majority opinion held that the Constitution's free exercise of religion clause did not bar the federal government from harvesting timber in and building a road through a national forest area that Native Americans used for religious purposes.
1988	*Hustler Magazine v. Falwell*	This unanimous ruling by eight justices was considered a landmark case for freedom of speech. It involved a case in which the Reverend Jerry Falwell sued *Hustler Magazine* for publishing a fake satirical advertisement poking fun at him and his deceased mother. The Court ruled in favor of the magazine, maintaining that satire and parody were protected forms of free speech.

Year	Case	Significance
1988	*Thompson v. Oklahoma*	The Court, in a 5-3 ruling, vacated the death sentence of a fifteen-year-old who was tried as an adult and convicted of murder. The justices ruled that imposing the death penalty against juveniles under the age of sixteen was a form of cruel and unusual punishment.
1988	*Webster v. Doe*	This decision allowed a former Central Intelligence Agency (CIA) employee to sue the CIA for firing him because he was a homosexual, which the CIA claimed made him a threat to national security. In a 6-2 ruling, the justices concluded that dismissed employees could sue the CIA if they believed their constitutional rights had been violated.
1989	*Allegheny County v. Greater Pittsburgh American Civil Liberties Union (ACLU)*	Writing for the majority, Justice Blackmun held that displaying a nativity scene inside a Pittsburgh, Pennsylvania, courthouse endorsed religion and, therefore, violated the Constitution's establishment clause separating church and state. This decision differed from the 1984 ruling in *Lynch v. Donnelly*, which held that a nativity scene that was part of a secular Christmas display for commercial purposes was constitutional.
1989	*Sable Communications of California, Inc. v. Federal Communications Commission*	Sable Communications, a provider of "dial-a-porn" telephone services both in and outside the metropolitan Los Angeles area, challenged a federal law that banned these sexually oriented calls. The Court ruled that the federal law was unconstitutional because it violated the free speech rights of pornographers.
1989	*Texas v. Johnson*	In a 5-4 decision, the Court overturned a Texas law that made the desecration of the American flag illegal. The justices maintained that flag burning was a form of symbolic speech and protected under the First Amendment.
1989	*Webster v. Reproductive Health Services*	This opinion upheld a Missouri law that prohibited the use of state funds to pay for abortions; the law also determined that life began at conception and mandated that unborn children should have the same rights and privileges available to other persons. Prochoice advocates maintained that by upholding this law, the Court seriously compromised the landmark *Roe v. Wade* (1973) decision, which legalized abortion.

Eddith A. Dashiell

■ Literature: Best-Selling U.S. Books

1980 Fiction
1. *The Covenant,* James A. Michener
2. *The Bourne Identity,* Robert Ludlum
3. *Rage of Angels,* Sidney Sheldon
4. *Princess Daisy,* Judith Krantz
5. *Firestarter,* Stephen King
6. *The Key to Rebecca,* Ken Follett
7. *Random Winds,* Belva Plain
8. *The Devil's Alternative,* Frederick Forsyth
9. *The Fifth Horseman,* Larry Collins and Dominique Lapierre
10. *The Spike,* Arnaud de Borchgrave and Robert Moss

1980 Nonfiction
1. *Crisis Investing: Opportunities and Profits in the Coming Great Depression,* Douglas R. Casey
2. *Cosmos,* Carl Sagan
3. *Free to Choose: A Personal Statement,* Milton and Rose Friedman
4. *Anatomy of an Illness as Perceived by the Patient,* Norman Cousins
5. *Thy Neighbor's Wife,* Gay Talese
6. *The Sky's the Limit,* Dr. Wayne W. Dyer
7. *The Third Wave,* Alvin Toffler
8. *Craig Claiborne's Gourmet Diet,* Craig Claiborne with Pierre Franey
9. *Nothing Down,* Robert Allen
10. *Shelley: Also Known as Shirley,* Shelley Winters

1981 Fiction
1. *Noble House,* James Clavell
2. *The Hotel New Hampshire,* John Irving
3. *Cujo,* Stephen King
4. *An Indecent Obsession,* Colleen McCullough
5. *Gorky Park,* Martin Cruz Smith
6. *Masquerade,* Kit Williams
7. *Goodbye, Janette,* Harold Robbins
8. *The Third Deadly Sin,* Lawrence Sanders
9. *The Glitter Dome,* Joseph Wambaugh
10. *No Time for Tears,* Cynthia Freeman

1981 Nonfiction
1. *The Beverly Hills Diet,* Judy Mazel
2. *The Lord God Made Them All,* James Herriot
3. *Richard Simmons' Never-Say-Diet Book,* Richard Simmons

4. *A Light in the Attic,* Shel Silverman
5. *Cosmos,* Carl Sagan
6. *Better Homes and Gardens New Cook Book*
7. *Miss Piggy's Guide to Life,* Miss Piggy as told to Henry Beard
8. *Weight Watchers 365-Day Diet Menu Cookbook*
9. *You Can Negotiate Anything,* Herb Cohen
10. *A Few Minutes with Andy Rooney,* Andrew A. Rooney

1982 Fiction
1. *E.T: The Extra-Terrestrial Storybook,* William Kotzwinkle
2. *Space,* James A. Michener
3. *The Parsifal Mosaic,* Robert Ludlum
4. *Master of the Game,* Sidney Sheldon
5. *Mistral's Daughter,* Judith Krantz
6. *The Valley of Horses,* Jean M. Auel
7. *Different Seasons,* Stephen King
8. *North and South,* John Jakes
9. *2010: Odyssey Two,* Arthur C. Clarke
10. *The Man from St. Petersburg,* Ken Follett

1982 Nonfiction
1. *Jane Fonda's Workout Book,* Jane Fonda
2. *Living, Loving, and Learning,* Leo Buscaglia
3. *And More by Andy Rooney,* Andrew A. Rooney
4. *Better Homes and Gardens New Cook Book*
5. *Life Extension: Adding Years to Your Life and Life to Your Years—A Practical Scientific Approach,* Durk Pearson and Sandy Shaw
6. *When Bad Things Happen to Good People,* Harold S. Kushner
7. *A Few Minutes with Andy Rooney,* Andrew A. Rooney
8. *The Weight Watchers Food Plan Diet Cookbook,* Jean Nidetch
9. *Richard Simmons' Never-Say-Diet Cookbook,* Richard Simmons
10. *No Bad Dogs: The Woodhouse Way,* Barbara Woodhouse

1983 Fiction
1. *Return of the Jedi Storybook,* Joan D. Vinge, adapter
2. *Poland,* James A. Michener
3. *Pet Sematary,* Stephen King

4. *The Little Drummer Girl*, John Le Carré
5. *Christine*, Stephen King
6. *Changes*, Danielle Steel
7. *The Name of the Rose*, Umberto Eco
8. *White Gold Wielder: Book Three of the Second Chronicles of Thomas Covenant*, Stephen R. Donaldson
9. *Hollywood Wives*, Jackie Collins
10. *The Lonesome Gods*, Louis L'Amour

1983 Nonfiction

1. *In Search of Excellence: Lessons from America's Best-Run Companies*, Thomas J. Peters and Robert H. Waterman, Jr.
2. *Megatrends: Ten New Directions Transforming Our Lives*, John Naisbitt
3. *Motherhood: The Second Oldest Profession*, Erma Bombeck
4. *The One Minute Manager*, Kenneth Blanchard and Spencer Johnson
5. *Jane Fonda's Workout Book*, Jane Fonda
6. *The Best of James Herriot*, James Herriot
7. *The Mary Kay Guide to Beauty: Discovering Your Special Look*
8. *On Wings of Eagles*, Ken Follett
9. *Creating Wealth*, Robert G. Allen
10. *The Body Principal: The Exercise Program for Life*, Victoria Principal

1984 Fiction

1. *The Talisman*, Stephen King and Peter Straub
2. *The Aquitaine Progression*, Robert Ludlum
3. *The Sicilian*, Mario Puzo
4. *Love and War*, John Jakes
5. *The Butter Battle Book*, Dr. Seuss
6. *"... And the Ladies of the Club,"* Helen Hooven Santmyer
7. *The Fourth Protocol*, Frederick Forsyth
8. *Full Circle*, Danielle Steel
9. *The Life and Hard Times of Heidi Abromowitz*, Joan Rivers
10. *Lincoln: A Novel*, Gore Vidal

1984 Nonfiction

1. *Iacocca: An Autobiography*, Lee Iacocca with William Novak
2. *Loving Each Other*, Leo Buscaglia
3. *Eat to Win: The Sports Nutrition Bible*, Robert Haas, M.D.
4. *Pieces of My Mind*, Andrew A. Rooney

5. *Weight Watchers Fast and Fabulous Cookbook*
6. *What They Don't Teach You at Harvard Business School: Notes from a Street-Smart Executive*, Mark H. McCormack
7. *Women Coming of Age*, Jane Fonda with Mignon McCarthy
8. *Moses the Kitten*, James Herriot
9. *The One Minute Salesperson*, Spencer Johnson, M.D., and Larry Wilson
10. *Weight Watchers Quick Start Program Cookbook*, Jean Nidetch

1985 Fiction

1. *The Mammoth Hunters*, Jean M. Auel
2. *Texas*, James A. Michener
3. *Lake Wobegon Days*, Garrison Keillor
4. *If Tomorrow Comes*, Sidney Sheldon
5. *Skeleton Crew*, Stephen King
6. *Secrets*, Danielle Steel
7. *Contact*, Carl Sagan
8. *Lucky*, Jackie Collins
9. *Family Album*, Danielle Steel
10. *Jubal Sackett*, Louis L'Amour

1985 Nonfiction

1. *Iacocca: An Autobiography*, Lee Iacocca with William Novak
2. *Yeager: An Autobiography*, Chuck Yeager and Leo Janos
3. *Elvis and Me*, Priscilla Beaulieu Presley with Sandra Harmon
4. *Fit for Life*, Harvey and Marilyn Diamond
5. *The Be-Happy Attitudes*, Robert Schuller
6. *Dancing in the Light*, Shirley MacLaine
7. *A Passion for Excellence: The Leadership Difference*, Thomas J. Peters and Nancy K. Austin
8. *The Frugal Gourmet*, Jeff Smith
9. *I Never Played the Game*, Howard Cosell with Peter Bonventre
10. *Dr. Berger's Immune Power Diet*, Stuart M. Berger, M.D.

1986 Fiction

1. *It*, Stephen King
2. *Red Storm Rising*, Tom Clancy
3. *Whirlwind*, James Clavell
4. *The Bourne Supremacy*, Robert Ludlum
5. *Hollywood Husbands*, Jackie Collins
6. *Wanderlust*, Danielle Steel
7. *I'll Take Manhattan*, Judith Krantz

8. *Last of the Breed*, Louis L'Amour
9. *The Prince of Tides*, Pat Conroy
10. *A Perfect Spy*, John Le Carré

1986 Nonfiction

1. *Fatherhood*, Bill Cosby
2. *Fit for Life*, Harvey and Marilyn Diamond
3. *His Way: The Unauthorized Biography of Frank Sinatra*, Kitty Kelley
4. *The Rotation Diet*, Martin Katahn
5. *You're Only Old Once*, Dr. Seuss
6. *Callanetics: Ten Years Younger in Ten Hours*, Callan Pinckney
7. *The Frugal Gourmet Cooks with Wine*, Jeff Smith
8. *Be Happy—You Are Loved!*, Robert H. Schuller
9. *Word for Word*, Andrew A. Rooney
10. *James Herriot's Dog Stories*, James Herriot

1987 Fiction

1. *The Tommyknockers*, Stephen King
2. *Patriot Games*, Tom Clancy
3. *Kaleidoscope*, Danielle Steel
4. *Misery*, Stephen King
5. *Leaving Home: A Collection of Lake Wobegon Stories*, Garrison Keillor
6. *Windmills of the Gods*, Sidney Sheldon
7. *Presumed Innocent*, Scott Turow
8. *Fine Things*, Danielle Steel
9. *Heaven and Hell*, John Jakes
10. *The Eyes of the Dragon*, Stephen King

1987 Nonfiction

1. *Time Flies*, Bill Cosby
2. *Spycatcher: The Candid Autobiography of a Senior Intelligence Officer*, Peter Wright with Paul Greengrass
3. *Family: The Ties That Bind . . . and Gag!*, Erma Bombeck
4. *Veil: The Secret Wars of the CIA, 1981-1987*, Bob Woodward
5. *A Day in the Life of America*, Rick Smolan and David Cohen
6. *The Great Depression of 1990*, Ravi Batra
7. *It's All in the Playing*, Shirley MacLaine
8. *Man of the House: The Life and Political Memoirs of Speaker Tip O'Neill*, Thomas P. O'Neill, Jr., with William Novak
9. *The Frugal Gourmet Cooks American*, Jeff Smith
10. *The Closing of the American Mind*, Allan Bloom

1988 Fiction

1. *The Cardinal of the Kremlin*, Tom Clancy
2. *The Sands of Time*, Sidney Sheldon
3. *Zoya*, Danielle Steel
4. *The Icarus Agenda*, Robert Ludlum
5. *Alaska*, James A. Michener
6. *Till We Meet Again*, Judith Krantz
7. *The Queen of the Damned*, Anne Rice
8. *To Be the Best*, Barbara Taylor Bradford
9. *One: A Novel*, Richard Bach
10. *Mitla Pass*, Leon Uris

1988 Nonfiction

1. *The Eight-Week Cholesterol Cure*, Robert E. Kowalski
2. *Talking Straight*, Lee Iacocca with Sonny Kleinfield
3. *A Brief History of Time: From the Big Bang to Black Holes*, Steven W. Hawking
4. *Trump: The Art of the Deal*, Donald J. Trump with Tony Schwartz
5. *Gracie: A Love Story*, George Burns
6. *Elizabeth Takes Off*, Elizabeth Taylor
7. *Swim with the Sharks Without Being Eaten Alive*, Harvey MacKay
8. *Christmas in America*, David Cohen, editor
9. *Weight Watchers Quick Success Program Book*, Jean Nidetch
10. *Moonwalk*, Michael Jackson

1989 Fiction

1. *Clear and Present Danger*, Tom Clancy
2. *The Dark Half*, Stephen King
3. *Daddy*, Danielle Steel
4. *Star*, Danielle Steel
5. *Caribbean*, James A. Michener
6. *The Satanic Verses*, Salman Rushdie
7. *The Russia House*, John Le Carré
8. *The Pillars of the Earth*, Ken Follett
9. *California Gold*, John Jakes
10. *While My Pretty One Sleeps*, Mary Higgins Clark

1989 Nonfiction

1. *All I Really Need to Know I Learned in Kindergarten: Uncommon Thoughts on Common Things*, Robert Fulghum
2. *Wealth Without Risk: How to Develop a Personal Fortune Without Going Out on a Limb*, Charles J. Givens
3. *A Woman Named Jackie*, C. David Heymann

4. *It Was on Fire When I Lay Down on It*, Robert Fulghum
5. *Better Homes and Gardens New Cook Book*
6. *The Way Things Work*, David Macaulay
7. *It's Always Something*, Gilda Radner
8. *Roseanne: My Life as a Woman*, Roseanne Barr
9. *The Frugal Gourmet Cooks Three Ancient Cuisines: China, Greece, and Rome*, Jeff Smith
10. *My Turn: The Memoirs of Nancy Reagan*, Nancy Reagan with William Novak

■ Literature: Major Literary Awards

Nobel Prizes in Literature

1980: Czesław Miłosz, Poland and United States
1981: Elias Canetti, United Kingdom (born in Bulgaria)
1982: Gabriel García Márquez, Colombia
1983: William Golding, United Kingdom
1984: Jaroslav Seifert, Czechoslovakia
1985: Claude Simon, France
1986: Wole Soyinka, Nigeria
1987: Joseph Brodsky, United States (born in the Soviet Union)
1988: Naguib Mahfouz, Egypt
1989: Camilio José Cela, Spain

Pulitzer Prizes

1980

Fiction: *The Executioner's Song* by Norman Mailer
Drama: *Talley's Folly* by Lanford Wilson
History: *Been in the Storm So Long: The Aftermath of Slavery* by Leon F. Litwack
Biography: *The Rise of Theodore Roosevelt* by Edmund Morris
Poetry: *Selected Poems* by Donald Justice

1981

Fiction: *A Confederacy of Dunces* by John Kennedy Toole
Drama: *Crimes of the Heart* by Beth Henley
History: *American Education: The National Experience, 1783-1876* by Lawrence A. Cremin
Biography: *Peter the Great: His Life and World* by Robert K. Massie
Poetry: *The Morning of the Poem* by James Schuyler

1982

Fiction: *Rabbit Is Rich* by John Updike
Drama: *A Soldier's Play* by Charles Fuller
History: *Mary Chestnut's Civil War* edited by C. Vann Woodward
Biography: *Grant: A Biography* by William McFeely
Poetry: *The Collected Poems* by Sylvia Plath

1983

Fiction: *The Color Purple* by Alice Walker
Drama: *'night, Mother* by Marsha Norman
History: *The Transformation of Virginia, 1740-1790* by Rhys L. Isaac
Biography: *Growing Up* by Russell Baker
Poetry: *Selected Poems* by Galway Kinnell

1984

Fiction: *Ironweed* by William Kennedy
Drama: *Glengarry Glen Ross* by David Mamet
History: No award
Biography: *Booker T. Washington: The Wizard of Tuskegee, 1901-1915* by Louis R. Harlan
Poetry: *American Primitive* by Mary Oliver

1985

Fiction: *Foreign Affairs* by Alison Lurie
Drama: *Sunday in the Park with George* by Stephen Sondheim and James Lapine
History: *Prophets of Regulation* by Thomas McCraw
Biography: *The Life and Times of Cotton Mather* by Kenneth Silverman
Poetry: *Yin* by Caroline Kizer

1986

Fiction: *Lonesome Dove* by Larry McMurtry
Drama: No award
History: *. . . the Heavens and the Earth: A Political History of the Space Age* by Walter A. McDougall
Biography: *Louise Bogan: A Portrait* by Elizabeth Frank
Poetry: *The Flying Change* by Henry Taylor

1987

Fiction: *A Summons to Memphis* by Peter Taylor
Drama: *Fences* by August Wilson
History: *Voyagers to the West: A Passage in the Peopling of America on the Eve of the Revolution* by Bernard Bailyn
Biography: *Burning the Cross: Martin Luther King, Jr., and the Southern Christian Leadership Conference* by David J. Garrow
Poetry: *Thomas and Beulah* by Rita Dove

1988

Fiction: *Beloved* by Toni Morrison
Drama: *Driving Miss Daisy* by Alfred Uhry
History: *The Launching of Modern American Science, 1846-1876* by Robert V. Bruce

Biography: *Look Homeward: A Life of Thomas Wolfe* by David Herbert Donald

Poetry: *Partial Accounts: New and Selected Poems* by William Meredith

1989

Fiction: *Breathing Lessons* by Anne Tyler

Drama: *The Heidi Chronicles* by Wendy Wasserstein

History: *Battle Cry of Freedom: The Civil War Era* by James M. McPherson; *Parting the Waters: America in the King Years, 1954-1963* by Taylor Branch

Biography: *Oscar Wilde* by Richard Ellmann

Poetry: *New and Collected Poems* by Richard Wilbur

National Book Awards

1980

Autobiography, Hardcover: *Lauren Bacall by Myself* by Lauren Bacall

Autobiography, Paperback: *And I Worked at the Writer's Trade: Chapters of Literary History, 1918-1978* by Malcolm Cowley

Biography, Hardcover: *The Rise of Theodore Roosevelt* by Edmund Morris

Biography, Paperback: *Max Perkins: Editor of Genius* by A. Scott Berg

Children's Book, Hardcover: *A Gathering of Days: A New England Girl's Journal, 1830-1832* by Joan W. Blos

Children's Book, Paperback: *A Swiftly Tilting Planet* by Madeleine L'Engle

Current Interest, Hardcover: *Julia Child and More Company* by Julia Child

Current Interest, Paperback: *The Culture of Narcissism* by Christopher Lasch

Fiction, Hardcover: *Sophie's Choice* by William Styron

Fiction, Paperback: *The World According to Garp* by John Irving

First Novel: *Birdy* by William Wharton

General Nonfiction, Hardcover: *The Right Stuff* by Tom Wolfe

General Nonfiction, Paperback: *The Snow Leopard* by Peter Matthiessen

General Reference Book, Hardcover: *The Complete Directory* edited by Elder Witt

General Reference, Paperback: *The Complete Directory of Prime Time Network TV Shows: 1946-Present* by Tim Brooks and Earle Marsh

History, Hardcover: *The White House Years* by Henry A. Kissinger

History, Paperback: *A Distant Mirror: The Calamitous Fourteenth Century* by Barbara W. Tuchman

Mystery, Hardcover: *The Green Ripper* by John D. MacDonald; *Stained Glass* by William F. Buckley, Jr.

Poetry: *Ashes* by Philip Levine

Religion/Inspiration, Hardcover: *The Gnostic Gospels* by Elaine Pagels

Religion/Inspiration, Paperback: *A Severe Mercy* by Sheldon Vanauken

Science, Hardcover: *Godel, Escher, Bach: An Eternal Golden Braid* by Douglas Hofstadter

Science, Paperback: *The Dancing Wu Li Masters: An Overview of the New Physics* by Gary Zukav

Science Fiction, Hardcover: *Jem* by Frederik Pohl

Science Fiction, Paperback: *The Book of the Dun Crow* by Walter Wangerin, Jr.

Translation: *Hard Labor* by Cesare Pavese, edited by William Arrowsmith; *Complete Critical Prose and Letters* by Osip Mandelstam, edited by Jane Gary Harris and Constance Link

Western: *Bendigo Shafter* by Louis L'Amour

1981

Autobiography/Biography, Hardcover: *Walt Whitman* by Justin Kaplan

Autobiography/Biography, Paperback: *Samuel Beckett* by Deirdre Bair

Children's Book, Fiction, Hardcover: *The Night Swimmers* by Betsy Byars

Children's Book, Fiction, Paperback: *Ramona and Her Mother* by Beverly Cleary

Children's Book, Nonfiction, Hardcover: *Mali—Oh Boy! Babies* by Alison Cragin Herzig and Jane Lawrence

Fiction, Hardcover: *Plains Song* by Wright Morris

Fiction, Paperback: *The Stories of John Cheever* by John Cheever

First Novel: *Sister Wolf* by Anne Arensberg

General Nonfiction, Hardcover: *China Men* by Maxine Hong Kingston

General Nonfiction, Paperback: *The Last Cowboy* by Jane Kramer

History, Hardcover: *Christianity, Social Tolerance, and Homosexuality* by John Boswell

History, Paperback: *Been in the Storm So Long: The Aftermath of Slavery* by Leon F. Litwack

Poetry: *The Need to Hold Still* by Lisel Mueller

Science, Hardcover: *The Panda's Thumb: More Reflections on Natural History* by Stephen Jay Gould

Science, Paperback: *The Medusa and the Snail* by Lewis Thomas

Translation: *The Letters of Gustave Flaubert* by Gustave Flaubert, translated by Francis Steegmuller; *Evening Edged in Gold* by Arno Schmidt, translated by John E. Woods

1982

Autobiography/Biography, Hardcover: *Mornings on Horseback* by David McCullough

Autobiography/Biography, Paperback: *Walter Lippmann and the American Century* by Ronald Steel

Children's Book, Fiction, Hardcover: *Westmark* by Lloyd Alexander

Children's Book, Fiction, Paperback: *Words by Heart* by Ouida Sebestyen

Children's Book, Nonfiction: *A Penguin Year* by Susan Bonners

Children's Book, Picture Book, Hardcover: *Outside Over There* by Maurice Sendak

Children's Book, Picture Book, Paperback: *Noah's Ark* by Peter Spier

Fiction, Hardcover: *Rabbit Is Rich* by John Updike

Fiction, Paperback: *So Long, See You Tomorrow* by William Maxwell

First Novel: *Dale Loves Sophie to Death* by Robb Forman Dew

General Nonfiction, Hardcover: *The Soul of a New Machine* by Tracy Kidder

General Nonfiction, Paperback: *Naming Names* by Victor S. Navasky

History, Hardcover: *People of the Sacred Mountain: A History of the Northern Cheyenne Chiefs and Warrior Societies, 1830-1879* by Father Peter John Powell

History, Paperback: *The Generation of 1914* by Robert Wohl

Poetry: *Life Supports: New and Collected Poems* by William Bronk

Science, Hardcover: *Lucy: The Beginnings of Humankind* by Donald C. Johanson and Maitland A. Edey

Science, Paperback: *Taking the Quantum Leap: The New Physics for Nonscientists* by Fred Alan Wolf

Translation: *In the Shade of Spring Leaves* by Higuchi Ichiyo, translated by Robert Lyons Danly; *The*

Ten Thousand Leaves: A Translation of The Man'Yoshu, Japan's Premier Anthology of Classical Poetry translated by Ian Hideo Levy

1983

Autobiography/Biography, Hardcover: *Isak Dinesen: The Life of a Storyteller* by Judith Thurman

Autobiography/Biography, Paperback: *Nathaniel Hawthorne in His Time* by James R. Mellow

Children's Book, Fiction, Hardcover: *Homesick: My Own Story* by Jean Fritz

Children's Book, Fiction, Paperback: *A Place Apart* by Paula Fox; *Marked by Fire* by Joyce Carol Thomas

Children's Book, Nonfiction: *Chimney Sweeps* by James Cross Giblin

Children's Book, Picture Book, Hardcover: *Miss Rumphius* by Barbara Cooney; *Doctor De Soto* by William Steig

Children's Book, Picture Book, Paperback: *A House Is a House for Me* by Mary Ann Hoberman, illustrated by Betty Fraser

Fiction, Hardcover: *The Color Purple* by Alice Walker

Fiction, Paperback: *Collected Stories of Eudora Welty* by Eudora Welty

First Novel: *The Women of Brewster Place* by Gloria Naylor

General Nonfiction, Hardcover: *China: Alive in the Bitter Sea* by Fox Butterfield

General Nonfiction, Paperback: *National Defense* by James Fallows

History, Hardcover: *Voices of Protest: Huey Long, Father Couglin, and the Great Depression* by Alan Brinkley

History, Paperback: *Utopian Thought in the Western World* by Frank E. Manuel and Fritzie P. Manuel

Original Paperback: *The Red Magician* by Lisa Goldstein

Poetry: *Selected Poems* by Galway Kinnell; *Country Music: Selected Early Poems* by Charles Wright

Science, Hardcover: *"Subtle Is the Lord . . ."* : *The Science and Life of Albert Einstein* by Abraham Pais

Science, Paperback: *The Mathematical Experience* by Philip J. Davis and Reuben Hersh

Translation: *Les Fleurs du Mal* by Charles Baudelaire, translated by Richard Howard

1984

Fiction: *Victory over Japan: A Book of Stories* by Ellen Gilchrist

First Work of Fiction: *Stones for Ibarra* by Harriet Doerr

Nonfiction: *Andrew Jackson and the Course of American Democracy, 1833-1845* by Robert V. Remini

1985

Fiction: *White Noise* by Don DeLillo

First Work of Fiction: *Easy in the Islands* by Bob Shacochis

Nonfiction: *Common Ground: A Turbulent Decade in the Lives of Three American Families* by J. Anthony Lukas

1986

Fiction: *World's Fair* by E. L. Doctorow

Nonfiction: *Arctic Dreams* by Barry Lopez

1987

Fiction: *Paco's Story* by Larry Heinemann

Nonfiction: *The Making of the Atom Bomb* by Richard Rhodes

1988

Fiction: *Paris Trout* by Pete Dexter

Nonfiction: *A Bright Shining Lie: John Paul Vann and America in Vietnam* by Neil Sheehan

1989

Fiction: *Spartina* by John Casey

Nonfiction: *From Beirut to Jerusalem* by Thomas L. Friedman

Newbery Medal for Best Children's Book of the Year

1980: *A Gathering of Days: A New England Girl's Journal, 1830-1832* by Joan W. Blos

1981: *Jacob Have I Loved You* by Katherine Paterson

1982: *A Visit to William Blake's Inn: Poems for Innocent and Experienced Travelers* by Nancy Willard

1983: *Dicey's Song* by Cynthia Voigt

1984: *Dear Mr. Henshaw* by Beverly Cleary

1985: *The Hero and the Crown* by Robin McKinley

1986: *Sarah, Plain and Tall* by Patricia MacLachlan

1987: *The Whipping Boy* by Sid Fleishman

1988: *Lincoln: A Photobiography* by Russell Freedman

1989: *Joyful Noise: Poems for Two Voices* by Paul Fleischman

Canadian Library Association Book of the Year for Children

1980: *River Runners* by James Houston

1981: *The Violin-Maker's Gift* by Donn Kushner

1982: *The Root Cellar* by Janet Lunn

1983: *Up to Low* by Brian Doyle

1984: *Sweetgrass* by Jan Hudson

1985: *Mama's Going to Buy You a Mockingbird* by Jean Little

1986: *Julie* by Cora Taylor

1987: *Shadow in Hawthorn Bay* by Janet Lunn

1988: *A Handful of Time* by Kit Pearson

1989: *Easy Avenue* by Brian Doyle

■ Music: Popular Musicians

Groups and performers followed by an asterisk (*) are subjects of their own entries in *The Eighties in America*.

Act	Members	Notable 1980's Songs	Notable Facts
Paula Abdul		"Forever Your Girl," "Opposites Attract," "Straight Up"	Originally a Los Angeles Lakers cheerleader and a choreographer, Abdul would later star as a judge with Simon Cowell and Randy Jackson on the hit television talent show *American Idol*.
Bryan Adams*		"Cuts like a Knife," "Heaven," "Summer of '69"	Adams's first single was a 1979 disco song, "Let Me Take You Dancing."
Aerosmith	Steven Tyler, Joe Perry, Tom Hamilton, Joey Kramer, Brad Whitford	"Angel," "Janie's Got a Gun," "Love in an Elevator"	In 1986, Tyler and Perry appeared on Run-D.M.C.'s rap cover of Aerosmith's 1976 hit "Walk This Way."
Air Supply	Russell Hitchcock, Graham Russell	"All Out of Love," "Making Love out of Nothing at All," "The One That You Love"	Hitchcock and Russell met in a production of *Jesus Christ Superstar.*
Asia	John Wetton, Geoff Downes, Steve Howe, Carl Palmer	"Don't Cry," "Heat of the Moment," "Only Time Will Tell"	Asia was a "supergroup" consisting of members of the Buggles, Yes, King Crimson, and Emerson, Lake & Palmer.
Bananarama	Sarah Dallin, Siobhan Fahey, Keren Woodward	"Cruel Summer," "I Heard a Rumor," "Venus"	Bananarama's first single, "Aie A Mwana," was produced by the ex-Sex Pistol Paul Cook.
The Bangles	Susanna Hoffs, Debbi Peterson, Vicki Peterson, Michael Steele	"If She Knew What She Wants," "Manic Monday," "Walk like an Egyptian"	Vicki Peterson joined Susan Cowsill of the Cowsills and Peter Holsapple, a former member of the dBs, to form the Continental Drifters during the 1990's.
Beastie Boys	Mike Diamond, Adam Horovitz, Adam Yauch	"Hey Ladies," "She's on It," "(You Gotta) Fight for Your Right (to Party!)"	The Beastie Boys' 1986 album *License to Ill* was one of the biggest-selling debuts of all time.
Pat Benatar		"Hit Me with Your Best Shot," "Love Is a Battlefield," "We Belong"	In the early 1970's, Benatar studied with a voice teacher from the Juilliard School of Music.
Blondie*	Debbie Harry, Chris Stein, Frank Infante, Jimmy Destri, Clem Burke, Nigel Harrison	"Call Me," "The Tide Is High," "Rapture"	Lead singer Harry made a successful transition to acting, enjoying featured roles in several films of the 1980's.

Act	Members	Notable 1980's Songs	Notable Facts
Bon Jovi*	Jon Bon Jovi, Dave Bryan, Richie Sambora, Alec John Such, Tico Torres	"Born to Be My Baby," "Livin' on a Prayer," "You Give Love a Bad Name"	Jon Bon Jovi addressed the Oxford Union debating society in 2001.
David Bowie		"China Girl," "Let's Dance," "Modern Love"	Bowie starred in the stage play *The Elephant Man* from July, 1980, to January, 1981.
Bobby Brown		"My Prerogative," "Roni," "Rock Wit'cha"	A former member of New Edition, Brown later became tabloid fodder as the (eventually former) husband of Whitney Houston.
Jackson Browne		"Lawyers in Love," "Somebody's Baby," "Tender Is the Night"	Browne's 1985 hit "You're a Friend of Mine" featured the playing of Bruce Springsteen's saxophonist Clarence Clemons and the backing vocals of Browne's then-girlfriend, actress Daryl Hannah.
Belinda Carlisle		"Heaven Is a Place on Earth," "I Get Weak," "Mad About You"	Carlisle was the lead singer of the Go-Go's and later married Morgan Mason, the son of actor James Mason.
The Cars	Ric Ocasek, Benjamin Orr, Elliot Easton, Greg Hawkes, David Robinson	"Drive," "Shake It Up," "You Might Think"	The cover of the Cars' *Candy-O* album featured a painting by the pin-up girl artist Alberto Vargas.
Peter Cetera		"After All," "Glory of Love," "The Next Time I Fall"	Cetera was the lead singer of Chicago from 1969 to 1985.
Cher*		"If I Could Turn Back Time," "Just like Jesse James," "We All Sleep Alone"	Cher won the Academy Award for Best Actress for her role in the 1987 film *Moonstruck*.
Chicago	Robert Lamm, Lee Loughnane, James Pankow, Walter Parazaider, Danny Seraphine, Chris Pinnick, Bill Champlin, Jason Scheff	"Hard Habit to Break," "Hard to Say I'm Sorry," "You're the Inspiration"	Chicago was originally named Chicago Transit Authority, after the city's rail and bus management agency.
Phil Collins		"Against All Odds (Take a Look at Me Now)," "One More Night," "Sussudio"	With the help of a supersonic Concorde airplane, Collins performed at both London's Wembley Stadium and Philadelphia's JFK Stadium as part of the fund-raising concert Live Aid on July 13, 1985.

Act	Members	Notable 1980's Songs	Notable Facts
The Commodores	Lionel Richie, William King, Ronald LaPread, Thomas McClary, Walter Orange, Milan Williams	"Lady (You Bring Me Up)," "Nightshift," "Oh No"	The Commodores' 1985 hit "Nightshift" was a tribute to the late soul singers Marvin Gaye and Jackie Wilson.
Christopher Cross		"Arthur's Theme (Best That You Can Do)," "Ride like the Wind," "Sailing"	Cross won five Grammy Awards in 1981, including Best New Artist, Album of the Year, and Best Song and Record of the Year (for "Sailing").
Culture Club*	"Boy George" O'Dowd, Michael Craig, Roy Hay, Jon Moss	"Church of the Poison Mind," "Do You Really Want to Hurt Me?," "Karma Chameleon"	Before forming the group that would become Culture Club, Boy George was briefly a member of the band Bow Wow Wow.
Def Leppard	Joe Elliott, Rick Allen, Steve Clark, Phil Collen, Rick Savage	"Armageddon It," "Love Bites," "Pour Some Sugar on Me"	Drummer Allen played on a specially created drum kit after losing his left arm in a 1984 car accident; guitarist Clark died of an alcohol-related illness in 1991.
Dire Straits	Mark Knopfler, Alan Clark, Guy Fletcher, John Illsley, David Knopfler, Terry Williams, Pick Withers	"Money for Nothing," "Romeo and Juliet," "Walk of Life"	Dire Straits's 1985 hit "Money for Nothing" became famous for the high-rotation screening of its computer-animated video on MTV and notorious for the appearance of the word "faggot" in one of the verses.
Thomas Dolby		"Hyperactive," "I Scare Myself," "She Blinded Me with Science"	Contrary to rumor, Dolby was not born in Cairo, Egypt, but in London, England.
Duran Duran*	Simon LeBon, Nick Rhodes, Andy Taylor, John Taylor, Roger Taylor	"Hungry like the Wolf," "The Reflex," "Rio"	The unrelated Andy and John Taylor were also members of the "supergroup" Power Station.
Gloria Estefan & Miami Sound Machine	Gloria Estefan, Emilio Estefan, Juan Avila, Enrique Gracia	"Anything for You," "1-2-3," "Falling in Love (Uh-Oh)"	Estefan's father was a bodyguard for the former Cuban president Fulgencio Batista.
Eurythmics	Annie Lennox, Dave Stewart	"Sweet Dreams (Are Made of This)," "Here Comes the Rain Again," "Would I Lie to You?"	The husband of Bananarama's Siobhan Fahey, Stewart has produced recordings for Bob Dylan, Tom Petty, Mick Jagger, and the Ramones.

Act	Members	Notable 1980's Songs	Notable Facts
Fleetwood Mac	Lindsey Buckingham, Mick Fleetwood, John McVie, Christine McVie, Stevie Nicks, Billy Burnette, Rick Vito	"Everywhere," "Hold Me," "Little Lies"	Fleetwood Mac's "Don't Stop" was used as the theme of Bill Clinton's 1992 presidential campaign.
Foreigner	Lou Gramm, Dennis Elliott, Mick Jones, Rick Wills	"I Want to Know What Love Is," "Urgent," "Waiting for a Girl like You"	Two of Foreigner's biggest hits feature contributions from the saxophonist Junior Walker and the New Jersey Mass Choir, "Urgent" and "I Want to Know What Love Is," respectively.
Samantha Fox		"I Wanna Have Some Fun," "Naughty Girls (Need Love Too)," "Touch Me (I Want Your Body)"	Fox first came to fame as a topless model in England.
Aretha Franklin		"Freeway of Love," "I Knew You Were Waiting (for Me)," "Sisters Are Doin' It for Themselves"	During the 1980's, Franklin recorded hit duets with the Eurythmics, George Michael, and Elton John.
Glenn Frey		"The Heat Is On," "Smuggler's Blues," "You Belong to the City"	A member of the Eagles, Frey appeared as the owner of a professional football team in the 1996 film *Jerry Maguire*.
Peter Gabriel		"Big Time," "Shock the Monkey," "Sledgehammer"	The original lead singer of Genesis, Gabriel's first three solo albums were each titled simply *Peter Gabriel*.
The J. Geils Band	Peter Wolf, Jerome Geils, Stephen Jo Bladd, Seth Justman, Danny Klein, Magic Dick Salwitz	"Centerfold," "Freeze-Frame," "Love Stinks"	Lead singer Wolf was married to actress Faye Dunaway from 1974 to 1979.
Genesis	Tony Banks, Phil Collins, Mike Rutherford	"That's All," "Tonight, Tonight, Tonight," "Invisible Touch"	Rutherford also scored several 1980's hits as the leader of Mike + the Mechanics.
Debbie Gibson		"Foolish Beat," "Lost in Your Eyes," "Only in My Dreams"	Gibson won $1,000 in a songwriting contest with a song that she had written at age twelve, "I Come from America."
The Go-Go's*	Belinda Carlisle, Charlotte Caffey, Gina Schock, Kathy Valentine, Jane Wiedlin	"Our Lips Are Sealed," "Vacation," "We Got the Beat"	The Go-Go's portrayed an all-male dance band in their 1984 "Turn to You" video.

Act	Members	Notable 1980's Songs	Notable Facts
Guns n' Roses*	Axl Rose, Saul "Slash" Hudson, Izzy Stradlin, Steven Adler, Duff McKagan	"Paradise City," "Sweet Child o' Mine," "Welcome to the Jungle"	Guns n' Roses' 1993 album *The Spaghetti Incident?* consists of covers of the band's favorite punk songs.
Hall & Oates		"Kiss on My List," "Maneater," "Out of Touch"	By 1984, Daryl Hall and John Oates had eclipsed the Everly Brothers as the most successful duo in rock history.
Heart	Ann Wilson, Nancy Wilson, Mark Andes, Denny Carmassi, Howard Leese	"All I Wanna Do Is Make Love to You," "Never," "These Dreams"	Nancy Wilson is married to the journalist, author, and filmmaker Cameron Crowe.
Don Henley		"The Boys of Summer," "Dirty Laundry," "The End of the Innocence"	Along with fellow members of the Eagles, Henley was inducted into the Rock and Roll Hall of Fame in 1998.
Bruce Hornsby & the Range	Bruce Hornsby, David Mansfield, George Marinelli, John Molo, Joe Puerta	"Mandolin Rain," "The Valley Road," "The Way It Is"	During the 1990's Hornsby occasionally played keyboards on tour with the Grateful Dead.
Whitney Houston*		"How Will I Know," "I Wanna Dance with Somebody (Who Loves Me)," "Saving All My Love for You"	Houston's 1985 hit "The Greatest Love of All" was originally a hit for George Benson and the theme song to the Muhammed Ali biopic *The Greatest* in 1977.
The Human League	Philip Oakey, Joanne Catherall, Suzanne Sulley	"Don't You Want Me," "(Keep Feeling) Fascination," "Human"	Before breaking through in the United States, the Human League had enjoyed a string of hits, including "Boys and Girls" and "Love Action," in England.
Billy Idol		"Dancing with Myself," "Rebel Yell," "White Wedding"	Idol was the lead singer of the English punk band Generation X.
INXS	Michael Hutchence, Garry Beers, Andy Farris, Jon Farris, Tim Farris, Rick Pengilly	"Devil Inside," "Need You Tonight," "New Sensation"	The cue-card-tossing sequence of INXS's 1987 video "Need You Tonight/Mediate" was a take-off on "Subterranean Homesick Blues," the opening sequence of *Don't Look Back*, a documentary about Bob Dylan released in 1965.
Janet Jackson		"Control," "Miss You Much," "Nasty"	Jackson acted in the television situation comedies *Good Times* and *Diff'rent Strokes* from 1977 to 1982.

Act	Members	Notable 1980's Songs	Notable Facts
Michael Jackson*		"Beat It," "Billie Jean," "Wanna Be Startin' Somethin'"	Jackson's 1982 album *Thriller* is the second-biggest-selling album of all time.
Joan Jett and the Blackhearts	Joan Jett, Ricky Byrd, Lee Crystal, Thommy Price, Gary Ryan	"Crimson and Clover," "I Hate Myself for Loving You," "I Love Rock 'n Roll"	Jett costarred with Michael J. Fox, Michael McKean, and Gena Rowlands in the 1987 film *Light of Day*.
Billy Joel		"Tell Her About It," "Uptown Girl," "We Didn't Start the Fire"	Joel played piano on the Shangri-Las' 1964 hit "Leader of the Pack."
Elton John		"I Don't Want to Go on with You like That," "I Guess That's Why They Call It the Blues," "I'm Still Standing"	Originally a hit in the 1970's as a tribute to Marilyn Monroe, John's "Candle in the Wind" would become an even bigger hit in 1997 when rewritten as a tribute to the late Princess Diana.
Journey*	Steve Perry, Jonathan Cain, Gregg Rolie, Neal Schon, Steve Smith, Ross Valary	"Don't Stop Believin'," "Open Arms," "Who's Crying Now"	Schon and Rolie first played together as members of Santana; Cain, who replaced Rolie in 1981, was also a member of The Babys and Bad English.
Kool & the Gang	James "J. T." Taylor, Robert "Kool" Bell, Ronald Bell, George Brown, Robert Mickens, Claydes Smith, Dennis Thomas, Earl Toon	"Celebrate," "Cherish," "Misled"	Kool & the Gang's "Celebrate" was used as the theme song of the 2004 Democratic Convention.
Cyndi Lauper*		"Girls Just Want to Have Fun," "Time After Time," "True Colors"	Lauper's "True Colors" was featured prominently in a 1980's Kodak advertisement; a version by Kasey Chambers was used as the theme song of the 2003 Rugby World Cup.
John Lennon*		"(Just like) Starting Over," "Watching the Wheels," "Woman"	Lennon, a former Beatle, was assassinated on December 8, 1980, in New York City.
Huey Lewis & the News	Huey Lewis, Johnny Calla, Mario Cipollina, Bill Gibson, Chris Hayes, Sean Hopper	"Do You Believe in Love," "I Want a New Drug," "The Power of Love"	Lewis played harmonica on 1970's solo albums by the pub-rock pioneers Nick Lowe and Dave Edmunds.
Kenny Loggins		"Danger Zone," "Footloose," "I'm Alright"	During the 1970's, Loggins was one half of the hit duo Loggins & Messina.

Act	Members	Notable 1980's Songs	Notable Facts
Loverboy	Mike Reno, Paul Dean, Matt Frenette, Doug Johnson, Scott Smith	"Hot Girls in Love," "Lovin' Every Minute of It," "Working for the Weekend"	Loverboy is one of the biggest-selling Canadian bands of all time.
Paul McCartney		"Coming Up (Live at Glasgow)," "Ebony and Ivory," "No More Lonely Nights"	Beginning with 1997's *Standing Stone*, McCartney composed and released a series of orchestral albums that became classical music best-sellers.
Madonna*		"Into the Groove," "Like a Prayer," "Live to Tell"	Madonna was the top female singles artist of the 1980's, with twenty top-forty hits, seventeen of which reached the top ten and seven of which reached number one.
Richard Marx		"Angelia," "Hold on to the Nights," "Right Here Waiting"	Prior to his solo success, Marx sang backup on albums by Lionel Richie, Chicago, Peabo Bryson, Teddy Pendergrass, and Julio Iglesias.
John Mellencamp*		"Hurts So Good," "Jack and Diane," "R.O.C.K. in the U.S.A. (A Salute to 60's Rock)"	From 1976 to 1982, Mellencamp released albums under the name John Cougar, a pseudonym selected by his manager Tony DeFries.
Men at Work	Colin Hay, Greg Ham, John Rees, Jerry Speiser, Ron Strykert	"Down Under," "It's a Mistake," "Who Can It Be Now?"	"Down Under" became famous for introducing Australian terms such as "crombie," "chunder," and "Vegemite sandwich" to the American pop charts.
George Michael*		"Faith," "Father Figure," "I Want Your Sex"	Michael performed "Somebody to Love" with the surviving members of Queen at the Freddie Mercury Tribute in 1992.
Milli Vanilli	Fabrice Morvan, Rob Pilatus (actually John Davis, Brad Howe, Charles Shaw)	"Blame It on the Rain," "Girl I'm Gonna Miss You," "Girl You Know It's True"	Morvan and Pilatus became notorious for not singing on "their" recordings and having to return their 1989 Best New Artist Grammy Award. Pilatus died of a drug overdose in 1998.
The Moody Blues	Justin Hayward, John Lodge, Graeme Edge, Patrick Moraz, Ray Thomas	"I Know You're Out There Somewhere," "The Voice," "Your Wildest Dreams"	In 1986 members of the British band Mood Six portrayed the young Moody Blues in the video for "Your Wildest Dreams."

Act	Members	Notable 1980's Songs	Notable Facts
Mötley Crüe*	Vince Neil, Tommy Lee, Mick Mars, Nikki Sixx	"Dr. Feelgood," "Girls, Girls, Girls," "Smokin' in the Boys Room"	Lee became tabloid fodder in the 1990's because of his marriages to—and divorces from—actresses Heather Locklear and Pamela Anderson.
Willie Nelson		"Always on My Mind," "On the Road Again," "To All the Girls I've Loved Before"	In the 1980's and 1990's, Nelson, Johnny Cash, Waylon Jennings, and Kris Kristofferson were members of The Highwaymen, a country music band.
New Kids on the Block	Jon Knight, Jordan Knight, Joey McIntyre, Donnie Wahlberg, Danny Wood	"Hangin' Tough," "This One's for the Children," "You Got It (The Right Stuff)"	New Kids on the Block's 1989 album *Hangin' Tough* sold more than eight million copies and included five top-ten hits.
Olivia Newton-John		"Heart Attack," "Physical," "Suddenly"	Newton-John is the granddaughter of the Nobel Prize-winning physicist Max Born.
Stevie Nicks		"Edge of Seventeen (Just like a White Winged Dove)," "Leather and Lace," "Stop Draggin' My Heart Around"	As a member of Fleetwood Mac, Nicks was inducted into the Rock and Roll Hall of Fame in 1998.
Billy Ocean		"Caribbean Queen (No More Love on the Run)," "Get Outta My Dreams, Get into My Car," "There'll Be Sad Songs (to Make You Cry)"	Although considered a 1980's artist, Ocean scored his first top-forty hit, "Love Really Hurts Without You," in 1976.
Robert Palmer		"Addicted to Love," "I Didn't Mean to Turn You On," "Simply Irresistible"	The trademark of Palmer's popular 1980's videos was the use of glamorous models as his backing band.
Ray Parker, Jr.		"Ghostbusters," "I Still Can't Get Over Loving You," "The Other Woman"	In 1984, Parker was sued for by Huey Lewis, who claimed that Parker's "Ghostbusters" plagiarized Lewis's "I Want a New Drug."
Pet Shop Boys	Chris Lowe, Neil Tennant	"Always on My Mind," "West End Girls," "What Have I Done to Deserve This?"	Prior to his musical career, Tennant was an editor at Marvel Comics and *Smash Hits* magazine.

Act	Members	Notable 1980's Songs	Notable Facts
Tom Petty & the Heartbreakers	Mike Campbell, Howie Epstein, Stan Lynch, Tom Petty, Benmont Tench	"Free Fallin'," "I Won't Back Down," "Refugee"	With Bob Dylan, George Harrison, Jeff Lynne, and Roy Orbison, Petty also was a member of the Traveling Wilburys.
Pointer Sisters	Anita Pointer, June Pointer, Ruth Pointer	"I'm So Excited," "Jump," "Neutron Dance"	During the 1970's the Pointer Sisters became the first black female act to perform at the Grand Ole Opry.
The Police*	Gordon "Sting" Sumner, Stewart Copeland, Andy Stewart	"Don't Stand So Close to Me," "Every Breath You Take," "Every Little Thing She Does Is Magic"	Sumner acquired the nickname Sting because of his preference for wearing a yellow and black shirt in his early days as a musician.
Prince*		"Little Red Corvette," "1999," "When Doves Cry"	Under pseudonyms such as "Christopher and Alexander Nevermind," Prince wrote hits for the Bangles, Sheena Easton, and other performers.
R.E.M.*	Michael Stipe, Peter Buck, Bill Berry, Mike Mills	"The One I Love," "Radio Free Europe," "Stand"	R.E.M. became figureheads of the Athens (Georgia) sound, the popularity of which contributed to the popularity of other locality-specific underground acts, such as the Replacements (Minneapolis) and Nirvana (Seattle).
REO Speedwagon	Kevin Cronin, Neal Doughty, Alan Gratzer, Bruce Hall, Gary Richrath	"Can't Fight This Feeling," "Keep on Loving You," "Live Every Moment"	REO Speedwagon took its name from a high-speed fire engine.
Lionel Richie*		"All Night Long (All Night)," "Penny Lover," "Stuck on You"	Before launching his solo career in 1982, Richie was the lead singer of The Commodores.
The Rolling Stones	Mick Jagger, Keith Richards, Ron Wood, Charlie Watts, Bill Wyman	"Emotional Rescue," "Mixed Emotions," "Start Me Up,"	The Rolling Stones' 1981 hit "Waiting on a Friend" featured the saxophone playing of jazz great Sonny Rollins.
Sade		"Never as Good as the First Time," "Smooth Operator," "The Sweetest Taboo"	Sade (pronounced "Shar-day") was born Helen Folasade Adu in Ibadan, Nigeria.
Bob Seger and the Silver Bullet Band	Bob Seger, Drew Abbott, Chris Campbell, Craig Frost, Charlie Martin, Alto Reed, Robyn Robbins	"Against the Wind," "Like a Rock," "Shakedown"	Seger's "Like a Rock" was used in a long-running series of advertisements for Chevrolet trucks.

Act	Members	Notable 1980's Songs	Notable Facts
Rick Springfield		"Don't Talk to Strangers," "I've Done Everything for You," "Jessie's Girl"	Besides being a teen idol in the 1970's, Springfield also portrayed Dr. Noah Drake in the soap opera *General Hospital.*
Bruce Springsteen & the E-Street Band*	Bruce Springsteen, Roy Bittan, Clarence Clemons, Gary Tallent, "Miami Steve" Van Zant, Max Weinberg	"Born in the U.S.A.," "Hungry Heart," "Glory Days"	In 1986 Springsteen's forty-song *Live/1975-1985* became the only boxed set to reach number one on *Billboard*'s album chart.
Starship	Mickey Thomas, Grace Slick, Don Baldwin, Craig Chaquico, Aynsley Dunbar, Pete Sears	"Nothing's Gonna Stop Us Now," "Sara," "We Built This City"	Thomas's first Top 40 appearance was as the lead singer on Elvin Bishop's 1976 hit "Fooled Around and Fell in Love."
Styx	Dennis DeYoung, Tommy Shaw, Chuck Panozzo, John Panozzo, James Young	"The Best of Times," "Mr. Roboto," "Too Much Time on My Hands"	Styx's 1983 album *Kilroy Was Here* was an anticensorship concept album, inspired in part by accusations that the band was encoding evil messages into its songs.
Donna Summer		"Cold Love," "She Works Hard for the Money," "The Wanderer"	Summer revamped her 1970's bad-girl image by publicizing her conversion to Christianity with the song "I Believe in Jesus" in 1980 and recording two albums with the Christian producer Michael Omartian in 1983 and 1984.
Tears for Fears	Roland Orzabal, Curt Smith	"Everybody Wants to Rule the World," "Shout," "Sowing the Seeds of Love"	Orzabal and Smith based their group's name and some of their songs on the primal scream theories of psychotherapist Arthur Janev.
Thompson Twins	Tom Bailey, Alannah Currie, Joe Leeway	"Doctor! Doctor!," "Hold Me Now," "Lay Your Hands"	The Thompson Twins named themselves after the detectives Thompson and Thompson in the European comic strip *The Adventures of Tintin.*
Toto	Bobby Kimball, David Hungate, Steve Lukather, David Paich, Jeff Porcaro, Steve Porcaro, Fergie Fredericksen	"Africa," "Rosanna," "Stranger in Town"	The real-life subject of "Rosanna" was the actress Rosanna Arquette.
Tina Turner*		"Break Every Rule," "Private Dancer," "What's Love Got to Do with It"	Turner costarred with Mel Gibson in the 1985 film *Mad Max Beyond Thunderdome.*

Act	Members	Notable 1980's Songs	Notable Facts
U2	Paul "Bono" Hewson, Dave "The Edge" Evans, Adam Clayton, Larry Mullen, Jr.	"I Still Haven't Found What I'm Looking For," "Where the Streets Have No Name," "With or Without You"	The briefcase with the lyrics for U2's 1981 album *October* was stolen, requiring Bono to come up with lyrics in the studio. The briefcase was found and returned to Bono in 2004.
Van Halen*	David Lee Roth, Eddie Van Halen, Michael Anthony, Alex Van Halen, Sammy Hagar	"Jump," "Panama," "Why Can't This Be Love"	Both Van Halen brothers were trained in classical music as children.
Steve Winwood		"Higher Love," "Valerie," "While You See a Chance"	As a teenager Winwood sang lead and played organ on the Spencer Davis Group's 1967 hits "Gimme Some Lovin'" and "I'm a Man."
"Weird Al" Yankovic*		"Eat It," "I Love Rocky Road," "I Want a New Duck"	Yankovic's career as rock's premier parodist was launched when his "My Bologna," a parody of the Knack's "My Sharona," was played on the nationally syndicated Dr. Demento radio show in 1979.
ZZ Top	Billy Gibbons, Dusty Hill, Frank Beard	"Gimme All Your Lovin," "Legs," "Sharp Dressed Man"	ZZ Top's best-known videos were mini triumph-of-the-underdog narratives that featured the band members and a trio of glamorous women as fairy godparents.

Arsenio Orteza

■ Music: Grammy Awards

This list includes winners of Grammy Awards in major categories. "Album of the Year" awards the artist who performed the album. "Record of the Year" awards the producer and artist, while "Song of the Year" awards the songwriter. An asterisk (*) following a name or group indicates the presence of a full-length entry in *The Eighties in America*.

1980

Album of the Year: *Christopher Cross*, Christopher Cross

Record of the Year: "Sailing," Michael Omartian (producer), Christopher Cross (artist)

Song of the Year: "Sailing," Christopher Cross (songwriter and artist)

Best New Artist: Christopher Cross

Best Pop Vocal Performance, Female: "The Rose," Bette Midler

Best Pop Vocal Performance, Male: "This Is It," Kenny Loggins

Best Pop Performance by a Duo or Group with Vocal: "Guilty," Barbra Streisand and Barry Gibb

Best Rock Vocal Performance, Female: *Crimes of Passion*, Pat Benatar

Best Rock Vocal Performance, Male: *Glass Houses*, Billy Joel

Best Rock Performance by a Duo or Group with Vocal: *Against the Wind*, Bob Seger and the Silver Bullet Band

Best R&B Vocal Performance, Female: "Never Knew Love Like This Before," Stephanie Mills

Best R&B Vocal Performance, Male: "Give Me the Night," George Benson

Best R&B Performance by a Duo or Group with Vocal: "Shining Star," Manhattans

Best R&B Song: "Never Knew Love Like This Before," James Mtume and Reggie Lucas (songwriters), Stephanie Mills (artist)

Best Country Vocal Performance, Female: "Could I Have This Dance?," Anne Murray

Best Country Vocal Performance, Male: "He Stopped Loving Her Today," George Jones

Best Country Performance, Duo or Group: "That Lovin' You Feeling Again," Emmylou Harris and Roy Orbison

Best Country Song: "On the Road Again," Willie Nelson (songwriter and artist)

Best Jazz Fusion Performance, Instrumental or Vocal: "Birdland," The Manhattan Transfer

Best Jazz Vocal Performance, Female: *A Perfect Match: Ella and Basie*, Ella Fitzgerald

Best Jazz Vocal Performance, Male: "Moody's Mood," George Benson

Best Jazz Instrumental Performance, Soloist: *I Will Never Say Goodbye*, Bill Evans

Best Jazz Instrumental Performance, Group: *We Will Meet Again*, Bill Evans

Best Jazz Instrumental Performance, Big Band: *On the Road Again*, Count Basie

1981

Album of the Year: *Double Fantasy*, Jack Douglas, John Lennon*, and Yoko Ono (producers), John Lennon* and Yoko Ono (artists)

Record of the Year: "Bette Davis Eyes," Val Garay (producer), Kim Carnes (artist)

Song of the Year: "Bette Davis Eyes," Donna Weiss and Jackie DeShannon (songwriters), Kim Carnes (artist)

Best New Artist: Sheena Easton

Best Pop Vocal Performance, Female: *Lena Horne: The Lady and Her Music*, Lena Horne (artist)

Best Pop Vocal Performance, Male: *Breakin' Away*, Al Jarreau

Best Pop Performance by a Duo or Group with Vocal: "Boy from New York City," The Manhattan Transfer

Best Rock Vocal Performance, Female: "Fire and Ice," Pat Benatar

Best Rock Vocal Performance, Male: "Jessie's Girl," Rick Springfield

Best Rock Performance by a Duo or Group with Vocal: "Don't Stand So Close to Me," The Police

Best R&B Vocal Performance, Female: "Hold On, I'm Comin'," Aretha Franklin

Best R&B Vocal Performance, Male: "One Hundred Ways," James Ingram

Best R&B Performance by a Duo or Group with Vocal: *The Dude*, Quincy Jones

Best R&B Song: "Just the Two of Us," Bill Withers, Ralph MacDonald, and William Salter (songwriters), Grover Washington, Jr., and Bill Withers (artists)

Best Country Vocal Performance, Female: "9 to 5,"
Dolly Parton

Best Country Vocal Performance, Male: "(There's)
No Getting Over Me," Ronnie Milsap

Best Country Performance, Duo or Group:
"Elvira," The Oak Ridge Boys

Best Country Song: "9 to 5," Dolly Parton
(songwriter and artist)

Best Jazz Fusion Performance, Instrumental or
Vocal: *Winelight*, Grover Washington, Jr.

Best Jazz Vocal Performance, Female: *Digital III at
Montreaux*, Ella Fitzgerald

Best Jazz Vocal Performance, Male: "Blue Rondo a
la Turk," Al Jarreau

Best Jazz Vocal Performance, Duo or Group:
"Until I Met You (Corner Pocket)," The
Manhattan Transfer

Best Jazz Instrumental Performance, Soloist: *Bye
Bye Blackbird*, John Coltrane

Best Jazz Instrumental Performance, Group: *Chick
Corea and Gary Burton in Concert, Zurich, October,
28, 1979*, Chick Corea and Gary Burton

Best Jazz Instrumental Performance, Big Band:
Walk on the Water, Gerry Mulligan

Video of the Year: *Michael Nesmith in Elephant Parts*,
Michael Nesmith

1982

Album of the Year: *Toto IV*, Toto (producer and
artist)

Record of the Year: "Rosanna," Toto (producer
and artist)

Song of the Year: "Always on My Mind," Johnny
Christopher, Mark James, and Wayne Carson
(songwriters), Willie Nelson (artist)

Best New Artist: Men at Work

Best Pop Vocal Performance, Female: "You Should
Hear How She Talks About You," Melissa
Manchester

Best Pop Vocal Performance, Male: "Truly," Lionel
Richie*

Best Pop Performance by a Duo or Group with
Vocal: "Up Where We Belong," Joe Cocker and
Jennifer Warnes (artists)

Best Rock Vocal Performance, Female: "Shadows
of the Night," Pat Benatar

Best Rock Vocal Performance, Male: "Hurts So
Good," John Cougar Mellencamp*

Best Rock Performance by a Duo or Group with
Vocal: "Eye of the Tiger," Survivor

Best R&B Vocal Performance, Female: "And I
Am Telling You I'm Not Going," Jennifer
Holliday

Best R&B Vocal Performance, Male: "Sexual
Healing," Marvin Gaye

Best R&B Performance by a Duo or Group with
Vocal (tie): "Let It Whip," Dazz Band, and
"Wanna Be with You," Earth, Wind, & Fire

Best R&B Song: "Turn Your Love Around," Bill
Champlin, Jay Graydon, and Steve Lukather
(songwriters), George Benson (artist)

Best Country Vocal Performance, Female: "Break
It to Me Gently," Juice Newton

Best Country Vocal Performance, Male: "Always on
My Mind," Willie Nelson

Best Country Performance, Duo or Group:
Mountain Music, Alabama

Best Country Song: "Always on My Mind," Johnny
Christopher, Mark James, and Wayne Carson
(songwriters), Willie Nelson (artist)

Best Jazz Fusion Performance, Instrumental or
Vocal: *Offramp*, Pat Metheny

Best Jazz Vocal Performance, Female: *Gershwin
Live!*, Sarah Vaughn

Best Jazz Vocal Performance, Male: *An Evening with
George Shearing and Mel Tormé*, Mel Tormé

Best Jazz Vocal Performance, Duo or Group:
"Route 66," The Manhattan Transfer

Best Jazz Instrumental Performance, Soloist: *We
Want Miles*, Miles Davis

Best Jazz Instrumental Performance, Group: *More
Live*, Phil Woods Quartet

Best Jazz Instrumental Performance, Big Band:
Warm Breeze, Count Basie

Video of the Year: *Physical*, Olivia Newton-John

1983

Album of the Year: *Thriller*, Michael Jackson* and
Quincy Jones (producers), Michael Jackson*
(artist)

Record of the Year: "Beat It," Michael Jackson*
and Quincy Jones (producers), Michael
Jackson* (artist)

Song of the Year: "Every Breath You Take," Sting*
(songwriter), The Police (artists)

Best New Artist: Culture Club*

Best Pop Vocal Performance, Female: "Flashdance:
What a Feeling," Irene Cara

Best Pop Vocal Performance, Male: *Thriller*,
Michael Jackson*

Best Pop Performance by a Duo or Group with Vocal: "Every Breath You Take," The Police

Best Rock Vocal Performance, Female: "Love Is a Battlefield," Pat Benatar

Best Rock Vocal Performance, Male: "Beat It," Michael Jackson*

Best Rock Performance by a Duo or Group with Vocal: *Synchronicity*, The Police

Best R&B Vocal Performance, Female: *Chaka Khan*, Chaka Khan

Best R&B Vocal Performance, Male: "Billie Jean," Michael Jackson*

Best R&B Performance by a Duo or Group with Vocal: "Ain't Nobody," Rufus and Chaka Khan

Best R&B Song: "Billie Jean," Michael Jackson* (songwriter and artist)

Best Country Vocal Performance, Female: "A Little Good News," Anne Murray

Best Country Vocal Performance, Male: "I.O.U.," Lee Greenwood

Best Country Performance, Duo or Group: *The Closer You Get*, Alabama

Best Country Song: "Stranger in My House," Ronnie Milsap (songwriter)

Best Jazz Fusion Performance, Instrumental or Vocal: *Travels*, Pat Metheny

Best Jazz Vocal Performance, Female: *The Best Is Yet to Come*, Ella Fitzgerald

Best Jazz Vocal Performance, Male: *Top Drawer*, Mel Tormé

Best Jazz Vocal Performance, Duo or Group: "Why Not!," The Manhattan Transfer

Best Jazz Instrumental Performance, Soloist: *Think of One*, Wynton Marsalis

Best Jazz Instrumental Performance, Group: *At the Vanguard*, Phil Woods Quartet

Best Jazz Instrumental Performance, Big Band: *All in Good Time*, Rob McConnell and the Boss Brass

Best Video, Short Form: "Girls on Film/Hungry Like the Wolf," Duran Duran*

Best Video Album: *Duran Duran*, Duran Duran*

1984

Album of the Year: *Can't Slow Down*, James Anthony Carmichael and Lionel Richie* (producers), Lionel Richie* (artist)

Record of the Year: "What's Love Got to Do with It," Terry Britten (producer), Tina Turner* (artist)

Song of the Year: "What's Love Got to Do with It," Graham Lyle and Terry Britten (songwriters), Tina Turner (artist)

Best New Artist: Cyndi Lauper*

Best Pop Vocal Performance, Female: "What's Love Got to Do With It," Tina Turner*

Best Pop Vocal Performance, Male: "Against All Odds (Take a Look at Me Now)," Phil Collins

Best Pop Performance by a Duo or Group with Vocal: "Jump (For My Love)," The Pointer Sisters

Best Rock Vocal Performance, Female: "Better Be Good to Me," Tina Turner*

Best Rock Vocal Performance, Male: "Dancing in the Dark," Bruce Springsteen*

Best Rock Performance by a Duo or Group with Vocal: *Purple Rain: Music from the Motion Picture*, Prince* and the Revolution

Best R&B Vocal Performance, Female: "I Feel for You," Chaka Khan

Best R&B Vocal Performance, Male: "Caribbean Queen (No More Rain on My Love)," Billy Ocean

Best R&B Performance by a Duo or Group with Vocal: "Yah Mo B There," James Ingram and Michael McDonald

Best R&B Song: "I Feel for You," Prince* (songwriter), Chaka Khan (artist)

Best Country Vocal Performance, Female: "In My Dreams," Emmylou Harris

Best Country Vocal Performance, Male: "That's the Way Love Goes," Merle Haggard

Best Country Performance, Duo or Group: "Mama, He's Crazy," The Judds

Best Country Song: "City of New Orleans," Steve Goodman (songwriter), Willie Nelson (artist)

Best Jazz Fusion Performance, Instrumental or Vocal: *First Circle*, Pat Metheny Group

Best Jazz Vocal Performance: *Nothin' but the Blues*, Joe Williams

Best Jazz Instrumental Performance, Soloist: *Hot House Flowers*, Wynton Marsalis

Best Jazz Instrumental Performance, Group: *New York Scene*, Art Blakey and the Jazz Messengers

Best Jazz Instrumental Performance, Big Band: *88 Basie Street*, Count Basie

Best Video, Short Form: "David Bowie," David Bowie

Best Video Album: *Making Michael Jackson's "Thriller,"* Michael Jackson*

1985

Album of the Year: *No Jacket Required*, Hugh Padgham and Phil Collins (producers), Phil Collins (artist)

Record of the Year: "We Are the World," Quincy Jones (producer) and USA for Africa* (artist)

Song of the Year: "We Are the World," Lionel Richie* and Michael Jackson* (songwriters), USA for Africa* (artist)

Best New Artist: Sade

Best Pop Vocal Performance, Female: "Saving All My Love for You," Whitney Houston*

Best Pop Vocal Performance, Male: *No Jacket Required*, Phil Collins

Best Pop Performance by a Duo or Group with Vocal: "We Are the World," Quincy Jones (producer), USA for Africa* (artist)

Best Rock Vocal Performance, Female: "One of the Living," Tina Turner*

Best Rock Vocal Performance, Male: "The Boys of Summer," Don Henley

Best Rock Performance by a Duo or Group with Vocal: "Money for Nothing," Dire Straits

Best R&B Vocal Performance, Female: "Freeway of Love," Aretha Franklin

Best R&B Vocal Performance, Male: *In Square Circle*, Stevie Wonder

Best R&B Performance by a Duo or Group with Vocal: "Nightshift," Commodores

Best R&B Song: "Freeway of Love," Jeffrey Cohen and Narada Michael Walden (songwriters), Aretha Franklin (artist)

Best Country Vocal Performance, Female: "I Don't Know Why You Don't Want Me," Roseanne Cash

Best Country Vocal Performance, Male: "Lost in the Fifties Tonight (In the Still of the Night)," Ronnie Milsap

Best Country Performance, Duo or Group: *Why Not Me*, The Judds

Best Country Song: "Highwayman," Jimmy L. Webb (songwriter), Waylon Jennings, Willie Nelson, Johnny Cash, and Kris Kristofferson (artists)

Best Jazz Fusion Performance, Instrumental or Vocal: *Straight to the Heart*, David Sanborn

Best Jazz Vocal Performance, Female: *Cleo Laine at Carnegie: The Tenth Anniversary Concert*, Cleo Laine

Best Jazz Vocal Performance, Male: "Another Night in Tunisia," Bobby McFerrin and Jon Hendricks

Best Jazz Vocal Performance, Duo or Group: *Vocalese*, The Manhattan Transfer

Best Jazz Instrumental Performance, Soloist: *Black Codes from the Underground*, Wynton Marsalis

Best Jazz Instrumental Performance, Group: *Black Codes from the Underground*, Wynton Marsalis Group

Best Jazz Instrumental Performance, Big Band: *The Cotton Club: Original Motion Picture Soundtrack*, Bob Wilber and John Barry

Best Music Video, Short Form: "We Are the World: The Video Event," Tom Trbovich (director), Quincy Jones (producer), USA for Africa* (artist)

Best Music Video, Long Form: *Huey Lewis and the News: The Heart of Rock and Roll*, Bruce Gowers (director), Huey Lewis and the News (artist)

1986

Album of the Year: *Graceland*, Paul Simon (producer and artist)

Record of the Year: "Higher Love," Russ Titleman and Steve Winwood (producers), Steve Winwood (artist)

Song of the Year: "That's What Friends Are For," Burt Bacharach and Carole Bayer Sager (songwriters), Dionne Warwick, Elton John, Gladys Knight, and Stevie Wonder (artists)

Best New Artist: Bruce Hornsby and the Range

Best Pop Vocal Performance, Female: *The Broadway Album*, Barbra Streisand

Best Pop Vocal Performance, Male: "Higher Love," Steve Winwood

Best Pop Performance by a Duo or Group with Vocal: "That's What Friends Are For," Dionne Warwick, Elton John, Gladys Knight, and Stevie Wonder (artists)

Best Rock Vocal Performance, Female: "Back Where You Started," Tina Turner*

Best Rock Vocal Performance, Male: "Addicted to Love," Robert Palmer

Best Rock Performance by a Duo or Group with Vocal: "Missionary Man," Eurythmics

Best R&B Vocal Performance, Female: *Rapture*, Anita Baker

Best R&B Vocal Performance, Male: "Living in America," James Brown

Best R&B Performance by a Duo or Group with Vocal: "Kiss," Prince* and the Revolution

Best R&B Song: "Sweet Love," Anita Baker, Gary Bias, and Louis A. Johnson (songwriters), Anita Baker (artist)

Best Country Vocal Performance, Female: "Whoever's in New England," Reba McEntire

Best Country Vocal Performance, Male: *Lost in the Fifties Tonight*, Ronnie Milsap

Best Country Performance, Duo or Group: "Grandpa (Tell Me 'bout the Good Old Days)," The Judds

Best Country Song: "Grandpa (Tell Me 'bout the Good Old Days)," Jamie O'Hara (songwriter), The Judds (artist)

Best Jazz Fusion Performance, Instrumental or Vocal: *Double Vision*, David Sanborn and Bob James

Best Jazz Vocal Performance, Female: *Timeless*, Diane Schuur

Best Jazz Vocal Performance, Male: "'Round Midnight," Bobby McFerrin

Best Jazz Vocal Performance, Duo or Group: "Free Fall," 2 + 2 Plus

Best Jazz Instrumental Performance, Soloist: *Tutu*, Miles Davis

Best Jazz Instrumental Performance, Group: *J Mood*, Wynton Marsalis

Best Jazz Instrumental Performance, Big Band: *The Tonight Show Band with Doc Severinsen*, The Tonight Show Band with Doc Severinsen

Best Music Video, Short Form: "Brothers in Arms," Dire Straits

Best Music Video, Long Form: *Bring on the Night*, Michael Apted (director), Sting* (producer and artist)

1987

Album of the Year: *The Joshua Tree*, Brian Eno and Daniel Lanois (producers), U2* (artist)

Record of the Year: "Graceland," Paul Simon (producer and artist)

Song of the Year: "Somewhere out There," Barry Mann, Cynthia Weil, and James Horner (songwriters), Linda Ronstadt and James Ingram (artists)

Best New Artist: Jody Watley

Best Pop Vocal Performance, Female: "I Wanna Dance with Somebody (Who Loves Me)," Whitney Houston*

Best Pop Vocal Performance, Male: *Bring on the Night*, Sting*

Best Pop Performance by a Duo or Group with Vocal: "I've Had (The Time of My Life)," Jennifer Warnes and Bill Medley

Best Rock Vocal Performance, Solo: *Tunnel of Love*, Bruce Springsteen*

Best Rock Performance by a Duo or Group with Vocal: *The Joshua Tree*, U2*

Best R&B Vocal Performance, Female: *Aretha*, Aretha Franklin

Best R&B Vocal Performance, Male: "Just to See Her," Smokey Robinson

Best R&B Performance by a Duo or Group with Vocal: "I Knew You Were Waiting (for Me)," Aretha Franklin and George Michael*

Best R&B Song: "Lean on Me," Bill Withers (songwriter), Club Nouveau (artist)

Best Country Vocal Performance, Female: "'80's Ladies," K. T. Oslin

Best Country Vocal Performance, Male: *Always and Forever*, Randy Travis

Best Country Performance, Duo or Group: *Trio*, Dolly Parton, Linda Ronstadt, and Emmylou Harris

Best Country Performance, Duet: "Make No Mistake, She's Mine," Ronnie Milsap and Kenny Rogers

Best Country Song: "Forever and Ever, Amen," Don Schlitz and Paul Overstreet (songwriters), Randy Travis (artist)

Best Jazz Fusion Performance, Instrumental or Vocal: *Still Life (Talking)*, Pat Metheny Group

Best Jazz Vocal Performance, Female: *Diane Schuur and the Count Basie Orchestra*, Diane Schuur

Best Jazz Vocal Performance, Male:"What Is This Thing Called Love," Bobby McFerrin

Best Jazz Instrumental Performance, Soloist: *The Other Side of Round Midnight*, Dexter Gordon

Best Jazz Instrumental Performance, Group: *Marsalis Standard Time, Volume I*, Wynton Marsalis

Best Jazz Instrumental Performance, Big Band: *Digital Duke*, Mercer Ellington

Best Performance, Music Video: *The Prince's Trust All-Star Rock Concert*, Anthony Eaton (producer), various artists

Best Concept, Music Video: "Land of Confusion," Jim Yukich and John Lloyd (directors), Jon Blair (producer), Genesis (artist)

1988

Album of the Year: *Faith*, George Michael* (producer and artist)

Record of the Year: "Don't Worry, Be Happy," Linda Goldstein (producer), Bobby McFerrin (artist)

Song of the Year: "Don't Worry, Be Happy," Bobby McFerrin (songwriter and artist)

Best New Artist: Tracy Chapman

Best Pop Vocal Performance, Female: "Fast Car," Tracy Chapman

Best Pop Vocal Performance, Male: "Don't Worry, Be Happy," Bobby McFerrin

Best Pop Performance by a Duo or Group with Vocal: *Brasil*, The Manhattan Transfer

Best Rock Vocal Performance, Female: *Tina Live in Europe*, Tina Turner*

Best Rock Vocal Performance, Male: "Simply Irresistible," Robert Palmer

Best Rock Performance by a Duo or Group with Vocal: "Desire," U2*

Best Hard Rock/Metal Performance, Vocal or Instrumental: *Crest of a Knave*, Jethro Tull

Best Rap Performance: "Parents Just Don't Understand," DJ Jazzy Jeff and the Fresh Prince

Best R&B Vocal Performance, Female: "Giving You the Best That I Got," Anita Baker

Best R&B Vocal Performance, Male: *Introducing the Hardline According to Terence Trent D'Arby*, Terence Trent D'Arby

Best R&B Performance by a Duo or Group with Vocal: "Love Overboard," Gladys Knight and the Pips

Best R&B Song: "Giving You the Best That I Got," Anita Baker, Randy Holland, and Skip Scarborough (songwriters) and Anita Baker (artist)

Best Country Vocal Performance, Female: "Hold Me," K. T. Oslin

Best Country Vocal Performance, Male: *Old 8 × 10*, Randy Travis

Best Country Performance, Duo or Group: "Give a Little Love," The Judds

Best Country Vocal Collaboration: "Crying," Roy Orbison and k. d. lang

Best Country Song: "Hold Me," K. T. Oslin (songwriter and artist)

Best Jazz Fusion Performance, Instrumental or Vocal: *Politics*, Yellowjackets

Best Jazz Vocal Performance, Female: *Look What I Got!*, Betty Carter

Best Jazz Vocal Performance, Male: "Brothers," Bobby McFerrin

Best Jazz Vocal Performance, Duo or Group: "Spread Love," Take 6

Best Jazz Instrumental Performance, Soloist: *Don't Try This at Home*, Michael Brecker

Best Jazz Instrumental Performance, Group: *Blues for Coltrane: A Tribute to John Coltrane*, Cecil McBee, David Murray, McCoy Tyner, Pharoah Sanders, and Roy Haynes

Best Jazz Instrumental Performance, Big Band: *Bud and Bird*, Gil Evans and the Monday Night Orchestra

Best Performance, Music Video: "Where the Streets Have No Name," Meiert Avis (director), Ben Dossett and Michael Hamlyn (producers), U2* (artists)

Best Concept, Music Video: "Fat," Jay Levey (director), Susan Zwerman (producer), Weird Al Yankovic* (artist)

1989

Album of the Year: *Nick of Time*, Don Was (producer), Bonnie Raitt (artist)

Record of the Year: "Wind Beneath My Wings," Arif Mardin (producer), Bette Midler (artist)

Song of the Year: "Wind Beneath My Wings," Jeff Silbar and Larry Henley (songwriters) and Bette Midler (artist)

Best New Artist: Milli Vanilli (revoked)

Best Pop Vocal Performance, Female: "Nick of Time," Bonnie Raitt

Best Pop Vocal Performance, Male: "How Am I Supposed to Live Without You," Michael Bolton

Best Pop Performance by a Duo or Group with Vocal: "Don't Know Much," Linda Ronstadt and Aaron Neville

Best Rock Vocal Performance, Female: *Nick of Time*, Bonnie Raitt

Best Rock Vocal Performance, Male: *The End of the Innocence*, Don Henley

Best Rock Performance by a Duo or Group with Vocal: *Traveling Wilburys, Volume I*, Traveling Wilburys

Best Hard Rock Performance: "Cult of Personality," Living Colour

Best Metal Performance: "One," Metallica

Best Rap Performance: "Bust a Move," Young MC

Best R&B Vocal Performance, Female: *Giving You the Best That I Got*, Anita Baker

Best R&B Vocal Performance, Male: "Every Little Step," Bobby Brown

Best R&B Performance by a Duo or Group with Vocal: "Back To Life," Soul II Soul featuring Caron Wheeler

Best R&B Song: "If You Don't Know Me by Now," Kenny Gamble and Leon Huff (songwriters) and Simply Red (artist)

Best Country Vocal Performance, Female: *Absolute Torch and Twang*, k. d. lang

Best Country Vocal Performance, Male: *Lyle Lovett and His Large Band*, Lyle Lovett

Best Country Vocal Performance, Duo or Group: *Will the Circle Be Unbroken, Volume II*, Nitty Gritty Dirt Band

Best Country Vocal Collaboration: "There's a Tear in My Beer," Hank Williams, Jr., and Hank Williams, Sr.

Best Country Song: "After All This Time," Rodney Crowell (songwriter and artist)

Best Jazz Fusion Performance, Instrumental or Vocal: *Letter from Home*, Pat Metheny Group

Best Jazz Vocal Performance, Female: *Blues on Broadway*, Ruth Brown

Best Jazz Vocal Performance, Male: *When Harry Met Sally*, Harry Connick, Jr.

Best Jazz Vocal Performance, Duo or Group: "Makin' Whoopee," Dr. John and Rickie Lee Jones

Best Jazz Instrumental Performance, Soloist: *Aura*, Miles Davis

Best Jazz Instrumental Performance, Group: *Chick Corea Akoustic Band*, Chick Corea Akoustic Band

Best Jazz Instrumental Performance, Big Band: *Aura*, Miles Davis

Best Music Video, Short Form: "Leave Me Alone," Michael Jackson*, Jim Blashfield (director), Frank DiLeo, Jerry Kramer, Jim Blashfield, and Paul Diener (producers), Michael Jackson* (artist)

Best Music Video, Long Form: *Rhythm Nation 1814*, Dominic Sena, Jonathan Dayton, and Valerie Faris (directors), Aris McGarry, Jonathan Dayton, and Valerie Faris (producers), Janet Jackson (artist)

■ Sports: Winners of Major Events

Athletes whose names appear with an asterisk (*) are subjects of their own full-length essays within *The Eighties in America*.

Major League Baseball

World Series

1980: Philadelphia Phillies (National League) 4, Kansas City Royals (American League), 2
1981: Los Angeles Dodgers (NL) 4, New York Yankees (AL) 2
1982: St. Louis Cardinals (NL) 4, Milwaukee Brewers (AL) 3
1983: Baltimore Orioles (AL) 4, Philadelphia Phillies (NL) 1
1984: Detroit Tigers (AL) 4, San Diego Padres (NL) 1
1985: Kansas City Royals (AL) 4, St. Louis Cardinals (NL) 3
1986: New York Mets (NL) 4, Boston Red Sox (AL) 3
1987: Minnesota Twins (AL) 4, St. Louis Cardinals (NL) 3
1988: Los Angeles Dodgers (NL) 4, Oakland A's (AL) 1
1989: Oakland A's (AL) 4, San Francisco Giants (NL) 0

All-Star Games

1980: National League 4, American League 2
1981: National League 5, American League 4
1982: National League 4, American League 1
1983: American League 13, National League 3
1984: National League 3, American League 1
1985: National League 6, American League 1
1986: American League 3, National League 2
1987: National League 2, American League 0 (13 innings)
1988: American League 2, National League 1
1989: American League 5, National League 3

American League Most Valuable Players

1980: George Brett*, Kansas City Royals
1981: Rollie Fingers, Milwaukee Brewers
1982: Robin Yount, Milwaukee Brewers
1983: Cal Ripken, Jr., Baltimore Orioles
1984: Willie Hernandez, Detroit Tigers
1985: Don Mattingly, New York Yankees
1986: Roger Clemens, Boston Red Sox
1987: George Bell, Toronto Blue Jays
1988: Jose Conseco, Oakland A's
1989: Robin Yount, Milwaukee Brewers

National League Most Valuable Players

1980: Mike Schmidt, Philadelphia Phillies
1981: Mike Schmidt, Philadelphia Phillies
1982: Dale Murphy, Atlanta Braves
1983: Dale Murphy, Atlanta Braves
1984: Ryne Sandberg, Chicago Cubs
1985: Willie McGee, St. Louis Cardinals
1986: Mike Schmidt, Philadelphia Phillies
1987: Andre Dawson, Chicago Cubs
1988: Kirk Gibson*, Los Angeles Dodgers
1989: Kevin Mitchell, San Francisco Giants

American League Rookies of the Year

1980: Joe Charboneau, Cleveland Indians
1981: Dave Righetti, New York Yankees
1982: Cal Ripken, Jr., Baltimore Orioles
1983: Ron Kittle, Chicago White Sox
1984: Alvin Davis, Seattle Mariners
1985: Ozzie Guillen, Chicago White Sox
1986: Jose Canseco, Oakland A's
1987: Mark McGwire, Oakland A's
1988: Walt Weiss, Oakland A's
1989: Gregg Olson, Baltimore Orioles

National League Rookies of the Year

1980: Steve Howe, Los Angeles Dodgers
1981: Fernando Valenzuela*, Los Angeles Dodgers
1982: Steve Sax, Los Angeles Dodgers
1983: Darryl Strawberry, New York Mets
1984: Dwight Gooden, New York Mets
1985: Vince Coleman, St. Louis Cardinals
1986: Todd Worrell, St. Louis Cardinals
1987: Benito Santiago, San Diego Padres
1988: Chris Sabo, Cincinnati Reds
1989: Jerome Walton, Chicago Cubs

National Basketball Association (NBA)

Championships
1980: Los Angeles Lakers 4, Philadelphia 76ers 2
1981: Boston Celtics 4, Houston Rockets 2
1982: Los Angeles Lakers 4, Philadelphia 76ers 2
1983: Philadelphia 76ers 4, Los Angeles Lakers 0
1984: Boston Celtics 4, Los Angeles Lakers 3
1985: Los Angeles Lakers 4, Boston Celtics 2
1986: Boston Celtics 4, Houston Rockets 2
1987: Los Angeles Lakers 4, Boston Celtics 2
1988: Los Angeles Lakers 4, Detroit Pistons 3
1989: Detroit Pistons 4, Los Angeles Lakers 0

NBA Most Valuable Players
1980: Kareem Abdul-Jabbar, Los Angeles Lakers
1981: Julius Erving, Philadelphia 76ers
1982: Moses Malone, Houston Rockets
1983: Moses Malone, Philadelphia 76ers
1984: Larry Bird*, Boston Celtics

1985: Larry Bird*, Boston Celtics
1986: Larry Bird*, Boston Celtics
1987: Magic Johnson*, Los Angeles Lakers
1988: Michael Jordan, Chicago Bulls
1989: Magic Johnson*, Los Angeles Lakers

NBA Rookies of the Year
1980: Larry Bird*, Boston Celtics
1981: Darrell Griffith, Utah Jazz
1982: Buck Williams, New Jersey Nets
1983: Terry Cummings, San Diego Clippers
1984: Ralph Sampson, Houston Rockets
1985: Michael Jordan, Chicago Bulls
1986: Patrick Ewing, New York Knicks
1987: Chuck Person, Indiana Pacers
1988: Mark Jackson, New York Knicks
1989: Mitch Richmond, Golden State Warriors

College Basketball

National Collegiate Athletic Association (NCAA) Championships
1980: Louisville 59, UCLA 54
1981: Indiana 63, North Carolina 50
1982: North Carolina 63, Georgetown 62
1983: North Carolina State 54, Houston 52
1984: Georgetown 84, Houston 75
1985: Villanova 66, Georgetown 64
1986: Louisville 72, Duke 69
1987: Indiana 74, Syracuse 73
1988: Kansas 83, Oklahoma 79
1989: Michigan 80, Seton Hall 79 (overtime)

National Invitational Tournament (NIT)
1980: Virginia 58, Minnesota 55
1981: Tulsa 86, Syracuse 84
1982: Bradley 67, Purdue 58
1983: Fresno State 69, DePaul 60
1984: Michigan 83, Notre Dame 63
1985: UCLA 65, Indiana 62
1986: Ohio State 73, Wyoming 63
1987: Southern Mississippi 84, La Salle 80
1988: Connecticut 72, Ohio State 67
1989: St. John's 73, Saint Louis 65

Professional Football

National Football League (NFL) Championships
1980: Oakland Raiders 27, Philadelphia Eagles 10
1981: San Francisco 49ers 26, Cincinnati
    Bengals 21
1982: Washington Redskins 27, Miami Dolphins 17
1983: Los Angeles Raiders 38, Washington
    Redskins 9
1984: San Francisco 49ers 38, Miami Dolphins 16
1985: Chicago Bears 46, New England Patriots 10
1986: New York Giants 39, Denver Broncos 20
1987: Washington Redskins 42, Denver Broncos 10
1988: San Francisco 49ers 20, Cincinnati
    Bengals 16
1989: San Francisco 49ers 55, Denver Broncos 10

NFL Most Valuable Players
1980: Brian Sipe, Cleveland Browns
1981: Ken Anderson, Cincinnati Bengals
1982: Mark Moseley, Washington Redskins
1983: Joe Theismann, Washington Redskins
1984: Dan Marino, Miami Dolphins
1985: Marcus Allen, Los Angeles Raiders
1986: Lawrence Taylor*, New York Giants
1987: John Elway*, Denver Broncos

1988: Boomer Esiason, Cincinnati Bengals
1989: Joe Montana*, San Francisco 49ers

Canadian Football League (CFL) Gray Cup Winners
1980: Edmonton Eskimos 48, Hamilton
    Tiger-Cats 10
1981: Edmonton Eskimos 26, Ottawa
    Renegades 23
1982: Edmonton Eskimos 32, Toronto
    Argonauts 16
1983: Toronto Argonauts 18, British Columbia
    Lions 17
1984: Winnipeg Blue Bombers 47, Hamilton
    Tiger-Cats 17
1985: British Columbia Lions 37, Hamilton
    Tiger-Cats 24
1986: Hamilton Tiger-Cats 39, Edmonton
    Eskimos 15
1987: Edmonton Eskimos 38, Toronto
    Argonauts 36
1988: Winnipeg Blue Bombers 22, British
    Columbia Lions 21
1989: Saskatchewan Rough Riders 43, Hamilton
    Tiger-Cats 40

College Football

Heisman Trophy Winners
1980: George Rogers, South Carolina
1981: Marcus Allen, University of Southern
    California
1982: Herschel Walker, Georgia
1983: Mike Rozier, Nebraska
1984: Doug Flutie, Boston College
1985: Bo Jackson*, Auburn
1986: Vinny Testaverde, Miami (Florida)
1987: Tim Brown, Notre Dame
1988: Barry Sanders, Oklahoma State
1989: Andre Ware, Houston

National Hockey League (NHL)

Stanley Cup Winners
1980: New York Islanders 4, Philadelphia Flyers 2
1981: New York Islanders 4, Minnesota North Stars 1
1982: New York Islanders 4, Vancouver Canucks, 0
1983: New York Islanders 4, Edmonton Oilers 0
1984: Edmonton Oilers 4, New York Islanders 1
1985: Edmonton Oilers 4, Philadelphia Flyers 1
1986: Montreal Canadiens 4, Calgary Flames 1
1987: Edmonton Oilers 4, Philadelphia Flyers 3
1988: Edmonton Oilers 4, Boston Bruins 0
1989: Calgary Flames 4, Montreal Canadiens 2

Hart Memorial Trophy (NHL MVP)
1980: Wayne Gretsky*, Edmonton Oilers
1981: Wayne Gretsky*, Edmonton Oilers
1982: Wayne Gretsky*, Edmonton Oilers
1983: Wayne Gretsky*, Edmonton Oilers
1984: Wayne Gretsky*, Edmonton Oilers
1985: Wayne Gretsky*, Edmonton Oilers
1986: Wayne Gretsky*, Edmonton Oilers
1987: Wayne Gretsky*, Edmonton Oilers
1988: Mario Lemieux*, Pittsburgh Penguins
1989: Wayne Gretsky*, Los Angeles Kings

Boxing

World Heavyweight Champions
John Tate
    (October 20, 1979-March 31, 1980)
Mike Weaver
    (March 31, 1980-December 10, 1982)
Michael Dokes
    (December 10, 1982-September 23, 1983)
Gerrie Coetzee
    (September 23, 1983-December 1, 1984)

Greg Page
    (December 1, 1984-April 29, 1985)
Tony Tubbs
    (April 29, 1985-January 17, 1986)
Tim Witherspoon
    (January 17, 1986-December 12, 1986)
James Smith
    (December 12, 1986-March 7, 1987)
Mike Tyson*
    (March 7, 1987-February 11, 1990)

Auto Racing

Indianapolis 500 Winners
1980: Johnny Rutherford
1981: Bobby Unser
1982: Gordon Johncock
1983: Tom Sneva
1984: Rick Mears

1985: Danny Sullivan
1986: Bobby Rahal
1987: Al Unser
1988: Rick Mears
1989: Emerson Fittipaldi

Tennis

Major Tournament Champions

Year	Australian Open	French Open	Wimbledon	U.S. Open
Men				
1980	Brian Teacher	Björn Borg	Björn Borg	John McEnroe*
1981	Johan Kriek	Björn Borg	John McEnroe*	John McEnroe*
1982	Johan Kriek	Mats Wilander	Jimmy Connors	Jimmy Connors
1983	Mats Wilander	Yannick Noah	John McEnroe*	Jimmy Connors
1984	Mats Wilander	Ivan Lendl	John McEnroe*	John McEnroe*
1985	Stefan Edberg	Mats Wilander	Boris Becker	Ivan Lendl
1986	no competition	Ivan Lendl	Boris Becker	Ivan Lendl
1987	Stefan Edberg	Ivan Lendl	Pat Cash	Ivan Lendl
1988	Mats Wilander	Mats Wilander	Stefan Edberg	Mats Wilander
1989	Ivan Lendl	Michael Chang	Boris Becker	Boris Becker
Women				
1980	Hana Mandlikova	Chris Evert	Evonne Goolagong	Chris Evert
1981	Martina Navratilova*	Hana Mandlikova	Chris Evert	Tracy Austin
1982	Chris Evert	Martina Navratilova*	Martina Navratilova*	Chris Evert
1983	Martina Navratilova*	Chris Evert	Martina Navratilova*	Martina Navratilova*
1984	Chris Evert	Martina Navratilova*	Martina Navratilova*	Martina Navratilova*
1985	Martina Navratilova*	Chris Evert	Martina Navratilova*	Hana Mandlikova
1986	no competition	Chris Evert	Martina Navratilova*	Martina Navratilova*
1987	Hana Mandlilkova	Steffi Graf	Martina Navratilova*	Martina Navratilova*
1988	Steffi Graf	Steffi Graf	Steffi Graf	Steffi Graf
1989	Steffi Graf	Arantxa S. Vicario	Steffi Graf	Steffi Graf

Golf

Major Tournament Champions (Men)

Year	British Open	Professional Golf Association (PGA) Championship	The Masters	U.S. Open
1980	Tom Watson*	Jack Nicklaus	Seve Ballesteros	Jack Nicklaus
1981	Bill Rogers	Larry Nelson	Tom Watson*	David Graham
1982	Tom Watson*	Raymond Floyd	Craig Stadler	Tom Watson*
1983	Tom Watson*	Hal Sutton	Seve Ballesteros	Larry Nelson
1984	Seve Ballesteros	Lee Trevino	Ben Crenshaw	Fuzzy Zoeller
1985	Sandy Lyle	Hubert Green	Bernhard Langer	Andy North
1986	Greg Norman	Bob Tway	Jack Nicklaus	Raymond Floyd
1987	Nick Faldo	Larry Nelson	Larry Mize	Scott Simpson
1988	Seve Ballesteros	Jeff Sluman	Sandy Lyle	Curtis Strange
1989	Mark Calcavecchia	Payne Stewart	Nick Faldo	Curtis Strange

Major Tournament Champions (Women)

Year	U.S. Open	Ladies Professional Golf Association (LPGA) Championship
1980	Amy Alcott	Sally Little
1981	Pat Bradley	Dnna Caponi
1982	Janet Alex	Jan Stephenson
1983	Jan Stephenson	Patty Sheehan
1984	Hollis Stacy	Patty Sheehan
1985	Kathy Baker Guadagnino	Nancy Lopez
1986	Jane Geddes	Pat Bradley
1987	Laura Davies	Jane Geddes
1988	Liselotte Neumann	Sherri Turner
1989	Betsy King	Nancy Lopez

Horse Racing

Triple Crown Races

Year	Kentucky Derby	Preakness	Belmont Stakes
1980	Genuine Risk	Codex	Temperance Hill
1981	Pleasant Colony	Pleasant Colony	Summing
1982	Gato Del Sol	Aloma's Ruler	Conquistador Cielo
1983	Sunny's Halo	Deputed Testamony	Caveat
1984	Swale	Gate Dancer	Swale
1985	Spend a Buck	Tank's Prospect	Creme Fraiche
1986	Ferdinand	Snow Chief	Danzig Connection
1987	Alysheba	Alysheba	Bet Twice
1988	Winning Colors	Risen Star	Risen Star
1989	Sunday Silence	Sunday Silence	Easy Goer

■ Time Line

Additional dates on legislation, U.S. Supreme Court cases, films, television shows, plays, literature, popular music, and sports can be found in other appendixes.

1980

International events: (Mar. 24) Archbishop Oscar Romero is killed by gunmen while celebrating mass in San Salvador; at his funeral six days later, forty-two people are killed amid gunfire and bombs. (Apr. 7) The United States severs diplomatic relations with Iran and imposes economic sanctions in response to Iran's capture of fifty-two American hostages on November 4, 1979. (Apr. 15-Oct. 31) About 125,000 Cubans enter the United States, arriving in boats departing from Mariel Harbor; many of the exiles had been released from Cuban jails and mental health facilities. (Aug. 7-14) Lech Wałęsa leads the first of many strikes at the Gdansk shipyard in Poland; the strikes will spur the formation of Solidarity, an independent trade union. (Sept. 22) Saddam Hussein, prime minister of Iraq, invades Iran, setting off an eight-year war between the two countries. (Nov. 20) The Gang of Four, a group of Chinese Communist Party leaders, is tried for its role in the Cultural Revolution.

Government and politics: (Feb. 2) The National Broadcasting Company (NBC) breaks the news that the Federal Bureau of Investigation (FBI) has set up Abscam, a sting operation in which FBI agents posed as Arab businessmen and offered American politicians money to perform favors for a nonexistent Arab sheik. (Mar. 3) Pierre Trudeau returns to office as prime minister of Canada after a nine-month absence. (May 20) In a referendum, Quebec voters reject a proposal for the province to become independent from Canada. (Jul. 16) Former California governor and actor Ronald Reagan is nominated for president at the Republican National Convention in Detroit. (Aug. 14) At the Democratic National Convention in New York City, President Jimmy Carter accepts his party's nomination for another term in office. (Nov. 4) Reagan carries forty-four states to defeat Carter in the presidential election.

Military and war: (Apr. 24-25) Operation Eagle Claw, a commando mission in Iran to rescue American hostages, is aborted after mechanical problems ground the rescue helicopters; the failed rescue operation results in the deaths of eight American servicemen.

Society: An advertisement featuring fifteen-year-old model Brooke Shields—in which she whispers "You know what comes between me and my Calvins? Nothing!"—is banned from the airwaves. Mattel introduces black and Hispanic Barbie dolls. (Jun. 1) Comedian Richard Pryor is badly burned as he tries to freebase cocaine.

Business and economics: 3-M introduces a new product, Post-it note, and begins selling it throughout the United States. By the end of the year, the unemployment rate in the United States exceeds 10 percent. (Dec. 12) Apple Computer makes its initial public offering, trading its stock at twelve dollars per share.

Transportation and communications: Japan passes the United States as the world's largest automaker. (Jun. 1) Cable News Network (CNN), the first all-news network, goes on the air.

Science and technology: (Mar. 1) The Voyager 1 space probe sends the first high-resolution images of Saturn back to scientists and confirms the existence of Janus, one of Saturn's moons. (May 18) Mount St. Helens erupts in Washington, killing fifty-seven people and causing three billion dollars in damage. (Jun. 16) In its ruling in *Diamond v. Chakrabarty*, the Supreme Court allows patents to be issued on living organisms.

Environment and health: RU-486, the abortion pill, is released in France. The U.S. Food and Drug Administration (FDA) warns pregnant women to restrict or eliminate caffeine consumption. (Sept. 22) Procter and Gamble Company announces a recall of its Rely brand tampons after federal studies conclude their use increases chances of toxic shock syndrome.

Arts and literature: *The Covenant*, a novel by James A. Michener, and *Crisis Investing: Opportunities and Profits in the Coming Great Depression*, by Douglas R. Casey, are the year's best-selling fiction and nonfiction books. (Apr.) Norman Mailer's *The Executioner's Song*, playwright Lanford Wilson's *Talley's Folly*, and *Selected Poems* by Donald Justice are among the year's Pulitzer Prize winners. (Dec. 17)

Amadeus opens on Broadway, where it runs for 1,181 performances; the drama will receive 1981 Tony Awards for Best Play (playwright Peter Shaffer), Best Actor (Ian McKellan), and Best Director (Peter Hall).

Popular culture: *The Empire Strikes Back* earns $290 million at the box office. (Sept. 23) Reggae musician Bob Marley plays his final live performance at the Stanley Theater in Pittsburgh, Pennsylvania. (Nov. 21) Millions of viewers tune into the television program *Dallas* to learn who shot lead character J. R. Ewing, the largest audience for a television show up to that point.

Sports: (Jan. 20) The Pittsburgh Steelers become the first National Football League (NFL) team to win four Super Bowls, defeating the Los Angeles Rams, 31-19. (Feb. 22) In what is called the Miracle on Ice, the U.S. hockey team defeats the Soviet Union in the semifinals of the Winter Olympics; the United States goes on to win the gold medal. (Mar. 21) President Jimmy Carter announces that the United States will boycott the 1980 Summer Olympics in Moscow. (Apr. 21) Rosie Ruiz wins the Boston Marathon but is later exposed as a fraud and stripped of her medal. (Jul. 19-Aug. 3) The Summer Olympic Games are held in Moscow. (Oct. 21) The Philadelphia Phillies win their first World Series, beating the Kansas City Royals, 4-1, in game 6.

Crime: (May 7) Paul Geidel, convicted of second-degree murder in 1911, is released from prison in Beacon, New York, after 68 years and 245 days, the longest time ever served by an American inmate. (Oct. 15) Terrorist James Hoskins forces his way into a Cincinnati, Ohio, television studio, holding nine employees hostage for several hours before releasing them and taking his own life. (Dec. 8) Former Beatle John Lennon is shot and killed outside his New York City apartment by Mark David Chapman, a deranged fan.

1981

International events: (May 13) Pope John Paul II is shot and nearly killed by Mehmet Ali Agca, a Turkish gunman, as he enters St. Peter's Square in Rome to address a general audience. (May 21) Socialist François Mitterrand becomes president of France. (Oct. 6) Egyptian president Anwar Sadat is assassinated during a parade by army members who were part of the Egyptian Islamic Jihad organization, a group opposed to his negotiations with Israel. (Dec. 13) Polish president Wojciech Jaruzelski declares martial law in response to growing government opposition by the Solidarity trade union.

Government and politics: (Jan. 19) Officials from the United States and Iran sign an agreement to release fifty-two American hostages after 444 days of captivity. (Jan. 20) Ronald Reagan becomes the fortieth president of the United States; minutes after his inauguration, Iran releases the fifty-two American hostages. (Mar. 30) President Reagan is shot in the chest outside a Washington, D.C., hotel by John Hinckley, Jr.; two police officers and Press Secretary James Brady are also wounded. (Aug. 19) President Reagan appoints Sandra Day O'Connor to be the first woman justice of the U.S. Supreme Court.

Military and war: (Aug. 19) Libyan leader Muammar al-Qaddafi sends two fighter jets to intercept two U.S. fighter jets over the Gulf of Sidra; the American jets destroy the Libyan fighters. (Aug. 31) A bomb explodes at the U.S. Air Force base in Ramstein, West Germany, injuring twenty people.

Society: Pac-Man, a Japanese video arcade game, is introduced in the United States. (Jul.) Christine Craft, an anchorwoman on a Kansas City television station, is demoted to reporter after focus group research concludes she is "too old, too unattractive, and wouldn't defer to men." (Jul. 29) Lady Diana Spencer marries Charles, Prince of Wales.

Business and economics: G. D. Searle and Company begins selling NutraSweet, the brand name for aspartame, an artificial sugar, after the FDA approves the product. (Jan. 21) The first De Lorean, a stainless steel sports car with gull-wing doors, moves off the production line.

Transportation and communications: (Mar. 6) Walter Cronkite signs off for the last time after anchoring the *CBS Evening News* for nineteen years. (Aug. 3) The Professional Air Traffic Controllers Organization (PATCO) goes on strike. (Aug. 5) President Reagan fires 11,359 striking air traffic controllers who ignore his order to return to work. (Aug. 7) The *Washington Star* ceases operations after 128 years of publication. (Sept. 26) The Boeing 767 airliner makes its debut flight.

Science and technology: (Mar. 19) Three workers are killed and five are injured during a test of the space shuttle *Columbia.* (Aug. 12) IBM begins selling a personal computer at a base price of $1,565.

Environment and health: (Jun. 5) The Centers for Disease Control and Prevention (CDC) report that five homosexual men in Los Angeles have a rare form of pneumonia seen only in patients with weakened immune systems, the first recognized cases of acquired immunodeficiency syndrome (AIDS). (Dec. 28) The first American test-tube baby, Elizabeth Jordan Carr, is born in Norfolk, Virginia.

Arts and literature: *Jane Fonda's Workout Book* is released and remains number one on *The New York Times* best-seller list for more than a year. (May 6) A jury of architects and sculptors unanimously selects Maya Lin's design for the Vietnam Veterans Memorial in Washington, D.C. (Dec.) A review in *Artforum* launches the career of artist Jean-Michel Basquiat.

Popular culture: (Jan. 12) *Dynasty,* a television soap opera about wealthy Denver-based oil family the Carringtons, premieres and becomes a smash hit. (Apr. 18) The rock band Yes splits up but regroups in 1983. (Aug. 1) Music Television (MTV) goes on the air. (Sept. 19) Simon and Garfunkel perform "The Concert in New York City's Central Park," a free show attended by almost half a million people. (Oct. 15) Heavy metal band Metallica is formed in Los Angeles.

Sports: (Apr. 18) A minor league baseball game between the Rochester Red Wings and the Pawtucket Red Sox becomes the longest professional baseball game in history, lasting eight hours and twenty-five minutes; the final one of the game's thirty-three innings is played on June 23. (Aug. 9) Major League Baseball (MLB) players end their strike as the All-Star Game is held in Cleveland's Municipal Stadium. (Sept.) John McEnroe defeats Björn Borg in the final game of the U.S. Open tennis tournament, becoming the first player since the 1920's to win three consecutive U.S. Open men's singles titles.

Crime: (Jun. 21) Wayne Bertram Williams is arrested and charged with two murders; he is later convicted of murdering twenty-three of the thirty children and young adults slain in the Atlanta child murders. (Aug. 24) Mark David Chapman is sentenced to twenty years to life imprisonment after being convicted of murdering John Lennon in New York City.

1982

International events: (Mar. 10) The United States places an embargo on Libyan oil imports in response to Libya's alleged support of terrorist groups. (Apr. 25) Israel completes its withdrawal from the Sinai Peninsula according to the terms of the Israel-Egypt Peace Treaty. (Jun. 6) Forces under the command of Israeli defense minister Ariel Sharon invade southern Lebanon; following this attack, the United Nations Security Council demands that Israel withdraw its troops from Lebanon. (Nov. 14) Lech Wałęsa, the leader of Poland's outlawed Solidarity movement, is released after eleven months in prison.

Government and politics: (Apr. 17) By proclamation of Queen Elizabeth II, Canada patriates its constitution and is granted full political independence from the United Kingdom. (Jun. 8) President Reagan becomes the first American chief executive to address a joint session of the British Parliament. (Jun. 30) The Equal Rights Amendment (ERA) falls short of the thirty-eight states needed to pass; Phyllis Schlafly and other leaders of the Religious Right take credit for its defeat. (Oct. 27) Dominion Day is officially renamed Canada Day.

Military and war: (Apr. 2) Argentina invades the British-controlled Falkland Islands. (Apr. 4) The government of the Falklands surrenders and the islands are placed under Argentinian control. (Apr. 5) A British Royal Navy task force sails to South America to recapture the Falklands. (Jun. 14) The Falklands War ends, when Argentina agrees to formally surrender to the United Kingdom.

Society: In response to a Gallup Poll question, 51 percent of Americans say they do not view homosexuality as normal. (Mar. 5) Comedian John Belushi dies of cocaine and heroin abuse in a Los Angeles hotel. (May 1) More than 100,000 people attend the first day of the 1982 World's Fair in Knoxville, Tennessee. (Jun. 5) The first Rubik's Cube World Championships are held in Budapest, Hungary. (Oct. 1) The Epcot theme park at Walt Disney World is opened to the public.

Business and economics: (Jan. 8) AT&T agrees to divest itself into more than twenty regional subdivisions, commonly known as Baby Bells. (Feb. 19) The De Lorean automobile factory in Belfast, Northern Ireland, is put into receivership; the company will fold in 1983. (Jul. 23) The International Whaling Commission decides to end commercial whaling by 1985-1986.

Transportation and communications: (May 2) The Weather Channel debuts on American cable television. (Sept. 15) The first issue of *USA Today*, a national newspaper published by the Gannett Company, goes on sale.

Science and technology: (Sept. 19) Scott Fahlman, a computer scientist at Carnegie Mellon University, posts the first emoticons—symbols for smiley faces designed to distinguish serious posts from jokes. (Oct. 1) Sony sells its first consumer compact disc (CD) player. (Dec. 26) The computer is named *Time* magazine's Man of the Year, the first time that the award is given to a nonhuman.

Environment and health: (Sept. 29-Oct. 1) Seven people in the Chicago area die after ingesting Tylenol capsules laced with potassium cyanide. (Dec. 2) In an operation at the University of Utah, Barney Clark, a sixty-one-year-old retired dentist, becomes the first person to receive a permanent artificial heart. (Dec. 3) A final soil sample taken from the site of Times Beach, Missouri, is found to contain three hundred times the safe level of dioxin. (Dec. 23) The Environmental Protection Agency (EPA) recommends the evacuation of Times Beach because of its high levels of dioxin contamination.

Arts and literature: (Apr.) John Updike's novel *Rabbit Is Rich*, Charles Fuller's *A Soldier's Play*, and Sylvia Plath's *The Collected Poems* are awarded Pulitzer Prizes. (Oct.) Gabriel García Márquez receives the Nobel Prize in Literature. (Oct. 7) *Cats*, a musical play based on *Old Possum's Book of Practical Cats* and other poems by T. S. Eliot, opens on Broadway, where it will eventually run for a record 7,485 performances.

Popular culture: The film *E.T.: The Extra-Terrestrial* tops the box office, with $310 million worth of ticket sales. *The New York Times* declares Grandmaster Flash and the Furious Five's "The Message" to be "the most powerful pop record of the year." By the end of the year, twenty-two million copies of the board game Trivial Pursuit will be sold in the United States. (Jan. 20) Ozzy Osbourne bites the head off of a live bat that is thrown at him while he is performing. (Feb. 1) *Late Night with David Letterman*, a comedy and talk show, premieres on NBC. (Dec. 1) Michael Jackson's *Thriller* is released and will eventually sell twenty million copies, making it the second biggest-selling album in entertainment history.

Sports: (Feb. 24) Wayne Gretzky of the Edmonton Oilers scores his seventy-seventh goal of the National Hockey League (NHL) season, breaking the previous record of seventy-six. He will go on to score ninety-two goals that season, which remains the record. (May 8) French-Canadian racing driver Gilles Villeneuve is killed during qualifying runs for the Belgian Grand Prix. (May 30) In what Indianapolis Motor Speedway historian Donald Davidson and public address announcer Tom Carnegie later call the greatest moment in the track's history, Gordon Johncock wins his second Indianapolis 500 race over Rick Mears by 0.16 second, the closest finish to that date. (May 30) Cal Ripken, Jr., of the Baltimore Orioles plays the first of what will become his record-breaking streak of 2,632 consecutive baseball games.

Crime: (Jan. 6) "Freeway Killer" William Bonin, who along with several accomplices may have murdered as many as thirty-six people, is convicted of fourteen murders in California. (Mar. 16) Claus von Bülow is found guilty of the attempted murder of his wife, socialite Sunny von Bülow. (Jul. 16) The Reverend Sun Myung Moon is sentenced to eighteen months in prison and fined $25,000 for tax fraud and conspiracy to obstruct justice.

1983

International events: (Mar. 5) Bob Hawke is elected prime minister of Australia. (May 17) Lebanon, Israel, and the United States sign an agreement on Israeli withdrawal from Lebanon. (Jun. 9) Conservative Margaret Thatcher wins another term as prime minister of the United Kingdom with 42 percent of the popular vote. (Jul. 20) The government of Poland announces the end of martial law and grants amnesty to political prisoners.

Government and politics: (Feb. 13) President Reagan proclaims 1983 "The Year of the Bible." (Feb. 24) A special commission of Congress releases a report criticizing Japanese American internment during World War II. (Mar. 8) President Reagan calls the Soviet Union an "evil empire." (Apr. 12) Harold Washington is the first African American to be elected mayor of Chicago. (Nov. 3) The Reverend Jesse Jackson announces his candidacy for the 1984 Democratic Party presidential nomination.

Military and war: (Mar. 23) President Reagan announces his Strategic Defense Initiative (SDI), a proposal to develop technology that can intercept enemy missiles; the media dub his proposal "Star Wars." (Apr. 18) The U.S. embassy in Beirut, Lebanon, is bombed and sixty-three people are killed. (Oct. 19) Maurice Bishop, the prime minister of Grenada, and forty others are executed in a military coup; the People's Revolutionary Army forms a military government to rule the country. (Oct. 23) Suicide truck-bombings destroy both the French and the U.S. Marine Corps barracks in Beirut, killing 241 American servicemen, 58 French paratroopers, and 6 Lebanese civilians. (Oct. 25) U.S. troops invade Grenada at the behest of Eugenia Charles of Dominica, a member of the Organization of American States; after the invasion, the prerevolutionary government is restored to power.

Society: Cabbage Patch Kids mania takes off after the soft-sculpture dolls are placed on the market; by the end of the year, nearly three million dolls will be sold, exceeding the previous record for first-year doll sales by more than one million. (Sept. 17) Vanessa Williams becomes the first African American to be crowned Miss America. (Oct. 4) The first Hooters restaurant opens in Clearwater, Florida.

Business and economics: Mortgage interest rates, which exceeded 16 percent in 1981, drop to 12 percent by the end of the year. The juice box becomes a new brown bag and lunch box option after Ocean Spray begins to sell cranberry juice in boxes. (Jun.) McDonald's introduces Chicken McNuggets, small pieces of breaded chicken deep-fried in oil.

Transportation and communications: (Apr. 15) American Public Radio is founded; the network will become Public Radio International in 1994. (Sept. 5) Tom Brokaw becomes lead anchor for *NBC Nightly News.*

Science and technology: (Jan. 26) The Lotus 1-2-3 spreadsheet program is released for IBM-PC compatible computers. (Apr. 7) Space shuttle *Challenger* astronauts F. Story Musgrave and Donald H. Peterson perform the first space shuttle space walk, which lasts four hours and ten minutes. (Jun. 18) Sally Ride, a crew member aboard *Challenger*, becomes the first American woman astronaut. (Aug. 30) Guion Bluford, the first African American astronaut, is among the crew of *Challenger.* (Oct. 25) The first version of Microsoft Word software is introduced under the name Multi-Tool Word.

Environment and health: (Jan.) A scientist at the Pasteur Institute in Paris isolates a virus that he believes is the original infecting microorganism of AIDS. (Feb. 23) The EPA announces that it will buy out and evacuate the dioxin-contaminated community of Times Beach, Missouri. (Mar. 9) Amid scandal, Anne Burford resigns as head of the EPA.

Arts and literature: *Return of the Jedi Storybook* is the year's best-selling fiction book. (Jan. 2) The musical *Annie* is performed for the last time after 2,377 shows on Broadway. (Apr.) Alice Walker's novel *The Color Purple* receives the Pulitzer Prize.

Popular culture: "Down Under" by Men at Work, "Africa" by Toto, and "Baby, Come to Me" by Patti Austin and James Ingram are among the year's most popular songs. (Feb. 28) The television series *M*A*S*H* presents its final episode, "Goodbye, Farewell, and Amen"; it becomes the highest-rated episode in television history. (Jul. 21) Diana Ross stages a free concert in Central Park for 800,000 people, enduring the severe weather; she vows to return the next day—and keeps her promise.

Sports: (Jan. 22) Björn Borg retires from tennis after winning five consecutive Wimbledon championships. (Jul. 24) George Brett, third baseman for the Kansas City Royals, is expelled from a baseball game in Yankee Stadium after charging an umpire who called him out for having more pine tar on his bat than is technically allowed. (Dec. 13) The Denver Nuggets and the visiting Detroit Pistons combine for a National Basketball Association (NBA) record 370 points, with Detroit winning in triple overtime, 186-184.

Crime: (Feb. 18) Thirteen people are killed in an attempted robbery in Seattle, Washington.

1984

International events: (Jun. 6) Indian troops storm the Golden Temple at Amritsar, the Sikhs' holiest shrine, killing about three hundred people. (Aug. 21) Half a million people in Manila, Philippines, demonstrate against the government of Ferdinand Marcos. (Sept. 26) The United Kingdom and the People's Republic of China sign an initial agreement to return Hong Kong to China in 1997. (Oct. 31) Indian prime minister Indira Gandhi is assassinated by two Sikh security guards; the killing sparks riots in New Delhi, and about 2,700 Sikhs are killed.

Government and politics: (Feb. 29) Canadian prime minister Pierre Trudeau announces his retirement. (Jun. 30) John Turner becomes Canada's seventeenth prime minister. (Jul. 12) At its national convention in San Francisco, the Democratic Party nominates Walter Mondale for president and Geraldine Ferraro for vice president—the first woman nominated to that position. (Aug. 23) President Reagan and Vice President George H. W. Bush are nominated for second terms at the Republican National Convention in Dallas. (Sept. 4) The Progressive Conservative Party of Canada, led by Brian Mulroney, wins 211 seats in the House of Commons, forming the largest majority government in Canadian history. (Nov. 6) President Reagan defeats Mondale with 59 percent of the popular vote, the largest percentage since Richard Nixon's 61 percent victory in 1972.

Military and war: (Feb. 26) The U.S. Marines pull out of Beirut, Lebanon.

Society: (Jun. 3) A unanimous Supreme Court upholds a Minnesota law that bars private clubs from discriminating against women. (Jul. 23) Vanessa Williams becomes the first Miss America to resign, surrendering her crown after nude photos of her are published in *Penthouse* magazine. (Oct.) The National Parent-Teacher Association (PTA) sends a letter to thirty record labels and the Recording Industry Association of America (RIAA) in which it proposes that labels be placed on recordings with "explicit lyrics or content."

Business and economics: (Jan. 1) AT&T divests into twenty-four independent regional units. (Jan. 24) The first Apple Macintosh computer goes on sale. (Nov. 4) Michael Dell, a student at the University of Texas, founds PCs Limited, which sells IBM-compatible personal computers built from stock components; the company will eventually change its name to Dell Computers.

Transportation and communications: Deregulation by the Federal Communications Commission (FCC) enables the first infomercials to appear on television. (Jun. 22) Virgin Atlantic Airways makes its debut flight.

Science and technology: (Jan. 5) Richard Stallman starts to develop GNU, a free software mass collaboration project. (Feb. 7) Astronauts Bruce McCandless II and Robert L. Stewart make the first untethered space walk. (Aug. 30) The space shuttle *Discovery* takes its maiden voyage. (Oct. 5) Marc Garneau, an astronaut on the space shuttle *Challenger*, becomes the first Canadian in space.

Environment and health: (Oct. 26) Physicians at Loma Linda University Medical Center perform the first animal-to-human transplant in a newborn, when they place a baboon's heart into the chest of Baby Fae, a twelve-day-old infant. (Dec. 3) A chemical leak from a Union Carbide pesticide plant in Bhopal, India, kills more than 1,000 people and injures from 15,000 to 22,000 others, of whom 6,000 will later die from their injuries.

Arts and literature: William Gibson coins the term "cyberspace" in his novel *Neuromancer*. Other novels published in 1984 include *Bright Lights, Big City*, by Brat Packer author Jay McInerney, and *The Hunt for Red October*, by Tom Clancy. (Apr.) *Ironweed* by novelist William Kennedy, *Glengarry Glen Ross* by playwright David Mamet, and *American Primitive* by poet Mary Oliver are among the year's Pulitzer Prize winners. (Oct. 11) *Ma Rainey's Black Bottom* opens on Broadway; playwright August Wilson will later receive the New York Drama Critics Circle Award for Best Play.

Popular culture: The first all-rap radio format is introduced at Los Angeles radio station KDAY. Run-D.M.C. is the first rap group to have an album certified gold. (Sept. 14) The first MTV Video Music Awards are held in Radio City Music Hall, New York City, where "You Might Think" by the Cars is named Video of the Year. (Sept. 20) *The Cosby Show* premieres on NBC.

Sports: (Feb. 8) The 1984 Winter Olympics open in Sarajevo, Yugoslavia. (May 8) The Soviet Union announces that it will boycott the 1984 Summer Olympics in Los Angeles. (May 8) The longest game in MLB history begins; the game between the Milwaukee Brewers and the Chicago White Sox will be played over the course of two days and twenty-five innings, with a total time of eight hours and six minutes. (Jul. 4) Richard Petty wins his two-hundredth career NASCAR victory at the Firecracker 400 in Daytona, Florida. (Jul. 28-Aug. 12) The 1984 Summer Olympics are held in Los Angeles.

Crime: (Mar. 22) Teachers at the McMartin Preschool in Manhattan Beach, California, are charged with Satanic ritual abuse of the school-children; the charges are later determined to be completely unfounded and are dropped. (Jul. 18) James Oliver Huberty sprays a McDonald's restaurant in San Ysidro, California, with gunfire, killing twenty-one people before he is shot and killed. (Dec. 22) While riding in a New York City subway car, Bernhard Goetz shoots four African American youths who try to steal from him.

1985

International events: (Mar. 11) Mikhail Gorbachev becomes the general secretary of the Soviet Communist Party and de facto leader of the Soviet Union. (Mar. 16) Associated Press reporter Terry Anderson is taken hostage in Beirut; he is eventually released on December 4, 1991. (Oct. 7) The cruise ship *Achille Lauro* is hijacked in the Mediterranean Sea by four Palestinian terrorists; one passenger, American Leon Klinghoffer, is killed.

Government and politics: (Jan. 20) President Ronald Reagan is privately sworn in for a second term in office. (May 5) President Reagan joins German Chancellor Helmut Kohl for a controversial funeral service at a cemetery in Bitburg, Germany, which contains the graves of fifty-nine men who served in the S.S. during World War II. (Nov. 19) President Reagan and Soviet leader Mikhail Gorbachev meet for the first time in Geneva, Switzerland.

Military and war: (Feb. 16) Israel begins withdrawing troops from Lebanon.

Society: (May) Tipper Gore, the wife of then-Senator Albert Gore, and Susan Baker, wife of then-Treasury Secretary James Baker, among others, organize the Parents Music Resource Center (PMRC) to educate parents about lyrics that are "sexually explicit, excessively violent, or glorify the use of drugs and alcohol"; the group eventually persuades the Recording Industry Association of America (RIAA) voluntarily to place warning stickers on recordings it deems indecent or inappropriate for minors. (Jun. 4) The Supreme Court, ruling in *Wallace v. Jaffree*, strikes down an Alabama law that allowed public school teachers to hold a one-minute period of silence for "meditation or voluntary prayer" each day. (Sept. 30) "Shock jock" Howard Stern is fired from radio station WNBC-AM in New York City for his comedy sketch "Bestiality Dial-a-Date."

Business and economics: (Apr. 23) Coca-Cola changes its formula and introduces New Coke; the new product receives an overwhelmingly negative response, and within three months the company puts its original formula back on the market. (Oct. 18) The Nintendo home entertainment system, an eight-bit video game counsel, is introduced to the North American market.

Transportation and communications: (Jan. 7) Saturn Corporation, a subsidiary of General Motors, is founded in response to the American popularity of Japanese cars. (Jun. 17) The Discovery Channel, which provides documentary-like programming about science, history, and other topics, airs on cable television. (Dec. 1) Ford begins selling its Taurus model, which in the mid-1990's will become the best-selling car in the United States.

Science and technology: (Nov. 20) Microsoft Corporation releases Windows 1.0, the first version of its Windows software program. (Sept. 1) A joint American-French expedition locates the wreck of the *Titanic.*

Environment and health: (Feb. 19) William J. Schroeder becomes the first artificial heart patient to leave the hospital. (Mar. 4) The FDA approves a blood test for AIDS, which has been used since then to screen all blood donations in the United States. (Oct. 2) Actor Rock Hudson dies, the first major public figure to die of AIDS.

Arts and literature: *The Accidental Tourist* by *Anne Tyler, The Mammoth Hunters* by Jean Auel, and *Lake Wobegon Days* by Garrison Keillor are published. (Mar. 28) *Biloxi Blues*, a new comedy by Neil Simon, opens on Broadway; the play will win 1985 Tony Awards for Best Play, Best Featured Actor in a Play (Barry Miller), and Best Direction of a Play (Gene Saks). (Nov. 26) President Reagan sells the rights to his autobiography to Random House for a record three million dollars.

Popular culture: *Back to the Future* is the year's top-grossing film. (Jan. 28) USA for Africa, a group of musicians who include Michael Jackson, Stevie Wonder, Lionel Richie, Bob Dylan, Willie Nelson, Bruce Springsteen, Tina Turner, and Paul Simon, record "We Are the World" to raise money for Ethiopian famine victims. (Jul. 13) Live Aid concerts in Philadelphia and London raise millions of dollars for Ethiopian famine relief.

Sports: (Mar. 6) Boxer Mike Tyson makes his professional debut in Albany, New York, fighting a match in which he wins by a first-round knockout. (Mar. 31) WrestleMania, an annual wrestling pay-per-view event, debuts at Madison Square Garden in New York City. (Jul.) For the fourth year in a row, Martina Navratilova is the champion ladies singles tennis player at Wimbledon; she will capture two more championships, in 1986 and 1987.

Crime: (Feb. 9) U.S. drug agent Enrique Camarena is kidnapped and murdered in Mexico; his body is discovered on March 5. (May 11) The FBI brings charges against the suspected heads of the five New York City Mafia families.

1986

International events: (Jan. 20) The United Kingdom and France announce their plans to build a rail tunnel under the English Channel. (Feb. 7) President Jean-Claude ("Baby Doc") Duvalier flees Haiti after twenty-eight years of family rule. (Feb. 25) President Ferdinand Marcos of the Philippines goes into exile, and Corazon Aquino becomes the first Filipino woman president. (Mar. 26) An article in *The New York Times* charges that Kurt Waldheim, former United Nations secretary general and a candidate for president of Austria, may have been involved in Nazi war crimes during World War II.

Government and politics: (Oct. 11) President Reagan and Soviet leader Mikhail Gorbachev meet in Reykjavík, Iceland, to discuss how they can reduce their intermediate missile stocks in Europe. (Nov. 3) The Iran-Contra affair begins when a Lebanese magazine reports that the United States has been secretly selling weapons to Iran in order to secure the release of seven American hostages held by pro-Iranian groups in Lebanon. (Nov. 25) Attorney General Edwin Meese announces that profits from covert weapons sales to Iran were illegally diverted to the anticommunist Contra rebels in Nicaragua. (Nov. 26) President Reagan denies his involvement in the Iran-Contra scandal and appoints three people to a special review board, later called the Tower Commission, to investigate the affair.

Military and war: (Apr. 15) At least fifteen people die after United States' planes bomb targets in Tripoli, Libya, and that nation's Benghazi region.

Society: (Jan. 20) Martin Luther King Day, a federal holiday honoring the civil rights leader, is ob-

served for the first time. (May 25) At least five million people participate in Hands Across America, forming a human chain from New York City to Long Beach, California, to raise money to combat homelessness and hunger. (Jul. 5) After an extensive refurbishing, the Statue of Liberty is reopened to the public. (Oct. 28) The centennial of the Statue of Liberty's dedication is celebrated in New York Harbor.

Business and economics: (Jan. 9) Kodak stops making instant cameras after losing a patent fight with Polaroid. (Oct. 9) News Corporation, Rupert Murdock's media company, completes its acquisition of the Metromedia group of broadcasting stations and launches the FOX Broadcasting Company. (Nov. 11) Sperry Rand and Burroughs merge to form Unisys, the world's second-largest computer company.

Transportation and communications: (Jul. 1) Seaboard System Railroad and Chessie System, Inc., merge to create CSX Transportation, a railroad company serving the East Coast. (Aug. 31) Aeroméxico Flight 498 collides with a small Piper aircraft over Cerritos, California, killing sixty-seven passengers and fifteen people on the ground.

Science and technology: (Jan. 12) The space shuttle is launched with the first Hispanic astronaut, Dr. Franklin R. Chang-Diaz. (Jan. 19) Brain, the first personal computer virus, begins to spread. (Jan. 28) The space shuttle *Challenger* disintegrates seventy-three seconds after its launch, killing its crew of seven astronauts, including schoolteacher Christa McAuliffe. (Feb. 9) Halley's comet reaches its closest point to the Sun during its second visit to the solar system in the twentieth century. (Feb. 19) The Soviet Union launches the Mir space station. (Dec. 23) The aircraft *Voyager* completes the first nonstop circumnavigation of the Earth by air without refueling in nine days, three minutes, and forty-four seconds.

Environment and health: About twenty-four million Americans are regularly performing aerobics, 90 percent of them women. Geneticists begin discussing the possibility of mounting a project to sequence the human genome. (Apr. 26) A reactor at the Chernobyl nuclear plant in Ukraine explodes, killing thirty-one people; thousands of other people are exposed to excessive amounts of radiation, and radioactivity renders large areas of Ukraine and Belarus uninhabitable.

Arts and literature: Stephen King's *It*, Tom Clancy's *Red Storm Rising*, and James Clavell's *Whirlwind* are the year's three top-selling fiction books. (Oct.) Wole Soyinka of Nigeria is awarded the Nobel Prize in Literature. (Oct.) *World's Fair*, a novel by E. L. Doctorow, and *Arctic Dreams*, a nonfiction book by Barry Lopez, receive National Book Awards.

Popular culture: *Top Gun*, starring Tom Cruise, is the top-grossing film of the year. (Apr. 21) During a highly publicized television show, journalist Geraldo Rivera opens gangster Al Capone's secret vault but finds only a bottle of moonshine. (Sept. 19) The film *Blue Velvet* is released, establishing David Lynch as a major American director. (Sept. 27) A tour bus carrying heavy metal band Metallica crashes in Sweden, killing their bassist, Cliff Burton.

Sports: (Apr. 29) Boston Red Sox pitcher Roger Clemens becomes the first pitcher in history to strike out twenty batters during a nine-inning game, defeating the Seattle Mariners. (May 24) The Montreal Canadiens defeat the Calgary Flames in five games to win the Stanley Cup. (Jul. 27) American cyclist Greg LeMond wins the Tour de France. (Nov. 22) Mike Tyson earns his first world boxing title by defeating Trevor Berbick in Las Vegas.

Crime: (Aug. 20) Patrick Sherrill, an employee of the U.S. Postal Service in Edmond, Oklahoma, kills fourteen of his coworkers before committing suicide. (Dec. 20) Three African Americans are assaulted by a group of white teenagers in the Howard Beach neighborhood of Queens, New York; one of the victims, Michael Griffith, is run over and killed by a motorist as he tries to flee the attackers.

1987

International events: (Apr. 27) The U.S. Department of Justice declares Austrian president Kurt Waldheim to be an "undesirable alien." (Jun. 10) During a visit to Berlin, President Reagan challenges Soviet premier Mikhail Gorbachev to tear down the Berlin Wall. (Dec. 8) The first Intifada, a Palestinian uprising against Israeli rule, begins in the Gaza Strip and West Bank. (Dec. 8) President Reagan and Soviet premier Gorbachev sign the Intermediate-Range Nuclear Forces (INF) Treaty.

Government and politics: (Feb. 26) The Tower Com-

mission, which has been investigating the Iran-Contra affair, criticizes President Reagan for failing to control his national security staff. (Mar. 4) In an address to the nation on the Iran-Contra affair, President Reagan acknowledges that his dealings with Iran "deteriorated" into an arms-for-hostages deal. (May 8) Allegations that Senator Gary Hart had an extramarital affair with Donna Rice force Hart to drop out of the race for the Democratic presidential nomination. (Sept. 17) Televangelist Pat Robertson announces his candidacy for the 1988 Republican presidential nomination. (Oct. 23) By a vote of 58-42, the U.S. Senate rejects President Reagan's nomination of former Solicitor General Robert Bork to the Supreme Court. (Nov. 18) U.S. Senate and House committees release reports charging President Reagan with "ultimate responsibility" for the Iran-Contra affair.

Military and war: (May 17) While patrolling the Persian Gulf, the USS *Stark* is struck by two missiles from an Iraqi Mirage fighter; thirty-seven sailors are killed and twenty-one others are injured in the explosion. (Oct. 19) U.S. warships destroy two Iranian oil platforms in the Persian Gulf.

Society: (Mar.) ACT UP, an activist organization demanding increased resources to fight AIDS, is founded in New York City. (Mar. 19) Televangelist Jim Bakker, head of PTL Ministries, resigns after admitting that he had an affair with church secretary Jessica Hahn. (May 5) The Assemblies of God defrocks Bakker. (Jun. 19) In *Edwards v. Aguillard*, the Supreme Court declares unconstitutional a Louisiana law requiring that Creation science be taught in all public schools that teach evolution. (Oct. 14-16) Jessica McClure, an eighteen-month-old child, falls down a well in Midland, Texas, and is rescued fifty-eight hours later, a real-life drama watched by millions of American television viewers.

Business and economics: (Jan. 31) The last Ohrbach's department store closes in New York City after sixty-four years in business. (Mar. 2) Chrysler Corporation acquires American Motors Corporation. (Jul. 17) The Dow Jones Industrial Average closes above the 2,500 mark for the first time, at 2,510.04. (Oct. 19) On Black Monday, the Dow Jones Industrial average falls 508 points, or almost 23 percent, while stock markets in other countries experience similar declines.

Transportation and communications: (Aug. 4) The FCC rescinds the Fairness Doctrine, which required radio and television stations to "fairly" present controversial issues. (Aug. 16) Northwest Airlines Flight 255 crashes as it takes off from Detroit Metropolitan Airport, killing all but 1 of its 156 passengers.

Science and technology: (Feb. 23) Supernova 1987A is observed—the first supernova visible to the naked eye since 1604. (Sept. 7-21) The world's first conference on artificial life is held at Los Alamos National Laboratory in New Mexico.

Environment and health: (May 11) The first heart-lung transplant is performed in Baltimore. (Aug. 4) The World Commission on Environment and Development, also known as the Brundtland Commission, publishes a report, *Our Common Future*, which seeks to discuss the environment and development as a single issue. (Dec. 29) Prozac, an antidepressant, becomes available in the United States.

Arts and literature: *Beloved*, a novel by Toni Morrison, is nominated for both the National Book Award and the National Book Critics Circle Award; it does not win either award but receives the 1988 Pulitzer Prize for fiction. *The Bonfire of the Vanities*, Tom Wolfe's novel about New York City in the 1980's, is published in book form after being serialized in *Rolling Stone*. (Mar. 12) *Les Misérables* opens on Broadway; it later wins eight 1987 Tony Awards, including Best Musical.

Popular culture: (Jan. 3) Aretha Franklin becomes the first woman inducted into the Rock and Roll Hall of Fame. (Apr. 19) The Simpsons, an animated dysfunctional family, make their first appearance on *The Tracy Ullman Show*. (Jul. 1) The first Edgefest, an annual rock festival that primarily promotes Canadian music, is staged at Molson Park in Barrie, Ontario.

Sports: (Jan. 25) The New York Giants defeat the Denver Broncos, 39-20, in Super Bowl XXI, winning the NFL championship for the first time since 1956. (Mar. 29) WrestleMania III is held at the Pontiac Silverdome in Pontiac, Michigan, setting the North American indoor attendance record at 93,173. (Apr. 30) NASCAR driver Bill Elliott sets the record for fastest lap at Talladega Motor Speedway at 211 miles, or 340 kilometers, per hour. (Oct. 25) Winning only eight-five games in the regular season, the Minnesota Twins surprise baseball fans by defeating the St. Louis Cardinals to win the World Series.

Crime: (Jan. 13) Fat Tony and Carmine Peruccia, two members of the New York City Mafia, are sentenced to one hundred years in prison for racketeering. (Jul. 4) A court in Lyon, France, sentences former Gestapo boss Klaus Barbie to life imprisonment for crimes against humanity.

1988

International events: (Jan. 1) Soviet premier Mikhail Gorbachev initiates perestroika, a program of economic restructuring. (May 15) The Soviet Union withdraws from Afghanistan after more than eight years of war. (Aug. 20) The Iran-Iraq war ends; an estimated one million people were killed in the eight-year conflict. (Nov. 15) An independent state of Palestine is proclaimed at the Palestinian National Council meeting in Algiers. (Dec. 2) Benazir Bhutto is sworn in as prime minister of Pakistan, the first woman to head the government of an Islamic country.

Government and politics: (Feb. 3) The House of Representatives denies President Reagan's request for $36.25 million to support the Nicaraguan Contras. (Feb. 12) Anthony Kennedy is appointed to the Supreme Court. (Jul. 20) The Democratic National Convention in Atlanta nominates Michael Dukakis for president and Senator Lloyd Bentsen for vice president. (Aug. 18) The Republican National Convention in New Orleans nominates Vice President George H. W. Bush for president and Senator Dan Quayle for vice president. (Oct. 5) During a vice presidential debate, Quayle maintains that he has as much government experience as John F. Kennedy did when he ran for president in 1960; Bentsen, his Democratic opponent, elicits a positive audience response when he replies, "Senator, I knew Jack Kennedy. I served with Jack Kennedy. Jack Kennedy was a friend of mine. Senator, you're no Jack Kennedy." (Nov. 8) Bush is elected president of the United States. (Nov. 21) Brian Mulroney and the Progressive Conservative Party of Canada win a second majority government.

Military and war: (Mar. 8) Two U.S. Army helicopters collide in Fort Campbell, Kentucky, killing seventeen servicemen. (Jul. 3) Iran Air Flight 655 is shot down by missiles launched from the USS *Vincennes*. (Nov. 22) The initial prototype of the stealth fighter is unveiled in Palmdale, California.

Society: (Jan. 1) The Evangelical Lutheran Church in America is founded, creating the largest Lutheran denomination in the United States. (Feb. 21) During his program, televangelist Jimmy Swaggart admits to committing an unspecified sin; his sin is later revealed to be an affair with a prostitute. (Mar. 6) Students at Gallaudet University, a school for the deaf, go on strike to protest the appointment of a nondeaf university president.

Business and economics: (Jul. 14) Volkswagen closes its Westmoreland County, Pennsylvania, plant—the first factory built by a foreign automaker in the United States—after ten years of operation. (Sept. 5) The Robert M. Bass Group, with two billion dollars of federal aid, agrees to buy American Savings and Loan Association, the largest thrift in the United States. (Oct. 30) Philip Morris purchases Kraft Foods for $13.1 billion. (Nov. 30) Kohlberg Kravis Roberts & Co. buys RJR Nabisco for $25.07 billion.

Transportation and communications: (Dec. 21) Pan Am Flight 103 is blown up by Libyan terrorists over Lockerbie, Scotland, killing 270 people.

Science and technology: Microsoft passes Lotus to become the world's largest software company. Microsoft begins developing its Windows NT (new technology). (Sept. 29) The National Aeronautics and Space Administration (NASA), which had grounded flights after the *Challenger* disaster, resumes space shuttle flights by launching the space shuttle *Discovery.*

Environment and health: Congress bans smoking on domestic air flights that are less than two hours long. The FDA approves the marketing of Viaspan, an isotonic solution used to preserve donated livers in a viable state before transplantation. (May 16) U.S. Surgeon General C. Everett Koop states in a report that the addictive properties of nicotine are similar to those of heroin and cocaine. (Jul. 6) The first reported medical waste on beaches in the New York area, including hypodermic needles and syringes possibly infected with the AIDS virus, wash ashore on Long Island; subsequent medical waste discoveries on beaches in Coney Island and in Monmouth County, New Jersey, force the closure of numerous New York-area beaches.

Arts and literature: *The Lyre of Orpheus,* the third novel in Robertson Davies' Cornish Trilogy, is published amid favorable reviews from critics. (Jun. 11) A concert at London's Wembley Stadium, featuring stars from the fields of music, comedy, and film, celebrates the seventieth birthday of imprisoned African National Congress leader Nelson Mandela.

Popular culture: For the first time ever, compact discs (CDs) outsell vinyl recordings. Oprah Winfrey has the highest-rated television talk show in the United States. *Who Framed Roger Rabbit,* the first film to combine live actors and animated characters, is the top-grossing film of the year. (Apr. 11) *The Last Emperor,* directed by Bernardo Bertolucci, wins nine Academy Awards.

Sports: (Jan. 29) The Midwest Classic Conference, a college athletic organization, is founded. (Feb. 13-28) The 1988 Winter Olympics are held in Calgary, Alberta, Canada. (Aug. 9) The Chicago Cubs play their first-ever night game at home in Wrigley Field, defeating the New York Mets, 6-4. (Sept. 17-Oct. 2) The Summer Olympic Games are held in Seoul, South Korea. (Oct. 15) An injured Kirk Gibson hits a dramatic home run to win the first game of the World Series for the Los Angeles Dodgers, defeating the Oakland A's by a score of 5-4; the Dodgers go on to win the series in five games.

Crime: (Mar. 16) Lieutenant Colonel Oliver North and Vice Admiral John Poindexter are indicted on charges of conspiracy to defraud the United States because of their roles in the Iran-Contra affair. (Nov. 11) Police in Sacramento, California, find a body buried in the lawn at the boardinghouse of sixty-year-old Dorothea Puente; six more bodies are eventually found, and Puente is convicted of three murders and sentenced to life in prison.

1989

International events: (Jan. 18) The Communist Party of Poland votes to legalize Solidarity. (Apr. 15) Students from Beijing, Shanghai, Xian, and Nanjing, China, begin protesting in Tiananmen Square. (May 20) The Chinese government declares martial law in Beijing in response to the Tiananmen Square protests. (May 30) Student protesters in Tiananmen Square unveil a statue, the Goddess of Democracy. (Jun. 4) The final standoff between student protesters and the military takes place in Tiananmen Square. (Nov. 9) The Berlin Wall falls as East Germany opens checkpoints, allowing its citizens to freely travel to West Germany; celebrating Germans begin tearing down the wall. (Nov. 17) The Velvet Revolution begins in Czechoslovakia as a peaceful student demonstration in Prague is severely repelled by police. (Nov. 28) With other communist regimes falling all around it and with growing street protests, the Communist Party of Czechoslovakia announces that it will relinquish its monopoly on political power. (Dec. 29) Václav Havel is elected president of Czechoslovakia, the country's first noncommunist leader in more than forty years.

Government and politics: (Jan. 20) George H. W. Bush becomes the forty-first president of the United States. (Feb. 10) Ron Brown is elected chairman of the Democratic National Committee, the first African American to lead a major political party. (Nov. 7) David Dinkins becomes the first African American mayor of New York City, while Douglas Wilder of Virginia is the first elected African American governor.

Military and war:. (Feb. 23) The Senate Armed Services Committee rejects President Bush's nomination of John Tower for secretary of defense.

Society: (Mar. 14) President Bush bans the importation of assault weapons into the United States. (Jun. 1) The SkyDome stadium, now known as Rogers Centre, opens in Toronto. (Sept. 5) During his first televised news conference, President Bush holds up a bag of cocaine purchased at Lafayette Park, across the street from the White House.

Business and economics: (Mar. 9) A strike forces Eastern Air Lines into bankruptcy. (Aug. 7) Federal Express buys Flying Tigers, originally a volunteer group of pilots who fought in World War II. (Oct. 13) In what is later called the Friday the Thirteenth Minicrash, the Dow Jones Industrial Average plummets 190.58 points to close at 2,569.26, most likely a result of the collapsing junk bond market.

Transportation and communications: (Mar. 1) The United States ratifies the Berne Convention, an international treaty on copyrights. (Mar. 4) Time, Inc., and Warner Communications announce plans to merge and create Time Warner.

Science and technology: (Mar. 23) Stanley Pons and Martin Fleischmann announce that they have achieved cold fusion at the University of Utah. (Jul. 26) A federal grand jury indicts Cornell University student Robert Tappan Morris, Jr., for releasing a computer virus, making him the first person to be prosecuted under the 1986 Computer Fraud and Abuse Act. (Aug. 25) Voyager II flies past the planet Neptune and its moon Triton.

Environment and health: (Feb. 14) Union Carbide agrees to pay the Indian government $470 million for the damages caused in the 1984 chemical leak disaster in Bhopal. (Mar. 24) The *Exxon Valdez* oil tanker runs aground, spilling 240,000 barrels, or 11 million gallons, of oil into Prince William Sound in Alaska.

Arts and literature: (Feb. 14) Iranian leader Ayatollah Khomeini encourages Muslims to kill author Salman Rushdie for writing his novel *The Satanic Verses*; Khomeini later offers a three-million-dollar bounty for Rushdie's murder. (Jun. 12) The Corcoran Gallery of Art in Washington, D.C., removes an exhibit of erotic photos by Robert Mapplethorpe.

Popular culture: (Apr. 16) The *Dilbert* comic strip is syndicated for the first time. (Jul. 5) The sitcom *Seinfeld* premieres on television. (Nov. 15) Disney's *The Little Mermaid* is released in theaters. (Dec. 17) The first full-length episode of *The Simpsons* airs on FOX.

Sports: (Apr. 2) Hulk Hogan defeats Randy Savage to become the World Wrestling Federation champion. (May 25) The Calgary Flames win their first Stanley Cup with a 4-2 victory over the Montreal Canadiens. (Aug. 24) Baseball player Pete Rose consents to a lifetime ban from the sport following allegations of illegal gambling; he also is barred from induction into the Baseball Hall of Fame.

Crime: (Jan. 24) Serial killer Ted Bundy is executed in Florida. (Apr. 19) A Central Park jogger is brutally attacked during an evening run in the New York City park. (Aug. 20) Lyle and Erik Menendez murder their wealthy parents in the den of the family's Beverly Hills home. (Dec. 6) In the worst single-day massacre in Canadian history, a twenty-five-year-old man who hates women goes to the École Polytechnique in Montreal and kills fourteen women, injures thirteen others, and then shoots himself.

Rebecca Kuzins

■ Bibliography

This bibliography lists books containing substantial material about a wide variety of topics pertaining to the 1980's. Additional works, and especially works on narrower subjects, can be found in the "Further Readings" notes at the end of every essay in *The Eighties in America*.

Books are listed under the following seven categories:

1. General Works

Carroll, Peter. *It Seemed Like Nothing Happened: America in the 1970's.* New Brunswick, N.J.: Rutgers University Press, 1990. Carroll examines the 1970's and explains why the decade was more significant than it appeared at the time. This history of the previous decade provides background information for better understanding the events of the 1980's.

Johnson, Haynes. *Sleepwalking Through History: America in the Reagan Years.* New York: W. W. Norton, 1991. Johnson argues that the United States in the 1980's was lulled to sleep by Ronald Reagan, while the country's ills, particularly the gap between the rich and the poor, intensified. He condemns Reagan for weakening America's constitutional system and for lowering public concern about the nation's problems.

2. Politics and Politicians

Collins, Robert M. *Transforming America: Politics and Culture During the Reagan Years.* New York: Columbia University Press, 2006. While America had a growing pride in itself during Ronald Reagan's presidency, the country also became more divided. Collins examines the source of both the pride and the division, focusing his explanation on Reagan. He also discusses other issues, including what he views as a divide between religious and secular forces. Includes photographs and a short bibliography.

Cook, Ramsay. *Teeth of Time: Remembering Pierre Elliott Trudeau.* Montreal: McGill-Queen's University Press, 2006. Cook, a longtime friend and political supporter of Trudeau, reflects on the private life and public career of the former Canadian prime minister. Cook examines the political issues, including constitutional reform and nationalism, which Trudeau strove to address throughout his lifetime.

Craig, Barbara Hinkson, and David M. O'Brien. *Abortion and American Politics.* Chatham, N.J.: Chatham House, 1993. The authors chronicle the political controversy surrounding abortion rights, describing the interaction between states, the federal government, interest groups, the Supreme Court, Congress, and the president. The book covers the period between the Supreme Court rulings in *Roe v. Wade* (1973) and *Planned Parenthood v. Casey* (1992).

Shilts, Randy. *And the Band Played On: People, Politics, and the AIDS Epidemic.* New York: Penguin, 1988. This work examines the early history of the AIDS epidemic, from the disease's origin until 1984, when the United States began making serious efforts to combat the illness. Shilts argues that the conservative Reagan administration and the American public, including gay leaders, tried to sweep the epidemic under the rug, which resulted in a delay in treating the disease.

Tygiel, Jules. *Ronald Reagan and the Triumph of American Conservatism.* New York: Longman, 2006. This book explores how Ronald Reagan symbolized the accomplishments of the conservative political movement. Tygiel discusses Reagan's achievement, failings, and the issues he failed to address.

3. Race

Carter, Dan T. *From George Wallace to Newt Gingrich: Race in the Conservative Counterrevolution, 1963-1994.* Baton Rouge: Louisiana State University Press, 1996. This study of the role of racial issues in American conservative politics includes valuable information about presidents Ronald Reagan and George H. W. Bush's response to these issues.

Edsall, Thomas Byrne, with Mary D. Edsall. *Chain Reaction: The Impact of Race, Rights, and Taxes on American Politics.* New York: W. W. Norton, 1992. The Edsalls argue that the Democrats had become the minority political party by the early 1990's because of three factors: race, civil rights, and taxes. They focus on how these factors turned many working-class and middle-class white people against the Democrats, providing a detailed analysis of the presidential elections from 1964 to 1988.

Hacker, Andrew. *Two Nations: Black and White, Separate, Hostile, Unequal.* New York: Charles Scribner's Sons, 2003. Hacker does not buy into the argument that race no longer matters in America; he argues persuasively that this issue continues to have an impact upon the country. He cites statistics to demonstrate that racism is a major reason for the disparities in income and crime and other differences between black and white Americans.

Laham, Nicholas. *The Reagan Presidency and the Politics of Race: In Pursuit of Colorblind Justice and Limited Government.* Westport, Conn.: Praeger, 1998. Laham looks at racial issues during the Reagan presidency. He argues that Ronald Reagan's desire to reduce the enforcement of civil rights laws was not motivated by racism but by the president's desire to limit the role of government.

Nagel, Joane. *American Indian Ethnic Renewal: Red Power and the Resurgence of Identity and Culture.* New York: Oxford University Press, 1997. Nagel argues that Americans are now more willing to identify themselves as Native Americans or American Indians than they were in the past. She attributes this, in part, to the Civil Rights movement of the 1960's, but she identifies other reasons for the resurgence in Native American culture in the last half of the twentieth century.

Nightingale, Carl Husemoller. *On The Edge: A History of Poor Black Children and Their American Dreams.* New York: Basic Books, 1993. Nightingale argues that both left-wing and right-wing politicians misunderstand the causes of black poverty. He indicts the role of the media and Americans' conspicuous consumption as the reasons for this indigence.

4. Supreme Court

Davis, Derek. *Original Intent: Chief Justice Rehnquist and the Course of American Church-State Relations.* Buffalo, N.Y.: Prometheus Books, 1991. Davis examines the Rehnquist Court during its initial years, focusing on its rulings regarding church-state relations. He argues that William H. Rehnquist endangered religious freedom by allowing state aid to religion. The book also includes a brief examination of the other justices who served on the Court in the early 1990's.

O'Connor, Sandra Day, and H. Alan Day. *Lazy B: Growing up on a Cattle Ranch in the American Southwest.* New York: Random House, 2003. O'Connor, whom Ronald Reagan appointed to the Supreme Court, and Day, her brother, recall their youth on the Lazy B cattle ranch.

Schultz, David A., and Christopher E. Smith. *The Jurisprudential Vision of Justice Antonin Scalia.* Lanham, Md.: Rowman & Littlefield, 1996. Schultz and Smith examine the first ten years of Scalia's service on the Supreme Court. They argue that there is not one consistent vision that has motivated Scalia, and that Scalia's extreme right-wing nature has prevented him from forming coalitions or remaking the law as much as he could have. The authors do not accept Scalia's word that his opinions follow the direct writing of the Constitution, or what is known as textualism; they critique Scalia's opinions to demonstrate how they often divert from a strictly textual interpretation.

Schwartz, Bernard. *The Ascent of Pragmatism: The Burger Court in Action.* Reading, Mass.: Addison-Wesley, 1990. Schwartz, who wrote a well-received book on Chief Justice Earl Warren, argues that the Burger Court was more a continuation of the Warren Court than a significant departure from it. He contends that Chief Justice Warren E. Burger was not the effective leader of the Court, as one might expect a chief justice to be, but that the Court was led by the more centrist justices. In addition to examining the Court as a whole, Schwartz also looks at the contribution of each justice.

Tushnet, Mark V. *A Court Divided: The Rehnquist Court and the Future of Constitutional Law.* New York: W. W. Norton, 2005. Tushnet describes the divisions within the Rehnquist Court, examining the views of the individual justices. He suggests that the centrists on the Court, especially Anthony Kennedy and Sandra Day O'Connor, played a significant role. While more focused on the 1990's, the book also devotes significant attention to the 1980's.

_____. *Making Constitutional Law: Thurgood Marshall and the Supreme Court, 1961-1991*. New York: Oxford University Press, 1997. Thurgood Marshall was one of the most liberal members of the Supreme Court in the 1980's, and Tushnet locates the source of Marshall's liberalism, describing his views on a variety of constitutional issues. The book also provides an overview of the Court and the justices who served with Marshall.

Van Sickel, Robert W. *Not a Particularly Different Voice: The Jurisprudence of Sandra Day O'Connor*. New York: Peter Lang, 1998. In 1981, O'Connor was the first woman appointed to the Supreme Court. This book argues that rather than providing a liberal break with tradition because of her gender, O'Connor continued to expound the Court's conservative and centrist philosophies. Van Sickel suggests that O'Connor's legal views and opinions were not shaped by her gender, but by her tendency to follow precedent and to avoid constitutional questions, wherever possible.

Yarbrough, Tinsley. *Rehnquist Court and the Constitution*. New York: Oxford University Press, 2001. While the course of the Rehnquist Court was not always consistent, it had a huge influence upon America, beginning in the 1980's. Yarbrough tries to explain how and why the Court reached its decisions, noting that its opinions generally continued past precedent. However, the Court broke new ground on economic issues, striking down more regulations on business and commerce than its predecessors.

5. Foreign Policy and Events

Andrew, Arthur. *The Rise and Fall of a Middle Power: Canadian Diplomacy from King to Mulroney*. Toronto: Lorimer, 1993. Andrew, a former Canadian ambassador, argues that Canadian power has been declining since its peak in the mid-1960's. He maintains that Canada could choose to reassert its power, but as of the early 1990's the country had become dependent on and subservient to the wishes of other nations, including the United States.

Bell, Coral. *The Reagan Paradox: American Foreign Policy in the 1980's*. New Brunswick, N.J.: Rutgers University Press, 1990. Bell describes the gap between Ronald Reagan's spoken goals for international relations and how he actually conducted foreign policy.

Farber, David. *Taken Hostage: The Iran Hostage Crisis and America's First Encounter with Radical Islam*. Princeton, N.J.: Princeton University Press, 2006. In his chronicle of the Iranian hostage crisis, Farber examines the rise of radical Islam and the impact of the crisis upon the United States. The effect of the crisis, Farber argues, cannot be explained without describing the general mood of melancholy that affected America in the 1970's.

Gaddis, John Lewis. *The United States and the End of the Cold War: Implications, Reconsiderations, Provocations*. New York: Oxford University Press, 1994. Gaddis examines the reasons for the end of the Cold War and reconsiders some of the significant figures in that struggle. He also describes the post-Cold War world, arguing that the end of the war did not mean the end of world conflict.

Garthoff, Raymond L. *The Great Transition: American-Soviet Relations and the End of the Cold War*. Washington, D.C.: Brookings Institution Press, 1994. This book analyzes U.S.-Soviet relations under presidents Ronald Reagan and George H. W. Bush. Garthoff argues that the United States was unnecessarily provocative toward the Soviet Union and downplays the United States' role in "winning" the Cold War.

Hahn, Peter L. *Crisis and Crossfire: The United States and the Middle East Since 1945*. Washington, D.C.: Potomac Books, 2005. This work provides a short introduction to the United States' policy in the Middle East during the last sixty years. In addition to discussing America's relations with Iraq, the book also examines the Israeli-Palestinian conflict and America's dependence upon the region's oil.

Karsh, Efraim. *The Iran-Iraq War, 1980-1988*. Oxford, England: Osprey, 2002. This brief history of the war describes the major battles and the tactics that Iran employed to repel Iraq. Includes a chronology, time line, and photographs.

Karsh, Efraim, and Inari Rautsi. *Saddam Hussein: A Political Biography*. New York: Grove Press, 2003. This biography of Hussein focuses on how he consolidated and maintained political power in Iraq, concluding with his role in the first Persian Gulf War. It also details his reasons for starting a war with Iran and invading Kuwait.

LeoGrande, William M. *Our Own Backyard: The United States in Central America, 1977-1992.* Chapel Hill: University of North Carolina Press, 2000. LeoGrande focuses on El Salvador and Nicaragua in his discussion of Central America, examining how these countries were shaped by the Cold War. He also discusses the United States' policy in Central America and how the Vietnam War affected America's involvement in that region.

North, Oliver. *Under Fire: An American Story.* New York: HarperCollins, 1992. Oliver North was heavily involved in the Iran-Contra affair, and in this autobiography he defends that operation and his participation in it.

Sick, Gary. *All Fall Down: America's Tragic Encounter with Iran.* Lincoln, Nebr.: iUniverse.com, 2001. Sick, a former aide who worked for the National Security Council and focused on Iran during the Carter administration, presents this blow-by-blow account of the Iran hostage crisis. He places the incident in context by reviewing American policy toward Iran before the crisis, including the activities of the Nixon administration.

_____. *October Surprise: America's Hostages in Iran and the Election of Ronald Reagan.* New York: Random House, 1991. Sick argues that Reagan supporters managed to maneuver the Iranians into waiting until after the November, 1980, elections to release the hostages, in return for arms and other concessions after Reagan was elected. The claims are controversial, but Sick's position in the National Security Council during the Reagan, Carter, and Ford administrations bolsters his claims.

Thornton, Richard C. *The Reagan Revolution, I: The Politics of U.S. Foreign Policy.* New York: Simon & Schuster, 1987. Thornton describes foreign policy in the early years of the Reagan administration, focusing on Ronald Reagan's opposition to the Soviet Union.

Walsh, Lawrence. *Firewall: The Iran-Contra Conspiracy and Cover-Up.* New York: W. W. Norton, 1998. Walsh, the independent prosecutor in the Iran-Contra investigation, maintains that President Ronald Reagan knew about the affair and that the cover-up protected Reagan from any legal ramifications.

Woodward, Bob. *Veil: The Secret Wars of the CIA, 1981-1987.* New York: Simon & Schuster, 2005. This work, by one of the reporters who broke the Watergate story, focuses on the Central Intelligence Agency (CIA) during the Reagan administration. It presents a picture of the CIA as dangerously active under the leadership of William Casey, and this picture embroiled the book in controversy. Woodward also maintains that the CIA was actively involved in the Iran-Contra affair.

6. Culture and Entertainment

Cullen, Jim, and Daniel Cullen. *Born in the U.S.A.: Bruce Springsteen and the American Tradition.* New York: HarperCollins, 1997. In the 1980's, many people used Bruce Springsteen's song, "Born in the U.S.A.," as a rallying cry for Americans. Cullen examines the roots of the song and many others written by Springsteen and places Springsteen within American musical and literary traditions.

Freiberger, Paul, and Michael Swaine. *Fire in the Valley: The Making of the Personal Computer.* Berkeley, Calif.: McGraw-Hill, 1999. This work chronicles the early days of Silicon Valley, beginning in the 1950's, with the creation of large computers such as UNIVAC, as well as discussing the birth of the personal computer in the 1970's. Freiberger and Swaine focus on important figures in the computer's development, including Bill Gates and Doug Englebart.

Fuller, Linda K. *The Cosby Show: Audiences, Impact, and Implications.* Westport, Conn.: Greenwood Press, 1992. *The Cosby Show* was one of the most popular television programs in the 1980's, and Fuller examines the reasons for this popularity, along with the show's effect on the television marketplace and the nationwide image of African Americans. She also surveys people in other countries in order to demonstrate the show's worldwide impact.

Kallen, Stuart A. *A Cultural History of the United States Through the Decades: The 1980's.* San Diego, Calif.: Lucent Books, 1998. This overview of the United States during the 1980's not only examines popular culture but also discusses the Reagan Revolution and the Cold War. It features information about AIDS, music, women's rights, technology, science, and the start of the computer revolution.

Mansour, David. *From Abba to Zoom: A Pop Culture Encyclopedia of the Late Twentieth Century.* Kansas City,

Mo.: Andrews McMeel, 2005. The encyclopedia contains thousands of entries regarding television, gadgets, fads, and music of the 1980's.

Rettenmund, Matthew. *Totally Awesome 80's: A Lexicon of the Music, Videos, Movies, TV Shows, Stars, and Trends of That Decadent Decade.* New York: St. Martin's Griffin, 1996. This work is more of a listing than an analysis, as Rettenmund provides a list of the best in each category included in his title. He also discusses the changing vocabulary and other trends, along with the popular culture figures of the period.

Wills, Gary. *Under God: Religion and American Politics.* New York: Simon & Schuster, 1990. Wills argues that America has always been a Christian nation and that the election of 1988 reflected this fact. He covers a wide variety of topics in this book, moving from the Scopes trial through the 1980's. While acknowledging the importance of religion, Wills also holds that the separation of church and state is good for both the state and the church.

7. Homosexuality

Rutledge, Leigh. *The Gay Decades: From Stonewall to the Present.* New York: Plume, 1992. As the title suggests, this book covers gay history in the United States from the 1969 Stonewall riot until the late 1980's. Rutledge goes beyond simply focusing on gays and lesbians to also discuss public figures and others who have shaped gay culture. As the author admits, this work focuses more on gay men than on lesbians.

Shawyer, Lois. *And the Flag Was Still There: Straight People, Gay People, and Sexuality in the U.S. Military.* New York: Haworth Press, 1995. Although American homosexuals argued for greater civil rights in the 1980's and obtained some changes in the 1990's, the issue of gays in the military remains unresolved. Shawyer examines the issue, arguing that the United States should drop its ban on homosexuals in the military. Shawyer played a significant role in persuading Canada to drop its ban, and she brings that experience to bear in her book.

Scott A. Merriman

■ Web Sites

In selecting the following Web sites, efforts have been made to identify sites of broadest interest to readers and those most useful in providing additional links. Attention has also been given to representative examples of more specialized sites, such as pages on individual personages and events.

AIDS

In Their Own Words: NIH Researchers Recall the Early Years of AIDS
http://aidshistory.nih.gov/home.html

Created by the National Institutes of Health (NIH), this Web site recounts the AIDS epidemic of the 1980's from the government's perspective. It includes documents and images about the disease, along with a time line, oral history transcripts, and links to related sites.

Ryan White.com
http://www.ryanwhite.com/index.html

Dedicated to Ryan White, the site includes an extensive discussion about the boy who was diagnosed with AIDS at the age of thirteen and who gained international recognition for his subsequent fight to remain in school. It features supplemental material about his mother's life and links to information about AIDS research and prevention.

Crises and Disasters

Avoiding Disaster: The Importance of Having a Disaster Plan
http://iml.jou.ufl.edu/projects/spring01/Hogue/index.html

The *Exxon Valdez* Oil Spill
http://iml.jou.ufl.edu/projects/spring01/Hogue/exxon.html

Johnson & Johnson's Tylenol
http://iml.jou.ufl.edu/projects/spring01/Hogue/tylenol.html

Designed as part of a 2001 University of Florida research project, these sites summarize the effects of several major corporate crises, including the Exxon Valdez oil spill and the Tylenol tampering scare, both of which occurred in the 1980's. These sites analyze how the corporations managed these crises and discuss the long-term public impact of these events.

BBC News: One Night in Bhopal
http://news.bbc.co.uk/1/hi/programmes/bhopal/default.stm

This page from the British Broadcasting Corporation (BBC) News site examines the 1984 Bhopal chemical spill—the worst industrial disaster in history. An estimated three thousand people died from a chemical leak at a factory owned by Union Carbide, an American company. The site includes video and audio coverage and reports the stories of survivors, some 500,000 of whom still suffer from aftereffects.

Government and Law

American Experience—Jimmy Carter
http://www.pbs.org/wgbh/amex/carter/

Created to accompany an episode of the Public Broadcasting Service's (PBS) program *American Experience*, this site provides information about Jimmy Carter's life before, during, and after his presidency, as well as a discussion of the episode and a teacher's guide. It includes a time line, photos of Carter and his family, and an in-depth examination of some of the issues of his presidency, including his attempts to bring peace to the Middle East and to end the Iranian hostage crisis.

Canadian Constitutional Documents: A Legal History
http://www.solon.org/Constitutions/Canada/English/index.html

The 1980's saw a great deal of constitutional change in Canada, not the least of which was the Canada Act of 1982, in which Britain relinquished the power to change Canada's laws, including its constitution. This site contains the text of the act, in both English and French, describes the previous legislation that the act amended, and summarizes the act's impact upon Canada.

The Canadian Encyclopedia
http://www.thecanadianencyclopedia.com/index.cfm?PgNm=Homepage&Params=A1

While this Web site is in no way limited to the 1980's, it provides a wealth of information about Canada during that decade. It features articles written by a variety of individuals, including academics, about Canadian history, and a search engine to enable users to retrieve information.

Famous Trials

http://www.umkc.edu/famoustrials

This Web site covers fifty famous trials, ranging in time from 339 B.C.E. to 2006. It includes two American trials from the 1980's: that of John Hinckley, Jr., who attempted to assassinate President Ronald Reagan, and the McMartin Preschool teachers charged with sexually abusing students.

From Cheers to Jeers: The Mulroney Years

http://archives.cbc.ca/IDD-1-73-1469/politics_economy/ brian_mulroney/

This page is part of the Prime Ministers' Gallery created by the Canadian Broadcasting Corporation (CBC). It focuses on former Prime Minister Brian Mulroney, including video and audio clips about him, as well as teacher lesson plans. The page chronicles how Mulroney was at first highly regarded, but later left office in disgrace.

Ronald Reagan Presidential Library

http://www.reagan.utexas.edu

This Web site is a good place for both serious researchers and more casual learners to retrieve information about Reagan. It explains how one can gain access to Reagan's presidential papers and features biographies of Reagan and his wife Nancy.

Ten Greatest Canadians—Pierre Elliot Trudeau

http://www.cbc.ca/greatest/top_ten/nominee/trudeau-pierre.html

Trudeau is frequently called one of the greatest prime ministers, and the Canadian Broadcasting Corporation (CBC) named him one of the ten greatest Canadians for his charisma, flair, and impact upon Canada. This page from a CBC Web site discusses his accomplishments, failures, and brilliant return to politics in the early 1980's. It includes a time line and links to multimedia materials.

United States Senate Committee on the Judiciary Hearing 99-1067: Hearings Before the Senate Committee on the Judiciary on the Nomination of Justice William Hubbs Rehnquist to be Chief Justice of the United States, July 29, 30, 31, and August 1, 1986

http://www.gpoaccess.gov/congress/senate/judiciary/ sh99-1067/browse.html

The complete text of the 1986 hearings in which the Senate Judiciary Committee considered President Ronald Reagan's promotion of William H. Rehnquist from associate to chief justice of the Supreme Court. This site is useful for students researching legal history in the 1980's, as Rehnquist's role as chief justice helped move the Court in a more conservative direction.

Walter Mondale

http://www.spartacus.schoolnet.co.uk/USAmondale.htm

Created by Spartacus Educational, a British organization that designs Web sites for history instruction, this page focuses on Mondale, the unsuccessful presidential candidate in 1984, who also served as Jimmy Carter's vice president. Unlike some treatments of Mondale, this biography covers his life before he became vice president and after his 1984 presidential run.

Military

The Invasion of Grenada

http://www.historyguy.com/Grenada.html

This Web site looks at the United States' invasion of Grenada in 1983. It examines the background, causes, consequences, and casualties of the conflict, along with links to related sites.

Lessons Learned: Iran-Iraq War

http://www.fas.org/man/dod-101/ops/war/docs/3203/

This document, compiled by the U.S. Marine Corps in 1990, analyzes the Iran-Iraq war, which was fought from 1980 to 1988 and in which the United States' backed the Iraqi government of Saddam Hussein. The instability from this war prompted Hussein to later invade Kuwait and significantly shaped subsequent events in the region. In addition to an overview of the conflict, there are sections on strategy, tactics and operations, and chemical weapons, among other features.

Marine Attack in Lebanon
*http://www.nytimes.com/learning/general/onthisday/
991023onthisday_big.html#headlines*

A reproduction of the front page of *The New York Times* for October 24, 1983, containing a report of the previous day's bombing of an American Marine Corps barracks in Beirut, Lebanon, where American forces were on a peacekeeping mission. About 230 people were killed in the attack.

"The Panama Invasion Revisited: Lessons for the Use of Force in the Post Cold War Era"
http://www.mtholyoke.edu/acad/intrel/gilboa.htm

This Web site, hosted by Mt. Holyoke University, contains an article from the *Political Science Quarterly* examining the United States' 1989 invasion of Panama. The article focuses on then-Panamanian leader Manuel Noriega, who was captured in the invasion, brought to the United States, and tried for criminal drug operations.

Saddam Hussein
*http://topics.nytimes.com/top/reference/timestopics/
people/h/saddam_hussein/index.html?inline=nyt-per*

This Web site from *The New York Times* surveys the life, reign, and death of Saddam Hussein, former dictator of Iraq. In the 1980's, Hussein was supported by the United States, who later declared war to overthrow his regime. The Web site chronicles Saddam's rise, leadership of Iraq, and fall from power and includes a time line, links to related articles, and photographs.

Pop Culture and Entertainment

AllMusic
http://www.allmusic.com

A compendium of material on all types of music, this site contains detailed information on many musicians and bands from the 1980's. It includes biographies, discographies, and lists of musicians who influenced each performer and band.

The Amazing 80's: 1980-1989
http://library.thinkquest.org/J0111064/80home.htm

A generic site on the 1980's, featuring information on entertainment, events, fads and fashions, inventions, and sports heroes. Though each section contains only a short list of items or individuals, this is a good beginning for further research.

BBC-Cult—I Love the 80's
http://www.bbc.co.uk/cult/ilove/years/80sindex.shtml

The British Broadcasting Corporation (BBC) hosts this site dedicated to the 1980's. It is organized by year, with each year featuring information about television, games, and toys. For those who think they really know the 1980's, a quiz is included, and there also are trivia questions and a photo gallery.

Big Hair Metal and Glam Rock
http://www.bighairmetal.com/

One of the biggest rock music fads of the 1980's was heavy metal, and bands performing this type of music were famous for having "big hair." This site features pages of information about Van Halen, Mötley Crüe, Pat Benatar, and other big hair metal bands and performers.

The Eighties Club: The Politics and Pop Culture of the 1980's
http://eightiesclub.tripod.com/index.htm

This is an in-depth look at the 1980's, with some material on the politics and headlines of the period. It includes a good deal of information on Ronald Reagan, with reprints of many of his speeches and numerous essays about him. It also contains sections on films and music, an encyclopedia of the 1980's, and a time line.

80's Memories, Fads, and Events
http://www.tripletsandus.com/80's/memories.htm

This site combines information, nostalgia, and fun. It offers users a chance to play vintage 1980's videos games online, including Frogger and Space Invaders, discusses why Generation X is a bad name for the generation that grew up in the 1980's, and includes a list of slang and fads from the decade.

80's Movies Rewind
http://www.fast-rewind.com/

This Web site covers hundreds of movies from the 1980's, ranging from well-known films to cult classics. It is primarily created by film fans, is frequently updated, and includes links to other sites.

The 80's Server
http://www.80s.com/default.html

Unlike other sites that deal with 1980's pop culture, *The 80's Server* provides links to sites that sell period memorabilia, including music. It also links to several places where users can play games related to the 1980's, as well as other sites about music, films, television shows, and sporting events of the era.

Film History of the 1980's
www.filmsite.org/80sintro.html

As the title suggests, this site contains a list of popular films, including a section on Academy Award winners, from the 1980's. Though the list is not comprehensive, it offers an idea of what was popular at the time. Some films have links to reviews.

Wide World of Sports Highlights—1980's
*http://espn.go.com/abcsports/wwos/milestones/
    1980s.html*

This Web site lists a large number of milestones and highlights in 1980's sports that were covered on the television program *Wide World of Sports*. The sports covered range from hockey to women's volleyball, skiing, and gymnastics.

Religion

Defining Evangelicalism
www.wheaton.edu/isae/defining_evangelicalism.html

A history of the evangelical movement in the United States, including an explanation of how the term "evangelical movement" was used in the 1980's. It also contains a discussion of the movement's interaction with politics beginning in the 1980's.

The Political Mobilization of the New Christian Right
http://are.as.wvu.edu/lebeau1.htm

Authored by Bryan LeBeau, chair of Creighton University's history department, this Web site discusses the right-wing religious movement, with analysis of the conservative Christian political mobilization that began in the 1980's. It also discusses the scandals that reduced the movement's power.

Soviet Union

Cold War
http://www.cnn.com/SPECIALS/cold.war/

This Web site accompanied the Cable News Network's (CNN) special series on the Cold War. The site provides historical perspective about the war's origins and its end in the late 1980's. Its list of declassified documents will be of particular interest to the more serious student of history.

Cold War International History Project
*http://wilsoncenter.org/
    index.cfm?topic_id=1409&fuseaction=topics.home*

This project, administered by the Woodrow Wilson International Center for Scholars, provides source documents, particularly those from the Soviets, about the Cold War. It also features links to information about relevant events, documents, publications, and other information about the conflict.

Perestroika and the Soviet Military: Implications for U.S. Policy
http://www.cato.org/pubs/pas/pa133.html

Perestroika was the restructuring undertaken by the Soviet Union during the 1980's in a last-ditch attempt to save the nation's economy. This article, written in 1990 by a retired American military official before the collapse of the Soviet Union, examines perestroika's impact on American foreign policy; it also suggests what the United States should do to maximize its position in the world.

Scott A. Merriman

■ Glossary

This list is a representative collection of words and phrases that were either first used or gained prominence during the 1980's in the United States. (n. = noun; adj. = adjective; adv. = adverb; v. = verb; exp. = expression)

AIDS, n. The acronym for the disease acquired immunodeficiency syndrome.

airhead, n. An ignorant or foolish individual.

amped, adj. Excited.

anorexia nervosa, n. A serious eating disorder that primarily afflicts teenage girls and young women and involves self-starvation.

bag, v. To take or steal something.

barf bag, n. A very offensive person.

Barney, n. A male who is considered unattractive.

Beemer, n. A BMW automobile.

bimbette, n. A female who is considered either stupid or sexually promiscuous.

Bite me, exp. An expression meaning "Kiss my ass."

Black Monday, n. The day in October, 1987, when the stock market plummeted more than five hundred points.

bling, n. Luxurious items such as jewelry.

blood, n. Friendship.

blow off, v. To let pass or to skip.

bodacious, adj. Attractive.

boho, n. Someone who is considered to be an artist or a bohemian.

bohunk, n. A very dumb athlete.

boink, v. To have sex.

bone, v. To engage in sexual activity.

boogie, v. To leave.

boom box, n. A portable stereo player.

boy toy, n. A good-looking male who is under the control of an older woman.

bring-down, n. Sad news.

bro, n. A male relative or friend with whom someone has established a close bond.

bulimia, n. A serious eating disorder that afflicts primarily teenage girls and young women and involves the gorging and purging of food.

bunk, adj. Nonsense or insincere bluster.

bust rocks, v. To exert oneself.

butt ugly, adj. Physically unattractive.

Cabbage Patch Kids, n. An extremely popular brand of doll created by Xavier Roberts and manufactured by Coleco.

camcorder, n. A portable video recording device.

cap, n. A bullet.

Care Bears, n. A popular set of characters created by American Greetings that appeared on greeting cards, on television, in feature films, and as stuffed teddy bears.

CD, n. The acronym for compact disc.

CD-ROM, n. The acronym for compact disc read-only memory.

cheese, n. Money.

cheesy, adj. Shabby or clichéd.

choice, adj. Very good.

chopper, n. A motorcycle that has been customized.

clock, v. To punch.

clydesdale, n. A large all-American male.

CNN, n. The acronym for Cable News Network.

cordless telephone, n. A portable telephone that works through the use of radio waves.

couch potato, n. Someone who spends a great deal of time watching television.

crack, n. A very addictive form of cocaine.

crackass, adj. Something that is considered to be cheap.

crib, n. The place where someone lives.

crusty, adj. Filthy.

cyberpunk, n. A popular science-fiction genre that primarily depicts alienated characters living in a world of high technology.

dead presidents, n. Money.

deep shit, n. A lot of trouble.

deke, v. To fake a person out.

dickhead, n. Someone who is considered to be a fool.

dinero, n. Money.

dink, n. The acronym for dual income, no kids.

dipstick, n. Someone who is considered to be a fool.

dis, v. To say something offensive or disrespectful to someone.

disposable cameras, n. Inexpensive cameras made to be used only once.

do lunch, v. To make an appointment to have lunch.

Donkey Kong, n. A popular video game released by Nintendo.

Don't have a cow, exp. To ask someone to stay calm.

dork, n. Someone who does socially inappropriate things.

douchebag, n. A reprehensible person.

downsize, v. To lay off employees.

duh, exp. That is dumb.

dump on, v. To criticize someone.

dweeb, n. A person who is socially inept.

earthbound, adj. Traditional or old-fashioned.

Eat my shorts, exp. A retort to criticism.

ecstasy, n. The street name for the psychedelic drug methylenedioxymethamphetamine, or MDMA.

ESPN, n. The acronym for Entertainment and Sports Programming Network.

evil empire, n. A term used by President Ronald Reagan to describe the Soviet Union.

family values, n. The so-called moral compass of a society, often used to promote a conservative or traditional ideology.

Farm Aid, n. A charity concert held for the benefit of American farmers.

Five-O, n. A police officer.

for sure or **fer sure**, exp. Of course.

fresh, adj. Something very new.

frosted, adj. Mad or angry.

Gag me with a spoon, exp. That is disgusting.

gangbanger, n. An active member of a street gang.

gear, n. Clothes.

geek, n. A person who is not cool or socially popular.

Generation X, n. A generation that began to have influence on popular culture during the 1980's.

genetic fingerprinting, n. The ability to distinguish one individual from another through the scientific testing of the individuals' deoxyribonucleic acid (DNA).

Get bent, exp. Go away.

Get with the program, exp. To do what is considered proper.

glasnost, n. A Russian term employed by Soviet leader Mikhail Gorbachev that means "openness."

go postal, v. To go crazy.

Great Communicator, n. Used as a term of respect for the communication skills of President Ronald Reagan.

grody to the max, adj. Very disgusting.

hacker, n. A person who is very good at using computers.

hair band, n. A hard rock band in which the members of the band have long frizzy hair.

hardcore, n. A loud, rebellious, and aggressive form of punk music.

have a cow, v. To get upset.

hellacious, adj. Stupendous.

high-five, v. To slap the palm of someone else with your palm when it is stretched above the head.

HIV, n. The acronym for human immunodeficiency virus.

homeboy, n. A good friend.

hoops, n. Basketball.

hoser, n. A person who is considered irritating or without any redeeming qualities.

house, n. A type of dance music played at warehouse parties.

I'm so sure, exp. A statement of sarcastic disbelief.

in a New York minute, adv. Happening with speed.

infomercial, n. A television informational program that is really no more than a lengthy paid advertisement for a product.

issues, n. Problems.

JAP, n. The acronym for Jewish American Princess.

Jarvik-7, n. An artificial heart designed by Dr. Robert K. Jarvik.

joanie, n. A girl who is considered to be awkward or boring.

Just Say No, exp. A slogan initiated by First Lady Nancy Reagan to encourage individuals to avoid getting involved with illegal drugs.

kegger, n. A beer party.

kickass, adj. Outstanding.

killer, adj. Outstanding.

Kiss my grits, exp. Another way of saying "kiss my ass."

kryptonite, n. A definite weakness.

lame, adj. Of disappointing quality.

laptop, n. A portable personal computer.

like, exp. Used as an interjection, "like" serves as a meaningless word when repeated many times in casual speech.

liposuction, n. A surgical procedure by which fat is sucked out of a patient.

Live Aid, n. A charity rock concert held for the purpose of raising money for famine-ravaged Ethiopia.

Macintosh, n. A personal computer manufactured by Apple.

major, adj. Extremely good.

Make me barf, exp. Stating displeasure with a situation.

Make my day, exp. Telling someone to go ahead and do what they were going to do, with the understanding that they will then suffer the consequences for their actions.

mall chick, n. A girl who likes to spend many hours at the mall.

max out, v. Take to the limit.

Me Generation, n. A generation that is preoccupied with the self.

moonies, n. The religious followers of the Reverend Sun Myung Moon.

moonwalk, n. A backsliding dance move made popular by Michael Jackson.

MS-DOS, n. The acronym for Microsoft disk operating system.

MTV, n. The acronym for Music Television.

neoexpressionism, n. An art movement that promoted bold figurative painting.

new wave, n. A music genre that emphasized a pop sound through the use of synthesizers.

no way, adv. Definitely not going to happen.

nuke, v. To heat something in the microwave.

NutraSweet, n. A popular artificial sweetener.

oink, n. The acronym for one income, no kids.

out to lunch, adj. Crazy.

Pac-Man, n. A popular video game.

PC, n. The acronym for both personal computer and political correctness.

perestroika, n. A Russian term associated with Soviet leader Mikhail Gorbachev that means "reconstruction."

perp, n. A criminal.

PMRC, n. The acronym for Parents' Music Resource Coalition.

poser, n. Someone pretending to be something that they are not.

pound, v. To drink to an extreme.

preppie, n. Someone who acts superior to others.

Prozac, n. An antidepressant drug prescribed for a variety of psychological disorders.

ralph, v. To vomit.

Reaganomics, n. The term used to describe President Ronald Reagan's free market economic policies.

real, v. Excellent.

Rogaine, n. The brand name for minoxidil, which is used as a topical drug for the treatment of male pattern baldness.

rollerblades, n. A style of roller skates, also known as inline skates.

RU-486, n. The commonly used name for the synthetic compound mifepristone, which is used for the medical termination of early intrauterine pregnancy.

Rubik's cube, n. A popular mechanical puzzle.

rule, v. To be amazing.

rush, n. A stimulating experience.

Rust Belt, n. A term used to describe the manufacturing region of the United States, as so many of these companies went out of business.

safe sex, n. A set of practices employed by persons engaging in sexual activity in order to protect themselves against sexually transmitted diseases (STDs).

scope, v. To examine closely.

scumbag, n. A disgusting person.

Shit happens, exp. Bad things or problems are always going to pop up in one's life.

Shop 'til you drop, exp. Shopping until one can no longer physically shop anymore.

ska, n. A musical style strongly influenced by reggae.

slam dancing, n. A dance form whereby participants literally crash into one another.

space cadet, n. Someone who is out of touch with reality.

space shuttle, n. A reusable spacecraft used to transport people into space.

Speedos, n. A pair of men's swimming trunks that fit snugly.

stagflation, n. The combination of stagnating economic growth and rising prices.

Star Wars, n. The common name for the Strategic Defense Initiative (SDI) proposed by President Ronald Reagan.

stoked, adj. Excited.

suck face, v. To French kiss.

sucks, v. To be not up to the job or occasion.

sweet, adj. Very nice.

ta-tas, n. Female breasts.

to the max, adv. To go to the limit.

toasted, adj. Drunk.

toss your cookies, v. To vomit.

totally awesome, adj. Amazing.

Trivial Pursuit, n. A popular board game in which participants must answer popular culture and general knowledge questions.

tubular, adj. Reaching greatness.

USFL, n. The acronym for United States Football League.

UVs, n. The acronym for ultraviolet rays of the sun.

Valley girl, n. A rich teenage girl from the San Fernando Valley section of Los Angeles.

veg, v. To take it easy.

Walkman, n. A popular portable audio player manufactured by Sony.

wannabe, n. A person who has ambitions of being like someone else.

warped, adj. Something disturbing or very weird.

whack, v. To kill.

Whatever, exp. It is of no consequence.

Where's the beef?, exp. A hamburger advertising slogan that also was used in the political arena to ask the question "Where's the substance?"

wicked, adj. Fantastic.

wig out, v. To lose control of one's emotions.

wigged, adj. Insane.

Windows, n. A hugely popular computer operating system created by Microsoft.

yes way, adv. Possibly going to happen (stated after "no way").

Yo, exp. Hello.

You're toast, exp. You're in a lot of trouble.

yuppie, n. The acronym for young urban professional or young upwardly mobile professional.

zapper, n. The remote control of a television.

zeek, n. An extremely uncool person.

zip it, v. Shut up.

Jeffry Jensen

■ List of Entries by Category

Subject Headings Used in List

African Americans

Affirmative action
Africa and the United States
African Americans
Atlanta child murders
Basquiat, Jean-Michel
Beloved
Brawley, Tawana
Break dancing
Central Park jogger case
Color Purple, The
Cosby Show, The
Crack epidemic
Do the Right Thing
Gangs
Griffith-Joyner, Florence
Hawkins, Yusef
Hip-hop and rap
Holmes, Larry
Horton, William
Houston, Whitney
Howard Beach incident
Jackson, Bo
Jackson, Jesse
Jackson, Michael
Jazz
Johnson, Magic

Kincaid, Jamaica
Leonard, Sugar Ray
Lewis, Carl
Martin Luther King Day
Miami Riot of 1980
MOVE
Mr. T
Multiculturalism in education
Murphy, Eddie
Nation of Yahweh
Naylor, Gloria
Prince
Public Enemy
Racial discrimination
Rice, Jerry
Richie, Lionel
Run-D.M.C.
Taylor, Lawrence
Thomas, Isiah
Turner, Tina
Tyson, Mike
Washington, Harold
Welfare
Williams, Vanessa L.
Wilson, August
Winfrey, Oprah
World music

Art & Architecture

Architecture
Art movements
Basquiat, Jean-Michel
Deconstructivist architecture
Gehry, Frank
Gentrification
Neoexpressionism in painting
Pei, I. M.
Performance art
Photography
Rock and Roll Hall of Fame
Schnabel, Julian
SkyDome
Vietnam Veterans Memorial
Xanadu Houses

Asian Americans

Air India Flight 182 bombing
Asian Americans
Boat people
Hwang, David Henry
Immigration to Canada
Immigration to the United States
Japan and North America
Joy Luck Club, The
Martial arts

Minorities in Canada
Multiculturalism in education
Pei, I. M.
Racial discrimination
Stockton massacre
Vietnam Veterans Memorial
World music

Business
Advertising
Affirmative action
Age discrimination
Air traffic controllers' strike
Apple Computer
AT&T breakup
Baseball strike of 1981
Book publishing
Business and the economy in Canada
Business and the economy in the
  United States
Chrysler Corporation federal rescue
De Lorean, John
Fax machines
401(k) plans
Glass ceiling
Globalization
Iacocca, Lee
Income and wages in Canada
Income and wages in the United
  States
Meritor Savings Bank v. Vinson
Microsoft
Mommy track
Power dressing
Savings and loan (S&L) crisis
Scandals
Sexual harassment
Tamper-proof packaging
Turner, Ted
Ueberroth, Peter
Unions
Voicemail
Wall Street
Women in the workforce
Yuppies

Canada
Aboriginal rights in Canada
Adams, Bryan
Agriculture in Canada
Air India Flight 182 bombing
Bourassa, Robert
Business and the economy in Canada
Canada Act of 1982

Canada and the British
  Commonwealth
Canada and the United States
Canada Health Act of 1984
Canada-United States Free Trade
  Agreement
Canadian Caper
Canadian Charter of Rights and
  Freedoms
Chrétien, Jean
Davies, Robertson
Demographics of Canada
École Polytechnique massacre
Education in Canada
Elections in Canada
Europe and North America
Film in Canada
Foreign policy of Canada
Fox, Michael J.
Garneau, Marc
Gibson, William
Gimli Glider
Gretzky, Wayne
Handmaid's Tale, The
Harp seal hunting
Health care in Canada
Hockey
Immigration to Canada
Income and wages in Canada
Inflation in Canada
Japan and North America
Jennings, Peter
Lemieux, Mario
Lévesque, René
Literature in Canada
Meech Lake Accord
Middle East and North America
Minorities in Canada
Mulroney, Brian
National Anthem Act of 1980
National Energy Program (NEP)
Ocean Ranger oil rig disaster
Olson, Clifford
Quebec English sign ban
Quebec referendum of 1980
Religion and spirituality in Canada
Richler, Mordecai
Sauvé, Jeanne
Schreyer, Edward
Shamrock Summit
SkyDome
Soviet Union and North America
Toronto bathhouse raids of 1981
Trudeau, Pierre

Turner, John
Unemployment in Canada
Vancouver Expo '86

Court Cases & the Law
Bork, Robert
Bowers v. Hardwick
Hustler Magazine v. Falwell
Meritor Savings Bank v. Vinson
O'Connor, Sandra Day
People's Court, The
Rehnquist, William H.
Roberts v. United States Jaycees
Supreme Court decisions
Thompson v. Oklahoma
Tort reform movement
Webster v. Reproductive Health Services

Crime & Punishment
Air India Flight 182 bombing
America's Most Wanted
Atlanta child murders
Berg, Alan
Bonin, William
Brawley, Tawana
Central Park jogger case
Crime
Domestic violence
Dupont Plaza Hotel fire
École Polytechnique massacre
Gangs
Goetz, Bernhard
Goldmark murders
Hawkins, Yusef
Horton, William
Howard Beach incident
Lennon, John
Lucas, Henry Lee
McMartin Preschool trials
Missing and runaway children
Nation of Yahweh
New Mexico State Penitentiary Riot
Night Stalker case
Olson, Clifford
Organized crime
Pan Am Flight 103 bombing
People's Court, The
Post office shootings
Rape
Reagan assassination attempt
Rose, Pete
San Ysidro McDonald's massacre
Scandals
Sexual harassment

Stockton massacre
Terrorism
Tort reform movement
Tylenol murders
U.S. Senate bombing

Disasters

AIDS epidemic
Cerritos plane crash
Challenger disaster
Cold Sunday
Day After, The
El Niño
Exxon Valdez oil spill
Heat wave of 1980
Hurricane Hugo
Loma Prieta earthquake
MGM Grand Hotel fire
Mount St. Helens eruption
Natural disasters
Nuclear winter scenario
Ocean Ranger oil rig disaster
Sioux City plane crash
Times Beach dioxin scare
Twilight Zone accident
Yellowstone National Park fires

Economics

Black Monday stock market crash
Business and the economy in Canada
Business and the economy in the
    United States
Canada-United States Free Trade
    Agreement
Consumerism
Economic Recovery Tax Act of 1981
Farm Aid
Farm crisis
Food Security Act of 1985
401(k) plans
Gentrification
Globalization
Home shopping channels
Income and wages in Canada
Income and wages in the United
    States
Inflation in Canada
Inflation in the United States
Junk bonds
Military spending
National Energy Program (NEP)
Reaganomics
Recessions
Savings and loan (S&L) crisis

Social Security reform
Tax Reform Act of 1986
Unemployment in Canada
Unemployment in the United States
Welfare

Education

Affirmative action
Bennett, William
Closing of the American Mind, The
Drug Abuse Resistance Education
    (D.A.R.E.)
École Polytechnique massacre
Education in Canada
Education in the United States
Information age
Just Say No campaign
McMartin Preschool trials
Magnet schools
Mainstreaming in education
Multiculturalism in education
Nation at Risk, A
National Education Summit of 1989
Political correctness
School vouchers debate
Standards and accountability in
    education
Stockton massacre

Environmental Issues

Agriculture in Canada
Agriculture in the United States
Air pollution
Biopesticides
Cancer research
Cold Sunday
El Niño
Environmental movement
Exxon Valdez oil spill
Food Security Act of 1985
Harp seal hunting
Heat wave of 1980
Malathion spraying
Mount St. Helens eruption
Nuclear Waste Policy Act of 1983
Nuclear winter scenario
Ozone hole
Radon
Spotted owl controversy
Superfund program
Times Beach dioxin scare
Water pollution
Watt, James G.
Yellowstone National Park fires

Film

Academy Awards
Action films
Airplane!
Aliens
Back to the Future
Big Chill, The
Blade Runner
Blue Velvet
Brat Pack in acting
Breakfast Club, The
Bridges, Jeff
Broderick, Matthew
Cher
Close, Glenn
Colorization of black-and-white films
Comedians
Costner, Kevin
Cruise, Tom
Do the Right Thing
Douglas, Michael
Empire Strikes Back, The
Epic films
E.T.: The Extra-Terrestrial
Fast Times at Ridgemont High
Fatal Attraction
Film in Canada
Film in the United States
Flashdance
Ford, Harrison
Fox, Michael J.
Full Metal Jacket
Gere, Richard
Ghostbusters
Gibson, Mel
Hannah, Daryl
Heaven's Gate
Hoffman, Dustin
Horror films
Hughes, John
Hurt, William
Kiss of the Spider Woman
Last Temptation of Christ, The
Little Mermaid, The
Martin, Steve
Multiplex theaters
Murphy, Eddie
Murray, Bill
Nicholson, Jack
On Golden Pond
Ordinary People
PG-13 rating
Platoon
Raging Bull

National Energy Program
National Minimum Drinking Age Act
    of 1984
Nuclear Waste Policy Act of 1983
Quebec English sign ban
Tax Reform Act of 1986
Tort reform movement

Literature
Auel, Jean M.
Beattie, Ann
Beloved
Bonfire of the Vanities, The
Book publishing
Boyle, T. Coraghessan
Brat Pack in literature
Children's literature
Clancy, Tom
Closing of the American Mind, The
Color Purple, The
Confederacy of Dunces, A
Cyberpunk literature
Davies, Robertson
Dworkin, Andrea
Erdrich, Louise
Gibson, William
Handmaid's Tale, The
Heidi Chronicles, The
Henley, Beth
Hwang, David Henry
Irving, John
Joy Luck Club, The
Keillor, Garrison
Kincaid, Jamaica
King, Stephen
Literature in Canada
Literature in the United States
Ludlum, Robert
Mamet, David
Miller, Sue
Minimalist literature
Naylor, Gloria
Oates, Joyce Carol
Poetry
Richler, Mordecai
Shepard, Sam
Steel, Danielle
Theater
Third Wave, The
Torch Song Trilogy
Tyler, Anne
White Noise
Wilson, August

Military & War
Beirut bombings
Cold War
Full Metal Jacket
Goldwater-Nichols Act of 1986
Grenada invasion
Intermediate-Range Nuclear Forces
    (INF) Treaty
Iran-Contra affair
Libya bombing
*M*A*S*H* series finale
Military ban on homosexuals
Military spending
North, Oliver
Panama invasion
Platoon
Poindexter, John
Rambo
Stealth fighter
Strategic Defense Initiative (SDI)
Tower Commission
USS *Stark* incident
USS *Vincennes* incident
Vietnam Veterans Memorial
Weinberger, Caspar
West Berlin discotheque bombing

Music
Adams, Bryan
Blondie
Bon Jovi
Boy George and Culture Club
Broadway musicals
Cats
Cher
Classical music
Compact discs (CDs)
Country music
Devo
Duran Duran
Farm Aid
Flashdance
Glass, Philip
Go-Go's, The
Grant, Amy
Guns n' Roses
Heavy metal
Hip-hop and rap
Houston, Whitney
Jackson, Michael
Jazz
Journey
Lauper, Cyndi
Lennon, John

Little Mermaid, The
Live Aid
Madonna
Mellencamp, John Cougar
Michael, George
Mötley Crüe
MTV
Music
Music videos
New Wave music
Osbourne, Ozzy
Parental advisory stickers
Phantom of the Opera, The
Pop music
Prince
Public Enemy
R.E.M.
Richie, Lionel
Rock and Roll Hall of Fame
Run-D.M.C.
Springsteen, Bruce
Star Search
Sting
Synthesizers
Talking Heads
Teen singers
This Is Spinal Tap
Turner, Tina
US Festivals
USA for Africa
U2
Van Halen
Vangelis
Women in rock music
World music
Yankovic, Weird Al

Native Americans
Aboriginal rights in Canada
Cher
Erdrich, Louise
Harp seal hunting
Indian Gaming Regulatory Act of
    1988
Minorities in Canada
Multiculturalism in education
Native Americans
Turner, Tina
World music

People
Adams, Bryan
Anderson, Terry
Atwater, Lee

Turner, Ted
Turner, Tina
Tyler, Anne
Tyson, Mike
Ueberroth, Peter
Valenzuela, Fernando
Vangelis
Washington, Harold
Watson, Tom
Watt, James G.
Weaver, Sigourney
Weinberger, Caspar
White, Ryan
Williams, Robin
Williams, Vanessa L.
Wilson, August
Winfrey, Oprah
Wright, Jim
Yankovic, Weird Al

Politics & Government

Abscam
Atwater, Lee
Bennett, William
Bentsen, Lloyd
Bork, Robert H.
Bourassa, Robert
Bush, George H. W.
Canada Act of 1982
Canada-United States Free Trade
    Agreement
Canadian Charter of Rights and
    Freedoms
Chrétien, Jean
Claiborne, Harry E.
Conch Republic
Congressional page sex scandal of
    1983
Conservatism in U.S. politics
Dukakis, Michael
Elections in Canada
Elections in the United States,
    midterm
Elections in the United States, 1980
Elections in the United States, 1984
Elections in the United States, 1988
Ferraro, Geraldine
Flag burning
Food Security Act of 1985
Gender gap in voting
Haig, Alexander
Hart, Gary
Horton, William
Iran-Contra affair

Jackson, Jesse
Just Say No campaign
Kirkpatrick, Jeane
Koop, C. Everett
LaRouche, Lyndon
Lévesque, René
Liberalism in U.S. politics
Meech Lake Accord
Meese, Edwin, III
Mondale, Walter
Moral Majority
Mulroney, Brian
National Anthem Act of 1980
National Energy Program
North, Oliver
O'Connor, Sandra Day
O'Neill, Tip
Poindexter, John
Quayle, Dan
Quebec English sign ban
Quebec referendum of 1980
Reagan, Nancy
Reagan, Ronald
Reagan assassination attempt
Reagan Democrats
Reagan Revolution
Regan, Donald
Rehnquist, William H.
Robertson, Pat
Sauvé, Jeanne
Scandals
Schreyer, Edward
Schroeder, Pat
Shultz, George P.
Social Security reform
Spotted owl controversy
Statue of Liberty restoration and
    centennial
Sununu, John H.
Supreme Court decisions
Tanner '88
Tower Commission
Trudeau, Pierre
Turner, John
U.S. Senate bombing
Washington, Harold
Weinberger, Caspar
Wright, Jim

Popular Culture

Aerobics
Airplane!
Auel, Jean M.
Baby Jessica rescue

Back to the Future
Bloom County
Brat Pack in acting
Brat Pack in literature
Break dancing
Breakfast Club, The
Cabbage Patch Kids
Comedians
Comic strips
Dallas
Dance, popular
Diets
Dynasty
Empire Strikes Back, The
E.T.: The Extra-Terrestrial
Fads
Fashions and clothing
Fast Times at Ridgemont High
Flashdance
Food trends
Gallagher
General Hospital
Generation X
Ghostbusters
Hairstyles
Hands Across America
Herman, Pee-Wee
Hip-hop and rap
Hobbies and recreation
Home shopping channels
Home video rentals
Infomercials
Keillor, Garrison
King, Stephen
Knoxville World's Fair
Leg warmers
Louisiana World Exposition
Married . . . with Children
Martial arts
Max Headroom
Miami Vice
Mommy track
Mr. T
MTV
Mullet
Music
New Coke
Pac-Man
Peller, Clara
Photography
Pop music
Power dressing
Preppies
Raiders of the Lost Ark

Rambo
Simmons, Richard
Slang and slogans
Star Search
Starbucks
Steel, Danielle
Tabloid television
Teen singers
Television
Toys and games
Trivial Pursuit
Valley girls
Vancouver Expo '86
Video games and arcades
Wave, the
When Harry Met Sally . . .
World Wrestling Federation
Yankovic, Weird Al
Yuppies

Religion & Spirituality

Bakker, Jim and Tammy Faye
Evangelical Lutheran Church in
   America
Falwell, Jerry
Goldmark murders
Grant, Amy
Heritage USA
Hubbard, L. Ron
Hustler Magazine v. Falwell
Jewish Americans
Last Temptation of Christ, The
Moral Majority
Nation of Yahweh
Religion and spirituality in Canada
Religion and spirituality in the
   United States
Robertson, Pat
Swaggart, Jimmy
Televangelism

Science & Technology

Apple Computer
Archaeology
Artificial heart
Astronomy
Bioengineering
Biopesticides
CAD/CAM technology
Camcorders
Cancer research
Car alarms
Cell phones
Challenger disaster

Colorization of black-and-white
   films
Compact discs
Computers
Cosmos
Cyberpunk literature
Disposable cameras
DNA fingerprinting
Doppler radar
Fax machines
Fetal medicine
Garneau, Marc
Genetics research
Halley's comet
Information age
Inventions
Medicine
Microsoft
Nobel Prizes
Nuclear winter scenario
Ozone hole
Pac-Man
Ride, Sally
Robots
Science and technology
Science-fiction films
SETI Institute
Space exploration
Space shuttle program
Star Trek: The Next Generation
Superconductors
Synthesizers
Tamper-proof packaging
Third Wave, The
Titanic wreck discovery
Tron
Video games and arcades
Virtual reality
Voicemail
Voyager global flight
Who Framed Roger Rabbit

Sexuality

ACT UP
AIDS epidemic
Androgyny
Bowers v. Hardwick
Congressional page sex scandal of
   1983
Fatal Attraction
Flynt, Larry
Handmaid's Tale, The
Homosexuality and gay rights
Hudson, Rock

Kiss of the Spider Woman
Louganis, Greg
Military ban on homosexuals
Pornography
Rape
Sexual harassment
Shields, Brooke
Swaggart, Jimmy
Torch Song Trilogy
Toronto bathhouse raids of 1981
Williams, Vanessa L.

Social Issues

Aboriginal rights in Canada
Abortion
ACT UP
Affirmative action
African Americans
Age discrimination
AIDS epidemic
AIDS Memorial Quilt
Asian Americans
Berg, Alan
Biological clock
Boat people
Bonfire of the Vanities, The
Bowers v. Hardwick
Brawley, Tawana
Central Park jogger case
Comic Relief
Consumerism
Crack epidemic
Craft, Christine
Demographics of Canada
Demographics of the United States
Disability rights movement
Do the Right Thing
Domestic violence
Drug Abuse Resistance Education
   (D.A.R.E.)
Dworkin, Andrea
École Polytechnique massacre
Farm Aid
Farm crisis
Feminism
Flag burning
Flynt, Larry
Gallaudet University protests
Gangs
Generation X
Gentrification
Glass ceiling
Goetz, Bernhard
Goldmark murders

Handmaid's Tale, The
Hawkins, Yusef
Homelessness
Homosexuality and gay rights
Horton, William
Howard Beach incident
Hustler Magazine v. Falwell
Immigration Reform and Control Act of 1986
Immigration to Canada
Immigration to the United States
Indian Gaming Regulatory Act of 1988
Jewish Americans
Just Say No campaign
Latinos
Live Aid
McKinney Homeless Assistance Act of 1987
Marriage and divorce
Martin Luther King Day
Meritor Savings Bank v. Vinson
Miami Riot of 1980
Military ban on homosexuals
Minorities in Canada
Missing and runaway children
Mommy track
Mothers Against Drunk Driving (MADD)
MOVE
Nation of Yahweh
National Minimum Drinking Age Act of 1984
Native Americans
Political correctness
Pornography
Prozac
Psychology
Racial discrimination
Rape
Roberts v. United States Jaycees
Sexual harassment
Skinheads and neo-Nazis
Spotted owl controversy
Third Wave, The
thirtysomething
Thompson v. Oklahoma
Toronto bathhouse raids of 1981
Tort reform movement
USA for Africa
Wall Street
Webster v. Reproductive Health Services
Welfare
Williams, Vanessa L.

Women in the workforce
Women's rights

Sports
Arena Football League
Baseball
Baseball strike of 1981
Basketball
Bird, Larry
Boitano, Brian
Boxing
Brett, George
Decker, Mary
Elway, John
Football
Gibson, Kirk
Golf
Goodwill Games of 1986
Gretzky, Wayne
Griffith-Joyner, Florence
Hershiser, Orel
Hockey
Holmes, Larry
Jackson, Bo
Johnson, Magic
Lemieux, Mario
LeMond, Greg
Leonard, Sugar Ray
Lewis, Carl
Louganis, Greg
McEnroe, John
Miracle on Ice
Montana, Joe
Navratilova, Martina
Olympic boycotts
Olympic Games of 1980
Olympic Games of 1984
Olympic Games of 1988
Play, the
Retton, Mary Lou
Rice, Jerry
Rose, Pete
Ryan, Nolan
SkyDome
Soccer
Sports
Taylor, Lawrence
Tennis
Thomas, Isiah
Turner, Ted
Tyson, Mike
Valenzuela, Fernando
Watson, Tom
Wave, the

Television
Bakker, Jim and Tammy Faye
Brokaw, Tom
Cable television
Cagney and Lacey
Cheers
Children's television
CNN
Colorization of black-and-white films
Comedians
Cosby Show, The
Craft, Christine
Dallas
Day After, The
Designing Women
Dynasty
Facts of Life, The
Falwell, Jerry
Family Ties
Fox, Michael J.
FOX network
General Hospital
Golden Girls, The
Hill Street Blues
Home shopping channels
Infomercials
Jennings, Peter
L.A. Law
Letterman, David
Magnum, P.I.
Married . . . with Children
*M*A*S*H* series finale
Miami Vice
Miniseries
Moonlighting
MTV
Murphy, Eddie
Murray, Bill
Music videos
Network anchors
Pauley, Jane
Rather, Dan
Rivera, Geraldo
St. Elsewhere
Sitcoms
Soap operas
Star Search
Star Trek: The Next Generation
Tabloid television
Talk shows
Tanner '88
Televangelism
Television
thirtysomething

Turner, Ted
Williams, Robin
Winfrey, Oprah
Wonder Years, The

Terrorism
Air India Flight 182 bombing
Anderson, Terry
Beirut bombings
Berg, Alan
Canadian Caper
Iranian hostage crisis
Klinghoffer, Leon
Libya bombing
Pan Am Flight 103 bombing
Terrorism
Tylenol murders
West Berlin discotheque bombing

Theater & Dance
Ballet
Break dancing
Broadway musicals
Cats
Dance, popular
Flashdance
Heidi Chronicles, The
Henley, Beth
Hip-hop and rap
Hwang, David Henry
Jackson, Michael
Literature in Canada
Literature in the United States

Madonna
Mamet, David
Performance art
Phantom of the Opera, The
Shepard, Sam
Theater
Torch Song Trilogy
Wilson, August

Transportation
Air India Flight 182 bombing
Air traffic controllers' strike
Car alarms
Cerritos plane crash
Chrysler Corporation federal rescue
De Lorean, John
Gimli Glider
Iacocca, Lee
Minivans
Pan Am Flight 103 bombing
Sioux City plane crash
Stealth fighter
Voyager global flight

Women's Issues
Abortion
Affirmative action
Auel, Jean M.
Biological clock
Cagney and Lacey
Central Park jogger case
Color Purple, The
Craft, Christine

Designing Women
Domestic violence
Dworkin, Andrea
École Polytechnique massacre
Fatal Attraction
Feminism
Ferraro, Geraldine
Gender gap in voting
Glass ceiling
Go-Go's, The
Golden Girls, The
Handmaid's Tale, The
Heidi Chronicles, The
Henley, Beth
Madonna
Marriage and divorce
Meritor Savings Bank v. Vinson
Mommy track
O'Connor, Sandra Day
Pauley, Jane
Pornography
Power dressing
Rape
Ride, Sally
Roberts v. United States Jaycees
Sauvé, Jeanne
Sexual harassment
Turner, Tina
Valley girls
Webster v. Reproductive Health Services
Women in rock music
Women in the workforce
Women's rights

The Eighties
in America

■ Photo Index

■ Personages Index

Page numbers in **boldface** type indicate full articles devoted to the topic.

■ Subject Index

Page numbers in **boldface** type indicate full articles devoted to the topic.